Legal Secretary's Complete Handbook

Also by Mary A. De Vries:

Secretary's Standard Reference Manual and Guide.

Private Secretary's Encyclopedic Dictionary, Second Edition (revisor).

Complete Secretary's Handbook, Fourth Edition (revisor).

The Prentice-Hall Complete Secretarial Letter Book.

Legal Secretary's Complete Handbook

Third Edition

by

Besse May Miller

Revised by

Mary A. De Vries

Prentice-Hall, Inc.   Englewood Cliffs, N.J.

Prentice-Hall International, Inc., *London*
Prentice-Hall of Australia, Pty. Ltd., *Sydney*
Prentice-Hall of Canada, Ltd., *Toronto*
Prentice-Hall of India Private Ltd., *New Delhi*
Prentice-Hall of Japan, Inc., *Tokyo*
Prentice-Hall of Southeast Asia Pte. Ltd., *Singapore*
Whitehall Books, Ltd., *Wellington, New Zealand*

© 1953, 1970, 1980, by

Prentice-Hall, Inc.

Englewood Cliffs, N.J.

15 14 13 12 11 10

Library of Congress Cataloging in Publication Data

Miller, Besse May.
  Legal secretary's complete handbook.

  Includes index.
  1. Legal secretaries—United States—Handbooks,
manuals, etc. I. De Vries, Mary Ann. II. Title.
KF319.M54 1980   651'.9' 34   79-22516
ISBN 0-13-528562-3

Printed in the United States of America

Preface to the

Third Edition

Many changes in the law are subtle—they happen almost without notice. Sometimes, of course, the changes are more dramatic, and almost everyone knows about them. But either way, it is clear that there are changes occurring all the time, and the successful legal secretary makes it her business to know what they are and how they affect her work.

This revised Third Edition of *Legal Secretary's Complete Handbook* has done your homework for you. Here you will find all the important changes in law and the practice of law that have taken place in recent years, with specific explanations of how these changes affect your duties in the law office. Every fact and figure has been thoroughly examined by highly qualified attorneys, paralegals, legal secretaries, and other experts. Essential new material has been added, and other vital information has been completely revised and updated. In short, every effort possible has been devoted to making this the most accurate, up-to-date, and useful reference available to the legal secretary, paralegal, and other law office personnel.

Although all important topics covered in the previous edition have been retained, some material has been completely reorganized to improve its effectiveness and to make it easier for you to locate facts and figures. For example:

Part 1 now includes eight chapters pertaining to general duties in the law office: Working in a Law Office; Contacts with Clients and Other

Callers; Reminder Systems and Practices; Filing in the Law Office; Handling Legal and Business Correspondence; How to Keep Books and Records; Using References in Legal Research; and Preparing Material for Printing.

Part 2 has three chapters that concern the preparation of legal instruments and documents: Handling Legal Instruments; How to Prepare Legal Papers; How to Handle Affidavits, Powers of Attorney, and Wills.

Part 3 offers all you need to know about preparing court papers in four chapters: Understanding Courts and Their Functions; Handling Court Papers; How to Prepare Court Papers; How to Handle Records on Appeal, Briefs, and Citations.

Part 4 has five chapters that show you how to assist in specialized practice: Assisting in Partnership Formation and Incorporation; Acting as Corporate Secretary; Assisting in Real Estate Practice and Foreclosures; Assisting with Probate and Estate Administration; Handling Commercial Collections.

Part 5 has been totally revised to include a convenient collection of essential legal facts and secretarial aids: Forms of Address, Honorary and Official Positions; Latin Words and Phrases; Glossary of Legal Terms; State Requirements for Ages of Testator and Number of Witnesses to Will; Courts of Record and Judicial Circuits; Authentication of Instruments; Notaries Public; Statutes of Limitation in Number of Years; Official Reports and How They Are Cited; Reporters of National Reporter System; Approved Method of Citing Compilations of Statutes and Codes.

A wealth of *new information* has been introduced covering everything from new features on office machines to working for a trial lawyer. To name just a few of the many new topics you will find:

> • duties of the paralegal • what happens in a courtroom • how to handle a caller who wants free advice on the phone • using loose-leaf services • guidelines in partnership formation • all about computerized research • keeping a forms file • what you should know about treatises • how to handle law students seeking part-time and summer jobs • new equipment that will make your work easier • and much more.

Just as important are the many *changes* that have been made to increase the usefulness of the information presented in the previous edition. To give you a few examples of the countless items that have been revised and updated:

> • the latest form of real property description • Latin words and phrases that no longer are italicized • the growing use of

machines in dictation and transcription ● new rules for addressing women ● how to know whether to make copies by copier or typewriter ● changes in the law regarding the right of lawyers to advertise ● current accounting terms to use in keeping books and records ● the difference between eminent domain and condemnation ● new state requirements for ages of testator and number of witnesses to will ● and many more.

Numerous documents are illustrated throughout the book, with detailed instructions for their preparation. In addition, specific directions are given for the steps to follow in processing the document, for instance: where to send it, whether to get it notarized, what records to keep, and so on. Sample letters are also shown for situations where the document must be transmitted by mail. In other words, you will find everything you need to know both to handle your routine duties and to understand the technicalities pertinent to the legal profession.

This Third Edition of the *Legal Secretary's Complete Handbook* shows you how to do every job in the law office easier and faster. It discusses every aspect of legal office procedures and describes the various duties and responsibilities in a clear, to-the-point manner. The wide range of legal information will be invaluable for beginning and experienced legal secretaries, paralegals, and other co-workers in the legal profession. Whether your work deals with the general practice of law or a specialized field, you will find this volume the most important reference tool on your desk.

Mary A. De Vries

Acknowledgments

Many professional people and organizations made important contributions to the Third Edition of the *Legal Secretary's Complete Handbook,* providing a rich supply of practical advice, guidance, literature, and encouragement.

This is particularly true of one person who devoted countless hours of her time and professional knowledge to ensure the accuracy and completeness of each revised chapter: Carolyn W. Baldwin, attorney, Murphy & McLaughlin, Laconia, New Hampshire. In addition to reviewing thousands of facts and figures found throughout this "one volume library" of essential data, Ms. Baldwin provided new information in important areas such as partnership formation and court procedures. Her expert counsel has been invaluable, and I am indeed grateful for her help. Appreciation is also extended to the firm of Murphy & McLaughlin for supporting these efforts, and to Charlene Morin, legal secretary at Murphy & McLaughlin, who further assisted our work with her suggestions for corrections, changes, and other improvements.

The value of this edition has been greatly increased through the specific review work, research activities, and other contributions made by attorneys, paralegals, legal secretaries, association directors, and numerous other individuals who shared our desire to make this edition as useful as possible. Among the many professionals who generously gave time and information to this project are David Fogg, CPA, of Nathan Wechsler & Company in Concord, New Hampshire; Attorney Stephen R. Goldman and Paralegal Robert Bonsall of the Rinden Professional Association in Concord, New

Hampshire. Other individuals and organizations also made our task easier by supplying current literature and information. Some provided illustrations for us to use throughout the text. My sincere thanks to each one, including President Harriet C. Sharp, Director of Public Relations Mary Ann Stevenson, and Executive Administrator Maxine M. Dover of the National Association of Legal Secretaries in Tulsa, Oklahoma; President Nancy Siegel and Executive Director Jeanne Kowalski of the National Federation of Paralegal Associations in Washington, D.C.; Executive Director William R. Fry of the National Paralegal Institute in Washington, D.C.; and Executive Director Leo E. Smith of the Commercial Law League of America in Chicago, Illinois. We also acknowledge, with thanks, the contribution of the Franklin Pierce Law Center Library in Concord, New Hampshire, which provided the sources for much of our research efforts.

M.A. De V.

CONTENTS

Preface to the Third Edition **5**

Part I General Duties in the Law Office

1. Working in a Law Office **25**

You and the Lawyer: 1.1. The law-office team 25. 1.2. Ethics in the law office 25. 1.3. Legal training 26. 1.4. Requirements for admission to the bar 26. 1.5. Law degrees 27. 1.6. Specialization in the law field 27. 1.7. Building a practice 28. 1.8. The lawyer's outside activities 30. 1.9. The lawyer's relationship with clients 31. 1.10. Fees 31.

Organization and Personnel of a Law Firm: 1.11. Kind of business organization 32. 1.12. Personnel in a law office 32. 1.13. The secretary's duties 33. 1.14. Deportment 34.

The Law Office: 1.15. Layout 34. 1.16. The furniture 35. 1.17. Equipment 35. 1.18. Stationery supplies 36.

A New Matter: 1.19. New case report 37. 1.20. What the secretary does 37. 1.21. Routing of new case report 38.

Typing and Dictation in the Law Office: 1.22. The secretary's loose-leaf formbook 40. 1.23. Importance of understanding dictated material 40. 1.24. Errors in the dictation 41. 1.25. Pairs of words that cause confusion 42. 1.26. Recurring phrases, clauses, and paragraphs 43. 1.27. Special outlines for unusual words 43. 1.28. Take-ins 43. 1.29. Testimony 44.

2. Contacts with Clients and Other Callers **49**

2.1. Introduction to the client 49. 2.2. Basic precepts 50.

Contacts in Person: 2.3. Contacts in person with clients 50. 2.4. Client calls without an appointment 51. 2.5. Stranger who wants legal advice 52. 2.6. A client is early for an appointment 53. 2.7. Hysterical clients 53. 2.8. Invitations from clients 54. 2.9. Presents and payment for work 54. 2.10. Client wants to see a file 54. 2.11. Salesmen and job hunters 55.

Contacts over the Telephone: 2.12. Importance of telephone contacts 56. 2.13. Rules of telephone courtesy 56. 2.14. Placing calls for the lawyer 56. 2.15. Long distance, or toll, calls 57. 2.16. When clients place toll calls 59. 2.17. Answering calls for the lawyer 59. 2.18. Making notes of incoming calls 59. 2.19. Screening calls for the lawyer 60. 2.20. Finding the purpose of a call 61. 2.21. The caller who wants legal advice over the phone 62. 2.22. An irate client calls 62. 2.23. Client or prospective client asks what a fee will be 63. 2.24. Your telephone conversation 63. 2.25. Desk telephone lists 63.

3. Reminder Systems and Practices **65**

The Diary: 3.1. What is a diary? 65. 3.2. Diaries you should keep 67. 3.3. How to make up diaries 67. 3.4. How to make entries about legal work

68. 3.5. How to obtain information for entries 68. 3.6. Checklist of entries to make in diary 69. 3.7. Tickler card file 70. 3.8. Use of tickler card file with diary 70. 3.9. Checklist of entries of work accomplished 71.

Follow-up Files: 3.10. Necessity for follow-up files 71. 3.11. Checklist of material to be placed in follow-up files 71. 3.12. Equipment for follow-up system 72. 3.13. Arrangement of folders for follow-up 72. 3.14. Operation of the follow-up system 72. 3.15. How to handle material in the daily follow-up file 73. 3.16. Follow-ups on a small scale 73. 3.17. Tickler card file for follow-up 73.

Reminding the Lawyer of Things to Be Done: 3.18. Necessity for reminder 75. 3.19. How to remind the lawyer of appointments 75. 3.20. Reminders showing appointments for a month 75. 3.21. How to remind the lawyer of things to be done 75. 3.22. How to remind the lawyer of court work 78.

4. Filing in the Law Office **79**
    4.1. Classification of files 79.

Numerical System of Filing Applied to Clients' Files: 4.2. What is the numerical system of filing? 80. 4.3. How to use the numerical system in a law office 81. 4.4. Assigning numbers according to type of case 84. 4.5. How to transfer numerical files 84.

Alphabetical System of Filing Applied to Client's Files: 4.6. What is the alphabetical system of filing? 85. 4.7. How to use the alphabetical system 85. 4.8. How to transfer alphabetical files 86.

Other Files: 4.9 Personal file 86. 4.10. General correspondence file 87. 4.11. Periodicals, bulletins, and so on 87.

Physical Setup of Files: 4.12. Preparation of material for filing 87. 4.13. How to type index tabs and labels 88. 4.14. How to arrange the papers in the file folders 89. 4.15. Preparation for closing a file 90. 4.16. Extra copies and printed papers, drafts 90. 4.17. Control of material taken from the files 90.

Information Storage and Retrieval Systems: 4.18. Electronics and the law office 96.

5. Handling Legal and Business Correspondence **99**
    5.1. Styles of letter setups 99. 5.2. Opinion letters 102. 5.3. Punctuation 103. 5.4. Subject line 104. 5.5. How to type the dateline 104.

The Address: 5.6. Forms of address 104. 5.7. Business titles or position 106. 5.8. Forms for addressing women 107. 5.9. How to type the street address 107.

Salutations: 5.10. How to type the salutation 108. 5.11. Forms of salutation 109. 5.12. Forms of salutation in letters addressed to women 109.

The Complimentary Close: 5.13. How to type the complimentary close 110.

Signature: 5.14. How to type the signature 110.

Miscellaneous Suggestions About Correspondence: 5.15. Envelopes 111. 5.16. Attention line 112. 5.17. Identification line 112. 5.18. Personal notation 112. 5.19. Reference line 112. 5.20. Mailing notation 113. 5.21. Enclosure mark 113. 5.22. Copy distribution notation 113. 5.23. Postscript 114. 5.24. Heading on succeeding pages 114. 5.25. Enclosures 114.

Some Concrete Aids in Letter Writing: 5.26. Suggested techniques 115. 5.27. Trite terms to be avoided 115. 5.28. Unnecessary words and phrases 118. 5.29. Two words with the same meaning 119. 5.30. Favorite words and expressions 119. 5.31. Big words versus one-syllable words 120. 5.32. Sentence length 120.

Telegrams: 5.33. How to send a telegram 120. 5.34. How to type a telegram 121. 5.35. How to send the same message to multiple addresses 121. 5.36. How to send a telegram to a person on a train 122. 5.37. How to send a telegram to a person on a plane 122. 5.38. Punctuation 122. 5.39. Paragraphing 122. 5.40. Mixed groups of letters and figures 122. 5.41. How to type a telegram when work is in the machine 122.

Letters the Secretary Writes

Letters Written over the Secretary's Signature: 5.42. Acknowledgment of correspondence received during employer's absence 123. 5.43. Letters making reservations 126. 5.44. Letters calling attention to an error in an account 128. 5.45. Reply to notice of meeting 129. 5.46. Letters calling attention to omission of enclosures 130. 5.47. Follow-up letters 130.

Letters the Secretary May Write for Employer's Signature: 5.48. Letters of appreciation 131. 5.49. Letters of sympathy 132. 5.50. Letters of congratulations 133. 5.51. Letters of introduction 135. 5.22. Letters of invitation 136. 5.53. Letters of acceptance 137. 5.54. Letters of declination 138.

6. How to Keep Books and Records **139**

How to Keep Books in the Law Office: 6.1. System of bookkeeping in the law office 139. 6.2. Books required 139. 6.3. Basic principles of double-entry bookkeeping 140. 6.4. Simple rules to remember 140. 6.5. Cash journal 141. 6.6. General ledger 142. 6.7. Subsidiary ledger 143. 6.8. Posting to the general ledger 145. 6.9. Explanation of cash journal entries and posting 145. 6.10. Trial balance 154. 6.11. Taking a trial balance of accounts receivable 155. 6.12. Profit and loss statement 155. 6.13. Drawing account 158. 6.14. Payroll record 158. 6.15. Capital account 158.

Time and Cost of Professional Services: 6.16. Records required to find time and cost of service 158. 6.17. Finding the cost of a lawyer's time 158. 6.18. Daily time sheet 159. 6.19. Posting the time charges 159.

Billing the Client: 6.20. Preparation of the bill 161. 6.21. Charges made to clients 163. 6.22. How the amount of the bill is calculated 163. 6.23. Petty cash fund 163.

7. Using References in Legal Research **165**

Statutes and Codes: 7.1. Compilation of laws 165. 7.2. How to find a law 166.

Reports of Decided Cases: 7.3. Scope and organization of reports 166. 7.4. How to use the reports and reporters 168. 7.5. How to find alternate citations 168. 7.6. Other publications of decisions 169. 7.7. Loose-leaf services 169.

Books That Classify the Law

American Digest: 7.8 Organization of the digest system 171. 7.9 How to use the digest system 171.

Shepard's Citations: 7.10. Purpose of Shepard's Citations 172. 7.11. How to use Shepard's Citations 172.

Illustrative Case

Corpus Juris Secundum System: 7.12. Scope and organization of system 174. 7.13. How to use Corpus Juris Secundum System 175. 7.14. How to cite 176. 7.15. American Jurisprudence and American Law Reports 176.

Form Books: 7.16. Practice manuals 176. 7.17. Books of legal form 176. 7.18. Treatises 177. 7.19 Basic reference books 177. 7.20. Computerized legal research 177.

Reference Facilities for Checking Names and Addresses: 7.21. Useful reference books 178.

8. Preparing Material for Printing **179**

Preparing the Manuscript: 8.1. Rules for typing manuscripts 179. 8.2. Checking the manuscript 181. 8.3. Marking copy 183. 8.4. How to estimate length of copy 185. 8.5. Working with others 186. 8.6. Procedure 186. 8.7. Importance of correcting galley and page proofs 187. 8.8. Reading the proof 187.

PART II   Preparing Legal Instruments and Documents

9. Handling Legal Instruments **193**

9.1. What is a legal instrument? 193. 9.2. Parties to an instrument 193. 9.3. How to type legal instruments 194.

Execution of an Instrument: 9.4. What is "execution" of an instrument? 196. 9.5. Testimonium clause 196. 9.6. Signatures 197. 9.7.

How to fit the signatures on the page 198. 9.8. Sealing an instrument 198. 9.9. Attestation clause 199.

Acknowledgments: 9.10. Importance of acknowledgments in the law office 201. 9.11. Laws governing acknowledgments 201. 9.12. Essentials of an acknowledgment 203. 9.13. How and where to type the acknowledgment 206. 9.14. Who may make an acknowledgment 206. 9.15. Who may take an acknowledgment 206. 9.16. Authentication 207.

Notaries Public: 9.17. What is a notary public? 207. 9.18. Following the letter of the law when you notarize a paper 208. 9.19. Details to observe when you notarize a paper 209.

Recording Legal Instruments: 9.20. Purpose in recording instruments 210. 9.21. Distinction between recording and filing 210. 9.22. What the secretary or paralegal does 210.

10. How to Prepare Legal Papers **213**

10.1. Number of copies 213. 10.2. Paper 213. 10.3. Margins 214. 10.4. Paragraphs 214. 10.5. Numbering pages 214. 10.6. Marginal and tabular stops 215. 10.7. Tabulated material 215. 10.8. Responsibility and distribution line 215. 10.9. Line spacing 216. 10.10. Standard rules for spacing 216. 10.11. Space for fill-ins 217. 10.12. Underscoring 217. 10.13. Quotations and other indented material 218. 10.14. Drafts 220. 10.15. Correction of errors 220. 10.16. Copying 221. 10.17. Collating 222. 10.18. Conforming 222. 10.19. Ditto marks 222. 10.20. Legal backs 223. 10.21. How to make corrections on bound pages 226. 10.22. Printed law blanks 227.

11. How to Handle Affidavits, Powers of Attorney, and Wills **229**

Affidavits: 11.1. What is an affidavit? 229. 11.2. Distinction between affidavit and acknowledgment 229. 11.3. Essentials of an affidavit 230. 11.4. Authentication 230. 11.5. Preparation of affidavit 230.

Powers of Attorney: 11.6. What is a power of attorney? 232 11.7. Parties to a power of attorney 232. 11.8. Forms of powers of attorney 232. 11.9. Statements and clauses 232. 11.10. Directions for the preparation of a power of attorney 233.

Wills: 11.11. What is a will? 233. 11.12. Who are the parties to a will? 234. 11.13. Forms and kinds of wills 235. 11.14. Printed forms of wills 235. 11.15. Pattern of the contents of wills 235. 11.16. Title 236. 11.17. Introductory paragraph 236. 11.18. Revocation clause 236. 11.19. Text, or body 236. 11.20. Payment of debts and funeral expenses 237. 11.21. Dispositive clauses 237. 11.22. Trust provisions 237. 11.23. Residuary clause 237. 11.24. Appointment of executor 237. 11.25. Appointment of guardian 238. 11.26. Precatory provisions 238. 11.27. Testimonium, or signature, clause 238. 11.28. Attestation clause and witnesses' signatures

238. 11.29. Typing a will 238. 11.30. Signature page and preceding page of a will 240. 11.31. How to gauge and test the page length 242. 11.32. Witnessing a will 242. 11.33. Certifying copies of wills 243. 11.34. Capitalization and punctuation 244. 11.35. "Do's and don'ts" in preparing a will 244. 11.36. Codicil 245. 11.37. Red-inking a will 245.

PART III Preparing Court Papers

12. Understanding Courts and Their Functions **249**
        12.1. The word "court" 249. 12.2. Court procedure 250. 12.3. What happens in court 250. 12.4. Court personnel 252. 12.5. American court system 253. 12.6. Jurisdiction 255. 12.7. Inferior courts 257. 12.8. Superior courts 257. 12.9. Courts of special jurisdiction 257. 12.10. Courts of intermediate review 258. 12.11. Supreme appellate courts 258. 12.12. Distinction between equity and law 259. 12.13. Judges and justices 260. 12.14. The trial lawyer 261. 12.15. Clerk of the court 261. 12.16. Clerk's index system 262. 12.17. Clerk's permanent record book 262. 12.18. Clerk's minute books 263. 12.19. Court calendar and calendar number 263. 12.20. Calendar call 263. 12.21. Term of court 264. 12.22. How to keep a progress record of court matters 264. 12.23. Physical features of a suit register 265. 12.24. Loose-leaf binder for the suit register 265. 12.25. File folder used for progress record 265. 12.26. Portable tray or cabinet for the suit register 265. 12.27. How to file the record sheets 265. 12.28. When and how to open a case in the suit register 267. 12.29. What to enter 267. 12.30. Form and sufficiency of record 267. 12.31. Closing the record of a case 271.

13. Handling Court Papers **273**
        Parties to an Action: 13.1. Party bringing or defending a law suit 273. 13.2. Parties to a cross action 274. 13.3. Party intervening 274. 13.4. Parties on appeal 274. 13.5. Amicus curiae 274. 13.6. Who may be parties to a law suit 275.
        Verifications: 13.7. What is a verification? 277. 13.8. Who may verify a pleading? 277. 13.9. Forms of verification 277. 13.10. How to type a verification 278. 13.11. How to administer the oath to person verifying a pleading 280.
        How to Type Court Papers: 13.12. Paper 282. 13.13. Heading or caption 282. 13.14. How to type the caption 283. 13.15. Captions on papers filed in federal district courts 292. 13.16. Indentations 292. 13.17. Number of copies 292. 13.18. Numbering pages 292. 13.19. Conforming copies 292. 13.20. Legal backs for court papers 292. 13.21. Folding 295. 13.22. Printed litigation blanks 295.
        Practice and Procedure 13.23. The secretary's responsibility 295. 13.24. Variations in practice and procedure 296.

14. How to Prepare Court Papers **297**
        Summons and Complaint: 14.1. Plaintiff's first pleading 297. 14.2.

Analysis of a complaint 298. 14.3. How to prepare the complaint 299. 14.4. The summons 301. 14.5. How to prepare the summons 301. 14.6. Return day of summons 303. 14.7. Alias summons; pluries summons 303. 14.8. What to do about the summons and complaint 304.

The Answer: 14.9. Defendant's first pleading 305. 14.10. Analysis of an answer 305. 14.11. How to prepare the answer 305. 14.12. Methods of service of answer on plaintiff's attorney 308. 14.13. What to do about the answer 310.

Notice of Appearance: 14.14. Analysis of a notice of appearance 310. 14.15. How to prepare a notice of appearance 310. 14.16. What to do about the notice of appearance 313.

Notice of Trial; Note of Issue: 14.17. Noticing a case for trial 313. 14.18. When the notice must be served 313. 14.19. Note of issue—preparation 313. 14.20 Notice of trial—preparation 314. 14.21. What to do about the notice of trial or note of issue 315.

Stipulations: 14.22. Analysis of a stipulation 317. 14.23. How to prepare a stipulation 317. 14.24. What to do about stipulations 319.

Demurrers: 14.25. Analysis of a demurrer 319. 14.26. How to prepare the demurrer 320. 14.27. What to do about a demurrer 324.

Demand for Bill of Particulars, Bill of Particulars, Interrogatories, and Motion to Make Pleading More Definite: 14.28. Demand for bill of particulars 324. 14.29. Parts of demand for bill of particulars 324. 14.30. How to prepare the demand for bill of particulars 325. 14.31. What to do about the demand for bill of particulars 327. 14.32. Parts of bill of particulars 328. 14.33. How to prepare the bill of particulars 328. 14.34. What to do about the bill of particulars 328. 14.35. Interrogatories 328. 14.36. Motion to make the pleading more definite 330.

Notices: 14.37. Analysis of a notice 330. 14.38. How to prepare a notice 330. 14.39. Backing and binding of notices 332. 14.40. Service of notice 332.

Motion and Notice of Motion: 14.41. What is a motion? 336. 14.42. Return day of motion 338. 14.43. Information you need to prepare a notice of motion 338. 14.44. What to do about the notice of motion and affidavit 339.

Affidavit for Use in Court: 14.45. Analysis of affidavit 339. 14.46. How to prepare an affidavit for court use 340.

Orders: 14.47. Analysis of an order 342. 14.48. How to prepare an order 342. 14.49. What to do about an order 344.

Findings of Fact and Conclusions (or Rulings) of Law: 14.50 What the "findings of fact and conclusions (or rulings) of law" are 346. 14.51. How to prepare findings of fact and conclusions (or rulings) of law 347. 14.52. What to do about findings of fact and conclusions (or rulings) of law 347.

Instructions to the Jury: 14.53. What an instruction to the jury is 348. 14.54. How to prepare an instruction to the jury 348.

Judgments and Decrees: 14.55. What judgments and decrees are 348. 14.56. How to prepare a judgment or decree 349. 14.57. Number of copies 349. 14.58. What to do about a judgment or decree 349.

15. How to Handle Records on Appeal, Briefs, and Citations **353**

15.1. Rules of the reviewing court 353. 15.2. Methods for review by a higher court 354. 15.3. Diary entries 354. 15.4. Change in caption of case 355. 15.5. Designation of parties to an appeal 355. 15.6. Notice of appeal 356. 15.7. Service on opposing counsel 356.

Contents and Preparation of the Record on Appeal: 15.8. What is a record on appeal? 357. 15.9. Assignment of errors and instructions to the clerk 357. 15.10. Who prepares the record 359. 15.11. How to prepare the record 359. 15.12. Format and make-up of record 360. 15.13. Binding, volumes, and title 360. 15.14. Certification, filing, and service 360.

The Brief: 15.15. Nature of a brief 360. 15.16. Preliminaries to preparing the brief 361. 15.17. Time element 361. 15.18. Preparation of the brief 361. 15.19. Application for oral argument 363. 15.20. Procedure when having a brief printed 367.

Citations: 15.21. What is a citation? 370. 15.22. How to take citations in shorthand 370. 15.23. Accuracy of citations 370. 15.24. Official reports and the National Reporter System 371. 15.25. How to cite a constitution 371. 15.26. How to cite statutes and codes 372. 15.27. How to cite cases in official reports and reporters 372. 15.28. Named reporters 374. 15.29. String citations 374. 15.30. How to cite an unpublished case 374. 15.31. How to cite slip decisions 374. 15.32. How to cite treatises 374. 15.33. How to cite law reviews 375. 15.34. How to cite legal newspapers 375. 15.35. Underscoring and italicizing 375. 15.36. Spacing of abbreviations 375. 15.37. Placement of citations 375. 15.38. Illustrations of citations 376.

PART IV Assisting in Specialized Practice

16. Assisting in Partnership Formation and Incorporation **381**

Corporations: 16.1. What is a corporation? 382. 16.2. Steps in the organization of a corporation 383. 16.3. Who may form a corporation? 384. 16.4. State of incorporation 384. 16.5. Memorandum preliminary to preparation of incorporating papers 384. 16.6. Reservation of name 385. 16.7. Incorporation papers 387. 16.8. Preparation of the articles of incorporation 387. 16.9. Execution of the incorporation papers 390. 16.10. Filing the incorporation papers and payment of fees 392.

Organization Meetings: 16.11. Necessity and purpose of organization meeting 393. 16.12. Preparation for the organization meeting 393. 16.13. Corporate outfit 393. 16.14. Waiver of notice of organization meeting 394.

16.15. Preparation of bylaws 394. 16.16. Minutes of first meeting of incorporators 394. 16.17. Minutes of first meeting of directors 394. 16.18. Resolution opening a bank account 395. 16.19. Preparation of stock certificates 398.

Partnerships: 16.20. What is a partnership? 398. 16.21. How a partnership is formed 398. 16.22. Preparation of partnership agreement 399.

17. Acting as Corporate Secretary **401**

17.1. Information folder 402.

Corporate Meetings: 17.2. Kinds of meetings 402. 17.3. Preparations for meetings 402. 17.4. Meeting folder 403. 17.5. Notice of stockholders' meeting 403. 17.6. Waiver of notice of stockholders' meeting 403. 17.7. Quorum at a stockholders' meeting 404. 17.8. Proxies and proxy statement 404. 17.9. Notice of directors' meeting 405. 17.10. Quorum at directors' meeting 405. 17.11. Preservation of notice 405. 17.12. The agenda 406. 17.13. Reservation and preparation of the meeting room 406. 17.14. Directors' fees 406. 17.15. Material to take to meetings 407. 17.16. Drafting resolutions before meetings 407. 17.17. Preparations for taking notes at meetings 408. 17.18. Taking notes at meetings 408.

Minutes: 17.19. The minute book 409. 17.20 Arrangement of contents of combined minute book 410. 17.21. Contents of minutes 410. 17.22. Preparation of draft of minutes 411. 17.23. How to prepare minutes in final form 411. 17.24. Correction of errors in minutes 412. 17.25. Certified extract of minutes 412. 17.26. Indexing of minutes 413.

Issuance and Transfer of Stock of a Small Corporation: 17.27. Authority to issue certificate 415. 17.28. Stock certificate book 415. 17.29. Original issue and transfer of stock 415. 17.30. Issuance of certificate of stock 417. 17.31. Transfer of certificate 417. 17.32. Separate form of assignment 418.

The Corporation Calendar: 17.33. Need for a corporation calendar 419. 17.34. How to keep the corporation calendar 420. 17.35. Where to get dates for the corporation calendar 420.

Change of Corporate Name: 17.36. Details when corporate name is changed 421.

Specimen Corporate Forms: No. 1. Minutes of first meeting of incorporators of a corporation 421. No. 2. Waiver of notice of first meeting of incorporators 423. No. 3. Waiver of notice of first meeting of directors 423. No. 4. Notice of annual meeting of stockholders 423. No. 5. Notice of special meeting of stockholders, indicating purpose of meeting 424. No. 6. Affidavit of secretary that notice of annual meeting of stockholders was mailed 424. No. 7. Affidavit of secretary of publication of notice of stockholders' meeting 424. No. 8. Proxy for special meeting of stockholders 425. No. 9. Notice of special meeting of directors, specifying purposes 425. No. 10. Minutes of annual meeting of directors 425. No. 11. Resolution of directors authorizing sale and issue of stock to persons determined by executive committee 427. No. 12. Resolution of directors amending a particular bylaw upon authorization of stockholders 427. No. 13. Directors' resolution accepting resignation of a member of board 427. No. 14. Directors' resolution accepting resignation of officer 428. No. 15. Directors' resolution expressing gratitude for services of resigning officer 428. No. 16. Blanket resolution of directors authorizing issuance of duplicate certificate in event of loss 428. No. 17. Excerpt of minutes showing adoption of minutes of previous meeting as corrected 428. No. 18. Resolution of directors (or stockholders) extending sympathy upon death of associate 428.

18. Assisting in Real Estate Practice
and Foreclosure **431**

18.1. Pattern followed for each instrument 431.

Real Property Descriptions: 18.2. How land is described 432. 18.3. Section and township description 432. 18.4. Metes and bounds description 434. 18.5. The plat system 434. 18.6. How to type real property descriptions 436. 18.7. How to check land descriptions 436.

Deeds: 18.8. What is a deed? 437. 18.9. Parties to a deed 437. 18.10. Forms of deeds 437. 18.11. Kinds of deeds 438. 18.12. Printed forms of deeds 438. 18.13. Checklist of information needed to fill in form 440. 18.14. Typed deeds 441. 18.15. Statements and clauses in deeds 441. 18.16. Revenue stamps and state taxes 443. 18.17. How to cancel the stamps 443. 18.18. Recording 443. 18.19. How to prepare a deed 443.

Mortgages: 18.20. What is a mortgage? 445. 18.21. Parties to a mortgage 445. 18.22. Designation of the parties 445. 18.23. Forms of mortgages 446. 18.24. Purchase money mortgage 446. 18.25. Printed mortgages 447. 18.26. Checklist of information needed to fill in mortgage or deed of trust 447. 18.27. Typed mortgages and deeds of trust 448. 18.28. Statements and clauses in mortgages 448. 18.29. State tax 450. 18.30. How to prepare a mortgage 450.

Leases: 18.31. What is a lease? 451. 18.32. Parties to a lease 452. 18.33. Classification of leases 452. 18.34. Printed forms 452. 18.35. Standard lease clauses 452. 18.36. Checklist of standard clauses in commercial leases 455. 18.37. Style of typed lease 456. 18.38. Execution, acknowledgment, and recording of lease 457. 18.39. How to prepare a lease 457.

Purchase and Sale Agreements: 18.40. What is a purchase and sale agreement? 457. 18.41. Necessity for a purchase and sale agreement 458. 18.42. Types of contracts of sale of land 458. 18.43. Parties to a purchase and sale agreement 459. 18.44. How to prepare a purchase and sale agreement 459. 18.45. Checklist of information necessary to fill in form

459. 18.46. Earnest money 460. 18.47. Escrow for the sale of real property 460.

Title Closings and Evidence of Title: 18.48. What is a title closing? 461. 18.49. Evidence of title 461. 18.50. Abstract of title 461. 18.51. Opinion of title 463. 18.52. Certificate of title 464. 18.53. Title insurance policies 464. 18.54. Torrens certificate 464. 18.55. Preparations for closing 464.

Preparation of Closing Statement: 18.56. What is a closing statement? 466. 18.57. How to calculate adjustments 467. 18.58. Example of calculation of tax adjustment 467. 18.59. Example of calculation of interest adjustment 467. 18.60. Example of calculation of insurance adjustment 471. 18.61. Example of calculation of rent adjustment 471. 18.62. Miscellaneous payments 471. 18.63. Suggested form of closing statement 472.

Foreclosure Actions: 18.64. What is a foreclosure action? 473. 18.65. Papers necessary for institution of foreclosure action 473. 18.66. Information needed to prepare papers in foreclosure action 474. 18.67. Venue 474. 18.68. Parties to a foreclosure action 474. 18.69. Fictitious names 474. 18.70. Description of note or bond 475. 18.71. Description of mortgage 475. 18.72. Description of property 475. 18.73. When is a mortgage considered in default 476.

Procedure in Foreclosure Action: 18.74. Title search for foreclosures 476. 18.75. Preparation of complaint 476. 18.76. Number of copies 477. 18.77. Lis pendens 477. 18.78. Preparation of notice of lis pendens 478. 18.79. Preparation of summons 478. 18.80. Filing and service of summons, complaint, and lis pendens 478. 18.81. Follow-up of process service 480. 18.82. Party sheet 480. 18.83. Other steps in foreclosure proceedings 481. 18.84. Checklist of what to do in foreclosure action 482.

**19. Assisting with Probate and
Estate Administration** **483**

19.1. Distinction between executor and administrator 483. 19.2. The lawyer's part in the administration of an estate 484.

Probate of Will: 19.3. The executor's right to act 484. 19.4. Probate of will 485. 19.5. Parties to a probate proceeding 485. 19.6. Copy of will and affidavit 487. 19.7. Petition for probate of will 487. 19.8. Transfer tax affidavit 493. 19.9. Citation and waiver in probate proceeding 493. 19.10. How to prepare a waiver of citation 493. 19.11. How to prepare a citation 495. 19.12. Preparations for hearing 495. 19.13. Notice of probate 498. 19.14. Deposition of witnesses to the will 498. 19.15. Oath of executor 498. 19.16. Decree admitting will to probate 499. 19.17. Letters testamentary 499. 19.18. Notice to creditors 500.

Appointment of Administrator: 19.19. Application for letters of administration 500. 19.20. Parties 500. 19.21. Who has prior right to letters of administration 500. 19.22. Necessary papers in application for letters of administration 501. 19.23. How to prepare petition; oath; designation of clerk 501. 19.24. Renunciation 506. 19.25. Citations 506. 19.26. Notice of application for letters of administration 508. 19.27. Letters of administration 508.

20. Handling Commercial Collections **509**

20.1. Commercial law lists 509. 20.2. Office procedures affecting collections 510. 20.3. How to file collection matters 510. 20.4. Filing system 510. 20.5. Acknowledgment of claim 514. 20.6. Collection letters 515. 20.7. Reports to the forewarder 516. 20.8. Installment payments 516. 20.9. Record of collections 516. 20.10. Remitting 517. 20.11. Fees 517. 20.12. Forwarding an item for collection 517.

Uncontested Suit: 20.13. When the lawyer recommends suit 518. 20.14. Summons and complaint 519. 20.15. Preparation and service of summons and short-form complaint 519. 20.16. Checklist of information needed to draw summons and complaint in suit on a collection item 519. 20.17. Judgment by default 520. 20.18. How to prepare a judgment by default 520.

PART V *Legal Facts and Secretarial Aids*

Forms of Address: Honorary and Official Positions: United States Government Officials 527. State and Local Government Officials 531. Court Officials 533. United States Diplomatic Representatives 534. Foreign Officials and Representatives 535. The Armed Forces/The Army 537. The Armed Forces/The Navy 538. The Armed Forces/Air Force; Marine Corps; Coast Guard 539. Church Dignitaries/Catholic Faith 540. Church Dignitaries/Jewish Faith 534. Church Dignitaries/Protestant Faith 543. College and University Officials 545. United Nations Officials 547.

Latin Words and Phrases: 549

Glossary of Legal Terms: 557

State Requirements for Age of Testator and Number of Witnesses to Will: 600

Courts of Record and Judicial Circuits: I. Federal Courts of Record in the United States and Their Members 602. II. State Courts of Record in the United States and Their Members 602. III. Judicial Circuits and the States and Territories in Each Circuit 609. IV. States and Territories and Judicial Circuit in Which Each Is Located 610.

Authentication of Instruments: 611

Notaries Public: 612

Statutes of Limitations in Number of Years: 614

Official Reports and How They Are Cited: 616

Reporters of National Report System: 618

Approved Method of Citing Compilations of Statutes and Codes: 620

Index **623**

Legal Secretary's
Complete Handbook

PART 1

GENERAL DUTIES

IN THE LAW OFFICE

1   Working in a Law Office

2   Contacts with Clients and Other Callers

3   Reminder Systems and Practices

4   Filing in the Law Office

5   Handling Legal and Business Correspondence

6   How to Keep Books and Records

7   Using References in Legal Research

8   Preparing Material for Printing

1

Working in a

Law Office

An understanding of what a law office is like—how it functions—its personnel—is needed as a basis for an intelligent performance of your duties. This chapter describes (1)what is expected of you in a law office; (2) the training and effort necessary for a lawyer to build a worthwhile practice; (3) the organization and personnel of a law firm; (4) the physical aspects of a law office; (5) the customary processing of a new matter when it is received by a law firm, before any work is done on it; and (6) the distinctive features of typing and dictation in a law office.

YOU AND THE LAWYER

1.1. The law-office team. Whether you work for one or several attorneys, you are part of the law-office team. To pull your share of the load, you must understand the lawyer's work and must take an interest in and think about it, so you will be able to do more than what is expected of you. You must be loyal and discreet and be governed by high standards in all of your actions. A secretary, in addition to being able to take shorthand rapidly and transcribe it accurately, or to transcribe from machine dictation, must have initiative, administrative ability, judgment, and a deep sense of responsibility.

1.2. Ethics in the law office. You are bound by the same code of ethics as your employer. You cannot solicit business for the lawyer; you must regard everything you know about a client or a case as confidential. You must never divulge the contents of a written document in the office, without permission from the lawyer. You must never talk outside the office about a case, even if the talk is merely an anecdote. Frequently you may be tempted to entertain friends with interesting tidbits about socially prominent clients, but you must always resist the temptation. Irreparable harm can result from mentioning anything about what is transpiring in a case. For example, suppose a lawyer dictates an application for injunction against removal of certain property from the county, so he or she can levy upon it. If you should mention this, the owner of the property, especially in a small town, might hear about it and remove the property before the judge signs the injunction. Information received from clients in the course of your work is a *privileged communication* (see page 41). To help you understand this matter of ethics more fully, write to the American Bar Association, 1155 East 60th Street, Chicago, Illinois 60637, for a copy of their code of professional responsibility.

1.3. Legal training. A lawyer spends many years in training for admittance to the bar. This usually includes four years in college, three years in law school, and a state examination. A practicing lawyer finds that competition is keen; practice is arduous for almost all lawyers and not always lucrative. The profession is overcrowded in large metropolitan areas; every year thousands drop out of the race and go into business or another profession because they cannot earn a living in the practice of law. Yet, thousands of young men and women enter law school every year, with the hope of eventually achieving a foothold in this honorable and fascinating profession. Those who succeed must face increasing demands upon them and thus they require the full cooperation and assistance of every member of the law-office team.

1.4. Requirements for admission to the bar. Each state has its own requirements for admission to the bar. In every state the requirements include four factors: academic training, legal training, moral character, and belief in and loyalty to the form of the United States government.

In almost all states the applicant for admission to the bar must take an examination, even though he or she is a law school graduate. Graduates of a few schools have been admitted without examination in some states. Admission to practice in one state does not license the attorney to practice in another state. He or she must comply with the rules that each state has for admission of an "attorney applicant." However, many states will admit an attorney from another state without examination after he or she has practiced a specified time, provided the applicant meets other requirements. Some states require the attorney applicant to take an examination.

License to practice in one or more states does not admit the lawyer to practice in the federal courts. To be admitted to practice in the United State Supreme Court, an attorney must have practiced three years in the highest court in his state or territory. A member of the bar moves the attorney's admission in open court. Requirements for admission to the federal courts of appeal and district courts vary with the circuit and the district.

An attorney may obtain special permission to argue a particular case before a court in which he or she is not licensed to practice. This often happens in criminal cases when the accused wants a nationally famous criminal lawyer to represent him in the state in which he is to be tried.

1.5. Law degrees. The law degrees obtainable and the abbreviations of them follow. Notice that in some cases the abbreviation of the Latin word *juris,* meaning law, is used. (LL.D. is sometimes conferred as an honorary degree.)

Bachelor of Laws	LL.B; B.L.
Bachelor of Civil Law	J.C.B.; B.C.L.
Master of Laws	LL.M; M.L.
Doctor of Laws	LL.D; J.D.
Doctor of Law	Jur. D.
Doctor of Civil Law	J.C.D.; D.C.L.
Juris Civilis Doctor	J.C.D.
Doctor of Jurisprudence	J.D.
Juris Doctor	Jur. D.; J.D.
Jurum Doctor	J.D.
Doctor of Juristic Science	J.S.D.
Doctor of Both Laws	J.U.D.

Traditionally, after three years of study, law schools have conferred a bachelor's degree, generally the LL.B. But in recent years, in recognition of the length of study required, some schools now confer a J.D. or its equivalent.

1.6. Specialization in the law field. General practioners in law, as in medicine, are gradually disappearing. Specialization in law is more prevalent in large cities than in small places. If you work for a specialist or are assigned to a particular department in a large firm, your work will probably be in only one field: corporation law (chapters 16 and 17); real estate matters and foreclosures (chapter 18); probate matters (chapter 19); or some other specialized field such as taxation, administrative law and practice, or domestic relations.

The trend toward specialization results from the lawyer's inclination and liking for a special field and from the human impossibility of becoming expert in every field. Specialization is a great timesaver for both the lawyer and the staff. The lawyer who handles a tax matter as incidental to his or her other practice must spend hours doing research on a problem that a tax specialist could dispose of in a few minutes, because the specialist deals with the same problem every day.

1.7. Building a practice. Graduating from law school and being admitted to the bar do not mean the lawyer will succeed in building a worthwhile practice. He or she must have not only the necessary training and knowledge of law, but a personality that will attract clients, gain their confidence, and hold them.

Traditionally, lawyers were not permitted to advertise under the Canons of Ethics or the more recent Code of Professional Responsibility of the American Bar Association, but the U. S. Supreme Court has struck down this prohibition as unconstitutional. State courts and bar associations are working together now to establish standards and guidelines for advertising. However, lawyers have always been able to engage in practices such as sending out an announcement card stating that he or she is engaged in the practice of law at a certain address. The lawyer also sends these announcements when he or she joins a new firm or moves the offices. Figure 1.1 illustrates an announcement when the lawyer first enters practice; figure 1.2, when he or she resumes practice; and figure 1.3, when he or she moves the offices. It is helpful for the secretary to compile and maintain a permanent list of people to whom

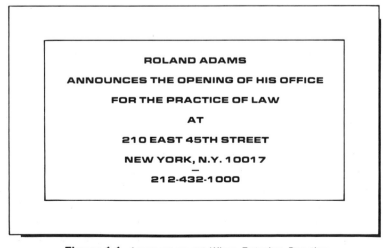

ROLAND ADAMS

ANNOUNCES THE OPENING OF HIS OFFICE

FOR THE PRACTICE OF LAW

AT

210 EAST 45TH STREET

NEW YORK, N.Y. 10017

212-432-1000

Figure 1.1. *Announcement When Entering Practice.*

One West Avenue
Chicago, Illinois 60616

Donald T. Lewis, having completed his term as a
Justice of the Supreme Court of the State of Illinois, announces
his return to the practice of law with the firm of

Wilson & Lewis

January 15, 198-   *312-665-4000*

Figure 1.2. *Announcement When Resuming Practice.*

DOUGLAS, HART & MORRIS

ANNOUNCE THE REMOVAL OF THEIR OFFICES TO

400 MARKET STREET

SAN FRANCISCO, CALIFORNIA 94105

WHERE THEY WILL CONTINUE THE GENERAL PRACTICE

OF LAW UNDER THE FIRM NAME OF

DOUGLAS, HART, MORRIS & WEBER

AUGUST 1, 198-   415-010-1000

Figure 1.3. *Announcement of Removal of Offices.*

announcements may be sent. Keep the list on 3- by 5-inch index cards and enter regularly any additions or changes that come to your attention.

The cards may be mailed to the groups listed below.

1. *Friends and acquaintances.* You will have to depend largely upon the lawyer to compile this list originally, but you can maintain it by

adding the names of contacts he or she makes that you know about and by keeping the addresses on the list up-to-date.

2. *Members of the local bar.* You can probably obtain this from the classified telephone directory. Volumes I through V of *Martindale-Hubbell Law Directory* contain a list of lawyers and their addresses in the United States and Canada. Every law library (chapter 7) and almost every law office have this directory, which contains a wealth of useful information about law and lawyers in various jurisdictions. Time spent becoming familiar with its organization and contents is well worthwhile. Also, local, county, and state bar associations usually publish lists of their members, and each law office should have a copy of the list or lists of local lawyers.

3. *County officials.* Each state publishes a "bluebook," directory, register, or roster, which contains the names of county officers, state officers, judges, members of the senate and house, and names of departments and administrative offices. Probably a more accessible source for the names of county officials is the clerks' office in the county courthouse.

4. *Classmates.* You can get the names and addresses of the lawyer's college and law-school classmates from the permanent secretary of his or her class. If there is no permanent class secretary, write to the alumni secretary who will refer you to the proper source for the information or send it to you.

5. *Other lawyers.* The names of lawyers in other localities with whom your employer is personally acquainted should be put on the announcement list.

6. *Clients.* The name of each client should be added to the announcement list.

1.8. The lawyer's outside activities. The legal profession is a public service; its purpose is the administration of justice. Therefore, the lawyer's first interest in outside activities is usually the work of his bar association—that is his duty as a member of the profession. But the lawyer also takes a wholehearted interest in civic affairs—the school, church, charities, and any movement that will improve the community in which he or she lives. The lawyer's position in the community demands that he or she participate in its affairs. Participation is the lawyer's duty; paralegals, legal secretaries, and other personnel should make it theirs. You should read the reports of the bar association and keep abreast of what is going on locally and nationally. Be always on the alert for news items that will interest the lawyer and call them to his or her attention. You will soon learn that the lawyer appreciates your interest and your willingness to help by doing things beyond the scope of your actual duties.

1.9. The lawyer's relationship with clients. A lawyer is a fiduciary. His or her relationship with a client is one of trust and confidence. The lawyer represents a client's interest to the best of his or her ability. The lawyer does not use his or her position of trust and confidence to further personal or private interests. The lawyer never discusses the client's business with outsiders but considers it strictly confidential. So sacred is the relationship between lawyer and client that information given to the lawyer by the client is a *privileged communication*, that is, the lawyer cannot be compelled to testify concerning it.

1.10. Fees. A fairly standard charge is made in many communities for certain items of work, including drawing deeds, mortgages, examining abstracts, evicting tenants, obtaining default divorces, foreclosing mortgages, organizing corporations, and probating estates, providing these matters have no unusual complications. Bar associations sometimes publish sample fee schedules for services performed by attorneys. The legal secretary should have a copy of the local bar association's schedules on hand so the attorney can consult them when necessary. Otherwise, there is no standard basis for determining the amount of a fee; each office has its own method. The time element is a large factor. For that reason, an accurate record of the time spent on each item is important.

The type of fee charged is important to you for record and bookkeeping purposes (chapter 6). Fees are classified as follows:

1. *Single retainer.* The client retains the lawyer for a specific case and agrees to pay a specified fee. Frequently part of the retainer is paid in advance.

2. *Yearly retainer.* Many organizations are constantly in need of legal advice and have numerous legal matters to be looked after. They retain lawyers on an annual basis. When a client is on a yearly retainer basis, you should know whether a specific matter is covered by the retainer or is to be charged for separately.

3. *Contingent fee.* In certain types of cases, the lawyer may agree to take a case for a client for a percentage of the amount recovered. The fee is contingent upon the successful outcome of the case. Contingent fees are customary in personal injury cases, especially if the client is unable to pay for the lawyer's time except out of the damages he or she might recover.

4. *Forwarding fee.* Frequently a case is referred to a lawyer by an out-of-town firm. Often, although not always, a percentage of the fee earned is sent to the forwarding attorney. The American Bar Association, however, does not approve of the forwarding fee.

5. *Collection charges.* The collection of commercial items is a special branch of law practice (chapter 20). There is a standard charge for collection cases, based on a percentage of the amount collected, with an additional fee if suit is necessary.

ORGANIZATION AND PERSONNEL OF A LAW FIRM

1.11. Kind of business organization. Formerly state statutes did not permit lawyers to incorporate—a lawyer either practiced alone or entered into a partnership with one or more lawyers. Many states now permit lawyers to form professional corporations or professional associations. The lawyer's highly personal obligation to his or her client is not affected by incorporation.

A law firm frequently consists of a senior partner or partners, a junior partner or partners, and associate lawyers. Even if a lawyer does not have a partner, he or she frequently has associates. They are paid a salary and do not share in the firm's profits, nor are they responsible for its obligations. You will notice that when lawyer's names are listed on the letterhead of a law firm or on the door of a law office, a line separates one group of names from another group. The names below the line are the names of associate lawyers who are not members of the firm.

In any law firm, whether large or small, a designated partner is responsible for the smooth functioning of the organization. Generally this partner is called the "managing partner." All of the service departments—stenographic, accounting, filing, maintenance of court docket—are under his or her supervision.

1.12. Personnel in a law office. One of the many compensations of working in a law office is the type of people with whom you are associated. The prestige and dignity of a law office demand that every position in the firm be filled by a person of intelligence and refinement. The personnel might consist of:

Partners
Associate lawyers
Managing clerk
Law clerks
Docket clerks
Office manager

Paralegals
Supervisor of secretaries and stenographers
Supervisor of equipment and machines
Secretaries
Stenographers
Proofreaders
Receptionist
Bookkeepers
Clerks
File Clerk
Mail Clerks
Telephone operators
Automatic typewriter operators
Computer operators
Office boys and pages

The number of persons in each position depends upon the size of the firm and the volume of work. Several of the positions are filled by the same person if the volume of work is small.

Paralegals, or legal assistants, have become important additions to the personnel of a law firm in recent years. Paralegals usually have a college background including paralegal studies or they may have completed a private paralegal training program. Some firms prefer to train their most experienced legal secretaries to become paralegals. In any case, the paralegals' education and training enable them to help lawyers perform many tasks, such as handling legal research and analyses, drafting and preparing legal documents, interviewing clients and witnesses, and organizing and maintaining dockets and files. Since the field is new and still evolving, paralegal duties vary widely from office to office; members of the profession are found in all sectors of society— law firms, courts, business and financial institutions, governement, and so on.

1.13. The secretary's duties. In a small law office, the work and responsibilities of all the service departments fall on the secretary. In a large office, some of the responsibilities are hers; in any event, she should be familiar with them so she can cooperate properly with other departments. In addition to stenographic work, the secretary in a law office has some or all of the following duties and responsibilities:

1. Writing letters (chapter 5)
2. Making appointments (chapters 2 and 3)
3. Taking telephone calls (chapter 2)
4. Filing (chapter 4)

5. Maintaining the diary and tickler file (chapter 3)

6. Keeping account of charges, disbursements, and collections (chapter 6)

7. Following office cases on court calendars (chapter 12)

8. Proofreading (chapter 8)

9. Maintaining the court docket or suit register (chapter 12)

10. Making reservations (chapter 5)

11. Ordering supplies (chapter 1)

12. Greeting clients (chapter 2)

1.14. Deportment. The dignity of a law firm should be maintained at all times by its personnel. An impression of refinement is reflected in (1) knowledge of professional customs and practices, (2) good manners, and (3) personal appearance.

The customs and practices in the legal profession that secretaries, paralegals, and other members of the law-office team should know are covered throughout this book.

Anyone who has aspired to work in a law office must have good manners, and politeness, friendliness, graciousness, and consideration for others should be well-established habits.

THE LAW OFFICE

1.15. Layout. The ideal suite of law offices consists of a reception room, a workroom, a library, a file room, a conference room, and a series of private offices. The reception room, workroom, and file room may be combined as a general office; the law books may be in various offices; there may be no conference room, but each lawyer *always* has a private office. The confidential nature of legal matters and the desire of clients for privacy demand this. Paralegals also may have individual offices, especially when they are expected to deal directly with clients. Glass partitions so common to business offices are not used in law offices because they do not ensure privacy. Large law offices usually have a series of private suites, consisting of an office for the lawyer and an office for the secretary who is assigned to him or her. Lawyers sometimes share an office suite, each lawyer conducting his or her practice as a sole practitioner.

Here are some suggestions you can make about the layout of a suite of law offices when you are asked for ideas:

1. If the workroom is also the waiting room, arrange the furniture so

it is not necessary for people passing in and out of the general office to enter the part used as a workroom.

2. The secretary should be located as near as possible to the lawyer to whom she is assigned.

3. Paralegals often need private quarters since their duties may involve confidential matters such as interviewing clients and prospective clients.

4. A private exit from the lawyer's private office is desirable so a client does not have to leave through the waiting room where other clients are waiting. It also affords the lawyer an opportunity to go and come without being observed.

1.16. The furniture. One piece of furniture that requires special comment is the *legal blank cabinet*. Every law office uses a large variety of printed legal forms or blanks. They must be kept in good condition and must be quickly available for use. There are many cabinets designed for this special purpose.

As in any office, secretarial desks are preferable to typewriter desks if the person using the desk has any clerical work to do.

1.17. Equipment. In addition to the equipment in almost every office, certain items are practically indispensable in a modern law office: a copyholder, an electric typewriter, a calculator, a photocopier, and dictating equipment; some large offices also require computers, automatic typewriters, and information storage and retrieval equipment.

Electric typewriters are basic to the modern law office, and many offices select models with the latest features, such as self-correcting devices and interchangeable typefaces. Photocopiers, too, are essential for efficient legal work. Most law offices now use copiers to make accurate and legible copies in lieu of carbon copies. However, the secretary should always ask to be certain copier copies are permissible for the work in question.

Many secretaries use a copyholder, which has an adjustable line-spacing attachment that decreases the possibility of skipping or repeating lines when doing copy work. The attachment is operated by depressing a lever with the right little finger. This movement soon becomes as automatic as depressing the space bar on a typewriter. Another advantage of the copyholder is that it is placed back of the typewriter and holds the paper in front of you, thus avoiding the strained position necessary when copying from material placed on the side of the desk. There are several makes of copyholders, but they all work on the same general principle.

1.18. Stationery supplies. In addition to the usual stationery used for correspondence, law offices have many kinds of paper for legal work. Often it is the secretary's responsibility to order stationery and other office supplies. To be certain such items are reordered in adequate time before the supply is depleted, it is important to maintain accurate records of the quantity on hand at all times, with projected reorder dates clearly marked on the calendar as a reminder. The stationery supplies used for various purposes in a typical law office follow:

"Legal cap" is white paper, 8″ by 13″ or 8½″ by 14″, with a wide ruled margin at the left and a narrow ruled margin at the right. It is used for court papers and for legal instruments, such as agreements, contracts, and the like. Substance 16 is used for the original or ribbon copy. Legal cap, substance 20, is preferable for the original of wills. In some states legal cap has numbers along the left margin. Copies are made by copier, on bond or onion skin, or with carbon sets.

"Legal-size" paper, plain without the ruled margins, same substance as the legal cap, is also used for legal instruments of various kinds and for court papers in some jurisdictions. The type of paper preferred by courts varies in different jurisdictions, even within a single state. Consult the clerk of court to determine proper sizes for court papers.

Short white paper, approximately 8″ by 10½″, with ruled margins, substance 16, is used for briefs and law memoranda.

Short white paper, approximately 8″ by 10½″, plain without ruled margins, is used for legal documents that are not written on long paper. The choice varies with the office.

"Manuscript covers" are of a heavy colored paper, often blue, about 25 percent cotton fiber. Legal instruments and court papers are bound in them.

Legal-size covers, with or without the firm name, are used for binding legal instruments and court papers. Legal-size covers with printed panels are frequently used for binding court papers. These covers are referred to as *backs*, because they cover only the back of the paper bound in them.

White covers, with or without the firm name engraved on them, are used for binding wills.

Short covers, with or without the firm name, are used for binding briefs, law memoranda, and legal instruments typed on short paper. They are double and are bound at the side.

Legal-size yellow manifold is used for drafts.

Legal scratch pads are pads of 8½″ by 14″ yellow paper, with ruled margin and lines. See that there is always one on the lawyer's desk and one in his or her briefcase. The lawyer uses these pads for making notes, writing drafts in longhand, and the like.

"Firm letterheads," 8½" by 11", substance 24, 20, or 16, are used for the original of firm correspondence. Some firms also have an 8½" by 7½" letterhead for short letters.

"Continuation sheets," loosely called second sheets, of the same substance as the letterheads are used for additional pages of a letter. They do not have a letterhead on them but usually have the firm name engraved or printed on them.

"Firm letterheads" often marked "copy," on unglazed onion skin, substance 9, may be used for copies of correspondence. Other copies are made on the office copier.

Colored onion skin or yellow manifold may be used for the file copy of correspondence.

"Executive letterheads," 6" by 7", engraved with the attorney's name, are used for the attorney's personal correspondence. This paper frequently has a kid finish.

"Monarch" size envelopes, 3⅞" by 7½" are used with the executive stationery. No 6¾ (3⅝" by 6½") and No. 10 (4⅛" by 9½") envelopes fit the 8½" by 11" letterheads.

Envelopes of heavy manila stock (about 40 pounds), 3½" bottom flap, 3½" top flap gummed solid, with a ¾" scored shoulder also gummed, are used for mailing bulky documents and papers that can be folded.

A NEW MATTER

1.19. New case report. When a new matter is received in a law office, it must be processed in a routine manner before the lawyer actually begins to work on it. In the well-organized law office, a new case report is made immediately on every matter received. The lawyer who interviews the client obtains the following information:

1. Name, address, and telephone number of the client
2. Name of opposing party, and his or her address and telephone number, if known
3. Attorney for opposing party, if any

Occasionally these data are given to the secretary by the client as he or she leaves the office, but it is usually more diplomatic for the lawyer to make a note of the information.

1.20. What the secretary does. The secretary's first job is to get the information from the lawyer as soon as the client leaves the office, so she can make up a new case report. The reports also call for one or more of the following items of information, which the lawyer should indicate to the secretary.

1. The general nature of the case, whether general litigation, probate, foreclosure, etc.

2. Whether the case is on an annual retainer basis or is a single case. This affects the bookkeeping (chapter 6).

3. Whether the client is new or old.

4. Whether stenographic services are to be billed separately or included in the overall fee.

5. Name of the junior partner or associate and the paralegal to be assigned to the case.

Printed forms are provided for new case reports. Frequently the lawyer makes out the reports, because they call for very little writing. Two types of forms are illustrated in figures 1.4 and 1.5. Notice that the form illustrated in figure 1.5 even has a space in which the attorney indicates whether or not the client is to be added to the firm announcement list described on page 28. When the report is filled out, it is ready to be routed.

MORGAN, BURBANK & CHAMBERS
REPORT OF NEW CASE OR MATTER
MUST BE TYPEWRITTEN

Date:

Name of Client:

CLASSIFICATION

☐ General Litigation

☐ Corporate and Financial

☐ Indiv. Pers., Trust

Address:

☐ Estate and Litigation as to Estate

Title of Case or Matter:

REAL ESTATE

☐ General

Court:

☐ Certiorari

Member in Charge:

☐ Dispossess

Assistant:

☐ Foreclosure

(CHECK AND RETURN PROMPTLY)

1. Charge Register:........................ 2. Managing Clerk:........................ 3. Bookkeepers:........................

4. Budget Committee:........................ 5. Files:........................

Figure 1.4. *New Case Report.*

1.21. Routing of new case report. The routing procedure varies with the office, but the following order of routing is practical and can be adapted to the requirements of any office. If you are a secretary in a small office, instead of routing the new case report you will take the steps indicated by this procedure.

HALL and DOBB
NEW CASE REPORT

File No.

Received by...

For Credit of...   Date..

Attorney receiving a new case will fill out this blank, sign it, and then send it to Files.
Files will assign the file number, index under the names given in 1 to 4; note any instructions as to filing in 5; initial

here........................and send to Assistant Managing Partner.

Assistant Managing Partner will assign attorneys, initial, etc. and send to the Accounting Department.
Accounting Department will see that the report is properly filled out, service ledger cards made, open a service ledger

account, and initial here..   ....
                                          Submitted by   Verified by

Accounting Department will list on weekly summary and initial here..

	Add to Firm Announcement List		Billing		Client	
Estimated Value of Case $_____			Retainer or Continuing	Single Cases	New	Old
Nature of Case	Yes ☐ No ☐		☐	☐	☐	☐

1. Name of Client...

    Address..

    ....

2. Title of Case...

    ....

3. Opposing Party...

    Address..

    ....

4. Additional Names (if any) ....

    that should be indexed..

    (Additional names should be given where the name of the person referring the case or the name of a person with whom there is to be much correspondence does not appear in 1, 2, or 3 above.)

5. Filing Instructions (if any)...

6. Remarks ....

Received by Assistant Managing Partner:.........................Date................................at...................

Attorney Responsible..

Assistant Assigned..

Junior Assigned...

Will case be litigated?

No ☐

Yes ☐

Doubtful ☐

2900 2-51 C.S.P. FORM 1A

From Reginald Heber Smith, Law Office Organization. *Courtesy American Bar Association Journal.*

Figure 1.5. *New Case Report—Another Form.*

1. File department. File number is assigned and a file opened. File clerk initials. (chapter 4)

2. Accounting department. Ledger sheet for the client and case is opened, after which disbursements may be made for and charged to the case. (chapter 6) Bookkeeper initials.

In an extremely large firm, there might be other departments or committees to which the report should be routed.

The new case is then returned to the filing department and filed. The mechanics of processing the case have been completed, and the attorney, the paralegal, and the secretary are ready to work on it. The matter might consist of drawing an instrument (Part 2), in which event the file will soon be closed (chapter 4); or it might involve litigation (part 3) that extends over a period of years; or it might be a matter in a specialized field of law (part 4), such as organizing a corporation (chapter 16). Regardless of the nature of the case, you, as secretary, will handle the dictation and typing (chapter 1), and, very probably, you will have contact with the client either in person or by telephone (chapter 2).

The subsequent chapters of this book will show you how to do in a professional manner any task that might arise in connection with the case.

TYPING AND DICTATION IN THE LAW OFFICE

1.22. The secretary's loose-leaf formbook. Every secretary in a law office should have a loose-leaf binder to hold copies of each kind of instrument used frequently in her office. The copy will show not only the style in which the instrument should be typed, but also the wording used by the lawyer for whom she works. Reference to your own loose-leaf book is much quicker than reference to a practice manual or to the file of a case that contains a similar instrument. Arrange the papers alphabetically according to the name of the instrument, or, if you prefer, break them down into litigation and nonlitigation papers. The binder should be legal size. It may be made out of heavy Manila stock.

1.23. Importance of understanding dictated material. Dictation is taken in shorthand at least part of the time in most law offices. However, mechanical dictating equipment is taking over an increasing portion of this work. These machines free the secretary for other work while the lawyer is dictating and allow the lawyer to dictate at time and places when the secretary is not available.

A well-trained legal stenographer could take dictation and transcribe it accurately without a notion of the meaning of the sentences, but she would consider her job boring and arduous. The dictated material is rarely monotonous and is intensely interesting to the secretary who understands what is being dictated. One of the objects of this book is to clarify what would otherwise be jargon to you.

Another difficult feature of dictation in a law office is the length of the material dictated. Frequently, dictation on one matter lasts three or four hours. Here, again, an understanding of what is being dictated changes the arduous task into a pleasant one. Being able to follow the lawyer's thought also enables you to take dictation more rapidly and to transcribe more accurately, thus saving time and eliminating rewrites.

1.24. Errors in the dictation. As a rule lawyers are excellent dictators. They think clearly and express themselves fluently, thus enabling the secretary to follow their trend of thought. However, sentences in legal work are long and involved and the best of dictators sometimes makes errors in grammar and sentence structure. Some of the responsibility for the English in the document is yours, and it is up to you to catch obvious errors. One of the most common errors is the omission of a main verb or a conjunction when a parenthetic clause intervenes. To detect an inaccuracy in sentence structure, read the independent clause in the sentence without the intervening subordinate clauses or parenthetic material. If you are following the dictator's thought, you will immediately realize something is wrong with the sentence. At the first break in the dictation, you should call the sentence to the dictator's attention, because you cannot supply the omission.

As an example, analyze the following sentence.

The courts below have decided, [although this plaintiff failed to bring her action within the time limit because an alternative remedy, which as against the employer was exclusive, was apparently granted to her by a statute] yet the courts are powerless to afford her any relief if under the express terms of the statute the action is now barred.

The words in brackets are parenthetic. During dictation the stenographer places a comma after *decided* and mentally awaits the objective clause that should follow. Without the intervening parenthetic clause, the sentence reads: "The courts below have decided, yet the courts are powerless. ..." In this instance, the dictator evidently intended to follow the material in brackets with the conjunction *that;* but, intent on the point he or she was making, the dictator lost sight of the sentence structure. The secretary immediately realizes the sentence is incomplete, but she cannot supply the word, because the dictator might have intended to say "... decided ... against the plaintiff, yet the court ...," instead of simply "... decided that ...." Thus, in such cases, call the omission to the lawyer's attention.

Another common error, and one you can easily detect and correct, is the repetition of the conjuction *that* in introducing a single clause when a phrase or clause intervenes between *that* and the clause it introduces. For example, in the sentence cited above, the dictator might easily have preceded and followed the bracketed material with *that,* instead of omitting it.

Another common slip on the part of the dictator that you must guard against is calling the plaintiff "defendant" and vice versa. You are more likely to detect this slip when transcribing your notes, or listening to machine dictation, than when taking dictation. If you have any doubt about which is accurate, check with the dictator.

1.25. Pairs of words that cause confusion. Many words used frequently in legal dictation sound alike and look alike when written in shorthand. Some of them have similar but not exact meanings and it is difficult to judge from the sense which is the correct word. A list of pairs of words that are confusing follows. It is limited to words used frequently in legal work and does not include words the secretary should have become thoroughly familiar with in school or in other fields of work, for example, *affect, effect*. Definitions of the words in this list that have a special legal significance are included in the glossary of legal terms in part 5. Do the following with reference to the pairs of words given below.

1. Fix firmly in your mind the meaning of each, particularly differences between meanings that are similar.

2. If the shorthand outlines for a pair of words are similar, make up a variation for one and become familiar with it.

3. When you are taking dictation, be particularly careful about the formation of the outlines for these words.

abjure, adjure	drawer, drawee
act, action	estop, stop
adverse, averse	in re, in rem
apperception, perception	interpellate, interpolate
arraign, arrange	judicial, judicious
atonement, attornment	jura, jurat
avoid, void	malfeasance, misfeasance,
avoidable, voidable	nonfeasance
case, cause	mandatary, mandatory
casual, causal	payor, payee
casualty, causality	persecute, prosecute
cite, site	plaintiff, plaintive
collision, collusion	precedence, precedents
comity, committee	prescribe, proscribe
cost, costs	presence, presents
corporal, corporeal	return, writ
descent, dissent	situate, situated
defer, differ	state, estate
depositary, depository	status quo, in statu quo
devisable, divisible	theron, therein

devisor, devisee	therefor, therefore
disburse, disperse	tortious, tortuous
dower, dowry	transferor, transferee
	vendor, vendee

1.26. Recurring phrases, clauses, and paragraphs. Many phrases, clauses, and short paragraphs are used over and over again in legal work. The lawyer's familiarity with them causes him or her to dictate them at a high rate of speed. Often, the lawyer will not dictate the entire clause or paragraph but will dictate only the first few words and the secretary completes it when transcribing. These phrases, clauses, and paragraphs vary with the field of practice and the wording varies with the state and, to a lesser extent, with the office. As soon as you recognize one that is used in your office, make up an abbreviated shorthand outline for it. Also, you should memorize the wording so you will not have to refer to a form when transcribing your notes. Throughout this book attention is called to phrases, clauses, and paragraphs that recur in legal work.

1.27. Special outlines for unusual words. In legal dictation, an unusual word that is difficult to write in shorthand might be repeated many times in the dictation of one matter. It might be a proper name or a scientific term. The first time the word is dictated make up an abbreviated outline and use that outline throughout the dictation. For example, the dictation might be about *thaumaturgy,* involving a *Mr. Kopooshian.* If you make a note that your shorthand symbol for "thau" stands for thaumaturgy, and your symbol for K stands for Kopooshian, your speed will not be reduced by writing these difficult words.

1.28. Take-ins. Frequently in legal work a dictator will tell the stenographer to "take in" certain material, meaning for her to copy it. The take-in might be quoted material from a text or testimony, in which case the take-in is indented and quoted. (See chapter 10.) Or the take-in might be a portion of a printed form or other document, the wording of which is applicable to the document that is being dictated. When the take-in is material of this kind, it follows the rest of the dictation just as if it were original dictation instead of a take-in.

The lawyer's instructions. Every office has a system of marking books, documents, drafts, and the like to indicate to the typist what is to be copied, and you will be expected to learn and follow that system. The marks are made very lightly in pencil and should be erased with an art gum eraser after the material has been proofread. The following is a practical system of marking material to be copied.

1. The signs < > indicate that the matter within them is to be omitted.

2. A number in a circle indicates that the matter to be copied begins or ends at that point. Odd numbers indicate the beginning; even numbers the end. Thus ①—② would mean copy from the point marked①to the point marked ②.

3. Crosses (XX) indicate that the matter between them is to be underscored.

4. To signify that something once erased, or marked for omission, is to remain, the word *stet* is written in the margin and dots are placed under the word or words to be retained. (Printers use this method of marking.)

Figure 1.6 illustrates a page marked for copying.

1.29. Testimony. Many occasions arise when the secretary in a law office is required to take the testimony of a person under oath. The testimony is usually in question and answer form and is referred to as a *deposition.* Counsel for both sides are present at the examination. You must take the testimony verbatim and transcribe it verbatim, without editing even glaring grammatical errors. If the exchange of questions and answers is too rapid and you fall behind in your notes, raise your left hand as a signal to the attorney conducting the examination to slow down. This might be embarrassing to you, but it is essential that every word of the testimony be reported accurately. Depositions are often tape-recorded, although it is desirable to have a stenographer record the proceedings at the same time. The tape can be used as a backup to ensure accuracy. Occasionally depositions are videotaped for use in court, but a written record is also usually made.

In taking testimony use a notebook that has a vertical line down the center of the page. Divide each half of the page into three columns by lightly pencilled vertical lines in the positions shown in figure 1.7. (It is assumed that you customarily write only to the dividing line, treating each column as a separate page.)

Notes of the questions by the examining attorney are placed on the page in the same position as notes are ordinarily placed. Each question begins at the extreme left of the page, extends to the center, and, if it takes more than one line, continues at the extreme left of the next horizontal line.

Notes of the witness' answer begin at the right of the first vertical line and extend to the center line. If more than one line is necessary, the answer continues on the next horizontal line at the right of the first vertical line. The witness' answers never extend to the left of that line.

Notes of the interpolations by opposing counsel begin at the right of the second vertical line and extend to the center line. If more than one line the sink and suddenly became dizzy and after reaching his room he vomited for about two hours. He reported that Dr. Smith was called who only talked with his daughter-in-law and did not examine him but pronounced with a grin "indigestion." Mr. Jorn called another doctor, a Dr. Palmer, who made a thorough examination and said it was not indigestion. Mr. Jorn also related that when he became dizzy at the sink that his daughter-in-law in a sassy fashion told him to get away as though his sickness was not altogether unexpected. He also reported that she had tampered with a bottle of his medicine. Was Mr. Jorn's process of thinking on the subject of his being poisoned by his son's wife so fantastic that it could reasonably be denominated as insane delusion? A complete answer to this inquiry can be found in the case of Owen v. Crumbaugh, 228 Ill. 380, at page 401, 81 N.E. 1044, at page 1051, 119 Am. St.Rep. 442, 10 Ann.Cas. 606, where the court used this language: "Whatever form of words is chosen to express the legal meaning of an insane delusion, it is clear, under all of the authorities, that it must be such an aberration as indicates an unsound or deranged condition of the mental faculties, as distinguished from a mere belief in the existence or nonexistence of certain supposed facts or phenomena based upon some sort of evidence. A belief which results from a process of reasoning from evidence, however imperfect the process may be or illogical the conclusion, is not an insane delusion. An insane delusion is not established when the court is able to understand how a person situated as the testator was might have believed all that the evidence shows that he did believe and still have been in full possession of his senses. Thus, where the testator has actual grounds for the suspicion of the existence of something in which he believes, though in fact not well founded and disbelieved by others, the misapprehension of the fact is not a matter of delusion which will invalidate his will. Stackhouse v. Horton, 15 N.J.Eq. 202; Potter v. Jones, supra [20 Or. 239, 25 P. 769, 12 L.R.A. 161]; Martin v. Thayer, 37 W.Va. 38, 16 S.E. 489; Mullins v. Cottrell, supra [41 Miss. 291]."

[2, 3] The trial judge wrote a short memorandum opinion giving his reasons for sustaining the validity of testator's will. It was his observation that the lay witnesses who testified for the defendant had a better opportunity to observe the testator than the doctors who appeared for the plaintiff, and accordingly their opinions were entitled to greater weight. The chancellor's findings should not be disturbed unless they are palpably wrong. A careful reading of the record convinces us we cannot so hold. The trial judge who sees and hears witnesses is in a much superior position to find the truth than the reviewing court who has before it only the printed page. Well worth repeating in this connection is the language of the Judge of the Supreme Court of Missouri in the case of Creamer v. Bivert, 214 Mo. 473, 113 S.W. 1118, 1120. "He (Trial Court) sees and hears much we cannot see and hear. We well know there are things of pith that cannot be preserved in or shown by the written page of a bill of exceptions. Truth does not always stalk boldly forth naked, but modest withal, in a printed abstract in a court of last resort. She oft hides in nooks and crannies visible only to the mind's eye of the judge who tries the case. To him appears the furtive glance, the blush of conscious shame, the hesitation, the sincere or the flippant or sneering tone, the heat, the calmness, the yawn, the sigh, the candor or lack of it, the scant or full realization of the solemnity of an oath, the carriage and mien. The brazen face of the liar, the glibness of the schooled witness in reciting a lesson, or the itching overeagerness of the swift witness, as well as honest face of the truthful one, are alone seen by him. In short, one witness may give testimony that reads in print, here, as if falling from the lips of an angel of light, and yet not a soul who heard it, nisi, believed a word of it; and another witness may testify so that it reads brokenly and obscurely in print, and yet there was that about the witness that carried conviction of truth to every soul who heard him testify."

We are of the opinion that the decree entered herein should be affirmed.

· Decree affirmed.

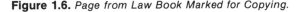

Figure 1.6. *Page from Law Book Marked for Copying.*

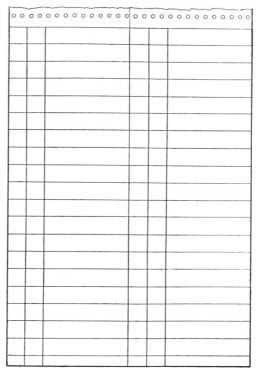

Figure 1.7. *Notebook Ruled for Question and Answer Testimony.*

is necessary, the interpolation continues on the next horizontal line at the right of the second vertical line. Remarks by opposing counsel never extend to the left of that line.

Notes of actions that must be indicated, such as marking exhibits for identification, are enclosed in brackets, thus distinguishing them from notes of the testimony. They are written in the same position as notes of the questions by the examining attorney.

Notes are written on the right half of the page in the same manner as on the left half, the center vertical line representing the left edge.

The preceding method of arranging the shorthand notes on the page of the notebook increases your speed by eliminating the writing of "Q" and "A," punctuation after the questions and answers, and the name of the opposing counsel when he or she makes an objection. It also facilitates reading back.

A transcription of testimony is shown in figure 1.8.

JAMES T. WATSON

DIRECT EXAMINATION BY MR. ADAMS:

    Q. Mr. Watson, what is your full name?

A. James T. Watson.

    Q. What is your address? A. 440 Ninth Avenue, White Plains,

New York.

    Q. Where are you employed, sir? A. R.V. Edwards Co., 150 Fifth

Avenue, New York City.

    Q. How long have you been employed there?

A. Since 1963.

    Q. What is your position at Edwards? A. Salesman.

    Q. Do you know Mrs. Mary Gray, the plaintiff in this action?

  A. Not too well; I know her as a customer.

    Q. In April, 19—, did you see her when she brought in the necklace

to Edwards? A. No.

    Q. What officer or employee did see her?

A. Another salesman.

    Q. What is his name? A. William A. Burke.

    Q. You don't know what he said to her concerning

the work to be done?

(Continued on following page)

(Continued from preceding page)

MR. DAVIS: I object to the form of that question.

A. No, only from our records.

Q. What records do you have with you that show the delivery of the necklace to Edwards?

[Mr. Watson produces record and Mr. Adams studies it.]

MR. ADAMS: I offer that in evidence.

MR. DAVIS: Can I see that?

MR. ADAMS: Certainly, I thought you had already seen it.

MR. DAVIS: It should not be admitted in evidence but should be marked for identification.

[Marked Plaintiff's Exhibit 1 for Identification.]

Q. Mr. Watson, with reference to plaintiff's exhibit marked Exhibit 1 for identification on your examination, do you recognize the handwriting in pencil on the notations on that exhibit? A. Yes, sir, that's Mr. Burke's.

MR. ADAMS: I have no further questions at this time. Mr. Foy, would you like to cross-examine?

Figure 1.8. *Transcription of Question and Answer Testimony.*

2

Contacts with Clients

and Other Callers

Every caller is a potential client, and every client with a small claim is a potentially valuable client. Because of the importance of contacts with clients and other callers, all members of the law-office team must constantly strive to maintain the proper attitude and conduct in handling contacts both in person and by telephone.

Certain situations requiring tact and diplomacy arise repeatedly in the course of the secretary's contacts with clients and other callers. Basic precepts govern the handling of these situations, but the application of the precepts varies with your personality, the office in which you work and the individual client or caller. In this chapter, we give fundamental instructions and make suggestions about how to handle certain difficult phases of contacts in person and over the telephone.

2.1. Introduction to the client. In law offices where the "team" spirit prevails, the lawyer always introduces the client to the paralegal assigned to the case and to the lawyer's secretary in the same manner that he or she makes a social introduction. Except in cases of women, dignitaries, and older persons, a basic rule in making introductions is that lower ranking persons are introduced *to* higher ranking persons, which means the name of the person of higher occupational status is mentioned first. A secretary is always introduced *to* an executive (Mr. Ross, this is my secretary Jeanne Franklin). The lawyer explains to the client that the secretary always knows where to reach him or her; that if the client telephones when the lawyer is out, the secretary will answer any questions or get the asnwer from another member of the firm. In an emergency she will get in touch with the lawyer. In addition, the lawyer explains to the client that he or she has the utmost confidence in the secretary and that she necessarily knows about the client's problem. The client gradually comes to know the secretary personally and to have a high regard and respect for her efficiency. The secretary's contacts thus promote the goodwill of the client and are of inestimable value to the lawyer.

2.2. Basic precepts. Good manners, judgment, and discretion should control your attitude in contacts with clients and other callers. Your tone of voice should always be warm, cordial, and respectful, without subservience. The tone of voice is especially important over the telephone, because you cannot show your interest by your facial expressions. Guard against the tendency to let your voice become mechanical and without expression.

On a new job the lawyer will probably give you explicit instructions about certain clients, but he or she will expect you to observe the following precepts without instructions.

1. Find out the name of a caller and the purpose of the call.
2. Never discuss with one client the affairs of another.
3. Guard against letting your knowledge of a client's legal difficulties color your attitude toward the client.
4. Never give legal advice.
5. Maintain the goodwill of the caller and make his or her contact with the firm pleasant and satisfactory.
6. Judge which clients the employer will welcome, which he or she wants to avoid, which should be seen by another lawyer in the firm, and which you should take care of yourself.
7. Make explanations to those callers whom the lawyer will not see, without antagonizing the caller.
8. Be prepared to handle emotional or difficult callers.

CONTACTS IN PERSON

2.3. Contacts in person with clients. You should be prepared to handle certain situations that occur frequently in law offices. You might make a mistake, but you may be sure the lawyer will back you up in the presence of a visitor. If the lawyer thinks you have made a mistake, he or she will tell you so privately and will point out to you how you should have handled the matter. Typical situations are:

1. A client calls without an appointment, and the lawyer cannot see him.

2. A client calls without an appointment, but the lawyer will see him.

3. A stranger wants legal advice.

4. A client is early for an appointment.

5. A client is hysterical.

6. A client invites you to dinner.

7. A client gives you a present or offers payment for work done for him.

8. A client wants to see a file.

9. A salesman wants to see the lawyer.

Suggestions are given here on how to meet the foregoing situations.

2.4. Client calls without an appointment. The client, Ms. Franklin, calls to see Mr. Perry, the attorney.

Secretary: Good afternoon. May I help you?
Ms. Franklin: Yes, I'm Marsha Franklin. I'd like to see Mr. Perry. Is he in?

Lawyer cannot see the client

Secretary: Yes, he's here, but he'll be with a client until after closing time. Could anyone else help you?

Ms. Franklin: No, I have to see him. I'm from out of town so I didn't make an appointment because I didn't know when I'd get here. It would only take a little while.

Secretary: I'm very sorry, but he asked me not to interrupt him or make any more appointments for this afternoon. Could you come some other day? I'd be glad to make a future appointment.

Ms. Franklin: Well, I don't know when I'll be back this way again, and it's very important.

From this point, the secretary must depend on her own judgment about whether the client is someone the lawyer would want to make an exception for or whether she should dismiss the client as inoffensively as possible. If she has been the secretary for a long time, she may be able to induce the client to see another lawyer in the office or to handle the matter temporarily herself. The important thing is to follow orders without offending the client.

If she is a new secretary, she should probably excuse herself and ask another lawyer in the firm to come out and speak to the client. The other lawyer could also tell her whether Mr. Perry should be notified that Ms. Franklin is there. The new secretary should hesitate to take the responsibility of turning away an out-of-town client. Under the circumstances, no reasonable attorney could censure a secretary for letting him or her know a client is in the office. If the client were not from out of town, the secretary should insist politely but firmly that she cannot disobey her instructions.

Lawyer will see the client

Secretary: I'm sorry I didn't note your name on Mrs. Hall's appointment book for today. What time did you have an appointment?

The secretary knows the client did not have an appointment, but this is a diplomatic way of bringing to his attention that he should always make an appointment in advance. It also prompts him to tell the secretary the amount of time the interview will require. Of course, the secretary's voice should be especially friendly and courteous.

Mr. Watson: I didn't have an appointment today, but I'll take only a few minutes of her time.
Secretary: I'm sure Mrs. Hall will be gald to see you for a few minutes, Mr. Watson. Won't you have a seat? Would you care to look at the paper while you're waiting?

The phrase "for a few minutes," said without emphasis, lets the client know the lawyer has other appointments and that he should be brief.

If Mrs. Hall is alone when Mr. Watson arrives without an appointment, after asking him to be seated, take the file to Mrs. Hall and tell her that Mr. Watson is waiting and would like to see her for a few minutes.

If Mrs. Hall is in conference and you know she will be finished within a short time, inform the client of this and ask him to wait. If you expect Mrs. Hall to be busy for some time and you know it is all right for you to interrupt her, ring her on the interoffice phone and ask if she would come outside to see Mr. Watson for a few minutes. If Mrs. Hall cannot be interrupted for some time, make this suggestion to the client:

Secretary: I'm sorry, Mrs. Hall isn't free right now. Do you have some other business in town you could attend to and come back in about one hour?

2.5. Stranger who wants legal advice. Someone the secretary has never seen before comes into the office. The following conversation might take place.

Secretary: How do you do. May I help you?
Mr. Jones: I'd like to see Mr. Smith.

Secretary: May I have your name please?

Mr. Jones: Jones—Robert A. Jones.

Secretary: I don't believe you have an appointment, do you, Mr. Jones?

Mr. Jones: No.

Secretary: Have you consulted Mr. Smith before?

Mr. Jones: No, I haven't.

Secretary: May I ask who referred you to him?

Up to this point, the secretary does not know whether Mr. Jones is calling about a legal matter or not, but the answer to her last question should enable her to classify the caller.

Mr. Jones: A friend of mine, George King—Mr. Smith handled a case for him once.

Secretary: Oh, yes, Mr. King. And may I ask the nature of your problem, Mr. Jones?

Mr. Jones: I had an automobile accident last week.

Secretary: I'm sorry to hear that. I'm sure Mr. Smith can help you, but he isn't free right now. Could I make an appointment for you to see him later today, say, 4:45 this afternoon?

Mr. Jones: Couldn't I wait now?

Secretary: I'm afraid he'll be busy for some time, and then he has another appointment. It would be better if you could come back. Would tomorrow be more convenient?

Mr. Jones: No, I guess this afternoon would be better.

Secretary: I'm sorry Mr. Smith can't see you now but I'll put you down for 4:45 this afternoon.

Mr. Jones: I'll be here then.

You should also get the telephone number of the visitor so if the lawyer cannot keep the appointment you can notify him at once. When the appointment is made for several days in advance, give the client the attorney's card as a reminder. The telephone conversation with the stranger who telephones for an appointment (page 56) is also applicable to a call in person.

2.6. A client is early for an appointment. A nuisance in a law office is the client who always arrives considerably ahead of appointment time and expects to carry on a conversation with the secretary until time for the appointment. You should offer the client a paper or a magazine and continue with your work. Discussion with the client not only is a waste of your employer's time; it is not good form. Of course, this suggestion does not mean you should be unfriendly or refuse to acknowledge remarks made by the client; it does mean you should discourage the client from conversing with you.

2.7. Hysterical clients. Sometimes a distraught client becomes hysterical in the office. If the client is a woman, take her to the rest room and make an effort to calm her. Since hysteria can be brought on by discussing the case with the secretary while waiting for the appointment, the secretary must try to direct the conversation away from the client's immediate concern. If the client is a man, the secretary may want to ask a male paralegal or other office personnel to help her.

2.8. Invitations from clients. A basic rule of office conduct is that office life and social life must be kept apart. This rule is particularly applicable to the contact between a lawyer's secretary and his or her clients. If the social contact proves disagreeable in any way, the unpleasantness may be reflected in the professional contact, and may even result in loss of the client. The secretary, therefore, should not accept social invitations from clients whom she has met in the lawyer's office. You may make an exception to this rule and accept an invitation from a client whom you have known a long time, provided you first ask the lawyer if he or she thinks it is all right for you to accept the invitation.

2.9. Presents and payment for work. Often the secretary is required to do some special work for out-of-town clients or associate counsels and is offered a present or payment for the work. Gifts of candy, cigarettes, and the like may be accepted without permission from the lawyer. It is also appropriate to accept Christmas presents, with your employer's consent, provided they are not very expensive. You should never accept expensive personal gifts from a client.

You do not accept payment for work done for a client or associate counsel when the work is done on the lawyer's time. When client or counsel requests you to work overtime or at night on a special job not connected with your work, you are entitled to payment. You should consult your employer before agreeing to do the work. The acceptance of payment for work done after hours on a matter connected with your job requires careful consideration. It is permissible, although not always desirable, to accept payment, provided you are offered a lump sum and are not asked the price of your services, and provided your employer is willing. Many secretaries feel that extra payment by the client or associate counsel is in the nature of a gratuity and do not wish to accept it for this reason. On the other hand, clients and associate counsel are genuinely appreciative of the extra effort on their behalf and are merely trying to show their gratitude. Refusal of their offer might easily offend them. You, of course, should be guided entirely by the extent of the service and your employer's views.

2.10. Client wants to see a file. Frequently a client stops in the office to look over papers in a file. It is not usually necessary to disturb the lawyer for this reason. Ask the client exactly what papers he would like to examine, remove them from the file, and hand them to him, if he is entitled to see them. He is entitled to examine papers that are his, such as a mortgage or deed. He is also entitled to examine other papers of which he has personal knowledge or which are of public record, such as court papers and transcripts of testimony taken in his presence. He is not entitled to examine the lawyer's working papers, correspondence about his case, or any other papers of which he does not have personal knowledge. Never hand an entire file to a client without express permission. Of course, he is not supposed to take any papers out of the office, unless the lawyer says that he may. Even then it is better to make a copy of the document for the client, if appropriate, and keep the original in the office.

2.11. Salesmen and job hunters. Salesmen are frequent visitors to law offices. You will soon learn to distinguish between those the lawyer is interested in seeing and those who are not welcome.

Law book salesmen. Law books, services, and periodicals are tools with which a lawyer works, and he or she buys them readily. Almost all lawyers are interested in seeing the salesmen who sell this material, if time permits. You will soon become familiar with the names of the various publishing houses and with their salesmen. Unless instructed otherwise, you can let the law book salesman see the lawyer at the time of his call, if convenient, or you can make a future appointment for him. It is to the advantage of the salesman to talk to the lawyer when he or she is not distracted or pressed for time. If you make an appointment the lawyer cannot keep, be punctilious in notifying the salesman before he comes to the office. Remember that the salesman's time is worth money and his services are useful to the lawyer.

Other salesmen. Although practically all office buildings have large signs prohibiting salesmen, they occasionally get into your office. They read the name of the firm on the door and walk in and ask to see one or more members of the firm. Often there is no visible means of detecting that the caller is in this class. When you ask the stranger who referred him to the attorney (see page 53), he will probably be evasive if he is selling and will tell you that he will require only a few minutes time. A rule that must be strictly observed is: never let a stranger into the lawyer's private office unless you are positive he is not a salesman.

Job hunters. Law students seeking part-time or temporary work and other job hunters may stop at the office and ask to see one of the lawyers. If no positions are available, inform the job hunter of this, briefly describe the situation in your law office, and invite the job hunter to leave a resume for future reference. If the person insists on speaking with an attorney, and one of the lawyers is free, you can ring that lawyer on the interoffice phone and ask if he or she is able to speak with the applicant for a few minutes. If no one is free to see the job hunter, advise the appropriate attorney later that someone stopped by and show him or her a copy of the resume before filing it.

CONTACTS OVER THE TELEPHONE

2.12. Importance of telephone contacts. Telephone contacts are of paramount importance in a law office. The secretary must know how to answer and makes calls smoothly, how to talk into the instrument, and how to take messages for the lawyer, as well as what to say. Here, in addition to the fundamentals of telephone techniques, examples are given on handling telephone calls in the following situations:

1. A stranger calls for an appointment but is reluctant to divulge the nature of his or her business.
2. An irate client telephones while the lawyer is out.
3. A client or prospective client asks the fee for certain services.

2.13. Rules of telephone courtesy. The following simple rules constitute the basis of courteous and efficient telephone usage:

1. Answer calls promptly.
2. When you leave your desk, arrange for someone to take your calls. Leave word where you can be reached and when you will return.
3. Keep pad and pencil handy.
4. In asking a caller to wait, say, "Will you please hold the line while I get the information," and wait for the reply. Then press the "hold" button. When you return to the telephone, thank the caller for waiting. If it will take you some time to get the information, offer to call back.
5. If you have to put down the receiver for any reason, do it gently.
6. Do not interrupt or be impatient. Listen attentively. Do not make the other party repeat because of your inattention.
7. Do not try to talk with a cigarette or pencil in your mouth.
8. When you have finished talking, say, "Thank you, Mr. Smith," or "Goodbye," pleasantly and replace the receiver gently. Let the caller hang up first.

2.14. Placing calls for the lawyer. Although many attorneys prefer to place their own calls, you should know the proper procedure to place the call for your employer. The correct practice to follow when you place calls for the lawyer has developed from expediency. When *you* place the call, it is your privilege to get the person called on the wire before connecting your employer. Assume that you are calling Miss Hardy for the lawyer, Mr. MacDonald. When you get Miss Hardy's secretary on the wire, you say, "Is Miss Hardy there, for Mr. MacDonald?" Then Miss Hardy's secretary will put her employer on and trust to your good judgment and care to see that Mr. MacDonald comes on the line promptly. (When she calls your employer, you reciprocate the courtesy.) When Miss Hardy comes on the line, say "Just a moment for Mr. MacDonald," press the "hold" button, and inform Mr. MacDonald which line to pick up for Miss Hardy's call.

You must be extremely careful not to keep the person called waiting for the lawyer to take the call. On the other hand, it is your job to see that the lawyer does not hold the phone needlessly. When you are calling a person whose secretary is cooperative and dependable, there is no difficulty because you and she can connect your employers simultaneously.

There is an exception to this procedure. If you call a close friend or a person to whom deference is due by the lawyer, connect the lawyer as soon as you talk to the secretary at the other end of the line. Tell the lawyer that the person he or she is calling will be on the line immediately and let the lawyer receive the call direct. Some secretaries follow this procedure at all times.

2.15. Long distance, or toll, calls. A record must be kept of every long distance, or toll, call that is placed from your office. These calls are usually made on behalf of a client and are charged to his or her account. Always ask the operator to tell you the amount of the charge and make a memorandum immediately. Figure 2.1 illustrates a useful printed form.

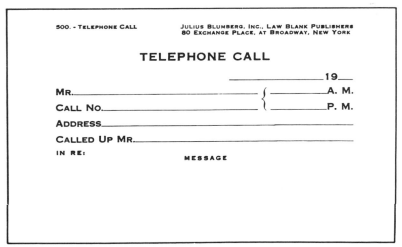

Courtesy Julius Blumberg, Inc.

Figure 2.1. *Record of Toll Telephone Call.*

525   JULIUS BLUMBERG, INC., LAW BLANK PUBLISHERS
80 EXCHANGE PLACE AT BROADWAY, NEW YORK

RECORD OF TELEPHONE CALLS

Month of..19___

Date	Telephone No.	Name and Address	Time	Remarks

Courtesy Julius Blumberg, Inc.

Figure 2.2. *Record of Telephone Calls.*

After you fill in the details, give it to the lawyer who made the call so he or she can initial it. As secretary, you may have the authority to initial it for the lawyer. The form is then sent to the bookkeeper. If you keep the books, you should have a folder for telephone memoranda, against which you can check the bill and make the charges to the clients' accounts. Many offices also have the operator keep a record of *all* outgoing calls. A handy form for keeping this kind of record is illustrated in figure 2.2.

2.16. When clients place toll calls. Clients frequently ask permission to place a telephone call. Quite often these calls are toll calls and the question of payment for them might present an embarrassing situation. The thoughtful client immediately suggests payment, but many excellent clients simply do not think about payment. Keep a record of these calls and bill the client for them, unless special circumstances make it more diplomatic for the law firm to charge the call to overhead.

2.17. Answering calls for the lawyer. If a secretary calls and tells you that her employer wants to speak with a certain lawyer in your office, ask her to wait a moment and announce the call to the lawyer. Say to the secretary, "One moment, please," and tell the lawyer that Mr. Harris of ABC is calling." The lawyer will then pick up the phone and wait until Mr. Harris is connected with him or her. Or perhaps the other secretary has learned that you are cooperative and she puts Mr. Harris on the line at the same time that you connect the call with your employer.

2.18. Making notes of incoming calls. It is important that the lawyer be informed of every call that comes in for him or her whether or not the caller leaves a message. Do not depend upon memory for this, but make a note immediately. If your office does not have printed forms for this purpose, you might suggest that some be ordered. Most are inexpensive and are convenient, easy-to-read, and neat. Figures 2.3 and 2.4 illustrate useful forms. Keep a pad of the form on your desk—and on the desk of everyone in the office who takes telephone messages.

TELEPHONE MESSAGE	DATE_____
TO_____	HOUR_____
FROM_____	TEL. NO._____

FORM 500X — JULIUS BLUMBERG, INC., 80 EXCHANGE PLACE AT BROADWAY, NEW YORK

Figure 2.3. *Telephone Message Memo.*

To_____

A.M.
Date_____Time_____P.M.

WHILE YOU WERE OUT

Mr._____

of_____

Phone_____

TELEPHONED		PLEASE CALL HIM	
CALLED TO SEE YOU		WILL CALL AGAIN	
WANTS TO SEE YOU		RETURNED CALL	

Message_____

_____

_____

_____

_____

Operator

No. 585—Julius Blumberg, Inc., 80 Exchange Place, New York

Figure 2.4. *Telephone Message Memo—Another Form.*

2.19. Screening calls for the lawyer. A lawyer usually expects his or her secretary to screen calls; otherwise the calls do not go through the secretary but are put through directly to the lawyer.

A polite way of asking who is calling is, "May I tell Miss Adams who is calling?" Or, "May I ask who is calling?" A legitimate caller seldom objects to giving his or her name.

If the caller does not want to give his name, you have the right to insist, politely but firmly, that he do so. As a matter of fact, you have no right to put through calls without first screening them, when this is expected of you, and without learning that the lawyer is willing to talk. If the caller insists upon withholding his name you might say, very politely,

"I'm very sorry, but Miss Adams has someone with her at the moment. If you'd rather not give your name, I'd suggest you write to Miss Adams and mark your letter 'personal,' I'll be glad to see that she gets it promptly."

2.20. Finding the purpose of a call. A secretary is usually expected to find out why a person wants an appointment with her employer. This frequently poses a delicate problem in the law office, because callers are often reluctant to disclose the nature of their legal business. However, knowledge of what the client wants frequently enables the secretary to save considerable time, not only for the lawyer but also for the prospective client. This situation is illustrated by the following conversation between a secretary and Mr. Goldman, the caller.

Secretary: Samuels and Rolff. (The practice in answering the telephone varies. In some offices, the practice is to answer the telephone with the number.)

Mr. Goldman: This is Henry Goldman. I'd like an appointment to see Mr. Samuels, please.

Secretary: I'm Carol Smith, Mr. Samuels secretary, and I'll be happy to arrange an appointment for you. What date and time would you like to see Mr. Samuels?

Informing the caller that you are the lawyer's secretary gives the client an opening to tell you the nature of his or her business. But this caller did not respond in the manner the secretary desired.

Mr. Goldman: I'd like to see him on Tuesday afternoon, say around 2 o'clock.

Secretary: Mr. Samuels will be busy part of the afternoon on Tuesday, Mr. Goldman. About how long will you need for your appointment?

This gives the caller another opportunity to state the nature of his business, but Mr. Goldman is rather elusive.

Mr. Goldman: I won't need more than an hour of his time. How about two to three?

Now comes the difficult part. You must find out what the caller wants and you must do it diplomatically. The "voice with a smile" is especially important here.

Secretary: In connection with a client's visit, Mr. Goldman, it's often necessary for Mr. Samuels to have certain forms or information available. So I'll have everything ready for your appointment on Tuesday, could you give me a general idea about the nature of your business? I don't need to know any of the details, of course, just a brief statement.

By giving him a good reason for your inquiry and assuring him that you are not interested in details, you have asked him, in a gracious and courteous manner, for a statment concerning his appointment.

Perhaps he says he wants a divorce. You know Mr. Samuels will not handle the case but that it will be turned over to a junior member of the firm.

Secretary: Mr. Davis of this office usually handles those matters and confers with Mr. Samuels when necessary. It would really be better for you to see Mr. Davis on Tuesday. If that's satisfactory, I'll arrange the appointment with Mr. Davis instead of Mr. Samuels.

Or perhaps Mr. Goldman says he has a small collection matter he wants Mr. Samuels to handle. Your office does not handle collections except for retainer clients.

Secretary: I'm sorry, Mr. Goldman. As much as Mr. Samuels would like to help you, he doesn't handle collections. However, Mr. Robert Ames, a young member of the bar located in this building, would no doubt be happy to handle the matter for you. Would you like his telephone number?

There are innumerable situations, but by exercising discretion and diplomacy you will soon be able to handle them all.

2.21. The caller who wants legal advice over the phone. Sometimes a caller wants to ask the lawyer for his or her legal opinion over the phone. Lawyers can rarely answer a legal question without thoroughly understanding the problem that gives rise to it. Try to find out the general nature of the problem presented, and if it is an area handled by the lawyer, suggest that the caller make an appointment to see the lawyer. Explain that the lawyer will need to discuss the problem in more detail before he or she can be of help. This way the caller should take the hint that free legal advice cannot be obtained over the phone. If the caller asks for *your* legal opinion, tell him or her you are sorry but you are not able to answer the questions, that it will be necessary for the caller to discuss the problem with an attorney.

2.22. An irate client calls. Occasionally a client who is annoyed about something telephones while the lawyer is out. It is usually advisable to avoid making explanations to him. Simply tell him that you will ask the lawyer to call as soon as he or she returns—and make sure you tell the lawyer about the call. No matter how expert a secretary you are, how tactful and diplomatic, some things must be handled by the lawyer, and annoyed clients belong at the top of the list.

2.23. Client or prospective client asks what a fee will be. Many clients and prospective clients try to find out over the telephone what the lawyer will charge for certain services. A lawyer's secretary should *never* quote fees; that is for the lawyer to do. In fact, the lawyer does not even like to quote fees until he or she is thoroughly familiar with the amount of work involved. For example, the fee for drawing a simple will is not as much as the fee for drawing a will that involves a trust. When a client asks you what a fee will be, offer to make an appointment with the lawyer. If the client does not want an appointment, offer to have the lawyer call him.

2.24. Your telephone conversation. If you have to make a telephone call for the lawyer, plan your conversation before placing the call. Know your facts. Know the points you want to cover. If necessary, have an outline of them before you while you talk. Have all records and other material before you. This is particularly important on out-of-town calls.

Identify yourself immediately to the person to whom you are speaking, thus, "This is Carol Smith, Mrs. Newton's secretary," or, "This is Carol Smith at Boyle and Matthews."

Keep your telephone conversation brief but not to the point of curtness. Take time to address people by their names and title and to use expressions of consideration, like "Thank you," "I'm sorry," and "I beg your pardon."

2.25. Desk telephone lists. You should keep on your desk an up-to-date directory of the name, address, and telephone number of each of the following:

Law Business Numbers
Attorneys associated in current cases (temporary listing)
Attorney available for various kinds of matters your office does not handle
Attorneys on opposite side of current cases (temporary listing)
Auctioneers
Bonding companies
Collection agencies
Consuls
Court reporters
Courts
Custodians
Deputy sheriffs
Detectives
Engineers
Engravers
Fast printing and copying services

Handwriting experts
Investigators
Law journals
Law stationers
Libraries
Marshals
Newspapers
Photographers
Printers
Process servers
Translators

Office Administration Numbers
Airlines
Building manager or superintendent
Emergency calls (Fire, Police, Ambulance, etc.)
Express office
Messenger service
Post Office
Railroads
Residence of employees in your office
Stationer (office supplies)
Telegraph office
Time of day
Travel agency
Typewriter and equipment repairs
Weather

Lawyer's Personal Telephone Numbers
Bank
Dentist
Doctors
Family (residence and business)
Florist
Friends whom he calls frequently
Garage
Insurance broker
Organizations to which he belongs
Services (dry cleaner, tailor, etc.)
Stock broker
Stores that he trades with
Theater ticket agency

3

Reminder Systems

and Practices

In a law office, certain things must be done at certain times. The need for an infallible system of reminders is imperative, because failure to take legal action at the time required might have irreparable consequences. *For any reminder system to function properly, the secretary must keep it accurately and must refer to it each day.*

Three reminder systems are described in this chapter: (1) the diary, (2) the card tickler, and (3) follow-up files, none of which is a complete substitute for the other. Suggestions are also made for methods of reminding the lawyer of his or her appointments and things to do.

THE DIARY

3.1. What is a diary? A diary is not only a record of future appointments and work to be done but also a daily record of what is actually accomplished. It is kept from year to year and furnishes a permanent record of appointments, dates that cases were tried, and time spent with clients in or out of office or in court. The diary has a separate page printed for each day in the year. Many standard yearbooks are designed for lawyers and are entirely satisfactory. The important thing is that they should have space for work actually done and the time consumed doing it as well as space for appointments and matters to be attended to. In many law offices, especially those in which several attorneys practice, time records and charges are kept on charge sheets (see chapter 6). In such instances it is not necessary to use a diary that provides space for work done and time consumed.

Figure 3.1 illustrates a page from a lawyer's diary. See also the Daily Page, illustrated in chapter 6 (Figure 6.4), which serves as an

Saturday, APRIL 20		112th Day

9:45 – Dept. 2 – Hill v. Pruitt   Trial

11:00 – Mr. J.D. Franklin   (Jr. 7491)

(ax. – 7230 – chg. Dennis v. City)

4:30 – Construction Committee Meeting

Last day to file Op. Br. – Yale V. City
Pay jury fee Deposit – Clifford v. Morris

Clients Name and Address	Work Done	Time
Hill (John V.) 115 Hilltop Lane	Briefing Trial	2 hrs. 4 hrs.

Figure 3.1. *Page from Lawyer's Diary.*

appointment book and as a convenient place to record all services and charges connected with a client's business. Chapter 12 describes suit registers, or court dockets. These are progress records of litigation; advance entries in the diary are essential as reminders to take the necessary action.

3.2. Diaries you should keep. Two diaries are required, one for the lawyer and one for you, but the entries are not completely duplicated. In the lawyer's diary, enter all of his or her appointments and important days to remember, such as a spouse's birthday. If the important days are not noted, the lawyer may inadvertently make conflicting engagements. Do not enter in the lawyer's diary items that are merely reminders to you, such as days on which checks should be written. Watch the lawyer's diary closely for appointments he makes without telling you.

In your diary, enter notations of your own business activities and appointments, as well as the lawyer's appointments and the things you will have to remind him or her about.

If you are responsible for following court cases for more than one lawyer, as well as being responsible for personal matters for a member of the firm, it will be less confusing to keep all court matters in a separate diary.

3.3. How to make up diaries. Keep a list of items that go in the diary year after year (see section 3.6). As soon as diaries for the forthcoming year are available, enter all of the recurring items, events, and appointments under the appropriate date. In preparing the diaries, work from the list, not from the previous year's diary, because dates for events change. For example, if the board meetings of a corporation client are held on the first Monday of every month, the actual dates vary from year to year. In making an entry, be certain the date is not Sunday or a holiday. Enter notations of additional appointments and things to do as soon as you learn about them.

Enter time-consuming tasks that must be done by a certain date sufficiently *in advance* to permit the work to be finished on time. Also make an entry under the date on which the action must be taken. The practice of making advance entries is very important and will save you and the lawyer the strain of having to prepare material on short notice. It is not usually necessary to make advance entries in the lawyer's diary— you can remind him or her of work to be done. (See page 75.) Underline important due dates and deadlines in red.

When dates call for presents or cards, enter a reminder in *your* diary, about ten days before the date, as well as on the date. Christmas presents and card lists should be brought up about six weeks before Christmas, the exact time depending upon local shopping conditions.

Advance notice of payments of large sums should also be entered in the diary. The lawyer's funds might be low, or he or she might want to negotiate a renewal of a loan.

3.4. How to make entries about legal work. Under the date upon which a step must be taken, make an entry setting forth (1) the title of the matter, (2) the time and place for the step, and (3) the nature of the act to be performed, fully described. If you keep the diary for more than one lawyer, also include the initials of the lawyer or lawyers interested. The third example of entries, below, indicates that a brief must be prepared. This entry should also be made under an advance date (see above), with a notation of the date the briefs must be ready. Form the habit of making entries in the diary immediately upon learning that they should be made. *Allow no telephone calls or other interruptions to interfere.*

Examples of entries:

> Jonathan Maxwell Estate—pay on account New York Estate Tax to obtain benefit of 5% discount.
> RSF

> R. V. Robertson Co.—Clerk's Office, U. S. Court-house, Foley Square—Order to show cause returnable why certain claims should not be compromised.
> NEL

> Dixon v. Rogers (both actions)—Last day to serve and file reply briefs.
> RFS:NEL

3.5. How to obtain information for entries. Information necessary to make these entries is obtained in various ways:

1. Observe the dates and the places mentioned in papers that your firm prepares and in those served on it by opposing counsel. For example, an order in the R. V. Robertson Co. case would read in part:

"ORDERED that the plaintiff or his attorney show cause, ... at the office of the Clerk of the United States District Court for the Southern District of New York in the United States Court House, Foley Square, Borough of Manhattan, City of New York, on the 18th day of July, 19.., at 10:30 o'clock in the forenoon...."

Obviously, you know that a diary entry should be made under date of July 18 and that the place is the Clerk's Office, U.S. Court House, Foley Square.

2. Observe the date a notice is served on your office, or your office serves a notice.

3. Calculate the time prescribed by law or rules of law for answering, replying to, or moving to dismiss or correct a pleading when a pleading is

served on your office. You can get this information from the practice rules of the court.

4. Calculate the time for taking any step when the time limit for that step runs from some other act of which you have notice.

5. *Ask the lawyer or the firm's managing attorney for diary dates whenever you do not have them or do not know how to calculate them.*

It would be impossible to set forth here all of the instances and time limits that affect litigation; not only are they numerous, but they vary with the state. Knowledge of them is gained by experience and study. The lawyer is responsible for knowing them and instructing you accordingly; *you* are responsible for making notations in the diary in accordance with his or her instructions and for asking the lawyer to give you those instructions. A few diaries have an appendix of timetables of procedure and court rules for specific states, which are very helpful to the legal secretary.

3.6. Checklist of entries to make in diary. Here is a checklist of the items that the secretary usually enters in the appropriate diary:

Appointments
    Clients, in and out of office
    Doctor and dentist
    Social, evening and daytime

Court Work
    Return dates on summons, orders to show cause and the like
    Deadlines for filing pleadings and serving copies on opposing counsel
    Deadlines for serving notices in probate court
    Hearings
    Pretrial conferences with court and opposing counsel
    Trial dates

Family Dates
    Anniversaries
    Birthdays
    Mother's Day
    Father's Day

Holidays
    Christmas
    Memorial Day
    Easter
    Election Day
    Independence Day
    Labor Day
    New Year's Day
    Religious holidays
    Thanksgiving
    Valentine's Day

Meetings
> Board of directors meetings
> Club meetings
> Committee meetings
> Stockholders' (also called shareholders') meetings
> Bar association meetings

Payment Dates
> Bar association dues
> Contributions
> Insurance premiums
> Interest on notes payable and maturity dates
> Periodic payments, such as salaries, rent, allowances to children, tuition, and the like

Renewal Dates
> Automobile registration
> Driver's license
> Hunting and fishing licenses
> Subscriptions to periodicals

Tax Dates
> Federal income tax returns and payment dates for clients and for the lawyer's personal tax
> Federal estate tax returns for clients
> Social security tax returns and payments
> State and local taxes
> Unemployment tax and disability contribution returns and payments
> Withholding tax returns and payments

3.7. Tickler card file. A tickler card file has a tabbed guide for each month of the year and 31 tabbed guides, one for each day of the month. The daily guides are placed behind the current month guide. Memoranda are made on cards or slips, which are filed behind the daily guide according to the date on which the matter is to be brought up.

3.8. Use of tickler card file with diary. Generally, secretaries in law offices do not like to depend upon tickler cards as reminders for deadlines, hearings, trial dates, and other legal work. It is too easy to lose or misplace a small 3″ by 5″ card or slip, and the resulting damage might be irreparable. Furthermore, tickler cards to not constitute a permanent record of the day's activities as a diary does.

Tickler cards can be used in conjunction with a diary very satisfactorily. They reduce the work necessary in making diary entries. Recurring items can be put on one card, and the card can be moved from week to week, month to month, or year to year. Thus, if a certain check is made out each Friday, you can make one card and move it each week, instead of making 52 entries in your diary. Also, you can put all necessary information on the card so you or anyone else can attend to the task without referrring to any other material. Tickler cards are also particularly useful for indefinite date follow-ups. If the lawyer has told you he or she wants to do a certain job sometime within the next few months, you can make a card and move it from time to time if the lawyer does not do the task when you first bring it to his or her attention.

A tickler card file *does not* take the place of a diary for noting appointments. All appointments, even regularly recurring ones, should be entered in the diary; otherwise, whenever you want to make an appointment you will have to look not only in the diary but also at the tickler.

Refer to the diary every afternoon for the following day and to the tickler each morning.

3.9. Checklist of entries of work accomplished. The purpose of making entries in the diary of work accomplished and time consumed is to charge the client for the work. Therefore, any time consumed in behalf of a client should be entered unless a separate time sheet is kept. This time includes:

Dictation
Appointments
Conferences
Closings
Interviewing witnesses
Trials
Hearings
Arguments
Research
Some telephone calls
Some stenographic work

FOLLOW-UP FILES

3.10. Necessity for follow-up files. If all the matters in a law office that had to be followed were entered in the diary, it would become so cluttered it would lose its usefulness. Therefore, follow-up, or tickler, files are a useful supplement to the diary. A notation or reminder, usually a carbon copy, is placed in the tickler file while the material itself remains in its proper place in the regular files. If the material itself is placed in the follow-up file instead of in the regular file, it cannot be located if it is needed before the follow-up date.

3.11. Checklist of material to be placed in follow-up files. Court cases are preferably followed through the diary, but the following matters are generally followed through follow-up files rather than through the diary:

1. Matters that are referred to other lawyers, law clerks, or paralegals in the office for information, comment, or action
2. Correspondence or memoranda awaiting answer
3. Collection letters (see chapter 20)
4. Covering letter enclosing documents sent by registered mail, until receipt is received
5. Requests for acknowledgements of documents, and so on
6. Receipts for documents left with court clerks or other officials for recording
7. Letters to Register of Deeds, or other officials, enclosing papers for recording, to be kept until papers are returned and delivered to client
8. Letters to abstract company

3.12. Equipment for follow-up system. Numerous styles of equipment for follow-up purposes are on the market, but many secretaries to busy lawyers have found the follow-up file system described here to be practical, efficient, and time saving. (See also section 4.18)

The only equipment necessary is a file drawer and file folders. Make a set of file folders consisting of (a) 12 folders labeled from January through December, (b) 31 folders labeled from 1 through 31, and (c) 1 folder marked "Future Years." If you have a heavy volume of follow-up material, it is advisable to have two sets of folders labeled by days—one for the current month and one for the succeeding month.

Tabbed guides marked 1 through 31 and removable separators tabbed with the months will make it easier to locate a particular folder, but these are not necessary to the efficient functioning of the system.

3.13. Arrangement of folders for follow-up. Arrange the folders labeled by days in numerical order in the front of the file. Place in these the follow-up material for the current month. The folder labeled for the current month is at the back of the other monthly folders ready to receive any material to be followed up in the same month next year. Immediately following the numerical daily folders is the folder for the coming month, followed by the folder for the succeeding month, and so on.

3.14. Operation of the follow-up system. 1. Make an extra copy of correspondence or memoranda that require a follow-up, preferably on paper of a different color. Mark on the extra carbon the date on which it is to be followed up. When there is no carbon copy of material for follow-up, write a brief memo for the tickler file. For example, if your employer gives you a newspaper clipping and tells you to bring it to his or her attention on the 30th of the month, prepare a tickler memo (on the same color paper as the follow-up carbon copy of correspondence) for follow-up on the 30th, but file the clipping so you can put your hands on it if your employer wants it before the 30th. The memo should indicate where the material is filed. File any pertinent papers in the regular files.

2. Place material that is to be followed up in the current month in the proper date folders. Each day transfer the empty daily folder back of the folder for the coming month. Thus you always have 31 daily folders for follow-ups, part of them for the remaining days in the current month and part of them for the first part of the coming month. Place material that is to be followed up more than 30 or 31 days in the future in the proper month folder, regardless of the day of follow-up. See figure 3.2, which is a diagram of the arrangement of folders on April 16. On that day, material to be followed up from April through May is placed in daily folders; material to be followed up after May is placed in the proper month folder.

3. On the first of each month, transfer the material from the folder for that month into the folders labeled by days. To avoid filing material for follow-up on Saturdays (if the office closes), Sundays, or holidays, reverse the folders for those days so that the blank side of the label faces the front of the file. Notice in figure 3.2 that the folders for April 17, 18, 24, and 25 and May 1, 2, 8, and 9 are blank. The empty folder for the current month is then transferred to the rear of the other month-by-month folders.

3.15. How to handle material in the daily follow-up file. Each day when you examine your follow-up file you will find that a large part of the material has been answered without a follow-up. Destroy these carbons or memoranda. If a heavy schedule keeps you from giving attention to all the material in the daily folder, mark the less important items for follow-up at a later date.

Move indefinite follow-ups forward from week to week until a definite date is established or until the matter is completed. This procedure is often referred to as "coming-back."

3.16. Follow-ups on a small scale. When you have only a small amount of correspondence or other matters to follow up, a set of follow-up file folders is not necessary. Mark the carbons with the follow-up date and file them chronologically in one folder, with those marked for the earliest follow-up on top.

3.17. Tickler card file for follow-up. A tickler card file is as useful as follow-up file folders for any type of material except correspondence. You can type a notation for yourself on a card and place it in a tickler card file as easily as you can type a memorandum and put it in a file folder. However, if you are typing correspondence anyway, it is easier simply to make an extra carbon copy for the follow-up file folders. Tickler cards are most suitable for things such as reminders of payment or expiration dates, for example, insurance premium due dates.

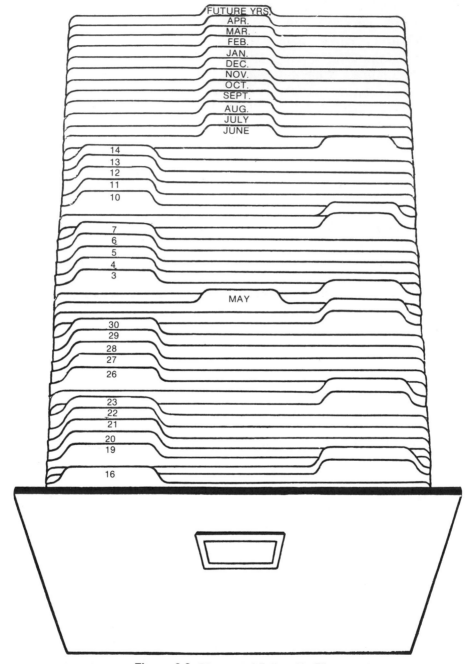

Figure 3.2. *Diagram of Follow-Up Files.*

REMINDING THE LAWYER OF THINGS TO BE DONE

3.18. Necessity for reminder. It is advisable for a secretary in a new job to ask the lawyer if he or she likes to be reminded of things to be done and if he or she has a preference as to the method. The lawyer's diary shows appointments and things to do. For many lawyers, placing the diary open at the current date in a conspicuous place on his or her desk is sufficient.

3.19. How to remind the lawyer of appointments. In the late afternoon, or the first thing in the morning, place on the lawyer's desk a typed schedule of his or her appointments, giving all pertinent information. Memorandum paper about 6" by 9" is desirable for this purpose. Before the time of the appointment give the lawyer the file and other material he or she will need for it.

3.20. Reminders showing appointments for a month. Many lawyers like to see the month's engagements at a glance. There are calendars designed for this purpose, usually on cardboard about 9" by 11". Figure 3.3 is an illustration of such a calendar. Note that under the arrangement of dates on this calendar, every Sunday in the month is on the top row, every Monday on the next row, and so on.

3.21. How to remind the lawyer of things to be done. To remind the lawyer of a task, place the file on his or her desk, with a memorandum if necessary. For example, if a real estate closing is scheduled for the 29th and papers must be drawn for it, put the file on his desk about the 27th with a memo that the closing is scheduled for the 29th.

If the lawyer told you he or she wants to do a certain thing in connection with a matter, attach a reminder to the file. For example, suppose the lawyer told you, "If we don't receive that information from Robinson by Friday, I want to obtain a stipulation postponing his case another week." On Friday, if the information has not been received, you type a memo, "You wanted to obtain a stipulation to postpone this case," and attach it to the Robinson file before placing it on the lawyer's desk. It might be even better for you to type the stipulation and give it to the lawyer with the file. This procedure would depend on your experience and the lawyer's wishes in connection with delegating such duties to you.

Some lawyers make a practice of calling their secretaries into their office the first thing every morning to dispose of the correspondence and to discuss pending matters and things to be done. This is the ideal arrangement. For the discussion, you take with you a list of things to be done and any material pertaining to them, as well as your notebook.

DECEMBER

Sunday, 6th	Sunday, 13th	Sunday, 20th	Sunday, 27th
Monday, 7th	Monday, 14th	Monday, 21st	Monday, 28th
Tuesday, 8th	Tuesday, 15th	Tuesday, 22nd	Tuesday, 29th
Wednesday, 9th	Wednesday, 16th	Wednesday, 23rd	Wednesday, 30th
Thursday, 10th	Thursday, 17th	Thursday, 24th Thanskgiving Day	Friday, 31st
Friday, 11th	Friday, 18th	Friday, 25th	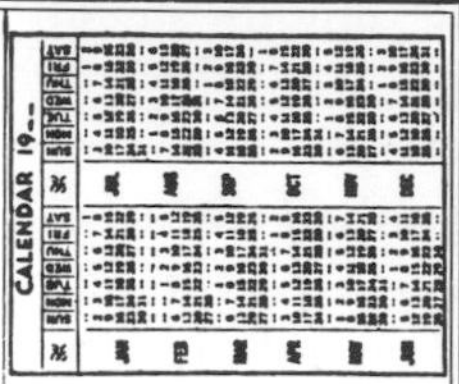
Saturday, 12th	Saturday, 19th	Saturday, 26th	

Tuesday, 1st
Wednesday, 2nd
Thursday, 3rd
Friday, 4th
Saturday, 5th

CALENDAR 19__

Figure 3.3. Appointment Calendar for a Month.

MORGAN, BURBANK & CHAMBERS
Managing Clerk's Department

To .. Mr. Ross. . . . .

Reference   Jones vs. Almond

Time: November 12,   **19 -- .** at   10 A.M.

Place: County Court House, Department B

Action

    Last day to

    Motion   for order dismissing complaint

    Settlement of

    Examination of

    Hearing

    Trial

    Argument

    . . . .

. . . . JTV . . . .
               Managing Clerk

Dated November 9 . . . . . ,   **19 --**

(Please note below disposition of matter and return to Managing Clerk.)

Attended and argued in support of motion.

Decision reserved.

               B. M. R.

Figure 3.4. *Notice of Diary Entry.*

3.22. How to remind the lawyer of court work. In a large office a diary of court cases is maintained by the managing clerk under the supervision of the managing attorney. Although each lawyer in charge of a matter is presumed to know its status, it is the duty of the managing clerk to follow the status of the matter, to furnish information regarding the status, and to aid in securing prompt and orderly disposition of court matters. In a comparatively small office, you, as secretary to the senior partner or to the managing partner, may have this responsibility.

From your diary records, send a written notice to the lawyer in charge, sufficiently in advance to permit him or her to make preparations necessary to take the indicated step. Figure 3.4 is a printed form, filled out, that is used for this purpose. Mimeographed, photocopied, or typed slips would also serve the purpose. The lawyer in charge of the matter should return the written notice to you with a notation of the action taken.

Another method of reminding the lawyers in your office about pending court work is to type the entries from your diary each week for two weeks in advance, making as many copies as necessary to circulate among the lawyers. In an office with numerous attorneys, the list would be mimeographed or photocopied. Each lawyer then checks the cases in which he or she is interested. You will recall that the diary entries include the initials of the interested lawyers.

If you are secretary to a lawyer who receives a notice from the managing clerk, or from the secretary to the managing partner, check your diary and see that preparations necessary to take the required action are made.

4

Filing in the

Law Office

Lawyers usually want specific file folders, papers, or letters in a hurry, and one of your most important duties is to produce them promptly. No matter what system of filing you use, the accuracy with which you file determines whether you will be able to find the desired material without extended searching and fumbling. Remember that a paper misplaced even temporarily causes embarrassment to you and to the lawyer and can mean a lost client.

Your filing system should be so well organized that someone besides you can find papers when needed. You might know where a paper is because you put it there, but no one else will be able to locate it. "Memory" filing is not a filing system.

In this chapter we classify the material to be filed and describe the methods appropriate to the material. We also tell how to prepare the material for filing and how to arrange the papers so disorderly files and unnecessary searching will be avoided.

4.1 Classification of files. It is expedient to segregate files pertaining to clients' business from files pertaining to personal and office administration matters. The following classification of files is appropriate for the typical law office:

1. *Clients' business.* Files in this category include all matters relating to clients, with the exception of commercial collections when handled in volume. Some offices separate the material into litigation and nonlitigation matters. Other offices segregate files relating to a

particular field of law if a large part of the practice is in a specific field. Still other offices segregate matters relating to a retainer client with a large volume of business. The least confusing method is to keep all the files of each client together. However, most offices segregate inactive client files from the active ones (see section 4.5).

Since clients' files constitute by far the major part of the files in a law office, the detailed explanations in this chapter of the numerical and alphabetical systems of filing relate to clients' files.

2. *Commercial collections.* When a fair volume of commerical collections is handled, the files are segregated from other clients' business because of the close follow-up on these cases. Chapter 20, "Handling Commercial Collections," describes fully the system of filing used for these cases.

3. *Personal files.* The lawyer's personal file contains material relating to the lawyer's personal business matters, correspondence, and outside activities, such as bar association committees.

4. *General correspondence* files. This is the miscellaneous or "catch-all" file. It contains all material not relating to clients' business or to the lawyer's personal matters. Office administration material, such as personnel applications and records, correspondence about office equipment, correspondence with law book publishers, and the like would be placed in this file. Correspondence about a case the lawyer does not accept would be filed here.

5. *Periodicals, bulletins, and so on.* Every office accumulates pamphlets, booklets, periodicals, and the like that contain information likely to be needed in the future.

6. *Subsidiary files.* You will need files (other than the general correspondence files) for material such as sample legal blanks. Some secretaries keep sample forms in a loose-leaf notebook; others prefer to keep such material in file folders.

NUMERICAL SYSTEM OF FILING
APPLIED TO CLIENTS' FILES

4.2. What is the numerical system of filing? Under the numerical system of filing, each file is given a number, and the folders are arranged in numerical sequence. This is an indirect filing system since it must be used in connection with a cross-index. The subject and number of each file are put on an index card, and the cards are arranged alphabetically. The advantages of the numerical system are the rapidity and accuracy of refiling and the opportunity for unlimited expansion. The disadvantages are the maintenance of the auxiliary card index and the necessity of making two searches, one of the index and one of the files, whenever papers or folders are withdrawn.

4.3. How to use the numerical system in a law office. A method of numerical filing used successfully in law offices is to give a key number to a client instead of to a case. Each case for that client is given the client's key number plus an identifying number or letter. An explanation of how to set up and maintain a filing system of this kind follows. There are variations in the details, but to point them out here would only cause confusion.

1. Assign a key number to the client in numerical sequence. His or her general file has this number. Then assign an identifying *number* to each matter that is litigation and an identifying *letter* to each matter that is not litigation. For example, Client Sloan & McKinley, Inc. has a file of general correspondence, a profit-sharing plan for employees, and a suit against The Baker Co. You give the general file the number 85, the profit-sharing file the number 85-A. and the suit the number 85-1. The next suit will be 85-2. (If you prefer, you might identify all files by number or letter instead of using numbers for the suits and letters for the nonsuit files, but the number and letter system segregates the client's court matters from his nonlitigation matters in the file cabinet and in the card index.)

2. Make index cards under each name that appears in connection with the matter. In some instances, for example, estate matters, your client's name does not appear in the subject of the file; nevertheless a card should be made in the client's name.

Type on the card the title of the case, the number assigned to it, and the client's name if it does not appear in the title. In a matter of litigation the card under the defendant's name will read *defendant ads. plaintiff*, instead of plaintiff vs. defendant. If the matter is not a suit or claim, type on the card, in addition to the client's name, an identifying description of the subject matter. For example:

Sloan & McKinley, Inc.
Profit-sharing Plan

It is not necessary but you might also make a card under the subject, which would read:

Profit-sharing Plan
Sloan & McKinley, Inc.

Make index cards and cross-index cards freely, and be liberal in the information that you type on them. They are the key to your filing system and eventually justify the time consumed in typing them. Figures 4.1, 4.2, and 4.3 illustrate three types of index cards. Figures 4.1 and 4.2 are printed especially for law ofices. See page 90 for an explanation of the entries on 4.3.

3. File the index cards alphabetically. When there is more than one card under a client's name, place them in this order: general card, nonlitigation cards arranged alphabetically according to subject, litigation cards arranged alphabetically according to opposing party. Suppose a client has a general file and five other files. The cards will be arranged as follows:

Sloan & McKinley, Inc.	52
Sloan & McKinley, Inc.—Arbitration	52-B
Sloan & McKinley, Inc.—Legislation	52-C
Sloan & McKinley, Inc.—Profit-sharing Plan	52-A
Sloan & McKinley, Inc. vs. Harvey	52-2
Sloan & McKinley, Inc. ads. Watson	52-1

Smith, John
  ads

James Hall (Client)

Document File	Correspondence File	Printed Papers	Storage
152-1	152-1		

Figure 4.1. *File Index Card.*

If the client's cases are numerous, you might put a guide card between the litigation and nonlitigation cards to facilitate locating the desired card.

4. File the folders in numerical sequence according to key number. If there is more than one file for a client, arrange those bearing identifying letters in alphabetical sequence; follow with those bearing identifying numbers in numerical sequence. Thus, in the cabinet, all files pertaining to one client are together; all of his or her nonlitigation matters are together, and all suits and claims are together.

Harvey, William				81 - 5
v. Baxter, Marie				
Correspondence	DOCUMENTS	PRINTED PAPERS	GENERAL SAFE	
81 - 5	81 - 5	Cabinet 2		
Cabinet #2 - Extra copies of briefs, case on appeal, etc.				

Figure 4.2. *File Index Card—Another Form.*

White, John B.	395-1
vs Daniels Pipe Blue Book Paper File Duplicates	

Figure 4.3. *File Index Card—Another Form.*

5. Keep a card showing the key number to be assigned to the next client in front of the index box.

6. When a client brings a case to the office, give the client a key number and assign the case an identifying letter or number. Reserve the key number, without identifying letters or numbers, for the client's general correspondence should it become desirable to have a file of that nature for him or her.

7. Reserve a key number for miscellaneous clients, who might want a letter written for them or have some small matter involving only one or two papers. These matters can be filed under the same key number, but all necessary index cards should be made.

4.4. Assigning numbers according to type of case. When files are separated according to type of case, a group of numbers is set aside for each category. For example, cases involving litigation will be numbered 1 through 199; probate cases, 200 through 399, and so on. The client does not have a key number. A list of available numbers is kept for each category, and the number of a closed file is placed on the appropriate list and used again.

Another method of numbering when files are separated according to type of case is for each category to have a separate sequence of numbers. There might be, for example, a Claim 485 and a Probate 485. Different colored labels or folders should be used for each category.

4.5. How to transfer numerical files. Apparently it is against the lawyer's conscience to destroy a file. Consequently all available space in the office is used for retired files, and the overflow is sent to a warehouse, or to the attic, or to any place where space is available. The procedure followed by many firms is to retain in the office as many closed files as space permits and from time to time to send the oldest closed files to outside storage, replacing them in the office with more recently closed files. When there are retired files in the office, the active files might be kept in the top drawers of the filing cabinets and the retired files in the lower drawers. The retired files are referred to only occasionally, and by using the top drawers for active files, stooping and bending are eliminated. We use the words *closed* and *retired* interchangeably here.

Law files are not retired periodically but are closed when the matter is presumably completed. A file opened in 1979 might be completed and ready for retirement in 1980, whereas a case opened in 1970 might remain active until 1985 or longer.

Ideally you should process a file for retirement as soon as you are informed that the matter has been completed, without permitting an accumulation. But this is a job that secretaries are inclined to postpone until there is a lull in the work. As soon as you are informed that the matter has been completed, stamp the file jacket "closed." Then when time permits, you can go through your filing cabinets and withdraw all closed cases and process them for retirement. Use old jackets for storage files.

Here are the steps in processing a file for retirement or storage.

1. Withdraw from the active index all cards relating to the closed case. Stamp the cards "Closed" with a small rubber stamp. If you wish you might also stamp the date on the card. You will notice that the index card illustrated in figure 4.1 has a column for this purpose, and the card shown in figure 4.2 has a column that can be designated *storage*.

2. Withdraw from the active files all jackets or folders holding papers that relate to the completed case. Your index card will indicate whether there are extra copies or printed papers that have been removed from the regular filing cabinet. (See figure 4.2.) The documents in the safe will not be sent to storage. They will be returned to the client, or other appropriate disposition will be made of them.

3. Keep your index of closed files separate from your index of active files. (Some offices, however, prefer to keep cards for inactive files in the master file so the secretary need look only in one place to see if something is active or inactive.)

4. If your policy is to segregate active and inactive cards, file the index cards in the closed card index, alphabetically, just as they were filed in the current index.

5. File the closed files in the transfer cabinets numerically just as they were filed in the active files.

ALPHABETICAL SYSTEM OF FILING
APPLIED TO CLIENTS' FILES

4.6. What is the alphabetical system of filing? Under the alphabetical system of filing, the folders are filed alphabetically according to name or subject. A cross-index is not necessary with this system of filing but can be used if desired. The principal advantage of the alphabetical system of filing is that it is not necessary to look up a file number in a cross-index when papers or folders are filed or withdrawn. The disadvantages are that the system does not lend itself to expansion as readily as the numerical system and requires more shifting of folders. The alphabetical system is also widely used in law offices.

4.7. How to use the alphabetical system. Each client has a general folder and each of his or her matters has a separate folder. All matters of a specific client are filed under the client's name. The order of arrangement of the various folders is similar to that of the index cards in a numerical system: The general folder comes first and is followed by the nonsuit files arranged alphabetically according to subject. These are followed by the litigation files arranged alphabetically according to opposing party. The various matters of Client Rossiter & Grossberg, Inc. might be labeled and filed as follows:

> Rossiter & Grossberg, Inc.—General
> Rossiter & Grossberg, Inc.—Arbitration—T.F. Lewis
> Rossiter & Grossberg, Inc.—Arbitration—J.B. Maxwell
> Rossiter & Grossberg, Inc.—Profit-sharing Plan
> Rossiter & Grossberg, Inc. ads. Goldman, Inc.
> Rossiter & Grossberg, Inc. vs. Donaldson Sound Systems, Inc.

If the active files of a client are very numerous, they might be numbered and a card index made of that client's files.

Another method of using the alphabetical system in a law office is to file under the name of the plaintiff, whether or not the plaintiff is the client. Lawyers have a tendency to think of suits and claims in terms of plaintiff vs. defendant. Nonlitigation matters are filed under the name of the client. When this method of filing is followed, cross-index cards are desirable. Make the index cards in the name of the client and others connected with the case and show on the card under which name the folder is filed.

4.8. How to transfer alphabetical files. When alphabetical files are closed or transferred to storage, cross-index cards *must* be made. The simplest method of transferring them is to assign the file a transfer number and make cross-index cards for each party connected with the matter. The files are then placed in the storage files in numerical order. This avoids shifting of files.

Some offices transfer alphabetically. The file drawers are then numbered and the drawer number in which the file is placed is indicated on the cross-index cards. Each year's transferred files may be filed together alphabetically. However, this entails shifting of files from drawer to drawer unless ample space under each letter is kept open for files to be stored under that letter in the future.

OTHER FILES

4.9. Personal file. The personal file is a combination name and subject file, and the alphabetical system of filing is used for it. A twenty-five division alphabetical guide will probably be sufficient; no cross-index is needed.

Make a folder for each letter of the alphabet. File the correspondence under the first letter of the correspondent's last name, according to date. Thus correspondence with Mrs. Pomeroy and with Mr. Hill will be in the same folder. If the lawyer has prolific correspondence with a certain person, make a separate folder for that correspondent. Also, make a separate folder for each separate business matter and outside activity. Thus, if the lawyer is on the Grievance Committee of the American Bar Association, there will be a folder labeled: "American Bar Association— Grievance Committee," and the folder will be filed under the letter *A*. Should the material for any particular subject become voluminous, withdraw it from the alphabetical file and file it under a guide of its own.

Close these files periodically by moving them to another drawer in the office where they will be available for reference if necessary. The correspondence folders can probably be transferred intact, or several letters of the alphabet combined in one folder to save space. However, it will probably be necessary to go through the subject folders, such as the "American Bar Association—Grievance Committee" folder, and extract material that is pertinent to the forthcoming year. Transfer the closed files from the office to storage when they are several years old, to make room in the office for the more recent personal files. (See also section 4.18.)

4.10. General correspondence file. The alphabetical system should be used for this file. It is operated in the same manner as the personal files. File according to the name of the correspondent. The division of the alphabetical guide needed will depend upon the volume of miscellaneous material. No card index is necessary.

Close and transfer these files periodically by the same method that you close and transfer the lawyer's personal files.

4.11. Periodicals, bulletins, and so on. File these alphabetically according to subject. The filing cabinet used for them need not be fireproof, and a twenty-five division alphabetical guide will be sufficient. This material will consist of government bulletins, advertisements, catalogues, announcements of changes in law firms, announcements from law schools, and any other material of this nature that the lawyer wishes to keep. Periodically you should go through the file and discard material that is out of date.

PHYSICAL SETUP OF FILES

4.12. Preparation of material for filing. To prepare material for filing, do the following:

1. Segregate papers belonging in different files; client's matters; personal; general correspondence.

2. Check to see if the lawyer has initialed the paper for filing. (In offices with more than one attorney, there should be a hard and fast rule that no paper is to be filed until the responsible attorney has initialed it.)

3. Check through all papers that are clipped or stapled together to see whether they should be filed together.

4. Remove all paper clips.

5. Mend torn papers with cellophane tape.

6. See that all legal documents have been conformed.

7. Mark on all court papers the date they were filed with the clerk of the court or served upon opposing counsel. (This information may have been stamped by the clerk of the court on the back of the paper and so may not be evident when the paper is fastened to the folder unless noted on the face of the paper.)

8. Note on the paper where it is to be filed. For numerical files, write the key and identification numbers in the upper right-hand corner; for a name file, underline the name in colored pencil; for a subject file, write the subject in colored pencil in the upper right-hand corner or underline it in colored pencil if it appears on the paper.

9. Punch a hole or holes in the *exact* place where the paper should be fastened to the folder. An electric gadget that punches holes in the paper is a valuable timesaver when thick documents must be stapled into folders.

10. When fastening the paper in the folder, check the number and name on the paper being filed with the number and name on the folder.

11. Sort unfiled material into categories and keep it nearby in one or more folders to save time in searching for unfiled items.

12. Fold oversized papers so the written material is on the outside, easily read without having to remove the paper and open it.

13. Use follow-up files (see chapter 3) to avoid needless searching for items needing follow-up.

14. File the latest material at the front of loose-leaf books to avoid paging through everything when searching for current items.

4.13. How to type index tabs and labels. For best results in typing tabs, guides, and folder labels, observe the following rules:

Use the briefest possible designations. Abbreviate, omitting punctuation whenever possible. Index tabs need to be legible only at normal reading distance. Guide labels should be legible at two or three feet. File drawer labels should be legible at six feet.

Use initial caps whenever needed. Full caps, especially in elite and pica type, do not increase the legibility of label designations; they decrease the amount of light background around the letters and make reading more difficult. Do not underline.

Folder labels. The most important part of a folder label is the eighth of an inch immediately below the scoring (the place at which the label is folded for positioning on the folder tab). Frequently this space is the only part visible in the file. Therefore, start at the first typing space below the scoring. Typing should begin in the first or second typing space from the left edge of the label, except for one or two chapter designations. If this is done, all folder labels in the file drawer will present an even left margin.

Use initial caps and indent the second and third lines so the first word of the first line will stand out.

In typing labels for a numbered subject or name file, leave space between the number and first word; type the subject in block form. Avoid exceptionally long file numbers if possible.

Guide labels. For file guide labels, use the largest type available. Begin the typing as high on the label as the guide tabs will permit. Center one- and two-chapter designations. Start all other designations in the second typing space from the left edge. Use abbreviations or shortened forms and omit punctuation, except for large numbers such as 10,000.

File-drawer labels. In preparing labels for file drawers, use the largest type available. Center the typing on the label and leave a double space above and below detailed reference information. It is better to print file drawer labels because type is not legible at a distance.

4.14. How to arrange the papers in the file folders. A file in a law matter consists of at least two parts: correspondence and formal documents, whether they be court papers or legal instruments such as agreements, leases, and the like. Each file must have a correspondence folder and a document folder, both of which are kept together in the file jacket. It does not matter what kind of "folder" is used, as long as it has enough firmness to serve as a backing sheet to which the papers may be fastened with a brad or other fastener that permits removal when desired. Correspondence and papers are both filed in their respective folders according to date, usually with the latest on top, although some lawyers prefer the reverse order. Always keep the correspondence folder on top of the document folder in the jacket.

A file might consist of more than two parts. Separate folders are required for briefs and law memoranda; drafts; extra copies; miscellaneous memoranda, such as interoffice memos, notes made by the lawyer, and so on. If a file contains both legal instruments (agreements, contracts, and the like) and court papers, a separate folder is made for each. If a case has papers filed in more than one court, a separate folder is made for each court. A law file might also contain a folder for "hold papers," that is, papers belonging to the client other than those kept in the safe. The "hold papers" should not be fastened in the folder. Always indicate on the index card the folders that are made up in each case. For example, the index card illustrated in figure 4.3 indicates that a blue book, a file for duplicates, and a paper file have been made in the case. (*Blue book* denotes, in the office whose card is illustrated, the folder in which important papers, such as wills and agreements, are filed; *paper file* denotes the folder for miscellaneous memoranda.)

As a file grows, it is broken down into volumes, with all letters together in one or two folders, all court papers together, and so on. Law files frequently become so voluminous that two or more jackets are required. All of the jackets in a particular case should have the same number. On each jacket, write the classification of the contents of that jacket—that is, the folders that are in the jacket—so you will not have to open more than one jacket to find the desired papers. Some offices make a separate index card for each jacket.

Figure 4.4 illustrates another kind of folder used for matters that will not become too voluminous. The outside cover gives a full history of the case from opening to closing. Every step in the litigation is shown on the cover so information required in a hurry is available at a glance.

A similar folder, generally used for contract or real estate matters, is illustrated in figure 4.5. The folder in figure 4.6 can be adapted for special documents like cases on appeal, briefs, and memoranda of law.

4.15. Preparation for closing a file. When closing a file, go through it carefully and remove all paper clips, pins, and the like. This procedure eliminates the possibility of storing papers that do not belong in that particular file. Quite often a misplaced paper is found, and removal of the clips reduces the size of the file. If a file has several jackets, you might be able to combine the contents into one jacket. Papers and folders in a closed file may be packed more tightly than those in an active file.

4.16. Extra copies and printed papers, drafts. A legal file usually contains extra copies and drafts of various documents. These should have separate folders. Extra copies, especially of printed papers, quickly become voluminous and impede the process of filing. Whether you have 5 or 50 cases with voluminous extra copies, try to set aside an extra filing cabinet or drawer for them. You may file them in the same order as the regular file. Notice that the index cards illustrated in figures 4.1 and 4.2 have a column headed "Print Papers." Indicate in this column (or elsewhere on the index card if you use another kind) that extra copies have been removed from the regular file. The same procedure may be followed with voluminous drafts.

4.17. Control of material taken from the files. To control folders taken from your files, use guides the same height as the file folders but of

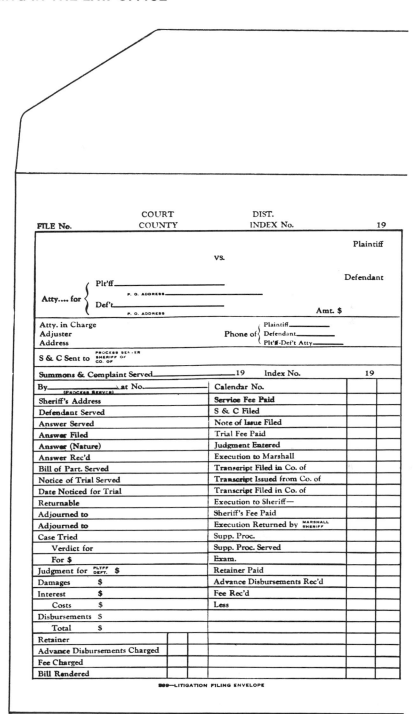

Figure 4.4. *Litigation Filing Envelope.*

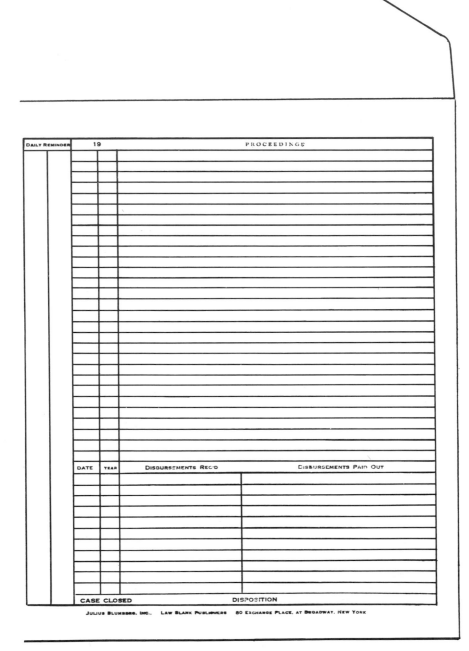

Figure 4.4. *Continued.*

JULIUS BLUMBERG, INC. LAW BLANK PUBLISHERS   80 EXCHANGE PLACE AT BROADWAY, NEW YORK

S 59B - Docket Envelope

File # _____ Closing Date _____ Place _____

Client _____ Phone _____

Client's Address _____

Property _____ Municipality _____

Map _____ Block _____ Lot _____

(Seller) (Buyer) Atty. _____ Phone _____

Purchase Price or Mortgage $

	Prep.	Ord.	Recvd.	Rec.	Bk.	Pg.	Delvd.
Contract							
County Search							
Tax & Assessment Search							
Planning Board Search							
Improvement Search							
Corp. Status Report							
Trenton Search							
Estate or Inher. Tax							
Prelim. Title Binder							
Survey (or Affidavit)							
Chancery Abstract							
Tenement House Bd.							
Mtg. Estoppel Letter							
Tax Bills							
Fuel Verification							
Water Adjustment							
Rent							
Fire Policy Adj.							
Liability Policy Adj.							
Fire Policies or End.							
Liability Policy or End.							
U. S. Revenue Stamps							
Deed							
Affidavit of Title							
Corp. Resolution							
Bond							
Mortgage							
Cancellation-Dischge. of Mtg.							
Satisfaction or Release—Mtg.							
Escrow							
Final Title Cert.							
Title Ins.							
Miscl.							

Courtesy *Julius Blumberg, Inc.*

Figure 4.5. *Docket Envelope—Litigation or Real Estate.*

Caption_____ File #_____

Court:_____ Phone_____

Plaintiff Atty._____ Phone_____

Defendant Atty._____ Phone_____

Doctor_____ Phone_____

Insurance Co._____ Phone_____

Adjuster_____ Phone_____

Settlement Offered On_____ $_____

Docket #_____ Case #_____

Cplt. Filed_____ Summons Svd_____

Ans. Due_____ Served_____

Demand For Jury_____ Served_____

Def. Interrog. Srvd._____ Ans. Due_____ Ans. Svd._____

Plaint. Int. Svd_____ Ans. Due_____ Ans. Svd_____

Deposition Notice_____ Taken_____ Recd. Transcript_____

Motions_____

Atty's Conference_____ Pretrial Date_____

Weekly Call_____ Date of Trial_____

Notification to Client_____ Subpoenas_____

Determination_____ Judgment Ent._____ Executed_____

Motion New Trial_____ Not. Appeal Filed_____

Settled_____ Releases_____

Miscl.

Figure 4.5. *Continued.*

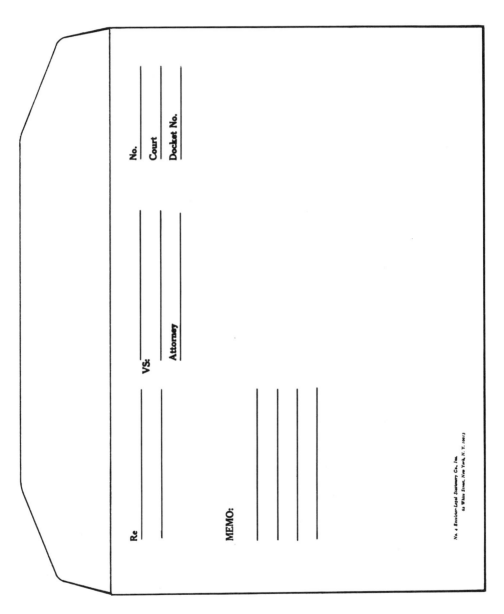

Figure 4.6. *Multi-purpose Docket Envelope.*

different-colored stock, with the word *out* printed on the tab. The *out* guide provides space on which to make an entry of the date, the material taken, who has it, and date it should be returned. Place the guide in the files where the removed material was located.

A secretary in a private office does not put an *out* guide in her file every time she withdraws material for the lawyer. She uses the guide under these circumstances: (1) Someone outside her immediate office wants the material. (2) The lawyer expects to take the material out of the office, say, when he or she goes on a trip. (3) She expects her employer to keep the material a week or so, say, to prepare a brief.

When a paper is removed from a folder, make a note of the removal and insert it in the folder. Many law offices have a rule (and it is a good one) that no one may remove a paper from a folder except the person responsible for the filing. However, some large offices have a check-out system whereby a 3- by 5-inch card must be filled out by anyone removing a file other than the secretary or her employer.

INFORMATION STORAGE AND RETRIEVAL SYSTEMS

4.18. Electronics and the law office. Electronic innovations are designed to save time in a law office. Automated card filing units, record retrieval systems, and the like have been developed by many companies with a view toward saving the lawyer time, money, and space.

Information storage and retrieval devices are available in a wide variety of sizes and capabilitites. Some provide high-density storage and rapid retrieval for active index cards used as a cross-reference to cases or account data. The card carriers are arranged in ferris-wheel fashion. As the operator presses a button, the carrier with the card tray is moved to operator's position in about three seconds. Reference is easier; vital records are protected against tearing, bending, and soiling; and records are always within immediate reach.

In another unit, the operator touches the keyboard and within seconds the desired slide or frame is delivered to the desk area ready for reference, revision, updating, insertion, or withdrawal. The visible margin of each card combined with colored signals ensure positive interpretation and evaluation. This combination assures faster retrieval and saves valuable executive and secretarial time.

Automated records retrieval system for case files and client records are geared to the law office that has an active filing operation consisting of six or more file cabinets. From a seated or standing position the operator touches a button and carriers for letter, legal, or larger sized folders rotate in either direction and stop in front of the operator for rapid media withdrawal or addition. Not only does this save time, it can also save the law office up to 50 percent floor space and ensure better client service and relations.

Some systems such as microfilming reduce data for storage on film. Rapid retrieval brings the film to a machine where it is magnified for reading. Certain models will produce a photocopy of the document being read.

Sophisticated storage and retrieval equipment is a must for large offices that need to move massive amounts of file material quickly and easily. For detailed information, consult trade catalogs and write to manufacturers for literature on current models.

5

Handling Legal and

Business Correspondence

The written communication that goes out of a law office represents the lawyer and his or her firm. If the composition is awkward or confusing and if the mechanical presentation is careless, inaccurate, or unpleasing to the eye, the lawyer's good work is apt to suffer and might be lost. The secretary can greatly enhance the effectiveness of all written communication by setting it up attractively and typing it accurately and neatly.

5.1. Styles of letter setups. The style in which letters are usually set up in the law office are the full-block (figure 5.1), block (figure 5.2), semiblock (figure 5.3), and official (figure 5.4). The official style is used frequently for informal letters written to personal acquaintances.

Full-block style. The distinguishing feature of the full-block style of letter is that there are no indentations; all structural parts begin flush left. Very few typewriter adjustments are needed. The complimentary close and dateline, for example, are aligned with the paragraphs at the extreme left rather than shifted to the right. Open punctuation is used.

Block style. The block style is the most widely used style in a business letter. The inside address and the paragraphs are blocked flush with the left margin. The salutation and attention line, if any, are also positioned flush left. However, the dateline and reference line are flush right and the complimentary close is placed slightly to the right of center page. Both lines of the signature are aligned with the complimentary close. Open punctuation is used.

𝒩ational 𝒜ssociation of 𝓛egal 𝒮ecretaries
(INTERNATIONAL)
ADMINISTRATIVE OFFICES
3005 EAST SKELLY DRIVE, SUITE 120 · TULSA, OKLAHOMA 74105

April 5, 19--

REPLY TO:

Mr. Carl B. Ryan
Ryan Communications Center
2216 East 20th Street
Chicago IL 60616

Dear Mr. Ryan:

Re: Full-Block Style of Letter

This is an example of the full-block style of letter, used in many
law offices because it is the most efficient letter form. Preparation
of this style saves time and energy.

As you see, there are no indentations. Everything, including the date
and the complimentary close, begins at the extreme left. This uniformity
eliminates several mechanical operations in typing letters. Open
punctuation is used in the inside address.

Since the dictator's name is typed in the signature, it is not considered
necessary to include his or her initials in the identification line.

Sincerely yours,

James P. Trout

dj

Figure 5.1. *Full-Block Style of Letter.*

Semiblock style. The distinguishing feature of the semiblock style is
that all structural parts of the letter begin flush with the left margin, but
the first line of each paragraph is indented five to ten spaces. Carry-over
lines in the address are indented three spaces. All lines of the typed

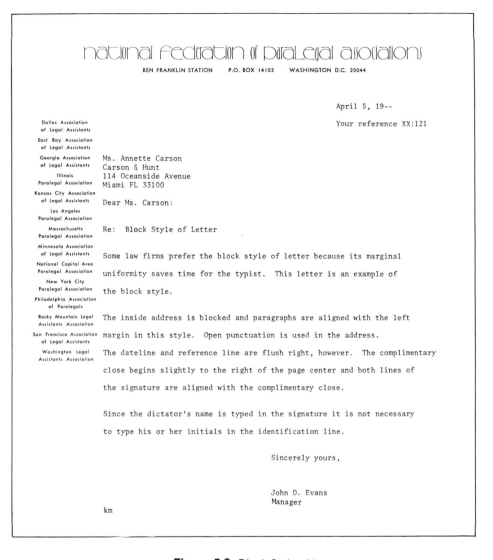

Figure 5.2. *Block Style of Letter.*

signature are aligned with the complimentary close. The dateline is typed flush with the right margin. Open punctuation is used.

Official style. The official style is often used for personal letters written on executive-size letterhead. The distinguishing feature of the

---

THE **NATIONAL PARALEGAL INSTITUTE,** INC.

2000 P ST. N.W., 6th FLOOR, WASH., D.C. 20036

202-872-0655(6)

William R. Fry
Executive Director

April 5, 19--

Messrs. Adams and Smith
35 Fifth Avenue
New York NY 10003

Dear Sirs:

           Re: Semiblock Style of Letter

    This is an example of the semiblock style of letter. Many law firms choose it because it combines utility with an attractive appearance.

    As you can see, the inside address is blocked. The first line of each paragraph is indented ten spaces. As in all letters, there is a double space between paragraphs. The dateline is flush with the right margin, two or four spaces below the letterhead. The subject line is two spaces below the salutation and is centered. The complimentary close begins slightly to the right of the page center. All lines of the signature are aligned with the complimentary close. Open punctuation is used in the address.

    The dictator's initials do not appear in the indentification line since his or her name is typed in the signature. The typist's initials often appear on the carbon copy only.

                    Sincerely yours,

                    Jennifer Clark
                    Correspondence Manager

Figure 5.3. *Semiblock Style of Letter.*

official style of letter is that the inside address is placed below the signature, flush with the left-hand margin, instead of before the salutation. The address is blocked. The identification line and enclosure notations, if any, are typed two spaces below the last line of the address.

5.2. Opinion letters. Opinion letters are formal letters giving a professional opinion to a client on some legal question. Each law firm has its own method of setting them up, usually in the style that is used for ordinary letters. These letters are generally signed manually by a partner

MURPHY & McLAUGHLIN
ATTORNEYS AT LAW
635 MAIN STREET
LACONIA, NEW HAMPSHIRE 03246

MICHAEL C. MURPHY
PHILIP T. MC LAUGHLIN
CAROLYN W. BALDWIN

TELEPHONE
(603) 524-4404

April 5, 19--

Dear Mrs. Baker:

This letter is an example of the official style. It is used in
many personal letters written by lawyers and looks unusually well on
the executive-size letterhead.

The structural parts of the letter differ from the semiblock style
only in the position of the inside address. The salutation is placed
two to five spaces below the dateline, depending on the length of the
letter. The inside address is written in block form, flush with the
left margin, from two to five spaces below the final line of the signature.
Open punctuation is used in the address. This style of letter usually
does not have a subject line. The identification line, if used, should
be placed two spaces below the last line of the address and the enclosure
mark two spaces below that.

Since the dictator's name is typed in the signature, his or her
initials are not needed in the identification line. The typist's initials
often are on the carbon copies of the letter only.

Sincerely yours,

George E. Thomas

Mrs. Jane W. Baker
The Office Supply House
18 Hillside Avenue
Minneapolis MN 55405

Figure 5.4. *Official Style of Letter.*

with the firm name, because they represent advice from the firm, not merely from the lawyer who dictated the letter. Usually the dictator's initials do not show on the orginal but do show on the office copies.

5.3. Punctuation. Either mixed or open punctuation may be used in the structural parts of a letter. *Mixed punctuation* means no end-of-line punctuation in the inside address. However, you do use a colon after the salutation and a comma after the complimentary close. *Open punctuation* means the omission of punctuation marks after the inside address, salutation, and complimentary close, unless a line ends in an abbreviation. Open punctuation is used most often with the full-block style of letter.

5.4. Subject line. In any letter, a subject line makes it unnecessary for the writer to devote the first paragraph of the letter to a routine explanation of its subject. In correspondence about law matters the subject line is a necessity as well as a convenience. The correspondence is often filed according to the subject and not according to the name of the correspondent, and, frequently, it is difficult to deduce from the letter the matter to which it refers. Since the subject is actually part of the body of the letter, it should follow the salutation. Preferably, it is centered two spaces below the salutation, and is preceded by *Re* or *In re* (see Latin Words and Phrases, part 5), which may be followed by a colon, or not, as desired.

5.5. How to type the dateline. 1. Date the letter the day it is dictated, not the day it is typed, unless instructed otherwise. If you date the letter the day it is transcribed, adjust references to time made in the dictation, such as "today" or "yesterday."

2. Type the date conventionally, all on one line.

3. Do not use *d, nd, rd, st,* or *th* following the day of the month.

4. Do not abbreviate or use figures for the month.

5. Do not spell out the day of the month or the year, except in very formal letters.

Right	*Wrong*
November 15, 19..	November 15th, 19..
	11/15/..
	Nov. 15, 19..
	November fifteenth, Nineteen hundred and ....

THE ADDRESS

5.6. Forms of Address. A person's name is important. If it begins with *Mac*, it should be written that way, not *Mc.* The same is true of firms and companies. Some law firms omit the comma between names of the members of the firm (for example, *Bell Wilson Nelson Adams*); others insert the ampersand between each name (*Bell & Wilson & Nelson & Adams*).Some companies include *Company, Co., The, Inc.,* or *&* as part of the official name. It is your duty to write a name the way the owner writes it. Never take a chance and write it the way you think it should be written—verify it from incoming correspondence, the file, or some other source. (See reference facilities in chapter 7.)

Titles. For the correct forms of addressing persons in official or honorary positions, see Forms of Address, part 5. Generally, the following forms apply:

1. Always precede a name by a title, unless initials indicating degrees or *Esquire* follow the name. The use of a business title or position or of *Sr.* or *Jr.* after a name does not take the place of a title.

Right	*Wrong*
Mr. David Henderson, President	David Henderson, President

2. *Esquire* or *Esq.* never precedes a name and is never used with any other title, not even with *Mr.* In business correspondence *Esquire* or *Esq.* is used only to address high-ranking professional men who have no other title, but the practice is different in law offices. Many law offices always address a lawyer as *Esquire.* You, of course, must be guided by the instructions of the dictator. Clerks of courts and justices of the peace are properly addressed as *Esquire.* Although *Esquire* is traditionally a title for men, it is now being used for women in the legal profession as well. It is preferable not to use *Esquires* after a firm name composed of two or more surnames.

Right	*Wrong*
Dr. John W. Parsons	Dr. John W. Parsons, Esq.
Ralph S. Manley, Esquire	Mr. Ralph S. Manley, Esquire
Harold M. Davis, Jr., Esq.	Mr. Harold M. Davis, Jr., Esquire
Anne J. Smith, Esq.	Ms. Anne J. Smith, Esq.

The title *Esq.* is commonly used in England and her colonies. There it is the proper title to use in addressing the heads of business firms, banking executives, doctors, and the like.

Correct in England
Jacob McHenry, Esq., President
Jonathan Holt, Esq., M.D.

3. *Messrs.* is used for addressing a firm of attorneys, as *Messrs. Jackson, Bell & Hunt.* It may be used in addressing a business firm of men, or men and women, when the names denote individuals, but not in addressing corporations or other business organizations that bear impersonal names.

Right	*Wrong*
Messrs. Jackson Fry Dennis	
Attorneys at Law	
Martin Fenwick & Sons	Messrs. Martin Fenwick & Sons

4. Initials or abbreviations indicating degrees and other honors are sometimes placed after the name of the person addressed. Use only the initials of the highest degree; more than one degree may be used, however, if the degrees are in different fields. In that case, place the degree pertaining to the person's profession first. A scholastic title is not used in combination with the abbreviation indicating that degree, but another title may be used in combination with abbreviations indicating degrees.

Right	*Wrong*
Janis E. Lewis, Ph.D.	Janis E. Lewis, A.B., A.M., Ph.D.
Dr. Morris Glass (*preferred*)	Dr. Morris Glass, M.D.
or	Professor Robert E. Kline, Ph.D.
Morris Glass, M.D.	
The Reverend Maxwell B. Hart, D.D., LL.D.	
Professor Robert E. Kline	

5.7. Business titles or position. 1. The designation of a business position follows the name. It does not take the place of a title.

Right	*Wrong*
Mr. John King, President	John King, President
	President John King

2. Do not abbreviate business titles or positions, such as president, secretary, and sales manager. *Mr.* (or *Mrs., Miss,* or *Ms.*) precedes the individual's name, even when the business title is used. If a person's business title is short, place it on the first line; if it is long, place it on the second line.

Ms. Donna Ullman, President	Ms. Donna Ullman
Ullman & Prince Company	Advertising Manager
1000 West Avenue	Ullman & Prince Company
Cleveland, OH 44100	1000 West Avenue
	Cleveland OH 44100

The modern trend, however, is to omit the business title, particularly if it makes the address run over four lines.

3. Hyphenate a title when it represents two or more offices.

Right	*Wrong*
Secretary-Treasurer	Secretary Treasurer

4. If a letter is addressed to a particular department in a company,

place the name of the company on the first line and the name of the department on the second line.

5. In addressing an individual in a firm, corporation, or group, place the individual's name on the first line and the company's name on the second line.

5.8. Forms for addressing women. 1. *Firm composed of women.* In addressing a firm composed of women either married or unmarried, use *Mesdames* or *Mmes.*

2. *Unmarried woman.* Use *Miss* or *Ms.* when you are addressing an unmarried woman. When you do not know whether she is married or unmarried, use *Ms.*

3. *Married woman.* Socially a married woman is addressed by her husband's full name preceded by *Mrs.* In business, she may be addressed either by her husband's name or by her given name and her married name, preceded by *Mrs.* Use the form she prefers if you know it.

4. *Widow.* Socially a widow is addressed by her husband's full name preceded by *Mrs.* In business either her husband's full name or her given name and her married name, preceded by *Mrs.* is correct. Use the form that she prefers if you know it.

5. *Divorcee.* If a divorcee retains her married name, the title *Mrs.* is preferable to *Miss.* If she uses her maiden name, she may use either *Miss* or *Mrs.* In business she may be addressed by her given name combined with her married name or by both her maiden and married names. Follow the form she prefers if you know it. Socially she is addressed by her maiden name combined with her married name.

6. *Wife of a titled man.* Do not address a married woman by her husband's title. Address her as *Mrs. James A. Altman* or *Mrs. J.A. Altman.* If she is addressed jointly with her husband, the correct form is *Dr. and Mrs. James A. Altman, Judge and Mrs. Donald Phillips.*

7. *Professional women.* Address a woman with a professional title by her title, followed by her given and last names. A married woman sometimes uses her maiden name and, if so, should be addressed by it. In social correspondence her title is sometimes dropped in addressing her and her husband.

When you do not know whether an addressee is a man or a woman, use the form of address appropriate for a man. *Women in official or honorary positions are addressed just as men in similar positions, except that Madam, Mrs., Ms., or Miss replace Sir or Mr.* See Forms of Address, part 5.

5.9. How to type the street address. The inside address and the addresss on the envelope are the same. The following instructions for writing it are standard, although various authorities give different rules for writing the address.

1. Do not precede the street number with a word or a sign.

Right	*Wrong*
60 Fourth Avenue	No. 60 Fourth Avenue
	# 60 Fourth Avenue

2. Spell out the numerical names of streets and avenues if they are numbers of 12 or under. When figures are used, do not follow with *d, st,* or *th.* Use figures for all house numbers except *One.* Separate the house number from a numerical name of a thoroughfare with a space, a hyphen, and a space.

> 16 West Tenth Street
> 16 West 13 Street
> One Ninth Avenue
> 2 Sixth Avenue
> 143 - 91 Street

3. If a room, suite, or apartment number is part of the address, it should follow the street address. This position facilitates mail delivery. If the address is an office building instead of a street, the suite number may precede the name of the building.

Right	*Wrong*
600 Tulip Drive, Room 214	Room 214, 600 Tulip Drive
2020 O'Shea Building	

4. Never abbreviate the name of a city. States, territories, and possessions should be abbreviated by their official two-letter designations (IL, OH, CA, etc.).

5. The zip code should appear on the last line of the address following the city and state. Not less than two nor more than six spaces should be left between the last letter of the state and the first digit of the code.

6. Even if there is no street address, keep the city and state on the same line.

7. Use a post-office box number if you have it instead of the street address.

SALUTATIONS

5.10. How to type the salutation. 1. Capitalize the first word, the title, and the name. Capitalize *dear* when it is used as the first word of the salutation.

2. Use a colon following the salutation. A comma is used only in social letters, particularly in those written in longhand.

3. *Mr., Mrs., Ms.,* and *Dr.* are the only titles that are abbreviated.

5.11. Forms of salutation. See Forms of Address, part 5, for the correct salutation to use in letters to people in official or honorary positions. The form of salutation varies with the tone of the letter and the degree of acquaintanceship between the lawyer and the client. The trend today is toward the less formal salutation.

1. If the letter is addressed to an individual, make the salutation singular, for example, *Dear Sir.* If the letter is addressed to a company or group, make it plural, for example, *Gentlemen* or *Dear Sirs.* The latter is preferable when addressing a firm of lawyers.

2. Never use a designation of any kind after a salutation.

Right	*Wrong*
Dear Mr. Wilson:	Dear Mr. Wilson, C.P.A.

3. The salutation in a letter addressed to an organization composed of men and women is *Ladies* and *Gentlemen*; to a man and woman, *Dear Sir and Madam*; to a married couple, *Dear Mr. and Mrs. Nash, Dr. and Mrs. Nash,* or *Dr. and Mr. Nash.*

4. Never use a *business* title or designation of position in a salutation. (Honorary and official titles are frequently used in salutations. See Forms of Address, part 5.) However, some lawyers address others in their profession as *Dear Brother Jones* or *Dear Sister Smith.*

Right	*Wrong*
Dear Mr. Franklin:	Dear Secretary:
	Dear Secretary Franklin:

5. If a letter addressed to a firm of lawyers is to the attention of an individual lawyer, the salutation is to the firm, not to the individual.

6. Follow a title with the surname.

Right	*Wrong*
Dear Professor Johnston:	Dear Professor:

5.12. Forms of salutation in letters addressed to women. 1. Do not use *Miss, Mrs.,* or *Ms.* as a salutation unless it is followed by a name.

Right	*Wrong*
Dear Miss MacDonald:	Dear Miss:
Dear Ms. MacDonald:	Dear Ms:
Dear Madam:	

2. If the letter is addressed to a firm of women, the salutation is *Ladies* or *Mesdames*. Do not use "Dear" or "My dear" with either of these salutations.

3. The salutation to two women with the same name is:

Dear Mesdames Smith (if married)
Dear Misses Smith (if unmarried)

When in doubt whether the addressee is a man or woman, use the salutation appropriate for a man. *For the correct form of salutation in letters addressed to women holding official or honorary positions, see Forms of Address, part 5.*

THE COMPLIMENTARY CLOSE

5.13. How to type the complimentary close. See Forms of Address, part 5, for the correct complimentary close to use in letters to people in official or honorary positions.

The form of complimentary close varies with the tone of the letter and the degree of acquaintanceship between the lawyer and the client. In the interchange of letters between lawyer and client, observe how the client closes the letter and be guided by his or her taste.

SIGNATURE

5.14. How to type the signature. Firms of attorneys frequently sign letters manually with the firm name, particularly if the letter expresses a professional opinion or gives professional advice. In some offices the firm name is typed on the letter and the lawyer who dictated it signs his or her name, thus:

BLACK, HALL & POINTER

By *Edgar R. Black*

A letter signed in the firm name, whether manually or typed, is written in the first person plural, not the singular.

Many letters are signed by the dictating attorney or by a partner without having the firm name appear in the signature. The purpose of typing a signature is to enable the recipient of the letter to decipher a difficult signature. There is no need, therefore, for the lawyer's name to be typed in the signature if it appears on the letterhead.

If a firm has alternate forms of signatures, the dictator will indicate his or her preference.

1. Type the firm name in capitals exactly as it appears on the letterhead.

2. If the signature of the dictator is typed, type it exactly as the dictator signs his or her name.

Right	*Wrong*
Richard P. Miller	*Richard P. Miller*
Richard P. Miller	R.P. Miller

3. The typed signature should never extend beyond the right margin of the letter.

4. No title except *Miss* or *Mrs.* precedes either the written or typed signature.

MISCELLANEOUS SUGGESTIONS ABOUT CORRESPONDENCE

5.15. Envelopes. The items in the address on the envelope are the same as those on the inside address (see page 104 et seq.). Figure 5.5 shows

---

```
Editorial Services                              SPECIAL DELIVERY
P.O. Box 504
Bull Shoals, AR 72619




                        Southern Diamond Cutters

                        400 Third Avenue

                        New York NY 10016



Attention Mrs. Lois Fenton
```

Figure 5.5. *Block Style of Address with Correct Placement of Attention Line*

an acceptable and commonly used style of address. It also shows the correct placement of the attention line and mailing notation.

Even if there is no street address, keep the name of the state on the same line as the name of the city. Use the proper two-letter postal abbreviation for the state. Write the name of a foreign country in capitals on the envelope; use initial capitals in the inside address.

5.16. Attention line. Strictly business letters addressed to a firm are often directed to the attention of an individual by the use of an *attention line*, in preference to addressing the letter to the individual. This practice marks the letter as a business rather than a personal letter and ensures that it will be opened in the absence of the individual to whom it is directed.

Type the attention line two spaces below the address. The word *of* is not necessary. The attention line has no punctuation and is not underscored. When a letter addressed to a firm has an attention line, the salutation is *Gentlemen* because the salutation is to the firm, not the individual. It is permissible to direct the letter to the attention of an individual without including his given name or initials, if they are unknown.

Preferable   Attention Mr. Henry R. Walters
Permissible   Attention Mr. Walters

5.17. Identification line. The indentification line shows who dictated the letter and who typed it. The only purpose of the identification is for reference by the firm *writing* the letter. It does not belong on the original of a letter, but many firms have the line typed on the original because it saves time.

The usual position of identification marks is two spaces below or on a line with the last line of the signature, flush with the left margin. If the dictator's name is typed on the letter, there is no need for his initials to appear in the identification marks.

5.18. Personal notation. A letter or envelope should not be marked "Personal" or "Confidential" as a device to ensure its delivery to a busy person. These words should be used only when no one but the addressee is supposed to see the letter. Type the word *Personal* or *Confidential* four spaces above the address. (In the official style of letter place the personal notation at the top of the letter.) You may underline the notation to catch the eye. The notation is also typed, in solid caps underlined, on the envelope, two spaces above the address.

5.19. Reference line. If a file reference is given in an incoming letter, include a reference line in your reply. Place your own reference beneath the incoming reference. When letterheads have a printed notation such as *In reply please refer to*, type the reference line after it. Otherwise, type it about four spaces beneath the date.

> Your file 2211
> Our File 7085
> or
> June 19, 19..
> Our Order 77C

5.20. Mailing notation. When a letter is sent by any method other than regular mail, type a notation of the exact method on the envelope, in the space below the stamps and above the address. Make a similar notation on the carbon copy of the letter.

5.21. Enclosure mark. When a letter contains enclosures, type the word *Enclosure* or the abbreviation *Enc.* flush with the left-hand margin one or two spaces beneath the identification line. If there is more than one enclosure, indicate the number. If the enclosures are of special importance, identify them. If an enclosure is to be returned, make a notation to that effect.

RPE:es   RPE:es   RPE:es
Enclosure   Enc. 2   Enc. Cert. ck. $2,350
                                    Mtge.—Fenton to Struthers
RPE:es
Enc. Policy 35 4698-M (to be returned)

The secretaries in a well-known law firm in the East follow the practice of placing an asterisk in the margin of the letter opposite the line that refers to the enclosure. This eliminates the possibility of forgetting to indicate at the bottom of the letter that there are enclosures.

5.22. Copy distribution notation. When a copy is to be sent to another person, type the distribution notation flush with the left-hand margin, below all other notations. If space permits, separate it from the other notations by two spaces.

SRE:NG
Enclosure
Copy to Mr. J.V. Buford

The abbreviation *c.c.* or *cc* may be used instead of *Copy to*. In the simplified form of letter neither is used.

Blind-copy notation. Type the blind-copy notation in the upper left-hand portion of the letter *on the carbons only*. This indicates that the addressee of the letter does not know that a copy was sent to anyone.

5.23. Postscript. When it is necessary to add a postscript to a letter, type it two spaces below the identification line or the last notation that is on the letter. The left margin of the postscript should be indented five spaces from the left margin of the letter itself. You may include or omit the abbreviations "P.S." Type the dictator's initials after the postscript.

5.24. Heading on succeeding pages. Law firms generally have continuation sheets, loosely called second sheets, with the firm name, but no address, engraved on them for use when a letter runs more than one page. If your office does not have engraved continuation sheets, use a plain sheet of the same size and quality as the letterhead. Type enough descriptive matter at the top of the succeeding pages to make them recognizable if they should become separated from the first page. The name of the addressee, the number of the page, and the date should be sufficient.

5.25. Enclosures. When it is necessary to fasten enclosures together or to a letter, use staples. The U.S. Postal Service objects to pins or metal clips because the pins injure the hands of postal employees and the clips tend to damage post office canceling machines.

1. *Enclosures the size of the letter.* These are easily folded and inserted, with their accompanying letters, into commercial envelopes of the ordinary size. If the enclosure consists of two or more sheets, staple them together but do not fasten the enclosed material to the letter. Fold the enclosure, then fold the letter, and slip the enclosure inside the last fold of the letter. Thus when the letter is removed from the envelope, the enclosure comes out with it.

2. *Enclosures larger than the letter.* These include briefs, abstracts, and other legal documents too large to fit into a commercial envelope of ordinary size. They are generally mailed in large manila envelopes. Enclosures of this kind may be handled in one of three ways.

a. The letter is inserted with the enclosure in the large envelope, which is sealed. In this case first-class postage is charged for both the letter and the enclosure.

b. A combination envelope is used. This is a large envelope with a flap that is fastened by a patent fastener of some kind, *but not sealed*. A smaller envelope of commercial size is affixed on the front of this envelope in the process of manufacture. The letter is inserted into the small envelope and the flap is sealed. Postage is affixed to the large envelope at third-class rate and to the small envelope at first-class rate.

c. The enclosure may be sent, *unsealed*, in one envelope and the letter, *sealed*, in another. In this case, of course, the letter should not refer to an enclosure but should state that the material is being sent by third-class mail.

3. *Enclosures smaller than the letter.* When enclosures are considerably smaller than the letter, staple them to the letter in the upper left-hand corner, on top of the letter. If two or more such enclosures are sent, put the smaller one on top.

SOME CONCRETE AIDS IN LETTER WRITING

We do not all have the talent that makes an outstanding letter writer, but we can improve the style and effectiveness of our own letters by studying those written by experts. Careful planning and highly developed techniques make those letters outstanding. This section will help you develop techniques that will improve the quality and persuasiveness of your letters.

5.26. Suggested techniques. The language of a letter should be natural, just as though the writer were talking to the reader. Unfortunately, lawyers are frequent offenders against this basic requirement of letter writing, and their staff are inclined to follow their style.

Here are six suggestions that will help you write letters in simple, straightforward language. When you draft a letter for your own or the lawyer's signature, if you will follow these suggestions he or she will probably be favorably impressed by the clarity and effectiveness of your letter.

1. Never use stilted or trite phrases.
2. Avoid unnecessary words or phrases.
3. Do not use two words with the same meaning for emphasis.
4. Avoid favorite words or expressions.
5. Do not use big words.
6. Use short sentences.

5.27. Trite terms to be avoided. Here is a list of expressions that are stilted or trite and hence not good usage.

Acknowledge receipt of. Use *we received*.

Advise. Used with too little discrimination and best reserved to indicate actual advice. Often *say* or *tell* is better.

BAD: We *wish to advise* that your case has been set for trial on November 15.
BETTER: We *are happy to tell* you that your case has been set for trial on November 15.

As per; per. Correctly used with Latin words: *per annum* and *per diem.*

> ALLOWABLE: $5 *per* page.
> BETTER: $5 *a* page.
> BAD: As *per* our telephone conversation.
> BETTER: *In accordance with* our telephone conversation.
> BAD: *Per* our agreement.
> BETTER: *According to* our agreement.

At all times. Often used with little meaning. Better to use *always.*

> POOR: We shall be pleased to talk with you *at all times.*
> BETTER: We will *always* be happy to welcome you at our office.

At this time. Also unnecessary in most cases. Try *at present* or *now.*

> POOR: We wish to advise that we have no further information *at this time.*
> BETTER: We are sorry to tell you we have no further information *at present.*

At your convenience; at an early date. Trite, vague, and unnecessary in most cases. Be specific.

> INDEFINITE: Please notify us *at an early date.*
> BETTER: Please let us know *within ten days* (or *by the first of next month*).
> VAGUE: We should appreciate hearing from you *at your convenience.*
> BETTER: We would appreciate hearing from you *by the tenth of* _____.

Beg. Avoid such expressions as *beg to state, beg to advise, beg to acknowledge,* and so on.

> POOR: In answer to yours of the 10th inst., *beg to state.* . . .
> BETTER: In answer (or response; or reply) to your letter of May 10, *we are pleased.* . . .

Contents carefully noted. Contributes little to a letter.

> POOR: Yours of the 5th received and *contents carefully noted.*
> BETTER: The instructions outlined in your letter of June 5 have been followed in every detail.

Duly. Unnecessary.

> POOR: Your request has been *duly* forwarded to our offices in Washington.
> BETTER: Your request has been forwarded to our offices in Washington.

Enclosed please find. Needless and faulty phraseology. The word *please* has little meaning in this instance. And the word *find* is improperly used.

> POOR: *Enclosed please find* draft of the contract.
> BETTER: *We are enclosing* (or *we enclose*) a draft of the contract.

Esteemed. Too flowery and effusive.

> POOR: We welcomed your *esteemed* favor of the 9th.
> BETTER: Thank you for your letter of April 9.

Favor: Do not use the word *favor* in the sense of letter, order, or check.

"Thank you for your *letter* (not *favor*) of October 5."

Handing you. Out of place in correspondence today.

POOR: We are *handing you* herewith affidavit made by Mr. R.M. Davis.
BETTER: We *enclose* affidavit made by Mr. R.M. Davis.

Have before me. A "worn-out" expression.

POOR: I *have before me* your complaint of the 10th.
BETTER: *In answer* (or *response;* or *reply*) to your letter of November 10 .... .

Hereto. Trite.

POOR: We are attaching *hereto* a copy of the agreement.
BETTER: We are attaching *to this letter* a copy of the agreement.

Herewith. Often redundant.

POOR: We enclose *herewith* a copy of the charter.
BETTER: We are happy to enclose a copy of the charter.

In re. Avoid except in subject line. Use *regarding* or *concerning.*

POOR: *In re* our telephone conversation of this morning. ...
BETTER: *Supplementing* (or *confirming;* or *regarding*) our telephone conversation of this morning. ...

Inst. Avoid the abbreviation of the word *instant,* and the word *instant* itself.

POOR: Your favor of the 6th *inst.* (or *instant*). ...
BETTER: Your letter of *June 6* ....

Our Mr. Becker. Say, *our associate Mr. Becker,* or just *Mr. Becker.*

POOR: *Our Mr. Becker* will call on you next Tuesday, May 10.
BETTER: *Our associate Mr. Becker* will call on you next Tuesday, May 10.

Proximo. A Latin word meaning *on the next.* Better to give the exact name of the month.

POOR: The meeting will be held on the 10th *prox.* (or *proximo*).
BETTER: The meeting will be held *December 10.*

Recent date. Vague and unbusinesslike. Better to give the exact date.

VAGUE: Your letter of *recent date.*
DEFINITE: Your letter of *June 2.*

Same. A poor substitute for one of the pronouns *it, they,* or *them.*

POOR: Your letter of the 5th received. We will give *same* our immediate attention.
BETTER: Thank you for your letter of March 5. We will make the requested arrangements immediately.

State. Often too formal. Better to use *say* or *tell*.

> POOR: We wish to *state*. ...
> BETTER: We are happy to *tell* you. ...

Take pleasure. A trite expression. Better to say *are pleased, are happy,* or *are glad*.

> POOR: We *take pleasure* in arranging reservations for you.
> BETTER: We *are happy* to make arrangements for you.

Thanking you in advance. Discourteous and implies that your request will be granted.

> POOR: Kindly mail me any information you may have concerning the ARS bill.
>   *Thanking you in advance* for the favor, I remain
>   Yours truly,
> BETTER: I will appreciate any information you may have concerning the ARS bill.
>   Sincerely yours,

Ultimo. A Latin word meaning *the preceding month*. No longer used in modern correspondence.

> POOR: Yours of the 9th *ultimo* (or *ult.*) received.
> BETTER: We have received your letter of *June 9*.

Under separate cover. Rather meaningless. Better to be specific and give the method of shipping.

> POOR: We are sending you *under separate cover* a copy of the record.
> BETTER: We are happy to send you *by insured parcel post* a copy of the record.

Valued. Too effusive and suggestive of flattery. Better to omit.

> POOR: We appreciate your *valued* suggestion given to Mr. McCall.
> BETTER: We appreciate your suggestion given to Mr. McCall.

Wish to say; wish to state; would say. All are examples of needless, wordy phraseology. Simply omit.

> POOR: Referring to your letter of the 10th, *wish to say* that we cannot make the necessary arrangements before the first of December.
> BETTER: In response to your letter of March 10, we regret we cannot make the necessary arrangements before December 1.

5.28. Unnecessary words and phrases. Many letter writers add unnecessary words to their phrases because of an erroneous idea that the padding gives emphasis or rounds out a sentence. For example, letter writers frequently speak of "*final* completion," "*month* of January," or "*close* proximity." The completion must be final or it is not complete; January must be a month; incidents in proximity must be close. Here is a list of some padded phrases frequently used in business letters. The italicized words are *totally* unnecessary.

The material came *at a time* when we were busy.
Houses appreciate *in value* with time.
During *the year of* 1980.
The radio cost *the sum of* $60.
At a theatre party *held* in New York.
We will send your stationery *at a* later *date*.
In about three months' *time*.
The problem *first* arose when the machine malfunctioned.
A *certain* book entitled *Day's End.*
The *close* proximity of your shop.
He arrived at *the hour of* noon.
There is merit to both *of them*.
In *the state of* Illinois.
The jar is made *out* of glass.
During *the course of* our conversation.
Perhaps it may be better to leave now.
His uniform *and invariable* policy is.
Someone *or other* is at fault.
I am now *engaged in* writing a book.
He entered by *means of* the elevator.
The car sells for *a price of* $8,000.

5.29. Two words with the same meaning. Some letter writers think that if one word does a job, two words add emphasis. Actually, the second word makes the thought less effective. Here are a few examples of "doubling."

> sincere and good wishes
> the first and foremost
> appraise and determine the worthwhile things
> our experience together and contacts in a civic association
> deeds and actions
> feeling of optimism and encouragement
> we refuse and decline
> unjust and unfair manner
> advised and informed
> at once and by return mail
> immediately and at once
> we demand and insist
> right and proper consideration
> assume obligation or responsibility

5.30. Favorite words and expressions. Avoid acquiring favorite words or expressions. They become habitual, and your letters sound cut and dried. For example, a lawyer might easily overwork the word "records." One letter might say, "According to our records, the grace period will expire next Monday," and the next, "The enclosed is for your records." A skillful letter writer would simply say, "The grace period will expire next Monday," and "The enclosed copy is for you."

5.31. Big words versus one syllable words. Some people think a large vocabulary of big words marks them as learned; but simple, short words do the best job. This statement does not mean a large vocabulary is not an asset. The more words you have, the more clearly and forcibly you can express yourself. But never use words of many syllables unless there is a reason for it. Why say "propertied interests" when you mean "rich people," or "utilize" for "use," or "annihilate" for "wipe out," or "transcend" for "go beyond," or "prior to" for "before."

5.32. Sentence length. Since the aim of a letter is to transfer a thought to the reader in the simplest manner with the greatest clarity, avoid long, complicated sentences. Lawyers probably disregard this technique of good letter writing more than any other people. Break up overlong, stuffy sentences by making short sentences out of dependent clauses. Here is an example (101 words):

> Believing the physical union of the two businesses to be desirable and in the best interests of the stockholders of each corporation, the Boards of Directors have given further consideration to the matter and have agreed in principle upon a new plan that would contemplate the transfer of the business and substantially all of the assets of the *A* Company to *B* in exchange for shares of common stock of *B* on a basis that would permit the distribution to the *A* Company stockholders of one and one-half shares of *B* common stock for each share of *A* Company common stock.

Rewritten in four sentences and reduced to 70 words, this becomes:

> The Boards of Directors of both companies thought a merger desirable and in the best interests of the stockholders. They finally agreed on a new plan. The business and substantially all assets of the *A* Company will be transferred to *B* in exchange for *B* common stock. *A* Company stockholders will get one and one-half shares of *B* common stock for each share of *A* Company common stock.

TELEGRAMS

5.33. How to send a telegram. Although telegraph messages are often sent over the phone, many large law offices have their own teleprinter, over which messages are sent directly to the telegraph office. The classes of domestic service are *fast telegram* (quickest and most expensive of all classes), *mailgram* (wired to the post office and delivered in the next regular mail), and *night letter* (the least expensive class, delivered the morning of the next business day). Contact your local Western Union office for current charges and other information. Cables to foreign countries are sent by *full-rate message* (the standard fast service) and *letter telegram* (overnight and least expensive service). Other classes of foreign service include *shore-to-ship and ship-to-shore radio, radio photo service,* and *overseas Telex service.* Contact one of the international carriers in your area for current charges and other information.

5.34. How to type a telegram. 1. The number of copies depends on the requirements of your office. Four is the usual number.

a.   The original for pickup by the telegraph messenger.

b.   A carbon copy for confirmation by mail.

c.   A carbon copy for your file.

d.   A carbon copy for the telegraph account file against which the charges may be checked.

2. Check the class of service—domestic service in the upper left corner, international service in the upper right corner—in the form provided on the telegraph blank. Also type the class of service two spaces above the address.

3. Type the date and hour in the upper right corner two spaces above the address.

4. Omit the salutation and complimentary close.

5. Double-space the message.

6. Do not divide a word at the end of a line.

7. Use caps and small letters and punctuate just as you would any other material. Use caps only for code words.

8. In the lower left-hand corner type:

a.   The dictator's initials and yours.

b.   Whether the message is to be sent "Charge," "Paid," or "Collect."

c.   Address and telephone number of your firm, unless printed on the blank.

9. If the telegram is to be charged, type the name of the charge account in the space provided on the blank.

5.35. How to send the same message to multiple addresses. If you want to send the same message to a number of people, type the telegram only once. List the names and addresses on a special sheet obtainable from the telegraph company (or on a plain sheet). Above the list type "Please send the attached message to the following 12 (whatever the number is) addresses."

5.36. How to send a telegram to a person on a train. If you want to reach someone who is on a train, send the telegram in care of the conductor. Give the name of the passenger, the train name or number and the direction in which it is traveling, car and reservation number, station and arrival time, city and state.

> Mr. John R. Winslow
> Care of Conductor
> The Congressional, Northbound
> Car 156, Roomette 12
> Due Broad Street Station, January 10, 7:18 P.M.
> Philadelphia, Pennsylvania

The telegram may be sent to any point en route where the train makes a stop.

5.37. How to send a telegram to a person on a plane. You may send a message to an airport to be delivered to a plane passenger. Give the name of the passenger, the name of the airline, the flight number and direction in which it is traveling, airport and arrival time, city and state.

> William King, Passenger
> United Airlines
> Flight 56, Westbound
> Due La Guardia Airport, May 12, 10:23 A.M.
> Flushing, New York

5.38. Punctuation. There is no charge for punctuation marks in telegrams between points in the United States: The words *Stop, Comma,* and the like are charged for.

5.39. Paragraphing. Telegrams written in paragraphs are transmitted in paragraphs at no extra cost.

5.40. Mixed groups of letters and figures. Mixed groups of letters, figures, affixes, and the characters $, /, &, %, #, ' (indicating feet or minutes) and " (indicating inches or seconds) are counted at the rate of five characters, or fraction thereof, to the word in messages between points in the United States and between points in Mexico. Thus, "one hundred" is counted as two words, but 100 is counted as one word; $34.50, as one word (the decimal is not counted); but 1000th (six characters) is counted as two words.

5.41. How to type a telegram when work is in the machine. Always transcribe a telegram as soon as it is dictated. Often a rush telegram will be given to you when you have other work in the typewriter, but it is not necessary to remove the work to type the telegram. Follow this procedure:

1. Backfeed the paper and carbons in the machine until the paper shows a top margin of about two inches.

2. Insert the first sheet of the telegram behind the material you are typing, against the paper table, just as if nothing were in the typewriter.

3. To make carbons of the telegram, insert the second sheet of the telegram against the coated side of the carbon paper already in the machine. Thus, the second sheet of the telegram is between the carbon and the second sheet of your letter. Do the same for each carbon you have in the typewriter. (You must insert a sheet for each carbon in your machine to prevent the typing from showing on the carbon copies of your work.) For additional copies add carbon sheets in the usual manner. Many firms, however, prefer to make photocopies of telegrams rather than carbon copies.

4. Turn the platen knob until the telegram blanks are in position for typing.

5. After typing the message, backfeed until you can remove the telegram from the machine.

6. Forward feed to the point at which you stopped writing your letter or other work and continue with your typing.

LETTERS THE SECRETARY WRITES

Of necessity, the lawyer's dictation time is limited. He or she must spend most of the time in conferences, in court, or in research. So the time reserved for dictating must be used for the more important work—contracts, briefs, examinations, and the like. The lawyer cannot afford to use that time for personal notes, letters of congratulations, complaints to stores he or she deals with, and so on.

The secretary must be prepared to take over this chore when possible. She should be able to get out a reservation letter, answer an invitation, set an appointment—on her own. The specimen letters set out below cover almost every type of miscellaneous communication the lawyer's secretary will be called upon to type from time to time—whether under her signature or her employer's. Once she selects the type of letter she needs, the rest is only a matter of typing.

LETTERS WRITTEN OVER THE SECRETARY'S SIGNATURE

5.42. Acknowledgment of correspondence received during employer's absence. Acknowledgment of a letter received during your employer's absence is a business courtesy. These letters fall into two classes: (1) an acknowledgment without answering the letter, and (2) an acknowledgment that also answers the letter.

Acknowledgment without answer. The pattern for these letters is simple.

1. Say that your employer is out of the city or away from the office.
2. Give the expected date of his or her return.
3. Assure the writer that his or her message will receive attention when your employer returns.
4. If the delay may cause inconvenience to the writer, add a note of apology.

Do not refer to your employer's illness when explaining his or her absence from the office, unless the addressee knows the lawyer is ill. Say, "Because of Mr. Bentley's absence from the office, he will not be able to attend. ..."

Dear Mr. Sloan:
    As Mrs. Franklin is away from the office this week, I'm acknowledging your letter of January 6 concerning the housing project. I'll bring it to her attention as soon as she returns and I know she will contact you promptly.
    Please accept my apologies for this unavoidable delay.
                      Sincerely yours,

Acknowledgment that also answers. The important factor in answering, as well as acknowledging, a letter during your employer's absence is to *know the facts.* Here is a suggested pattern:

1. Identify the incoming letter.
2. Say that your employer is away.
3. State the facts that answer the letter.
4. If appropriate, or desirable, say that your employer will write when he or she returns.

Dear Mrs. Smith:
    Your letter reminding Mr. Williams of the Rotary Club luncheon on October 17 has arrived during his absence from the office.
    Mr. Williams plans to return to Louisville the 17th and expects to attend the luncheon. If there are any changes in his plans, I'll let you know immediately.
                      Sincerely yours,

Letters concerning appointments. Here is a pattern a letter arranging an appointment should follow:

1. Refer to the purpose of the appointment.

2. Suggest, or ask the person to whom you are writing to suggest, the time, place, and date.

3. Ask for a confirmation of the appointment.

Employer asks for appointment: You want to fix the time.

Dear Mr. Jefferson:

Mr. Black will be in Los Angeles for a few hours on Tuesday, March 22. He would like to discuss with you the recent Supreme Court decision in the McNally case.

Will it be convenient for Mr. Black to call at your office at three o'clock on March 22?

Sincerely yours,

You have to let the other person fix the time.

Dear Mrs. Kennedy:

Mr. Billings is returning from Canada the end of this week and would like to discuss with you the result of his conference with the president of the Kittering Corporation.

Would you please ask your secretary to telephone me at 624-9200 and let me know when it will be convenient for you to see Mr. Billings? Thank you.

Sincerely yours,

You ask someone to come in to see your employer: You want to fix the time.

Dear Mr. Penman:

Mr. Adams would like to see you on Monday, February 27, at two o'clock in his office, Room 201, to complete arrangements for the rental of your summer cottage.

Please let me know whether this time is convenient. Thank you very much.

Sincerely yours,

You have to let the other person fix the time.

Dear Ms. Farrington:

The papers in connection with the trust you are creating for your daughter are now complete, except for your signature. Mr. Lewis would like you to come to his office early next week to sign them. Would you please telephone me when it will be convenient for you to do this?

Thank you.

Sincerely yours,

Reply to letter asking your employer for an appointment. You fix a definite time.

Dear Mr. Smith:

Mrs. Benjamin will be glad to see you on Monday, December 27, at two o'clock in her office, Room 1000, to discuss with you the program for the annual convention. She will be looking forward to seeing you then.

Sincerely yours,

You want to let the other person fix the time.

Dear Ms. Glass:

Mr. Logan will be glad to see you some time during the week of March 3, to talk over the installation of the elevator in his residence at 20 West 20 Street.

If you will telephone me at 221-1000 we can arrange a time that will be convenient for you and Mr. Logan. Thank you.

Sincerely yours,

Your employer signs the letter.

Dear Mr. Birdsell:

I'll be happy to talk with you when you are in Denver next week. Would it be convenient for you to come to my office at ten o'clock Thursday morning, November 5? I believe this hour would give us the best opportunity to discuss your project without interruption.

It will be a pleasure to see you again.

Cordially yours,

You have to postpone fixing a definite time.

Dear Mr. Edwards:

This is in answer to your letter asking for an appointment with Mr. Finley.

He's away from the office now and is not expected back until the end of the month. However, I'll write to you just as soon as I know when he will be able to see you.

Sincerely yours,

You have to say "no" politely.

Dear Mr. Shotts:

Mrs. Smith has considered very carefully all that you said in your letter of December 21. If there were any possibility that a meeting with you would be helpful she would be glad to see you. However, she does not believe that would be the case and has asked me to let you know and to thank you for writing.

Sincerely yours,

5.43. Letters making reservations. Although many reservations are made by telephone (using toll-free numbers listed in the yellow pages), a capable secretary is also prepared to compose letters making reservations.

Plane. The points to cover in a letter making a plane reservation are:

1. Name and position of person desiring reservation
2. Flight and date on which space is desired
3. Schedule of flight
4. Air card number (if any)
5. Confirmation

Gentlemen:

Mr. Allan Robbins of Robbins, Barkley & Wentworth would like to reserve space to Los Angeles on flight 26 out of Chicago on Saturday, November 24. Our schedule shows this flight leaves at 9:45 a.m., Central Standard Time, for Los Angeles and arrives at 10:00 a.m., Pacific Standard Time. Mr. Robbins is holder of air travel card 72910.

Please confirm this reservation immediately by wire. Thank you.

Sincerely yours,

Train. A letter making a train reservation includes:

1. Name and position of person desiring reservation
2. Accommodation desired
3. Point of departure and destination
4. Date and time
5. Name of train, if known
6. Arrangement for delivery of tickets
7. Confirmation
8. Arrangement for payment

Gentlemen:

Please reserve a bedroom for Mrs. Martha Vinton, president of Vinton & Vinton, Inc., on train no. 600 from Chicago to Los Angeles, leaving Chicago Saturday, November 27, at 3:00 p.m. Mrs. Vinton will call for the tickets at the Chicago station on November 24. Please confirm this reservation by wire as soon as possible.

If you will send the invoice for the tickets to this office, we will remit at once. Thank you.

Sincerely yours,

Hotel. When you write for hotel reservations for your employer include the following information:

1. Accommodations desired
2. Name of person for whom reservation is requested
3. Date and time of arrival
4. Probable date of departure
5. Request for confirmation

Also inquire about checking-out time.

Gentlemen:

Please reserve for Mr. Rudy Mannox a corner bedroom and bath, preferably a southeastern exposure, beginning Monday, December 14. Mr. Mannox will arrive early in the evening of the 14th and plans to leave the morning of December 20.

Please confirm this reservation by wire. Thank you.

Sincerely yours,

5.44. Letters calling attention to an error in an account. In calling attention to an error in an account, avoid giving the impression you are complaining. These letters fall into four classes: (1) when the amount of an item is incorrect; (2) when the total is incorrect; (3) when returned merchandise has not been credited; (4) when an item not purchased is charged to the account. (The illustrations here relate to personal accounts but can be adapted to business accounts.)

When the amount of an item is incorrect. Here is a workable outline that covers the necessary points.

1. Give the name and number of the account.

2. Describe the item and tell how it is incorrect.

3. State your version of what the item should be, giving any documentary information you have.

4. Ask for a corrected statement *or* enclose check for the correct amount and ask that the error be rectified on the account.

Gentlemen:

The June statement of Mr. Elton Randall's account #15836 shows a charge of $9.80 on May 5 for stationery. Evidently the figures were transposed in posting. The amount should be $8.90, as shown by sales slip #62405-J. Please verify this correction and credit Mr. Randall's account with 90 cents.

I've deducted $0.90 from the amount of the statement and enclose Mr. Randall's check for the balance of $98.53.

Sincerely yours,

When the total is incorrect. Follow the same pattern as when the amount of an item is incorrect.

Gentlemen:

The June statement of Mrs. Frank Hudson's account #15836 shows a balance of $56.90. I believe this amount should be $46.90.

The debits and credits shown on the statement agree with Mrs. Hudson's records. I would appreciate it, therefore, if you would check your total again. If you find that the statement should not be for $56.90, please send Mrs. Hudson a corrected statement. Thank you.

Sincerely yours,

When returned merchandise has not been credited. Follow the same pattern as when the amount of an item is incorrect.

Gentlemen:

On May 4 Mr. Harold White, whose account number is 15863, returned for credit a pair of bookends purchased from you on May 2. The price was $27.50, including tax.

Mr. White's June statement does not show this credit. A credit slip was given to him, but unfortunately, it has been misplaced. Mr. White would appreciate it if you would verify the credit and send him a corrected statement.

In the meantime, I'm enclosing Mr. White's check for $146.25, the amount of the statement less the price of the returned merchandise.

Sincerely yours,

When an item not purchased is charged to the account. These letters should include the following points:

1. Name and number of the account
2. Description of the item charged in error, including the price and the date charged
3. Any additional pertinent information that you have
4. A request that the charge be investigated
5. A request for a corrected statement

Gentlemen:

The June statement of Ms. June Cooper's account #14825 shows a charge of $5.85 on May 15 for three pairs of hose. Ms. Cooper charged three pairs of hose for $5.85 on May 10 and three pairs for the same amount on May 20, but she did not charge any hose on May 15. The six pairs that she bought were properly charged to her account.

Ms. Cooper does not know why the charge was made against her account. Please investigate and let her know what happened. Naturally, she is concerned that someone might have used her account without her permission.

If the charge was made through clerical error, please send a corrected statement. Thank you.

Sincerely yours,

5.45. Reply to notice of meeting. Sometimes the secretary knows whether her employer plans to attend a meeting; at other times, she must find out what his or her plans are. Her letter covers the following points:

1. Repeat the time, date, and place of the meeting.
2. Say whether the employer plans to attend the meeting.
3. Give a reason if he or she does not plan to attend.

Dear Mr. Brown:

Mr. Morris plans to be present at the meeting of the Finance Committee on Tuesday, October 26, at 9:30 a.m., in your office.

Sincerely yours,

Dear Mr. Brown:

Mr Morris has the notice of the meeting of the Finance Committee on Tuesday, October 26, at 9:30 a.m. Unfortunately, previous business appointments will prevent him from attending this meeting.

Sincerely yours,

5.46. Letters calling attention to omission of enclosures. When an enclosure mentioned in an incoming letter is omitted, you should notify the sender. Here is the pattern your letter should follow:

1. Identify the incoming letter and enclosure.

2. State that the enclosure was omitted.

3. Ask that the enclosure, or a copy of it, be sent to you.

Dear Ms. Boyd:

In your letter of March 3 to Mr. Pearson you said you were enclosing a copy of the tentative program for the meeting of the Sales Executives Club to be held in May. The program, however, was not enclosed.

Since Mr. Pearson's reply to your letter will be governed by the tentative program, I would appreciate it if you could send a copy of the program right away.

Thank you very much.

Sincerely yours,

5.47. Follow-up letters. If correspondence in your follow-up file is not answered by the follow-up date, trace the letter for a reply. Your letter should cover the following points:

1. Identify the letter. Identification by date is not sufficient because your correspondent does not know what you are writing about.

2. Offer a reason for the recipient's failure to reply, without casting reflection on him or her.

3. Enclose a copy of your original letter, unless it was very short. If so, simply repeat the contents in your follow-up letter.

Copy of original letter not enclosed.

Gentlemen:

On February 2 we ordered from you six copies of your latest bulletin on "Practicing Attorneys' Letter" but we have not yet had an acknowledgment of the order.

As our first order evidently went astray, please consider this a duplicate.

Sincerely yours,

Copy of original letter enclosed. (As this is a follow-up of a letter requesting a favor, it is written for your employer's signature.)

Dear Mr. Fonda:

In the rush of work you probably have not had time to answer my letter of October 25 about using some of your practice ideas in our <u>Bar Association Journal</u>, with credit to you. On the chance this letter did not reach you, I'm enclosing a copy of it.

I would like very much to include your ideas in the next issue. This will be possible if I have your reply by December 15.

Thanks very much.

Sincerely yours,

LETTERS THE SECRETARY MAY WRITE
FOR EMPLOYER'S SIGNATURE

5.48. Letters of appreciation. A letter of appreciation should reflect genuine sincerity and honest gratitude; it should not reflect merely the writer's desire to conform with the rules of etiquette. The tone should be one of friendly informality.

Dear Ms. Wyckoff:

I want to thank you for having given so freely of your time yesterday in talking with Fred Duxbury, the young man I recommended to you for a sales position with your firm.

I talked with him again this morning, and he is enthusiastic over the prospect of joining your organization. He was particularly impressed by what you told him, and he appears eager to tackle the job.

Although I've grown wary of recommending people, I cannot help feeling in this case I was justified in suggesting that you meet Mr. Duxbury.

Sincerely yours,

For assistance to firm, club, or association.

Dear Mr. Hardy:

The Society for Advancement of Management is deeply indebted to you for your inspiring remarks made at its annual conference. The members of the society will long remember your message as having contributed immeasurably to the success of the meeting.

As chairman of the conference, I'm particularly indebted to you for your kindness in agreeing to speak. I sincerely hope the society will be honored again at some future conference by your presence on the speaker's platform.

I also look forward to having lunch with you in the near future and hearing more about your ideas.

Sincerely yours,

For hospitality.

Dear Mr. Cartwright:

This is my first day back in the office after my long northern trip.

Everything considered, it was an extremely pleasant trip, and the luncheon visit with you in Buffalo helped to make it so. Thank you again for rearranging your plans on such short notice to include me in your day.

I hope something will bring you through the South before the year is over and that you will include a day in Birmingham.

Sincerely yours,

For message of congratulations.

Dear Tom:

I appreciate your kind words about my efforts to guide the recent Credit Management program. It was a lot of fun, and I only hope that all the participants in our discussion enjoyed this exchange of ideas as much as I did.

Your making a special effort to attend, despite adverse circumstances, made me feel very good. I was glad you were able to be there, since it's likely we will be working together on similar programs for a long time to come. I hope so.

Thanks again for your thoughtful note, Tom.

Cordially,

For message for sympathy.

Gentlemen:

On behalf of the personnel of Stone & Westerly, I want to thank you for your kind letter of sympathy upon the death of our president Mr. Jonas MacIntyre.

It's true that this organization has sustained a shock and a great loss in the sudden passing of Mr. MacIntyre. But by holding to the high standards he represented, we believe we will be paying him the most appropriate tribute.

Your friendship, as manifested in your letter, gives us encouragement as we undertake this task.

Very sincerely yours,

5.49. Letters of sympathy. In any letter written to express sympathy, sincerity and tact are the most important qualities. Avoid words or sentiments that could distress the reader. Do not philosophize upon the meaning of death or quote scripture or poetry. A letter of condolence and sympathy should not be long and involved. Decision as to the length is based upon (1) the degree of friendship between writer and reader; (2) the situation that prompts the letter; and (3) the tastes and temperament of the reader.

Upon death.

Dear Mrs. Cullen:

Every member of our firm was shocked and saddened at the sudden death of your husband.

Although sympathy is small consolation, even when it comes from the hearts of those who share your sorrow, I want you to know how keenly John's loss is felt by everyone here. I don't need to tell you of the respect and admiration in which he was held by all who worked with him.

Other members of the firm join me in this expression of our deep sympathy. We only wish it were within our powers to alleviate the sadness that has come to you and your family.

Very sincerely yours,

Upon personal injury or illness.

Dear Mr. Wilson:

I just learned of your painful injury and want to send you my best wishes for a speedy recovery.

Since you will be confined to your home for a few days, I believe you will enjoy reading a new book that has given me a number of pleasant hours. I'm sending it along with this note.

Cordially yours,

5.50. Letters of congratulations. The outstanding qualities of an expression of congratulations are (1) brevity, (2) naturalness of expression, and (3) enthusiasm. Trite, stilted phrases indicate a lack of sincerity and destroy the individuality of the letter.

The following illustrations of congratulatory messages are suitable for numerous occasions that occur frequently in business.

Upon professional or civic honor.

Dear Mr. Guyote:

I was very glad to learn you are the new secretary of the Omaha Chamber of Commerce. I can think of no one better qualified for this important work, and I know you will make an outstanding success of it.

Whenever I can be of assistance in any way, you'll find me glad to cooperate.

Cordially yours,

Upon promotion.

Dear Mr. Moore:

I just learned of your appointment as division superintendent of the Santa Fe Railroad.

At a time when you have such good reason to be proud and happy, may I add my sincere congratulations. I was very glad to hear of your promotion and wish you every success in your new position.

Cordially yours,

Upon retirement from business.

Dear Ms. Forest:

Twenty-eight years of helpful counsel to your associates and wise leadership in your community is a record of service that few people achieve. It's also a record that deserves a sincere word of gratitude from those you've helped so generously during all these years.

We will miss your steady hand, but we know how fully you've earned the first leisure time of your entire twenty-eight years in Mansfield.

Congratulations on your outstanding record of service and best wishes for many happy years ahead.

Sincerely yours,

Upon speech, article, or book.

Dear Mr. Conwell:

Last night I read your excellent article in the June issue of The American Banker. You've presented the soundest treatment of bank credit problems I've ever seen.

I congratulate you on this fine article. Many others, I'm sure, have learned as much from your constructive analysis as I have.

Cordially yours,

Upon outstanding community service.

Dear Mayor Fry:

As a citizen of Oakland, I want to express my sincere appreciation for the many things you've done to make it a better city in which to live.

Probably yours has seemed like a thankless task at times, but the satisfaction of a big job well done is no small reward in itself.

Certainly that satisfaction is yours in abundant measure, and also the pleasure of knowing that you have the gratitude of every citizen who stands for honest and efficient city government.

Sincerely yours,

Upon business anniversary.

Dear Mr. Shell:

On the eve of your fortieth business anniversary, I want to extend to you my congratulations on your record of achievement and my sincere best wishes for the future.

Your forty years in business represent not only a career of the highest ethical standards, but also one of genuine service to this community. You have won the respect, confidence, and admiration of the people of Clinton, and you have every right to be proud of the reputation you've earned.

Yours sincerely,

Letters of seasonal good wishes.

Dear Mrs. Larson:

The association with you during the past year has been so enjoyable that I want to send you this word of good wishes for a happy and successful 19___.

I hope the coming year will afford more opportunities for pleasant contacts between your firm and mine and that I'll have the pleasure of further visits with you from time to time.

Sincerely yours,

5.51. Letters of introduction. The letter of introduction may be prepared for direct mailing to the addressee or for delivery in person by the one introduced. In the latter case the envelope should be left unsealed as a courtesy to the bearer. When there is sufficient time for the letter to reach its recipient before the arrival of the person introduced, the preferable practice is to send the note directly to the addressee.

The letter is ordinarily written in a spirit of asking a favor. It should include:

1. The name of the person being introduced
2. The purpose or reason for the introduction
3. All relevant and appropriate details, personal or business
4. A statement that any courtesy shown will be appreciated by the writer

Introducing a personal friend.

Dear Jim:

My good friend and former neighbor Don Parker will present this note to you when he stops in Omaha on his way to the Pacific Coast.

Don is head of the advertising staff of Fall River Air Service, and I am sure you and he will have much to discuss. In fact, it's because I think you both will enjoy a visit that I'm writing.

I'll appreciate any courtesy you may extend to Don during his brief stop in Omaha. Thanks, Jim.

Sincerely yours,

Introducing a business or professional associate.

Dear Mr. Samson:

This letter will be handed to you by my friend and associate Harvey Lister, a well-known writer of articles on business.

Mr.Lister is preparing a book in which he hopes to outline the development of the textile industry during the last half century. He believes that through a talk with you he could obtain both information and inspiration that would be valuable to him in his work.

Since you are <u>the</u> authority on your particular phase of the industry, he has asked for an introduction to you. I'll appreciate any courtesies you may show him, and I know he will, too. Thanks very much.

Sincerely yours,

5.52. Letters of Invitation. The letter of invitation should be cordial and gracious in tone, entirely free of stilted formality. It should be complete in detail, telling *when*, and *where,* and, if the occasion is essentially business, *why*.

To attend banquet, luncheon, or entertainment.

Dear Suzanne:

Can you join me for lunch at the Fifth Avenue Hotel next Monday noon about 12:30 p.m.?

Anne Steele will be with me for the day, and I'd like to have you meet her. Aside from the fact that she is someone you would enjoy knowing, the contact might prove helpful from a business standpoint. Anne plans to add several new departments to their Boston and Worcester stores.

I'd have written you this note earlier, but I didn't learn until today that she would be in town next week. I hope you can make it.

Cordially,

To give address or informal talk.

Dear Mr. Connelly:

The subject of "How to Write Good Business Letters" is an interesting one to every business and professional person. For a long time I've intended, when it came my turn to arrange a program for the Businessmen's Club, to invite a real authority in the field to talk to the Club on that subject.

My turn came today, when I was asked to arrange the program for Tuesday noon, November 17. I know of no other person so well qualified as you to speak on the technique of writing business letters, and I'm hoping very much that you'll find it possible to accept my invitation.

Our luncheon meetings are held in the Banquet Room of Hotel Cleveland. They begin at 12:15 p.m. and are usually over about 1:30 p.m. The talks range from thirty to forty minutes.

If you can be our guest on the 17th, you'll receive a most enthusiastic welcome.

Sincerely yours,

5.53. Letters of acceptance. A personal letter accepting an invitation should convey appreciation and enthusiasm. If the invitation has left certain details—such as time and place—to the convenience of the recipient, the acceptance must deal specifically with these points. Otherwise, a brief note is sufficient.

Accepting invitation to banquet, luncheon, or entertainment.

Dear Jack:

I'll be delighted to be your guest at the Businessman's Club on Thursday, October 12. For several months I've hoped I might hear John Parson's widely discussed talk on "Personality in Client Contact," and the opportunity to hear it in your company will make it doubly enjoyable.

As you suggest, I'll be in the Claremont lobby a few minutes after twelve. Thanks for thinking of me.

Cordially,

Accepting hospitality for an overnight visit.

Dear Mr. McGuire:

Nothing could have been more welcome than your letter inviting me to stay with you during my weekend in Portland. I'm happy to accept.

It's very thoughtful of you and Mrs. McGuire to extend the hospitality of your home, and I look forward to seeing you next Saturday.

Sincerely yours,

Accepting speaking invitation.

Dear Mr. Walton:

I'll be happy to speak to the Rotary Club on Monday, June 26. Thank you for asking me.

The subject you suggest is quite satisfactory, and I'll do my best to give your members an interesting half-hour. I know that prompt adjournment is an important requirement of most luncheon clubs, and I assure you my remarks will be confined to the allotted time. I mention that point because long-winded speakers are among my pet aversions and quite probably you share my sentiments.

I'll be glad to meet you in the Biltmore lobby at twelve o'clock, and I look forward with pleasure to the visit with your club.

Cordially yours,

Accepting membership in professional or civic organization.

Dear Ms. Lane:

Your cordial invitation for me to join the American Business Writing Association pleases me very much, and I accept with pleasure.

I realize your membership includes many recognized authorities on the subject of business writing, both in academic ranks and in business circles. I'm highly complimented at the opportunity to become associated with such a group.

Sincerely yours,

Accepting invitation to serve on civic or professional committee or board.

Dear Mr. Faber:

I was both pleased and complimented to receive your letter yesterday.

It will be a pleasure to serve on the Planning Committee for the "Better Burlington" campaign, and I'm looking forward to a pleasant association with you and Ms. Harper in this work.

Yours sincerely,

5.54. Letters of declination. Letters of declination should include an expression of regret and an expression of appreciation for the invitation. An explanation of the circumstances that prevent acceptance helps to show that the regret is sincere. The message must combine cordiality with tact.

Declining invitation to banquet, luncheon or entertainment.

Dear Jerome:

Only this morning I accepted another invitation to be a guest at the Acceptance Banquet. This makes it impossible for me to enjoy your hospitality.

It's a pleasure, however, to know I'm going to see you during that week. Thank you for your kindness in remembering me in arranging your table.

Very sincerely yours,

How to Keep

Books and Records

Although the practice of law is a profession and not a business, the successful lawyer today practices his or her profession in a businesslike way. The lawyer maintains an orderly system of accounts that shows whether a fee is adequate for the time spent on a case, what percentage of overhead bears to his or her income, and the like. Of course, you will be punctilious in maintaining any system that has been established in your office. You also may make suggestions for the improvement of the system.

This chapter describes the fundamentals of bookkeeping in the lawyer's office. It also tells you how to keep records that will show the lawyer immediately the cost of his or her services.

HOW TO KEEP BOOKS IN THE LAW OFFICE

6.1. System of bookkeeping in the law office. In many law offices, you will find in operation a simple "double-entry" system of bookkeeping that you can maintain even though you have had little or no experience in keeping books. Although the books of account may vary in detail, the fundamental principles involved are the same. The following explanation will make it easier for you to follow the instructions of the person who describes the setup of the books to you.

6.2. Books required. In addition to checkbooks, the books usually maintained are a cash journal, a general ledger, and a subsidiary accounts receivable, or clients, ledger, all of which are usually maintained in loose-leaf post binders. The function of each is explained in this chapter.

6.3. Basic principles of double-entry bookkeeping. In every double-entry system, records are kept by accounts. An account is a formal record of related transactions kept in a general ledger. Entries are made in a book of original entry and are posted to the appropriate accounts in the ledger. Posting merely means tranferring items from a book of original entry to a ledger account. This posting process is greatly simplified by assigning each account a number and arranging the accounts in numerical order in the general ledger. Each account has a debit column and a credit column. The debit is the left-hand column and the credit is the right-hand column.

In double-entry bookkeeping every transaction must be recorded in two accounts—as a debit in one account and a credit in another.

Debits and credits. A few principles for debit and credit are all you need to learn to be able to keep the simple bookkeeping books that are ordinarily kept in a lawyer's office. Application of these rules will be explained later.

1. A debit *increases* asset accounts. Cash (bank account), accounts receivable, furniture and fixtures, and other property owned by the firm are assets.

2. A debit *increases* expense accounts, such as salaries, office supplies, and taxes.

3. A debit *decreases* the capital account. The money the lawyer puts into the bank when he or she opens a law office is shown in the capital account. It is decreased when the lawyer withdraws any of that money or when he or she incurs a loss in carrying on the practice.

4. A debit *decreases* an income account.

5. A debit *decreases* liability accounts. Accounts payable is a liability account. So is any other item the firm owes.

6. A credit does exactly the reverse of a debit.

These principles may be expressed as a formula as follows:

Debit —*Increases* assets and expense accounts.
    Decreases capital, income, and liability accounts.
Credit—*Decreases* assets and expense accounts.
    Increases capital, income, and liability accounts.

6.4. Simple rules to remember. Since almost all transactions in a law office involve either bank deposits or bank withdrawals, or charging clients for services and receiving payment from them, you will have no difficulty in making your entries if you remember the four rules that follow.

1. Cash received (bank deposits) is always debited to the bank account in which it is deposited and therefore must be credited to another account.

2. Cash payments (bank withdrawals) are always credited to the bank account on which the check is drawn and therefore must be debited to another account.

3. Accounts Receivable is always debited when bills for services are sent to a client, and the amount charged must be credited to the Services Charged account.

4. Accounts Receivable is always credited when a client pays for services, and the payment must be debited to the Services Charged account.

6.5. Cash Journal. In a law office the book of original entry commonly used is referred to as a *cash journal*. It is a chronological record of every cash or other transaction that passes through the office. It is, of course, supplemented by a record of the lawyer's time, referred to on page 158, from which billings are made. The usual journal sheet consists of from 16 to 18 columns, spread across two facing pages (see illustrations in section 6.9). Appropriate headings which will vary with the office, are written in the columns. An acceptable form of journal sheet has the lines numbered at each side to facilitate following the line across the sheet. In addition to space for date, description of item, and check number, the cash journal sheet in a law office will usually include the following columns, for the purposes indicated:

Cash (Firm Bank Account), debit. All deposits of moneys belonging to the firm are entered here.

Cash (Firm Bank Account), credit. All checks drawn on the firm bank account are entered here.

Trust Fund Account, debit. All receipts of moneys belonging to clients are entered here. Large advances by clients for expenses are also usually deposited in the trust account and, therefore, are entered in this column. Collections of commercial items for clients (chapter 20) are deposited to the trust account. Separate funds should be used when the firm is either executor or trustee of a client's estate or trust.

Trust Fund Account, credit. All checks drawn on the trust fund account are entered here.

Accounts Receivable, debit. All charges made to clients are entered here.

Accounts Receivable, credit. All payments made by clients are entered here.

Accounts Payable, debit. All payments made on accounts owed are entered here. Law firms have few outstanding accounts payable. Therefore this column is frequently omitted, and the payments on accounts owed are entered in the General Ledger (debit) column, from which the detail entry is posted to the debit column of the control account in the general ledger.

Accounts Payable, credit. All accounts owed are entered here. As indicated before, this column may be omitted and entries made instead in the General Ledger (credit) column, from which the detail entry is posted to the credit column of the control account in the general ledger.

Services Charged, debit. All payments made by clients for services are entered here.

Services Charged, credit. All charges made to clients for services are entered here.

General Ledger, debit, and General Ledger, credit. These columns are for accounts that do not have separate columns of their own, such as Furniture and Fixtures, Library, and Accounts Payable. Expenses that occur only occasionally, such as rent, insurance, and entertainment, are entered in the General Ledger column. The entries are posted in detail to the respective accounts in the general ledger.

Fees Earned. All income from fees is entered here. Only one journal column is necessary because all entries are credits.

Tax Expense. Taxes the firm pays are entered here. They include the firm's share of the social security tax, unemployment tax, use and occupancy tax, and others. All entries are debit entries.

Overhead expenses. There may be any number of columns for overhead expenses, such as Office Supplies, Utilities, and Telephone. The breakdown depends upon the need and the number of columns. All entries are debits.

Miscellaneous Expense. Expenses that cannot be readily classified and have no account of their own in the ledger are entered here. All entries are debits.

6.6. General ledger. The general ledger is a loose-leaf book containing all the accounts, including the control account for the individual clients accounts. The entries in the journal are posted to the accounts affected. The cash journal shows what transactions took place on a certain date, whereas the ledger shows the recorded status of each specific account at any time.

The accounts in the ledger are arranged numerically and grouped in the following order in the general ledger to facilitate the preparation of financial statements.

Assets (Bank Accounts, Furniture and Fixtures, Accounts Receivable, etc.)
Liabilities (Accounts Payable, Loans Payable, etc.)
Capital (Proprietorship)
Income
Expense

The general ledger will have accounts for the following columns shown in the cash journal (section 6.9): Cash (Firm Bank Account), Trust Fund Account, Accounts Receivable, Services Charged, Accrued Withholding Tax, Accrued Federal Insurance Contributions, Fees Earned, Tax Expense, Telephone, Office Supplies, Salaries, and Miscellaneous Expense in which any miscellaneous expense may be entered in detail. The general ledger will also have accounts for items that are entered in the General Ledger column, such as Rent, Insurance, Petty Cash, Accounts Payable, and others.

In addition, it will have some accounts that are not immediately affected by the journal. They will have been opened when the books were set up. Entries are usually made in them only once a year, when the books are closed. They generally include a Capital (proprietorship) account, Profit and Loss, Accumulated Depreciation, Depreciation, Bad Debts, and others. The closing entries, which are posted to these accounts, are usually made by the accountant.

6.7. Subsidiary ledger. The subsidiary accounts receivable ledger is the most important record in the law office—the accounts receivable are the lawyer's largest asset. The Accounts Receivable account in the general ledger is a "control" account; it summarizes the individual accounts in the subsidiary ledger. Its balance equals the sum of the balances of the individual accounts in the subsidiary accounts receivable ledger. The control account simplifies getting a trial balance and, especially, detecting any error that might be made in posting to the wrong side of the individual accounts that it controls. When the client's ledger sheets are the same size and shape as the sheets in the general ledger, the accounts receivable may be kept in a separate part of the general ledger. The accounts are kept in alphabetical order according to the client's name.

Unless a separate record is kept of the hours worked on a case (see page 159), it is desirable that the client's ledger sheet should have columns for this information. It should also have separate columns for disbursements and charges for services and a column for payments. Figure 6.1 shows a form of client's ledger sheet suitable for a law office.

Section 6.18 shows an attorney's daily time record. Information can be

Nature of Case: (3)
Escrow Agreement, Real Estate

Name of Client   Kenneth Harrison
Address   1800 Seventh Avenue
Berkeley, California 94710

Date	Lawyer	Hours		Description	Debits		Credits	Balance
		Partner	Staff		Disbursements	Service		(credit)
Mar.8	R.S.E.	1.25		Conference with client				
9				Abstract of title	20.			
12	L.E.T.		2.50	Examination of Abstracts				
13	R.S.E.	1.00		Conference with Smith Attorney				
14				Deposit for Trust			1,350.	(1,350.)
18	L.E.T.		2.50	Draft Agreement				
19	R.S.E.	1.25		Conference with Smith Attorney				
21	L.E.T.		1.00	Drawing deed				
23	R.S.E.	.50		Conference with client				
24	R.S.E.	1.25		Closing				
24	L.E.T.		1.25	Ch. R.D. Smith settlement	780.			(550.)
25				Services		550.		

Figure 6.1. *Client's Ledger Sheet*

picked up from that record and be brought into the client's ledger sheet (figure 6.1). Thus the ledger sheet will reflect the actual time spent by the attorney handling any particular phase of the matter.

As soon as a new case is received, open a ledger sheet for it and fill in all of the data shown in the heading of the account illustrated in figure 6.1. Because of the manner in which lawyers bill their clients, a separate sheet is opened for each case. Thus, a client with three cases pending would have three sheets in the ledger. When a case is disposed of, the sheet is removed from the active ledger. You can get the information necessary to open the account from the New Matter Report (see page 37, *et seq.*).

The column for disbursements and the column for services charged are debit items. Postings are made to these columns from the cash journal.

6.8. Posting to the general ledger. Recording the items from the cash journal to the affected accounts in the ledger is called *posting*. The items in the Accounts Receivable column should be posted daily to the client's subsidiary ledger account, so charges for disbursements are apparent when the lawyer decides to bill the client. (See page 161 for billing the client.) The other items may be posted monthly. The items in the General Ledger column must be posted individually to the accounts affected. Only the totals of the other columns are posted to the corresponding accounts.

Here is the procedure for posting from the cash journal to the accounts in the general ledger:

1. Total each column in the journal. Then total the debit columns and the credit columns. The totals of the debit and credit columns must equal each other. If they do not, you have made an error in the entries or in addition.

2. Post the totals from all columns except General Ledger to the corresponding accounts in the general ledger as a debit or credit, as indicated in the column. You have previously posted the individual items in the Accounts Receivable column to the respective clients' accounts. The total of the Accounts Receivable column is posted to the control account in the general ledger.

3. Post the individual items from the General Ledger column to the respective accounts in the general ledger, as a debit or credit, as indicated in the column. Place a check mark at each item to show that it has been posted.

4. Draw a double red line under the total of each column that has been posted. Your next entries will be below these lines and new totals will not include the figures above the red lines.

6.9. Explanation of cash journal entries and posting. A cash journal sheet is illustrated in figure 6.2. Each of the entries shown and the

	19—	Description	Ck. No.	Cash (Firm Bank Acc.) Debit	Credit
1	Apr. 11	Forward		3195 90	1900 00
2	15	Real Estate Co.—Rent	1132		800 00
3		Clerk of Court—for Henry Fowler	1133		6 00
4	16	Henry Fowler—Services			
5	17	Ck from Henry Fowler		306 00	
6		Ck from S. M. Jones-Real Est Escrow			
7	18	Title Abs Co—abs for S. M. Jones			
8	19	R. D. Smith—Jones Escrow matter	105		
9		S. M. Jones—Services			
10	20	Ellwood & Jones (S. M. Jones acct.)	106	220 00	
11	22	Ck. A. H. Brown—retainer		100 00	
12	23	A. H. Brown—Services			
13		Bell Telephone Co	1134		65 00
14		L. R. Ellwood—Drawing acct.	1135		833 33
15	30	Agnes Smith—salary	1136		271 02
16		Firm Bank Account	1137		2577 70
17		Petty Cash	1138		40 00
18					
19					
20					
21					
22					
29					
30					
31					
32					
33					
34					
35					
36				4171 90	4173 05

Figure 6.2. *Double-page Spread Journal Sheet (Left Edge).*

manner in which it is posted to the general and subsidiary ledgers is explained below. The entries will not normally be in the order in which they are shown here, but this order is presented for purposes of the explanation.

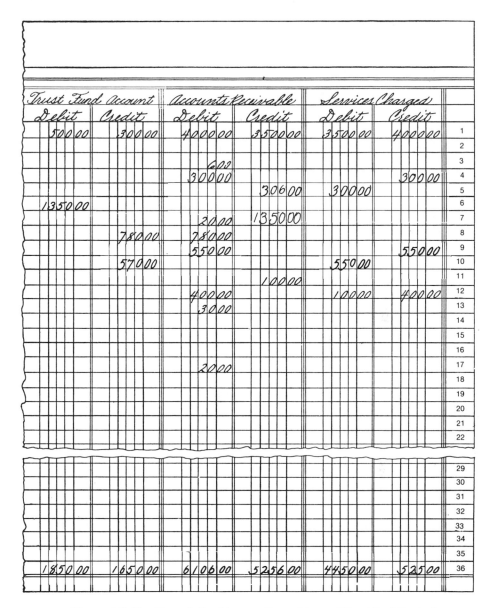

Figure 6.2. Continued. *Double-page Spread Journal Sheet (Left Center).*

Line 1. The balances are brought forward from the bottom of the preceding page of the journal.

Line 2. Check #1132 in the amount of $800, payable to the Real Estate Co. for rent is drawn on the firm bank account. It is entered in the credit

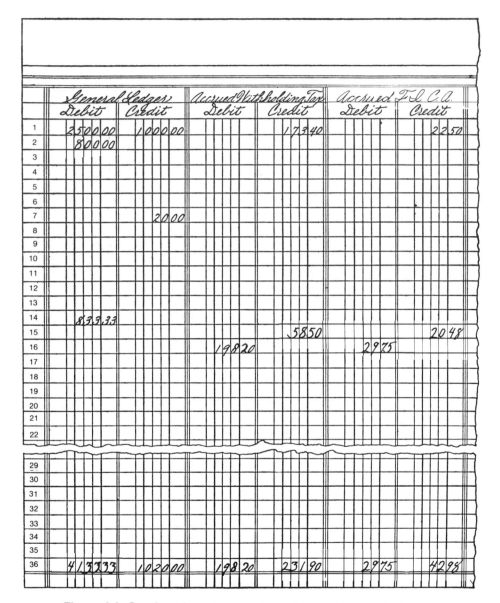

Figure 6.2. Continued. *Double-page Spread Journal Sheet (Right Center).*

column of the Firm Bank Account and in the debit column of General Ledger, because there is no column for rent expense.

At the end of the month all rent items will be posted to the debit column of the Rent account in the general ledger. The credit entry in the

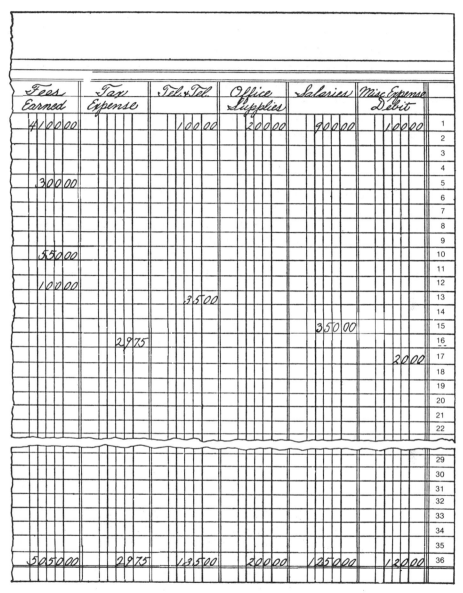

Fees Earned	*Tax Expense*	*Tel.+Tel.*	*Office Supplies*	*Salaries*	*Misc Expense Debit*	
410000		10000	20000	90000	10000	1
						2
						3
						4
30000						5
						6
						7
						8
						9
55000						10
						11
10000						12
		3500				13
						14
				35000		15
	2975					16
					2000	17
						18
						19
						20
						21
						22
						29
						30
						31
						32
						33
						34
						35
505000	2975	13500	20000	125000	12000	36

Figure 6.2. Continued. *Double-page Spread Journal Sheet (Right Edge).*

Firm Bank Account column will be included in the total that will be posted at the end of the month to the Firm Bank Account in the general ledger.

Line 3. Check #1133, in the amount of $6 is drawn on the firm bank account in favor of Clerk of the Court for the account of client Henry Fowler. It is entered in the credit column of the Firm Bank Account and in the debit column of Accounts Receivable.

It is posted from the journal to the debit Disbursement column in Henry Fowler's account in the subsidiary ledger. It will be included also in the total that will be posted at the end of the month to the debit column of the Accounts Receivable control account in the general ledger. The credit entry in the Firm Bank Account column will be included in the total that is posted at the end of the month to the credit column of the Firm Bank Account in the general ledger.

Line 4. Client Henry Fowler is charged $300 for services. This is not a cash transaction. The $300 for services is entered in the debit column of Accounts Receivable and in the credit column of Services Charged.

It is posted from the cash journal to the debit Services column in Henry Fowler's account in the subsidiary ledger. It will be included also in the total that will be posted at the end of the month to the debit column of the Accounts Receivable control account in the general ledger. The credit entry in the Services Charged column will be included in the total that will be posted at the end of the month to the credit column of the Services Charged account in the general ledger.

Line 5. Client Henry Fowler sends the firm a check for $306. It is entered in the debit column of the Firm Bank Account and in the credit column of Accounts Receivable.

The amount of $306 is posted in the credit column of Henry Fowler's account in the subsidiary ledger. It will be included also in the total that will be posted at the end of the month to the credit column of the Accounts Receivable control account in the general ledger, and in the total that will be posted at the end of the month to the debit column of the Firm Bank Account.

However, $300 of the $306 is for fees earned, which was previously credited to Services Charged. Therefore, $300 is entered in the debit column of Services Charged and in the credit column, Fees Earned.

The $300 will be included in the total that will be posted at the end of the month to the debit column of the Services Charged account in the general ledger. It will be included also in the total of the Fees Earned that will be posted at the end of the month to the credit of that account in the general ledger.

Line 6. Client S.M. Jones gives the firm a check for $1,350 as advance for expenses in a real estate matter. That amount is entered in the debit column of the Trust Fund Account and in the credit column of Accounts Receivable.

It is posted to the credit column of S. M. Jones's account for that particular case in the subsidiary ledger, and will be included also in the totals that will be posted at the end of the month to the debit column of the Trust Fund Account and to the credit column of the Accounts Receivable control account in the general ledger.

Line 7. An abstract of title was ordered for Jones and received, together with an invoice for $20. The $20 is entered in the debit column of Accounts Receivable and in the credit column of General Ledger.

The law firm pays the abstract company only once a month, but it is important that Jones's account be charged with $20 immediately. It is posted, therefore, to the debit Disbursements column of S. M. Jones's subsidiary ledger account immediately. It is also posted to the credit column of the abstract company's account in the general ledger. (If transactions with the abstract company are too few to justify a separate account in the general ledger, the $20 will be posted to the Accounts Payable account in the general ledger.) It will be included also in the total posted to the debit column of the Accounts Receivable control account at the end of the month.

Line 8. Check #105 for $780 is drawn on the Trust Fund Account to the order of R. D. Smith, in the Jones escrow matter. It is entered in the credit column of the Trust Fund Account and in the debit column of Accounts Receivable.

It is posted immediately to the debit Disbursement column of Jones's account in the subsidiary ledger and will be included in the total posted to the debit column of the Accounts Receivable control account at the end of the month, and in the total posted to the credit column of the Trust Fund Account at the end of the month.

Line 9. The Jones matter having been completed, Jones is charged $550 for services rendered. The charge is handled in the same manner as in line 4. However, Jones has money on deposit with the firm in the Trust Fund Account, and the charge of $550 will close out his account. A bill is sent to him showing no balance owing, and the ledger sheet for the case is transferred to an inactive account file.

Line 10. To obtain payment from Jones for the $550 service charge and the $20 disbursements, shown by his ledger account, check #106 for $570 is drawn on the Trust Fund Account in favor of the law firm. It is entered in the debit column of the Firm Bank Account and in the credit column of the Trust Fund Account.

The $570 will be included in the totals that will be posted at the end of the month to the debit column of the Firm Bank Account and to the credit column of the Trust Fund Account in the general ledger.

However, the $550, which represents fees earned, was previously credited to Services Charged. Therefore $550 is entered in the debit column of Services Charged and in the credit column, Fees Earned.

The $550 will be included in the totals that will be posted at the end of the month to the debit column of the Services Charged account in the general ledger, and in the total of the Fees Earned that will be posted at the end of the month to the credit column of that account in the general ledger.

Line 11. Client R. H. Brown pays an advance retainer of $100 on account of services to be rendered. This money represents fees earned *when earned*, but is not to be held in trust as was the $1,350 in the Jones matter (line 6). An advance retainer is also to be distinguished from a yearly retainer (see page 41, chapter 1), which is considered earned income immediately. The $100 advance retainer is entered in the debit column of the Firm Bank Account and in the credit column of Accounts Receivable. It is not yet fees earned nor a debit to Services Charged, because the services have not been rendered. Later when Brown is billed for services rendered, the $100 will represent a part of the bill (see line 12).

The $100 is posted immediately to the credit column in Brown's account in the subsidiary ledger and is included also in the totals that will be posted to the debit column of the Firm Bank Account and to the credit column of the Accounts Receivable control account in the general ledger.

Line 12. Client Brown is charged $400 for services rendered and is billed for that amount. The $400 is debited to Accounts Receivable and credited to Services Charged. It is posted immediately to Brown's ledger account and is also included in the totals posted to the respective general ledger accounts.

But the $400 includes $100 already collected (line 11). Therefore Services Charged is debited and Fees Earned is credited with $100. The amount is included in the totals posted to the respective general ledger accounts. (When the balance of $300 is paid, it will be handled in the same manner as any fee for services. See line 5.)

Line 13. Check #1134 payable to the telephone company is drawn on the firm bank account for $65 and entered in the credit column of the Firm Bank Account. Clients are charged with toll calls made in their behalf. Telephone bills must therefore be broken down to determine what part of the bill is telephone expense and what part must be charged to individual clients as disbursements. In this case, the breakdown shows $30 chargeable to clients and $35 to telephone expenses. In the cash journal, $30 is entered in the debit column of Accounts Receivable and the remaining $35 is entered in the debit Telephone and Telegraph Expenses column.

These amounts will be included in the totals posted at the end of the month to the debit of the Accounts Receivable control account, the debit of the Telephone Expense account, and the credit of the Firm Bank Account in the general ledger. From the breakdown of the telephone bill, the amount chargeable to each client is posted immediately in the debit Disbursements column of his account in the subsidiary ledger.

Line 14. Check #1135 in the amount of $833.33 is drawn on the firm bank account to the order of L. R. Elwood, one of the partners. It is entered in the credit column of the Firm Bank Account and in the debit General Ledger column.

It is posted to the debit side of Mr. Elwood's drawing account in the general ledger. The credit will be included in the total posted at the end of the month to the Firm Bank Account in the general ledger.

All entries in Mr. Elwood's account are debits until the end of the year, or other accounting period, when the profits of the firm are credited in accordance with the partnership agreement. Drawing accounts of the partners are not "expenses" for the purpose of figuring profit and loss, nor for income tax purposes. No tax is withheld from checks payable to the partners.

Line 15. Agnes Smith, a stenographer claiming only her own exemption and with no dependents, receives a salary of $700 per month, payable semimonthly. Using 1977 rates, a total of $78.98 is taken out of her salary each payday—$58.50 for the withholding tax and $20.48 for the Social Security Tax (FICA). A check for $271.02 ($350 - $78.98) is drawn on the firm bank account. It is entered in the Salaries expense column; $58.50 and $20.48 are entered in the credit columns of the Accrued Withholding and FICA accounts respectively.

The $58.50 and $20.48 will be included in the totals posted to the credit of Accrued Withholding and Accrued FICA accounts in the general ledger. They are also included in the total of the Salaries column that will be posted to the debit of the Salaries account in the general ledger. This procedure is followed for salaries paid all office employees, including associate lawyers who work for a salary, but not including the partners.

All entries in the Salaries account are debits, until the end of the year when the closing entries are made. Then the Salaries account is credited with the total of salaries for the year and the Profit and Loss account is debited with the same amount.

An individual salary account for each employee should also be kept. See page 158.

Line 16. Check #1137 for $257.70, payable to the Firm Bank Account, for payroll taxes is drawn on the firm bank account. (This amount is submitted to the Firm Bank with Federal Deposit Form 501.) It is entered in the credit column of the Firm Bank Account. The $198.20 and $29.75 previously withheld from employees are entered in the debit columns of Accrued Withholding and Accrued FICA accounts. The remainder, $29.75, represents the firm's share of the Social Security Tax (Federal Insurance Contribution) and is entered in the Tax Expense column.

The $257.70 will be included in the total that is posted to the credit of the Firm Bank Account in the general ledger; $198.20 and $29.75 will be included in the totals posted to the debit of the Accrued Withholding and Accrued FICA accounts; $29.75 will be posted as a debit to the Tax Expense account in the ledger.

Line 17. Check #1138 for $40 is drawn on the firm bank account to replenish the petty cash fund (see page 163) and is entered in the credit column of the Firm Bank Account. Petty cash payments are analyzed to determine what part of the expenditures is miscellaneous expense and what part must be charged to individual clients as disbursements. In this instance, the analysis shows that $20 was spent for items chargeable to the clients and $20 for items chargeable to miscellaneous expense. In the cash journal, $20 is entered in the debit column of Accounts Receivable and $20 is entered in the debit Miscellaneous Expenses column.

These amounts will be included in the totals posted to the debit of the Accounts Receivable control account, the debit of the Miscellaneous Expenses account, and the credit of the Firm Bank Account in the general ledger. From the analysis of the petty cash disbursements, the amount chargeable to each client is posted in the debit Disbursements column of his account in the subsidiary ledger.

6.10. Trial balance. The process of listing the titles of the accounts in the ledger and showing the balance of each, whether debit or credit, is known as *taking a trial balance.* The purpose is to determine whether the total debits equal the total credits and to establish a basic summary for financial statements.

Here are the steps in taking a trial balance.

1. Get the balance of each account in the general ledger by subtracting the total of the debits from the total of the credits, or vice versa if the debit total is larger than the credit total.

2. Enter the balance on the ledger sheet, in the explantion column on the debit side if the balance is a debit; in the explanation column on the credit side if the balance is a credit. You may keep a running record of the account by bringing down the totals in pencil in small figures at the end of each month.

3. Type at the top of a legal-size sheet, "Trial Balance as of (date)."

4. Type a list of the accounts, placing balances in two parallel

columns, debit balances in the left column and credit balances in the right.

5. Total the columns. They will equal one another unless you have made an error.

6.11. Taking a trial balance of accounts receivable. Whenever a trial balance is taken, the accuracy of the accounts in the clients' subsidiary ledger should also be proved. This is done by adding the debit balances and the credit balances, if any, and subtracting the credits from the debits. The result should be the same as the balance shown in the Accounts Receivable control account in the general ledger. If it is not, you have made an error in your posting or in your calculations.

In taking the balance of accounts receivable, remember that both the disbursement entries and the charges for services are debits, whereas the payments received are credits.

Services Charged account is in reality a reserve set aside for the collection of accounts receivable for services and should be in balance with the amounts that are receivable for services.

In taking off your trial balance of the accounts receivable, a separate listing should be made of the accounts receivable for advances made by the attorney for clients' expenses, indicated on the client's ledger sheet as Disbursements. After deducting from the total listing of all receivables the amount of receivables for expense, the balance should equal the credit balance in the Services Charged account, unless there are certain prepayments in the accounts receivable balances in the form of advance retainers or trust deposits. A glance at the illustrated cash journal will show that every debit to Accounts Receivable *for services rendered* is reflected in the credits to Services Charged.

6.12. Profit and loss statement. A profit and loss statement shows the lawyer whether he or she made a profit or lost money over a given period.

It also shows the amount of each type of expense. The accountant usually prepares this statement after he has closed the books for the period. However, you can at any time prepare a profit and loss statement as follows:

1. Take a trial balance as explained on page 154.

2. Take a sheet of paper and rule the right of the page with two columns for the insertion of figures. Entitle the sheet "Profit and loss statement for the period beginning (insert the date) and ending (insert the date)."

3. List the income accounts shown in the trial balance, carrying the figure for each account to the right column. Draw a line under the figures and show the total of the income accounts.

PAYROLL

NAME

ADDRESS   PHONE   SOCIAL SEC. NO.

NO. OF EXEMPTIONS

DATE 19	PERIOD PAID FOR	RATE	EARNINGS			DEDUCTIONS				NET PAID	CHECK NUMBER
			REGULAR	OTHER	TOTAL	W.H. TAX	FICA W.H.	OTHER W.H.	TOTAL		
JAN.											
TOTAL JANUARY											
FEB.											
TOTAL FEBRUARY											
MAR.											
TOTAL MARCH											
TOTAL 1ST QUARTER											

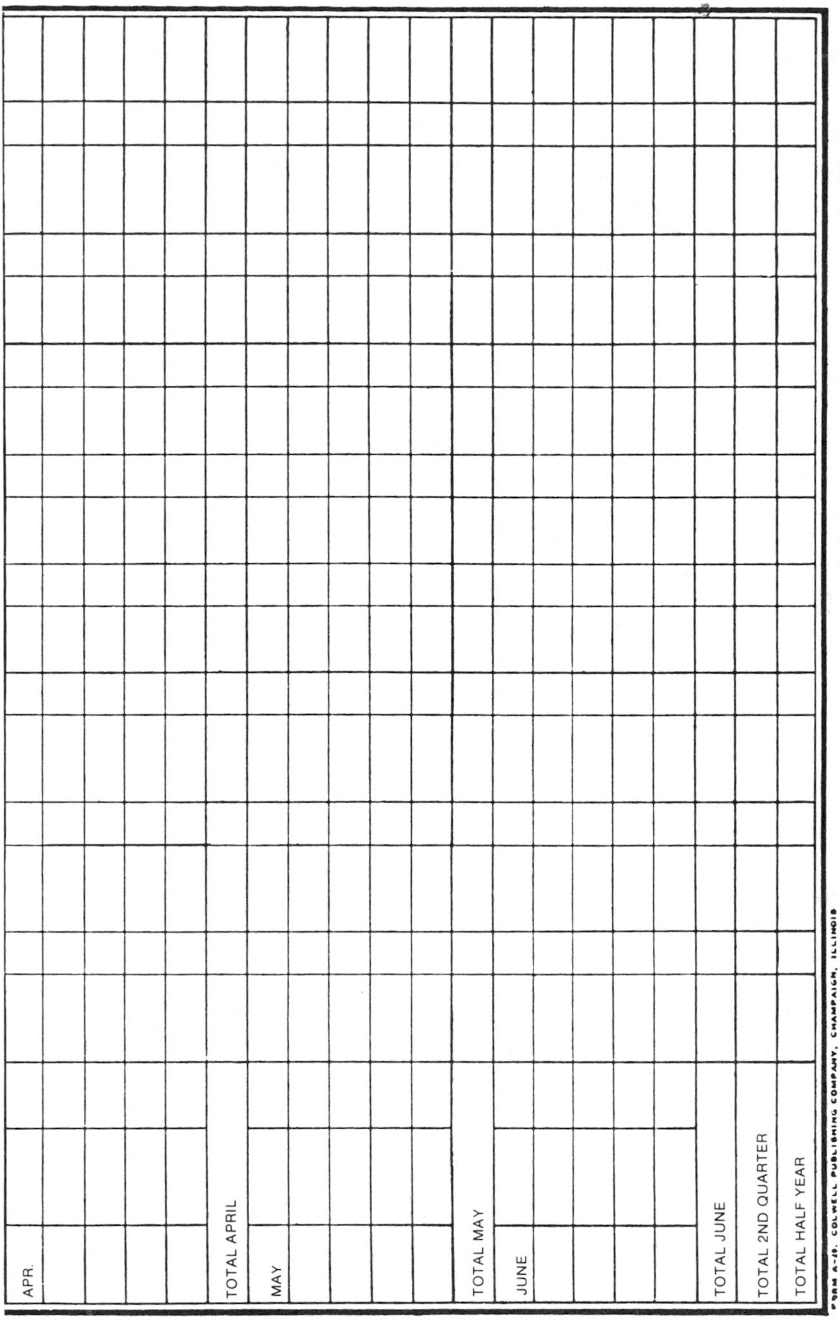

From Daily Log for Lawyers, Courtesy Colwell Publishing Company.

Figure 6.3. *Payroll Record.*

4. List the expense accounts shown in the trial balance, carrying the figure to the left column. Draw a line under the figures and show the total of the expense accounts.

5. Subtract. The balance shows the law firm's net profit or loss.

6.13. Drawing account. Each member of the firm has a drawing account. All of the entries are on the debit side. These accounts are closed out at the end of the accounting period, usually by the accountant.

6.14. Payroll record. An individual account for each employee should also be kept, to facilitate reports to the state and federal governments and the preparation of the withholding receipt that must be given to each employee. Figure 6.3 is a form suggested for this purpose when employees are paid weekly. The form provides space for recording and accumulating taxes withheld for remittance to the Internal Revenue Service and for the annual withholding statement. These entries are posted from the cash journal.

6.15. Capital account. It takes money to open a law office and operate it before the fees are received. The money the lawyer puts up for this purpose is known as *capital*. It is entered in the debit column of the Firm Bank Account and in the credit column of the Capital account. At the end of each year when the books are closed and the lawyer finds out whether he or she has made a profit or has lost money on the operation of the office, an entry is made to show the change in Capital account. A profit is posted to the credit of the Capital account and a loss to the debit. As previously mentioned, the accountant usually makes the closing entries.

TIME AND COST OF PROFESSIONAL SERVICES

6.16. Records required to find time and cost of service. The records required to ascertain the cost of the lawyer's service on a specific case are the following:

Daily time sheet
Client's ledger (kept in connection with bookkeeping)

6.17. Finding the cost of a lawyer's time. In figuring the profit and loss in a law office for accounting purposes, the lawyer's time is not counted, but the lawyer who practices his or her profession in a businesslike manner wants to know the cost of the time spent on a case. The fee charged may be more than the cost, giving the lawyer a profit, or it may be less, resulting in a loss. But at least the cost of the lawyer's time is a basis for a fair fee. Even when a client is on a yearly retainer or when the lawyer accepts a case on a contingent basis, he or she wants to know the cost.

The cost per hour of a lawyer's time is arrived at by adding the lawyer's drawing account to the overhead and dividing by the number of hours he or she expects to be working during the year. If there is more than one attorney practicing for the firm, the overhead is proportioned among them, including the associates, on the basis of their drawing accounts. The senior member of the firm, who has the largest drawing account, is thus charged with a larger proportion of the overhead than a junior member. This is as it should be since he or she has a better office, a higher paid secretary, and the like. Salaries paid associate attorneys are not included in overhead for the purpose of calculating the cost of services; the associate's cost to the firm is figured in the same manner as the cost of a partner's service.

Example: The firm of Davis & McKenzie is composed of two partners and a salaried associate. Senior Partner Davis draws $40,000 per year, Junior Partner McKenzie draws $28,000, and Associate Dennison is paid a salary of $22,000. The overhead is $67,500, or approximately 75 percent of the total paid the three lawyers. (The overhead figure is taken from the books, but Dennison's salary is deducted from that figure.) The overhead each lawyer is expected to carry bears the same relation to the total overhead that the amount paid him by the firm bears to the total paid all the lawyers. The overhead of each lawyer is, therefore, 75 percent of his earnings, or $30,000, $21,000 and $16,500 respectively. Each lawyer works 1,600 hours per year. Senior Partner's cost is approximately $43.75 per hour [($40,000 + $30,000) ÷ 1600]; Junior Partner's cost is approximately $30.63 per hour [($28,000 + $21,000) ÷ 1600]; and the associate's is approximately $24.06 per hour [($22,000 + $16,500) ÷ 1600].

6.18. Daily time sheet. To arrive at the cost of a job, each lawyer in the office should keep a daily time sheet. The diary illustrated in figure 3.1, chapter 3, can be used as a time record. Figure 6.4 illustrates another form. These forms do not provide for an estimated fee, but this is covered by the new matter reports illustrated in figures 1.4 and 1.5, chapter 1. In some offices the secretaries and stenographers also keep time sheets. The time spent on each matter is posted to the client's ledger account and is considered in calculating the fee.

6.19. Posting the time charges. Post the time charges to the client's ledger account (figure 6.1) from the daily time sheet, showing which lawyer did the work. When the lawyer is ready to fix the fee, he or she will ask for the time spent on the case by each attorney. The lawyer knows the cost per hour and can thus calculate the cost to the firm of the services rendered. The fee may be more or less than that cost.

TIME	Kind of Work	MATTER	TIME	Kind of Work	MATTER
9 a.m.			2 p.m.		
.10			.10		
.20			.20		
.30			.30		
.40			.40		
.50			.50		
10 a.m.			3 p.m.		
.10			.10		
.20			.20		
.30			.30		
.40			.40		
.50			.50		
11 a.m.			4 p.m.		
.10			.10		
.20			.20		
.30			.30		
.40			.40		
.50			.50		
12 m.			5 p.m.		
.10			.10		
.20			.20		
.30			.30		
.40			.40		
.50			.50		
1 p.m.			6 p.m.		
.10			Remarks:		
.20					
.30					
.40			Evening		
.50					
2 p.m.					

C—Consultation with client; I—Interview with others; T—Telephone conversation; D—Dictation; W—Work; L—Looking up Law; M—Miscellaneous

Courtesy Julius Blumberg, Inc.

Figure 6.4. *Attorney's Daily Time Sheet.*

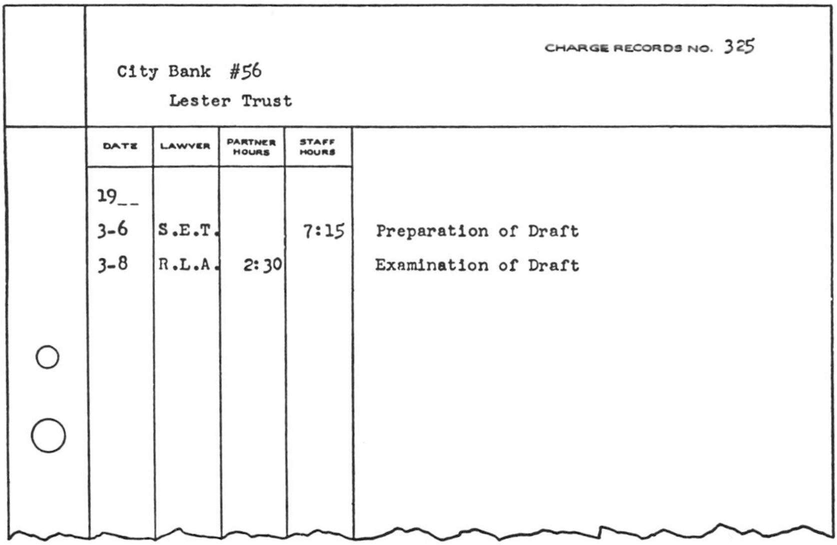

CHARGE RECORDS NO. 325

City Bank #56
Lester Trust

DATE	LAWYER	PARTNER HOURS	STAFF HOURS	
19__				
3-6	S.E.T.		7:15	Preparation of Draft
3-8	R.L.A.	2:30		Examination of Draft

Figure 6.5. *Service Ledger Sheet.*

Some law firms do not post the time to the client's ledger account but keep it on a service ledger sheet similar to those illustrated in figures 6.5 and 6.6. In that case, the lawyer calls for the time record when he or she is ready to bill the client. Only the disbursements, service charges, and payments appear on the client's ledger account. These time charge sheets may be kept in a loose-leaf ledger, or in a ledger tray. In a comparatively small office where the number of cases does not justify a separate tray, the time charge sheets may be kept in the same tray as the suit register sheets described in chapter 12.

BILLING THE CLIENT

6.20. Preparation of the bill. Instead of billing clients once a month, the usual practice in a law office is to bill them when a case is completed, unless it is a long, drawn-out matter. Then the client is billed at intervals. The lawyer will probably dictate the bill.

Law firms generally have printed bill heads; otherwise, they use letterheads. The general practice is to make an original and two copies—the original for the client, a copy for the case file, and a copy for the invoice file. The bills are usually numbered and filed in the invoice file according to number. If they are not numbered, they are filed according to date.

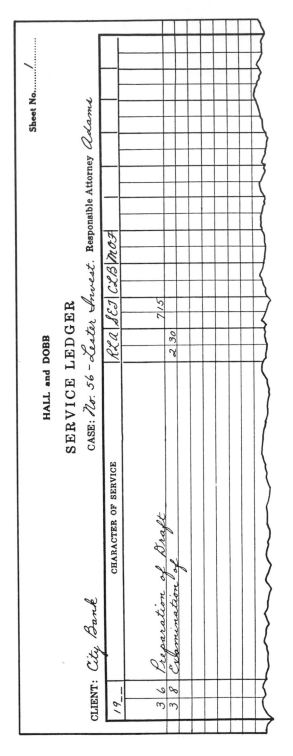

Figure 6.6. Service Ledger Sheet—Another Form.

6.21. Charges made to clients. Fees for services and disbursements made in behalf of a client are charged to his account. (See Client's Ledger Sheet, figure 6.1) The disbursements, which are itemized in the bill, include:

Recording fees
Court costs
Fee paid process servers
Revenue or documentary stamps
Postage, when for heavy airmail or registered documents; also when a special job requires mailing a large number of letters
Stenographic services when an out of the ordinary amount of clerical work is required
Long distance telephone calls
Telegrams
All fees paid for investigations, accountings, abstracts, etc.
Photostats, Xerox or other copies

6.22. How the amount of the bill is calculated. When the lawyer is ready to bill the client, he or she will want a report on the time costs. You will give him or her a report of the total number of hours spent on the case by each lawyer from the time the case was opened or from the date of the last bill. Each lawyer's time is listed separately, because the cost per hour varies with the lawyer. You can get this information from the client's service ledger sheet (figures 6.5 and 6.6), or from his account ledger sheet if the account shows the time record (figure 6.1). The lawyer knows the cost per hour of each member of the firm and of each associate lawyer (you might not) and calculates the cost accordingly.

He or she will also want a record of the advances made for the client, and the status of the account as a whole. The lawyer will get this from the client's account ledger sheet or you will give him or her a record of the disbursements. Whenever a client is billed, examine the current petty cash record to see if any expenditures have been made in his behalf; also examine records of toll telephone costs. After a client is billed, the lawyer cannot very well send him a bill for 50 cents for an item that you paid out of petty cash, but numerous small advances add up to sizable sums.

6.23. Petty cash fund. Keep a petty cash fund in the office to pay for any incidental expenses that may arise, such as recording fees and collect messages. The size of the fund will vary according to the demands made upon it, but it should be large enough to last about a month. Keep the money in a safe place because you are responsible for it. Never mix this money with your own funds; never make change from it unless you can make the exact change, and *never* borrow from it.

Keep a running record of expenditures made from the fund. As each expenditure is made, no matter how small, enter the date, the amount, purpose for which spent, and the client and case to which it is chargeable. When the petty cash fund gets low, add up the expenditures and write a check, payable to yourself, for the total—that is, the amount necessary to bring the petty cash fund up to its original figure. Attach the record to the check when you give it to your employer for his signature. Mark the record, "Paid—*(date)*—, Ck. No._____," initial, and file it. Then start a new running account for future expenditures from the fund.

7

Using References

in Legal Research

Without law books, the lawyer could not function. Before drawing an agreement, bringing a court action, undertaking to defend a law suit, advising a client—before making a move of any kind— the lawyer "looks up the law." The books that enable a lawyer to do his or her job efficiently are:

1. Statutes and codes
2. Reports of decided cases and administrative rulings
3. Books that classify the law
4. Form books
5. Treatises and loose-leaf services

STATUTES AND CODES

7.1. Compilations of laws. The laws enacted by the Congress of the United States and the various state legislatures are systematically sorted and arranged in chapters and subheads to facilitate their use. The compilations, known as *statutes* and *codes* usually contain, also, the Consitution of the United States and of the particular state. See page 620 for a list of compilations.

Every lawyer has the compilation of his or her own state; law firms that practice in several states have the compilations for those states; nearly all lawyers have the United States Code or, more commonly, one of the commercially produced annotated versions such as U.S. Annotated (West) or U. S. Code Service (Lawyer's Cooperative); law association libraries and law college libraries usually have the compilations of every state.

The compilations are kept up to date by pocket parts and supplements.

7.2. How to find a law. You should familiarize yourself with the arrangement of the compilation for your state. You will find that the preface contains useful explanatory material. Every compilation contains a general index, and some of them also have an index in each volume. The indexes vary in their completeness and usefulness, but with a little perseverance you will be able to find the desired section of the law. After you search the compilation, search the supplements and pocket parts, if any, and all session laws since the date of the latest supplement. The section of the law in which you are interested might have been amended or repealed since the compilation, or a new law on the subject might have been enacted.

When a law suit involves a statute, the court's judicial interpretation and construction of that statute becomes as much a part of the law as the statute itself. You will notice that the notes in annotated compilations (see figure 7.1) include references to the published opinions that relate to the statutes. If the compilation is not annotated, you will have to look elsewhere (see "Books That Classify the Law,"below), to locate judicial interpretations of the statutes.

REPORTS OF DECIDED CASES

7.3. Scope and organization of reports. When a point of law has once been settled by a judicial decision, it forms a precedent for the guidance of the courts in similar cases. The decisions are published in order that they may be readily accessible to the lawyers and the courts. Every practicing attorney must have access to the published reports of decisions in his own state, either in the official state reports or the appropriate reporter of the National Reporter System. See "Official Reports and the National Reporter System," page 371, *et seq.*

Preceding the opinion in a case is a brief statement of each point of law determined by the case. These statements are known as the *syllabus,* or the *headnotes.* In the reporters, the headnotes are numbered, and the part of the opinion that covers a particular headnote is numbered to correspond with the headnote number. Thus, if you are interested only in a statement made in headnote 3, you turn to the "[3]" in the opinion.

Each series of reports or reporters is numbered consecutively. Additional volumes of the reporters in the National Reporter System are

198.23   Personal liability of executor, etc.

If any executor shall make distribution either in whole or in part of any of the property of an estate to the heirs, next of kin, distributees, legatees or devisees without having paid or secured the tax due the state under this chapter, or obtained the release of such property from the lien of such tax he shall become personally liable for the tax so due the state, or so much thereof as may remain due and unpaid, to the full extent of the full value of any property belonging to such person or estate which may come into his hands, custody or control.

Historical Note

Derivation:

Comp.Gen.Laws Supp.1936, § 1342 (96).
Laws 1933, c. 16015, § 16.

Prior Laws:

For complete text of the Inheritance and Estate Tax Laws of 1931, see Appendix to this chapter.

Cross References

Apportionment of estate taxes, see § 734.041.
Determination of amount by commissioner and payment thereof as discharging executor, see § 198.19.

Law Review Commentaries

Vexing probate problems. Judge William C. Brooker, 31 Fla.Bar J. 75 (February 1957).

Library References

Taxation ☞890.   C.J.S. Taxation § 1169.

Notes of Decisions

I. Protection of tax liens

The commissioner of taxation, under his rule-making power contained in §§ 198.08 and 199.03, and granted to aid in the proper enforcement of said §§ 198.01 et seq., 199.01 et seq., should adopt rules and regulations designed to protect the state's interest through tax liens in bank account subject to payment to foreign personal representatives under circumstances which might well have the effect of a loss of the state's lien in this connection. 1959 Op.Atty.Gen. 059–7, Jan. 15, 1959.

Figure 7.1. *Excerpt from Annotated Compilation.*

published several times a year; volumes of the official state reports, less often. In arranging the books on the library shelf, leave an empty shelf, or part of a shelf, after the last volume of a series so you will not have to shift the books when additional volumes are received. Keep the advance sheets (see page 371) in consecutive order after the last volume of the series. When a new bound volume is received, destroy the advance sheets that are covered by it.

7.4. How to use the reports and reporters. Finding a case in a report or reporter when you have the volume and page number needs no explanation. Just be careful not to confuse the second series of a reporter with the first series. If the lawyer tells you that a case is in "76 Northeastern," he does not mean "76 Northeastern Second." Each report and reporter has a list of the cases cited in it with the cases arranged alphabetically under the name of plaintiff and defendent. For example, *Abbott v. Bralov* is also listed *Bralov; Abbot v.* Since a reporter covers more than one state, it contains a general table of all the cases reported, followed by a separate table for each state. Thus, if you know the volume and the name of either party to a case, you can easily find the page number where the opinion begins.

In the back of each reporter there is a digest of the cases reported in that volume, arranged according to subject. The lawyer might know the substance of a decision and the approximate time it was decided, but be unable to recall the name of the case. You can refer to the volume or volumes covering the approximate time of the decision and, under the appropriate subject in the digest, you will be able to locate the desired case. This might involve searching several volumes and is not a desirable method of research, but is sometimes necessary.

You can find the names of the justices of the appellate courts in the front of the reports and reporters.

The name and location of the attorneys in a case are given immediately following the syllabus, preceding the opinion.

7.5. How to find alternate citations. When the lawyer has a citation to a case in an unofficial reporter, he may require the official citation. Occasionally the reverse is true. There are several ways to find alternate citations to state court cases. (1) The table of cases in the state or regional digest generally gives alternative citations. Be sure you have the correct case when you look up the alternative citation; there are sometimes two or more cases under the same name. (2) The *National Reporter Blue Book* and the blue books for state and regional reporters are compilations of tables of alternate citations. The blue books generally are found only in relatively large libraries. (3) *Shepard's Citations* lists the alternate citations preceded by a lowercase "s" indicating "same case." Look up the citation you have in the appropriate volume of *Shepard's* to find the alternate citation by this method.

7.6. Other publications of decisions. In addition to state reports and the National Reporter System, there are several other types of publications of decisions.

Selected cases series, annotated. Selected cases series limit the cases reported to (1) decisions that deal with questions upon which there is a conflict of law; (2) decisions that deal with novel questions; and (3) decisions that are outstanding by reason of their treatment of the question involved and their review of the authorities. The decisions are reported in full, with headnotes, and are fully annotated. They thus may be used not only as a report of the decision, but as a guide to other cases in point and as a source of original research.

American Law Reports is the only current selected series of American cases. The series is the merger of, or successor to, all previous selective cases series. The following diagram shows the development that resulted in the current series. The diagram gives the abbreviations by which the publications are cited. The full titles, in the sequence in which they appear in the diagram, are:

> Lawyers' Reports Annotated
> Lawyers' Reports Annotated, New Series
> Lawyers' Reports Annotated, Third Unit
> American Decisions
> American Reports
> American State Reports
> American and English Annotated Cases
> American Annotated Cases
> American Law Reports

L.R.A.—>L.R.A. (N.S.)—>L.R.A. (3rd Unit)
Am. Dec—>Am. Rep.—>Am. State Rep.
⎱ Ann. Cas. ⎰ A.L.R.
Am. & Eng. Ann. Cas.

The volumes are identified by year of publication and by letter, thus 1916A, 1916B, etc.

Subject reports. Some reports publish only those decisions that relate to a particular subject or topic of law. Among the series of subject reports are the American Federal Tax Report (AFTR) and American Labor Cases (ALC).

7.7. Loose-leaf services. Most law firms that practice extensively in a particular area of the law, such as federal taxation, corporation law, labor law, environmental law, and the like, subscribe to one or more loose-leaf services in their areas of specialization. For example, Commerce Clearing House publishes *Standard Federal Tax Reporter, Poverty Law Reporter, Trade Regulation Reporter, Federal Energy Guidelines,* and many more. Bureau of National Affairs publishes *Labor Law Reporter, Family Law Reporter,* and *Environmental Law Reporter,* among others. Prentice-Hall publishes *The Prentice-Hall Federal Tax Service, State and Local Tax Services,* and a wide range of other services that deal with tax and/or labor laws. The Executive Reports division of Prentice-Hall also publishes a helpful periodical titled *The Creative Legal Secretary.* These loose-leaf services provide frequent updating of information in areas of the law that are constantly changing. They include reports of court decisions, both state and federal, reports of pertinent decisions of agencies, reprints and explanations of agency regulations, and text and summaries of proposed or enacted legislation in a particular field.

Another important loose-leaf service found in many law offices is *U.S. Law Week,* published by the Bureau of National Affairs, Inc. This service reports all U.S. Supreme Court decisions as soon as they are handed down and lists case names and docket numbers of all cases currently before the Court. It also summarizes important state and lower federal court decisions as they are handed down, along with federal agency rulings and federal statutes. Consult the "how to use" card in the general law section binder for detailed instructions on research in *Law Week.*

Your office will receive releases to be filed in each service to which the firm subscribes. These are usually issued weekly and should be filed promptly to keep the service up-to-date. Each release contains detailed filing instructions that must be followed meticulously to avoid mistakes.

BOOKS THAT CLASSIFY THE LAW

The books that classify the law enable the lawyer to pick from among the millions of cases those that are on point with the legal problem that confronts him or her. These books, because of their nature, are sometimes called *books of index.* They include digests, encyclopedias, texts, citators, and tables of cases. The lawyer uses them initially as a lead and also to direct him or her to other cases in point. Among the books most commonly used are the *American Digest,* state and regional digests, *Corpus Juris* and *Corpus Juris Secundum, American Jurisprudence,* and *Shepard's Citations.* Knowledge of how to use these books will enable you to use other books of index.

AMERICAN DIGEST

7.8. Organization of the digest system. Digests are published for every state and for all regional reporters except Northeast and Southwest. In addition, there is a *Federal Practice Digest* and a *Supreme Court Digest*. All state and federal cases are brought together in the American Digest System. Because of its broad scope, this system is awkward to use to find case law of a particular jurisdiction. The American Digest is cumulated into a Decennial Digest every ten years and supercedes the General Digest for that period. At the beginning of each ten-year period, a new General Digest Series begins. Each volume of the General Digest Series contains a reference to all the cases on every topic published during the period covered by that particular volume. Thus, each volume of the General Digest Series contains the topic *Judgment*. By the end of the ten-year period the General Digest may contain forty to fifty volumes, most of which must be searched to find all the cases on a given topic decided during the period since the last decennial cumulation.

A detailed fact index constitutes part of each digest. The index is contained in volumes entitled "Descriptive Word Index." The descriptive words are listed in black type in alphabetical order. Different situations involving the fact element are listed in lighter type and refer to the place in the digest where cases in point may be found. The reference is by means of topic and key number.

An analysis precedes each main topic. The digest of cases are grouped according to the point of law involved, and each point is given a key number. Each digest also contains a table of cases, by plaintiff and defendant, with complete citations to the National Reporter Systems and to official state reporters where they have been published. This is an alternative and often quicker way to find alternate citations than to use the blue books mentioned in section 7.5.

7.9. How to use the digest system. Suppose you are interested in the priority over other claims of an allowance by the executor to a widow.

The first step in finding the authorities through the digest system is to get the key number. There are three methods of getting the key number:

1. If you already have at least one case in point, from the key numbers in the headnotes in the reporters, which correspond to the key numbers in the digests
2. From the Descriptive Word Index
3. From the analysis that precedes each topic.

SHEPARD'S CITATIONS

7.10. Purpose of Shepard's Citations. To prove a point, the lawyer cites a decision contained in a published opinion. Before citing the case he or she wants to know something of its history and subsequent treatment. The lawyer is interested in knowing whether the case has been appealed to a higher court, whether it was affirmed or reversed; whether it has been followed in many other cases; and whether it has been overruled in a subsequent case. *Shepard's Citations* is designed to give the lawyer this information. It is quite easy to "shepardize" a case, and you will probably be asked to assist the lawyer with this research. A lawyer never cites a case as authority without first shepardizing it. *Shepard's* also shepardizes statutes, showing where they have been interpreted by state and federal courts.

7.11. How to use Shepard's Citations. An explanation of how to use *Shepard's* appears in the front of each volume, along with a list of abbreviations used. Figure 7.2 illustrates a page from the Federal Reporter Citations.

ILLUSTRATIVE CASE

*(Acknowledgment is made to Shepard's Citations, Inc.,
for this explanation.)*

Let us assume that by reference to a digest, encyclopedia, textbook or other unit of legal research, you have located the case of *Hanover Star Milling Co.* v. *Allen & Wheeler Co.,* reported in Volume 208 of the Federal Reporter on page 513, dealing among other things with the property right which a complainant has in a trademark.

Figure 7.2 is a reproduction from Shepard's Federal Reporter Citations. Note the volume of reports to which the citations apply, "Vol. 208," in the upper right-hand corner of the page.

An examination of the heavy face type numbers within the page locates the page number "—513—" in the seventh column of citations. This is the initial page of the case under consideration. Following this page number you will find the citation "sLRA1916D 136" indicating that the same case "s" is also reported in 1916D Lawyers Reports Annotated 136.

In obtaining the history of this case you will observe that upon appeal to the United States Supreme Court, it was affirmed "a" in 240 United States Reports "US" 403, 60 Lawyers Edition of United States "LE" 713, 36 Supreme Court Reporter "SC" 357, 1916 Decisions of the Commissioner of Patents " '16 CD" 265. Wherever there are parallel sets

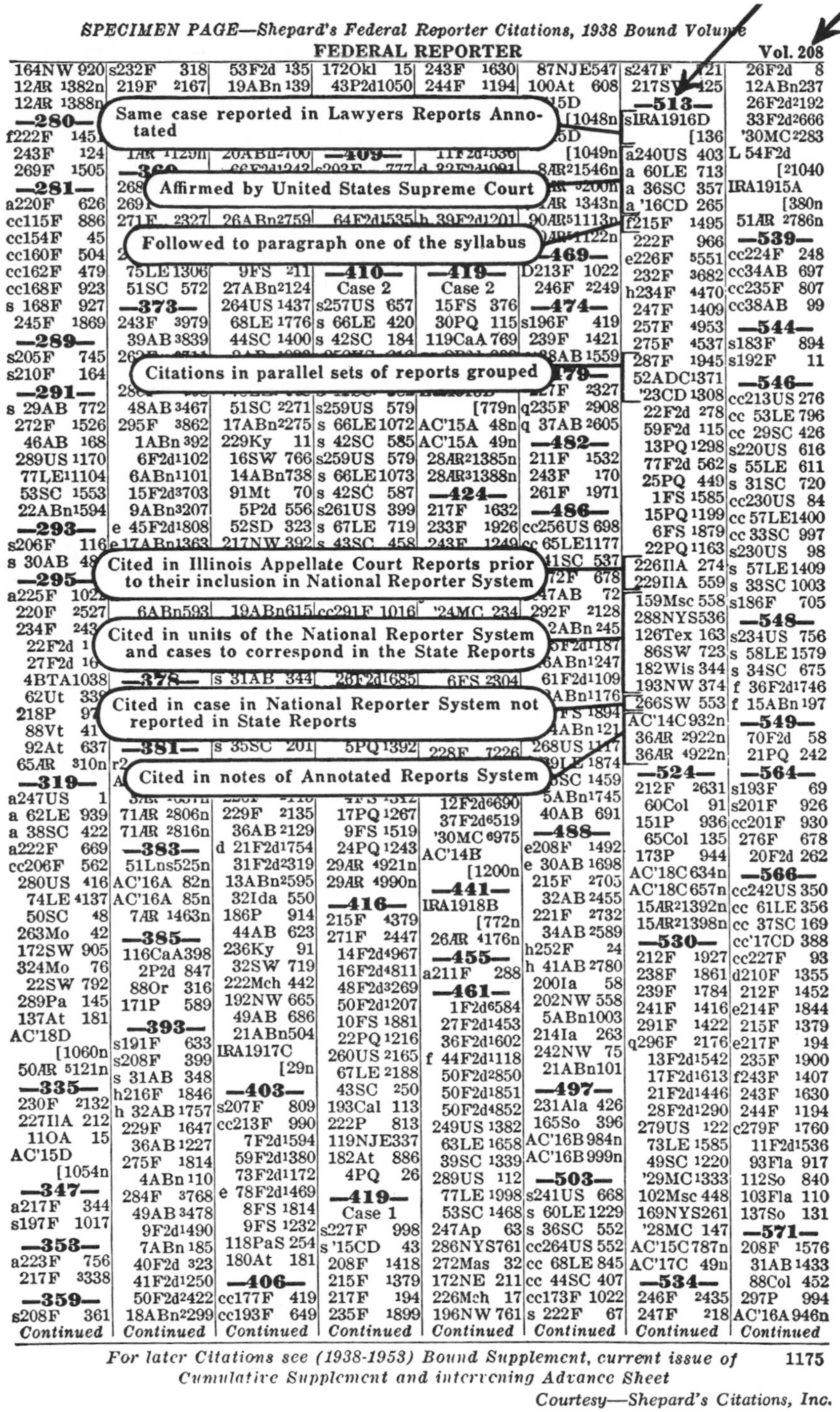

SPECIMEN PAGE—Shepard's Federal Reporter Citations, 1938 Bound Volume

FEDERAL REPORTER   Vol. 208

The specimen page shows columns of citation data with the following annotated callout boxes overlaid:

- Same case reported in Lawyers Reports Annotated
- Affirmed by United States Supreme Court
- Followed to paragraph one of the syllabus
- Citations in parallel sets of reports grouped
- Cited in Illinois Appellate Court Reports prior to their inclusion in National Reporter System
- Cited in units of the National Reporter System and cases to correspond in the State Reports
- Cited in case in National Reporter System not reported in State Reports
- Cited in notes of Annotated Reports System

Sample citation column entries include:

164NW 920 | s232F 318 | 53F2d 135 | 172Okl 15 | 243F 1630 | 87NJE547 | s247F 421 | 26F2d 8
12AR 1382n | 219F 2167 | 19ABn 139 | 43P2d1050 | 244F 1194 | 100At 608 | 217SW 425 | 12ABn237

—280— ... —513— ...

For later Citations see (1938-1953) Bound Supplement, current issue of
Cumulative Supplement and intervening Advance Sheet   1175

Courtesy—Shepard's Citations, Inc.

Figure 7.2. *Page from Shepard's Federal Reporter Citation.*

of reports covering the same citing case these citations immediately follow each other.

It is also to be observed that by examining the abbreviations preceding the citations, this case has been followed "f," explained "e," and harmonized "h" in subsequent cases in the Federal Reporter.

The next citation covers the reference "215F¹495." The small superior figure "1" in advance of the citing page number 495, indicates that the principle of law brought out in the first paragraph of the syllabus of the cited case is also dealt with in 215 Federal Reporter 495.

Assuming you are primarily interested in the principle covered in paragraph one of the syllabus, we find the additional citations that contain the superior figure "1" in advance of the citing page number include numerous other cases that deal with this particular point of law and are reported in the Federal Reporter; Federal Reporter, Second Series "F2d"; Federal Supplement "FS"; Appeal Cases District of Columbia "ADC"; Decisions of the Commission of Patents and United States Patents Quarterly "PQ."

In addition to the citations in point with paragraph one of the syllabus, there are several citations to other paragraphs of the syllabus of this case in cases reported in the Federal Reporter, Federal Reporter, Second Series, and in the notes "n" of the America Law Reports "ALR." Thus, the citations dealing with a point of law in any particular paragraph of the syllabus may be referred to instantly without examining every citation to the case.

This case has been cited by the courts of Illinois, New York, Texas, and Wisconsin. These citations are arranged alphabetically by the state reports with the corresponding reference in the National Reporter System. The citation 266 Southwestern Reporter (SW) 533 is a case decided in the Court of Civil Appeals of Texas and not reported elsewhere. This case has also been cited in the notes of 1914C Annotated Cases 932 (AC'14C932n).

By examining this same volume and page number in the 1938-1953 Bound Supplement, latest issue of the Cumulative Supplement, and intervening Advance Sheet, all subsequent citations to this case will be found.

CORPUS JURIS SECUNDUM SYSTEM

7.12. Scope and organization of system. The Corpus Juris Secundum System consists of Corpus Juris Secundum and Corpus Juris. The system is a complete statement of the body of American law in Encyclopedic form, broken down into approximately 430 titles. The authorities cited in the notes in the Secundum are the cases decided since that tile in Corpus Juris was written. If there are earlier cases on the point, footnote references in Corpus Juris Secundum direct the searcher to the precise page and note in Corpus Juris where they will be found. The absence of a footnote reference to Corpus Juris indicates there are no earlier cases. Thus, although the text of Corpus Juris is being superseded by Corpus Juris Secundum, Corpus Juris remains a vital part of the lawyer's library because of the footnotes.

The titles embraced by the system are alphabetically arranged. Judicially defined words, phrases, and maxims are alphabetically interspersed through the titles. The backbone of each volume shows the first and last words in that volume and also the volume number. Volume 72 of Corpus Juris is a complete descriptive word index to all volumes of Corpus Juris. Each volume of the Secundum has an index to the titles contained in that volume.

7.13. How to use Corpus Juris Secundum System. There are three methods of finding the discussion and supporting authorities in the Corpus Juris Secundum System.

1. *The fact, or descriptive, word index.* Find the descriptive word in the index to the title in the back of the volume. For example, if you are interested in the extent of an implied agency, your title would be *Agency*. In the index you will find "Implied agency," with the section and page number where implied agency is discussed. At the head of the section is an analysis of points covered in the section, which enables you to narrow your search.

Each volume of Corpus Juris does not contain an index. If the title in which you are interested has not been published in the Secundum, look for the descriptive word in Volume 72, "Descriptive-word Index and Concordance," of Corpus Juris.

2. *The general analysis preceding each title.* At the beginning of each title is an analysis, or breakdown, of the contents of the title. The topics are in boldface capitals and are numbered with roman numerals. Each of the topics has a subanalysis. Judge which topic should cover the point in which you are interested, and then look at the subanalysis for the specific point. "III Creation and Extent of Relation" should cover implied agency. In the subanalysis of that topic, you will find, "§ 24, Implied Agency—p. 1045."

If you cannot judge which topic should cover your problem, you can look at each of the subtopics, but this, of course, is a slower method of research.

3. *Words and phrases alphabetically arranged throughout the set.* If an important word or words in your problem can be picked out, you can

refer to those words in CJS and find cross-references to many related topics in which the words have meaning or importance.

7.14. How to cite. Cite by volume number, title, and page and section number.

> 57 C.J., Set-Off and Counterclaim, p. 376, § 22
> 24 C.J.S., Criminal Law, p. 147, § 1606

7.15. American Jurisprudence and American Law Reports. The Lawyers Co-operative Publishing Company has completely revised its encyclopedia, *American Jurisprudence,* and published it as a second edition, referred to as "AmJur 2^{d}". It is cross-referenced to American Law Reports (ALR) and to the Lawyers Edition (Law. Ed.) of the U.S. Supreme Court Reports. The format differs slightly from Corpus Juris and CJS, but it serves much the same purpose. Few law offices have both encyclopedias, but most have one of them.

FORM BOOKS

7.16. Practice manuals. Practice manuals contain forms of pleadings, which the lawyer usually follows when dictating. Since the wording of pleadings differs with the state, a practice manual is used only in the state for which it is prepared. With the aid of a practice manual you can draft many pleadings without dictation. The forms always indicate by italics, by parentheses, or in some other manner the wording that must be changed with each case, such as names, dates, and various clauses applicable to a particular situation, and the like. In addition to the complete forms, the manuals contain many clauses applicable to various circumstances, which may be substituted for the clauses contained in the complete form.

7.17. Books of legal forms. Books of legal forms contain forms of instruments and documents as distinguished from litigation papers. Although the statutes prescribe the wording of many instruments, books of legal forms are generally useful for all states. They call attention to statutory requirements and often given forms for each state. For example, *Current Legal Forms,* published by Matthew Bender, New York, one of the best known sets of legal forms, gives forms of acknowledgments, deeds, mortgages, and wills that meet the requirements of each state. It is a multivolume set, published in a loose-leaf format, and updated periodically. Some form books cover only forms in one particular field. For example, Corporation Forms, a service published by Prentice-Hall, Inc., contains forms covering every conceivable situation relating to the organization of a corporation. Numerous clauses, as well as complete forms, enable the user to pick out the appropriate clause to suit his purpose. In giving instructions for the preparation of a legal instrument, the lawyer will frequently tell you to copy certain forms or clauses from a form book.*

7.18. Treatises. Treatises expound the theory of the law in particular areas and cite key cases that illustrate the state of the law on a given point in various jurisdictions. Some are supplemented, usually annually, by pocket parts or paper supplements. Others are published in a loose-leaf post-binder format and are supplemented by replacement and added pages and sections at intervals as the publisher deems necessary. These supplements must be carefully filed as soon as they are received, just as the loose-leaf services are filed.

7.19. Basic reference books. There are a few books that provide basic information to all personnel in the law office. The following list may be supplemented in your office by essential books for the jurisdiction and specialty in which the firm practices. Always order the latest edition of any reference book.

1. *Legal Reserach in a Nutshell,* West, or *How to Find the Law,* West
2. *Ballentine's Law Dictionary,* Lawyers Co-operative, or *Black's Law Dictionary,* West
3. *Law Dictionary for Non-Lawyers,* West
4. *Webster's Collegiate Dictionary*
5. *A Uniform System of Citations,* Harvard Law Review
6. Court rules of the jurisdiction
7. *Legal Secretary's Encyclopedic Dictionary,* Prentice-Hall.

7.20. Computerized legal research. Large firms and major law libraries are now using automated legal research systems for some of their work. There are two major systems available: WESTLAW, produced by the West Publishing Company, and LEXIS, by Mead Data Central Corporation. WESTLAW involves searching the headnotes of the National Reporter System by computer. With LEXIS, the entire text of published judicial opinions is recorded in the computer's memory. Seaching these large data banks requires considerable training and knowledge of legal terminology.

---

*Sletwold's Manual of Documents and Forms for the Legal Secretary, 2nd ed. (Prentice-Hall) gives sample forms of legal documents and explanations covering their typing.

REFERENCE FACILITIES FOR CHECKING NAMES AND ADDRESSES

7.21. Useful reference books. The following reference books are useful for confirming the spelling of names and the accuracy of addresses:

New York City Official Directory
Official Guide of the Railways
Telephone directories
Zip Code Guide
The American Bar
The Bar Register
Congressional Directory
Directory of Directors in the City of New York
The Law List (British)
The Lawyer's List
Martindale-Hubbell's Law Directory
Moody's Manuals
State Legislative Manuals
Oficial Register of the United States
Polk's (Trow's) New York Co-partnership and Corporation Directory (Manhattan and Bronx)
Poor's Manuals
Rand McNally's Bankers Directory
World Almanac

8

Preparing Material

for Printing

The lawyer's secretary assists in the preparation of a wide variety of printed materials. Briefs, forms of deeds, mortgages, and other instruments used extensively for a special client, booklets and pamphlets, as well as office forms, pass through the secretary's hands at some of, if not all, their stages of production. He or she may be expected to get quotes; type manuscripts; mark copy for typesetting and printing; coordinate work with editors, artists, compositors, and printers; read galleys; and check page proofs and negative proofs. The following pages explain what you should know about composition if you are to help produce a good printing job economically.

PREPARING THE MANUSCRIPT

8.1. Rules for typing manuscripts. A piece of writing that is to be sent to a printer or compositor is called *manuscript* or *copy*. Copy should be typewritten, neatly and legibly, on sheets of paper of uniform size. Make carbon copies or photocopies for reference purposes, but always send the original to the printer.

In typing the manuscript, observe the following rules:

1. Keep the typewritten line down to about six inches.
2. Use double spacing, even for material that would be single spaced in a typed copy, except in tables.
3. Keep the right-hand margin as even as possible, to help you later in estimating the length of the copy.

4. Indent paragraphs five to ten spaces.

5. Type headings and subheadings in the position they are to occupy on the final printed page, and be uniform in your capitalization of them. (See also *Front matter,* below.)

6. Use one side only of the sheet.

7. Leave a margin of at least one inch on all four sides.

8. Keep the pages as nearly uniform in length as possible, to help you later in estimating the length of the copy.

9. Set off extracted or quoted material from the rest of the text by indenting it from the left margin or from both the left and the right margins. Indent lists of items in a similar manner. Space above and below extracts and lists to separate them from the rest of the text copy. Remember that permission to quote must be requested for copyrighted material. Use the credit line provided by the copyright owner as a footnote (see *Footnotes and bibliographies,* below).

10. Type any footnotes (which must always have corresponding references in the main text) either (a) at the foot of the page on which they occur; or (b) on a separate sheet at the end of the report or document (see *Footnotes and bibliographies,* below).

11. If references are made to material appearing in other parts of the manuscript, instruct the typesetter (on the manuscript) to carry a query on each successive proof, so you will be reminded to put in the correct page reference numbers when you receive the final page proofs.

Front matter. Front matter of a book, report, or some other larger document includes a title page and table of contents. There might also be a list of tables and/or illustrations and a preface or introduction. The *title page* should show the document's title, who is submitting it, and the date. Center items on the space left after any edge taken up by a binder. Keep at least four line spaces between each item and two spaces between additional lines in a single item. The *table of contents* should list chapter and topic numbers and titles to the left and page numbers to the right. Center it on the page area left after the binder edge. Set up a list of tables or illustrations in the same manner. A *preface* or *introduction* should be set up the same as a text page.

Footnotes and bibliographies. Use numbers if there are many footnotes; otherwise asterisks or symbols may be used. *Superior figures,* slightly raised from the line (for example [1]) or diagonals (for example /1/) may be used. Type the note at the bottom of the page (or collect all of them at the end of the document). For example:

1. John Doe, *Modern Law Offices* (Chicago: ABC Press, 1980).
2. Jane Smith, "Secretarial Techniques," *Law Journal,* June 1980, p. 7.

Bibliographies are always typed at the end of a document usually in alphabetical order. Indent the second and third lines instead of the first one. For example:

Doe, John. *Modern Law Offices.*
  Chicago: ABC Press, 1980.

Smith, Jane. "Secretarial Techniques."
  Law Journal, June 1980, p. 7.

Tables. Single-space tables on separate sheets. Use symbols or superior letters to mark footnotes in the body of the table and type the actual notes directly beneath the table. Refer to each table in the text (for example: "see table 3"). Give each table a number and title. Use only horizontal (not vertical) rules to set off column heads from the body of the table. Type items in the left column flush left with an initial capital only. Table titles and crossheads should be upper-lowercase throughout.

8.2. Checking the manuscript. Every piece of copy should be checked carefully for errors before it is sent to the printer. Checking saves time and money and contributes to a better finished product. *Read your manuscript over several times,* looking for errors. Remember that each error corrected on the typed manuscript will save the expense of resetting a line or even a whole paragraph. Here are some guides to follow as you read over the copy:

1. *Be consistent.* If a word can be spelled or abbreviated in more than one correct form, choose the one you prefer and use it consistently. On the first reading, make a list of your selections of optional spellings to guide you toward consistency.

2. Make *short corrections* by crossing out the incorrect word and writing the correction over it, not in the margin. The margin is used for instructions to the printer. To make *lengthy corrections,* cross out the incorrect matter and type the correct matter on a separate sheet of paper. Mark the correction as an insert and show clearly where it is to be inserted.

3. Use *proofreader's marks* (see figure 8.1) in correcting the manuscript. For example:

(a) To lowercase a capital letter, draw a diagonal line through it; to capitalize a lowercase letter, draw three lines under it.

(b) To start a new paragraph, insert a ⁋ sign; to run in material typed as a new paragraph, draw a line from the word starting the new paragraph to the last word of the preceding paragraph.

(c) To separate two words typed as one, draw a vertical line between them.

(d) To make deletions, use a heavy pencil and a ruler and neatly and heavily cross out what you do not want.

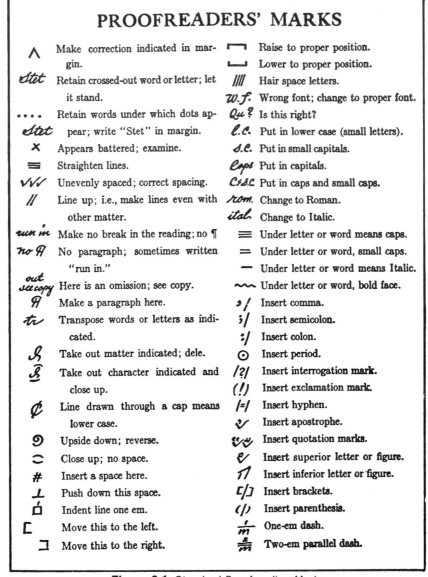

Figure 8.1. *Standard Proofreading Marks.*

(e) To retain material already crossed out, insert a row of dots beneath it and write the word "stet" in the margin beside it in a circle. Be sure, however, that the crossed-out material you wish to retain is legible; if there is any doubt, retype it as an insert.

4. *Number the pages* of your manuscript consecutively after all corrections and insertions have been made.

5. In checking the manuscript, do not indicate corrections to be made in the margins; make all changes within the lines of typing on the manuscript. (Correcting manuscript differs in this respect from correcting proof.)

8.3. Marking copy. Marking copy simply means telling the printer, clearly and concisely, what you want—you must never assume that the printer will know. Of course, to instruct the printer you must first know what you want yourself. This necessity entails planning.

Planning. In your planning, follow these steps:

1. Plan the size of the type area in relation to the size of the page. If you are to have page numbers and a running head—that is, a line heading on each page—include them in your estimated type area. One rule of thumb in planning a booklet, leaflet, or book is to make the inside margin (the one in the center of the book) the smallest margin, the top margin larger, the outside margin (the one at the outer edge of the page) larger than that, and the bottom margin the largest.

2. Decide what kind and size of type you want, and whether you want to use more than one kind and size of type (a different kind of type for headings, a different size for quotes, for example). Your printer will supply you with a specimen sheet or booklet showing the kinds and sizes of type he has. Type is measured by points. Each kind is available in different sizes. The same type faces appear in several styles, such as **boldface,** *italics,* and SMALL CAPS. The printer can advise you. Also, you may want to compare quality and costs by requesting samples and quotes from different compositors. *Hot type,* composition by use of hot metal such as linotype, is sometimes of higher quality. But *cold type,* such as IBM typewriter, is sometimes faster and more economical.

3. Determine the pica width and depth of the type area. A pica is an arbitrary printer's measure. There are approximately six picas to an inch. Type and space between lines (leading) are measured in points. There are 12 points to the pica.

4. Settle all other points of style. For example: (a) Will you center all headings or make them flush with the left-hand margin? (b) Do you want to use italics? (c) Do you want to use boldface type? (d) How do you want your quotations and citations set? Plan a consistent style and *stick to it.* Then mark your copy *consistently.*

How to mark copy. When you mark copy, remember that you get what you ask for and that you must mark clearly and accurately. Instruct the printer about the following points, all of which are illustrated in figure 8.2:

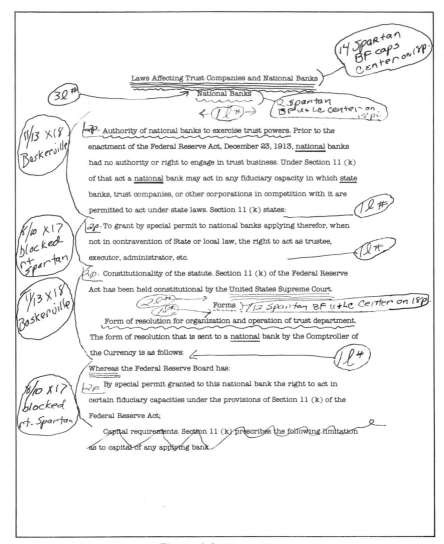

Figure 8.2. *Marked Copy.*

1. Underline all words or sections to be set in italics.
2. Draw a wavy line under the words or sections to be set in boldface.
3. Indicate what is to be set in capital letters and what in small capitals or a combination of capitals and small capitals. Draw three lines under letters to be set in all capitals. Draw two lines under letters to be set in small capitals.
4. Mark all headings in the desired size and style of type.
5. In the left-hand margin, mark the size and name of the body type

and the pica width of the type area, thus: 11/13 x 18 Baskerville, which calls for 11 point Baskerville type, leaded 2 points, set 18 picas wide. Your printer may use a numerical code instead of names for his types. If the code number for Baskerville were 97, you could write your instructions as 11/13 x 18/97.

6. Always *circle* instructions to the printer or compositor in the margin.

In marking copy, use proofreader's marks, shown in figure 8.1, whenever possible. These marks are a shorthand system that will save you time and will be recognized by compositors and printers.

8.4. How to estimate length of copy. You may estimate the length of copy by a count of (a) words or (b) characters. Both methods are described below, the character method first because it is the more accurate.

If you have followed the typing rules of keeping the right-hand margin fairly even and of writing the same number of lines on each page, you will find it easy to apply the following methods of estimating length of copy.

1. *Estimating by character count:*

(a) Measure the length of a typewritten line in inches.

(b) Multiply the result in step (a) by 10, if your typewriter type is pica; by 12, if it is elite. (Pica type has 10 characters, elite type 12 characters, to the inch.) This step gives you the number of characters to the line.

(c) Multiply the number of characters in a line, step (b), by the number of lines on a page of typewritten copy.

(d) Multiply the number of characters to a page, step (c), by the number of pages of typewritten copy.

Apply the following rules in counting characters: consider spaces between words and quotation marks and other punctuation as characters; count a short line at the end of a paragraph as a full line.

EXAMPLE: Suppose that each line of typewritten copy measures 6 inches. If your typewriter has pica type, the number of characters in a line will thus be 6 × 10, or 60. If each page contains 27 lines of type, there will be 1,620 characters on the page (27 × 60). If your manuscript has 5 pages, there will be 1,620 × 5, or 8,100, characters in the manuscript.

2. *Estimating by word count:*

(a) Find the average number of words to a line by counting the number of words in several lines and dividing this total by the number of lines counted.

(b) Multiply the average number of words to a line, step (a), by the number of lines to a page to get the average number of words per page.

(c) Multiply the average number of words to a page, step (b), by the number of pages.

Apply the following rules in counting words: count two short words as one word; count a long word as two words.

EXAMPLE: Suppose that in 5 typewritten lines you have counted 60 words, or 12 words to a line ($60 \div 5$). If each page contains 27 lines of type, there are an estimated 324 (27×12) words to a page. If your manuscript has 5 full pages, there are an estimated 1,620 (324×5) words in the manuscript.

If your copy cannot be typed uniformly for some reason, and you have difficulty estimating length, ask the compositor or printer for assistance.

8.5. Working with others. On occasion you may need to coordinate the work of artists, designers, photographers, copy editors, and others. This will necessitate not only reminding each person of respective deadlines, to keep the project on schedule, but also checking the work of others. For instance, when the manuscript you have typed is edited by another person, reread it carefully when it is returned to you. Be certain the editor's handwriting is legible and that his or her markings are clear and consistent. Similarly, when a designer or artist is responsible for selecting typefaces and determining matters such as spacing, margins, and so on, again, reread the manuscript carefully and see that all such design specifications are marked clearly and consistently throughout. Follow this procedure with anyone else who is involved in some stage of production. When someone's markings are confusing or illegible, ask for clarification before submitting the manuscript to the typesetter.

8.6. Procedure. The printer returns your original manuscript with at least two sets of the material set in type. The typset material may arrive in *galley proofs* or *page proofs*. Galley proofs are not yet divided into pages. Page proofs, however, are set up in actual pages, with running heads, folios, and so on already inserted. You may ask for more than two sets of galley proofs but if you ask for many there may be an extra charge. Read the proofs that have been marked by the printer carefully against the original manuscript, make all corrections on them and, after the lawyer has made any desired changes, return them to the printer.

When the manuscript has illustrations, tables, and the like, you (or an artist) should prepare a dummy for the printer to be returned with the corrected galleys, to be sure these breaks in the text fall where you want them.

A dummy consists of blank sheets of paper cut and folded to the size of a proposed leaflet, folder, booklet, or book, to indicate shape, size, and general appearance. The galley proofs are cut to size and pasted on the sheets. In preparing this dummy, you must make allowance for changes in lines resulting from your corrections on the galleys. Determine where you want illustrations to appear and mark appropriate spaces for them, labeling each position. Mark off margins, column areas, and so on before pasting copy onto the dummy sheets. Page dummies should not contain type corrections. Such markings are made on another set of galleys going back to the compositor. Keep facing dummy pages equal in length and avoid *widows,* or short lines, at the top of the page. Keep at least two lines of type after a subhead at the bottom of a page.

When the printer receives the corrected galleys, and the dummy if any, he or she makes the desired changes and sends you *page proofs.* If major changes are necessary in the page proofs, ask the printer for corrected page proofs. When you are satisfied that the proofs are perfect insofar as your work is concerned (see page 369), give them to the lawyer for his or her approval. The lawyer will mark them "O.K. to print" and initial them.

8.7. Importance of correcting galley and page proofs. The checking and reading of galley proofs is the second major step in the successful preparation of the printed work. As much care should go into the reading of proofs as went into the preparation of copy. The importance of this step is stressed because it is on the galley or page proofs that you get your last chance to make corrections before negatives and plates are made for printing.

Any corrections on galley or page proofs that deviate from the original manuscript sent to the printer are called *author's alterations.* These corrections are charged for at a penalty time rate. That is, the cost of setting a line at this stage is many times greater than the original cost. It can easily be seen, then, that excessive author's alterations make the job needlessly expensive. Also, there is the possibility that the printer will commit serious typographical errors in making trivial changes. Where time is an important factor, numerous corections can slow up the job considerably.

Before you begin to read the proof, familiarize yourself with proofreader's marks, which are standard and are understood by all printers. Figure 8.1 is an illustration of these marks, and figure 8.3 shows how they are used.

8.8. Reading the proof. On the proof you may find the printer's proofreading marks. They call for corrections of errors the typesetter has made. These corrections are made at the printer's own expense.

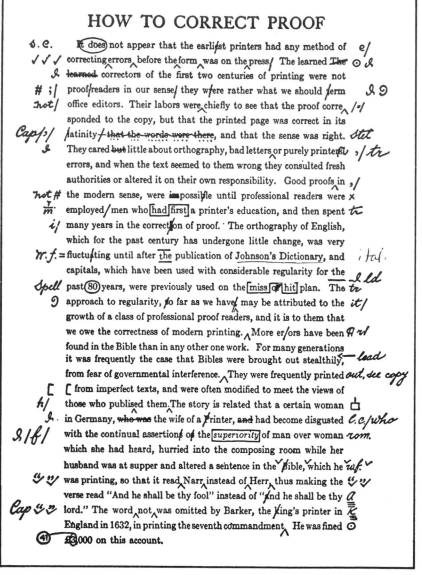

Figure 8.3. *Corrected Galley.*

Here is a checklist of errors to look for:

1. Spelling

2. Punctuation

3. Inconsistencies in spelling, punctuation, use of italics, boldface, capitals, and in paragraph indentions and spacing

4. Transpositions of lines

5. Page numbers

6. Continuity from page to page

If the material to be proofread is technical or lengthy, have someone read aloud the original manuscript to you (including punctuation marks, capitalization, italics, and so on) slowly enough so that you can follow the proof. Make all corrections in a neat, legible hand. Should the correction consist of more than several words, type it directly on the proof. If it is quite lengthy, type it on a separate sheet, label it "Insert 1," and mark the proof with the same words ("Insert 1") at the proper place of insertion. Attach the insert to the proof on which the insert is noted.

After galleys have been proofread and corrected by the compositor, you must check page proofs to be certain all errors in the galleys were actually corrected. You must see that the pages are of equal length, that footnotes are grouped properly, that illustrations are marked for the proper positions, that headings, including running heads and folios, are positioned properly, that the spacing around items such as tables and headings is correct, and so on. After final errors have been marked, return the pages to the compositor for final corrections.

PART 2

Preparing Legal Instruments
and Documents

9   Handling Legal Instruments
10 How to Prepare Legal Papers
11 How to Handle Affidavits, Powers of Attorney, and Wills

9

HaNdliNq LeGal INSTRUMENTS

Over three-fourths of a lawyer's practice relates to matters that are not litigated. This practice involves, among other things, the preparation of numerous legal instruments. In this chapter we give basic information about legal documents generally. Because you will probably have to notarize many of these legal instruments, we describe the duties of a notary.

9.1. What is a legal instrument? A *legal instrument* is a formal written document, such as a deed, bill of sale, lease, contract, or will. It gives formal expression to a legal act or agreement. Although both legal instruments and court papers are referred to as legal documents, a legal instrument is not to be confused with a court paper. A *court paper,* or *pleading* as it is called professionally (see chapter 13), constitutes a step in bringing or defending a law suit and is prepared and filed for the information of the court, whereas a legal instrument is designed for the use of the parties who sign it and constitutes evidence of the agreement between them. A legal instrument is not a step in a court action, but it is frequently the basis of one. If one of the parties to a legal instrument does not abide by its provisions, the other party may sue to enforce the provisions of the instrument. Copies of a legal instrument are used frequently as exhibits in court actions.

9.2. Parties to an instrument. Those who acquire a right, undertake an obligation, or give up a right, as evidenced by a written instrument, are the *parties* to the instrument. A party may be an individual, a partnership, or a corporation. Almost all instruments have two or more parties; but there are some, for example, assignments and powers of attorney, that have only one party. An acknowledgment is usually executed by the individual (attorney-in-fact) who accepts a power of attorney. All parties who have a common interest in the subject matter of the document are grouped together and are usually referred to throughout the instrument by a descriptive identification, instead of by name. An expression occasionally used is "party (parties) of the first part," "party (parties) of the second part." More commonly, the term may be a description such as *contractor, seller,* or any term appropriate to the party's interest in the subject matter of the instrument. There may be more than one party in a group designated by a descriptive term. You will notice that the instrument illustrated in figure 9.1 has two parties of the first part but only one of the second part.

Witness the hands and seals of the said parties this ______ day of

______________, 19______.

In the Presence of:

______________________________ L.S.

____

______________________________ L.S.

Buyers

____

______________________________ L.S.

Sellers

Figure 9.1. *Testimonium Clause, Signature and Seal for Individuals, Witnessed.*

9.3. How to type legal instruments. Although certain instruments, such as deeds and wills, are set up in a special style, the typewritten style of agreements or contracts generally varies only slightly, no matter what the subject matter is. Many specific instruments are illustrated throughout this book (see the index). Figure 9.2 illustrates a skeleton of a form of agreement used by many law offices. It is easily adaptable to any general agreement or contract. Always make duplicate originals for the parties to the contract and a copy for your file. If the lawyer wants an extra copy, he or she will tell you. Agreements may be typed on long or short paper, with or without the ruled margin. If the lawyer has a preference, he or she will specify it.

THIS AGREEMENT, entered into on the ___ day of
_____, 19—, by and between _____ CORPORATION,
a corporation organized and existing under and by virtue of
the laws of the State of _____, and having its office
at _____, _____, hereinafter referred to as
"_____," and THE _____ COMPANY, a corporation organized and existing under and by virtue of the laws of the
State of _____, and having its office at _____,
_____, hereinafter referred to as "_____,"

W I T N E S S E T H :

WHEREAS _____
_____; and

WHEREAS _____
_____
_____.

NOW, THEREFORE, in consideration of the premises
_____
_____,

IT IS AGREED:

1. _____
_____
_____ .

2. _____
_____.

IN WITNESS WHEREOF the parties hereto have on the
day and year first above written caused these presents to be

(Continued on following page)

(Continued from preceding page)

```
executed in their behalf and in their corporate names re-

spectively by their proper officers hereunto duly authorized

and their respective corporate seals to be hereto attached

by like authority.


(Corporate Seal)                         _____CORPORATION

                                    By _____
ATTEST:                                                   President


_____
               Secretary
                                    THE _____COMPANY

(Corporate Seal)
                                    By _____
                                                      Vice President
ATTEST:


_____
               Secretary
```

(Number page in center, one-half inch from bottom.)

Figure 9.2. *Agreement Between Two Corporations with Seals Attested.*

EXECUTION OF AN INSTRUMENT

9.4. What is "execution" of an instrument? Technically, *execution of an instrument* is doing that which is required to give effect or validity to the instrument and, therefore, includes signing and delivery. In law office parlance, execution more frequently refers merely to the signing of an instrument by the party or parties described in it. Legal instruments must be executed with a certain formality. Some or all of the following formalities attach to the exectuion of various instruments: sealing, witness or attestation, acknowledgment, and notarization, each of which is discussed below.

9.5. Testimonium clause. The *testimonium clause* is the clause with which an instrument closes. It immediately precedes the signature. It is a declaration by the parties to the instrument that their signatures are attached in testimony of the preceding part of the instrument. The testimonium clause is not to be confused with the *witness* or *attestation* clause (page 199). The testimonium clause relates to the parties themselves, whereas the witness or attestation clause relates to those who sign the paper as witnesses, not as parties to the instrument.

Quite often, the testimonium clause will guide you in setting up the signature lines. It will indicate (1) what parties are to sign the instrument; (2) what officer of a corporation is to sign; (3) whether the instrument is to be sealed; and (4) whether a corporate seal is to be attested. For example, from the following clause, which is a form commonly used, you know that the president of the corporation is to sign, that the seal is to be affixed, and that the secretary of the corporation is to attest the seal.

In WITNESS WHEREOF, The Bentley Corporation has caused its corporate seal to be hereto affixed, and attested by its secretary, and these presents to be signed by its president, this 26th day of October, 19...

On the other hand, from the following clause, also commonly used, you know that the instrument is not to be sealed.

IN TESTIMONY WHEREOF, the parties hereto have duly executed this agreement.

The introductory words to the testimonium clause, *in witness whereof, in testimony whereof,* and the like, are sometimes typed in solid caps. The word following is lowercase unless it is a proper name. A comma usually follows the introductory words.

9.6. Signatures. An instrument recites who will sign it. As a general practice, lines are typed for signatures. Type the first line of signature four spaces below the body of the instrument, beginning it slightly to the right of the center of the page. Type a line for the signature of each person who must sign the instrument. There are no special requirements for the spacing of signature lines, except that sufficient space should be allowed for the average-size handwriting and the lines should be evenly spaced. Three of four spaces between lines are practical.

Frequently the descriptive identification of the parties signing is placed under the signature lines, for example, "First Party," "Buyer," "Seller," "Parties of the First Part," or whatever identification was used in the instrument. The lawyer will probably instruct you as follows: "Two signature lines for parties of the first part, and one for the party of the second part," but you will know from the content of the instrument what signature lines are necessary. Figure 9.1 illustrates signature lines and identification of the parties.

When a corporation is a party to an instrument, the instrument is signed in the name of the corporation by the officer or officers authorized to execute it. Type the name of the corporation in solid caps, leave sufficient space beneath it for a signature, and type "By" and a line for signature. Under the signature line, type the title of the corporate officer who is going to sign the instrument. The testimonium clause usually recites the title of the officer who is supposed to sign the instrument. The corporate seal is placed at the left margin, parallel to the signature (see figure 9.2.)

When a partnership is a party, type the name of the partnership in solid caps, leave sufficient space beneath it for signature, and type "By" and a line for signature. Since partnerships do not have officers, there will be no title under the signature line.

9.7. How to fit the signatures on the page. Arrange the body, or text, of the instrument so at least two lines appear on the page with the signatures. The signatures must all be on the same page unless there are so many that they require more than a full page. To comply with these requirements you must gauge carefully the length of the material to be typed. This is not difficult if you are copying from a draft; otherwise, you might have to make a test copy and adjust your spacing accordingly. Here are methods by which you may lengthen or shorten the available typing space to fit the signatures on the page.

1. Leave wider or narrower top and bottom margins.

2. If you are using paper without ruled margins, leave wider or narrower left and right margins.

3. If the last line of a paragraph is full-length, adjust the right margin of that paragraph so at least one word carries over to another line, thereby taking up an extra line. Or, if a paragraph ends with one word on a line, adjust the margin so it is not necessary to carry over the one word, thereby saving a line of space.

4. Triple-space between paragraphs.

5. Leave less space between the test of the instrument and the signatures.

6. Leave less space between the signatures.

9.8. Sealing an instrument. Figure 9.2 illustrates signatures to a sealed corporate instrument. The practice of affixing a seal to an instrument originated in the days when only a few people could write their names. Written instruments were marked with sealing wax, which was impressed with a ring or other device. This seal was the mark of the person making the instrument and took the place of his signature. The process of affixing the seal is referred to as *sealing the instrument*, and the instrument then becomes a *sealed instrument*. Previously the sealed instrument had a twofold significance: (1) Under the statutes of limitations, the time during which suit could be brought on a sealed instrument was longer than on an unsealed instrument. (2) Suit on a contract could not be defended on the basis that it was without consideration, because the consideration of a sealed instrument could not be questioned. (If an instrument is to be sealed, the testimonium clause will so indicate.) Most jurisdictions have now abolished this distinction between sealed and unsealed instruments relating to the statute of limitations. In most instances, also, a mere recital that an instrument is sealed will not serve as substitute for the showing of consideration. In many jurisdictions, it is no longer necessary to seal deeds and wills or other documents signed by individuals. But the corporate seal retains its importance to attest to a corporate act.

A corporation's seal. Almost all corporations adopt a formal seal. It is engraved on a metal plate and impressed by this means upon the paper. The seal usually recites the name of the corporation and the year and state of incorporation. It is often kept in the custody of the clerk of the corporation who is, in many instances, the lawyer. The secretary may be responsible to see that the seal is properly filed and available when corporate documents requiring it are to be signed. As a practical matter, a corporation's bylaws usually provide that any instrument signed on behalf of the corporation will be impressed with the corporate seal. An officer of the corporation impresses the seal on the instrument when it is signed. In many cases the corporate secretary must bear witness, or "attest" to the fact that the imprint on the paper is the seal of the corporation. Whenever the testimonium clause recites that the seal is to be *attested*, type the ATTEST line on the left side of the page, opposite the signature lines, as shown below:

ATTEST _____
               Secretary

The attest by the officer of a corporation to its seal is not to be confused with the attestation or "witnesss" clause, which relates to the subscribing witnesses (see figure 9.3).

An individual's seal. The wax seal formerly used by individuals has been replaced by the word *seal* or *L.S.* (abbreviation for *locus sigilli,* meaning "place of the seal"), or any other scroll or mark. At the end of the signature lines on an instrument that must be sealed, type SEAL or L.S. in solid caps.

9.9. Attestation clause. Frequently the signatures to an instrument must be witnessed to make the instrument legal. The act of

```
                    IN WITNESS WHEREOF, we, the lessors and the
          lessee, have hereunto set our hands and seals to the fore-
          going lease, consisting of twenty-two pages (22), on this
          - - day of April 19--.


Signed, sealed, and delivered )
                               )
by lessors in the presence of:)
                               )
                               )
                               )
_____)
                               )                                    _____ L. S.
                               )
                               )
_____)                                   _____ L. S.
                               )                                            Lessors
Signed, sealed, and delivered )
                               )
by lessee in the presence of: )
                               )                                    _____ L. S.
                               )                                            Lessee
_____)
                               )
                               )
_____)
```

Figure 9.3. *Legend and Signature Lines for Two Groups of Witnesses.*

witnessing the signature to a written instrument, at the request of the party signing the instrument, is *attestation.* The witness is called a subscribing witness, because he signs his name as a witness. A legend or clause that recites the circumstances surrounding the signing of the instrument often precedes the signature of the attesting witnesses and is called the *attestation clause.* The wording of the attestation clause varies from a simple "In the presence of" to the rather lengthy clause used in wills (see figure 11.4).

The legend and the lines on which witnesses sign are written opposite the lines for the signatures of persons who will execute the instrument. When parties to an instrument do not sign at the same time, different people witness the signature. The instrument then carries signature lines for each of the witnesses, with an identification of the parties whose signatures each group is witnessing (see figure 9.3).

ACKNOWLEDGMENTS

9.10. Importance of acknowledgments in the law office. An acknowledgment is a familiar tool in the law office, and the staff should acquire an intimate knowledge of it. Technically, an *acknowledgment* is the act by which a person who executes a legal instrument declares to an officer, designated by statute, that he or she is the person who executed the instrument. In law office terminology, the term signifies both the declaration of execution and the officer's written certificate of the declaration. It is common practice for a legal instrument to carry a certificate of acknowledgment, because almost all states require the acknowledgment of an instrument before it can be recorded or filed. Furthermore, when an instrument is introduced in court as evidence, the certificate of acknowledgment is usually sufficient proof of the authenticity of the instrument.

9.11. Laws governing acknowledgments. Many states have adopted the Uniform Acknowledgment Act, and in these states the law governing the use of acknowledgments and the form of the certificate are

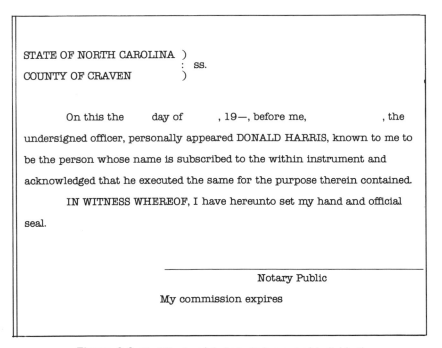

STATE OF NORTH CAROLINA)
: ss.
COUNTY OF CRAVEN)

On this the   day of   , 19—, before me,   , the undersigned officer, personally appeared DONALD HARRIS, known to me to be the person whose name is subscribed to the within instrument and acknowledged that he executed the same for the purpose therein contained.

IN WITNESS WHEREOF, I have hereunto set my hand and official seal.

_____
Notary Public

My commission expires

Figure 9.4. *Certificate of Acknowledgment of Individual.*

STATE OF NEW MEXICO)
               : ss.
COUNTY OF MORA   )

       I, MARY SMITH, a notary public in and for the said state and county, duly commissioned and sworn, hereby certify that JOHN COLE and PHYLLIS COLE, his wife, who are to me personally known, this day appeared before me personally, and severally acknowledged that they signed, sealed, and delivered the foregoing deed for the purposes therein stated. The said PHYLLIS COLE, wife of said JOHN COLE, being duly examined by me, separate and apart from her said husband, did declare that she signed, sealed, and delivered the said deed freely and voluntarily, and without compulsion by her said husband, with intention to renounce and convey all dower or other right, title, and interest in the property thereby conveyed, for the uses and purposes therein stated.

       IN WITNESS WHEREOF, I have hereunto set my hand and official seal this 30th day of April, 19—.

                                  ————————————————
                                      Notary Public

Figure 9.5. *Certificate of Acknowledgment by Husband and Wife— Separate Examination.*

similar. Otherwise, the law varies with the state. Some of the statutes are very precise in their requirements and they must be adhered to strictly. The acknowledgments illustrated in figures 9.4 through 9.8 show you how acknowledgments are set up when typed and will give you a general idea of the wording of various forms of acknowledgment. They are not supposed to be copied word for word. At first the lawyer will either dictate or make available to you a form of the acknowledgment he or she wants you to use. Make an extra copy for your loose-leaf book of forms for future reference when you are expected to type an acknowledgment without detailed instructions.

    A principle of law governing acknowledgments that you should remember is this: The law of the state where the instrument is to be

STATE OF MICHIGAN)
              : SS.:
COUNTY OF BARRY)

      I hereby certify that on this day before me, an officer duly authorized in the state aforesaid and in the county aforesaid to take acknowledgments, personally appeared WALTER HUTCHINS and ALLEN AVERY, to me known and known to be the persons described in and who executed the foregoing instrument as president and secretary, respectively, of Hartshorne Company, Inc., a corporation named therein, and severally acknowledged before me that they executed the same as such officers, in the name of and for and on behalf of the said corporation.

      IN WITNESS WHEREOF, I have hereunto set my hand and affixed my official seal this   day of September, 19—.

_____

Notary Public

My commission expires

Figure 9.6. *Certificate of Acknowledgment by Corporation—Two Officers.*

recorded or used, not the law of the state where the instrument is executed, governs. Thus, if your office is in New York and you prepare an instrument that is to be recorded in Florida, the form and wording follow the Florida statutes, although the certificate will show that the acknowledgment was made in New York. But if you send an instrument to Florida to be signed and returned for recording in New York, the certificate of acknowledgment will follow the New York law, although it will show that the acknowledgment was made in Florida.

    9.12. Essentials of an acknowledgment. Although acknowledgments vary with the state, they all have certain basic essentials. The following basic essentials are apparent in the acknowledgments illustrated in figures 9.4 through 9.8.

    Venue. An acknowledgment always begins with a recital of the venue, that is, the name of the state and county in which the

STATE OF ARIZONA)
               : ss.
COUNTY OF YUMA)

        On this   day of   , 19—, before me, Nancy Jones, notary public in and for said county and state, personally appeared ABRAHAM F. SCHOENFELD, known to me to be one of the partners of the partnership that executed the within instrument, and acknowledged to me that such partnership executed the same.

                     _____
                         Notary Public in and for said
                               County and State

Figure 9.7. *Certificate of Acknowledgment by Partnership.*

STATE OF OHIO)
               : SS.
COUNTY OF PIKE)

        On this the   day of   , 19—, before me,   , the undersigned officer, personally appeared HAROLD PETERSON, known to me to be the person whose name is subscribed as attorney-in-fact for MICHAEL M. HATFIELD, and acknowledged that he executed the same as the act of his principal for the purposes therein contained.
        IN WITNESS WHEREOF I hereunto set my hand and official seal.

                     _____
                                 Notary Public

Figure 9.8. *Certificate of Acknowledgment by Attorney-in-Fact.*

acknowledgment is made. In Kentucky, Massachusetts, Pennsylvania, and Virginia, the venue recites the name of the commonwealth instead of the state; in Louisiana, the parish instead of the county. Type the statement of the venue in solid caps, bracket it, and follow with *ss.,* the abbreviation for *scilicet* (*sc,* though correct, is not used in legal papers). The abbreviation may be caps or small letters. Like most abbreviations, it is followed by a period. Technically, a colon should also follow because scilicet means "to wit," but few law offices observe this technicality.

Date of acknowledgment. An acknowledgment always recites the date on which the acknowledgment is made. When you type the certificate of acknowledgment, leave blank spaces for the day of the month, and also for the name of the month if you are preparing the instrument near the end of the month. Although a client is supposed to sign and acknowledge an instrument on the 30th of April, he or she might not get into the office until the 1st day of May. The date of the acknowledgment does not necessarily coincide with the date of the instrument, but the date of an acknowledgment must *never* precede the date the instrument was signed.

Designation of person making acknowledgment. The name of the person making the acknowledgment always appears in the certificate. Type it in solid caps. If the person making the acknowledgment is making it in a capacity other than that of an individual, that capacity is also stated, but not in solid caps. For example, when a person makes an acknowledgment as secretary of a corporation, the designation is written, "... WILLIAM FOLEY, secretary of Fenton Instruments, Inc., ..." The person who makes the acknowledgment does not sign the certificate.

Signature and designation of officer taking acknowledgment. The officer who takes an acknowledgment signs the certificate. In typing the certificate, type a blank line for his or her signature four spaces beneath the body of the certificate. Type his or her title underneath the line. In many states the certificate also recites the name and full title of the officer taking the acknowledgment. If you do not know who is to take the acknowledgment, leave a blank space long enough for the average name to be inserted in handwriting.

Date of expiration of commission. Many states require that an acknowledgment taken by a notary public show the date of the expiration of his or her commission. On acknowledgments to be used in those states, which are listed in part 5, Notaries Public, type "My commission expires   , 19 ." two spaces below the signature. Notaries usually have a rubber stamp showing the expiration date of their commission, and the typed line is not necessary except as a reminder that the date of expiration must appear on the certificate.

Notary's seal. In almost all cases the certificate of acknowledgment must also bear the notary's seal, especially if the instrument is acknowledged outside the state where it is to be recorded. (See part 5, Notaries Public, for those states that require a notary's seal.) In some states, a justice of the peace may take an acknowledgment and swear witnesses. The requirements for becoming a justice of the peace differ slightly from those for becoming a notary public, as do the functions of the officer.

9.13. How and where to type the acknowledgment. Acknowledgments are usually double spaced. They follow the signatures. Although there is no rule of law governing the placement of an acknowledgment on the page, it is desirable that the entire acknowledgment be placed on the signature page of the instrument, even if single spacing is necessary to accomplish this. If the entire acknowledgment cannot be placed on the signature page it is preferable to type part of it on that page. In the case of some instruments, for example a power of attorney that authorizes the conveyance of any interest in real estate, it is practically mandatory to type the acknowledgment on the same page as the signatures. The suggestions given on page 198 for fitting signatures on the page are applicable to fitting the acknowledgment on the page.

9.14. Who may make an acknowledgment. Any person who signs an instrument is qualified to acknowledge it, and this person acknowledges it in the same capacity that he or she signed A person who signs an instrument in his own behalf acknowledges it as his act in his individual capacity (figure 9.4). If husband and wife sign, each makes an acknowledgment, but in almost all states only one certificate of acknowledgment is necessary (figure 9.4). See also page 209.

The officer of a corporation acknowledges that the corporation executed the instrument, and the acknowledgment associates the acknowledger with the corporation. In those states that require a corporate instrument to be signed by two officers, each officer acknowledges the instrument but both acknowledgments are included in the same certificate (figure 9.6).

A partner acknowledges that an instrument was executed by the partnership (figure 9.7).

An attorney-in-fact acknowledges that he signed the principal's name and his own as attorney-in-fact (figure 9.8).

A subscribing witness may also acknowledge an instrument. The wording of an acknowledgment by a subscribing witness differs considerably from an acknowledgment made by a party to the instrument. The lawyer will dictate the acknowledgment, or give you a form to follow.

9.15. Who may take an acknowledgment. The statutes in the various states designate the officers before whom an acknowledgment may be made, or who may "take acknowledgments." These officers include, among others, judges, clerks of courts, and notaries public. Usually the secretary or paralegal in a law office is appointed notary public, so he or she may take acknowledgments of clients to instruments prepared in the office. (See below for the qualifications and duties of a notary public.)

9.16. Authentication. As previously pointed out, instruments are frequently acknowledged in one state and recorded in another. Some states require that instruments acknowledged outside the state must have the notary's certificate of acknowledgment authenticated by a designated official, usually the clerk of the county court in which the notary public is registered. The clerk's *authentication* is a certification to the effect that the notary is authorized to take acknowledgments and that the signature on the certificate of acknowledgment is his or hers. The statutes usually prescribe the wording of the certificate of authentication. If your office is in a state that requires authentication of the notary's certificate, prepare the certificate of authentication in accordance with the statute in your state. (The lawyer will dictate it or give you a form to follow. Make a copy for your loose-leaf notebook.) Your letter forwarding the instrument for acknowledgment should point out that the authentication, as well as the certificate of acknowledgment, should be signed. (See part 5, Authentication of Instruments.)

NOTARIES PUBLIC

9.17. What is a notary public? A *notary public* is a commissioned officer of the state, whose powers and duties consist, among others, in administering oaths, certifying to the genuineness of documents, and taking acknowledgments. In some states a notary is authorized to act only in the county in which he or she is commissioned; in others the notary is qualified to act throughout the state. Almost all law offices have a notary public, and frequently the secretary or paralegal is the notary. Lawyers in some states, for example, New Jersey and New York, have de facto notarial authority, but they must generally qualify, register, and have a notarial seal or stamp. The eligibility requirements are not stringent, relating primarily to age and residence. If your office wants you to be commissioned as a notary, write to the official in your state who appoints notaries for an application blank. Part 5, Notaries Public, shows the official to whom to write in each state and whether a bond is required. The table also indicates those states that require a notary public to keep a record of his or her official acts. In some states, as will appear from the application blank, the application must be endorsed by a member of the legislature, a judge, or some other designated official.

After the commission is received, order a notary's seal and stamp. Then register your commission with the clerk of the court (or other designated official) in your county, so the officer can authenticate your certificate of acknowledgment on papers that are to be recorded in another state.

In some states, a justice of the peace performs many of the functions of the notary. The justice of the peace may administer oaths, take acknowledgments, and so forth. The requirements for eligibility and the means of acquiring the commission are similar to those for a notary. The justice of the peace may or may not have an official seal. He or she no longer has any judicial functions, although the justice of the peace may perform marriages. In other states, the justice of the peace is still a judicial officer. In either case, the functions and methods of appointment are entirely statutory.

9.18. Following the letter of the law when you notarize a paper. A commission as a notary public is a trust; it confers certain powers upon you as well as requiring that you perform certain duties. In exercising those powers and duties, you should observe punctiliously the "letter of the law." In a law office your principal duty as a notary public will be taking acknowledgments.

Notice that all of the certificates of acknowledgments previously illustrated (figures 9.4 through 9.8) recite that the person making the acknowledgment "personally appeared" before the notary. This is true of all forms of acknowledgments in every state. You, therefore, should never take an acknowledgment without the actual appearance of the individual making the acknowledgment. In fact, it is illegal to do so. If a client's wife signs an instrument at home and wants to acknowledge it over the telephone, politely but firmly decline to take the acknowledgment and state the reason for your refusal.

Acknowledgments also recite that the individual "acknowledged" that he or she signed the instrument. You do not administer an oath to a person making an acknowledgment, but ask: "Do you acknowledge that you signed this instrument?" or, "Do you acknowledge that you executed this instrument as attorney-in-fact for Henry J. Cromwell?" or a similar question, depending upon whether the acknowledgment is being made by an individual in his own behalf, an officer of a corporation, a partnership, or an attorney-in-fact.

Acknowledgments also recite that the notary knows, or has satisfactory evidence, that the person making it is the person "described in and who executed" the instrument. You must have satisfactory evidence of the identity of a person whose acknowledgment you take. Of course, in taking acknowledgments made by clients, you are not likely to have difficulty in this respect. A notary who willfully makes a false certificate that an instrument was acknowledged by a party to the instrument is guilty of forgery.

A certificate of acknowledgment also shows the date it is signed by the notary. You should never postdate or antedate a certificate. To do so constitutes fraud and deceit in the exercise of your powers.

Some states require that the wife be examined by the notary "separate and apart" from her husband. This is especially true with reference to instruments relating to real estate. If the state in which an instrument is to be recorded has this requirement, you should follow the statutory procedure strictly. Do not take the wife's acknowledgment in the presence of her husband. Figure 9.5 illustrates a certificate in a state requiring a separate acknowledgment by the wife.

9.19. Details to observe when you notarize a paper. You should exercise special care to see that documents you notarize are executed correctly. If the papers are not in conformity with the requirements of the office where they are to be recorded, they will be rejected. You do not read an instrument that you notarize, but you should read the acknowledgment and also glance over the instrument. Observe the following details when taking an acknowledgment:

1. If the instrument recites that it is "under seal," be sure that the signature to the instrument is followed by "L.S." or "Seal."

2. When a corporation is a party to an instrument, be sure the corporate seal is impressed on the instrument if required; seals are usually required on corporate instruments.

3. Fill in all blanks in the instrument and in the certificate of acknowledgment.

4. Be sure to show the date of the expiration of your commission, when required.

5. Be sure to impress your notarial seal on the certificate, when required. Part 5, Notaries Public, shows which states require a notary's seal on papers acknowledged within the state. All states require a seal on papers acknowledged in another state.

6. Be sure that rubber stamps used by you make legible imprints. A black stamp pad is preferable because the black ink photocopies more distinctly than other inks.

7. Be sure to have the clerk of the court (or other designated official) authenticate your certificate of acknowledgment if authentication is required.

RECORDING LEGAL INSTRUMENTS

9.20. Purpose in recording instruments. Legal instruments are frequently recorded in a public office, and the record is available to anyone who is interested. The purpose of recording the instruments is to protect the interests of all persons. For example, *A* wants to purchase some property from *B*. He learns from the public record that *C* holds a mortgage on the property. *A* purchases the property, but he makes legal arrangements that will protect not only his own interests but those of *C* as well.

9.21. Distinction between recording and filing. The terms *record* and *file* are used loosely. They are not synonymous and should not be used interchangeably. If an instrument is to be *recorded*, it is given to an official designated by the state statute. The official copies the instrument in a book, thereby preserving it perpetually. This record furnishes authentic evidence of the existence of the instrument. After the official records the instrument, he or she stamps upon it the date and the number and page of the record book in which it is recorded and returns it to the person who gave it to him or her, usually the lawyer. When a paper is *filed*, it is placed in the custody of a designated official, who enters upon the paper the date of its receipt and keeps it in his or her office, where it is available for inspection. Legal instruments are generally recorded, whereas court papers are are always filed. However, in some states certain legal instruments are filed and recorded in the abstract; that is, only a summary of the essential parts is recorded. The official designated to record legal instruments varies with the locality. He or she might be the county clerk, the town clerk, a register or recorder of deeds, or some other official.

Instruments that are recorded or filed are also appropriately indexed so the record or file can be easily located.

In most places, records are photocopied for recording or filing. Therefore, it is necessary that all instruments submitted for recording be typed with heavily inked ribbon, preferably black.

9.22. What the secretary or paralegal does. When the lawyer asks you to have an instrument recorded, be sure you know not only what official is to record it, but also *where* it is to be recorded. For example, although your office is located in Adam County and the client signs the paper there, if the instrument relates to property located in Brown County, the instrument must be recorded in Brown County, not in Adams County.

Your firm's name and address will probably appear on the legal back in which the instrument is bound. Before having the instrument recorded, write immediately above it, "Please record and return to:" If the firm's name and address are not printed on the legal back, type them on it.

If the instrument is to be recorded in a place located near your office, take it in person to the office of the proper official. He will give you a receipt for it and return it to your office when he has recorded it. You will have to pay a recording fee, which is fixed by the state statutes. In some places, the recording office will bill your firm periodically for recording. Otherwise, pay the fee out of petty cash or take a blank check to the recording office and fill in the amount when you are told what the recording fee will be.

When it is necessary to mail the instrument to the recording office, send it by registered mail, return receipt requested, with a covering letter. The letter should be addressed to the designated official and should describe the instrument sufficiently to identify it. You will also have to enclose a check for the fee or request that a bill be forwarded. The official may not record the instrument until the fee is received. A model letter for this purpose follows.

REGISTERED
RETURN RECEIPT REQUESTED   November 14, 19..
James P. Frost, Esquire
Clerk of the County Court
DeKalb, Illinois 60115

Sir:

We are enclosing for recording lease, dated November 14, 19.., between Hilary Ross and Edmond Butler.

If you will tell us the correct amount of your fee for recording this instrument, we will forward a check to you promptly.

Sincerely,
OAKLAND & RUBIN
By
   B. B. Oakland

Enclosure

Place the receipt from the recording official, or a copy of your covering letter to him, in your follow-up file so you may follow up if the instrument is not returned promptly. Allow about two weeks for the return of the instrument. When it is returned, send it to the client with a covering letter (unless, for some reason, the instrument is to be kept by the lawyer). After an instrument has been recorded, there is no need to forward it by registered mail.

How to Prepare

Legal Papers

One of the most common and most important duties in a law office is the preparation of legal papers. Printed forms are often used in drawing up legal instruments and some court papers. However, whether a preprinted form is available or whether you must prepare the legal paper from scratch, accuracy is essential in all cases. The directions in this chapter are general and apply to all legal papers. Directions that are peculiar to a specific document are given when that document is discussed.

10.1. Number of copies. An original, your file copy, and a varying number of carbon copies or photocopies of all legal documents are necessary. Frequently, one or more of the copies is to be a *duplicate original,* or *triplicate original*, which means it is to be signed and treated in all respects as though it were an original or ribbon copy. The dictator will tell you how many copies to make. Instructions are usually given in this manner: "Two and four," meaning an original, a duplicate original, and four copies; or, "One and five," meaning an original and five copies, no duplicate original being necessary. When copiers are available in the office, some offices make only the original carbon ribbon copy and then make the additional copies on the machine. If there is any doubt whether photocopies are permitted in a particular situation, check with the lawyer before proceeding.

10.2. Paper. Use heavyweight paper for the original or ribbon copy, and lightweight for the carbons, the weight depending on the number of copies. Duplicate and triplicate originals, if typed, are usually prepared on paper of the same substance as the ribbon copy. Today, however, additional originals are often prepared by copier. Some offices follow the practice of making the last carbon copy, which is the office copy, on heavy paper because it is more durable. Others use a distinctive color of paper for file copies.

The kind of paper used depends on the document being typed and also varies with the office. See the discussion of the specific document; also the list of stationery supplies in chapter 1.

10.3. Margins. Documents typed on legal-size paper are bound at the top; those on letter-size paper, at the left. Leave a margin of at least 1½" for binding.

Top margin. Begin typing either five or six double spaces from the top of the paper, but make a habit of always allowing the same number of spaces. By following this practice, you know that every page of a document starts at the same place on the paper and has the same number of typed lines.

Bottom margin. Leave a margin of approximately one inch at the bottom. With a margin of five double spaces at the top and an inch at the bottom, each legal-size page of typing will have 32 lines double spaced; each letter-size page (8½ by 11"), 24 lines.

In a neatly typed legal document, the typing on every page of manuscript ends exactly the same number of spaces from the bottom of the page. Carbon paper with a numbered margin, or a backing sheet with a numbered margin, will ensure an even bottom margin. If you do not have carbon paper with a numbered margin, or if you are making too many copies to use a backing sheet, mark lightly the place where the typing should end, before inserting the paper in the typewriter.

Left margin. Leave a margin on the left of approximately 1¼", or 1½" if the paper is to be bound on the left. On legal cap, begin typing one space to the right of the colored line that indicates the left margin.

Right margin. Leave a right margin of approximately one inch. On legal cap, this will place the margin approximately ⅝" to the left of the colored line that indicates the right margin. This allows a leeway of seven spaces between the right margin and the line. Avoid excessive hyphenation and also a ragged right margin.

Under no circumstances should the typing extend beyond the colored lines that indicate the margin.

10.4. Paragraphs. Indent paragraphs 10 spaces.

10.5. Numbering pages. Number pages of legal documents one-half inch from the bottom of the page, in the center of the line. The number should be preceded and followed by a hyphen, thus: -4-. If the first page is not numbered, the numbering begins with -2-. Be exact in placing the number; when the pages are collated the numbers should overlie one another.

10.6. Marginal and tabular stops. On a typewriter with pica type, and pica type is most frequently used in law offices, set your marginal and tabular stops as follows:

> Paper guide 0
> Left marginal stop 15
> Right marginal stop 75
> First tabular stop 25
> Second tabular stop 30
> Third tabular stop...... 35

With the stops set at these points, practically no adjustment of the typewriter will be necessary for margins, paragraph indentations, proper placement of quotations, and the like.

10.7. Tabulated material. When portions of a paper or letter are tabulated or itemized, the items are usually preceded by a number or letter in parentheses or followed by a period. Begin each line of the tabulated text two spaces to the right of the number. The first letter of each listed item is capitalized. When the sentences are incomplete, no punctuation is used after each item, as shown in figure 10.1. Full sentences, of course, would be followed by a period.

      I have revised the affidavit you returned, I hope in accordance with your recommendations. If you find it satisfactory as now drawn, may I ask you:

    1.   To swear to it before a notary and have him affix his seal and notarial stamp

    2.   To fill in the last column of Schedule B as to the months for which payments are in default on each vehicle

    3.   To return the affidavit with five forms of the conditional sale contract

---

Figure 10.1. *Tabulated Items.*

10.8. Responsibility and distribution line. In the upper left-hand corner, type a notation of the number of copies made, the date, the dictator's initials, and your initials.

Example: 2-3
                              7/23/..
                              ERJ:sm

This indicates that one original and a duplicate original and three copies, one of which is for the files, were made on July 23, 19.., and that the document was dictated by ERJ to sm. The binding covers the notation. It is not necessary to put the notation on any page except the first one. If a page of the document is retyped after the date shown, put a new responsibility line on that page. The identification data should appear on the file copy only of wills, minutes, proxies, and statistical statements.

In the upper right-hand corner of your file copy, indicate the distribution, thus:

1 orig. to JRA	7/24/..
1 orig. to MDE	"
1 copy to SRT	"
1 copy to LRS	"

The third copy that was made is your file copy.

10.9. Line spacing. As a rule all legal work is double spaced, although one and one-half spaces may be acceptable in some cases, for example, when a double-spaced acknowledgment will not fit on the page with signatures acknowledged. Usually quotations are single spaced.

Triple-space before and after all indented material. Also triple-space drafts.

It is permissible to single space an acknowledgment (page 206) to get it on the signature page.

10.10. Standard rules for spacing. Usage has established the following rules for spacing:

After a comma	1 space
After a semicolon	1 space
After every sentence	2 spaces
After a colon	2 spaces
Before or after a dash, which is two hyphens	No space
Before or after a hyphen	No space
Between quotation marks and the matter enclosed	No space
Between parentheses and the matter enclosed	No space
Between any word and the punctuation following it	No space
After an exclamation mark used in the body of a sentence	1 space
After a period following an abbreviation or an initial	1 space

After a period following a figure or letter at the beginning of a line in a list of items	2 spaces
Between dots used to show an ellipsis	No space
Between asterisks used to show an elipsis	1 space
Before and after x meaning *by,* for example, 3″ x 5″ card	1 space
Before or after an apostrophe in the body of a word	No space
Between the initials that make a single abbreviation, for example, C.O.D. (but see "Citations," in chapter 15)	No space

10.11. Space for fill-ins. When a date is to be filled in later, leave a space instead of typing a line for the fill-in.

June , 19..	3 spaces
This day of June, 19..	6 spaces

Do not leave the blank for a later fill-in at the end of a line, because it will not be noticeable.

10.12. Underscoring. *Underscoring,* or underlining, in typed material is equivalent to italics in printed material. The underlining is continuous and not broken at the spacing between words. The following uses of underscoring in legal work are recommended.

1. Underscore for emphasis. The dictator indicates when underscoring is to be used for emphasis.

2. Underscore material that is in italics in the original.

3. Underscore to indicate Latin words and phrases, or abbreviations of them. Words of other foreign languages are also underlined, but Latin is used most frequently in legal work.

4. Underscore titles of books, brochures, plays, movies, and paintings.

Exceptions. Do not underscore foreign words that have become a part of the English speech through continuous use. If in doubt, consult *Webster's.* You will note that parallel bars (‖) precede foreign words that occur frequently in speech and print in English but that are not yet completely Anglicized, as is shown by their being printed generally in italic type. In the list of Latin words and phrases in part 5, those that should not be underlined are in Roman type, whereas those that should be underlined are in italic type. You will notice that some words are in Roman when standing alone but are in italics when used in certain phrases. For example, the word *caveat* is not italicized, but the phrase *caveat emptor* is.

10.13. Quotations and other indented material. *Margins and paragraphs.* The left margin of quotations and other indented material should be five spaces to the right of the principal left margin; the beginning of a paragraph within the material should be indented an additional five spaces. If a quotation begins in the middle of a paragraph indentation is omitted.

The right margin of indented material may be even with the principal right margin or about five spaces to the left of it.

Short lines of indented material should be indented about fifteen spaces, thus:

> The American Bar
> The Bar Register
> The Lawyer's List

Line spacing. Quotations are usually single spaced, but this does not apply to all indented material. Triple-space before and after each quotation or other indented material; double-space between paragraphs of single-spaced indented material.

Quotation marks: When the material is indented, do not enclose it in quotation marks. When the material is *not* indented, but is part of the regular text, place double quotation marks at the beginning and end of the quotation and at the beginning of each new paragraph within the quoted material. Change double quotation marks in material you quote to single quotation marks, thus conforming to the rule that quotations within quotations should be enclosed in single quotation marks. Change single quotation marks in quoted material to double quotation marks.

Errors. Copy quotation exactly, even obvious errors. Indicate errors in the same way that you do in making an exact copy of any material (see 10.16, Copying).

Italics. If words in the original are in italics, underscore them. If words that are not in italics in the original are underscored at the direction of the dictator, the words "Italics ours" or "Emphasis ours" in parentheses are added at the end of the quotation. It frequently happens that part of a quoted passage is italicized and that the dictator wants to emphasize another part of it. In that case, put "italics theirs" in parentheses immediately following the italicized matter and add the words "Emphasis ours" in parentheses at the end of the quotation. In figure 10.2 the word *records* was italicized in the original. The rest of the underscoring was added by the dictator for emphasis.

How to show omissions. Omissions of part of a quotation are indicated by the use of ellipses. They may be points (dots) or asterisks

> The portinont part of the opinion rendered by the Copyright Office at
> our request reads as follows:
>
> > The Copyright Office does not undertake to pass upon his [the
> > author's] rights, leaving the question to the courts in case of
> > dispute. It simply _records_ (italics theirs) his claims, and by this
> > recording gives him certain rights provided his claims can be
> > substantiated....
> >
> > ... this [copyright] is taken out in the name of the publisher
> > rather than of the author, as the contract itself is really a
> > license to sell from the publisher to the author [sic]. It is also
> > the duty of the publisher to take all necessary steps to effect
> > renewals....
> >
> > An auther should be "guided" by his publisher in all
> > questions of copyright. (Emphasis ours.)
>
> We contend that this opinion strongly supports the contention of the
> petitioner.

10.2. *Exact (Chinese) Copy of Quoted Material.*

(stars) and are usually in groups of three. Preferably, there is a space between asterisks, but not between points. Some law offices that formerly used asterisks now use points, probably because they eliminate the necessity of using the shift key and, also, they look neater if the material contains many omissions. You will be guided by the practice in your office.

In using either points or asterisks, simply remember that they take the place of words, and place them accordingly. Thus, if a quotation begins in the middle of a sentence, there is no space between the quotation mark and the first ellipsis, but there is a space between the final ellipsis and the following word. If an entire sentence is omitted, four ellipses are used, the first being a period. Punctuation is placed in the same relation to the ellipses as if they were words.

You may indicate omission of one or more entire paragraphs by a line of ellipses, five spaces apart, or by four ellipses at the end of the last sentence preceding the omission. Some law offices use a single group of three asterisks in the center of the line instead of a full line.

Figure 10.2 illustrates a quotation with points showing omissions. (It also shows errors that were in the material being copied. See 10.16, Copying.) Note that the first paragraph begins in the middle; there are one or more paragraphs omitted after the first paragraph; the next paragraph begins and ends in the middle of a sentence; the last paragraph is quoted in full. Note that there are four points at the end of the second paragraph. The fourth one is a period, indicating the end of the sentence.

10.14. Drafts. Type drafts on an inexpensive grade of legal-size paper. Usually law offices provide an inexpensive yellow paper for this purpose. Make no carbon copies unless otherwise instructed. Lawyers expect to make changes in drafts; therefore, triple-space all dictated material. Extracts copied from books or other documents may be single spaced in the draft, because it is not necessary to make corrections in them. Leave wide margins. Type the date, the initials of the dictator and your initials, and the word DRAFT in capital letters in the upper left-hand corner of the first page. If there is a second or a third draft, indicate this fact. Follow the usual practices for form and style except with reference to line spacing and margins.

Crossing-out is permissible in typing a draft—in fact, it is preferable to erasing because it takes less time. Speed is more desirable than neatness, but accuracy must not be sacrificed. Although a lawyer expects to make changes in a draft, careless transcription of his or her dictation is annoying and is not tolerated any more than it would be in a final copy.

Before retyping a corrected draft, study the corrected page, noting:

1. Portions marked for omission
2. Additional material to be inserted
3. Transpositions
4. Corrections in spelling, punctuation, and the like

Note carefully the changes in each sentence before typing. Difficult handwriting between lines of typing and in the margins may often be deciphered quickly by referring to the scratched out typewriting, of which the handwritten matter is usually a revision.

10.15. Correction of errors. If an insertion or deletion does not jibe with the other material, you are misinterpreting it, or the lawyer has overlooked something. When you detect an error of this kind, or any error other than typographical, in a draft you are retyping, check with the lawyer. If you cannot locate the lawyer and you cannot get a clarification, use your judgment in making the change and call it to his or her attention when you return the work. As a general rule, no extensive corrections should be made in legal documents such as wills, agreements, and court papers. When the error involves more than a few letters, retype the page.

10.16. Copying. In *retyping* an unsigned draft, type it in correct form in accordance with the practices recommended in this book. But the practice is different when *copying* an executed document, signed letter, extracts from books, and in any case when an exact copy is required. The following instructions apply when you are typing an exact copy, sometimes called a *Chinese* copy (see figure 10.1).

1. Type the word COPY in the upper left-hand corner, under your initials and the date.

2. Copy exactly, even obvious errors, because the copy purports to be a "true and exact" copy.

3. Indicate obvious errors copied from the original as follows: (a) Underline an incorrect letter or figure. (b) Put "sic" in parentheses or brackets after apparently or obviously incorrect words or phrases. (c) Show an omission by a caret. If your typewriter does not have a caret, use the slanting bar and underscore key (/__).

> agreement entered into the 31<u>th</u> day of April. ...
> upon rec<u>ie</u>pt. ...
> I give, devise and bequest [sic] unto. ...
> meeting of the United ∧ Assembly in Paris. ...

4. Copy page for page and line for line as far as practicable.

5. When the document is completed, proofread (see chapter 8) it with some other person. That person reads aloud from the original copy while the typist checks the copy. The reader should indicate paragraphs, punctuation, underlining, full capitals, hyphens, and so on.

See page 43 for the method by which the lawyer gives instructions for copying certain material.

Punctuation and capitalization. Punctuation in legal documents should be handled the same way as it is with other material, such as correspondence (see chapter 5). However, there are a few exceptions to general rules of capitalization. Names, for instance, are usually typed in all capitals in legal papers. Often the first letter of words pertaining to specific papers are capitalized, such as Warranty Deed. Versus (v. or vs.) is generally typed in all lowercase letters. Court and venue names are usually typed in all capitals, as are the titles of legal papers, such as AGREEMENT. Your files will have many examples to follow if you are in doubt, and the lawyer will instruct you further when more than one procedure is permissible.

Test-writing. When retyping a page of a document that has had matter added to or taken from it, and the paragraph does not end at the bottom of the page, it may be necessary to make a test-write of the revised portion so the last line of the page will be full length.

Letterheads. When only part of a letterhead is copied, type across the top of the page, in solid caps, enclosed in brackets, the name of the firm [LETTERHEAD OF ....]. This is in addition to your initials, the date, and COPY in the upper lefthand corner.

10.17. Collating. Every legal paper of two or more pages should be collated. *Collating* is the process of organizing a set of pages in the correct sequence. The task is facilitated by the use of a rubber finger or a pencil eraser.

10.18. Conforming. After the original of a document is signed, conform the copies, that is, make them like the original. This includes writing in, or typing in signatures, dates, recording data, and notarial data inked or stamped on the original. In typing the signature, there is no need to type *Signed* in front of the typed copy. Do not be afraid to copy the signature of a judge or anyone else; you are not forging but only making a true copy. You should not try to imitate the signature. Conformed copies can also be made by using a photocopy machine. There is no need to "sign" copies made by photocopier.

When conforming an executed document bearing an official or a corporate seal, write in brackets at the left of the official or corporate signature the word [CORPORATE SEAL] if the seal is a corporate seal; [NOTARIAL SEAL] if the seal is that of a notary public; or [OFFICIAL SEAL] if the seal is that of any officer other than a notary public. Seals of individuals are indicated by SEAL unless written otherwise on the original.

When a county clerk's certificate is attached to an original document, it is advisable for you to find out from the lawyer whether a notation, such as:

```
{ County Clerk's Certificate
{ for _____ County, State
{ of _____ attached to
{ original.
```

is sufficient or whether the entire certificate must be copied and annexed to the conformed copies of the document. It is sometimes important to have a copy of the entire certificate, especially in cases where a certified copy of an original instrument is required.

10.19. Ditto marks. Ditto marks are not permissible in a legal document. They are used in exhibits and schedules but not in the document to which the exhibits and schedules are annexed. Ditto marks may sometimes be used in drafts to save time, but repeat the language in full when typing in final form.

10.20. Legal backs. Typed legal instruments and court papers are usually backed with a manuscript cover, called a *legal back*, of thick paper 8½″ or 9″ by 15″. Certain data, referred to as the *endorsement,* are typed on the back of the cover. An endorsed back of an agreement is illustrated in figure 10.3. The contents of the endorsement vary with the

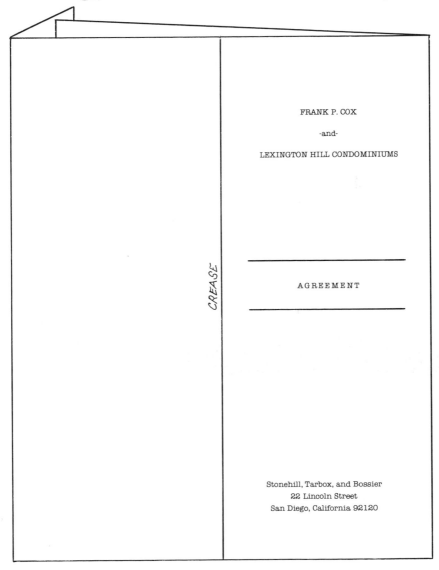

FRANK P. COX

-and-

LEXINGTON HILL CONDOMINIUMS

CREASE

AGREEMENT

Stonehill, Tarbox, and Bossier
22 Lincoln Street
San Diego, California 92120

Figure 10.3. *Legal Back for Agreement*

NOTICE OF ENTRY

Sir :- Please take notice that the within is a *(certified)*
true copy of a
duly entered in the office of the clerk of the within
named court on   19

Dated,

Yours, etc.,

Attorney for

Office and Post Office Address

To

Attorney(s) for

NOTICE OF SETTLEMENT

Sir :- Please take notice that an order

of which the within is a true copy will be presented
for settlement to the Hon.

one of the judges of the within named Court. at

on the   day of   19
at   M.
Dated,

Yours, etc.,

Attorney for

Office and Post Office Address

To

Attorney(s) for

Index No.   Year 19

Attorney for

Office and Post Office Address, Telephone

To

Attorney(s) for

Service of a copy of the within

is hereby admitted.
Dated,

....

Attorney(s) for

Figure 10.4. *Litigation Back (Outside Cover).*

instrument, but usually include a brief description of the instrument and
the names of the parties to it. Litigation backs (illustrated in figures 10.4
and 10.5) are used for backing up court papers like pleadings and motions.
Figure 10.4 is the outside cover. The attorney's name and address are
generally engraved or printed in the space provided. The inside cover
(figure 10.5) contains verifications, affirmations, and affidavits of
service. The appropriate ones are used for any particular case.

To type the endorsement:

STATE OF NEW YORK, COUNTY OF   CERTIFICATION BY ATTORNEY

    The undersigned, an attorney admitted to practice in the courts of New York State, certifies that the within
has been compared by the undersigned with the original and
found to be a true and complete copy.

Dated: ....

STATE OF NEW YORK, COUNTY OF   ATTORNEY'S AFFIRMATION

    The undersigned, an attorney admitted to practice in the courts of New York State, shows: that deponent is

the attorney(s) of record for
in the within action; that deponent has read the foregoing
and knows the contents thereof; that the same is true to deponent's own knowledge, except as to the matters therein
stated to be alleged on information and belief, and that as to those matters deponent believes it to be true. Deponent
further says that the reason this verification is made by deponent and not by

    The grounds of deponent's belief as to all matters not stated upon deponent's knowledge are as follows:

    The undersigned affirms that the foregoing statements are true, under the penalties of perjury.

Dated: ....

STATE OF NEW YORK, COUNTY OF   ss.:   INDIVIDUAL VERIFICATION

                                          , being duly sworn, deposes and says that
deponent is   the   in the within action; that deponent has
         read the foregoing   and knows the contents thereof; that
the same is true to deponent's own knowledge, except as to the matters therein stated to be alleged on information and
belief, and that as to those matters deponent believes it to be true.

Sworn to before me, this   day of   19   ....

STATE OF NEW YORK, COUNTY OF   ss.:   CORPORATE VERIFICATION

                                      , being duly sworn, deposes and says that deponent is the
         of ·   the corporation
named in the within action; that deponent has   read the foregoing
and knows the contents thereof; and that the same is true to deponent's own knowledge, except as to the matters therein
stated to be alleged upon information and belief, and as to those matters deponent believes it to be true.
This verification is made by deponent because
is a   corporation. Deponent is an officer thereof, to-wit, its
The grounds of deponent's belief as to all matters not stated upon deponent's knowledge are as follows:

Sworn to before me, this   day of   19   ....

STATE OF NEW YORK, COUNTY OF   ss.:   AFFIDAVIT OF SERVICE BY MAIL

being duly sworn, deposes and says, that deponent is not a party to the action, is over 18 years of age and resides at

That on the   day of   19   deponent served the within
upon   attorney(s) for
                         in this action, at
                                     the address designated by said attorney(s) for that purpose
by depositing a true copy of same enclosed in a postpaid properly addressed wrapper, in — a post office — official
depository under the exclusive care and custody of the United States post office department within the State of New York.

Sworn to before me, this   day of   19   ....

Figure 10.5. *Litigation Back (Inside Cover).*

STATE OF NEW YORK, COUNTY OF   ss.:   <u>AFFIDAVIT OF PERSONAL SERVICE</u>

being duly sworn, deposes and says, that deponent is not a party to the action, is over 18 years of age and resides at

That on the   day of   19   at No.
                                         deponent served the within

upon
the   herein, by delivering a true copy thereof to   h   personally. Deponent knew the
person so served to be the person mentioned and described in said papers as the   therein.
Sworn to before me, this   day of   19   --

Figure 10.5. *Litigation Back (Inside Cover) Continued.*

1. Lay the backing sheet on the desk as though for reading.

2. Bring the bottom edge up to approximately one inch from the top and crease.

3. Bring the creased end (which is now at the bottom) up to approximately one inch from the top. (You now have a fold with about one inch of the top edge of the backing sheet protruding beyond the fold.)

4. The surface of the folded sheet that is uppermost is the surface on which the endorsement is to be typed. (If the backing sheet has a printed panel or the firm's name on it, that portion of the sheet will be the uppermost surface.) Put a small pencil check in the upper *left*-hand corner of the surface.

5. Partially unfold and insert in typewriter so the pencil mark is on the upper *right*-hand corner of the surface when you type on it.

6. Do not type to the left of the crease (see figure 10.4). After typing the endorsement, turn down the top edge of the backing sheet about an inch (see step 3), crease, insert document in the crease, and staple. Fold the document and the backing sheet, creasing the documents to fit the creases in the backing sheet.

10.21. How to make corrections on bound pages. Frequently after a legal document is neatly bound, it is necessary to make a minor change on one of the pages. Corrections can be made on pages that are bound at the top without unstapling them. Insert a blank sheet of paper in the typewriter, as though for typing. When it protrudes about an inch above the platen, insert between it and the platen the unbound edge of the sheet to be corrected. Turn the platen toward you until the typewriter grips the sheet to be corrected. You can then adjust the bound sheet to the proper position for making the correction.

Corrections cannot be made on pages that are bound at the side without unstapling them.

10.22. Printed law blanks. Printed law blanks are widely used in drawing up legal instruments and some court papers. Law blank printers publish a catalogue showing the numbers and titles of the blanks that they print. Each law blank has its title and, usually, the printer's catalogue number, printed in small letters in the upper left-hand corner. The blanks are obtainable at almost any stationery store. Frequently the secretary or paralegal can fill in these blanks without any dictated instructions from the lawyer. When it is necessary to dictate the material to be inserted in the blanks, the usual manner of giving instructions is as follows:

The lawyer numbers in pencil the spaces to be filled in, 1, 2, 3, and so on. He or she then dictates the material that should be be typed in each numbered blank, thus eliminating any confusion about where each dictated insertion should be typed.

Observe the following suggestions about filling in law blanks, so the completed form will be neat and accurate:

Typing on ruled lines. Make certain that the typing is adjusted so the bases of letters with tails that extend below the line of type (g, p, and y) just touch the ruled line.

Date of printing. Printed forms bear a printer's mark showing the number of copies printed and the date of the printing. When filling in more than one copy, use forms that were printed at the same time, because a change might have been made in the form.

Registration of printing. Before attempting to fill in more than one blank form at a time by using carbon paper, make sure the printing on all copies registers exactly. To do this, place the edges of the forms together and hold to the light. You can then see whether the printed matter in one copy lies exactly over corresponding material in the other copy. The forms should be perfectly aligned without jogging. Otherwise, after inserting the forms and carbon in the typewriter, loosen your typewriter platen and adjust the edges of the forms. They must be exactly even or the typing will not be properly spaced on the copies.

Fill-ins on both sides of sheet. When making carbon copies of a form that has fill-ins on both sides of the sheet, take particular care to avoid having one side the ribbon copy and the other side the carbon copy, thus rendering the form unfit for execution. Double-sheet forms are particularly apt to cause trouble in this respect.

Small blanks. When the blanks on the form are small, fill in each form individually; do not use carbons. Be careful not to overlook any of the small blanks. In many forms they are not indicated by underlining, but only by a small space. Many of them call only for letters identifying the person or persons signing the document. For example, a printed mortgage form might include the following: "Said mortgagee —, —h— heirs or assigns." If there is more than one mortgagee, *s* is added to *mortgagee* and —h— becomes *their*. If there is only one mortgagee, the first blank is not filled in, and —h— becomes *her* or *his*.

"Z" ruling. Frequently the material typed on a printed form does not fill the space provided. To protect the instrument from alteration, draw a "Z" ruling, as illustrated below, with pen and ink in the unused space.

11

How to Handle Affidavits,

Powers of Attorney, and Wills

Chapters 9 and 10 gave basic information about legal instruments and how to prepare legal papers. This chapter reviews three representative instruments that are a part of the work in every law office.

AFFIDAVITS

11.1. What is an affidavit? An *affidavit* is a written statement of facts sworn to by the person making the statement in the presence of an officer authorized to administer the oath. A party making a statement in writing may *affirm* the statement in lieu of swearing to it in most jurisdictions. This right was originally reserved only for those whose religion forbade their taking an oath. The person making the affidavit is called the *affiant* or the *deponent*. The purpose of an affidavit is to help establish or prove a fact. Affidavits are used to prove, among other things, identity, age, residence, marital status, and possession of property. They are also an essential part of court motions (see chapter 14).

11.2. Distinction between affidavit and acknowledgment. An affidavit is a complete instrument within itself, but an *acknowledgment* is always part of, or rather an appendage to, another instrument. The purpose of an affidavit is to prove a fact, whereas the purpose of an acknowledgment is the declaration by the person making it that he or she signed this instrument to which the certificate of acknowledgment is attached. An affidavit is sworn to, but an acknowledgment is not. Both the person making an affidavit and officer administering the oath sign an affidavit; only the officer taking an acknowledgment signs it. An affidavit has a jurat, but an acknowledgment does not.

11.3. Essentials of an affidavit. Some affidavits are written in the first person and some in the third person, but they all have the following basic essentials.

Venue. When an affidavit is used in a court case, it is always preceded by the caption of the case (see figure 14.21). The affidavit itself begins with a recital of the venue.

Name of affiant. The name of the person making the affidavit is written in solid caps.

Averment of oath. The introduction to the affidavit avers that the affiant was sworn, or made the statement under oath.

Statement of facts. The body of the affidavit is a narrative of the facts that the affiant wants to state.

Signature of affiant. The affiant always signs the affidavit, even those that are written in the third person.

Jurat. A jurat is a clause in an official certificate attesting that the affidavit or deposition was sworn to at a stated time before an authorized officer. It is often referred to as the "sworn to" clause. The form of jurat varies slightly in the different states. In a few states, the jurat recites the title of the officer and the state, or state and county, in which he or she is authorized to act. In a few other states, the name of the affiant is repeated in the jurat. The most common form of jurat is:

Subscribed and sworn to (or affirmed) before me
this ____ day of _____, 19 __.

_____
Notary Public

Signature of notary. The notary signs immediately beneath the jurat. He also affixes his seal and the expiration date of his commission. In some states the expiration date precedes the signature.

11.4. Authentication. If the affidavit is to be used in a state other than that in which it is made, an *authentication* of the officer's signature and authority is sometimes necessary. The procedure is the same as when an acknowledgment is authenticated. (See chapter 9.)

11.5. Preparation of affidavit. Directions for the preparation of an affidavit for use in a court case are given on page 340. The directions given here apply to affidavits that are not to be used in a court case. (See figure 11.1.) Court requirements for legal- or letter-size paper can be determined from the clerk of the court in which the document is to be filed. Inquire about the number of copies to make.

STATE OF KENTUCKY)
: ss.
COUNTY OF ELTON)

    JOHN A. BARNES, being duly sworn, deposes and says:

    He is the Secretary of Timberlane Corporation, and that no stockholder of said Corporation has filed with the Secretary thereof a written request (other than such written request or requests as may have heretofore expired or been withdrawn) that notices intended for him shall be mailed to some address other than his address as it appears on the stock book of the said Corporation.

                                        _____
                                                 Secretary

Sworn to before me this

    day of   , 19—

_____
       Notary Public

Figure 11.1. *An Affidavit.*

    1. The venue is typed like the venue on an acknowledgment (chapter 9).

    2. Double-space.

    3. Type the affiant's name in solid caps.

    4. Make a signature line at the right for the affiant to sign.

    5. Usually the jurat is typed on the left half of the page (see figure 11.1), but in a few jurisdictions, the practice is to type it across the entire page.

    6. Type a signature line for the notary public (or other officer who is to administer the oath) immediately beneath the jurat, at the left margin of the page. If the jurat is typed across the page, type the signature line on the right half of the page.

    7. Beneath the signature line type the officer's title. In some states the officer's authority to act in the particular political subdivision is required. For example: Notary Public in and for the County of *Los Angeles*, State of California.''

8. Type "My commission expires   ." (when required) two spaces beneath the officer's title if the jurat is typed on the left half of the page. If the jurat is typed across the page, the expiration dateline is typed at the left margin, parallel to the officer's signature and title.

POWERS OF ATTORNEY

11.6. What is a power of attorney? A *power of attorney* is a written instrument giving authority to the agent appointed to act in the name and on behalf of the person signing it. Authority may be given to another to borrow money; collect debts; manage, lease, sell, or mortgage real estate; prosecute a suit at law; and for almost any other purpose. Frequently, a lawyer gives the secretary a power of attorney to sign his or her name to checks.

11.7. Parties to a power of attorney. The person who gives the authority to another to act for him or her is called the *principal*. The principal may be an individual, a corporation, or a partnership, but principals must be capable of performing the act they authorize another to perform for them.

The person to whom authority is given is the *agent*, or *attorney-in-fact*. The latter designation does not imply that the agent is a lawyer. An attorney-at-law may be an attorney-in-fact, but an attorney-in-fact is not necessarily an attorney-at-law.

11.8. Forms of powers of attorney. A power of attorney is either general or limited. A *general power of attorney* is broad in scope and enables the agent to transact almost any business for the principal, whereas under a *limited power of attorney*, the agent's power is limited to a specified act or acts.

11.9. Statements and clauses. Except with respect to the powers granted by the instrument, all powers of attorney are similar. No state requires a specific form. A power of attorney begins with the words *Know all men by these presents,* or simply *Know all men,* typed in solid caps. After a recital of the parties and their residence, the powers granted by the instrument are set forth. This portion of the instrument is most important and requires careful and expert phrasing so powers granted may be clearly and precisely defined. The lawyer dictates the recital of powers or gives you a special form to follow.

A power of attorney ends with a testimonium clause, which is similar to the testimonium clause in any instrument (see page 196). Those relating to real estate are always acknowledged.

11.10. Directions for the preparation of a power of attorney. Unless otherwise instructed, follow these directions when typing a power of attorney.

1. Make an original for the attorney-in-fact, a copy for the principal, and a copy for your files.
2. Use legal- or letter-size paper according to court requirements.
3. Place the responsibility marks on the office copy only.
4. Double-space.
5. Do not forget to have at least two lines of typing on the signature page.
6. Prepare signature line for the principal or principals only.
7. If the powers granted relate to the conveyance of real estate, the instrument must be prepared with the formalities required for a deed. Follow directions on page 443 *et seq.,* in chapter 18.
8. If the powers granted do not relate to real estate, ask the lawyer if the power of attorney is to be witnessed and acknowledged. If so, follow instructions in chapter 9.
9. Collate.
10. Endorse legal back (chapter 10) as illustrated in figure 11.2.
11. Check to see that the principal's signature agrees with the name typed in the instrument.
12. After the instrument is signed, and acknowledged if necessary, conform copies to original (see chapter 10).
13. If a power of attorney relates to real property, it is recorded like any conveyance. However, sometimes it is not recorded until the attorney-in-fact exercises the power granted. Ask the lawyer for instructions about recording.
14. The lawyer will tell you whether the original of the power of attorney is to be delivered directly to the attorney-in-fact or to the principal.
15. Make a notation on your office copy of the distribution of the orignal and copy.

WILLS

11.11. What is a will? A *will* is the disposal of one's property to take effect after death. At one time only real estate was disposed of by will, personalty being disposed of by testament. The distinction between the terms *will* and *testament* is no longer of legal significance, and the terms are frequently used interchangeably.

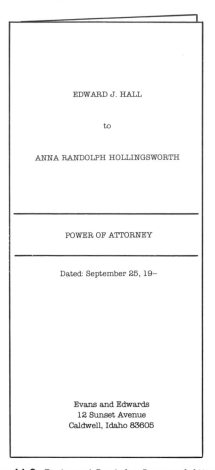

EDWARD J. HALL

to

ANNA RANDOLPH HOLLINGSWORTH

POWER OF ATTORNEY

Dated: September 25, 19--

Evans and Edwards
12 Sunset Avenue
Caldwell, Idaho 83605

Figure 11.2. *Endorsed Back for Power of Attorney.*

11.12. Who are the parties to a will? *Testator.* The only party to a will is the *testator*, or *testatrix* if a woman. The testator is the person who makes the will—who disposes of the property and issues the instructions to be carried out after his or her death. A testator must be of sound mind and of the age required by the state statutes. In the majority of states, the age requirement is 18. In some states the age requirement for the testator of personal property is lower than for the testator of real property; also some states lower the age requirement of a testatrix. Part 5, State Requirements for Ages of Testator and Number of Witnesses to Will, shows the age requirements in the various states.

The law of the state where the testator resides (his or her domicile) controls with respect to personalty, but with respect to real estate, the law of the state where the property is situated controls.

Frequently a man and his wife make a joint will in which case both sign the will as *joint testators.* Joint wills are not prepared as frequently today as they were a few years ago.

Beneficiaries. Beneficiaries are not parties to the will, but are the ones who benefit from it. Strictly speaking, a *devisee* is one to whom real estate is willed, whereas a *legatee* is one to whom personalty is bequeathed. Like the terms *will* and *testament, devisee* and *legatee* are frequently used interchangeably, but you will notice that the careful lawyer does not use the terms loosely in the wills he or she drafts.

11.13. Forms and kinds of wills. None of the states requires that a will and testament follow any specific wording, but the statutes do provide for certain formalities in its execution.

Oral wills, known as *nuncupative* wills, are recognized only under very limited circumstances in almost all of the states. Written wills are far more common. A will may be written entirely in the testator's handwriting and without the usual formalities of execution; such a will is called a *holographic* will and is acceptable in some 19 states. In other states, a handwritten will is admitted to probate only if it is executed with the same formalities required of typewritten wills. You will be concerned principally with the formal written will, typed and executed in the lawyer's office.

Reciprocal wills. Wills made by two or more persons with reciprocal testamentary provisions in favor of each other are called *reciprocal wills.* The term is used whether the testators make a joint will or separate wills. Husbands and wives quite often make reciprocal wills.

11.14. Printed forms of wills. Although it is possible to buy printed forms of wills, they are seldom, if ever, used in a law office. In the first place, clients regard the making of a will as a very serious matter and would not be favorably impressed by the use of a printed form. Then, too, the detailed contents of wills vary so greatly that the use of a printed form saves little time and effort.

11.15. Pattern of the contents of wills. Although no two wills are alike in detail, they are all drafted from similar patterns. The outline given below generally is followed in properly drawn wills. The explanation in the succeeding paragraphs will enable you to recognize each part and clause.

Title
Introductory paragraph
    Revocation clause
Body or text
    Payment of debts and funeral expenses

Dispositive clauses
    Devises
    Bequests
    Trust provisions
    Residuary clause
  Appointment of executor
  Appointment of guardian
  Precatory provisions
Testimonium clause
Signature and seal
Attestation clause
Witnesses' signatures

11.16. Title. The *title* merely identifies the document, as "Last Will and Testament of John Jones," or "First Codicil to the Last Will and Testament of John Jones." It is typed in solid caps, underscored, and arranged symmetrically, beginning about six double spaces from the top of the page. See figure 11.3.

11.17. Introductory paragraph. In the introductory paragraph, the testator sets forth his or her name and residence and recites that he or she does "hereby publish and declare this my Last Will and Testament." Introductory clauses also frequently recite the mental capacity of the testator to make a will, that is, "of sound mind and disposing memory."

11.18. Revocation clause. The *revocation clause* specifically revokes all former wills. Wills do not always include this clause, even though the testator has made other wills, because the act of executing a new will normally has the effect of revoking prior wills. The revocation clause is either a part of the introductory paragraph or is a separate paragraph, usually near the end of the will.

11.19. Text, or body. The *text,* or *body,* of the will disposes of the testator's property, appoints his or her executor, and expresses wishes of the testator that are not necessarily mandatory. The provisions in the body of the will are often referred to as *articles*, or *items*, and are numbered. There are no fast rules as to numbering schemes, but the following are among those commonly used.

In the center of the page: ARTICLE I, ARTICLE II, etc.; ITEM I, ITEM II, etc.; or I, II, etc.

At the side of the page: FIRST:, SECOND:, etc.; First:, Second:, etc,; or, in a short will, 1., 2., etc.

The various articles might have subparagraphs that are also numbered (1), (2), etc., or (a), (b), etc., and these in turn might be subdivided. If you use numbers for subparagraphs, use letters for sub-

subparagraphs. The left margin of sub-subparagraphs is usually indented about 10 spaces.

You must be consistent throughout the will in the numbering system you use and, also, on the lookout for inconsistencies in the lawyer's dictation in this respect. He or she might dictate, "Article I," and "Item 20." If a certain article contains more than 26 bequests, you should choose numbers, rather than letters, for the subparagraphs in all of the articles.

11.20. Payment of debts and funeral expenses. The first paragraph in the body of a will usually directs an executor to pay debts, expenses of last illness, and funeral expenses. This provision is normally not necessary, because the law requires the executor to pay these debts, but it is customarily included.

11.21. Dispositive clauses. The *dispositive clauses* are the provisions that express the testator's will as to what will be done with his or her property—the provisions that *dispose* of the property. Disposal of real property is a *devise*; disposal of personal property, a *bequest* or *legacy*. In a carefully drawn will, the testator will "give and devise" real property; "give and bequeath" personal property; and "give, devise and bequeath" both real and personal property.

11.22. Trust provisions. Many wills set up trusts, which are known as *testamentary trusts*. The testator wills property to an institution, or an individual, "in trust for the following purpose. ..." A testamentary trust is usually created when the testator wants the beneficiary to receive the income from it during his or her life, or until he or she reaches a certain age, or until the happening of some other contingency. Wealthy testators frequently set up endowment funds in trust for charitable and educational purposes. The trust provisions of many wills are very explicit and, therefore, quite lengthy. They constitute part of the dispositive provisions of the will.

11.23. Residuary clause. The *residuary clause* is that part of the will that disposes of all of the testator's property not otherwise devised or bequeathed, "... all the rest, residue, and remainder. ..." A residuary clause is an essential part of the will. Specific or general devises and bequests have priority over the residuary clause, and it is therefore the last dispositive provision of a properly constructed will. No set form of words is necessary.

11.24. Appointment of executor. Someone must see that the provisions of the testator's will are carried out after his or her death. The testator appoints an *executor* in his or her will for this purpose. The executor may be an individual or an institution, such as a bank. If the individual is a woman, she is the *executrix* (plural, *executrices*).

Frequently, the testator appoints more than one executor, or he or she may appoint an alternate, in the event of the incapacity or refusal of his or her first choice to act. Usually the paragraph naming the executor follows the dispositive provisions (bequests) of the will.

11.25. Appointment of guardian. If a testator is the surviving parent he or she will probably appoint a *guardian* of the "person and property" of his or her minor children. Or the testator might choose to appoint one guardian for the person of the children and another for their property. The paragraph appointing a guardian normally follows the paragraph appointing an executor.

11.26. Precatory provisions. *Precatory provisions* in a will are those in which the testator expresses words of desire, expectation, hope, or recommendation that certain action will be taken by the executor— generally in connection with establishing a trust for a named beneficiary. For example, testator may state that he "wishes and requests" or "has the fullest confidence in") his or her testator doing thus and so.

Unfortunately, expressions like these often result in litigation to determine testator's intention. Were these words meant to *impose an obligation* that testator must carry out, or were the words a mere recommendation that testator use his or her discretion in creating or not creating a particular trust?

The carefully drawn will should clearly spell out the testator's intentions rather than just use precatory provisions capable of more than one interpretation.

11.27. Testimonium, or signature, clause. The *testimonium,* or *signature, clause* to a will is similar to the testimonium clause in any written instrument (see page 196). Triple-space between the text of the will and the testimonium clause and *do not number it.*

11.28. Attestation clause and witnesses' signatures. All states require that a will be witnessed, but the required number of witnesses varies (see Part 5, State Requirements for Ages of Testator and Number of Witnesses to Will). The attestation clause (see page 199) to a will recites that the will was witnessed at the request of the testator and that it was signed by him or her in the presence of the witnesses, who subscribed their names in the presence of the testator and in the presence of each other. Holographic wills are seldom witnessed.

11.29. Typing a will. Figures 11.3 and 11.4 illustrate the first and last pages, respectively, of a will. The typing of a will offers a greater challenge to the typist than possibly any other typing she does. Many wills are short, but some are very long and involved, ranging from 10 to 50 or more pages, all of which is dictated. The lawyer chooses his or her words very carefully and the dictation, therefore, is not rapid. The

THE LAST WILL AND TESTAMENT OF

DAVID C. BRAUN

I, DAVID C. BRAUN, of Laconia, County of Belknap, State of New Hampshire, do hereby declare this my Last Will and Testament, and hereby revoke any and all wills and codicils heretofore made by me.

FIRST: I direct that all of my just debts and funeral expenses be paid as soon as practicable after my decease.

SECOND: I give and devise my farm located in the town of Meredith, County of Belknap, State of New Hampshire, to my son, Richard, and his heirs and assigns forever.

THIRD: I give and bequeath to my daughter, Anne, fifty (50) shares of common stock of United States Steel, Inc.

FOURTH: I give and bequeath the following sums of money to the following persons, to-wit:

(a) The sum of Seven Hundred Fifty Dollars ($750.) to Robert Jones of Allentown, Georgia.

(b) The sum of One Thousand Dollars ($1,000.) to Edna Jones of Ellisville, Florida.

FIFTH: I give and bequeath to the Merchants' Loan and Trust Company, a coporation, organized under the laws of

-1-

Figure 11.3. *First Page of Will*

transcription should cause no difficulty; the challenge lies in the typing of the final copy. There should be no erasures in names or amounts and no discernible erasures in other parts. Probate of wills has been refused when material provisions have been erased, because the courts could not tell whether the alteration was made before or after execution. The typing should begin and end at the same point on every page, except the last, and yet there must be continuity from page to page, which means that no page should end with a paragraph or with a sentence. The purpose of the continuity is to avoid the omission, or the possible insertion, of a page.

made in this will and including any property over which I have a power of
appointment, hereby defined as my residuary estate, I give, devise and
bequeath to my daughter, <u>Jane,</u> her heirs and assigns forever.

  IN WITNESS WHEREOF, I have signed my name at the end of this
my Last Will and Testament and affixed my seal this   day of May, 19—.

_____ [L.S.]

     The foregoing instrument, consisting of ten typewritten
     pages, including this page, was signed, published and
     declared by DAVID C. BRAUN to be his Last Will and
     Testament in the presence of us, who, at his request, in his
     presence and in the presence of each other, have subscribed
     our names as witnesses.

_____ of _____

_____ of _____

_____ of _____

(Number page in center, one-half inch from bottom.)

Figure 11.4. *Last Page of Will.*

Some lawyers go so far as to require that the last word on each page be
hyphenated. The placement of the signature with reference to the
testimonium and attestation clauses is of prime importance in a will.

  Frequently the lawyer will tell you to copy a certain paragraph from
another will, or from a skeleton form. Be on the lookout for differences
between the will you are typing and the form you are following, such as a
change from singular to plural or from *his* to *her*, and the like.

  11.30. Signature page and preceding page of a will. The
placement of the *signature* often presents a problem. Good practice makes
the solution obligatory in some respects, permissible in others.

  It is obligatory that at least one line of the testimonium clause be on
the same page as part of the will (see figure 11.5). In other words, a new
page cannot begin with the testimonium clause, because this

Figure 11.5. *One Line of Testimonium Clause on Page with Part of Text of Will.*

arrangement would increase the possibility of the loss of a page, or permit the insertion of a page without detection.

It is obligatory that at least one line of the attestation clause be on the page with the signature (see figure 11.6). The purpose of this requirement is to tie in the witnesses' signatures with that of the testator.

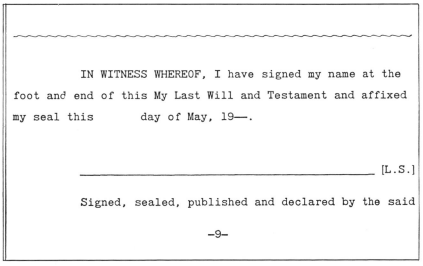

Figure 11.6. *One Line of Attestation Clause on Page with Signature.*

The most desirable setup of the signature page is to have at least three lines of text on the page with the testimonium clause, the signature, and the attestation clause and witnesses' signatures (see figure 11.4).

It is permissible, though not desirable, to have the signature and attestation clause on a page containing only one line of the testimonium clause.

11.31. How to gauge and test the page length. Unless a will is very short and simple, a draft, triple-spaced, is always typed.

1. Count the lines, exclusive of the testimonium clause, signature line, attestation clause, and witnesses' signatures.

2. Assume the draft is 15 pages, 25 lines to the page (drafts are triple-spaced), or a total of 375 lines.

3. Plan on a top margin of five double spaces and an inch margin at the bottom, on 13-inch paper; this will leave room for 32 lines of typing.

4. Divide the total number of lines by the lines per page. You will have 11 typewritten pages with 23 lines left over for the 12th page. A triple space between the test and a three-line testimonium clause, plus three spaces for the signature line places the signature line at the bottom of the page without room for any of the attestation clause. But it is obligatory that at least one line of the attestation clause be on the page with the signature. So, you must try another plan.

Plan on a top margin of six double spaces, instead of five, and type 31 lines to the page. This will give 12 typewritten pages with threee lines remaining for the 13th page. You then have ample room for the testimonium clause, the signature, the attestation clause, and the witnesses' signatures. (See figure 11.4 and section 9.7.)

Of course, in counting the lines in the draft, you must allow for interlineations and deletions that were made on the draft. If a paragraph is changed considerably, so you cannot tell how many lines it contains, retype it before counting the lines of your draft. You must also take into consideration triple spaces between articles or items, if you plan to use them. In the illustration in figure 11.5, there is a triple space between the title and the introductory paragraph; also, each article is separated from the preceding one by a triple space, making a total of six extra spaces, which is equivalent to three double spaces, on that page. Although the page length is 32 lines, that page actually has only 28 lines of typing. The extra spaces throughout the will must be added to the total number of lines.

11.32. Witnessing a will. When a will is drawn up and executed in your office, you will probably be asked to witness it. The procedure of witnessing a will is rather formal. The general practice is for the testator to "publish" the will in the presence of the witnesses by declaring that the document is his or her will. The testator also asks the witnesses to witness the signing of it. The testator not only signs the will but initials the left margin of the other pages. Each witness signs in the presence of the testator and of each other, and no one leaves the room while the will is being signed, witnessed, and sealed.[1] You will notice from figure 11.4 that space for the address of the witness is provided. The address is important because the witness will be called upon to prove the will after the testator's death.

11.33. Certifying copies of wills. It is customary in many law offices for the secretary to certify the copies of a will. This certification is not for the purpose of the formal affidavit required when the will is probated (see chapter 19) but is for authentication of the carbon copies made when the will was typed. Type the form of certification on the copies and, after the copies have been conformed to the original, sign the certification. The following is a form of certification to be used when the typist conforms the copies.

I certify that this carbon copy is one I typed simultaneously with the original will and that after the execution of the original, I conformed this copy to the original by adding the initials, date, signatures, and the addresses of the witnesses.

If someone other than the typist of the will conforms it, the form of certification to be signed by the typist should be changed to read:

I certify that this carbon copy is one I typed simultaneously with the original will and that after the execution of the original, this copy was conformed to the original by the addition of the initials, date, signatures, and the addresses of the witnesses.

Some large law firms use the following form of certification:

We, the undersigned, hereby certify that we have compared the foregoing copy with the original will of . . . . dated . . . . and find it to be a true and accurate copy thereof.

---

[1] The procedure in Louisiana is different. Generally, the will is not witnessed until after it is placed in an envelope, or other cover, that is closed and sealed. The testator presents the closed and sealed envelope to a notary public and three witnesses, declares that the envelope contains his testament, signed by him. The notary then superscribes the envelope, and he, the testator, and the witnesses sign the superscription. The superscription must state that the testator declared, in the presence of witnesses, that the testament was signed by him and written by him or another at his direction.

This last form of certification requires the reading of the will by three persons, or more if more than two copies are made. One person reads the original will aloud and signs the top line of the certification on each of the copies. Each person who follows a copy signs the second line of the certification on the copy she has followed.

11.34. Capitalization and punctuation. You will notice from figure 11.3 that the testator's name is written in solid caps, whereas all other names are underscored (preferably with red ink). The words *last will and testament* are written with initial caps in the will and in the attestation clause. In the phrases *make, publish and declare* and *give, devise and bequeath,* no comma precedes the conjunction *and.* Many lawyers prefer that *executor* and *trustee* be capitalized. You will notice from figure 11.4 that the words *in witness whereof* are written in solid caps and are followed by a comma. These arrangements are arbitrary but are followed extensively in law offices that give considerable attention to these details.

11.35. "Do's and don'ts" in preparing a will. Unless otherwise instructed follow these directions when preparing a will.

1. Type first in draft form unless the will is only a few pages.

2. In the final typing, make an original and two copies, the original and one copy for the testator and the other copy for your files. (If a bank or other institution is named executor, ask if an extra copy is to be made for it.)

3. Use either a very good quality, letter-sized bond paper or a very good legal cap (see chapter 1).

4. Place the responsibility line at the top of the office copy *only.* (See chapter 10.)

5. Double-space, except the attestation clause.

6. Type the same number of lines on each page, calculating the number of lines as suggested on page 242.

7. Number each page no more than one double space below the last line, except the last page, which should be numbered one-half inch from the bottom of the page.

8. Do not forget to precede and follow the page number with a hyphen. Type the hyphen preceding the number at 42 on the typewriter scale, if a pica type machine is used.

9. Triple-space between the text of the will and the testimonium clause.

10. Start the signature line at point 30 on the typewriter scale, if a pica, and continue the line to 67, writing the first bracket in [L.S.] or [SEAL] at point 68. These two scale points are important: the first to

accommodate a long signature and the second to permit a neat application of the seal. (It is customary to seal a will whether or not the statute requires it.)

11. If a wax seal is used, omit the typed seal. Have wax and ribbon available.

12. Single-space the attestation clause. Indent it three spaces from the regular left margin, indenting the first line five spaces. Type the attestation clause all the way over to the right ruled margin of the paper.

13. Start the first witness line three spaces below the attestation clause, at the left margin, and underscore for 25 spaces; then type "residing at" and underscore for another 25 spaces.

14. Triple-space between the witness lines.

15. Collate.

16. Check and double-check spelling of names.

17. Endorse the back as shown in figure 11.7, using back engraved with firm's name. Back the original and first carbon.

18. If real estate devised by the will is described, have someone compare the description with you.

19. Bind firmly and securely.

After the will is signed and witnessed:

20. Conform copies to original. (See chapter 10.)

21. Certify the copies as described on page 243.

22. If your office is to retain the original of the will for safekeeping, give the testator a receipt, signed in the firm's name by one of the lawyers or yourself, reading as follows: "The will of . . . . , dated . . . . , is in our possession for safekeeping."

23. Enclose the original in an envelope, marked "Last Will and Testament of . . . . , dated . . . ."

24. If an institution is named executor, forward conformed copy with covering letter.

25. If a copy of a former will by the testator is in your file, note on it that a later will, of a certain date, has been executed.

11.36. Codicil. After making a will, a testator might decide to change, delete, or add certain provisions. He or she does this by means of a *codicil,* which is a supplement to the will. A codicil is written and executed with the same formality as the will. It is not attached to the will, but should be placed in a separate envelope on which is typed, "Codicil to Last Will and Testament of . . . . , dated . . . ." A testator may make more than one codicil.

11.37. Red-inking a will. Some attorneys like to *red-ink* a will. The usual method of red-inking is as follows:

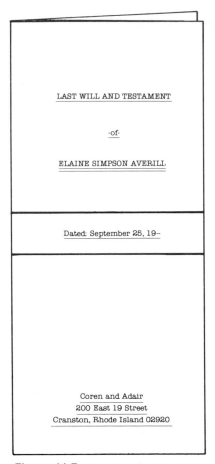

LAST WILL AND TESTAMENT

-of-

ELAINE SIMPSON AVERILL

Dated: September 25, 19–

Coren and Adair
200 East 19 Street
Cranston, Rhode Island 02920

Figure 11.7. *Endorsed Back for Will.*

Draw *double* red lines:

    Under the name of the testator in the introductory paragraph
        and on the cover

    Under each Article number

    Under "IN WITNESS WHEREOF"

Draw *single* red lines:

    Under each name appearing in the will

    Under "Executor" and "Trustee"

    Under everything appearing on the cover, including the
        engraved name of the law firm but excepting the name of
        the testator, which has double lines under it.

PART 3

PREPARING COURT PAPERS

12 Understanding Courts and Their Functions

13 Handling Court Papers

14 How to Prepare Court Papers

15 How to Handle Records on Appeal, Briefs, and Citations

12

Understanding Courts

and Their Functions

A large part of the work in a law office concerns the functions of the court. Therefore, an understanding of the organization of courts and their functions is not only desirable but necessary.

12.1. The word "court." The word *court,* as it relates to the practice of law, is commonly used in these senses:

1. *Court* refers to the persons assembled under authority of law, at a designated place, for the administration of justice. These persons are the judge or judges, clerk, marshal, bailiff, reporter, jurors, and attorneys, and they constitute a body of the government. Thus, the lawyer's secretary says that her employer "is in court this morning," meaning that he or she is appearing before this duly assembled body in the interest of a client. It is not necessary that all of these persons be present to constitute a court—court is frequently held without a jury.

2. The word refers to the authorized *assembly* of the persons who make up the court. Thus, we say, "Court will be held ..." meaning that the judge, clerk, attorneys and so on will gather together to administer justice. Or we say, "Judge Smith's court ...," meaning the clerk, attorneys, jurors, and so on over which Judge Smith presides.

3. *Court* refers to the judge or judges themselves, as distinguished from the counsel or jury. Thus, we have the expression, "In the opinion of the Court ...," "May it please the Court, ...," "The Court stated...." In this sense, the word is written with a capital, because it is personified when it stands for the judge.

4. The word *court* is used occasionally to refer to the chamber, hall, or place where court is being held. Thus, a spectator is present "at court," in the courtroom, but the defendant is "in court" because he or she is part of the assembly.

5. The name of a specific court always includes the word *court,* which is capitalized; for example, Probate Court, Essex County. Neither probate nor court is capitalized if reference is made to probate courts generally; for example, "Petitions for letters of administration are filed in probate courts."

12.2. Court procedure. Court proceedings are generally conducted for and in behalf of the litigants by attorneys-at-law. It is permissible for an individual party to a law suit to represent himself or herself in court [a corporation generally must appear by attorney], but a layman seldom has the required technical knowledge. Court actions consist of a series of written statements of the claims and defenses of the parties to a court action. These written statements are known professionally as *pleadings*.

In almost all states, a civil legal proceeding is commenced when the first pleading is filed with the clerk of the court by the person bringing the suit. The plaintiff—the person bringing the suit—makes a written statement in clear and concise language of the facts that caused him or her to bring the suit. The designation of this first pleading varies with the court; it might be called a *complaint,* a *declaration,* a *libel,* or a *petition.* In some states, the first pleading in an equity action is designated as a *bill in equity* or a *bill of complaint.* A summons, or its equivalent, is then issued and served upon the person against whom the action is brought—usually called the *defendant.* The defendant answers the summons and complaint, defending himself or herself by raising legal arguments or by denying the facts stated by the plaintiff in the complaint. When the case is finally submitted to the court for a decision, the judge decides controversies about legal points; a jury, or a judge acting in place of a jury, decides questions of fact. See chapter 14 for pleadings that might be filed in a civil action.

12.3. What happens in court. Court proceedings vary in elaborateness and formality from a simple hearing in the judge's office, called *chambers,* to a full-dress jury trial. A common feature of all court proceedings is the dignified demeanor of all participants and the respect accorded the presiding judicial officer.

In an informal hearing in chambers, only the judge (or on occasion the special master assigned), the litigants, and their attorneys are present. In a more formal courtroom hearing, the litigants, their attorneys, and the presiding judge will be joined by the clerk of court, the court reporter, and one or more bailiffs.

If you attend a jury trial, you are likely to see the following procedure at every session of the trial. Before the judge arrives, the plaintiffs and their attorneys and the defendants and their attorneys will be present in the courtoom along with the court reporter, a bailiff, and any members of the public who want to attend. All present stand while the jury is brought into the courtroom and seated in the jury box. Everyone then rises at the order of the bailiff and remains standing until the judge has entered the courtroom and is seated behind the bench.

The clerk declares the court in session and announces the first case to come before the court at this particular session. The plaintiff, if it is a civil case, or the prosecution, if it is a criminal case, begins by making an *opening statement.* This is a brief outline of the case to be presented and the evidence expected to be brought before the court. Sometimes the defense attorney will make an opening statement immediately after that of the prosecution or plaintiff. The prosecution or the plaintiff, again depending on whether it is a criminal or civil case, then presents the evidence he or she has to support his or her side of the case. Witnesses are called and questioned in turn by the plaintiff's attorney or the prosecution as the case may be.

When the prosecution has completed the questioning of a witness, the defendant's attorney has a turn to cross-examine the same witness. When the defendant has completed cross-examination, the prosecution or plaintiff may ask further questions of the witness on what is called *redirect examination.* Redirect is limited to questioning on matters brought up on cross-examination. Occasionally redirect examination is followed by a *recross-examination* by the defendant's attorney. Upon completion of the evidence for his or her side, the plaintiff or prosecution rests.

The same routine is followed for the defendant's *case in brief.* The attorney may make a brief opening statement and proceed to present the evidence. At the end of the defendant's evidence, the prosecution or plaintiff may present rebuttal witnesses. Evidence will be limited to matters raised by the defendant's witnesses. When both sides have completed presenting all their evidence, the attorneys present their *closing arguments* to the jury. The defendant argues first. He or she reviews the evidence presented and describes to the jury in detail his or her theory of the case and reasons for believing they should find in the defendant's favor. When the defendant has completed his or her argument, the prosecution or plaintiff then presents a closing argument.

Finally, before the jury retires to deliberate on the evidence, the judge *charges* the jury. He or she describes to the jury the issues they must decide and outlines for them the law of the jurisdiction, on which they must base their decision. After this, the jury retires to deliberate. They may upon occasion ask the judge for further instructions. Otherwise the case is complete when they return with their verdict. In a criminal case, the judge may sentence the defendant immediately upon the return of a guilty verdict, or he or she may defer sentencing.

12.4. Court personnel. *Judge.* The *judge* is responsible for the conduct of proceedings in the courtroom. Although the judge's rulings are subject to exception and appeal to a higher tribunal, they may not be actively questioned while the trial proceeds. As the evidence is presented, the judge rules on objections and makes certain limited instructions to the jury. After the evidence is completed, the judge instructs the jury about the law. If a trial is without a jury, the judge is also the finder of fact as well as the determiner of law.

Jury. The *jury* may consist of as few as six or as many as twelve individuals. Their function is to listen to the evidence, to make determinations of fact where testimony conflicts, and to apply the law as the judge gives it to them to the facts found.

Court reporter. The *court reporter* records verbatim every word spoken in the courtroom. Even conferences at the bench between the judge and attorneys are often recorded by the court reporter at the judge's request or at the request of the attorneys. A number of methods are currently in use for reporting court proceedings. The most common is the stenotype machine. There are court reporters who take down the proceedings in shorthand in the conventional way, too. A more recent innovation is a type of tape recorder in which the reporter repeats each word spoken into a special kind of microphone, identifying the speaker as he does so.

Clerk of court. The *clerk of court* is responsible for scheduling the trials and seeing that all matters in the court run smoothly. He or she is the administrative officer of the court. The clerk reads the indictment at the beginning of the trial, but may have no other spoken function during the trial. He or she is responsible for seeing that the jury is cared for and that their questions are relayed to the judge while they are deliberating.

Bailiffs. The *bailiffs* are responsible for preserving order in the court, under the direction of the clerk.

Attorneys. All *attorneys* are officers of the court. An attorney is responsible for presenting the evidence in the most favorable light for his or her client. The attorney must abide by the rules of the court and defer to the ruling of the judge whether or not he or she agrees with it at the time.

Plaintiff or prosecution. The *plaintiff* or *prosecution* initiates the law suit. He or she bears the burden of preparing the case and presenting the evidence to the jury to support the case.

Defendant. The *defendants* are not obliged to present any evidence. If the defendants believe the plaintiff's or prosecution's evidence is so weak that the jury cannot find in his or her favor, they may decline to present evidence on their own behalf. Ordinarily, however, defendants present evidence to show that the plaintiff's or prosecution's evidence is insufficient to support the case he or she is trying to make.

Witnesses. One or more *witnesses* may be called by either side in a law suit. Often witnesses are *sequestered,* that is, they are not permitted to come into the courtroom to hear testimony preceding theirs. They may testify voluntarily or they may be subpoenaed by either side. Each witness undergoes direct examination by the side that calls him and cross-examination by the oppostion. Some witnesses may be *expert witnesses,* hired by one side to bring testimony to the jury on matters beyond the experience of the ordinary person. Examples of people called as expert witnesses are doctors, engineers, psychiatrists, and so forth, depending on the type of case.

Plaintiffs and defendants. Both *plaintiffs* and *defendants* are usually present during the trial of their case. They may or may not testify in their own behalf. There is no requirement that they do so. Each can assist his or her attorneys in many ways, both during preparation of the case and during the trial itself, by supplying information about people and events involved.

12.5. American court system. The *American court system* consists of federal courts plus the various court systems of all of the states. The courts of the District of Columbia and Puerto Rico are part of the federal court system, although both are now organized along lines similar to state court systems. The Supreme Court of the United States is the highest tribunal in our land—it is the apex in the hierarchy of courts, both federal and state. There is no appeal from its decisions.

State courts. The system of *state courts* follows a fairly consistent pattern, indicated in part 5, Courts of Record and Judicial Courts. Each system consists of the state's highest appellate court and of courts of original jurisdiction, that is, courts where suits are initiated. States with a large volume of cases also have intermediary appellate courts to relieve the congestion of cases in the highest court. A case is brought and tried in a lower court and may be appealed to a higher court having appellate jurisdiction until it reaches the state's highest appellate court or, in some cases, the United States Supreme Court.

Under some of the state systems, the state is divided into circuits or districts with a court for each. Usually court is held in each county seat and the judges travel the "circuit" to the county seats to hold court. Other states have only one superior, or trial court, which is composed of geographical divisions. The distinction is reflected in the wording of the captions on court papers. For example, Mississippi is divided into 17 judicial circuits, with a separate court for each. The captions on the court papers read:

IN THE CIRCUIT COURT OF THE FIRST JUDICIAL DISTRICT
OF HINDS COUNTY, MISSISSIPPI

On the other hand, there is only one superior court of Massachusetts, which is composed of divisions according to counties. The captions on the court papers read:

COMMONWEALTH OF MASSACHUSETTS
ESSEX, ss   SUPERIOR COURT

In many jurisdictions the courts are also divided into parts, for the purpose of facilitating the court's work. There is no standard principle upon which the division is based. For example, the Chancery Court of Davidson County, Tennessee, is divided into Part One and Part Two, and members of the Nashville bar can bring their suits in either part. The caption designates the part. In Kings County, New York, Part One of the Supreme Court (which is the trial court in New York State) is the part in which all cases are called when they appear on the ready day calendar (see page 263). The judge presiding in Part I sends cases to the different trial parts. After a case is assigned to a certain part, that part is designated in the caption.

The courts in one state have no control over, or relation to, the courts in another state—the hierarchy in each state is complete. Federal district courts will apply the law of the state in which they sit in cases where federal law is not at issue. The United States Supreme Court is the final arbiter in all cases involving federal constitutional or statutory law.

Federal courts. When our country first adopted its Constitution, a rivalry and jealousy existed among the states that made up the Union, and between the federal government and the respective state governments. The citizens of one state were fearful that they would not receive a fair verdict from judge or jury in another state. The federal government feared that the state courts would not interpret and enforce the national laws to the best of their ability. To avoid any miscarriage of justice that might result from interstate antagonism, the Congress provided for a *federal system of courts* for the trial of cases involving federal laws and interstate commerce and, also, cases involving *diversity of citizenship*—cases brought by a citizen of one state against a citizen of another state.

The federal system of courts consists of the Supreme Court of the United States, 11 courts of appeal (ten numbered Circuits plus the District of Columbia Circuit), 90 district courts, a court of claims, a customs court, and a tax court. (See part 5, Courts of Record and Judicial Circuits.) The United States is divided into 11 judicial circuits—10 are comprised of several states each, and there is in addition the District of Columbia Circuit.

United States district court. The *district courts* are the trial courts of general federal jurisdiction. Each state has at least 1 district court, and some of the larger states have as many as 4. There is also a United States Small District Court in the District of Columbia. In all, there are 89 district courts in the 50 states, plus the 1 in the District of Columbia. In addition, the Commonwealth of Puerto Rico has a United States district court with jurisdiction corresponding to that of district courts in the various states.

At present each district court has from 1 to 27 federal district judgeships, depending upon the amount of judicial work within its territory. Only 1 judge is usually required to hear and decide a case in a district court, but in some kinds of cases, 3 judges must be called together to comprise the court. In districts with more than 1 judge, the judge senior in commission who has not reached his seventieth birthday acts as the chief judge. There are in all 385 permanent district judgeships in the 50 states and 15 in the District of Columbia. There are 3 judgeships in Puerto Rico. Except in certain territories, district judges hold their offices during good behavior as provided by Article 3, Section 1, of the Constitution. However, Congress may create temporary judgeships with the provision that when a vacancy occurs in that office, such vacancy will not be filled. Each district court has a clerk, United States attorney, a United States marshall, one or more United States magistrates, referees in bankruptcy, probation officers, and court reporters and their assistants.

Cases from the district court are reviewed by the United States Court of Appeals except that injunction orders and special three-judge courts, certain decisions holding acts of Congress unconstitutional, and certain criminal decisions may be appealed directly to the Supreme Court.

12.6. Jurisdiction. The laws of our country provide that certain causes of action (law suits, cases) must be brought in one court, others in another. The authority of a court to hear a particular cause of action and to render a binding decision is called *jurisdiction*. It is the lawyer's problem to determine in which court his or her client's case should be brought—which court has jurisdiction over it. To hear a case, a court must have jurisdiction *in personam* (of the person) or *in rem* (of the thing and subject matter jurisdiction).

In personam jurisdiction. This means a court must have jurisdiction over the *litigants* (the person or persons bringing the suit and those defending it). For example, if the litigants live in different cities in the same county, the county court, rather than a city or municipal court, has jurisdiction. A New York court does not have jurisdiction over a citizen of Mississippi in a suit brought by a New York citizen. Foreclosure actions can be brought only in the county where the property is located unless the Mississippi citizen is physically present and duly served with process in New York State. There are a number of exceptions to this rule, however. So-called long-arm statutes give a court jurisdiction over a citizen of another state who has done certain kinds of acts in the state where the court sits.

In rem jurisdiction. This means the court must have jurisdiction over the physical property, usually real estate, in controversy.

Subject matter jurisdiction depends upon several factors: nature of the case, amount involved, location of the property. For example, a magistrate's court has jurisdiction over a traffic violation but cannot try a person for murder. A suit for damages caused by an automobile collision cannot be brought in a probate court.

Some courts have original jurisdiction, whereas others have appellate jurisdiction. Suits are commenced and tried only in courts of original jurisdiction, which are usually the lower courts. After a case has been decided in a court of original jurisdiction, it may be brought into a higher court having appellate jurisdiction for another decision. Appellate courts have original jurisdiction over some matters.

The term *jurisdiction* is also used to refer to the *sphere* of a court's authority, as distinguished from the authority itself. Thus, we might say the jurisdiction of a district court is limited to that particular district; of a state supreme court, to that particular state. The decisions of a particular court prevail within that court's jurisdiction, although they might be in conflict with the decisions of a court in another jurisdiction—another sphere of authority.

Limitations on the jurisdiction of each court vary too much to attempt to give more than a general resume here. Furthermore, it is the lawyer's job to know in which court a particular action should be brought. But the secretary, paralegal, and other staff should have a general understanding of jurisdictional limitations so they will understand why a case is brought in a certain court. Any classification of courts is necessarily incomplete and, also, overlapping, but for our purpose we arbitrarily classify courts as (1) inferior, (2) superior, (3) courts of special jurisdiction, (4) courts of intermediate review, and (5) supreme appellate courts. The general jurisdiction of each class is given below.

12.7. Inferior courts. The most common *inferior courts* are justice courts, small claims courts, and a class of courts whose jurisdiction is confined to misdemeanors and violations of city ordinances. Courts of this class are variously called police, magistrate's, municipal, district, or recorder's courts. All inferior courts have a very narrow jurisdiction. In criminal matters, they are restricted to decisions on misdemeanors (minor infractions) and preliminary hearings or inquiries in felony cases. In civil actions, they have jurisdiction over actions involving small amounts only, the amount varying with the state. For example, in Texas, county courts have jurisdiction over claims of $500 or less; in Illinois, small claims courts have jurisdiction of claims for $1,000 or less. Inferior courts are usually courts not of record, that is, their proceedings are not recorded. Sometimes the judge of an inferior court is not a lawyer. The decisions of these courts are subject to review or correction by higher courts. Actually, circuit and district courts are "inferior" to appellate or supreme courts, but the term is usually applied to the courts of limited jurisdiction described here.

12.8. Superior courts. The highest state courts of original jurisdiction are *superior courts*. They are usually designated as circuit, district, or superior courts. (In New York the highest court of original jurisdiction is called the Supreme Court.) They have original jurisdiction in the first instance and are the courts where cases outside the jurisdiction of inferior courts are tried originally. They also have appellate jurisdiction over matters arising in inferior courts, in certain administrative tribunals, and, in many states, over probate matters. They control or supervise the lower courts by writs of error, appeal, or certiorari.

In some states, superior courts have one or more departments or divisions that have jurisdiction over special matters. For example, the Superior Court of New Jersey has a law division for the trial of actions at law and a chancery division for hearing equity matters; in California, a department of each superior court acts as a probate court. Other states have courts of special jurisdiction for probate matters.

12.9. Courts of special jurisdiction. *Courts of special jurisdiction* are courts of original jurisdiction over certain restricted matters. Some states have courts of special jurisdiction in some fields; other states, in other fields. The most common courts of special jurisdiction are probate courts, criminal courts, chancery courts, juvenile courts, county courts, and municipal courts in large cities.

Probate courts have jurisdiction over the probate of wills, administration of a decedent's estate, and guardianship of minors and insane people.

Criminal courts have original jurisdiction over criminal cases. Criminal trial courts may be called *oyer & terminer* (hear and determine).

Chancery courts have jurisdiction over equity or chancery matters and apply rules of chancery law. See page 259 for the distinction between equity and law.

Juvenile courts usually have exclusive original jurisdiction over all neglected, dependent, or delinquent children under eighteen.

County courts have widely diverse jurisdiction in the different states. For example, in Oregon, they are courts of criminal jurisdiction; in Florida, they have jurisdiction over misdemeanors, violations of city and county ordinances, and in civil actions where the amount in controversy does not exceed $2,500; in Mississippi, they have concurrent jurisdiction with circuit and chancery courts if the amount involved does not exceed $10,000.

Municipal courts in large cities are frequently courts of record and have concurrent jurisdiction with superior courts, if the amount involved does not exceed a stated sum, usually not more than $3,000.

12.10. Courts of intermediate review. As previously indicated, *courts of intermediate review* are established to relieve congestion in a state's highest appellate court. They are indicated in part 5, Courts of Record and Judicial Circuits, by an asterisk. Some states have more than one court of intermediate review. These courts exercise appellate jurisdiction only, except that in some states they have original jurisdiction to issue writs of mandamus, certiorari, habeas corpus, and the like. They have jurisdiction of matters of appeal from the final judgments, orders, or decrees of superior courts, usually in both law and chancery matters. The appellate jurisdiction of intermediate courts is frequently restricted. For example, the Georgia Court of Appeals, which is a court of intermediate review, does not have jurisdiction over appeals involving the Constitution of Georgia or of the United States. The appellate courts of Illinois do not have jurisdiction over criminal appeals other than misdemeanors. In New Jersey and New York, divisions of the superior court (New York's equivalent of superior courts is called Supreme Court) exercise intermediate jurisdiction.

12.11. Supreme appellate courts. There is only one *supreme appellate court* in each state. These courts are courts of last resort in their respective states. (In Oklahoma, the Criminal Court of Appeals, and in Texas, the Court of Criminal Appeals, are courts of last resort in criminal cases.) The jurisdiction of these courts is appellate, their original jurisdiction, if any, being limited to the issuance of writs of mandamus, certiorari, habeas corpus, and the like.

The highest court in 42 states is designated as the *Supreme Court.* The designations in the eight other states are as follows:

Connecticut	Supreme Court of Errors
Kentucky	Court of Appeals
Maine	Supreme Judicial Court
Maryland	Court of Appeals
Massachusetts	Supreme Judicial Court
New York	Court of Appeals
Virginia	Supreme Court of Appeals
West Virginia	Supreme Court of Appeals

12.12. Distinction between equity and law. The word *equity* means "fair dealing," and that is the purpose of the system of legal rules and procedures known as equity. Remedies at the common law in England were frequently inadequate to give the wronged party a fair deal. He would then take his case to the King's Chancellor, who tempered the strict letter of the law with fairness. As a result of this practice, chancery courts, in which equity is practiced, were established, presided over by a chancellor instead of a judge. Cases heard in equity are not tried before a jury, whether or not there is a formal separation of cases at law or in equity. A few states still have courts of chancery, as indicated in part 5, Courts of Record and Judicial Circuits. Other states do not separate cases in equity from cases at law, but apply equity principles when appropriate. In the majority of states, equity and law are organized under a single court, which has two dockets—one in equity and one in law.

Ordinarily, law actions have for their object the assessment of damages, but a court of equity goes further and attempts to prevent the wrong itself or to give the complainant what he or she bargained for. Among the more common equity actions are injunction suits, specific performance, partition suit, rescission of a contract, reformation of a contract, and all matters relating to trusts and trustees.

In the course of its development, equity has established certain fundamental principles or maxims, which the lawyer frequently uses in dictating briefs. Among these are the following.

1. *He who seeks equity must do equity.* If I seek the return of property I was induced to sell through fraud, I must offer to return the purchase price.

2. *He who comes into equity must come with clean hands.* If I induce you to breach a contract and to make one with me instead, and then you breach the contract with me, a court of equity will not compel specific performance of your contract with me.

3. *Equity will presume that to be done which should have been done.* If I unlawfully take possession of your cow, a calf from that cow will belong to you, because a court of equity will presume that I was holding the cow for you.

4. *Equity aids the vigilant, not those who slumber on their rights.* Where the statute of limitations (page 614) has not run, but a claimant has delayed unreasonably in bringing suit, a court of equity may bar the claim by reason of such delay.

5. *Equity follows the law.* Except where the common law is clearly inadequate, equity follows the precedents of the common law and the provisions of the statutes. Thus, if a deed is void by common law or statute, the mere fact that a holder has given valuable consideration for it will not make the deed valid in equity.

6. *Equity regards substance rather than form.* Common law is normally governed by legal form. Corporations, for example, are regarded in law as artificial beings, separate from their stockholders, directors, and officers. To accomplish justice, equity may disregard the corporate fiction and examine the substance of the dispute. For example, several men sold out a fish business and agreed not to go into the fish business in the same locality. They immediately formed a corporation to carry on a fish business in competition with the purchaser. The Court ignored the corporate entity and granted an injunction against the violation of the agreement not to compete.

12.13. Judges and justices. Insofar as power, authority, and duty are concerned, there is no distinction between a *judge* and a *justice*. The law in each state specifies whether the members of each court in that state will be designated as judges or justices. In the majority of states, the members of the highest appellate courts are called justices, whereas the members of the trial courts are judges. Part 5, Courts of Record and Judicial Circuits, shows the technical designation of the members of each court listed there.

The lawyer prepares orders and decrees for the court's approval. It is important, therefore, for you to know whether the technically correct designation of the Court is judge or justice, because these papers always contain the Court's title, either in the heading or in the signature. Almost all of them commence with a heading similar to the following:

EXAMPLE 1.
   Present:
      HONORABLE DAVID M. WILSON,
                        Justice.
EXAMPLE 2.
   Present:
      HONORABLE MARGARET R. MADISON,
            United States Dictrict Judge.

See page 342, *et seq.* for an explanation of orders and decrees; see figures 14.21, 14.22, and 14.23 for approved styles of setting them up.

It is also important for you to know whether a member of a court is a judge or a justice when writing and speaking to or about him or her. Part 5, Forms of Address, gives the correct forms of address, salutation, and complimentary close in letters to judges, justices, and clerks of courts, and also the correct form for referring to them in a letter and the correct form to use in speaking to or informally introducing them.

12.14. The trial lawyer. As with many professions, the legal profession is becoming increasingly specialized. In some countries, notably England, the legal profession is divided into two distinct categories: *barristers,* who actually try cases in court, and *solicitors,* who attend to other legal matters for their clients. In this country, we have no such formal separation. However, many lawyers do no trial work whatsoever, and others engage in litigation almost exclusively. Trial lawyers may further specialize in criminal or civil cases.

The secretary and paralegal who work with the trial lawyer may have closer contacts with the court than do those who work with attorneys who do not engage in active litigation. Whether the trial lawyer is involved chiefly in civil or criminal cases, the paralegal in particular may be involved in factual investigation, interviewing of witnesses, and preparation of certain documents for trial. The secretary to a trial lawyer will be required to keep track of the status of the case, at every stage, and to help the lawyer prepare for trial in whatever way the attorney directs.

12.15. Clerk of the Court. The secretary's and paralegal's contact with the court is chiefly through the *clerk*. Almost all correspondence is addressed to him or her (see the chart in Part 5 for the correct form of addressing clerks of courts); the clerk answers inquiries, written or telephoned, about pending court cases, court rules, the calendar, and any other matters pertaining to his or her office. The clerk of a court and the personnel in the clerk's office can be of considerable help to the lawyer's secretary and paralegal. It is frequently necessary to look up something in the records of the clerk's office or to telephone for information regarding a case. It behooves both secretary and paralegal to maintain cordial relations with the personnel in the clerk's office at all times.

Although the systems of keeping records in clerk's offices vary in detail because of statutory requirements and custom, they are fundamentally the same. A brief explanation of how these records are kept will contribute to the ability of all law-office personnel to deal effectively with the clerk's office.

12.16. Clerk's index system. The clerk receives all court papers—complaints, answers, amendments, motions, appearances, and the like. As soon as the summons and complaint, or other first pleading, is filed, the clerk assigns an *index number,* also called a *docket number* and an *action number,* to the case. The numbers are consecutive. In some courts, an initial is used to indicate the court in which the case is filed. For example, *S* for Superior, *C* for Circuit, *P* for Probate. In courts that have separate law and equity divisions, the letter *L* or the letter *E* will be a part of the index number. In some courts, the successive numbering of cases starts over at the beginning of each year, and the number includes the year. Thus, the index number might read 80S-1328, or 1328/80, or 1328-1980, indicating that the case was filed in 1980. When a clerk uses this system of numbering, the year is as important as any part of the number. The clerk keeps a cross-index of the cases, arranged alphabetically according to the name of the plaintiff, and, also, in some courts, a cross-index arranged according to the name of the defendant.

How to use the index number. 1. If you file the first pleading, get the index number from the clerk of the court or from the clerk's records so you may enter it in your office file. If an attorney in your office files the paper, he or she should get the number and give it to you. Ask for it. To find an index number in the clerk's records, look in the plaintiff's index under his or her name. You should procure the index number as soon as possible after it is assigned to a case.

2. After an index number is assigned to a case, you *must* type that number on all papers thereafter prepared in the case in that court. Before filing a paper or giving it to an attorney to file, check to see that the proper index number is endorsed on it, both on the paper itself and on the backing.

3. You must have the index number in order to get information about the status of a case.

12.17. Clerk's permanent record book. The permanent record book kept by the clerk of the court is usually called the *docket* or the *register*. It contains a record of all legal papers filed in the suit. The cases are entered consecutively according to index number, a case to a page. The clerk enters on the docket sheet the index number, the title of the case, the names and addresses of the attorneys, and the date the summons was served. He or she also enters on the docket sheet all subsequent proceedings.

How to use the register. Although the lawyer keeps his or her own record of the information in the clerk's register, it is sometimes necessary to consult the register to check on dates that papers were filed by opposing counsel. Besides, an attorney is frequently interested in the developments in a case in which he or she is not representing any of the litigants. The lawyer is usually interested in knowing the status of cases immediately preceding his or hers on the court calendar, to judge when his or her case will be reached.

If you want information on any case in court, look in the alphabetical index under the plaintiff's name and get the index number, unless you already have the number. Then turn to that page number in the docket and read the entries made there. If you want to read the original papers on file, give the clerk the index number and ask him or her to get them for you.

12.18. Clerk's minute books. The clerk enters abstracts of all court orders in a *minute book,* numerically according to index number. He or she might have separate books for law, chancery, divorce, and the like.

How to use the minute book. If you want any information about the court's orders in a case, you can get it by consulting the minute book. You must have the index number. Usually the clerk's office will give you the information over the telephone.

12.19. Court calendar and calendar number. The *court calendar* is a list of cases that are ready to be brought to the attention of the court. When Notice of Trial, or Note of Issue, is filed (see page 313), the clerk of the court assigns the case a *calendar number* and places it on the general court calendar. Successive numbers are given to successive cases. The purpose of the calendar number is to have the case come up for trial in its turn. Do not confuse it with the index number, which will continue to appear on papers prepared for the case. After the clerk gives a case a calendar number, it must await its turn to be called for trial in numerical order. From the cases on the general calendar, the clerk prepares a list of cases for the judge to try each day, or as fast as he or she can get to them. The cases on the list are "called" before the court on a certain date.

12.20. Calendar call. The list of cases to be called before the court is referred to as the *daily call* in courts where cases are called daily, and as the *weekly call* in courts where cases are called weekly. The lists may be published in the local law journal, so the lawyers will know when their cases are to be called before the court. Otherwise lists may be distributed to law offices by the clerk's office. Both sides are supposed to be in court when the case is called. If the plaintiff responds and the defendant does not appear, there will be a judgment or decree by default. If the defendant is ready and the plaintiff does not appear, the case will be dismissed for want of prosecution (DWP).

Answering the calendar call. In some offices the secretary or paralegal answers the calendar call to save the lawyer's time. The cases will be called by calendar number and by title. When your case is called, answer "Ready"; or when the lawyer is trying a case in another court, "Ready subject to engagement." Then explain to the court that the lawyer is trying a case in another court but will be available at a later hour. The lawyer will not send you to answer the calendar call if he or she is not ready and must ask for an adjournment. If the case has been settled out of court, you will answer, "Settled."

After all the cases on the list are called, they are called for trial, in turn. There is no need for the lawyer to sit through the trial of other cases. You, or whoever is answering the call for the lawyer, will wait in the courtroom until a reasonable time before the lawyer's case is about to be reached for trial, and then telephone him or her to come to court to try the case.

12.21. Term of court. The designated period prescribed by law during which a court may sit to transact business is known as a *term of court* or *term time.* The periods during the term when the court actually sits are known as *sessions.* The terms are usually designated by the time they commence, for example, *November term.* A term of court is also referred to in various jurisdictions as *general term* or *trial term,* meaning the term during which cases are tried.

12.22. How to keep a progress record of court matters. In every law office a record is kept of the progress of all matters pending in court, whether the matter is a litigated case, a foreclosure, an estate administration proceeding, or a special proceeding. This record saves time that would be required to examine all of the papers in the file. A quick examination of the record shows the status of the matter. Also, just before term time the lawyer can examine quickly the records of all pending cases as a double check on things to be done. The record is variously called a *suit register,* a *register of actions,* or a *docket,* but the objectives and procedure are the same. The following sections explain the procedure for keeping this record and refer to it, for convenience, as the suit register.

12.23. Physical features of a suit register. The progress record of an action is typed or written on forms designed for the purpose or on plain paper. The form or sheet used depends on where the records are kept. The records are commonly kept in (1) a loose-leaf binder, (2) the file folder, or (3) a portable tray or cabinet.

12.24. Loose-leaf binder for the suit register. Either an ordinary three-ring, letter-size binder or a post binder may be used for keeping the suit register. If the record is typed, the former is probably more expedient because the sheets are more easily removed for the purpose of typing the entries. Numerous types of forms for keeping the record are printed by various office supply houses and are on sale at local stationers. These forms are usually designed to fit a special loose-leaf binder, also manufactured by the supply house. Printed forms are not necessary, unless a special binder is used. In an ordinary loose-leaf binder, punched paper of durable quality, with reinfored edges, is adequate.

12.25. File folder used for progress record. Some offices keep progress records in the file folder, either by writing the entries on the folder itself or by typing them on a sheet placed in the front of the folder. If the record is kept on a loose sheet, a colored sheet is desirable because it is more easily distinguished from the other papers in the folder. Figure 12.1 illustrates a sheet appropriate for this purpose.

12.26. Portable tray or cabinet for the suit register. A portable cabinet or tray with a visible index is probably the least expensive facility for keeping the record. The cabinet is fireproof and has a lid that may be locked when the record is not being used. The visible index shows the name of the case, the attorney handling it, and the court index number. Celluloid tabs may be used to flag specific cases. The manufacturer of the cabinet or tray also makes available strips for the index and sheets for typing the record. The sheets are designed for numerous uses and have no printing on them except a ruled space at the left for the dates. They are of heavy stock paper and come in various sizes. Unless a wide carriage machine is available for typing the record, the sheets should be small enough to fit the carriage of a standard machine. The sheets are loose in the pocket provided for them and thus are easily removed for typing entries or for reference. The portable cabinets hold a large number of cases and, therefore, are not appropriate for offices with a light docket.

12.27. How to file the record sheets. The preferred method of filing the record sheets is alphabetically according to the first-named plaintiff, or the decedent in the case of an estate, or the principal

COURT_____

DOCKET NO._____

HALL and DOBB
10 SLATE STREET
BOSTON, MASS. 02178

OFFICE NAME_____

OUR FILE NO._____

SERVICES

VS.

ATTACHMENTS

DATE OF WRIT_____

RESPONSIBLE ATTY_____

ATTY. TO BE NOTIFIED_____

PLAINTIFFS ATTY._____

DEFENDENT ATTY._____

TRUSTEE ATTY._____

RETURN DAY_____

FORM OF ACTION_____

AD DAMNUM_____

NATURE OF CASE_____

COPY WITHIN	DATE FILED	DESCRIPTION	TRIAL LIST

Figure 12.1. *Progress Record Sheet.*

corporation or individual named in a special proceeding. In offices with a heavy docket, the estates and special proceedings might be segregated from the litigated cases. Some offices with extremely heavy dockets separate the records according to the court in which the case is pending. When a visible index is used, celluloid tabs of various colors can designate specific courts to permit quick selection of cases pending in a particular court.

12.28. When and how to open a case in the suit register. A suit register sheet is not opened on every matter in the office—only on court matters. Therefore, the record is opened when the first paper is filed in court or when a paper is served on your office, indicating that the case is pending in court. In opening the record, enter on the sheet (1) the court in which the action is pending; (2) the full title of the case, as it appears on the summons and complaint or other first paper filed; (3) nature of the proceeding, that is, "Suit on note," "Divorce," "Petition for letters of administration," and the like, as indicated by the new matter slip (page 37); (4) amount, if any, used for; (5) names, addresses, and telephone numbers of all opposing counsel; (6) name of the attorney in your office who is handling the matter; (7) court index number as soon as available; (8) calendar number, as soon as available.

All of the above information is put at the top of the record sheet. The entries follow, and each entry is dated at the left side of the sheet. Figure 12.2 illustrates a suit register record.

12.29. What to enter. Some offices record only court papers and orders in the suit register. The office record is then actually a duplicate of the court docket kept by the clerk of the court; hence, the name "office docket." Many offices enter all written, formal steps in connection with an action. It is often a matter of practice and judgment as to what to enter. Obviously, you would not enter, "Received phone call from plaintiff's attorney asking when we thought case would be reached; told him we had no definite estimate." That does not affect the progress of the case. But, also obviously, you would enter, "Served notice of trial for October 19.. Term," just as soon as the notice of trial was served on the opposing counsel. The best rule is to use your own judgment as to what actually affects the progress of the action and to enter too much rather than too little. If you are in doubt as to the advisability of making an entry, ask the lawyer in charge.

12.30. Form and sufficiency of record. In making entries in the suit register give complete information. Describe the matter entered with particularity, but not in great detail. Observance of the following directions will help you make complete and accurate entries:

1. Date all entries.
2. Avoid abbreviations.
3. When an action is commenced by the service of a summons only, open the record sheet immediately; but you cannot enter the nature and substance of the action until the complaint is received. Enter this information opposite the title as soon as the complaint is received.
4. When an answer or notice of appearance is served on your office,

SUPREME COURT—NEW YORK COUNTY

                     INDEX NO. 19000-19—

ATLANTIC CORPORATION,

           Plaintiff,

        -against-

JACKSON MILLS CORPORATION,

           Defendant.

- - - - - - - - - - - - - - - - - - - x

ACTION FOR $250,000 FOR BREACH OF CONTRACT FOR FAILURE TO COMPLETE DELIVERY OF JEEPS AND TRUCKS PURSUANT TO TERMS OF WRITTEN AGREEMENT DATED MAY 26, 19—.

John Barnes, Esq.,
Attorney for Plaintiff,
211 E/W 75th Street
New York, N.Y. 10019

Baker & Bookman,
Attorneys for Defendant
Partner in Charge: Mr. Hill
Principal Assistant: Ms. Jones

19—		
July	13	Summons and verified complaint served on defendant.
August	1	Obtained stipulation extending defendant's time to answer or move with respect to complaint to and including August 21, 19—.
	21	Served verified answer to complaint on attorney for plaintiff and obtained "copy received."
	21	Served demand for a verified bill of particulars.
	31	Signed stipulation extending plaintiff's time to serve on a verified bill of particulars to and including September 20, 19—.
Sept.	19	Gave "copy received" on plaintiff's verified bill of particulars.
	20	Served note of issue noticing this case for trial for the October 19— Term to be tried by Court with a jury on attorney for plaintiff and obtained "copy received"; filed original with County Clerk of New York County and obtained Index No. 19000-19—; filed copy with Trial Term Calendar Clerk, and obtained Jury Contract Calendar No. 17000.
Oct.	6	Ms. Jones attended on call of Contract Jury Reserve Calendar and this case was adjourned by consent to the Reserve Calendar of the Contract Jury Calendar for the November 19— Term.
Nov.	10	Ms. Jones attended on call of Contract Jury Reserve Calendar and this case was adjourned by consent to the Reserve Calendar of the Contract Jury Calendar for the February 19— Term.

(continued)

(continued)

19—

Feb.	9	Mr. Barnes attended on call of Contract Jury Reserve Calendar and requested the Court to set this case down for a day certain because two important witnesses must come from Japan; the Court marked this case for the head of the Ready Day Calendar for trial on March 5, 19—.
March	5	Mr. Barnes attended on call of Day Calendar and this case was assigned to Mr. Justice Carter, at Trial Term, Part X.
	5	Mr. Barnes reports that a jury was picked and the trial commenced at 2:00 P.M. and is to continue on March 6, 19– at 10:00 A.M.
	6	Mr. Barnes reports that the trial went on all day and is to continue on March 7, 19–.
	7	Mr. Barnes reports that plaintiff rested, Court reserved decision on motions to dismiss and defendant's case was commenced to be continued on March 8, 19–.
	8	Mr. Barnes reports that defendant rested, the usual motions for a directed verdict were made and decision reserved, both sides summed up to the jury and the Court is to charge the jury on March 9, 19– at 10:00 A.M.
	9	Mr. Barnes reports that after the Court's charge, the jury retired, and after four hours deliberation returned a verdict in favor of defendant, the Court denied plaintiff's motions to set the verdict aside and for a new trial, etc.
April	12	Entered judgment dismissing plaintiff's complaint with costs as taxed in the sum of $145.00.
	12	Served judgment with notice of entry and copy of bill of costs as taxed on attorney for plaintiff and obtained "copy received."
	17	Plaintiff paid judgment for costs as taxed amounting to $145.00 and we filed a satisfaction of said judgment.

Figure 12.2. *Suit Register Record.*

enter the name of the attorney, his address and telephone number, and the party he represents.

5. As soon as you know the court index number, enter it opposite the title. Also enter it on the index tab if you keep a record that has a visible index.

As a condition precedent to proper filing, the court index or docket number must be placed on every paper that is filed. The individual who files the paper on behalf of your office must get the index number from the clerk of the court or from his docket and give it to you so that you can enter it on the record. Make a practice of checking the suit register weekly for any missing index numbers.

6. Keep the entries opposite the title up to date, including index number, substitutions of attorneys, changes of addresses, office file number, and the like.

7. In describing petitions, orders, and stipulations, enter a notation as to when they are verified, signed, entered, or dated, respectively, and by whom.

8. When entering stipulations, enter, "Obtained stipulation..." if your office is granted something by it; enter "Signed stipulation..." if your office gives a right. For example, if your office represented the plaintiff, the entry of the stipulation illustrated in figure 14.10 would be:

Signed stipulation with Fenton & Jacobs, dated September 25, 19. , extending time of Creative Classics, Inc. to answer to October 13, 19...

If your office represented Creative Classics, Inc., the entry would read:

Obtained stipulation from Richards & Russell, dated September 23, 19.., extending time to answer to October 13, 19...

Some stipulations, for example a stipulation of discontinuance, are both "obtained" and "signed."

9. Enter the name of the attorney from your office who attends motions, calls of calendar at trials, hearings, arguments of appeals, and the like, and the disposition of the respective matters.

10. Enclose in quotation marks any entry from a law journal or similar publication with a reference to the date and page of the publication, because the date of the event is often different from the date upon which the event is announced in the publication.

11. When cases are settled out of court, enter the amounts paid, dates of payment, data concerning exchange of general releases, if any, and the like.

12. When judgment is entered, enter the amount of the judgment, the amount of costs, and payment received, if any.

13. Examine the diary (chapter 3) each day for the day just past, to be certain that a report and entry has been made for everything listed there.

12.31. Closing the record of a case. Do not close the record of a case in the suit register until you are reasonably certain that no further steps, such as appeal, collecting on a judgment, moving to vacate a judgment, recording a satisfaction, levying execution, and the like, are to be taken by either party. The time to appeal should always have elapsed before the case is closed.

Domestic relations cases where child custody, support, or alimony are involved are subject to being reopened for a considerable period— until the youngest child reaches majority in a matter of custody and support, or whenever there is a significant change in the circumstances of either party in any case.

As soon as a case is closed, remove the sheet on that case from the record file and place it in the designated place. This might be another loose-leaf book or a file cabinet. File the sheets alphabetically according to the first-name plaintiff, or the decedent in the case of an estate, or the principal corporation or individual named in a special proceeding. The closed sheets are kept indefinitely; some law offices have them bound from time to time.

13

Handling Court Papers

Pleadings and supporting papers, such as affidavits and bills of particulars, are commonly called *court papers* or *litigation papers,* as distinguished from the legal documents or instruments described in chapter 9. Court rules require that they be set up in a particular style.

An understanding of the various parties that may become involved in a legal action, and their designations, is essential to the preparation of a court paper. An explanation concerning the parties, therefore, is given first in this chapter. General instructions applicable to the preparation of all court papers follow. Detailed instructions for the preparation of specific papers are given in subsequent chapters.

PARTIES TO AN ACTION

13.1. Party bringing or defending a law suit. The party who brings a law suit—the one who has a cause of action—is the *plaintiff*. He or she is the one who complains. In some states, the party bringing the action is called the *complainant* when the suit is an action in equity. In most states, especially those whose rules of procedure follow the model of the federal rules, the party who brings an action in equity is no longer called the complainant, but is known as the plaintiff, just as in actions at law.

The party against whom suit is brought is the *defendant*.

13.2. Parties to a cross action. In some cases, defendant's interest cannot be defended properly by answering the plaintiff's complaint or by a counterclaim (see 567). For example, an airline and an airplane manufacturer were co-defendants in a wrongful death action. The complaint alleged that the plane was improperly designed and was not safe for its intended use. The airline claimed that if defective and hazardous conditions existed in the plane, they were caused by the failure of the airplane manufacturer to keep his guarantee that the plane would be free from defect in design.[1]

Under these circumstances, in almost all states the defendant (airline here) is permitted to *implead* the third party who becomes a third-party defendant. The party who is impled (airline manufacturer here) is the third-party defendant.

13.3 Party intervening. A law suit sometimes adversely affects a third party who is not a party to the litigation. If the Court permits, that person may become a party to the action by filing a *complaint in intervention,* and is called an *intervenor,* or in some states, the *third-party plaintiff.* For example, while negotiations for a contract were in progress, the employee who was negotiating the contract as agent for his employer suddenly quit the employer and closed the contract in his own behalf. The former employee later sued to enforce the contract. His former employer claimed that the former employee was his agent and was permitted to intervene to assert his interest in the contract. He became a party to the action as an *intervenor.*[2]

13.4. Parties on appeal. The party who loses a law suit or is dissatisfied with a judgment or court order may appeal to a higher court. See chapter 15 for designation of parties on appeal.

13.5. Amicus curiae. An *amicus curiae* (Latin for "friend of the court") is not strictly speaking a party to the law suit. He or she is a person who has no inherent right to appear in the suit but is allowed to participate to protect his or her own interests. Leave to file a brief as *amicus curiae* is frequently granted to a lawyer who has another case that will be affected by the decision of the Court in the pending case. An *amicus curiae* might also volunteer information for the benefit of the judge. For example, in adoption proceedings the guardian of a child might seek permission to appear as *amicus* for the purpose of presenting evidence about which the Court should be informed and that might lead the Court to refuse the order of adoption.

---

[1] Blue et al. v. United Air Lines, Inc. et al., 98 N.Y.S. (2d) 272.
[2] Patterson v. Pollock, et al., 84 N.E. (2d) 606.

13.6. Who may be parties to a law suit. A party to a law suit may be an individual, a partnership, a corporation, or an association.

Minors and incompetents. An individual ordinarily sues on his or her own behalf, but minors (frequently referred to as infants) and incompetents (persons of unsound mind or habitual drunkards) are legally incapable of bringing a legal action. If the minor or incompetent has a legally appointed guardian, the suit is often brought by the guardian. Otherwise, depending upon the state, a suit is brought on behalf of a minor or incompetent by his or her "next friend," or by a guardian *ad litem* appointed by the Court for the special purpose of the litigation. The fact that the plaintiff sues by his guardian or next friend is indicated in the caption of the case and is alleged in the pleadings. If a minor or an incompetent is defendant in a suit, he or she answers by a guardian *ad litem* or next friend. In Louisiana a minor is represented by a *Tutor*, and a mentally incompetent person, by a *Curator*.[3]

The expressions commonly used follow:

WILLIAM HENDRICKS, a minor, suing by his
father and next friend, ARNOLD HENDRICKS

JAMES LEWIS, guardian ad litem of
WILLIAM HENDRICKS, an incompetent

JILL NEWTON, by her next friend
LLOYD T. CRAFT

JEFFREY CROSS, by FRANCIS ADLER,
guardian by appointment of Orphans' Court of
Baltimore City

Executors, administrators, trustees. Often a plaintiff has a cause of action, not for a wrong against him in his individual capacity, but for a wrong against him in his representative capacity as executor, administrator, or trustee. The action is then brought by the plaintiff in that capacity. The capacity in which the action is brought is indicated in the caption and is stated in the introductory sentence of the pleadings. An executor (executrix, if a woman) sues "as executor of the last will and testament of Lynda Smith, deceased." An administrator (administratrix if a woman) sues "as trustee under will of Lynda Smith," or "as trustee under trust created by Lynda Smith." Actions are also brought against, and defended by, executors, administrators, and trustees of estates and trusts.

Husband and wife. In some actions if a married person sues, the spouse joins in the complaint. The caption indicates, and the first paragraph of the pleading declares, the relationship. If the husband has the cause of action, the suit is brought by John Rogers and Mary Rogers, his wife; if the wife has the cause of action, the suit is brought by Mary Rogers and John Rogers, her husband. The same practice is followed when a married person is sued. In the caption of all pleadings, except the complaint, and in the endorsements on the back of a court paper (page 292), the Latin phrase *ex uxor,* or *et ux.,* may be substituted for "and Mary Rogers, his wife"; *et vir* may be substituted for "and John Rogers, her husband."

Partnerships. When a party to an action is a partnership, that fact is indicated in the caption and declared in the first paragraph of the pleading.

Expressions similar to the following are used in the caption.

ADAM JACKSON and DAVID HAMMOND,
doing business as a partnership
under the name of JACKSON and HAMMOND,

KENNETH AVERY and DONALD PLANTE, d/b/a
AVERY & PLANTE, a partnership

MERVIN CARSON and ANDREW BOWKER, individually
and as co-partners doing business under
the firm name and style of BOWKER'S

The stock statement in the pleading is "... Henry Daniels and Joseph Farnsworth are now, and at all times mentioned were, co-partners, doing business under the fictitious firm name and style of Daniels-Farnsworth Company, a co-partnership, and have filed the certificate and published the notice as required by ... *(insert code or statute section).* ..."

Corporations. When a litigant is a corporation, its corporate existence is alleged in the first paragraph of the complaint. The wording of the allegation depends upon whether the corporation is a domestic corporation, that is, incorporated in the state where suit is brought, or a foreign corporation, that is, incorporated in a state other than that in which suit is brought.

In some states, a party's corporate existence is also indicated in the caption, as follows:

Domestic corporation
> WESTERN LOAN COMPANY, INC., a domestic
> corporation,

Foreign corporation
> WESTERN LOAN COMPANY, a corporation organized
> and existing under and by virtue of the laws of the State
> of _____.

VERIFICATIONS

13.7. What is a verification? A *verification* is a sworn statement by a qualified person that the allegations contained in a pleading are true. The statutes require that many pleadings and supporting papers be verified, and some law firms follow the practice of verifying all pleadings whether or not the statute requires it. The litigation papers commonly verified are:

Complaints
Answers
Petitions
Bills of particulars

If the complaint is verified, the answer *must* be verified.

A verification always recites the venue and always has a jurat, or "sworn to" clause. One of the duties of a notary public is to administer the oath to a person verifying a pleading. (See page 280 for directions about administering the oath.) The verification is usually written on a separate page, but you may type it on the last page of the pleading, or at least begin it on the last page, if you wish. No rule of law or court governs. Some legal backs have verifications printed on the inside, but the verifications are generally typed.

13.8. Who may verify a pleading? Generally the verification is by a party to the action, but under some conditions an agent or the attorney for a party to an action may verify a pleading. The attorney will tell you who is going to verify the pleading.

13.9. Forms of verification. There is a special form of verification appropriate for each capacity in which the person verifying the pleading (called the *deponent* or the *affiant*) might make a verification. Figures 13.1, 13.2, 13.3, and 13.4 illustrate verifications by an individual, an officer of a domestic corporation, an officer of a foreign corporation, and an attorney for a party to the action. They are included here to give you an understanding of the general content of a verification and to show you

```
STATE OF INDIANA )
                 : ss.
COUNTY OF KNOX   )


        ALBERT F. MAXWELL, being duly sworn, deposes and says: That he
is one of the defendants herein; that he has read the foregoing answer and
knows the contents thereof, and that the same is true of his own knowledge,
except as to the matters therein stated to be alleged upon information and
belief, and as to those matters he believes it to be true.


                                    _____  _____


Sworn to before me this
  21st day of June, 19--.



 _____
```

Figure 13.1. *Verification of Answer by Individual.*

how one should be set up. Use them as a pattern for making forms of verifications for your loose-leaf notebook of forms, but get a lawyer in your office to approve the wording of them or to dictate the forms he or she wants you to use. You will notice that if an agent or attorney verifies, he or she states, in addition to the allegation ordinarily used:

1. The grounds of the agent's or attorney's belief as to all matters not stated upon his or her knowledge.

2. Why the verification is not made by the party to the action.

The last two paragraphs of a verification by an attorney or an agent change with the facts, but otherwise the wording of the verifications as indicated in these illustrations remains practically the same in every action.

The venue of the verification depends, of course, on where the verification is made.

13.10. How to type a verification. Observe the following points with reference to the typing of verifications:

1. Although many typists leave no space between the longest line of

```
STATE OF MAINE      )
                    :  SS.
COUNTY OF OXFORD )


         LEONA J. CROWLEY, being duly sworn, deposes and says: That she is

the treasurer of Taylor & Benson, Inc., the plaintiff in the above entitled

action; that she has read the foregoing complaint and knows the contents

thereof; that the same is true of her own knowledge, except as to matters

therein stated to be alleged upon information and belief, and as to those

matters she believes it to be true.



                                        _____




Given under my hand and seal this

         day of September, 19--.



_____
         Notary Public
My commission expires
```

Figure 13.2. *Verification of Complaint by Officer of Domestic Corporation.*

typing and the bracketing of the venue, its appearance can be improved by leaving one or two spaces.

2. The abbreviation for scilicet (SS) may be lowercase or in caps, followed by a period or by a period and a colon.

3. There are three single spaces between the venue and the body of the verification.

4. The name of the deponent is in solid caps.

5. There are three spaces between lines of signature and the jurat, which is at the left of the page.

In figure 13.3, the month in the jurat, as well as the day of the month, is filled in by the notary. Whenever you prepare a paper for signature near the end of the month and are not certain that it will be signed before that month expires, leave the month blank, so it will not have to be changed if the verification is not sworn to until the following month.

STATE OF MARYLAND)
                   : SS.
COUNTY OF CHARLES)

     EDGAR O. BRECKENRIDGE, being duly sworn, deposes and says:

That he is a vice-president of Ferris Manufacturing Company, Inc., the

defendant in the above entitled action; that he has read the foregoing answer

and knows the contents thereof; that the same is true to his own knowledge,

except as to the matters therein stated to be alleged on information and

belief, and that as to those matters he believes it to be true.

     That this verification is made by deponent and not by defendant

because defendant is a foreign corporation organized under the laws of the

State of Delaware and deponent is an officer thereof, to wit: a vice-president;

that the sources of deponent's knowledge and the grounds of his belief as to

all matters therein alleged upon information and belief consist of _____

_____

_____

                                  _____

Sworn to before me this

    day of   , 19--.

_____

My commission expires

Figure 13.3. *Verification of Answer by Officer of Foreign Corporation.*

    13.11. How to administer the oath to person verifying a pleading. Unlike an acknowledgment of the execution of a legal instrument (chapter 9), the verification of a pleading must be sworn to. If you are a notary in a law office, it will be your duty to administer the oath to the person verifying the pleading. The proper procedure is to stand and raise your right hand and ask the verifier to do the same. Then administer the oath in the following, or similar, words: "Do you solemnly swear that the contents of the foregoing instrument subscribed by you are the truth, the whole truth, and nothing but the truth, so help you God?" The verifier should answer, "Yes" or "I do."

STATE OF KANSAS)
: ss.
COUNTY OF BARTON)

      WAYNE B. BOVEY, being duly sworn, deposes and says: I am an attorney at law and a member of the firm of Castle & Yale, attorneys for the plaintiff in the above entitled action. I have read the foregoing complaint and know the contents thereof and the same is true of my own knowledge except as to the matters therein alleged to be upon information and belief, and as to those matters I believe it to be true.

      This verification is made by deponent and not by plaintiff because plaintiff is a foreign corporation and none of its officers are within the City of Great Bend and County of Barton where I reside and have my offices for the transaction of business.

      The sources of my information and the grounds of my belief as to all matters in said complaint stated to be alleged upon information and belief are correspondence with persons representing plaintiff and an examination of a file with reference to this account.

      Subscribed and sworn to before me this   day of

    , 19--.

                         Notary Public

My commission expires

Figure 13.4. *Verification of Complaint by Attorney for Plaintiff.*

    If the verifier's religion forbids him or her to swear, use the word *affirm* instead of swear. The word *affirmed* should also be substituted for *sworn to* in the jurat.

    You will notice from the preceding illustrations of verifications that, again unlike acknowledgments (chapter 9), the verifier signs the verification as well as the instrument that precedes it. The jurat follows the verifier's signature. You, as notary public, will sign the jurat and affix your notary seal and show date your commission expires, if required in your state. (See part 5, Notaries Public.)

HOW TO TYPE COURT PAPERS

13.12. Paper. Pleadings and supporting papers, except those for which printed law blanks are used, may be typed on legal-size or regular 8½″ by 11″ paper, depending on the preference of the court. The clerk of court will indicate his or her preference in this matter. Paper size may differ from one court to another within a given state. However, the trend is toward 8½″ by 11″ size paper, with or without ruled margins.

13.13. Heading or caption. All court papers have a heading, or caption, which is written on every separate document, although several documents might be bound together. The caption consists of the following parts:

1. *Jurisdiction and venue.* Usually the *jurisdiction*, that is, the name of the court in which the case is brought, and the venue are recited together in phraseology similar to this:

IN THE DISTRICT COURT WITHIN AND FOR
CLARK COUNTY, STATE OF WASHINGTON
or
IN THE DISTRICT COURT OF ALBANY COUNTY
WYOMING

In a few states the venue is recited separately from the jurisdiction, thus:

```
STATE OF ILLINOIS )
                  : SS        IN THE CIRCUIT COURT
COUNTY OF COOK   )                 THEREOF
```

2. *The title of the case.* This gives the names and designation of the various parties to the action (page 273). The heading that appears on the summons and complaint is used throughout the action until it is appealed, unless (1) there should be a change of parties by amendment, or (2) there is more than one plaintiff or defendant. In the latter case, it is necessary to show only the first-named plaintiff and the first-named defendant, followed by appropriate words indicating that there are others, such as *et al., et ux., et vir.*

3. *The index number.* The index, docket, or action number is assigned by the clerk of the court (see page 262). Although it is not known at the time the first paper is filed in court, it must be included on all later papers.

4. *Title of the pleading.* Each litigation paper has a designation or title, such as Petition, Complaint, Notice of Trial, and the like. The common practice is to include the title in the heading or just beneath it. All offices do not follow this practice.

13.14. How to type the caption. Court rules specify the information that goes into the caption, but only a few courts regulate the style in which the caption must be typed. Twenty styles of captions are show in figure 13.5. One of them, perhaps with a slight variation, is appropriate for your office. Ask the lawyer to designate the one he or she wants you to follow. After the appropriate style has been indicated:

1. Note carefully the capitalization, punctuation, alignment, and spacing.

2. Notice the placement of each part of the caption with reference to the other parts. For example, in Style 5, the title of the document follows

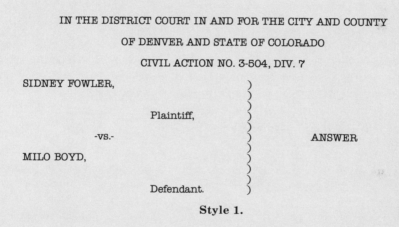

IN THE DISTRICT COURT IN AND FOR THE CITY AND COUNTY

OF DENVER AND STATE OF COLORADO

CIVIL ACTION NO. 3-504, DIV. 7

SIDNEY FOWLER,

Plaintiff,

-vs.- ANSWER

MILO BOYD,

Defendant.

Style 1.

IN THE SUPERIOR COURT OF THE STATE OF WASHINGTON
FOR KING COUNTY

EDNA WILLOW,

Plaintiff,

vs. No. 5786

CARL JONES, DEMURRER TO COMPLAINT

Defendant.

Style 2.

IN THE DISTRICT COURT OF THE STATE OF IOWA
IN AND FOR POLK COUNTY

ALAN STERLING,

                Plaintiff,   )
) No. _____

         vs.   )
MORRIS ALTURA,   )   PETITION
)

              Defendant.)

Style 3.

IN THE CIRCUIT COURT OF THE FIRST JUDICIAL DISTRICT

OF HINDS COUNTY, MISSISSIPPI

ELYDIA LYONS   PLAINTIFF)

      vs.   ) NO. _____

JEANNE CASS   DEFENDANT)

Style 4.

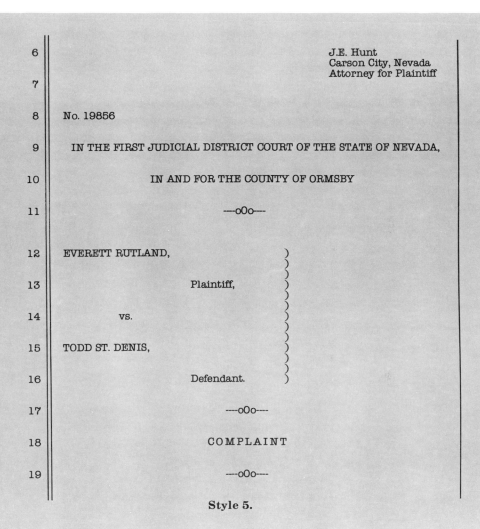

6	J.E. Hunt Carson City, Nevada Attorney for Plaintiff
7	
8	No. 19856
9	IN THE FIRST JUDICIAL DISTRICT COURT OF THE STATE OF NEVADA,
10	IN AND FOR THE COUNTY OF ORMSBY
11	---oOo---
12	EVERETT RUTLAND,)
13	Plaintiff,)
14	vs.)
15	TODD ST. DENIS,)
16	Defendant.)
17	----oOo----
18	COMPLAINT
19	----oOo----

Style 5.

JACKSON and HILL
ATTORNEYS AT LAW
108 West Avenue
WICHITA, KANSAS 67203

IN THE DISTRICT COURT OF SEDGWICK COUNTY,
KANSAS

STERLING J. MASON,			
Plaintiff	)		
	)		
vs.	)	No. _____	
	)		
SYLVIA IOSCO,	)	Div. No. _____	
Defendant	)		

Style 6.

NO. 3456

KEITH ORLEANS   :   SUPERIOR COURT

v.   :   COUNTY OF HARTFORD

RUSSELL DANVERS   :   APRIL   19--

Style 7.

STATE OF WISCONSIN   :   CIRCUIT COURT   :   MILWAUKEE COUNTY

OTTO F. NORTHUP,

                    Plaintiff

            vs.   COMPLAINT

JULIA ROCKWOOD,

                    Defendant.

Style 8.

IN THE CIRCUIT COURT, FOURTH
JUDICIAL CIRCUIT OF FLORIDA,
IN AND FOR DUVAL COUNTY.

---x

MERRILL PENDLETON,

                         Plaintiff,   NO. 3456

                                         ANSWER

        vs.

GRADY WALKER,

                         Defendant.

---x

Style 9.

IN THE DISTRICT COURT OF THE THIRD JUDICIAL DISTRICT OF THE

STATE OF IDAHO, IN AND FOR THE COUNTY OF ADA

---x

MARGOT SHIPLEY,

                         Plaintiff: No. _____

            -vs.-   COMPLAINT

SUZANNE ELKRIDGE,

                         Defendant.

---x

Style 10.

CIVIL DISTRICT COURT FOR THE PARISH OF ORLEANS

STATE OF LOUISIANA

No. . . . .   DIVISION . . . .   DOCKET . . . .

LOIS EASTON

VS.

ROBERT BLAINE COMPANY

TO THE HONORABLE, THE JUDGES OF THE CIVIL DISTRICT COURT FOR THE
PARISH OF ORLEANS, STATE OF LOUISIANA:

FILED: _____   _____
                                                          DEPUTY CLERK

Style 11.

THE STATE OF NEW HAMPSHIRE

Hillsborough, SS.   January Ten, 1978
Superior Court

_____

NATIONAL BANK AND TRUST	v.	COMMERCIAL BANK, JANE

NATIONAL BANK AND TRUST   v.   COMMERCIAL BANK, JANE
COMPANY, PAUL S. COLOGNE,   AMBOY, and LESTER
and HORACE NEWBERRY,   AMBOY
Executors of the Estate
of FREDERICK NEWBERRY,
deceased

_____

MOTION TO AMEND DECLARATION

Style 12.

PULASKI CIRCUIT COURT

JULES BRYON .... Plaintiff,

- vs. -   No. _____

EDWIN DEALE, ... Defendant.

COMPLAINT AT LAW

Style 13.

FRANKLIN CIRCUIT COURT

WALDO KNOX   PLAINTIFF

VS.   PETITION

MARTHA BINGHAM   DEFENDANT

Style 14.

SUPREME COURT OF THE STATE OF NEW YORK

COUNTY OF NEW YORK

--x

ROSE KAPLAN,   :   No. ....

                   Plaintiff,   :   COMPLAINT

          vs.   :

ANITA ADDIS,   :

                   Defendant.   :

--x

Style 15.

IN THE CIRCUIT COURT OF THE SEVENTH JUDICIAL DISTRICT

SANGAMON COUNTY, ILLINOIS

JOHN FISK,   )
)
            Plaintiff,   )
)   No. _____
      -vs-   )
)
MARTIN VASSAR,   )
)
            Defendant.   )

Style 16.

VIRGINIA:

IN THE LAW AND EQUITY COURT OF THE CITY OF RICHMOND

ORIN WALSH,

                                                    Plaintiff,

v.

ALBERT DUNSTABLE,

                                                    Defendant.

MOTION FOR JUDGMENT

Style 17.

STATE OF SOUTH DAKOTA   )   IN CIRCUIT COURT
) SS
COUNTY OF HUGHES   )   SIXTH JUDICIAL CIRCUIT

SAMUEL MUIR,   PLAINTIFF)
)
            -vs-   )   SUMMONS
)
CARROLL MORLEY,   DEFENDANT)

Style 18.

PERRY OAKLAND,   *   IN THE

                  Plaintiff   *   CIRCUIT COURT

         vs.   *   OF BALTIMORE COUNTY

THOMAS NORWAY,   *   IN EQUITY

                 Defendant   *   Docket No. 85, Folio 196

****

ANSWER

Style 19.

UNITED STATES DISTRICT COURT

EASTERN DISTRICT OF LOUISIANA

NEW ORLEANS DIVISION

JOANNA WHITE   :

            Plaintiff   :   No._____

        vs.   :   CIVIL ACTION

CHRISTOPHER CLARK   :

            Defendant   :

:::::::::::::::::::::::::::::::::

MOTION FOR EXTENSION OF TIME

Style 20.

Figure 13.5. *Caption of Paper Filed in a Federal District Court.*

the caption, whereas in Style 2, the title of the document is typed at the right of the title of the case.

3. Set your margins and tabular stops at the appropriate places on the typewriter scale and try to keep them there, so you will not have to change them each time you type a paper.

4. If in the style appropriate for your office the title of the case is set off by a box or other outline, form the habit of making all boxes the same width, or making all outlines at the same point on the typewriter scale. This habit facilitates typing the captions.

13.15. Captions on papers filed in federal district courts. It is mandatory that the caption on all papers filed in federal district courts set forth the name of the court, the title of the case, the file number, and the designation of the paper being filed. Usually the title of the case is boxed, although it is not mandatory that the caption be typed in any particular style. Style 20 in figure 13.5 illustrates a caption on a Motion for Extension of Time filed in a Federal District Court.

13.16. Indentations. Indent 10 spaces for paragraphs. Never block paragraph a court paper.

The left margin of quotations and other indented material should be five spaces to the right of the principal left margin; the beginning of a paragraph of indented material should be indented an additional five spaces.

The right margin of indented material should be approximately five spaces to the left of the principal right margin.

Spacing. Double-space the body of all court papers. Quotations and descriptions may be single spaced, but many courts prefer that this material also be double spaced.

Single-space names of parties in the caption.

Single-space the line of signature and address and, also, the name and address of opposing counsel, which appear on many court papers.

13.17. Number of copies. When typing court papers, always make an original for the court, a copy for each opposing party or his or her attorney, and a copy for your file. Some courts require an extra copy. It is frequently necessary to make additional copies and also duplicate originals. When this is the case, the dictator will tell you how many copies to make. If you are in doubt as to the number of copies needed, inquire.

13.18. Numbering pages. Number pages of court papers about one-half inch from the bottom in the center of the page.

13.19. Conforming copies. After the original and duplicate originals are signed, conform the copies (see page 222).

13.20. Legal backs for court papers. Papers that are filed in, or submitted to, a court, may be stapled in legal backs, similar to the backs on legal instruments (page 223). However, the trend is away from the use of legal backs for court papers. In a number of jurisdictions legal backs are reserved for documents such as wills and deeds that will be retained for long periods. The copy, or copies, that are served on opposing counsel may also be bound, but the office copy that you keep in your file is not. Before binding, collate the original and the copies. (Many courts now prefer that court papers not be bound in legal backs because they are awkward and bulky to file. Therefore, many firms now have ruled papers for such documents with the name and address of the firm printed to the left of the rule in the lower left-hand corner of the sheet.)

It is preferable that all copies of backs be ribbon copies; certainly no more than one carbon copy should be made at a time. Some law firms follow the practice of using backs of one color for the original and backs of another color for the copy to be served on the counsel. This avoids the possibility of filing the copy of the paper instead of the original in court.

Endorsement. The endorsement on the back of a court paper (see figure 13.6) includes:

1. *Index number.* Leave blank space for this until the number is ascertained.

2. *Name of the court.* Get this from the heading of the paper itself.

3. *Style of the case.* This is the same as the caption in the box. It is sometimes difficult to get a long title into the limited typing space provided on the back. This can be overcome in three ways:

    (1) Type only the name of the first plaintiff, or defendant, if there are more than one, and follow by *et al.,* the abbreviation for *et alius* and *et alii* meaning "and another," and "and others." It is inaccurate to use *et als.*

    (2) Substitute "etc." for a lengthy description of the parties. For example, "... constituting the Legal Committee, etc." would be substituted for "... constituting the Legal Committee of the Parent and Teachers Association of Henry County." Usually a title is shortened in this manner only at the direction of the attorney.

    (3) Loosen the platen and use variable spacing, thus gaining a line or two. This mars the appearance of the back but is sometimes necessary.

4. *Name of paper or papers stapled in the back.* When two or more papers are bound together, they must be bound in a certain order, but the back is not necessarily endorsed in that order. For example, an order and notice of entry are bound together, with the notice first, or on top, but the back is endorsed "Order and Notice of Entry." This wording of endorsements for specific papers, as well as the order in which they are

Figure 13.6. *Endorsed Back on Summons and Complaint.*

bound, will be given in the detailed instructions relating to each paper in subsequent chapters.

5. *Name and address of attorney filing the paper.* This is usually printed on the back. If it is not printed, type it. Some courts, especially in large cities, require that the telephone number also be included.

6. *Party represented.* The name and address of the attorney is followed by the designation of the party in whose behalf the paper is filed. For example, Attorneys for Defendant. However, if there is more than one defendant, and the paper is filed on behalf of only one of them, the name of the defendant must be given.

7. *Name of opposing counsel and designation of the party he or she represents.* The wording of the endorsement is:

> To Stephen Tower, Esq.
> Attorney for Defendant

Usually you cannot fill in the name of the opposing attorney on the summons and complaint, because at that stage of the proceedings you do not know who is going to represent a defendant.

Figure 13.6 illustrates a legal back with a printed panel for the endorsement.

Some law firms use backs without a printed panel for court papers as well as for other legal documents. Before typing an endorsement on a plain back, follow the instructions given on page 223 for typing backs to legal instruments, so the endorsement will be typed on the proper panel. Commence typing two single spaces from the top and leave only two spaces between the court heading and the box that contains the title of the case. Leave only two single spaces between the box and name and address of attorney. The purpose of typing with this spacing is to leave as much room as possible at the bottom of the panel for stamped and handwritten notations.

13.21. Folding. Court papers are customarily folded into document form before they are filed in court or served on opposing counsel. Your office copy is not usually folded. In many courts there is a trend away from document filing and over to flat filing, because the uselessness of folding legal papers into document form and then having to unfold them for reference is now widely realized. But the secretary should continue to use document folding for court papers until instructed to the contrary.

13.22. Printed litigation blanks. Printed forms for some court papers are available and, in many cases, it is preferable to use them. When they are used, the same care should be taken in filling them that is taken with all printed forms (page 227). When detailed instructions are given about specific pleadings and supporting papers in the subsequent chapters, you will be told if printed blanks are generally used.

PRACTICE AND PROCEDURE

13.23. The secretary's responsibility. The procedure in a civil action is highly technical and is the lawyer's responsibility. He or she will also dictate many of the pleadings in their entirety because their wording must be precise to meet statutory requirements. In many instances the paralegal will assist the lawyer in preparing pleadings. The secretary's responsibilities might consist of (1) keeping an accurate calendar and record of the proceedings; (2) preparing the pleadings in a workmanlike manner; and (3) relieving the lawyer of details.

13.24. Variations in practice and procedure. The rules of civil practice and procedure vary in detail not only in the various states but, to a lesser extent, in various jurisdictions within a state. A fundamental variation of interest is the requirement with respect to the service and filing of pleadings. For the purpose of this chapter the jurisdictions may be grouped in respect to service and filing as follows:

A. In the majority of jurisdictions, a copy of every pleading and supporting paper must be served on opposing counsel, and the original filed in court. When copy of the initial pleading is served with the summons, as is often the case, it is served on the defendant, because there is no counsel of record at that time.

B. In a few jurisdictions copies of pleadings and supporting papers do not have to be served on opposing counsel, but *a copy as well as the original must be filed in court.* Counsel withdraws the duplicate from court to learn the contents of the papers filed by opposing counsel. (All jurisdictions require service of the summons on the defendent.)

C. In a few jurisdictions, for example in New York Supreme Court, copies of pleadings are served on opposing counsel, but the originals are not filed in court until the case is at issue. The court has no indication that a law suit is pending until the case is ready to be set for trial. This does not apply to civil courts.

D. In some jurisdictions a copy must be served on opposing counsel, and an original and a copy filed in court.

The directions in chapter 14 are based on the practice in jurisdictions that fall within Group A. If a jurisdiction in which suit is filed falls within group B, C, or D, you can easily adapt the directions. Suppose the directions tell you to serve copy on opposing counsel and file the original in court, but your action is pending in a jurisdiction that falls within group B. You know that you need not serve a copy on opposing counsel but that you must file an original and copy in court. Or suppose the directions say to make three copies—an original for the court, a copy for opposing counsel, and a copy for your office file, but the jurisdiction is within group D. You know that you will have to make four copies, because a copy as well as the original must be filed in court. *Opposing counsel* refers to the counsel for each adverse party. Thus, if the rules require service on opposing counsel and there is more than one adverse party, sufficient copies of the paper are prepared to permit service of a copy on counsel for each party.

14

How to Prepare

Court Papers

This chapter, and the following one, discusses pleadings and supporting papers and describes how all court papers are prepared. The secretary and paralegal can adapt the illustrations given here to other pleadings and supporting papers. Keep in mind the variations in practice and procedure discussed on page 278, *et seq.* Remember, also, that local courts in some jurisdictions have requirements that are not statewide.

The Federal Rules of Civil Procedure, adopted by the federal courts in 1938, were designed to reduce the complexities of common law pleading. Under the federal rules, the distinction between law and equity is abolished in the pleadings and all initial pleadings are called *complaint*. The federal rules also abolished the demurrer, replacing it with a less formal *motion to dismiss*.

With a few notable exceptions, most states have adopted the Federal Rules of Civil Procedure, with some changes, for use in their own courts. Among the states that have not adopted a version of the federal rules are New York, California, and New Hampshire. The federal rules are, of course, used in all federal courts. Each federal court has some rules applicable only to its own jurisdiction. These differ from one district to another.

SUMMONS AND COMPLAINT

14.1. Plaintiff's first pleading. The *first pleading* by the plaintiff is a formal and methodical specification of the facts and circumstances surrounding the cause of action. It sets forth in detail the grounds upon which the plaintiff is suing the defendant, and asks the court for damages or other relief. The lawyer will usually dictate complaints, except very simple ones, because the facts and circumstances differ, although the phraseology is standard.

The plaintiff's first pleading is called the *complaint* in the majority of states; the *petition,* the *writ,* or the *declaration* in a few states. In those states where a distinction still exists between actions at law and in equity, the first pleading in equity actions is called the *bill of complaint* or *bill in equity*. (We use the term *complaint* to refer to the first pleading regardless of the terminology in the various states.)

14.2. Analysis of a complaint. Although complaints necessarily differ in detail, they follow a standard pattern. A complaint consists of the following parts:

1. *Caption.* (See chapter 13.) The caption to the complaint designates the court in which the action is brought and lists the full names of all plaintiffs and defendants. It does not show the clerk's index number because that is not available at the time the complaint is prepared.

2. *Introduction.* The opening paragraph of the complaint simply states, "The plaintiff, by his attorney, John Jones, complaining of the defendant, alleges as follows:" or words to that effect.

3. *Body.* The body of the complaint states the facts and circumstances that are the basis for the action. The complaint may contain one or more causes of action, each of which is a separate and complete division within itself. These divisions are referred to as *counts* in some jurisdictions. A cause of action, or count, is composed of one or more *allegations*. These are statements that the plaintiff expects to prove. Complaints in certain actions must contain standard allegations, which the lawyer dictates from memory or from a practice manual. For example, when a domestic corporation is the plaintiff, the allegation will allege the corporate status in a form similar to the following:

That at all times hereinafter mentioned, the plaintiff was and still is a domestic corporation, organized and existing under and by virtue of the laws of the State of
....

When a corporation is the defendant, the allegation is introduced by the words, "Upon information and belief..."

4. *Prayer.* The prayer, or "wherefore" clause, is the final paragraph of the complaint and "demands" judgment against the defendant for a specified sum, or, in equity actions, "prays" for other relief to which the plaintiff believes he or she is entitled. The language used in equity gives the prayer its name. The complaint will also demand interest if the action is for a definite amount of money owed by the defendant, as when the action is on a stated account or a promissory note.

5. *Signature.* Either the plaintiff or his or her attorney must sign the complaint. In some instances, both must sign the initial pleading. Usually the original must be signed manually. An exception is New York State where a typed or printed signature is sufficient. In federal courts, pleadings must be signed by an attorney in his or her individual name, not in the firm name.

6. *Verification.* The law in the various states specifies which complaints must be verified, but many lawyers follow the practice of having all complaints verified. The verification is signed before a notary public. (See "Verifications," page 277, *et seq.*)

14.3. How to prepare the complaint. Simple forms of complaint, such as complaints in actions for goods sold or in actions on promissory notes, are often left to the secretary or paralegal to draw, without dictation. At first the lawyer will give you a form to follow, but you will soon memorize the wording, especially if your office handles many cases of a particular kind of litigation. Make an extra copy of the complaint in each kind of action for your loose-leaf form book.

Figure 14.1 illustrates a complaint. Follow the general directions for the preparation of litigation papers (page 282, *et seq.*) The following directions relate specifically to the preparation of a complaint:

1. Make an original for the court, a copy for each defendant, and a copy for your files.

2. Number the counts or causes of action.

3. Number the allegations.

4. Type a line for signature and "Attorneys for Plaintiff" underneath it. (In New York, do not type the signature line; instead, type the firm name, followed by "Attorneys for Plaintiff" and the firm's address.)

5. The verification, when required, is typed preferably on the last page of the document or at least is started on the last page, but it may be typed entirely on a separate sheet. There is no rule of law about this. If the verification is printed on the inside of the legal back, the office copy will not have a verification. The lawyer will tell you who is to verify the complaint.

6. In large cities it is customary to follow the verification (or the signature if there is no verification) with the name, address, and telephone number of the firm representing the plaintiff.

7. When legal backs are used, endorse one (see the directions on page 293) for each copy of the complaint, except your office copy. In the space provided for the title of the document, type "Summons and Complaint." Staple after the summons is prepared.

8. Collate.

JMH:p 3/30/-- 1-2-1

IN THE CIRCUIT COURT OF THE ELEVENTH
JUDICIAL CIRCUIT OF FLORIDA, IN AND FOR
DADE COUNTY.

--x

GEORGE N. CARR and
HELEN R. CARR,

                        Plaintiffs,

           -vs.-   No. _____

PRINCE DISTRIBUTING CORPORA-
TION, a corporation, and CONTEM-
PORARY CLASSICS, INC., a
corporation,

                        Defendants.

--x

COMPLAINT

    Plaintiffs by their attorneys, Jones & Stevens, complaining of the defendants above named, allege:

FOR A FIRST CAUSE OF ACTION:

    1. That the plaintiffs _____

_____

_____.

    2. Upon information and belief, that _____

_____.

FOR A SECOND CAUSE OF ACTION:

    3. Plaintiffs repeat, reiterate _____

(Continued on following page)

(Continued from preceding page)

WHEREFORE, plaintiffs demand judgment against defendants for the sum of Five thousand three hundred twenty-five and 36/100 dollars ($5,325.36), with interest thereon from the 20th day of December, 19--, together with the costs and disbursements of this action.

Jones & Stevens
Attorneys for Plaintiffs

(If verification required, type on this page or on separate sheet.)

Figure 14.1. *Complaint.*

14.4. The summons. Strictly speaking, a *summons* is not a pleading, but it is an essential part of every law suit. It is the first paper that is served on the defendant, sometimes being served before the preparation of the complaint. It notifes the person named in the summons that suit has been brought against him or her and commands that person to appear in court or answer the complaint by a certain date. Although the secretary to the plaintiff's attorney prepares the summons, it is generally issued and signed by the clerk of the court.

A summons consists of the following parts:

1. Caption.
2. Body. This commands the defendant to answer the complaint within the time specified.
3. Signature and seal of the clerk of the court. (In New York the plaintiff's attorney issues the summons.)

14.5. How to prepare the summons. A printed form of summons (see figure 14.2) is used, unless there are numerous parties plaintiff or parties defendant.

1. If the name of a court is printed on the form, make certain that it is the court in which the action is being filed.
2. Make an original for the court, a copy for each defendant, and a

Form 1.902 RULES OF CIVIL PROCEDURE

Form 1.902   Summons

(Name of Court)

A. B.,
               Plaintiff,
          –vs–   CASE NO. _____
C. D.,
               Defendant.

SUMMONS

THE STATE OF FLORIDA:

To All and Singular the Sheriffs of said State:

YOU ARE HEREBY COMMANDED to serve this summons and a copy of the complaint or petition in the above styled cause upon the defendant _____
_____.

Each defendant is hereby required to serve written defenses to said complaint or petition on _____, plaintiff's attorney, whose address is _____, within 20 days after service of this summons upon you, exclusive of the day of service, and to file the original of said written defenses with the clerk of said court either before service on plaintiff's attorney or immediately thereafter. If you fail to do so, a default will be entered against you for the relief demanded in the complaint or petition.

WITNESS my hand and the seal of said Court on _____, 19__.

(Name of Clerk)
As Clerk of said Court

By _____
As Deputy Clerk

Figure 14.2. *Printed Form of Summons.*

Source: West Publishing Company, Boston, Massachusetts 02108.
Reproduced by permission of the publisher.

copy for your file. An extra copy of the summons must be filed in court in those jurisdictions that require an extra copy of pleadings to be filed.

3. The caption is exactly like that of the complaint. List names of all parties in full.

4. If there are numerous parties, type on legal-size paper instead of using a printed form. Copy the printed form exactly, making sure that all punctuation is included, because usually the statutes direct the form of a summons.

5. Put a legal back on a typed summons, so the affidavit of service can be filled in.

6. Endorse the back of the original summons and of each copy, unless the summons is stapled to the complaint. The endorsements need not list all the parties. It is sufficient to show the name of the first plaintiff and the name of the first defendant, with appropriate words indicating that there are others (see page 282).

14.6. Return day of summons. The civil practice and procedure codes and statutes provide the date by which, or the time within which, a defendant must respond to a summons, or at least file a notice of appearance. The final day for the defendant's appearance is designated as the *return day* of the summons. Thus, if the defendant is required to answer "within 20 days" from the service of the summons, the 20th day is the return day. In some jurisdictions certain days, designated as *return days* or *rule days,* are set aside for filing papers in court. In these jurisdictions the rules provide that the defendant must appear "by the next rule day," if the summons is served on him a certain number of days before rule day; otherwise, he must appear on the following rule day. Thus, the return date is always a rule day.

These return dates are very important and should always be *entered in your diary,* whether your office is serving the summons or has received a summons for a client.

How to compute the time. The statutes and codes also provide how the time should be computed. The usual method is to *exclude* the date from which the period begins to run, but to *include* the last day of the period. If it falls on Sunday or a legal holiday, the next business day is the return date. Intermediate Sundays or holidays are included in the computation, unless the period allowed is less than seven days. The period begins to run the day the summons is served, not the day it is dated. This method of computation of time applies to the time for filing all pleadings as well as to the return day of the summons.

14.7. Alias summons; pluries summons. If the original summons is not served on all of the defendants for any reason, the clerk will issue another summons, designated as an *alias summons.* It is prepared like the original summons, except that *alias* precedes *summons*. If the alias summons is not served, and it is necessary to issue a following summons, the third one is designated as a *pluries summons*.

14.8. What to do about the summons and complaint.

1. Prepare the complaint, and verification when required.

2. Have original complaint signed and verified, after approval by the lawyer.

3. Conform the copies.

4. Prepare summons.

5. Attach a copy of summons to each copy of complaint. Place the complaint against the inside of the cover, if one is used, so the verification printed on the inside cover will read as a continuation of the complaint. Put the summons on top of the complaint. Do not attach original summons to original complaint.

6. Open case in suit register (chapter 12) and make appropriate entry.

7. File original complaint in court, have clerk of court issue (sign, seal, and date) original summons, and pay required fee.

8. Conform copies of summons, by filling in date, name of clerk, and seal of court.

9. Make a note of the index number assigned by the clerk and put it on all subsequent papers prepared by you in that particular case.

10. Give original of summons, together with copy of summons and copy of complaint for each defendant, to process server for service on defendants. (In some jurisdictions, the copies are given to the clerk of the court at the time the original summons is issued, and he or she, in turn, delivers them to the sheriff for service.)

11. The summons illustrated in figure 14.2 has a space for the sheriff's return, which the sheriff fills in after serving the summons. If a process server is employed to make service, instruct him to get in touch with you as soon as he serves the summons and complaint, for the purpose of making affidavit of service. The affidavit should be made on the same day that service is made. If affidavit of service is on a separate sheet, it should have a regular caption, like that on the complaint, but if the affidavit is made on the back of the summons, no caption is necessary.

12. File original summons and proof of service in court. If the summons is not filed within the time permitted by the practice rules, a new summons must be served.

13. Mark on office copy date service is made and by whom.

14. *Enter in diary* return date of summons. Remember that the period begins to run the date the summons is served, not the date it is prepared.

15. If you are employed by the lawyer for defendant, *enter in diary* return day of summons. This is very important. Failure to answer by the date might mean a default judgment.

THE ANSWER

14.9. Defendant's first pleading. The modern summons contains a notice to the defendant to appear in court or to file and serve an answer to plaintiff's complaint within a specified time. If the summons directs the defendant to appear only, he or she may do so by filing an appearance with the clerk of the court (see page 310). If a copy of the complaint is served with the summons, the defendant is directed to file and serve his or her answer. The filing and service of an answer by the defendant constitute his or her appearance in court. Failure to obey the summons subjects the defendant to a judgment by default in favor of the plaintiff.

As soon as a client brings a summons to your office, *enter in your diary* the time by which he or she must appear or answer. It is your responsibility to see that no default judgment is taken against a client of your office because of your negligence.

14.10. Analysis of an answer. The *answer* is the defendant's formal written statement of his or her defense, signed by the defendant's attorney. It denies some, or all, of the allegations of the complaint and sets forth the grounds of the defendant's defense. It may also set up claims the defendant has against the plaintiff as *counterclaims*.

The answer consists of the following parts:

1. Caption
2. Introduction
3. Denials of allegations of the complaint
4. Counterclaims, if any
5. "Wherefore" clause; prayer, if answer contains a counterclaim
6. Signature of attorney for defendant
7. Verification if the complaint is verified

14.11. How to prepare the answer. The lawyer will dictate the answer to the secretary, but it is the secretary's responsibility to set it up in a workmanlike manner. Unless the lawyer indicates a preference, follow the style illustrated in figure 14.3.

1. Type on legal-size paper or 8½ by 11 paper, depending on the practice of the firm or the court.
2. Make an original for the court, a copy to serve on each plaintiff's attorney, and a copy for your file.

BMM:r 4/22/-- 1-2-1

IN THE CIRCUIT COURT OF THE ELEVENTH
JUDICIAL CIRCUIT OF FLORIDA, IN AND FOR
DADE COUNTY.

---x
                                                           :
GEORGE N. CARR and   :   Index No. 11660-19--
HELEN R. CARR,   :

                          Plaintiffs,   :

                 vs.   :

PRINCE DISTRIBUTING CORPORA-   :
TION, a corporation, and CONTEM-
PORARY CLASSICS, INC., a
corporation,

                          Defendants.   :
                                              :
---x

ANSWER

The defendant Prince Distributing Corporation, answering the
amended complaint herein by his attorneys, Parker & Madison.

    1.   Admits _____
_____
_____.

    2.   Denies that he has knowledge or information sufficient to form a
belief as to the allegations contained in the paragraph of the complaint
designated "SECOND."

(Continued on following page)

(Continued from preceding page)

FOR A FIRST SEPARATE AND COMPLETE
DEFENSE, DEFENDANT ALLEGES:

3. On information and belief _____

_____ .

FOR A SECOND SEPARATE AND PARTIAL
DEFENSE, DEFENDANT ALLEGES:

4. _____

_____ .

FOR A DISTINCT SEPARATE AND AFFIRM-
ATIVE DEFENSE AND BY WAY OF A
COUNTERCLAIM, DEFENSE ALLEGES:

5. _____

_____ .

WHEREFORE, defendant demands that the complaint be dismissed

with costs and asks judgment in the amount _____

_____ .

_____
Attorneys for Defendant
Prince Distributing
Corporation

(If verification required, type on this page or on separate sheet.)

Figure 14.3. *Answer.*

3. The caption is the same as that on the complaint, but if there are numerous parties the title of the case may be shortened on most

subsequent documents by adding *et al., et ux,* or *et vir.* However, some documents, like a judgment, will require the parties' names in full.

    4. The index number must appear on the answer, at the right of the box.

    5. The title of the document is "Answer."

    6. Number the paragraphs consecutively throughout, except the last paragraph, which is the "wherefore" clause. Do not start new series of numbers for the paragraphs in each separate defense.

    7. Type a line for signature of attorney.

    8. The answer must be verified if the complaint is.

    9. In some large cities, the attorney's name, address, and telephone number must appear after the verification, but usually this is not necessary. The attorney's address is on the legal back if one is used.

    10. When backs are required, endorse a legal back for each copy except your office copy. (See figure 14.4.) Notice that the endorsement differs from the endorsement on the complaint in that it shows the court's index number and the name of the attorney for the plaintiff, on whom a copy of the answer is served. When the complaint was prepared, the secretary for the plaintiff did not know the index number or who would represent the defendant.

    11. Collate and staple, in backs if they are used.

    12. After signature and verification, conform exactly.

14.12. Methods of service of answer on plaintiff's attorney. Although practice may vary with the jurisdiction, the answer is generally served on the plaintiff's attorney by (1) handing him a copy, or leaving it at his office with his clerk or other person in charge of the office; or (2) by mailing it to the attorney. No regular process server is necessary in the majority of jurisdictions. You, or a clerk in your office, may serve the papers.

    Proof of service. The attorney on whom the answer is served, or you if you are authorized, writes on the back of the original a receipt similar to the following:

Copy received. . . . . ^(date) . . . .

(Firm name)
. . . .

Attorneys for . . . . ^(name of client) . . . .

Many offices have rubber stamps for this purpose.

    Printed legal backs have printed on them an admission of service, which usually contains the words "due and proper" service, "timely"

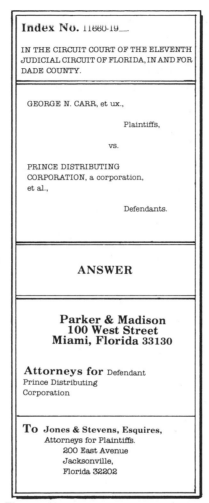

Figure 14.4. *Endorsed Back of Answer.*

service, or the like. When you accept service, be sure to strike out these words. Although you are authorized to accept service, it is not your responsibility to admit that it was due, proper, or timely.

In some jurisdictions, the attorney whose office is serving the answer endorses on the back of the original:

> I do hereby certify that copy hereof has
> been furnished to ....
> by mail (or delivery), this .... day
> of .... , 19 ...

14.13. What to do about the answer. 1. Prepare the answer, and verification, if required.

2. Have answer signed, and verified, after approval by the attorney.

3. Notarize verification.

4. See that copy is served on plaintiff's attorney.

5. Be sure that receipt of service is endorsed on back of original, or that affidavit of service is attached.

6. Conform your office copy.

7. File original, with admission of service in court, with fee if required.

8. Make entry in suit register of service and filing.

9. If you are employed by the attorney on whom the answer is served, make a notation on the back of your copy of the date and hour it was served; also make entry in suit register.

10. *Enter in diary* date by which next action must be taken.

NOTICE OF APPEARANCE

14.14. Analysis of a notice of appearance. In jurisdictions where a summons may be served on the defendant without a copy of the complaint, the defendant appears by filing a *notice of appearance* with the clerk of the court and serving a copy of it on the plaintiff's attorney. It is a statement that the defendant appears by his or her attorney. Thereafter, copies of all pleadings are served on the attorney appearing for the defendant, if service is required. In some jurisdictions, the notice of appearance is addressed to the attorney for the plaintiff; in others, to the clerk of the court. Figure 14.5 illustrates a typed notice of appearance in a common law case; figure 14.6, in an equity case.

14.15. How to prepare a notice of appearance. Many courts have a printed appearance form that they supply to attorneys who practice in their jurisdictions. These should be used when they are available. Otherwise, a stock printed form may be used or the notice may be typed on plain bond paper.

1. Prepare an original for the court, a copy to be served on opposing counsel, and a copy for your office file.

2. The caption is identical with that on the summons. If the title of the case is long, you may shorten it as described on page 293.

3. Type signature line for the attorney, with his or her address underneath. When a printed form is used, type the attorney's name

SUPREME COURT OF THE STATE OF NEW YORK

COUNTY OF NEW YORK

---x

ELDON McKAY,   :

                                        Plaintiff,   :

                    -against-   :

BARRY PARSONS,   :

                                        Defendant.   :

---x

SIR:

     PLEASE TAKE NOTICE that the defendant Barry Parsons hereby appears in the above entitled action and that we are retained as attorneys for him therein, and hereby demand that a copy of the complaint and of all other papers in this action be served on us at the office below designated.

Dated, New York, July 25, 19--.

                             Yours, etc.,

                                   WILLIAMS & WILLIAMS,
                                   Attorneys for Defendant,
                                   214 Madison Avenue,
                                   New York, N. Y. 10001

To:

        J. D. BAXTER, ESQ.,
        Attorney for Plaintiff,
        1007 East 17th Street,
        New York, N. Y. 10016

Figure 14.5. *Notice of Appearance in Common Law Case.*

UNITED STATES DISTRICT COURT

EASTERN DISTRICT OF NEW YORK

---x

ARNOLD JONES,   :

                                     Plaintiff,   :

            -against-   :   E 87-20

SHELLEY ART CENTER,   :

                                     Defendant.   :

---x

TO THE CLERK OF THE ABOVE COURT:

     We hereby enter our appearance as attorneys and solicitors for the
defendant SHELLEY ART CENTER in the above entitled suit.

Dated, New York, July 5, 19--.

                          Yours, etc.,

                            MICHAELS *&* FOLLETT
                            Attorneys for Defendant
                            Shelley Art Center,
                            1000 Third Avenue,
                            New York, N. Y. 10016

To:

     RODNEY BROWN, ESQ.
       Attorney for Plaintiff
       3040 Northwest Boulevard,
       New York, N. Y. 10017

THE CLERK OF THE UNITED STATES DISTRICT COURT,
   Eastern District of New York,
     Post Office Building
     Brooklyn, N. Y. 11201

Figure 14.6. *Notice of Appearance in Equity Case (Federal Court).*

underneath the line for signature so the opposing counsel will have no difficulty in deciphering the signature.

14.16. What to do about the notice of appearance. A notice of appearance is never verified, because it contains no statements of fact. Otherwise, your responsibilities with respect to the notice of appearance are the same as with respect to the answer. In some jurisdictions the notice of appearance is not served on opposing counsel; he or she learns from the court record that the appearance has been filed.

NOTICE OF TRIAL: NOTE OF ISSUE

14.17. Noticing a case for trial. A material point, raised by the pleadings, about which there is a controversy between the parties is an *issue.* The issue may be an *issue of fact* or an *issue of law.* When an issue is raised, it is said to be *joined,* and the case is *at issue.* Issue is deemed joined on the date the last pleading is served.

At any time after issue is joined, either party may have the case noticed for trial. In some jurisdictions a case is noticed for trial by the filing of a *note of issue* or *memorandum setting for trial;* in others, by the filing of a *notice of trial.* Some jurisdictions require both. In still other jurisdictions, a case is set for trial on motion of counsel. Whatever procedure, or by whatever name the notice is called, the purpose is to place the case on the trial calendar.

Notice of a case for trial does not mean it will be brought up for trial on that date or even at that term of court, but that it will be placed on the trial calendar to await its turn.

14.18. When the notice must be served. Note of issue or notice of trial must be served on opposing counsel a designated number of days before the term of court at which the case will be placed on the trial calendar. The requirement varies with the jurisdiction. Suppose a new term of court commences on the first Monday of the following month, which, let us say, is May 5. Practice rules require that the note of issue or notice of trial must be served 12 days, for example, before the commencement of the term. Therefore, the notice must be served by April 23. Service after that date will not give counsel 12 days' notice. Thus, if on April 25 the lawyer tells you to prepare a notice of trial, you know it will have to be for the June, not the May, term of court.

It is important for you to become familiar with this particular practice requirement; otherwise, you will not be able to prepare the note of issue or the notice of trial.

14.19. Note of issue—preparation. Note of issue is a printed form that you can easily complete without directions from the lawyer. Figure 14.7 illustrates a completed form.

Figure 14.7. *Note of Issue.*

Courtesy Julius Blumberg, Inc.

1. Make an original for the court, a copy to serve on each opposing counsel, and a copy for your file.

2. Telephone numbers of attorneys should be included in the note of issue and *must* be included in some jurisdictions.

3. Each sentence is a separate paragraph.

4. Do not staple in legal back, but endorse on printed from.

5. The back of the printed note of issue has forms for affidavit of personal service and of service by mail. After service is made, fill in the appropriate form. Figure 14.8 illustrates the back of a note of issue with affidavit of service by mail completed.

14.20. Notice of trial—preparation. The lawyer does not usually dictate a notice of trial. You can get the wording from a practice manual in your office. The wording varies slightly with the jurisdiction, and, in some jurisdictions, notice given by the plaintiff differs from notice given by the defendant. Notice of trial given by the plaintiff recites an intention to take an "inquest," whereas notice by the defendant recites that a motion to dismiss the complaint will be made. Memorize the wording in your jurisdiction to save time in the preparation of notices. Figure 14.9 illustrates a notice of trial.

State of New York, County of Kings   ss.:
 Elaine Smith,
being duly sworn, deposes and says: that deponent is
 secretary to   attorney for plaintiff
herein; is over 18 years of age; not a party to this
action; and resides at 216 East 17 Street,
 Borough of Brooklyn, New York. 11205
On the 25th   *day of*   April   19--
deponent served the within note of issue, on

 Jones Smith and Edwards,
          Esq.
attorney for the defendant   *in the within entitled*
action, by depositing a true and correct copy of the same
properly enclosed in a post-paid wrapper, in the Post-
Office—a-Branch-Post-Office—Station—Sub-Station—
Finance-Station—Letter-Box—Mail Chute—*Official*
Depository maintained and exclusively controlled by
the United States at
 45 Main Street, Brooklyn, N.Y. 11201
that being then the Post Office of the attorneys for
 plaintiff;   *directed to said attorneys for*
defendant, at No. 14 Congress Street,
 Brooklyn, N.Y. 11201
that being the address designated by him for that
purpose.

Sworn to before me this 25th
day of April,   *19--*

State of New York, County of   ss.:

being duly sworn, deposes and says: that deponent is
     attorney for
herein; is over 18 years of age; not a party to this
action; and resides at

On the   *day of*   19
deponent served the within note of issue, on

        Esq.,
attorney for   *herein, at his office at*

during his absence from said office by then and there
leaving a true copy of the same with

his partner; his clerk; therein; person having charge
of said office.

Sworn to before me this
day of   19

STATE OF NEW YORK

......................SUPREME......................COURT

COUNTY OF.....KINGS.........................

JOHN E. THOMPSON

           Plaintiff

    against

SMITH-ROGER, INC.

          Defendant

𝔑ote of 𝔍ssue

ELWOOD & ADAMS
Attorneys for Plaintiff
(Office and Post Office Address)
45 Main Street
Brooklyn, N.Y. 11201

    Attorney **for**

Courtesy Julius Blumberg, Inc.

Figure 14.8. *Back of Note of Issue.*

 1. Make an original for the court, a copy to serve on each opposing counsel, and a copy for your office file.

 2. Endorse legal backs, if used.

 3. Have attorney sign it.

14.21. What to do about the notice of trial or note of issue. 1. Prepare the note of issue or notice of trial, as the case may be.

 2. After the lawyer approves it, see that it is served on opposing counsel by the required date.

 3. Be sure that receipt of service is endorsed on back or that the printed form provided is properly completed.

MUNICIPAL COURT OF THE CITY OF NEW YORK

BOROUGH OF MANHATTAN: FIRST DISTRICT

--x
                                               :
GERALD KLINE,   :   No. 7834/--
                                               :
                             Plaintiff,   :
                                               :   NOTICE OF TRIAL
            -against-   :
                                               :
NORMAN ACKERMAN and HILL   :
MANUFACTURING COMPANY, INC.,   :
                                               :
                             Defendants.   :
                                               :
--x

SIRS:

      PLEASE TAKE NOTICE that the issues in this action will be brought to trial and an inquest taken therein at Part II of this Court, to be held at the Court House situated at No. 8 Reade Street, Borough of Manhattan, City of New York on the 24th day of November, 19–, at 10 o'clock in the forenoon of that day or as soon thereafter as counsel can be heard.

Dated, New York, November 8, 19–.

                                   Yours, etc.,

                                   RICHARDS & RUSSELL
                                   Attorneys for Plaintiff
                                   1069 West 39th Street,
                                   New York, N. Y. 10016

To:

      ROY TAYLOR, ESQ.
        Attorney for Defendant
        Fifth Avenue and 80th Street,
        New York, N. Y. 10028

      CLERK OF THE MUNICIPAL COURT OF
        THE CITY OF NEW YORK-
          Borough of Manhattan,
          First District.

Figure 14.9. *Notice of Trial Given by Plaintiff.*

4. Conform your office copy.

5. File original in court.

6. *Make diary entry.*

7. Make appropriate entry in suit register.

8. If you are employed by the counsel on whom notice is served, note on your copy date and hour of service; *make appropriate diary entry;* enter in suit register.

STIPULATIONS

14.22. Analysis of a stipulation. Attorneys for opposing parties frequently make agreements respecting certain phases of a law suit. The agreement might be an accommodation to opposing counsel, such as an extension of the time in which to file a pleading; or it might be an agreement that will save time in court, such as an agreement admitting certain facts. These agreements between counsel are called *stipulations.* A stipulation is usually an agreement among the attorneys for all the parties to an action. However, it may be simply an agreement between the attorney for the plaintiff and the attorney for a defendant, the other parties defendant not being interested in the particular stipulation. Although stipulations are filed in court (except in those few jurisdictions where no papers are filed until note of issue), the court is usually not required to approve the stipulation except in domestic relations cases.

A stipulation consists of the following parts:

1. Caption

2. Body

3. Dateline

4. Signatures of attorneys for all interested parties

14.23. How to prepare a stipulation. The wording of all stipulations about a particular step in the litigation is substantially the same. The lawyer does not usually dictate the simple stipulations. He or she will say, "Draw up a stipulation in the Jones case extending our time to answer until March 10"; or "Draw up a stipulation in the Smith case to set for trial on March 18." You can get the wording from a practice manual. Whenever you prepare a stipulation of a different kind, make an extra copy for your form file. Memorize the short forms to save time in preparing them. The lawyer will dictate some stipulations, such as those admitting certain facts.

It is customary for the attorney seeking the stipulation to prepare it. When typing it, follow the style shown in figure 14.10.

38

PREPARING COURT PAPERS

WGR:MH   9/25/--   (2)

IN THE COURT OF COMMON PLEAS OF ALLEGHENY COUNTY,

PENNSYLVANIA

ALAN R. EGLE and
PATRICIA Y. EGLE,   :
                                     :
                                     :
            Plaintiffs,   :
                                     :
       vs.   :   No. 223 October Term, 19--
                                     :
THE METROPOLITAN   :
CORPORATION and CREATIVE   :
CLASSICS, INC.,   :
                                     :
            Defendants.   :

STIPULATION

IT IS HEREBY STIPULATED AND AGREED by and between the

undersigned attorneys that the time for defendant Creative Classics, Inc., to

answer or otherwise plead to the Second Amended Complaint herein, filed

the 22nd day of September, 19--, be and the same hereby is extended to and

including the 13th day of October, 19--.

_____
            (Simon & Greene)
          Attorneys for Plaintiff

_____
            (Fenton & Jacobs)
         Attorneys for Defendant
           Creative Classics, Inc.

Dated: September 25, 19--.

Figure 14.10. *Stipulation Extending Time to Answer.*

1. Type on legal-size or regular paper according to the usage of the court.

2. Make an original for the court and a copy for all interested attorneys plus a file copy.

3. The caption is the same as that on the complaint, except that the style of the case may be shortened.

4. Type "IT IS HEREBY STIPULATED AND AGREED" in solid caps.

5. When there is more than one stipulation in the same document, type each in a separate paragraph.

6. Type a signature line for each attorney or firm of attorneys who are stipulating. Indicate the party represented by the stipulating attorney, thus: "Attorney for Defendant Bernard Lowe."

7. Endorse legal back, if used, for each copy of stipulation, including the copy for your office, unless you are instructed to back only the court copy, for purposes of economy.

14.24. What to do about stipulations. 1. Prepare the stipulation.

2. Ask the attorney to sign the original and all copies.

3. Deliver them to opposing counsel who is stipulating and ask for his or her signature on the original and your office copy, giving opposing counsel a copy that was signed at your office.

4. If the stipulation sets a date for future action, *make an entry in your diary*.

5. Make entry in suit register (see chapter 12).

6. If you are employed by the attorney who did not prepare the stipulation, *make an entry in your diary* and your suit register when you receive a copy of it.

DEMURRERS

14.25. Analysis of a demurrer. Many states have abolished demurrers, as such, but a *motion to dismiss for failure to state a case* is essentially the same thing. A *demurrer* or *motion to dismiss* is a pleading that raises an issue of law, not of fact. It objects to defects that are apparent from the pleading itself. Instead of denying facts alleged in the complaint, as an answer does, a demurrer to a complaint takes exception to the complaint because it is insufficient on some legal ground. For example, a defendant may demur to or move to dismiss a complaint on the ground that the plaintiff does not have legal capacity to sue. The defendant may also demur to the plaintiff's reply. But a demurrer is not a pleading to be used by the defendant only. A plaintiff may demur to the defendant's answer, or to a cross-complaint. Each cause of action (count), or each defense, is demurred to separately.

A stipulation consists of the following parts:

1. Caption
2. Introduction
3. Grounds of demurrer, each states separately
4. Signature of attorney
5. Attorney's certificate of good faith when required
6. Points and authorities

The statutes name the grounds for demurrer. These grounds usually include, among others, the following: (1) that the court has no jurisdiction; (2) that the plaintiff has no legal capacity to sue; (3) that the complaint (or answer) is ambiguous, unintelligible, uncertain. A demurrer is supported by legal points and authorities sustaining the grounds of demurrer.

14.26. How to prepare the demurrer. The statement of a specific ground for demurrer usually follows a standard form, with which you will quickly become familiar. Although the lawyer ordinarily will dictate the demurrer, he or she might ask you to follow a form. Unless otherwise instructed, follow figure 14.11 for style when typing a demurrer. Figures 14.12 and 14.13 illustrate the points and authorities supporting a demurrer.

1. Type on the size paper specified by the court.

2. Make an original for the court, a copy for the opposing party's counsel, and a copy for your file.

3. The caption is the same as that on the complaint, but you may shorten the title of the case.

4. The index number must appear on the demurrer, at the right of the box.

5. The title of the document is "Demurrer to Complaint," or "Demurrer to Answer," as the case may be.

6. Number the grounds of demurrer to each cause of action or count (or each defense) consecutively, beginning with "I."

7. Type a line for the attorney's signature.

8. There is no verification because a demurrer does not allege or aver facts.

9. Type the attorney's certificate of good faith in jurisdictions where it is required by the court rules. The certificate reads:

IN THE SUPERIOR COURT OF THE STATE OF CALIFORNIA

IN AND FOR THE COUNTY OF LOS ANGELES

AUDREY SLOANE,	)	No. 14788
Plaintiff,	)	
vs.	)	DEMURRER TO COMPLAINT
DOUGLAS SLOANE,	)	
Defendant.	)	

Comes now the above named defendant, DOUGLAS

SLOANE, and demurs to Count One of the Complaint on file herein

upon the following grounds and each of them:

I

That Count One of said complaint fails to state

facts sufficient to constitute a cause of action against

this defendant.

II

That Count One of said complaint fails to state

facts sufficient to constitute a cause of action against

this defendant in this, that it affirmatively appears there-

from that the purported cause or causes of action therein

set forth are barred by the provisions of §§ 339(1), 343

Figure 14.11. *Demurrer (First Page).*

1   IV

2   That Count One of said complaint is ambiguous

3   for each of the reasons heretofore set forth for its uncer-

4   tainty.

5   V

6   That Count One of said complaint is unintelli-

7   gible for each of the reasons heretofore set forth for its

8   uncertainty.

9   DEMURRER TO COUNT TWO

10   Defendant demurs to Count Two of said complaint

11   upon the following grounds and each of them:

12   I

13   (Continue as in the demurrer to Count One.)

14   WHEREFORE, this demurring defendant prays that

15   this demurrer be sustained without leave to amend and that

16   he be dismissed with his costs.

17   _____
                               JOSEPH SCHAEFFER
                               Attorney for Defendant

18   I hereby certify that this demurrer is filed in

19   good faith; that it is not filed for the purpose of delay,

20   and in my opinion the grounds are well taken.

21   _____
                               JOSEPH SCHAEFFER
                               Attorney for Defendant

Figure 14.12. *Demurrer (Last Page).*

POINTS AND AUTHORITIES

POINT ONE

A PARENT IS NOT BOUND TO COMPENSATE THE OTHER PARENT FOR THE VOLUNTARY SUPPORT OF HIS CHILD WITHOUT AN AGREEMENT FOR COMPENSATION.

Civil Code § 208

POINT TWO

AS BETWEEN THE PARENTS OF MINOR CHILDREN, THEIR RESPECTIVE OBLIGATIONS OF SUPPORT OF EACH OTHER AND TO THE MINOR CHILDREN MUST BE DETERMINED IN THE PROCEEDING FOR DIVORCE, AND IN THE ABSENCE OF SOME SPECIFIC PROVISION TO THAT EFFECT, THE FATHER WHO HAS BEEN DEPRIVED OF THE CUSTODY OF THE MINOR CHILDREN IS NOT OBLIGATED FOR THEIR SUPPORT.

Calegaris v. Calegaris, 4 Cal. App. 264, 87 Pac. 561;

Ex Parte Miller, 109 Cal. 643, 42 Pac. 428;

Lewis v. Lewis, 174 Cal. 336, 163 Pac. 42.

Respectfully submitted,

_____
JOSEPH SCHAEFFER
Attorney for Defendant

Figure 14.13. *Points and Authorities Supporting Demurrer.*

I hereby certify that this demurrer is filed in good faith and not for the purpose of delay. In my opinion the grounds are well taken.

_____
Attorney for   . . . .

10. Begin the points and authorities on a separate page.

11. Endorse a legal back, if used, for each copy except your file copy. The endorsement is similar to the endorsement on the back of the answer in that it shows the index number and the name of opposing counsel on whom a copy of the demurrer is served.

14.27. What to do about a demurrer. 1. Prepare the demurrer and points and authorities.

2. Staple original and copies in endorsed legal backs, if used.

3. Get attorney to sign original and copies, and also certificate of good faith if required.

4. Serve copy on attorney for opposing party.

5. See that admission of service is endorsed on back of original.

6. Conform your office copy.

7. File original in court, with fee if required.

8. Make entry in suit register of service and filing.

9. If you are employed by the counsel on whom the demurrer is served, make a notation on the back of your copy of the date and hour the demurrer was served, and an entry in the suit register.

DEMAND FOR BILL OF PARTICULARS, BILL OF PARTICULARS, INTERROGATORIES, AND MOTION TO MAKE PLEADING MORE DEFINITE

A complaint does not contain all the minute details or particulars of the plaintiff's claim against the defendant. The defendant is entitled to those details so he or she may interpose the proper answer and prepare to defend himself or herself in the trial of the case. Likewise, the plaintiff may need more definite information from the defendant before he or she can adequately defend the case. The methods by which this information is obtained vary with the state and also with the kind of action. This process is called *discovery*. The Federal Rules of Civil Procedure permit liberal discovery in federal courts, and many states have adopted similar discovery rules. However, some states permit more limited discovery than is allowed under the federal rules.

14.28. Demand for bill of particulars. Under the federal rules, the *demand for bill of particulars* was abolished, leaving the liberal discovery rules to accomplish this purpose. In jurisdictions that retain the motion, it is used to obtain the specific details of a claim made by one party against another, especially when the claim is based on an account. A party demands that the adverse party furnish him or her with a statement of the details, called a *bill of particulars,* within a specified time (or within the time provided by statute). He or she may ask the court for an order for the bill of particulars, in which case the procedure is like that in any other motion. The demand for bill of particulars is addressed to opposing counsel.

14.29. Parts of demand for bill of particulars. The demand for bill of particulars consists of the following parts:

1. Caption
2. Salutation
3. Introduction
4. Details demanded
5. Dateline
6. Signature of attorney demanding the bill
7. Name and address of attorney on whom the demand is made

14.30. How to prepare the demand for bill of particulars. Usually the lawyer dictates the demand for bill of particulars. Unless otherwise instructed, follow figure 14.14 for style.

1. Make an original for the court (some courts require an extra copy), copy to serve on each opposing counsel, and a copy for your file.

2. The caption is the same as that on the complaint; the title of the case may be shortened.

3. The salutation is to opposing counsel. It is typed in solid caps and reads:

SIRS: (if to a law firm)
SIR: (if to one lawyer)
or TO .... , ATTORNEY FOR .... :

In some jurisdictions the demand for bill of particulars is addressed to the party *and* his or her attorney.

4. Number consecutively and indent the details demanded.

5. Type the dateline at the left margin, three spaces beneath the last numbered paragraph.

6. Type a line for signature of attorney demanding the bill. Beneath the signature line, indicate the party he or she represents.

7. Type name and address of counsel to whom the demand is

JMH:p 8/23/-- 1-2

SUPREME COURT OF THE STATE OF NEW YORK

COUNTY OF RICHMOND

---x
                                                                    :
WARREN D. CANNON and   :
REGINA M. CANNON,   : No. _____
                                                                    :
                                                                    :
                                            Plaintiffs,   :
                                                                    :
                                                                    :
                    -against-   :
                                                                    :
                                                                    :
MODERN DIE COMPANY, and   :
C & M PRESS, INC.,   :
                                                                    :
                                                                    :
                                            Defendants   :
                                                                    :
---x

                    DEMAND FOR BILL OF PARTICULARS

SIRS:

        PLEASE TAKE NOTICE that the above named defendants hereby
demand that the plaintiffs serve upon the attorneys for the defendants
within ten days a Bill of Particulars showing in detail the following:

        (1) The date and the time of day of the occurrence as closely as
the plaintiffs can fix it.
        (2) Its location, identifying as closely as possible the display
counters and the place on the floor between them as described in
paragraph FIFTH of the complaint.

                                        (Continued on following page)

(Continued from preceding page)

---

        (3) A statement of the injuries and a description of those claimed to be permanent.

Dated, New York, August 23, 19--,

                     Yours, etc.,

                        JARRELL & GROSSET,
                        Attorneys for Defendants,
                        Box 2000,
                        New York, N. Y. 10006

TO:

TARA & TARA,
  Attorneys for Plaintiffs,
    4700 East Drive,
      New York, N. Y. 10016

Figure 14.14. *Demand for Bill of Particulars.*

addressed at the left margin, several spaces beneath the signature. If the attorney's name is given in the salutation, this is not necessary.

    8. There is no verification to a demand for bill of particulars.

    9. Endorse legal back, if used, for original and all copies except your office copy.

    10. Collate and staple in backs.

14.31. What to do about the demand for bill of particulars. 1. Prepare the demand for bill of particulars.

    2. Ask attorney to sign.

    3. See that copy is served on opposing counsel.

    4. Be sure that receipt or certificate of service is endorsed on back of original.

    5. Conform your office copy.

    6. *Make diary entry* of date bill of particulars must be served.

    7. File original in court.

    8. Make entry in suit register of service and filing.

    9. If you are employed by the attorney on whom the demand is

served, make notation on back of your copy of date and hour of service. *Enter in diary date by which bill of particulars must be served.* Also make entry in suit register.

14.32. Parts of bill of particulars. The bill of particulars (bill of discovery in equity proceedings) consists of the following parts:

1. Caption
2. Salutation
3. Introduction
4. Statements of particular details required by the demand for bill
5. Dateline
6. Signature of attorney
7. Name and address of attorney to whom the bill is addressed
8. Verifications in some jurisdictions

14.33. How to prepare the bill of particulars. Usually the lawyer dictates the bill of particulars. Follow figure 14.15 for style unless instructed otherwise. The bill of particulars is prepared like the demand for the bill, except that in almost all jurisdictions it *must* have a verification. The lawyer will tell you who is to verify the bill.

14.34. What to do about the bill of particulars. Your responsibilities with respect to the bill of particulars are the same as with respect to the demand for the bill. In addition, have the bill verified and notarize it before serving on opposing counsel.

14.35. Interrogatories. In most jurisdictions specific testimony may be obtained from either party by means of *interrogatories,* or written questions. Either party may file with the clerk interrogatories to be propounded to the adverse party, with an affidavit that the answers will be material testimony in the cause. The clerk then issues a copy of the interrogatories to be served upon the person to whom they are addressed or upon his or her attorney. The answers to the interrogatories must be verified.

How to prepare interrogatories. 1. Make an original, a copy for the person to whom they are addressed, and a copy for your files.

2. The caption is the same as on the complaint.

3. Number the interrogatories and begin each one on a new line. Many jurisdictions require that space be left after each question so the answer may be inserted directly on the original.

JMH:p 8/23/-- 1-2-1

JEAN M. DELURY and   *   IN THE
SARA R. DELURY,
        Plaintiffs   *   CIRCUIT COURT

                   *   OF BALTIMORE COUNTY

         vs.   *

WATSON INDUSTRIES and   *
WATSON SHIPPING, INC.,
                  *
        Defendants
                  *

*   *   * * *   *   *

BILL OF PARTICULARS

The following is a bill of the particulars of the plaintiffs' claim against the defendants, that is:

(a) The accident occurred on February 23, 19--, at approximately 9:30 a.m.

(b) The accident occurred in the aisle between the second and third counters from the entrance to defendants' store about midway between the ends of said counters and nearer to the third counter.

(c) The following amounts are claimed as special damages:

1.	Hospital bills	$ 1,758.03
2.	Physicians' services and medical supplies	1,023.50
3.	Nurses	1,160.00
4.	Household Assistance	904.60
5.	Transportation to hospital and doctor's office	43.10

(d) Plaintiffs reside at 200 West Plaza, Baltimore, Maryland.

        BRANHAM & WORLD
        Attorneys for Plaintiffs

(If verification is required, type on separate sheet.)

Figure 14.15. *Bill of Particulars.*

4. As the name implies, interrogatories are usually in the form of questions and each interrogatory is followed by a question mark.

5. Preferably the affidavit is typed on the last page of the interrogatories, but it may be on a separate page.

14.36. Motion to make the pleading more definite. In some jurisdictions, a party to an action obtains more specific information by filing a motion "to make the pleading more definite and certain." (See figure 14.16.) The procedure is like that in any other motion. The adverse party, if the court so orders, amends his or her pleading in accordance with the order. In many jurisdictions where liberal discovery is allowed, it proceeds without court order unless a party refuses to cooperate voluntarily.

NOTICES

14.37. Analysis of a notice. *Notice* has more than one meaning in the field of law, but we are concerned here with the notices that play an important part in the conduct of a law suit. In this sense, a notice is a formal written advice of an act to be done or required to be done. The notice is intended to apprise opposing counsel of some proceeding in which his or her interests are involved. Court rules require that opposing counsel be given this notice. (Sometimes notice is given to the party to the litigation, but more frequently to his counsel.) For example, if an attorney expects to move the Court for an order, notice of motion must be given opposing counsel. When the Court enters an order, judgment, or decree, the prevailing counsel must give notice of entry to other interested counsel. Notice of a contemplated proceeding is not given to opposing counsel when such notice would defeat the purpose of the proceeding. For example, when a judgment creditor in an attempt to collect a judgment moves the Court for an order attaching the debtor's bank account, he or she will not give notice to the debtor or his or her attorney. Recent U.S. Supreme Court rulings make *ex parte* prejudgment attachments very difficult to obtain. Notice and hearing are now usually required before a party's real or personal property may be attached.

14.38. How to prepare a notice. Printed forms are sometimes used for notices, but more frequently they are typed on regular or legal-size paper. The lawyer will dictate some notices, and parts of others, but you will be expected to draw many of them without dictation. Whenever you prepare a different kind, make a copy for your form book.

The following kinds of notices are illustrated in this and other chapters.

STATE OF SOUTH CAROLINA)
) IN THE COURT OF COMMON PLEAS
)
COUNTY OF RICHLAND)

Robert C. Woods,)
)
)
              Plaintiff,)
) MOTION TO MAKE COMPLAINT MORE
    vs.   )   DEFINITE AND CERTAIN
)
Winston V. Thomas,)
)
)
             Defendant.)

TO: Jestice & Skinner, Attorneys for the Plaintiff:

    You will please take notice that the undersigned as attorneys for the defendant will move before the Honorable Henry Sims, Judge of the Court of Common Pleas, at chambers on September 24, 19–, or as soon thereafter as counsel can be heard, for an Order directing that the complaint herein be made more definite and certain in the following particulars, by alleging:

    A.   The date and time of day of the accident alleged in paragraph four (4) of the complaint.

    B.   The location of the accident as alleged in paragraph four (4) of the complaint.

    C.   The length of time confined to a hospital, to a bed at home and to the house as alleged in paragraph seven (7) of the complaint.

                                  _____

                                  Hope and Nault
                                  Attorneys for the defendant.

Dated at Columbia, S.C. this

10th day of September, 19–.

Figure 14.16. *Motion to Make Pleading More Definite and Certain.*

Notice of Filing and Entry (figure 14.17)
Notice of Settlement (figure 14.18)
Notice to Take Deposition upon Oral Examination (figure 14.19)
Notice of Motion (figure 14.20)
Notice of Appearance (figures 14.5 and 14.6)

Follow these figures for style; the wording may vary slightly with the jurisdiction.

1. Make an original for the court, copy for opposing counsel, and a copy for your files.

2. The caption is the same as that on the complaint, but you may shorten the title of the case. Be sure to include the index number.

3. The notice is addressed usually to opposing counsel. The salutation is generally in one of the following forms:

    (a) SIR: (*or* SIRS: if opposing counsel is a firm)
    (b) PLAINTIFF and CLAXTON & HAYWARD,
        HIS ATTORNEYS:
    (c) TO:
        CLAXTON & HAYWARD, ESQS.
        Attorneys for John Stevens
        15 Albert Street
        Chicago, Illinois 60630

4. Type the dateline three spaces below the last line of the notice, at the left margin.

5. The attorney signs the notice.

6. The name and address of the attorney to whom notice is given should appear on the notice, either in the salutation or after the signature.

14.39. Backing and binding of notices. The original and copies of notices, except the office copy, are stapled in appropriately endorsed legal backs, like any other court paper. You will observe that many notices refer to an "annexed" or "attached" paper. When this is the case, the notice and the other paper are stapled together, with the notice on top, unless the other paper is to be signed by the judge. Whenever a group of papers are given to the judge for signature, any paper that he or she is supposed to sign is placed on top, so the judge will not have to search for the appropriate paper. In the endorsement on the back, the name of the annexed paper is placed first because it is the more important paper. Thus, we have a legal back endorsed, "Undertaking and Notice of Motion"; "Order and Notice of Entry"; "Affidavit and Notice of Motion"; "Proposed Order and Notice of Settlement."

14.40. Service of notice. Since the purpose of the notice is to give information to opposing counsel, the notice must be served on him or her

SRM:t 7/20/-- 1-4-1

SUPREME COURT OF THE STATE OF NEW YORK

COUNTY OF NEW YORK

---x

	:	
In the Matter of	:	
	:	
the Application of the	:	FILE NO.
		11,422-19--
PEOPLE OF THE STATE OF NEW YORK, by	:	
ROLAND EVANS, as Superintend-		
ent of Insurance of the State of New	:	
York, for an order to take possession		
of the property and rehabilitate the	:	
UNIQUE INSURANCE COMPANY	:	

---x

S I R S:

PLEASE TAKE NOTICE that an order of which the within is a copy

was duly filed and entered in the office of the Clerk of the County of New York

on the 17th day of July, 19--.

Dated, New York, July 20, 19--.

Yours, etc.,

Terrance & Cameron,
Attorneys for Petitioner,
Box 27050,
New York, N. Y. 10001

To:

JONATHAN WARD, ESQ.,
Attorney for Superintendent of Insurance,
100 Fifth Avenue,
New York, N. Y. 10005

(Continued on following page)

(Continued from preceding page)

> PHILIP STAEBLER, ESQ.,
>> Attorney for Unique Insurance Company
>> and the Reorganization Committee,
>> 85 East Avenue,
>> New York, N. Y. 10016

> LOUISE F. LAWFORD, ESQ.,
>> Attorney for certain Creditors of Unique
>> Insurance Company,
>> 1400 East Avenue,
>> New York, N. Y. 10016

> MESSRS. GRAY & PACKARD,
>> Attorneys for First State National Bank,
>> 200 Northeast Parkway,
>> New York, N. Y. 10017

(To be typed on one page.)

Figure 14.17. *Notice of Filing and Entry.*

STATE OF MICHIGAN

THE CIRCUIT COURT FOR THE COUNTY OF ALGER

```
-----------------------------------------------------------------------x
                                          :
PAXTON CORPORATION,                       :         Index No. 3548-L
                                          :
                        Plaintiff,        :
                                          :
           -against-                      :     NOTICE OF SETTLEMENT
                                          :
DAVID WOODHAVEN,                          :
                                          :
                        Defendant.        :
-----------------------------------------------------------------------x
```

To: CHISHOLM & WASHINGTON, ESQ.,
  Attorneys for Defendant,
    669 Canby Street,
      Muskegon, Michigan 49344

SIRS:

      PLEASE TAKE NOTICE that a proposed order, of which the annexed

is a true copy, will be submitted for signature and settlement to Honorable

Michael March, Justice, at the office of the Clerk of Special Term, Part II, at the Alger County Court House, Munising, Michigan, on the 11th day of July, 19--, at ten o'clock in the forenoon of that day.

Dated, Michigan, July 7, 19--.

Yours, etc.,

SHERMAN & COVE,
Attorneys for Plaintiff,
1147 Park Lane,
Muskegon, Michigan 49344

Figure 14.18. *Notice of Settlement.*

JMH: 7-1--- 1-1-1

UNITED STATES DISTRICT COURT

SOUTHERN DISTRICT OF NEW YORK

--x

LINVILLE CORPORATION,

                                    Plaintiff, : Index No. L 69-218

             -against-   : NOTICE TO TAKE
                                 : DEPOSITION UPON
                                 ORAL EXAMINATION

BOYINGTON DISCOUNT STORES, INC., :

                   Defendant. :

--x

SIRS:

      PLEASE TAKE NOTICE that at 10:00 o'clock in the forenoon on the 7th day of July, 19-, at the offices of Elman & Cooper, the plaintiff in the

(Continued on following page)

(Continued from preceding page)

above entitled action will take the deposition of Paul Manchester, president

of defendant Boyington Discount Stores, Inc., who resides at 20 Triangle

Lane, Long Island, New York, 11040 upon oral examination pursuant to the

Federal Rules of Civil Procedure, before an officer authorized by law to take

depositions. The examination will continue from day to day until

completed. You are invited to attend and cross-examine. The address of said

offices is 117 West 42nd Street, New York, N. Y. 10017.

Dated New York, July 1, 19–.

                        Yours, etc.,

                              LOWES & HILL,
                              Attorneys for Plaintiff,
                              117 West 42nd Street,
                              New York, N. Y. 10017

To:

        JEFFERSON & GRANVILLE,
        Attorneys for Defendant
        200 Lexington Avenue,
        New York, N. Y. 10016

(To be typed on one page.)

Figure 14.19. *Notice to Take Deposition Upon Oral Examination.*

(except in rare cases of *ex parte* attachment) and proof of that service filed in court. Generally notice may be served and receipt of copy or proof of service made in the same manner as service of an answer (see page 000). Enter the service and filing of notices in your suit register. If the notice refers to a date by which some action must be taken, *enter that date in your diary*. Be most meticulous about this entry, because the attorney's failure to take the required action might result in the loss of the law suit for his client. Remind the attorney of the entry in the same manner that you remind him of all diary entries (chapter 3).

MOTION AND NOTICE OF MOTION

    14.41. What is a motion? A *motion* is an application for an order addressed to the court or to a judge in his or her chambers by a party to a

IN THE CIRCUIT COURT OF THE SEVENTH JUDICIAL DISTRICT
SANGAMON COUNTY, ILLINOIS

JAMES R. KINLEY,   )
)
           Plaintiff   )
)
      vs.   )   NO. 431/--
)
RUFUS BENNINGTON,   )
)
         DEFENDANT)

NOTICE

TO:
    Margaret N. Hedrow,
    Illinois Building
    Springfield, Illinois 62705
       Attorney for Defendant

    PLEASE TAKE NOTICE that on 7th day of October, A.D. 19--, at 10:00
A.M., or as soon thereafter as counsel may be heard, we shall appear before
the Honorable WIlliam C. Yates, Judge of the Circuit Court, at Springfield,
Illinois, and shall present the motion, true copy of which is attached hereto.

    Dated this 18th day of September, A.D. 19--.

                              Enderlin and Dallas
                              First National Bank Building
                              Springfield, Illinois 62703
                              Attorneys for Plaintiff

    Received a true copy of the above notice, together with a copy of motion
attached thereto, this ____ day of September, A.D. 19--.

                              _____
                              Attorney for Defendant

Figure 14.20. *Notice of Motion.*

law suit. Whenever an attorney wants the court to take any action in a
pending case, he or she "moves" the court to take that action. Motions are
numerous and varied. They include:

Motion for Change of Venue
Motion to Strike
Motion for New Trial
Motion for Leave to Amend
Motion to Set Cause for Trial

Unless a motion is made during a hearing or trial, it is in writing. Notice of the motion is usually given to opposing counsel so he or she will have a chance to contest it.

In federal courts and in many other jurisdictions, the written notice to the attorney constitutes compliance with the requirement that a motion must be in writing. Thus, we will have the written notice of motion, but no written motion, the motion being made orally at the hearing. The *notice of motion* states the papers and proceedings upon which the motion will be brought and also the grounds of the motion. The supporting papers usually include an affidavit that is attached to the notice of motion.

Some jurisdictions have special terms of court at which all motions are heard. In crowded jurisdictions, the contested motions are heard in one part, and *ex parte* motions (see page 481), of which opposing counsel has no notice, are heard in another part. You should acquaint yourself with the part in which they are heard, if there is a disctinction in any of the courts in your locality.

14.42. Return day of motion. All notices of motion give the date the attorney will move the court for entry of the desired order. This date is the *return day* of the motion; the motion is *returnable* on that day. The practice rules provide that the notice must be served on opposing counsel a specified number of days, or a reasonable time, before the return day of the motion. Some jurisdictions that do not have special terms of courts for motions set aside certain days in the month as "motion day," on which days all motions are returnable. You should become familiar with (1) the motion days in the various courts and (2) how many days of notice are required.

14.43. Information you need to prepare a notice of motion. Figure 14.20 illustrates a notice of motion. They are prepared like other notices (page 330). The lawyer will dictate some notices of motions, but you should be able to prepare many of them upon instructions from him or her without dictation. You will need the following information:

1. Style of case. You can get this from the complaint or other papers in the file.

2. Papers and proceedings upon which the motion will be based. The lawyer usually dictates this.

3. Grounds upon which the motion will be made. The lawyer will

dictate these, except when they are standard. For example, a motion to strike is always on the ground that portions of the pleadings are "sham, irrelevant and redundant." (The standard wording of the clause varies with the court.)

4. Return day of motion (page 338). If you do not know how to calculate the return day, ask the lawyer.

5. Time motion will be heard. Usually court practice rules set aside a certain hour at which motions will be called. If you are not familiar with this time in the various courts, ask the lawyer or consult the rules. The notice will read "at .... o'clock in the ...... noon, or as soon thereafter as counsel can be heard."

6. Where the motion will be heard. Motions are usually heard in the court where the case is pending. In some jurisdictions specific terms, parts, departments, or divisions are set aside for motions.

7. Name of affiant and date of supporting affidavit, if the motion is based on an affidavit, as it usually is. The lawyer will give you this information. Very probably he or she will dictate the affidavit before instructing you about the notice.

14.44. What to do about the notice of motion and affidavit. A motion is frequently based upon an affidavit (see below), as appears from the wording of the notice. When this is the case, your responsibilities, after preparation of the notice and affidavit, are the following:

1. Endorse a legal back "Affidavit and Notice of Motion" and staple the papers together, placing the notice on top.

2. After approval by the lawyer, see that copy is served on opposing counsel.

3. See that receipt of service is on back of original. If the papers are served by mail, prepare certificate of service by mail.

4. *Enter return day of motion in your diary.*

5. Conform your office copy.

6. File original, with proof of service, in court.

7. Make entries in suit register of service and filing.

8. If you are employed by the attorney on whom the papers are served, make notation on back of your copy of date and hour of service. *Enter in diary return day of motion.* Also make entry in suit register.

AFFIDAVIT FOR USE IN COURT

14.45. Analysis of Affidavit. Affidavits, other than those for use in court cases, were discussed in chapter 11. That discussion is applicable to all affidavits. The content of an *affidavit* for use in court cases always relates to the case. If differs from verification in that the affiant swears that facts stated in the affidavit are true, whereas the verifier swears to the truth of statements made in a pleading to which the verification is attached.

An affidavit for use in court cases consists of the following parts:

1. Caption
2. Title
3. Venue
4. Body
5. Signature of affiant
6. Jurat
7. Signature and seal, or stamp, of notary public

14.46. How to prepare an affidavit for court use. Figure 14.21 illustrates an affidavit for use in court. It is prepared like any affidavit, with this important exception: It is preceded by a caption like the one on the complaint. If differs from a verification in form in that it is complete, with caption and legal back, whereas the verification is actually a part of the pleading that it verifies.

1. Use the size paper preferred by the court or what is customary in your office.

2. Make an original for court, copy for opposing counsel, and copy for your file.

3. The caption is the same as that on the complaint and includes the index number. The title of the case may be shortened.

4. The box is followed by the recital of the venue.

5. Type a line for signature.

6. The jurat is typed at the left of the page.

7. Type a line for the notary's signature.

8. Endorse a legal back, if one is used, for all copies except the office copy. The endorsement will depend on what the affidavit is about. It might be "Affidavit in Opposition," or "Affidavit of Service by Mail," or any one of a number of other subjects. If another paper is bound in the back with the affidavit, the endorsement will also include the title of that paper.

9. After approval by the lawyer, have affiant sign original affidavit.

10. Notarize original and conform copies.

JMH:p 12/15/- 2-1

IN THE CIRCUIT COURT OF THE FIRST JUDICIAL DISTRICT

OF HINDS COUNTY, MISSISSIPPI

ADAM SHALLOHE,	PLAINTIFF)	
	)	
	)	
VS.	)	NO. _____
	)	
	)	
	)	
RICHARD RAMSEY,	DEFENDANT)	

AFFIDAVIT OPPOSING MOTION

STATE OF MISSISSIPPI

COUNTY OF HINDS

GRANT F. RIGGS, being duly sworn, deposes and says: He is an attorney and counsellor at law, associated with the firm of Messrs. Hettinger & Pomona, attorneys for the defendant herein, and that he has knowledge of all of the facts hereinafter set forth.

[Set forth facts here.]

WHEREFORE, your deponent prays that plaintiff's motion be denied, with the costs of this motion.

_____

SWORN TO AND SUBSCRIBED before me, this the 15th day of December, 19--.

_____

Figure 14.21. *Affidavit in Opposition.*

ORDERS

14.47. Analysis of an order. Every direction of a court, judge, or justice, made or entered in writing and not included in a judgment or decree, is called an *order*. Orders are made upon motion of counsel. A judge who decides a motion may say to counsel, "Submit order," or, "Settle order on notice." If the judge directs prevailing counsel to "submit order," counsel will prepare the order and submit it to the court without service of a copy on opposing counsel. After the order is entered, prevailing counsel serves a copy on opposing counsel with a notice that it was filed and entered in the office of the county clerk (see figure 14.17).

If the judge tells counsel to "settle order on notice," the prevailing counsel is obliged to serve a copy of the proposed order on opposing counsel. Opposing counsel, in turn, is permitted to serve a "counterorder," which is his or her version of the judge's decision. On the date named in the order, the order and the counterorder are submitted to the judge, who will sign the order that he or she thinks embodies the terms of his or her decision. The judge might make changes in the order or decide to rewrite it entirely.

If an order is entered while the court is sitting, it is called a *court order*. If it is signed by a judge, or justice, in his or her chambers or elsewhere while the court is not in session, it is called a *judge's order*. Both have the same legal effect, but in many jurisdictions there is a distinction in the form and wording.

14.48. How to prepare an order. The caption of an order entered *while the court is sitting* usually differs from the caption of the pleadings in two respects (see figure 14.22):

1. It shows the term and name of the court, where the court is sitting, and the date, in a single-spaced legend at the right of the page.

2. The name of the presiding judge precedes the box. The order also has a space for the judge's signature and the initials of his title. Thus, U. S. D. J. (United States District Judge); J. S. C. (Justice of Supreme Court); J. C. C. (Justice of City Court); J. M. C. (Justice of Municipal Court), and so on. In some courts the word *enter* precedes the signature, thus:

Enter,

_____

J.S.C.

When an order is signed by a judge *while the court is not sitting*, the caption is similar to that on the complaint. "Enter" does not precede the

At a Special Term, Part II, of the
Supreme Court of the State of New
York, held in and for the County of
Kings, at the Courthouse thereof,
Fulton and Joralemon Streets, in the
Borough of Brooklyn, City of New
York, on the 18th day of July, 19--.

PRESENT:

HON. MILTON B. HUNTER,

Justice.

- -x

DONALD RUTHERFORD

Plaintiff

-against-

JEFFREY LANDIS

Defendant

- -x

On reading and filing the annexed stipulation and consent of the
attorney for the plaintiff, and the attorneys for the defendant, dated the 16th
day of July, 19--, and on motion of LOUIS BOWMAN, attorney for the plaintiff,
it is

ORDERED, that the testimony of the plaintiff, DONALD RUTHERFORD,
be taken as a witness in his own behalf, without the state, pursuant to the
terms of the said stipulation, by ANDREW MADDOCK, ESQ., Solicitor, residing
in Downport, County Down, Ireland, upon the interrogatories and cross-
interrogatories annexed to the said stipulation, and it is further

(Continued on following page)

(Continued from preceding page)

ORDERED, that after the taking of the said deposition the said

ANDREW MADDOCK return the same in a single packet securely sealed, by

registered mail, postage prepaid, to the County Clerk of Kings County, at the

courthouse, Fulton and Joralemon Streets, Borough of Brooklyn, City of New

York, 11201 U.S.A., and it is further

ORDERED, that the trial of the action be stayed until the return of the

said deposition.

ENTER

J.S.C.

Figure 14.22. *Court Order.*

signature as is the case with court orders in many courts. Type the judge's title in full instead of the initials. Figure 14.23 illustrates a judge's order.

Although an order to show cause is a court order, it is prepared like a judge's order.

In all other respects an order is set up and typed like the pleadings.

Endorse legal backs, if required, for all copies except your office copy. If a notice is attached to the order, as is frequently the case, endorse the back "Order and Notice of Entry" (or "Notice of Settlement," or whatever the notice is called). Place the copy of the order that the judge is to sign on top of the set of papers, but in the other sets place the notice on top.

14.49. What to do about an order. *When the judge instructs counsel to settle order on notice.*

1. Prepare the following three papers:
    a. *Proposed order.* Make an original for the court; two copies for each opposing counsel, one to be served with notice of settlement and one to be served after the order is entered.
    b. *Notice of settlement.* Make a copy for each opposing counsel and an office copy. The notice is not filed in court.
    c. *Notice of entry.* If the legal back has this notice printed on the inside, you will not have to type it. If you do type it, make a copy for each opposing counsel, and an office copy.

IN THE CIRCUIT COURT FOR JEFFERSON COUNTY, ALABAMA

JASPER FREIGHT LINES,   )
)
)
)
                 Plaintiff,   )
)
)
)
        v.   )   IN EQUITY
)   NO. 5487-X
)
LILLIAN STACY,   )
)
)
)
                 Defendant.   )

ORDER

The plaintiff above named having duly moved for an order

_____

_____

_____ ;

NOW, after reading and filing the _____

_____ ,

on motion of Page & Newton, Esqs., attorneys for the plaintiff, and no one

appearing in opposition thereto, it is hereby

ORDERED by the Court that _____

_____ .

Dated this 6th day of July, 19____.

_____
                Circuit Judge

Figure 14.23. *Judge's Order.*

2. Staple notice of settlement (figure 14.18) on top of proposed order, a copy for each opposing counsel. The legal back will be endorsed "Proposed Order and Notice of Settlement."

3. See that service is made on opposing counsel and that receipt of service is acknowledged on the original of the order.

4. *Enter in diary* the date the proposed order will be submitted to the court.

5. Make entry in suit register of service of notice of settlement.

6. Staple notice of entry (figure 14.17) on top of order, a copy for each opposing counsel. The legal back, if any, will be endorsed "Order and Notice of Entry."

7. The lawyer will take to court the original of the proposed order and the copies that are stapled with the notice of entry. The judge will "settle" the order and will make any necessary changes in pen and ink on the original of the order as submitted. If he or she signs and enters the order immediately, the lawyer will conform the copies to the order as entered.

8. If the judge does not sign the order immediately, make a follow-up *entry in your diary* and follow the law journal closely to see when the order is entered.

9. As soon as the order is signed, see that conformed copies with notice of entry are served on opposing counsel *immediately*. Prompt service of the settlement of order is very important, because opposing counsel's time to take an appeal begins to run when service is made, not when the order is entered.

10. Make entry in suit register of order and of service.

11. *Make entry in diary* of last day to appeal from order.

12. If you are employed by the attorney on whom notice of entry is served, make entries in the suit register *and in the diary*.

When the judge instructs counsel to submit order. It is not necessary to serve a copy of the order on opposing counsel before submitting it to the court or judge. No notice of settlement is necessary.

1. Make an original of the order for the court, a copy for opposing counsel, and an office copy.

2. Make copy of notice of entry for each opposing counsel and an office copy.

3. Proceed as in steps 6 through 12, above.

FINDINGS OF FACT AND CONCLUSIONS (OR RULINGS) OF LAW

14.50. What the "findings of fact and conclusions (or rulings) of law" are. At the trial of a case, certain facts are determined from the pleadings and evidence. Certain rules of law are applicable to those facts. After the trial of a case by the court without the jury, the court directs the attorneys to prepare a statement of the facts and applicable rules of law. This statement is designated *findings of fact and conclusions (or rulings) of law.* In other jurisdictions, the court directs counsel for both sides to prepare findings of fact and conclusions (or rulings) of law. In some jurisdictions, the court directs counsel for only one party to prepare the statement; opposing counsel then has a specified time within which to file objections and submit his or her proposed findings. The secretary's and paralegal's duties are the same in either situation.

14.51. How to prepare findings of fact and conclusions (or rulings) of law. The lawyer dictates the findings of fact and conclusions (or rulings) of law.

1. Make an original for the court, a copy for each counsel, and a copy for your file.

2. The caption is the same as on the complaint.

3. The document is entitled "Findings of Fact and Conclusions (or Rulings) of Law."

4. The findings of fact are enumerated, beginning with FIRST, or I.

5. The conclusions (or rulings) of law are enumerated, beginning with FIRST, or I.

6. The dateline is typed below the last conclusion (or ruling) of law, at the left margin.

7. Type a line for the judge's signature.

8. Endorse legal backs and all copies except your office copy.

14.52. What to do about findings of fact and conclusions (or rulings) of law.

1. As soon as the court directs counsel to prepare findings of fact and conclusions (or rulings) of law, *enter in diary* the date by which the statement must be prepared.

2. See that copy is served on opposing counsel. ("Judgment," page 348, is sometimes prepared and served at the same time.)

3. See that receipt of copy is acknowledged, or make an affidavit of service by mail.

4. *Enter in diary* date by which opposing counsel must file objections and submit his proposed findings.

5. The original, with proof of service on opposing counsel, is submitted to the judge who tried the case.

6. Make entry in suit register of service, submission to judge, signing, and filing.

INSTRUCTIONS TO THE JURY

14.53. What an instruction to the jury is. When a case is tried by a jury, the court instructs or *charges* it regarding the law applicable to the action. Counsel for both sides submit to the court instructions they want the court to give the jury. The court may give an instruction as proposed by counsel, may modify it, or may refuse to give it. Counsel may take exception to instructions given to the jury at the request of opposing counsel, or to a modification of, or refusal to give, an instruction that he or she proposed.

14.54. How to prepare an instruction to the jury. Many offices keep printed forms of stock instructions, but the lawyer will dictate others.

1. Make an original for the judge, a copy for opposing counsel, and an office copy.

2. Type each instruction on a separate sheet of paper.

3. Number each instruction for identification purposes.

4. Identify the party submitting the instructions, thus, "Plaintiff's Instruction No. ....." (This may be placed at the top or bottom of the charge; numbers are inserted later in the order in which the charge is given.)

5. There is no caption.

6. Instructions are not stapled in a legal back and are not endorsed.

JUDGMENTS AND DECREES

14.55. What judgments and decrees are. A decision by a court, after a trial or hearing, of the rights of the parties is a *judgment*. Broadly speaking, any adjudication by a court of law or of equity is considered a judgment, but technically an adjudication by a court sitting in equity is a *decree*. The words *judgment* and *decree* are often used synonymously by the statutes, especially in states where the civil procedure codes have abolished the formal distinction between law and equity. A decree usually directs the defendant to do or not to do some specific thing, as opposed to a judgment for money damages in a court of law. The sentence in a criminal case is the judgment.

A decree or judgment is *interlocutory* when it leaves unsettled some question to be determined in the future; for example, a temporary injunction is an interlocutory decree. A decree or judgment is *final* when it disposes of the case, leaving no question to be decided in the future. The parties, however, may appeal to a higher court from a final judgment or decree. The execution of the judgment is *stayed* pending the higher court's decision.

A judgment is sometimes entered "on the pleadings" upon motion of counsel, before a trial of the cause is reached. For example, the plaintiff moves the court to strike the answer of the defendant and direct judgment for the plaintiff. More frequently, judgment is not entered until the case has been tried and findings of fact have been made (page 346).

14.56. How to prepare a judgment or decree. In a few jurisdictions, the clerk of the court prepares the judgments, but usually the prevailing lawyer does. The lawyer will dictate the judgment or decree. A judgment is similar in style to a court order (figure 14.22). Follow figure 14.24 for the style of a decree.

14.57. Number of copies. It might be necessary to prepare extra copies, in addition to the usual original for the court, copy for each opposing counsel, and your office copy. The number of copies will depend upon the following factors:

1. Number of copies to be certified for delivery to the parties.

2. Whether service of copy is made on opposing counsel with notice of entry (see page 344) after judgment is entered as well as before the judgment is submitted to the court.

3. Kind of action.

You will have to ask the lawyer about the number of copies, or you might get the information from a practice manual. When you prepare a judgment in the various types of actions, you should familiarize yourself with the number of copies required.

14.58. What to do about a judgment or decree.

1. See that copy is served on opposing counsel. Notice is not usually attached, but findings of fact and conclusions of law (page 346) frequently accompany the judgment.

2. See that receipt of copy is acknowledged, or make affidavit of service by mail.

3. The lawyer will submit the original, with proof of service, to the judge who tried the case. If it is not signed immediately, *enter in diary* reminder to follow up.

4. When judgment has been signed and filed, the clerk of the court enters it. Check legal newspaper for book and page of entry, and note on office copy and in suit register. If entry is not made within a few days after the judgment was signed, check with the clerk of the court.

5. Serve notice of entry of judgment (see figure 14.17) on opposing

IN THE DISTRICT COURT IN AND FOR THE CITY AND COUNTY
OF DENVER AND STATE OF COLORADO
CIVIL ACTION NO. 3-504, Div. 7

CAROLINE BILLINGS FRY,	)	
	)	
Plaintiff,	)	
	)	
-vs-	)	INTERLOCUTORY DECREE IN DIVORCE.
	)	
DOUGLAS MONROE FRY,	)	
	)	
Defendant.	)	

THIS CAUSE, coming on to be heard on this 9th day of January, 19–,
upon its merits, the plaintiff being represented by Jones & Fairmount,
attorneys of record, and the defendant appearing by Crystal & Gwinner,
attorneys of record, and the Court having examined the full record herein,
finds that it has jurisdiction herein; and having heard the evidence and the
statements of counsel, the Court now being fully advised

DOTH FIND that a divorce should be granted to the
plaintiff herein upon the statutory grounds of _____

_____ .

IT IS ORDERED, ADJUDGED and DECREED by the Court, that an
absolute divorce should be granted to the plaintiff, and an Interlocutory
Decree of Divorce is hereby entered, dissolving the marriage of plaintiff and
defendant six months after the date of this Interlocutory Decree.

IT IS EXPRESSLY DECREED by the Court that during such six months
period after the signing of this Interlocutory Decree the

(Continued on following page)

(Continued from preceding page)

parties hereto shall not be divorced, shall still be husband and wife, and neither party shall be competent to contract another marriage anywhere during such period, and the Court during all of said period does hereby retain jurisdiction of the parties and the subject matter of this cause and upon motion of either party, or upon its motion, for good cause shown, after a hearing, may set aside this Interlocutory Decree.

It is further ORDERED, ADJUDGED and DECREED by the Court that defendant shall pay into the Registry of the District Court on the _____

_____ .

It is further ORDERED, ADJUDGED and DECREED by the Court that the sole care, custody and control of the minor children, Lester Douglas Fry and Julia Caroline Fry, is hereby awarded to the plaintiff as a suitable person to have such care and custody until the further order of the Court, with the defendant to have reasonable visitation rights.

The Court FURTHER DECREES that after six months from the date hereof this Interlocutory Decree shall be and become a Final Decree of Divorce and the parties shall then be divorced, unless this Interlocutory Decree shall have been set aside, or an appeal has been taken, or a writ of error has been issued.

Done in open Court this 9th day of January, 19--.

BY THE COURT,

Judge.

APPROVED AS TO FORM:

Crystal & Gwinner
Attorneys for Defendant.

Figure 14.24. *Interlocutory Decree of Divorce.*

counsel immediately after entry. In some actions it is necessary to serve another copy of the judgment with notice of entry. This extra copy was made at the time the original was typed.

    6. *Enter in diary* last day that opposing counsel may take an appeal.

    7. File original notice of entry with proof of service with court. Make entry in suit register.

15

How to Handle Records

on Appeal, Briefs,

and Citations

The party who loses a law suit, or who is dissatisfied with a judgment or court order or decree, may ask a higher court to review the decision of the lower court with the hope that the higher court will reverse or modify the lower court's decision. When a case is appealed, the lawyers for each party file a *brief* with the appellate court in support of their contentions. This chapter describes procedure for review by a higher court. It also gives the fundamentals that affect your part in the preparation of a brief. Illustrations show the appearance of typed and printed briefs.

15.1. Rules of the reviewing court. The procedure for taking a case to a higher court is governed by the rules of the highest state tribunal. These rules are based upon the civil practice acts or codes of civil procedure and are usually found in an appendix to the act or code. They may also be obtained in pamphlet form from the clerk of the appellate court or from the state judicial council. The United States Supreme Court makes the rules for appeals to it and, also, for appeals from federal district courts to federal courts of appeal.

You can easily find in these rules the information you should have to do your part of the appellate work in accordance with the court's requirements. The rules provide, among other things, for the following:

1. Methods for review
2. Content of the record on appeal
3. Form of testimony (question and answer, narrative, or abstract)
4. Preparation and format of record
5. Preparation and format of brief
6. Time allowed for filing and service of papers
7. Method of service on opposing counsel
8. Costs

15.2. Methods for review by a higher court. The method for review by the higher tribunal is by *appeal* from the lower court to the higher court, in the majority of states. In a few states, the method is by a petition to the higher court for a *writ of error*. At one time chancery cases were reviewed by means of an appeal and law cases by means of a writ of error. This distinction in appellate procedure now exists in very few states. Regardless of the method for review, the procedure is loosely referred to as *taking an appeal, appealing a case*. The use of the term *appeal* here embraces both appeals and writs of error.

A case may also be referred to a higher court, under special circumstances, by means of extraordinary writs, such as *certiori, mandamus, habeas corpus, prohibition, quo warranto,* and *stay writs.* These writs eliminate the necessity of hearings and trials in the lower court.

In some states the appeal is to an intermediate appellate court (see page 257) and thence to the highest state court. In states that do not have intermediary appellate courts (and in certain cases even if they do), the appeal is direct from the trial court to the highest court. The procedure for taking an appeal to an intermediate appellate court is similar to, but not exactly the same as, taking an appeal to the highest state tribunal. The main variations are in the details, such as the time allowed for the various steps taken, disbursements to be paid, whether the papers are to be typewritten or printed, and the size and quality of paper that is to be used. Check the rules of the intermediate appellate court.

15.3. Diary entries. The reviewing court's rules require that an appeal must be perfected according to a strict timetable. It is your duty to make diary entries of the schedule so there will be no slip-up on the part of your office. You should also note the progress of the appeal in the suit register (see chapter 12). The rules of some courts provide for return days of appeals, just as they do for pleadings (see page 338). Other courts consider the date upon which the record on appeal is filed as the date from which the time for filing motions and briefs will run. You can get the appropriate timetable from the reviewing court's rules, or the lawyer will give it to you. Dates by which the following steps must be taken should be entered in the diary:

1. Filing notice of appeal by appellant
2. Assignment of errors and instructions by appellant for making up transcript of record
3. Filing of additional instructions by appellee
4. Filing of record on appeal in reviewing court
5. Appellee's motion to quash or dismiss an appeal
6. Hearing of motions
7. Filing of appellant's brief
8. Filing of appellee's brief
9. Filing of appellant's reply brief

15.4. Change in caption of case. From the time the record is filed with the appellate court, the caption of the case changes. The caption on all motions and brief thereafter filed shows the name of the appellate court, and the designation of the parties shows their appellate status. The lower court's index number of the case is no longer indicated.

15.5. Designation of parties to an appeal. In almost all states the party appealing is referred to as the *appellant,* and the party opposing the appeal is referred to as the *appellee* or the *respondent.* When the defendant in the lower case is the appellant, the title of the case is reversed in the majority of the states. Thus, *John Smith v. Alfred Jones* becomes *Alfred Jones v. John Smith.* But this is not the practice in all states. Eight methods of designating parties on appeal in the caption are shown in figure 15.1. In cases where review is by petition for a writ, the party appealing is designated as the *petitioner* and the other party as the *respondent.*

Although the designation of the parties changes in the title of the case, the briefs sometimes refer to the parties by their designation in the lower court. (Some rules require this designation.) Or the brief might refer to a party by the lower court designation on one page and by the appellate court designation on the other. The change in designation is very confusing, and the lawyer might inadvertently refer to the defendant-appellant instead of plaintiff-appellant or to the plaintiff instead of plaintiff-in-error. Before the lawyer begins to dictate a brief to you, or you begin to transcribe a dictated brief or tape, fix firmly in your mind the designation of the parties in both the trial and appellate courts so you will observe any error in designation of parties.

STYLES OF DESIGNATION OF PARTIES ON APPEAL BY DEFENDANT TO
HIGHEST STATE COURT WHEN TITLE OF CASE IN LOWER COURT WAS

Joseph Smith, Plaintiff, vs. William White, Defendant

Style 1 (Names reversed)

William White,
    Appellant,
vs.
Joseph Smith,
    Appellee.

Style 5 (Names not reversed)

Joseph Smith,
    Appellee,
vs.
William White,
    Appellant.

Style 2 (Names not reversed)

Joseph Smith,
    Plaintiff and Respondent,
vs.
William White,
    Defendant and Appellant.

Style 6 (Names not reversed)

Joseph Smith,
    Respondent,
vs.
William White,
    Appellant.

Style 3 (Names not reversed)

Joseph Smith,
    Plaintiff and Appellee,
vs.
William White,
    Defendant and Appellant.

Style 7 (Names reversed)

William White,
    Appellant and Defendant,
vs.
Joseph Smith,
    Respondent and Plaintiff.

Style 4 (Names reversed)

William White,
    Plaintiff-in-Error
vs.
Joseph Smith,
    Defendant-in-Error.

Style 8 (Names reversed)

William White,
    Defendant Below, Appellant,
vs.
Joseph Smith,
    Plaintiff Below, Appellee.

Figure 15.1. *Methods of Designating Parties on Appeal in the Caption.*

15.6. Notice of appeal. Under the rules of a typical state, the filing of a *notice of appeal* with the clerk of the court whose order is appealed from gives the appellate court jurisdiciton, and an appeal is deemed to have commenced. The time usually allowed for filing a notice of appeal is 30 days (see the rules) after receipt of a copy of the judgment with notice of entry.

You can get the wording of the notice of appeal from the court rules or from a form book, or the lawyer will dictate it or give you a form to follow. Set it up in the same manner and use the same kind of paper as for other court papers.

1. Make an original, a copy for each appellee, and a copy for your files (but see 5 below).
2. The caption is the same as that on the pleadings.
3. Bind in a legal back, properly endorsed.
4. The attorney for the party who appeals signs the notice of appeal.
5. Serve a copy on counsel for appellee and file the original, with proof of service, with the clerk of the court. In some states the rules do not require service of notice of appeal on opposing counsel, but a copy is usually given to opposing counsel for his or her file. In other states the rules require that the notice be filed in duplicate, one containing the proof of service.

15.7. Service on opposing counsel. Service of all papers and notices required by the rules of the appellate court may be made by leaving them in the office of the opposing counsel during regular office hours with a person in charge of the office or by depositing them, securely sealed and postpaid, in the post office directed to such attorney at his or her usual post office address. Proof of service is made by affidavit. The lawyer's secretary will probably mail the document and, therefore, make the affidavit, when service is had by mail. Placing the properly sealed and addressed document in an "outgoing basket" to be dispatched by the mail clerk in your office is not compliance with the statute. You must actually do what the affidavit of service says. Figure 15.2 illustrates an affidavit of service by mail. If the wording of the affidavit used in your office differs, make an extra copy for your form book.

Notice that the affidavit is preceded by the caption of the case. When this affidavit is copied into the record on appeal, the caption will be omitted, but the recital of venue will be included.

CONTENTS AND PREPARATION OF THE RECORD ON APPEAL

15.8. What is a record on appeal? A *record on appeal* is a copy of the pleadings, exhibits, orders, or decrees filed in a case in the lower court, and a transcript of the testimony taken in the case. The purpose of the record is to inform the appellate court of what transpired in the lower court. The rules specify that the record must be abbreviated as much as possible, so the judges will not have to wade through a mass of extraneous material. The appellate court does not need to be informed about matters that are not pertinent to the decision of the questions before it. Furthermore, the larger the record, the more expensive it is.

15.9. Assignment of errors and instructions to the clerk. Within a certain number of days after the notice of an appeal is filed, the

IN THE CIRCUIT COURT OF THE ELEVENTH
JUDICIAL CIRCUIT OF FLORIDA, IN AND FOR
DADE COUNTY.

---x

JOSEPH SMITH,   :

                      Plaintiff,   :

              vs.   :   No. 13,670-C

WILLIAM WHITE,   :

                      Defendant.   :

---x

AFFIDAVIT OF SERVICE

STATE OF FLORIDA,)
                   : SS.
DADE COUNTY.   )

     Before the subscriber personally appeared LILLIAN MACKENZIE, who,
being first duly sworn, deposes and says that she is employed by Warner &
Oates and was so employed on January 8, 19--; that on said date she
personally placed in an envelope addressed to Merrill Webster, Esq., a true
copy of the foregoing Notice of Appeal; that said envelope, having been
properly addressed and sealed, with sufficient postage affixed thereto, was
deposited by her on said date in the United States Mails at Miami, Florida.

                                      _____

Subscribed and Sworn to Before Me
This 8th day of January, 19--.

_____
Notary Public, State of Florida
at Large.
My commission expires: 5/8/--.
(SEAL)

Figure 15.2. *Affidavit of Service by Mail.*

number being specified by the rules, the appellant files *assignments of error and directions to the clerk* for making up the transcript of record on appeal. The assignments of error and directions to the clerk may be combined in one document.

The purposes of an *assignment of errors* are to apprise the appellate court of the specific questions presented by the appellant for consideration and to inform the opposite party of the matters of error relied on, so discussion may be limited and concentrated on those points.

The *directions to the clerk* designate the portion of the proceeding and evidence to be included in the transcript of record—those portions pertinent to the questions before the appellate court. The appellee might consider that other portions of the record will throw light on the questions to be reviewed by the court. If so, the appellee files additional directions and cross-assignments.

In lieu of directions to the clerk the parties may file written stipulations with the clerk designating the contents of the record.

Preparation. The directions for preparing the notice of appeal apply also to assignments of error and instructions to the clerk (see page 356). The originals are filed with the clerk of the court, and copies are served on counsel for the appellee. Proof of service of these documents on opposing counsel is filed with the clerk and included in the transcript of record.

15.10. Who prepares the record. The clerk of the court or the appellant prepares the record from the directions to the clerk filed by the parties. The common practice is to employ a court reporter to make up the transcript, but the secretary to an attorney for the appellant sometimes prepares the record.

15.11. How to prepare the record. The instructions to the clerk will indicate to you the documents and evidence to be included in the record. You will copy them from the papers in the court file, which you may obtain from the clerk of the court. The following directions are applicable to the preparation of records in any state:

1. Omit formal parts of documents.
2. Copy pleadings in the order of filing.
3. In the center of the page, just above the pleading, put in solid caps the nature or kind of document, such as "Demurrer to Amended Complaint" (not simply "Demurrer").
4. Do not copy the caption of the pleadings.
5. Indicate the filing date of each pleading by typing "Filed" and the date at the end of the pleading. This information is usually stamped on the back of the document.
6. The first page in the record is a complete index that gives in chronological order the date of the filing of each instrument in the court

below, the name or character of the instrument, and the page of the record where it may be found. The index is prepared last.

15.12. Format and make-up of record. *Consult the rules.* They provide whether the record must be printed or typewritten, or either. They also specify the kind of paper, size of type, folio size, and the like. Here are the requirements in a typical state that permits a record to be either printed or typewritten. If directions refer to printed records, see chapter 8, "Preparing Material for Printing."

The following requirements also apply to briefs.

1. Black and distinct lettering
2. Type no smaller than small pica
3. Double spaced (this requirement is stated in terms of leading for a printed brief)
4. Margin no less than one inch
5. Quoted material indented and singled spaced (for a printed record this requirement is stated in terms of ems)
6. Opaque, white, unglossed paper
7. Legal cap is typewritten; 6 by 9 inch folio if printed

15.13. Binding, volumes, and title. The record is bound in pamphlets. If typewritten, the pamphlets are securely fastened; if printed, they are stitched. If the record consists of more than 200 pages, it should be bound in two or more volumes. The cover of each volume contains the style of the cause, the title of the appellate court, the title of the court from which the cause is appealed, and the names and addresses of counsel, and, if more than one volume, the number of the volume.

15.14. Certification, filing, and service. The record is certified by the clerk of the lower court and also verified by the clerk if he or she does not prepare it. A copy (or copies) is served on opposing counsel, and the original and required number of copies (see the rules) filed with the clerk of the appellate court, together with proof of service. The record must be filed within the time specified by the rules. A filing fee is required at the time the record is filed.

THE BRIEF

15.15. Nature of a brief. *Black's Law Dictionary* gives the following complete, yet concise, definition of a *brief*: "A written or printed document, prepared by counsel to serve as the basis of an argument upon a cause in an appellate court, and usually filed for the information of the court. It embodies the law which the counsel desires to establish, together with the arguments and authorities upon which he rests his contention." *Brief* is short for *brief of argument."*

The brief must contain a history of the appealed case, a statement of the questions or points involved, and the argument. The history is a concise statement of the essential facts without argument. It states the purpose of the litigation, contains a chronological enumeration of the pleadings, the issues, and the judgment of the trial court, giving references to applicable pages of the transcript. The questions or points should be stated as concisely as possible. Each one is numbered and set forth in a separate paragraph and is usually followed by a statement of whether it was answered in the negative or the affirmative by the trial court. The section of the brief entitled *Argument* contains a division for each of the questions involved, with discussion and citation of authorities.

15.16. Preliminaries to preparing the brief. Before the lawyer dictates the brief, he or she *briefs* cases to be used in support of his or her position. This means that the lawyer makes a summary, digest, or abstract of a case, quoting pertinent parts from the court's opinion. Although the lawyer will dictate notes of these abstracts to you, the dictation will consist principally of instructions to take in (see page 43) excerpts of the court's opinion. Type each summary on a separate sheet of paper. Put the name of the case and the citation at the top of the sheet, double-space the lawyer's language and indent and single-space the take-ins. No copy is necessary.

Check carefully the spelling of names and the volume and page number of each citation. After typing the notes, have someone read back the take-ins, if possible. This is especially important if the book quoted from is a borrowed book that must be returned before the final brief is written.

15.17. Time element. The court rules provide that the appellant must file his or her brief within a specified number of days after the record is filed, and that the appellee has a specified number of days thereafter to file his or her brief. The appellant then has an additional time in which to file a reply brief. The timing is close. If the brief is to be printed, there is a deadline by which the manuscript must reach the printer. Unfortunately, many lawyers are inclined to put off the preparation of a brief until the last minute, and there is nothing you can do about it except remind the lawyer of the date the brief must be filed.

15.18. Preparation of the brief. *Draft.* Type a rough draft of the dictated brief. Occasionally the lawyer will dictate part of a brief and then, because of other matters, be unable to complete the dictation for a day or two. In the meantime, you should transcribe the tape or your notes and place a copy on the lawyer's desk for reference when he or she is able to work again on the brief.

Number of copies. After the lawyer revises the draft, retype it making the number of copies required by the rules, unless the lawyer asks for a second draft. If the brief is to be printed, make an original and two copies—the original for the printer, one copy for the lawyer, and one for your files.

Format. Figure 15.3 illustrates a page from a typed brief, figure 15.4 from a printed brief. The rules governing the format of the record (see page 360) apply to briefs. Notice also the following points about the make-up of a brief:

1. The questions or points are typed in solid caps or printed in boldface.

2. When several cases are cited in support of the same proposition, they are placed one under the other unless they are in a quotation.

Index and list of authorities cited. A brief of more than 12 pages (consult the rules) must be indexed and prefaced by an alphabetical list of the authorities cited. These pages are numbered with small roman numerals. The index is actually a table of contents. Figure 15.5 illustrates an index; figure 15.6, the list of cases. In this list, the titles of the cases cited are not necessarily underscored or in italics. Underscoring of a long list of authorities takes considerable time.

Notice in the illustration (figure 15.6) that there is no volume and page number cited for the case of *City of Miami Beach v. Perrell.* It sometimes happens that a case is cited before the court's opinion is published in the reporter or even in the advance sheets. The page and volume numbers are then left blank. Should the opinion be published before the brief is filed, the reference may be inserted.

Cover and binding. The cover of the brief contains the name of the court, the style of the case, identification of the brief (the party filing it), and the name and address of the attorneys representing the party filing the brief. When the brief is typed on legal-size paper, use a legal back, endorsed with these items, and staple at the top. When the brief is typed on letter-size paper, use double covers and staple at the side. Some rules specify different colors for the backs of the appelant's brief, the appellee's brief, and the appellant's reply brief. Figures 15.7 and 15.8 illustrate brief covers.

Filing and service. The rules specify the number of copies of the brief that must be filed with the clerk of the appellate court and the number of copies that must be served on opposing counsel. Service on opposing

---

1

THE BROAD POWERS GIVEN UNDER THE WILL CLEARLY
INDICATE AN INTENTION TO PERMIT THE EXECUTORS
AND TRUSTEES TO MAKE THE PROPOSED TEN-YEAR
LEASE AND OTHER LONG-TERM LEASES

By the terms of Article EIGHT of the Last Will and

Testament of _____

_____

Article EIGHT reads in part as follows:

"I hereby give to my Executors or Executor and to
my Trustees or Trustee, as the case may be, and to such of
them and their successors or successor as shall qualify or
may be acting for the time being, full power, authority, and
discretion to manage and operate any property I may leave;
* * * and in general to do and perform all acts that seem to
them wise and necessary for the proper management,
investment, and reinvestment of my estate, it being my
intention and direction that they should have the widest
possible powers, authority, and discretion in relation
thereto." (Italics ours.)

Among the powers expressly conferred upon the Trustees

by the testator_____

_____

In Corse v. Corse, 144 N. Y. 569, 572, power to grant

leases for a term not limited _____

_____

See cases in point.

Goddard v. Brown, 12 R. I. 31, 46, 47 (1821);
Holland v. Bogardus-Hill Drug Co., 314 Mo. 214;
    284 S. W. 121;
Lord v. Roberts, 84 N. H. 517; 153 Atl. Rep. 1, 3;
Matter of Jones, 122 F. 2d 853.

Figure 15.3. *Page from Typed Brief.*

counsel may be by mail or in person. Proof of service must be made to the appellate court.

15.19. Application for oral argument. Although witnesses do not appear before appellate courts, the lawyers are permitted to argue the case before the court. In many cases the lawyer believes the brief is sufficient and does not choose to argue the case. In some states, if the lawyer wants to appear before the appellate court, he or she must make application for oral argument at the time the brief is filed. Copy of the

9

ARGUMENT.

PART I.

An Answer to the Spurious Questions Posed by the Appellants.

The Court can dispose of this case either on narrow technical grounds that will result in its being tried over again and appealed again, or on broad equitable principles. We hope it will choose the latter and thus effectvely put an end to this controversy that has already gone on too long and caused too much ill feeling in the Village.[1] The whole trend of modern judicial thought is away from decisions on pinpoints. This case was fully and fairly submitted to the Chancellor who gave the parties almost unlimited opportunity to present everything they had. The appellants failed miserably to establish any defense and are asking this Court to reverse the case on the sheerest technicalities.

The City's Brief.

The first, second, and fifth questions posed by the appellant, Miami Shores Village, can be treated together. They are:

"FIRST QUESTION.

May a property owner resort to the courts for relief from alleged oppressive zoning without first having exhausted the administrative remedies?

---

[1]See Plaintiff's Exhibits Nos. 10 and 11 in Appendix.

Figure 15.4. *Page from Printed Brief.*

INDEX

History of the Case 1

Appellants' Statement of the Questions Involved .. 4

Appellee's Statement of the Questions Involved:

    Question No. 1 4

    Question No. 2 5

Foreword 6

Argument—

    Part I. An Answer to the Spurious Questions
    Posed by the Appellants 9

        The City's Brief 9

           A Planning Board or Adjustment Board
           Would Have Had No Authority to
           Change the Zoning 12

    Question No. 1 23

    Part II. An Outline of the Position of the Prop-
    erty Owner and an Overall Discussion of the
    Case 25

        Estoppel 34

    Question No. 2 37

    Part III. A Detailed Discussion of the Evidence
    Containing References to the Transcript of Rec-
    ord 41

        The Testimony for the Plaintiff:

           Walter 42

           D. 49

           Leonard A. 55

           Adrian 58

           Lon 61

Figure 15.5. *Index to Brief.*

INDEX III

AUTHORITIES CITED

Allen v. *Avondale Co.* (1938), 135 Fla. 6, 185 So. 137 28

Barton v. *Moline Properties* (1935), 121 Fla. 683, 164 So. 551, 103 A. L. R. 725 30

City of Coral Gables v. *State ex rel. Worley* (1950), 44 So. 2d 298 18

City of Fort Lauderdale v. *Smith* (1950), 44 So. 2d 302 ... 107

City of Miami Beach v. *Daoud* (1942), 149 Fla. 514, 6 So. 2d 847 .... 50, 110

City of Miami Beach v. *First Trust Co.* (1950), 45 So. 2d 681 .... 31, 42, 50, 108

City of Miami Beach v. *Gulf Oil Corp.* (1940), 141 Fla. 642, 194 So. 236 100

City of Miami Beach v. *Perrell* (1951), ... So. 2d 11, 109

City of Miami Beach v. *Sun Oil Company* (1940), 141 Fla. 645, 194 So. 237 100

City of Miami Beach v. *Texas Company* (1940), 141 Fla. 616, 194 So. 368 98

Dade County v. *Thompson* (1941), 146 Fla. 66, 200 So. 212 29

De Carlo v. *Town of West Miami* (1950), 49 So. 2d 596 .... 12, 110

Downs v. *Kroeger* (1927), 200 Cal. 743, 254 P. 1101 29

Ehinger v. *State* (1941), 147 Fla. 129, 2 So., 2d 357 103

Forde v. *City of Miami Beach* (1941), 146 Fla. 676, 1 So. 2d 642 .... 32, 36, 37, 101

Glogger v. *Bell* (1941), 146 Fla. 1, 200 So. 100 100

Green Point Savings Bank v. *Board of Zoning Appeals* (1939), 281 N. Y. 534, 24 N. E. 2d 319 11

Harrington v. *Board of Adjustment, City of Alamo Heights* (Tex. 1939), 124 S. W. 2d 401 .... 11, 16

Figure 15.6. *List of Authorities Cited in Brief.*

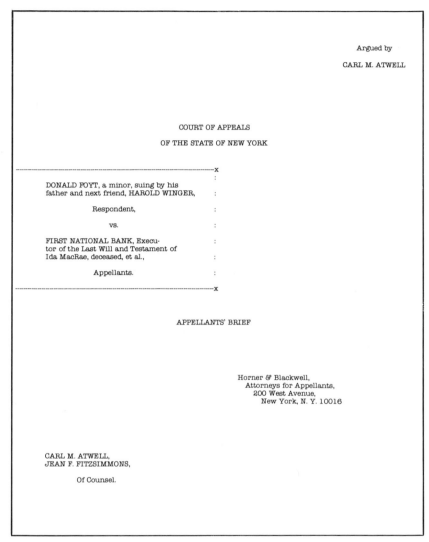

Argued by

CARL M. ATWELL

COURT OF APPEALS

OF THE STATE OF NEW YORK

---x
                                     :

DONALD FOYT, a minor, suing by his
father and next friend, HAROLD WINGER,   :

      Respondent,   :

        vs.   :

FIRST NATIONAL BANK, Execu-   :
tor of the Last Will and Testament of
Ida MacRae, deceased, et al.,   :

      Appellants.   :
---x

APPELLANTS' BRIEF

Horner & Blackwell,
Attorneys for Appellants,
200 West Avenue,
New York, N. Y. 10016

CARL M. ATWELL,
JEAN F. FITZSIMMONS,

   Of Counsel.

Figure 15.7. *Cover for Brief on Letter-Size, or Smaller, Paper.*

application is served on opposing counsel in the same manner that the brief is served.

15.20. Procedure when having a brief printed. Material for "Preparing Printing," chapter 8, tells you in detail how to prepare material for the printer and how to follow through until the material is in printed form. It also gives you the information you need about printing to be able to assume this responsibility efficiently. Figure 15.9 is a page of

IN THE SUPREME COURT OF FLORIDA

OCEANA ESTATES,

Appellant,

vs.

WATERFRONT DEVELOPMENT CORPORATION,

Appellee.

BRIEF OF APPELLEE

Edwards, Deland, and Moore,

704 Ocean Drive,

Miami, Florida 33143

Attorneys for Appellee.

Figure 15.8. *Cover for Printed Brief (6 x 9 inches).*

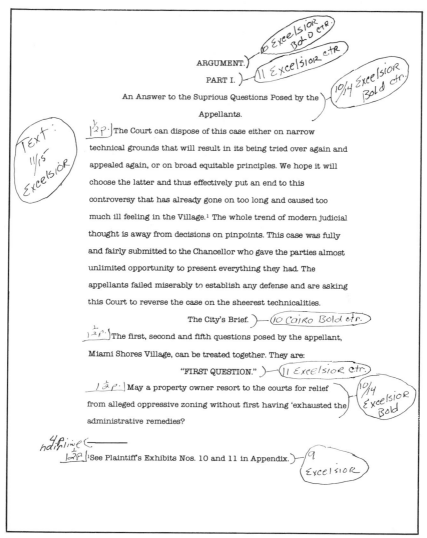

Figure 15.9. *Page of Manuscript from Brief, Marked for Printer.*

typed manuscript from a brief, marked for the printer in accordance with the directions given in chapter 8. (Figure 15.4 illustrates the same page after it is printed.) Printers who specialize in court work are usually familiar with the requirements of the court rules.

When the galley proofs are received, the lawyer will read the brief again and make any changes he or she desires. You have the following responsibilities:

1. Proofread for typographical errors (see chapter 8).

2. Check the makeup, for example, see that material that should be in boldface type is in boldface; that quotations are indented, and so on.

3. Compare the quotations with the source from which taken or, if this is impractical, with your manuscript.

4. Check the citations, preferably by reference to the cited case in the reporter; otherwise, against your manuscript.

5. Check the record references against the record itself.

6. Return the corrected proof to the printer with instructions for the number of copies to be printed, stock and color of cover, and the like.

CITATIONS

15.21. What is a citation? A *citation*[1] is a reference to an authority that supports a statement of law or from which a quotation is taken. Citations occur most frequently in briefs, law memoranda, and opinion letters. The lawyer speaks of *citing a case,* a *cited case, citing a report,* and the like. The references are principally to the following sources:

1.   Constitutions, statutes, codes

2.   Law reports

3.   Texts and periodicals

A useful publication to have when preparing materials that include citations is a booklet called *A Uniform System of Citation,* published by the Harvard Law Review Association in Cambridge, Massachusetts. The most recent edition is the 12th, published in 1976. However, some state supreme courts require a form of citation that differs from the Harvard system. Always check your own supreme court rules to see how the official state reporters should be cited in appellate briefs.

15.22. How to take citations in shorthand. It sometimes happens that citations, particularly volume, page, and section number, are incorrectly set down when dictation is rapid. The following procedure is recommended: Write down the volume number, allow a small space, and immediately write down the page or section numbers, going back to fill in the title of the volume. The memory more readily retains the title of the volume than it does the page or section number. In the citation of a case, it is more important to obtain the correct numbers and title of the book than the correct names of the parties. You may go to the law report and easily find the title of the case.

15.23. Accuracy of citations. The importance of accuracy of citations cannot be overemphasized. Check and doublecheck volume and page references and spelling of names. Check against the original

---

[1]Certain writs and summonses issued by courts are also known as citations.

reports, not against your notes or taped dictation. Check printed briefs against the original reports, not against manuscript. A judge is annoyed if he or she cannot find a case cited because you made a typographical error in the citation. Misspelling of the name of a well-known case marks the lawyer as either careless or ignorant. Errors in citations are always avoidable, and it is your responsibility to see that no reflection is cast upon the lawyer through your carelessness.

15.24. Official reports and the National Reporter System. All of the opinions of the highest state tribunals and of the United States Supreme Court, and many of the opinions of intermediary appellate courts, are published. Each appellate court has a reporter, whose duty it is to see that the opinions are published in bound form at intervals. The publication under the direction of the state reporter is considered the *official* report of the court's opinion. (See part 5, Official Reports and How They Are Cited.)

West Publishing Company publishes the opinions of the federal courts and the courts of every state, those of several states being published in the same bound volume. This system of reports, covering the entire country, is called the *National Reporter System.* Part 5, Reporters of the National Report System, shows the names of the reporters, how they are cited, and the courts covered by each. You will notice some of the reporters are designated "Second Series." The designation is for numbering purposes and indicates that the numbers of the volumes have started over with 1.

These reporters, which are "unofficial" reports of the courts' opinions, are published much sooner than the official reports. Some states have discontinued the publication of state reports and use the appropriate reporter of the *National Reporter System* as the official report. The Lawyer's Cooperative Publishing company also publishes the decisions of the United States Supreme Court. Their publication is called *Supreme Court Reports,* Lawyer's Edition, and is cited as L. Ed.

Before the opinions are published in bound volumes of the *National Reporter System,* they are published in weekly pamphlets known as *Advance Sheets.* (Some official reports also have advance sheets.) Thus, the lawyer is informed immediately of the courts in which he or she is interested. The page numbers in the advance sheets correspond with the page numbers that will appear in the bound volumes.

15.25. How to cite a constitution. Show the number of the article, or amendment, in roman numerals; the section number in arabic numerals. Give date if the constitution cited is not in force.

| U.S. Const. | Art. IV, §2 | Ga. Const. | Art. XI, §3 |
| U.S. Const. | Amend. VI, §2 | Ga. Const. | Art. II, §1 (1875) |

15.26. How to cite statutes and codes. Whenever full reference to a federal statute is necessary, cite date, chapter number, statute citation, and United States Code citation, thus: Section 1 of the Act of June 13, 1934, c. 482, 48 Stat. 948, 40 U.S.C. 276b. Compilations of state statutes and codes are cited by chapter, title, or section number. Part 5, Approved Method of Citing Compilations of Statutes and Codes, gives the approved form of citing the latest compilation in each state. The list is not exclusive—some states have more than one approved compilation.

When citing statutes and codes, observe these directions:

1. If a compilation in its preface gives the method of citing it, use that citation.

2. Where the date is incorporated in the title of the compilation, show it.

3. When statutes or codes of one state are cited outside of that state, the name of the state is always indicated for identification purposes. For example, lawyers in Kansas cite the Kansas General Statutes as "G.S." but outside of Kansas the citation is Kan. G.S.

4. When citing an act or law that has been repealed and no longer appears in the latest compilation, give the date of the compilation cited.

Ill. Rev. Stat. c. 114, §88 (1889)

15.27. How to cite cases in official reports and reporters. Cases in official reports and reporters are cited alike. Directions for citing cases must be considered in the light of applicable court rules. Some courts lay considerable emphasis on how cases should be cited and whether citation to the National Reporter System should be included. The following directions are the rules of thumb used in many law offices. Examples of citations are on pages 376 and 377.

Names of parties. 1. Cite the name of the case as it appears in the running head of the report, not as it appears at the beginning of the opinion. Do not abbreviate the first word.

2. When the United States is a party, do not abbreviate to *U. S.* unless it is part of the name of a government vessel. (See example 1.)

3. Do not substitute the initials of a government agency or a labor union for its full name in briefs. You may in other legal writings. (See example 2.)

4. Use the first name of railways, but abbreviate the balance. (See example 3.)

5. When *Co.* and *Inc.* are both part of a name omit the *Inc.*

6. When the names of parties change completely on appeal indicate the fact by the use of *sub nom.* (See example 4.) This direction does not apply when the names of the parties are merely reversed.

Volume and page. Cite the volume and page number of the report or reporter in which the opinion is published. The reference is to the entire opinion and gives the page at which the opinion begins. A *spot page reference* follows when it is desired to call attention to a particular page, such as one from which a quotation is taken. (See example 5.)

The designation "2d" *must* be included in the citation of a volume in a second series. A reference to 58 N. E. is not the same as a reference to 58 N. E. 2d.

Date. Show in parentheses the year the decision is handed down by the court. It appears at the beginning of the court's opinion. Both *A Uniform System of Citation* and *Practical Manual of Standard Legal Citations* place the date at the end of the citation (example 1), but lawyers, when writing briefs, frequently place it between the title of the case and the volume reference (example 5). Many lawyers do not show the date of the decision unless it is relevant to the argument.

Jurisdiction and court. When the name of the reporter does not indicate the jurisdiction, show the jurisdiction in parentheses preceding the date. (See example 6.) Also show the name of the court deciding the case if it is not the highest court in the state. (See example 7.) This is always necessary when only the unofficial reporter is cited.

Parallel citations. Both the official and unofficial reports should be cited if available. Cite the official report first. (See example 8.) When the case has not been published in the official reports, but will be in the future, cite the name of the official report, preceded and followed by blanks, thus, —Miss.—, 55 So. 2d 447. (See example 9.)

Federal courts. When citing cases decided by the federal courts of appeals, show the circuit in parentheses. (See example 10.) The District of Columbia circuit is indicated by *D. C.* (See example 11.) When citing cases decided in the federal district court, show the district, but not the division, in parentheses. (See example 12.)

Selective case series. In some law report series, such as *American Law Reports* and *Law Reports Annotated,* only certain cases are published. These series are cited by the year of publication, the *letter* of the volume (A, B, C, or D), and page. (See example 13.) In parallel citations, they follow the National Reporter citation. It is customary to cite selective case series in briefs for state courts but not in those for federal courts.

15.28. Named reporters. Old court reports carry the name of the reporter. When citing cases in the U. S. reports before volume 91, always cite by the volume number and name of the reporter, not by the subsequently assigned consecutive U. S. number. To cite these volumes by the U. S. number is considered bad form. The following are the names of the old court reports and the number of volumes they reported.

> 4 of Dallas (cited as 1 Dall. 10)
> 9 of Cranch (cited as 1 Cranch 10)
> 12 of Wheaton (cited as 1 Wheat. 10)
> 16 of Peters (cited as 1 Pet. 10)
> 24 of Howard (cited as 1 How. 10)
> 2 of Black (cited as 1 Black 10)
> 23 of Wallace (cited as 1 Wall. 10)

When citing state cases, follow the local practice. For example, in Massachusetts the early reports are often cited by the name of the reporter, whereas in North Carolina a rule of court requires that they be cited by the consecutive number. When the name reporter is used, indicate the jurisdiction and date in parentheses. (See example 14.)

15.29. String citations. When several cases are cited one after the other instead of on separate lines, the citation is referred to as a *string citation*. Separate the cases with a semicolon. (See example 15.)

15.30. How to cite an unpublished case. When citing a case that has not been reported, cite by name, court, the full date, and the docket number if known. (See example 16.)

15.31. How to cite slip decisions. Each opinion of the United States Supreme Court is published separately as soon as it is handed down. This form of publication is called a *slip decision*. Slip decisions are printed by the Government Printing Office and also by two unofficial publishers, Commerce Clearing House and U.S. Law Week. They are widely circulated and are frequently cited in briefs. Cite by number, court, date of decision, and source if unofficial. (See example 17.)

15.32. How to cite treatises. Cite by volume number (if more than one volume), author, title of the publication, page or section number, and the edition in parentheses. If the editor is well known, his or her name follows the edition. Underscore or italicize the title of the publication. (See example 18.)

Star Page. In a few well-known works, the paging of the original edition is indicated by stars in differently paginated editions. Cite by the star page. (See example 19.)

15.33. How to cite law reviews. Cite the volume and page number and the year. Underscore or italicize the title of the review. If an article is referred to, place it in quotation marks. Abbreviate *Law* (L.), *Review* (Rev.), and *Journal* (J.). See example 20.)

15.34. How to cite legal newspapers. When citing a case that has not been published in either the official or unofficial reports but has been published in a legal newspaper, give the name of the newspaper, the volume and page number, the column, the court, and the exact date of the decision. (See example 21.)

15.35. Underscoring and italicizing. Underscoring and italicizing vary with the law office, but the following directions, some of which are arbitrary, are based upon the practices followed by many lawyers:

1. Underscore the names of the parties.

2. In a printed brief, the underscoring of *v.* or *vs.* is optional. Continuous underscoring gives a more even appearance on the typed page and requires less care than breaking the underscoring at the desired points. Printers usually set the *v.* or *vs.* in roman.

3. When a previously cited case is referred to in the text of the brief by part of the title used as an adjective, italicize it.

Under the authority of the *Daoud* case the Court held...

When the reference is repeated under the same point of the brief, do not italicize it.

4. Italicize *case* or *cases* only when it is part of the usual name of the case.

5. It is preferable not to underscore words and expressions between citations of the same case that relate to its history, such as *affirmed, certiorari denied,* and the like. (See example 22.)

15.36. Spacing of abbreviations. In briefs and other legal writings, the general practice is to close up the citation, thus *N.E.2d.*

15.37. Placement of citations. Unless a citation is part of a quotation, it is indented and placed on the line following the quotation. If it runs over one line, the carry-over line is indented.

"... should be denied, as proposed allegations would add nothing to the equity of the bill."

Volunteer Security Co. v. *Dowl* (1947), 159 Fla. 767, 33 So. 2d 150, 152

When several citations are given in support of a point, list them one under the other (see figure 15.6).

15.38. Illustrations of citations. The following examples of citations illustrate the foregoing directions. Parts appearing in italics would be underscored on the typewriter. Apparent inconsistencies in the italics and in the placement of the dates in the examples demonstrate the variations in accepted practices. However, you should be consistent throughout a brief.

Example   **Citation**

1. *United States* v. *Texas & Pacific Motor Transport Co.,* 340 U. S. 450, 71 S. Ct. 422 (1951)

2. *United States* v. *Congress of Industrial Organization,* 335 U. S. 106, 68 S. Ct. 1349, 48 A. L. C. 1164, aff'g 77 F Supp. 355, 48 A. L. C. 559 (D. C. Cir. 1948)

3. *Nashville, C. & St. L. Ry.* vs. *Walters,* (1934) 294 U. S. 405, 55 S. Ct. 486

4. *Blaustein* v. *United States,* 44 F. 2d 163 (C.C.A. 3), certiorari denied *sub nom. Sokol* v. *United States,* 283 U. S. 838, 51 S. Ct. 486

5. *Dyett v. Turner,* (U.S.D.C., D.UTAH, Cent. DIV., 1968) 287 F. Supp. 113; 114

6. *Harrington* v. *Board of Adjustment, City of Alamo Heights,* (Tex. 1939) 124 S. W. 2d 401, 404

7. *Rayl* v. *General Motors Corp.,* (Ind. App. 1951) 101 N. E. 2d 433 *Janice* v. *State,* 107 N. Y. S. 2d 674 (Ct. Cl. 1951)

8. *People* v. *Davis,* 303 N. Y. 235, 101 N. E. 2d 479

9. *In re Fortune,* (1951) ——— Ohio St. ———, 101 N. E. 2d 174

10. *American Fruit Machinery Co.* v. *Robinson Match Co.,* 191 Fed. 723 (3rd Cir. 1911)

11. *Barbee* v. *Capital Airlines, Inc.,* (D. C. Cir. 1951) 191 F. 2d 507

12. *Standard Oil Co.* v. *Atlantic Coast Line R. Co.,* (W. D. Ky. 1926) 13 F. 2d 633

13. *Hanover Star Milling Co.* v. *Allen & Wheeler Co.,* 208 Fed. 513, 1916D L. R. A. 136 (7th Cir. 1913)

14. *Forward* v. *Adams,* 7 Wend. 204 (N. Y. 1831)

15. *Rubin* v. *Board of Directors of City of Pasadena,* (1940) 16 Cal. 2d 119, 104 P. 2d 1041; *Harrington* v. *Board of Adjustment, City of Alamo Heights,* (Tex.) 1939) 124 S. W. 2d 401; *Green Point Savings Bank* v. *Board of Zoning Appeals,* (1939) 281 N. Y. 534, 24 N. E. 2d 319

16. *Roe* v. *Doe,* No. 152 U. S. Sup. Ct., Jan. 10, 1952

17. *Jones* v. *Smith,* No. 40, U. S. Sup. Ct., No. 21, 1945 (15 U. S. Law Week)

18. 2 Pomeroy, *Equity Jurisprudence* §428 (5th ed., Symonds, 1941)

19. 2 Bl. Comm. *358

20. 42 *Yale* L. J. 419 (1933)

21. *Garden Park Apts., Inc.* vs. *Fletcher,* 127 N. Y. L. J. 703, col. 7 (Sup. Ct. Spec. Term Feb. 20, 1952)

22. *In re Morse,* (1928) 220 App. Div. 830, 220 N. Y. Supp. 858, rev'd on other grounds, 247 N. Y. 290, 160 N. E. 374

PART 4

Assisting in

Specialized Practice

16 Assisting in Partnership Formation and Incorporation

17 Acting as Corporate Secretary

18 Assisting in Real Estate Practice and Foreclosures

19 Assisting with Probate and Estate Administration

20 Handling Commercial Collections

16

Assisting in

Partnership Formation

and Incorporation

The work of forming a corporation and qualifying it to do business in more than one state is highly technical, requiring strict observance of specific state laws, and of federal laws if public issues of stock are involved.

The organization of a simple corporation with no public issues of stock is not particularly complicated and is a frequent assignment in every law office. The task offers the secretary and paralegal a chance to assume considerable responsibility, thereby relieving the busy lawyer. In the case of a complicated corporation, the lawyer may engage the services of a firm, such as The Prentice-Hall Corporation System, Inc., that specializes in incorporating, qualifying, and maintaining corporations. In that case, the secretary and paralegal have no part in the incorporating work.

A partnership is a much less formal entity than a corporation and may come into being without any legal consultation whatsoever. Most states have adopted the Uniform Partnership Act, which in general outlines the duties and obligations of partners to each other and particularly addresses partnership assets and debts when the partnership is dissolved. There are a number of instances in which a lawyer may be consulted before or after the formation of a partnership.

The partnership will probably want to register its partnership name with the Secretary of State. The name is reserved in the same manner as the name of a corporation.

The partners may want to draw up a formal agreement among themselves outlining the various duties and responsibilities of the partners. In partnerships where one or more of the partners is a so-called limited partner, it is most common to draw up a formal agreement indicating the nature of the limited partner's participation. Because a partnership is a less formal organization than a corporation, the lawyer will probably dictate the terms of any agreement to suit the circumstances.

The following sections examine the nature of partnerships and corporations and outline the duties of the law-office team in each case.

CORPORATIONS

16.1. What is a corporation? A *corporation* is a device for carrying on an enterprise. It is an entity, a "legal person," separate and apart from the persons who are interested in and control it. The state authorizes its existence and gives it certain powers. It also has certain powers that it gives itself, within the limits prescribed by the state, when it goes through the formalities of organization. A corporation has fundamental characteristics that make it the most popular form of business organization. Probably the most favorable aspect of the corporate form is the assurance of limited liability to the persons who put capital into the business. This means that an individual's personal assets cannot be reached to satisfy creditors of the corporation.

Corporations may be classified as public corporations, corporations not for profit, and corporations for profit, each class being organized under different statutes.

Public corporations include all the subdivisions of the state, such as cities, and towns, tax districts, and irrigation districts. They also include government-owned corporations, such as the Federal Deposit Insurance Corporation and Federal Savings and Loan Insurance Company.

Corporations not for profit are those organized for purposes other than the pecuniary gain of their members. Nonprofit corporations do not have capital stock or pay dividends. Those who are interested in and control the corporation are referred to as its members, rather than its stockholders or shareholders as in a corporation for profit. These corporations include religious, civil, social, educational, fraternal, charitable, and cemetery associations.

Corporations for profit, or *business corporations,* are corporations with capital stock that carry on an enterprise for profit. Business corporations fall into three groups: (1) banks and insurance companies, which are known as *moneyed corporations;* (2) corporations that furnish public utility services to the public, such as transportation, telephone and electricity, which are known as *public service corporations or public utilities;* and (3) corporations engaged in ordinary business pursuits, which are known as *private corporations.* The first two classes are subject to stricter governmental control than the private corporation.

Class (3) corporations fall into three categories: publicly owned corporations, close corporations, and professional corporations or associations. *The publicly owned corporation* sells its shares to members of the general public, either through the major stock exchanges or "over the counter." The *close corporation* is generally one that has a small group of stockholders (some states even permit only a single stockholder), often members of the same family, and all of whom are active in the business and constitute the board of directors and officers of the corporation. Many states now have special corporation laws that apply to this kind of corporation to make it easier for the corporation to operate. The *professional corporation,* in some states called the *professional association,* is one composed of a group of, say, doctors, lawyers, or dentists who practice their profession in corporate form as distinguished from individual or partnership form. Most states now have laws that permit various professions to incorporate their practices.

The organization procedure described in this chapter relates to a private business corporation, but it is adaptable to other corporations.

16.2. Steps in the organization of a corporation. To organize a corporation means to bring it into existence. Each state designates a specific department and official through which the lawyer must work. Certain steps are necessary. These involve routine procedure you can follow at the lawyer's direction without detailed instruction.

The usual steps in the organization of a corporation are:

1. Reservation of name
2. Preparation of incorporating papers
3. Execution of papers
4. Filing of papers
5. First meeting of incorporators
6. First meeting of directors

16.3. Who may form a corporation? Those who unite for the purpose of forming a corporation are *incorporators*. They tell the lawyer the kind of business the corporation will engage in and other details the lawyer needs to know before he or she begins the legal organization procedure. They also put up the capital for the corporation. Only natural persons may incorporate, although they may actually be representing a corporation or a partnership.

In many states a single incorporator is sufficient. A few states also require that one or more of the incorporators must be a resident of that state, or that the organization meeting of the corporation must be held in that state. In those states that so require, the incorporators are frequently *dummies*. They are not the principals who are actually interested in the organization of the corporation, but merely act for them until the organization meeting. Law office employees may act as dummy incorporators.

16.4. State of incorporation. A state in which a corporation is organized is the *state of incorporation*. A corporation is not necessarily incorporated under the laws of the state in which its executive office is located, especially if it is to carry on business in more than one state. Each state has a corporation law (see part 5, Incorporating Chart, for the name of the corporation law in each state) under which private business corporations for profit are organized. The laws of some states are more favorable to corporations generally than those of other states. The lawyer recommends the state whose laws are most favorable to the proposed corporation. The cost of incorporating and the tax laws in each state are also taken into consideration. Therefore, the lawyer for whom you work might organize a corporation under the laws of a state far removed from your office. Delaware is the leading incorporating state.

In the state of incorporation, a corporation is known as a *domestic* corporation; in all other states, as a *foreign* corporation. (Corporations organized outside the United States are referred to as *alien* corporations.) Thus, a corporation incorporated in Delaware is a domestic corporation there, but in New York and California, it is a foreign corporation. A corporation is sometimes incorporated in more than one state, but generally if it wants to carry on its business in another state, it qualifies to do business in that state as a foreign corporation.

16.5. Memorandum preliminary to preparation of incorporating papers. Each lawyer has his or her own method of giving instructions about the preparing of incorporating papers. A paralegal may do much of the routine work of preparing papers of a new corporation. A method commonly followed, and a very workable one, is the dictation of a preliminary memorandum. After the lawyer has a conference with the principals interested in forming a corporation, he or she dictates a memorandum of the conference. This memorandum covers all information necessary to the preparation of the charter. It will include:

1. State of incorporation.
2. The corporate name selected by the principals, usually first and second choice.
3. Nature of business in which the corporation proposes to engage. This clause is known as the *purpose clause.* The lawyer might direct you to a form in the form file or in a form book instead of dictating the clause.
4. Names and addresses of incorporators.
5. Names and addresses of directors.
6. Number of shares of stock each incorporator and director will hold, if any.
7. Designation of resident agent.
8. Location of principal office within the state of incorporation.
9. Fiscal year of the corporation.
10. Date for annual stockholders' meeting.[1]
11. Amount of capital with which the corporation will commence business (the corporation law in each state fixes a minimum amount).
12. Authorized capital stock and its breakdown (number of shares of common stock and of preferred stock; number of shares with par value, and the par value of each; number of shares of no par stock).
13. Designations, rights, preferences, and all other details relating to preferred stock. This clause in the charter is known as the *stock clause.* It is frequently quite complicated, and sometimes several drafts of it are written before its provisions satisfy the principals.

This memorandum will serve as the basis for the organization of the corporation. With the help of the memorandum and appropriate forms, you will be able to complete the organization of a simple corporation without detailed instructions from the lawyer.

16.6. Reservation of name. Deciding on a corporation's name is a serious matter, to which the incorporators and the lawyer give careful consideration. All of the states require that a corporation's name should indicate that it is a corporation by the use of *company, association, incorporated,* or similar words or abbreviations of them. Also, the majority of the states will not permit the use of the work *bank* or *trust* in the name of a corporation unless it is a banking institution. The chief importance of a name to the incorporators is that, as a business develops,

---

[1]The words *stockholders* and *shareholders* often are used interchangeably.

its name acquires a value in itself, representing to a great extent the goodwill of the company. The state laws and the courts generally protect the corporation's exclusive right to the use of its name. The state official will not accept for filing a charter or articles of incorporation, if the name of the proposed corporation so closely resembles that of a corporation existing in the state that deception or confusion might result. Therefore, as soon as the lawyer dictates the memorandum described in the preceding paragraph, he or she will tell you to find out if the choice of name is available, and, if so, to reserve it.

What to do to clear the name. Write to the designated state official and ask if the chosen name is available. You have to ascertain if the proposed name is available not only in the state of incorporation, but also in any states in which the corporation expects to qualify. If the organization of the corporation must be completed quickly, you might wire or at least ask the state official to answer by wire collect.

In some states the state official will reserve a name for a specified period for the payment of a fee or as a courtesy. In the states that require a fee enclose a check when you ask to have the name reserved. When you wire, send the check to the designated official as soon as you have a reply to your wire.

Your letter might read as follows:

The Honorable James R. Clark
Secretary of State of Vermont
Montpelier, Vermont 05053

Sir:

Re: Franklin J. King, Inc.

Will you please let us know whether the above styled name is available for a domestic corporation, which we are about to organize under the laws of your state.

If so, please reserve it for us for a statutory period. Enclosed is check for $5 in payment of reservation fee.

Please reply by wire, collect.

Sincerely yours,

Warner & Croft

If the incorporators expect to qualify as a foreign corporation in another state, the first paragraph will be changed to read:

"... foreign corporation, which we are about to qualify to transact business in your state."

If you wire, your telegram might read: "Wire collect whether Franklin J. King, Inc. is available for corporation."

16.7. Incorporation papers. The next step in the organization of a corporation is the preparation of the proposed *articles of incorporation*, to be submitted to the designated public official for approval. The articles determine what the corporation is authorized to do, and the corporation cannot function until it has been approved by the proper official. The articles of incorporation are sometimes called *charters, certificate of incorporation,* or *articles of association*, depending upon the terminology used in the state of incorporation. Some states provide a printed form that may be used; otherwise, the charter is drawn from models that have been approved by the public official with whom the papers must be filed. Your office will have, or you will accumulate, a form file from charters prepared for previous clients. These forms will serve as models in the preparation of the charter for a corporation in the process of organization.

The states have different requirements for the provisions of the charter, but all of the states require that they must contain special information with reference to the items set forth in the memorandum dictated to you by the lawyer.

16.8. Preparation of the articles of incorporation. The preparation of the average incorporation papers is largely routine, and you should be able to prepare it from the memorandum previously dictated, by using a form from your files as a model.

1. Find out the number of copies required by law in your state. *Make three extra copies* — one to be kept at the principal office of the corporation, one for your file, and one for the minute book. (In some states, an extra copy is required as an exhibit to the application for a permit to sell securities to the public. A copy of the charter must also be filed with the application to the Securities Exchange Commission if the stock is to be sold publicly.) Some states also require that a certified copy be filed in each county where the corporation owns real estate. You will also have to make an extra copy for some states in which the proposed corporation expects to qualify. Many states now accept a certificate of good standing from the appropriate official (usually the Secretary of State) of the state of incorporation.

2. Use either 8½" by 11" good quality bond paper or legal cap. The trend is toward the use of the letter-size paper, except in those states where printed forms prepared by the state are used. When letter-size paper is

used, the ribbon copy of the second typing is made on minute paper, thus saving the time required to copy the charter in the minute book.

3. If printed blank forms are used be sure they are of the same date of printing; otherwise, they might not be exact copies. When filling in the blanks, follow the instructions in chapter 10 for filling in any printed form.

4. When typing the charter, always use pica type and double-space it. These requirements are mandatory in nearly every state. Otherwise, there is no specific form in which the charter must be typed. Figures 16.1, 16.2, and 16.3 illustrate the first, second, and last pages of a charter and will serve as a model for style. The following details are customary, though not mandatory:

(a) The title of the document and name of the corporation are written in solid caps.

(b) The following words are written with initial caps whenever they refer to the corporation being organized: corporation, certificate of incorporation (or any other name by which the charter is known), board of directors, bylaws.

(c) The left margin of indented material is indented five spaces from the principal left margin, and the first line of an indented paragraph is indented five additional spaces. The right margin is also indented.

(d) Subindentations are indented an additional five spaces.

(e) Numbered or lettered items are indented.

(f) Purpose clauses are indented.

(g) Pages are numbered.

(h) Numbers are written out, followed by figures in parentheses.

5. Type a signature line for each signer.

6. In almost all states the charter is a sealed instrument (see page 198). If the state of incorporation requires the seals of the signers, type (L.S.) or (SEAL) after each signature line.

7. If an acknowledgment is required, type the certificate of acknowledgment in the form required by the state of incorporation. The venue will recite the state and county where the incorporators sign, not the state of incorporation. The rules that govern the acknowledgment of any instrument govern the acknowledgment of incorporation papers. Remember that some states require acknowledgments taken outside the state to be authenticated. Therefore, if the acknowledgment is to be taken in a state other than the state of incorporation, determine if authentication is necessary. If all incorporators sign at the same time, one certificate of acknowledgment is sufficient, but if they sign at

CERTIFICATE OF INCORPORATION

OF

FRANKLIN J. KING, INC.

———

We, the undersigned, for the purpose of associating to establish a corporation for the transaction of the business and the promotion and conduct of the objects and purposes hereinafter stated, under the provisions and subject to the requirements of the laws of the State of Vermont (particularly an act entitled "An Act Providing a General Corporation Law", approved March 10, 1899, and the acts amendatory thereof and supplemental thereto, and known as the "General Corporation Law of the State of Vermont"), do make and file this Certificate of Incorporation in writing and do hereby certify as follows, to wit:

FIRST: The name of the coporation (hereinafter called the Corporation) is

FRANKLIN J. KING, INC.

SECOND: The respective names of the County and of the City within the County in which the principal office of the Corporation is to be located in the State of Vermont are the County of Washington and the City of Montpelier. The name of the resident agent of the Corporation is The Prentice-Hall Corporation System, Inc. The street and number of said principal office and the address by street and number of said resident agent is 317-325 South State Street, Montpelier, Vermont 05053.

Figure 16.1. *First Page of Incorporation Papers.*

different times, there must be a separate acknowledgment for each. Some states do not require that all incorporators who sign must acknowledge the instrument.

8. Prepare a cover for each copy except the one that is on minute paper. The only typing on the cover is, "Certificate of Incorporation (or articles, or charter, as the case may be) of (name of corporation)."

THIRD: The nature of the business of the Corporation and the objects

or purposes to be transacted, promoted or carried on by it are as follows:

    To _____

    _____

    _____.

    To _____

    _____

    _____:

       (a) _____

       _____

       _____;

       (b) _____

       _____.

    To _____

    . _____ .

FOURTH: The name and place of residence of each of the

incorporators are as follows:

NAME	PLACE OF RESIDENCE
B. M. Morris	Montpelier, Vermont
R. T. Shoals	Montpelier, Vermont
J. K. Winslow	Montpelier, Vermont

FIFTH: The Corporation is to have perpetual existence.

SIXTH: _____

_____ .

-2-

Figure 16.2. *Second Page of Incorporation Papers.*

16.9. Execution of the incorporation papers. In a few states, all copies of the papers required to be filed with the designated public official must be ribbon copies, carbons not being acceptable. In others, an original and duplicate originals or triplicate originals are acceptable. Some states will accept an original and conformed copies.

If the papers are to be executed in your office, notify the incorporators that the papers are ready for signature and arrange a time for them to

IN WITNESS WHEREOF, we, the undersigned, being all of the incorporators hereinabove named, do hereby further certify that the facts hereinabove stated are truly set forth and accordingly have hereunto set our respective hands and seals.

Dated at Montpelier, Vermont

October 31, 19–

_____ (L.S.)

_____ (L.S.)

_____ (L.S.)

STATE OF VERMONT   )
) SS.:
COUNTY OF WASHINGTON)

BE IT REMEMBERED that personally appeared before me, Jacob Carter, a Notary Public in and for the County and State aforesaid, B. M. Morris, R. T. Shoals, and J. K. Winslow, all the incorporators who signed the foregoing Certificate of Incorporation, known to me personally to be such, and I having made known to them and each of them the contents of said Certificate of Incorporation, they did severally acknowledge the same to be the act and deed of the signers, respectively, and that the facts therein stated are truly set forth.

Given under my hand and seal of office this 31st day of October, A. D. 19–.

_____

Notary Public

-10-

Figure 16.3. *Last Page of Incorporation Papers.*

come in to sign. (It is advisable to do this as soon as you know when the papers will be ready, to avoid delay.) If some or all of the incorporators are to sign outside your office, forward the document with a covering letter.

Each original, duplicate original, and triplicate original must be signed, but the copies that are to be conformed need not be signed. The signature must be the same on each copy, and must be written exactly as in the document. Thus, if an incorporator signs his name, *A.B. Johnson*, his name should not be written *Adam B. Johnson* in the document.

When acknowledgments are required, take the acknowledgment of the incorporators who sign in your office and notarize all signed copies. Conform the unsigned copies.

16.10. Filing the incorporation papers and payment of fees. After the document has been executed, send the required number of copies to the proper state official, with a letter of transmittal and a check in payment of the organization tax and fees. Your letter of transmittal might read as follows:

Secretary of State
State of Vermont
Montpelier, Vermont 05053

Gentlemen:
Re: Franklin J. King, Inc.

     We are enclosing an original and two conformed copies of the Certificate of Incorporation of Franklin J. King, Inc. Please record the original of the Certificate in your offices and certify and return to us the conformed copies.

     We are also enclosing our check in the amount of $70, covering (1) the organization tax, $10; (2) filing fee, $25; (3) recording fee, $15; (4) certification of copy for recording, $10; and (5) certification of one extra copy, $10.

                            Sincerely yours,

                            Warner & Croft
Enclosures   (4)

If the charter is acceptable, the public official will retain the original. He or she will mark the copy, or copies, to show that the charter has been filed and endorse his or her approval upon it, or attach a certificate of approval to it, and return it, together with receipt for tax and fees, to your office. You will then do the following:

1. Conform your office copy, noting particularly the date of the official's filing marks. This date, rather than the date on which the charter was executed, is the date of incorporation.

2. Draw check for the local filing fee and file the certified copy of the charter in the appropriate local office if required.

3. Note on your office copy the date the papers were filed locally.

4. Paste the tax receipt in the minute book.

ORGANIZATION MEETINGS

16.11. Necessity and purpose of organization meeting. From a practical, as well as legal, standpoint, a corporation cannot transact its business until details of its organization are completed. Therefore, as soon as the charter is approved and filed with the proper authorities, and other mandatory requirements of the law are complied with, an organization meeting is held. The states do not all use the same terminology as to the participants in the organization meeting. There are at least four variations: (1) *incorporators;* (2) *incorporators and subscribers* (to the stock); (3) *shareholders* or *stockholders;* (4) *subscribers* (signers of the charter). In some states the organization meeting is a meeting of the directors named in the charter. The actions taken at organization meetings are routine and are usually agreed upon in advance by the principals organizing the corporation. Frequently, therefore, the meeting is not actually held but the minutes are prepared as though the meeting had been held.

16.12. Preparation for the organization meeting. The secretary and paralegal will have to make certain preparations for the organization meeting. These preparations include:

1. Obtaining a corporate outfit
2. Preparation of waiver of notice of meeting and obtaining signatures to it
3. Preparation of bylaws
4. Preparation of minutes of first meeting of incorporators
5. Preparation of minutes of first meeting of directors
6. Preparation of bank account resolution
7. Preparation of stock certificates

16.13. Corporate outfit. Simultaneously with the preparation of the papers, order a *corporate outfit.* This consists of a seal, minute book, stock certificate book, and a stock ledger, and may be obtained from any stationer who handles legal supplies. Some minute books contain printed forms for minutes and bylaws, but many lawyers object to the use of them. When you order the outfit, your letter should give all data necessary to the preparation of the seal and stock certificates. The following model letter indiates the necessary data.

Figure 16.4 illustrates the compact kind of corporation outfit that is available from most legal stationers.

City Stationery Company
803 33rd Street
Montpelier, Vermont 05053

Gentlemen:
Re: Franklin J. King, Inc.

Please forward to us immediately the following corporation supplies:

1. Hand Seal (FRANKLIN J. KING, INC., a Vermont corporation, Incorporated 19..)
2. Minute Book with Filler
3. Stock Certificate Book (minimum number of certificates)
4. Stock Ledger

For your convenience in preparing the stock certificates, we submit the following information: There are authorized to be issued 150 shares of capital stock (only one class authorized) having no par value, fully paid and nonassessable. FRANKLIN J. KING, INC., is a corporation of the State of Vermont and was incorporated in the year 19...

Please send your invoice when the supplies are mailed to us, and we will promptly forward our check in payment.

Sincerely yours,

Warner & Croft

If there are two classes of stock, it is advisable to send a copy of the charter with the order. The stationer can then get the preferred stock clause, which is printed on the back of the stock certificate, directly from the charter. The certificate of common stock will be one color; preferred stock, another.

16.14. Waiver of notice of organization meeting. The statutes require that the incorporators, directors, shareholders, or subscribers, as the case may be, must be given notice of the organization meeting, just as of any other meeting (see page 405), unless they waive notice. It is customary for them to waive notice of the organization meeting. It is your responsibility to prepare the waiver and obtain the signatures of the interested parties. Forms 2 and 3, on page 423, illustrate waivers of notice of first meeting of incorporators, and of first meeting of directors, respectively. Waivers are usually typed on legal cap.

Figure 16.4. *Corporation Outfit.*

16.15. Preparation of bylaws. The bylaws of a corporation are the rules adopted to govern the corporation, its offices, directors, and stockholders. Like the charter, the bylaws usually follow a more or less routine pattern. The lawyer will dictate special clauses or paragraphs peculiar to the corporation being organized and will dictate a memorandum that includes the following information:

1. Place of stockholders' meeting
2. Day and hour of annual meeting of stockholders
3. Time when notice of annual meeting of stockholders must be given (usually 10 days before meeting)
4. Who may call special meetings of stockholders (usually president, vice-president, or upon request two directors or holders of 25 percent of the outstanding stock)

5. Time when notice of special meeting of stockholders must be given (usually 10 days before meeting)

6. Percentage of stock that constitutes a quorum (usually a majority)

7. Place of directors' meetings

8. When regular directors' meetings are to be held

9. Time when notice of regular meetings of directors must be given (usually 3 to 5 days before the meeting)

10. Who may call special meetings of directors (usually president, vice-president, or upon request two directors)

11. Time when notice of special meetings of directors must be given (usually 3 to 5 days before the meeting)

12. Number of directors to constitute quorum

13. Officers who are to sign and countersign checks

14. Officers who are to sign and countersign stock certificates

15. When the fiscal year of the company ends

With the help of this memorandum and the organization papers, you will be able to follow a form and prepare the bylaws. Bylaws are too lengthy to be included here, but you may refer to any book of incorporating forms,[2] or you may obtain a printed copy of the bylaws of corporations that are listed on a stock exchange. Figure 16.5 shows how the bylaws should be set up. Letter-size paper is preferable.

16.16. Minutes of first meeting of incorporators. You can prepare minutes of the first meeting of incorporators without instructions from the attorney, by following a form. The purpose of the minutes is to place on record the filing date of the original of the charter; the filing date of a certified copy in the appropriate county office, where required; the election of directors; the presentation and adoption of the bylaws; and the authorization of the board of directors to issue capital stock of the corporation. Form 1 on page 421 is a form of minutes of the first meeting of a corporation. Detailed directions for the typing of minutes in final form are given on page 411. In a few states, including Maryland and Utah, corporations do not hold an incorporators' meeting but transact this business at the first meeting of directors, who are named in the charter.

16.17. Minutes of first meeting of directors. The purposes of the first, or organization, meeting of the board of directors are to elect officers, approve and ratify the acts of the incorporators, adopt a seal, approve the form of stock certificate, open a bank account, designate a resident agent,

---

[2]See *Prentice-Hall Corporation Forms,* published by Prentice-Hall, Inc., Englewood Cliffs, N.J. 07632.

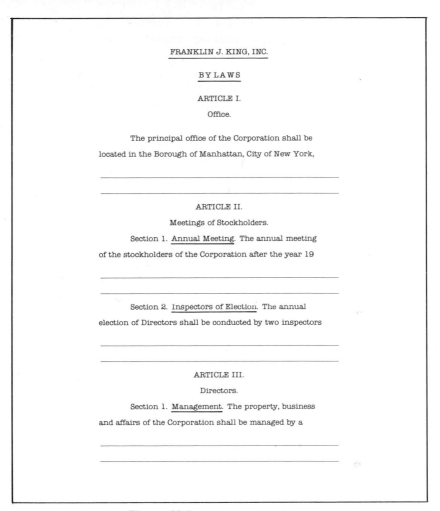

FRANKLIN J. KING, INC.

BYLAWS

ARTICLE I.

Office.

The principal office of the Corporation shall be
located in the Borough of Manhattan, City of New York,

_____

_____

ARTICLE II.

Meetings of Stockholders.

Section 1. Annual Meeting. The annual meeting
of the stockholders of the Corporation after the year 19

_____

_____

Section 2. Inspectors of Election. The annual
election of Directors shall be conducted by two inspectors

_____

_____

ARTICLE III.

Directors.

Section 1. Management. The property, business
and affairs of the Corporation shall be managed by a

_____

_____

Figure 16.5. *First Page of Bylaws.*

and to transact any other business that may properly come before the
meeting. The lawyer usually dictates the minutes of the organization
meeting of the board of directors. See page 411 for typing directions.

16.18. Resolution opening a bank account. The resolution of the
board of directors authorizing the opening of a bank account must
conform to the requirements of the bank in which the account is to be
carried. Banks usually have printed forms of these resolutions. Therefore,
obtain the forms and signature cards and fill them in before the meeting.
The necessary information is available from the memoranda dictated by
the lawyer immediately after his or her original conference with the
principals (pages 384 and 395). The signature cards and resolutions must

be signed by the proper individuals. See page 415 for procedure in handling resolutions prepared by outside organizations.

16.19. Preparation of stock certificates. The lawyer will tell you to whom stock certificates must be issued and the number of shares each stockholder must receive, or the preliminary memorandum dictated by him or her will give you this information. See page 000, *et seq.* for directions about issuance of stock. The certificate must be signed and sealed as required by the bylaws. In some instances when the incorporators are dummies, stock is issued to them and they, in turn, assign it to the actual incorporators. This procedure is not generally necessary, but if it is followed, prepare assignments of certificates in blank of any stock the dummies hold.

PARTNERSHIPS

16.20. What is a partnership? When two or more individuals undertake an enterprise together, without the formalities of incorporation, they form a partnership. A corporation, as a legal entity, may also be a member of a partnership.

There are two kinds of partners. A *full partner* shares in the profits and is fully liable for the debts of the partnership, both his or her personal assets and the partnership assets being reachable by creditors. The *limited partner* simply invests in the business but takes no part in the activities of the partnership. His or her share of the profits is specified by agreement and generally relates to the amount he or she has invested; the limited partner is liable for the losses of the business only to the extent of his or her investment.

16.21. How a partnership is formed. A partnership may be formed by a simple agreement between two or more parties to enter into a business together. Most partnerships, however, draw up an agreement among the partners, outlining their duties and liabilities throughout the existence of the partnership and at its termination. The partnership agreement will usually state:

1. The nature and place of business and the firm name
2. The time of beginning and the duration of the partnership
3. The contribution of each partner to the capital of the firm
4. The share of each in profits and losses
5. The powers of each partner in the conduct of the business
6. Provisions for its dissolution and the conclusion of its affairs

The agreement may be drawn up at any time, before or after the commencement of the business.

16.22. Preparation of partnership agreement. A partnership agreement is a much less formal document than the charter of a corporation. There are rarely state law requirements about how it must be presented. In essence, it is a written contract among the partners, its form being dictated by the number of persons involved, the type of business they are about to enter, and various other factors.

The first item might be the name of the partnership and a brief description of the type of business it plans to carry on. The second item might outline the duration of the partnership and make provisions for carrying on the business after the death or withdrawal of one of the partners. Additional sections might describe the place of business and the overall purpose of the business in as much detail as the partners wish. Another section might deal with capital investment in the business by various partners, followed by a formula for sharing profits and losses. The duties of the partners might be outlined in detail. The final sections might outline the way the partnership business will wind up after its dissolution.

The partnership name may be reserved with the Secretary of State in most states and registered to prevent another business from using the same name.

17

Acting As

Corporate Secretary

The lawyer works closely with the corporate secretary. He or she is frequently a director and officer of the corporation, and many responsibilities that are ordinarily those of the corporate secretary are delegated to the lawyer. He or she drafts resolutions and makes the preparations for holding directors' and stockholders' meetings. The lawyer prepares the minutes of meeting and submits them to the corporate secretary for his or her signature. The lawyer is also responsible for seeing that certain matters, such as lease renewal, are attended to at certain times.

The lawyer's secretary and paralegal will likely have the following duties and responsibilities pertaining to the affairs of a corporate client:

1. Making all preparations for corporate meetings
2. Recording the minutes of the meetings
3. Issuing certificates of stock and handling ordinary stock transfers, if the corporation is small
4. Making a record of important documents and safekeeping them
5. Keeping the corporation calendar
6. Looking after details if corporation changes its name

You will perform some of these duties on your own initiative without instructions from the lawyer; others you will undertake only under instructions from the lawyer and, at first, under his or her close supervision. If you are to be successful in the performance of these duties, you must be *thoroughly familiar with the bylaws* of the corporation.

17.1. Information folder. When the lawyer has the responsibilities listed in the preceding paragraph, it is advisable to keep an information folder (or loose-leaf notebook) pertaining to the corporation. The material in the folder makes available information needed at a moment's notice, without the necessity of removing a document from the safe or looking at the minute book or other records. The material will vary with the need, but ordinarily includes:

1. Schedule of stockholders' meetings (showing when annual meetings are to be held; how special meetings are called; notice required; what constitutes a quorum)
2. Schedule of directors' meetings (showing how called; notice required; what constitutes a quorum)
3. Dividends (chronological record of dividends paid)
4. Number of stockholders
5. Record of incorporation
6. Bylaws
7. States in which the corporation is doing business
8. List of bank accounts (showing where located; who may sign checks)
9. Abstracts of indentures (including abstracts of special agreements such as option to purchase property)

CORPORATE MEETINGS

17.2. Kinds of meetings. In addition to the organization meetings described in the preceding chapter, the kinds of corporate meetings are (1) annual stockholders' meetings, (2) special stockholders' meetings, (3) regular meetings of directors, (4) special meetings of directors, and (5) committee meetings.

17.3. Preparations for meetings. Preparations for meetings include the following activities:

1. Keeping a current meeting file
2. Sending notices of the meeting
3. Preparing the agenda
4. Reserving the meeting room and getting it ready
5. Arranging for payment of directors' fees
6. Preparing to record minutes

17.4. Meeting folder. Keep a current folder for each forthcoming meeting, with the name and date of the meeting noted on the cover or tab. Keep in the folder all papers and documents pertaining to matters to be discussed at the meeting. As matters to be taken up at the meeting come before the lawyer, he or she examines them, makes whatever notes are necessary, arranges the material for presentation at the meeting, and gives you the material. Shortly before the meeting, the corporate secretary might submit a list of items for the agenda. File this material, together with the material given you by the lawyer, in the current meeting folder and make up the agenda for the meeting from it (see page 406).

Also place in the meeting folder all copies of calls, notices of meetings, a list of those to whom the notice must be sent, drafts of resolutions to be taken up at the meeting, and possibly a skeleton of the minutes (see page 408). On the list of stockholders, show the number of shares owned by each.

In addition to the current material, keep in the folders on stockholders' and directors' meetings (1) a pamphlet copy of the corporation laws of the state in which the corporation is organized, (2) a copy of the corporation's charter and bylaws, with amendments, and (3) other papers of a similar nature that may be needed at any stockholders' or directors' meetings. After the meeting has taken place, remove the current papers and file them in their respective folders, leaving in the current file only the documents necessary for all meetings. The folder is then ready to receive papers for the next meeting.

17.5 Notice of stockholders' meeting. The bylaws tell how and when *notices of stockholders' meetings,* both annual and special, must be sent. The secretary must follow those provisions closely. The notices are usually in writing, and the secretary mails them to the stockholders a certain number of days before the meeting, *as specified in the bylaws.*

Form and content of notice. The notice of a stockholders' meeting may be in the form of a postcard or of an announcement sent in a sealed envelope. The notice should specify the date, the place, the hour at which the meeting is to be held, and the purpose of the meeting.

An example of a notice of the stockholders' annual meeting and an example of a special meeting notice are given on pages 423 and 424.

17.6. Waiver of notice of stockholders' meeting. Notices of meetings are sent to all stockholders who have the right to vote. However, in small corporations, the stockholders frequently *waive* notice. In that case prepare a waiver for the stockholders to sign either before or at the meeting. You can easily adapt Form No. 2 on page 423 as a waiver of notice of stockholders' meeting.

When a stockholder waives notice, indicate that fact on the list of stockholders that is kept in the current meeting folder.

17.7. Quorum at a stockholders' meeting. In a small corporation, the secretary has the responsibility of making sure that a quorum will attend the meeting; without a quorum the meeting cannot be held. If you have this responsibility, consult the bylaws to see what percentage of the stock ownership is needed to constitute a quorum. In business corporations the "majority" representation that is normally required is based upon shares of stock and not upon number of individual stockholders. For example, if a company has a total of 20 stockholders, 5 of whom own over half the stock, those 5 stockholders would constitute a majority. Thus, you see the necessity for indicating on the stockholders' list the number of shares owned by each.

17.8. Proxies and proxy statement. As it is impossible for all stockholders of a large corporation to attend meetings, it is customary for a stockholder who cannot attend to give some other person, or a committee, authority to vote his stock. This authority is known as a *proxy.* The word is also used to denote the person to whom the authority is given, and the form on which the authority is given. The proxy form is sent to each stockholder with the notice of meeting.

The Securities Exchange Commission requires a corporation whose stock is listed on a stock exchange to furnish a written proxy statement to each person whose proxy is being solicited. The proxy statement must set forth the nature of the matters to be voted on under the proxy, whether the person giving the proxy has power to revoke it, and other information relating to the proxy. Proxy statements are technical legal documents. The lawyer will dictate the statement to the secretary and ask for a draft. After the draft has been corrected, it must be retyped for the printer.

What the secretary does. Usually the secretary of a small corporation does not send proxies with the notice of meeting. However, if for any reason you anticipate that there will not be a quorum present, get proxies from stockholders who cannot attend, representing a sufficient number of shares to make up a quorum. As small corporations do not list their stock, a proxy statement is not required.

Although large corporations use printed proxy forms, proxies may be reproduced by any mechanical process. If only a few are required, type them on letter-size paper, either plain or with the corporation's letterhead, but not on the lawyer's letterhead. The office copier may also be used to duplicate the form. See page 425 for form.

The proxy need not be witnessed or notarized. The signature should agree with the name in the stock certificate. The signature lines of a proxy to be executed by a corporation should be prepared in the same manner as the signature to any instrument signed on behalf of a corporation (see page 197).

As each proxy is received, check the stockholders' list in the current meeting file to show that the proxy has been received.

17.9. Notice of directors' meeting. Follow the provisions of the bylaws in sending notices of meetings to directors. Even if notice of a regular meeting is not required by the bylaws, it is advisable to notify the directors of the meeting. If a special meeting is to be called, telephone or telegraph the directors to determine whether the time is convenient for all of them. Send a written notice after the time of the meeting is definitely fixed.

The list of the directors that is kept in the current meeting folder should be tabulated, with columns showing the date each was notified, the date a follow-up notice, if any, was sent, and the replies.

Form and content of notice. Notices of directors' meetings are usually typewritten on the corporation's letterhead. Printing or photocopying the notice on cards or paper slips, with blanks for the date, time, and place of the meeting, is a time-saving expedient. A light stock for card notices is preferable, since heavy stock is not suitable for insertion in the typewriter to fill in necessary information.

The notice is sent in the name of the corporate secretary. It should specify the date, the place, and the hour at which the meeting is to be held. Whether or not it is required by statute or bylaws, the notice of a special meeting should state the purpose for which it is held.

An example of a notice of a directors' special meeting specifying the purpose of the meeting is on page 425.

17.10. Quorum at directors' meeting. A directors' meeting cannot be held unless a quorum is present. Consult the bylaws for the number of directors necessary to constitute a quorum. A quorum at a directors' meeting differs from a quorum at a stockholders' meeting in that the representation is based upon the number of directors and not upon the amount of stock owned by them.

If you learn that a quorum will not be present, telephone those directors who expect to attend and arrange, with approval of the person calling the meeting, to have the meeting postponed. This is particularly important if the directors are coming from a distance.

A director cannot give a proxy for a directors' meeting. But corporate action may be taken without a formal directors' meeting when written consent is obtained from all or a majority of the directors.

17.11. Preservation of notice. Keep a copy of every notice of meeting, with the date of mailing noted on it, in the current meeting folder. If the notice has been published in the newspapers, keep a clipping of the published notice and the name of the publication and dates of publication.

17.12. The agenda. The *agenda* consists of an itemized list of matters to be brought up at a meeting. The secretary lists them from the accumulated material in the current meeting folder. The agenda should follow the order of business as set forth in the bylaws.

Here is a typical agenda prepared for a directors' meeting:

1. *Read minutes of last meeting.* (Attach a typewritten copy of the minutes of the previous meeting to the corporate secretary's copy of the agenda.)

2. *Submit the following statements:* (Here enumerate the reports of officers and committees to be presented to the meeting. Copies of the reports may be attached to the agenda.)

3. *Adopt resolution approving minutes of executive committee meetings.* (If minutes are long, copies may be made and attached to the agenda.)

4. *Business of the meeting.* (Here enumerate business to be acted upon indicating each item by a summary of the resolution that is required.)

Begin preparation of the agenda several days before the meeting. Have it completely in order the evening before the meeting. Prepare a copy for each director. Attach to the agenda the exhibits, supporting papers, reports, and the like that contain the information necessary to supply the groundwork for discussion.

17.13. Reservation and preparation of the meeting room. If a meeting is to be held in a room that is used for other purposes, notify the person who is responsible for the room to have it available at the time of the meeting. When you enter the date of the meeting in the corporation's calendar (see page 419), also enter at an earlier date a reminder to reserve the room. This should be done in ample time to avoid conflict, the time of the advance notice depending upon the demand for the room.

In preparing the room for the meeting, have it dusted, properly heated, and ventilated. See that sufficient costumers and coat hangers are available. Provide stationery, memorandum pads, pen and ink, and pencils for each person who is expected to attend the meeting. Have a supply of clips, pins, rubber bands on the table, and put an ash tray and matches at each place. If any special equipment, such as slide projectors, recorders, or display materials, is to be used at the meeting, be sure it is assembled and operational by the time the meeting begins.

17.14. Directors' fees. The fee payable to directors for attendance at a meeting is usually fixed by resolution adopted by the board of directors. When preparation for the meeting is the lawyer's responsibility, payment of the fees might be his or her responsibility also. In this case, arrange with the treasurer of the corporation to have the checks or cash at the meeting. If any payments are left over because of nonattendance, return them to the treasurer. Make the payments to the directors after the meeting, preferably enclosed in an envelope. Individual corporate policy will indicate how and when payment is to be made.

17.15. Material to take to meetings. Take the following material to directors' and stockholders' meetings:

1. Pamphlet copy of the corporation laws of the state in which the corporation is organized

2. Copy of the certificate of incorporation, with marginal notations of amendments and copies of them

3. Copy of the bylaws, with marginal notations of amendments and copies of them

4. Separate sheet for order of business

5. Rules and regulations of the corporation, if any, governing the conduct of meetings

6. Proof of the mailing of notices of the meeting and, where necessary, of publication

7. The original call for the meeting and, if there has been a demand for a call, the original of the demand

8. The minute book

9. The corporate seal

10. Current papers pertaining to the meeting (see page 403)

11. Blank affidavits, oaths, and the like

17.16. Drafting resolutions before meetings. The lawyer will dictate all resolutions involving legal technicalities, but there are many simple resolutions that you can draft yourself. The forms on page 427, *et seq.* are examples of resolutions that almost all corporations adopt. Draft all simple resolutions that are indicated by the agenda and submit them to the lawyer before typing in final form. Frequently the lawyer submits drafts of resolutions to the office or department of the corporation that originated the proposition, to ensure that the resolution expresses the correct view. Every secretary or paralegal who has any of the duties of a corporate secretary should have as part of his or her equipment a book of resolutions[1] as a guide to the form that the resolution should take.

Resolutions to satisfy outside person or organization. Certain actions may require the passage of a resolution in a form satisfactory to some

---

[1]See W. Sardell, *Encyclopedia of Corporate Meetings, Minutes, and Resolutions,* rev.ed. Englewood Cliffs, N.J.; Prentice-Hall, Inc. 1978.

outside person or organization. For example, the opening of a bank account by a corporation generally calls for passage of a resolution in the form required by the bank. If such a resolution is to come before the meeting, get the required form before the meeting. After the board passes the resolution, fill in the blanks. To avoid copying the resolution into the minutes, get two blank forms of the resolution and fill in both forms, pasting one copy into the minute book and making it a part of the minutes by reference. The original of the resolution, signed by the proper officers of the corporation, is filed with the bank. Of course, if you make extra copies of the minutes you will need extra copies of the blanks.

17.17. Preparations for taking notes at meetings. In advance of the meeting prepare either a skeleton of the minutes or a memorandum form for entering notes. The *skeleton,* or outline, is a rough draft of the minutes with the spaces to be filled in with details as they develop at the meeting. A skeleton is particularly useful when the program of a meeting is prearranged. Use the forms of minutes on pages 421 to 422 as a guide in preparing the skeleton.

Figures 17.1 and 17.2 show a memorandum form for entering notes. The memorandum includes the nature of the meeting (regular or special) and how notice was given (regular or personal) or whether waiver was secured, so a checkmark is all that is necessary to show the facts. The resolutions submitted to the meeting are numbered to correspond with the numbers of the resolutions on the memorandum. The notes on this memorandum supply the secretary with all the information necessary for writing minutes of the meeting.

17.18. Taking notes at meetings. Verbatim notes of a meeting are not generally necessary except at stockholders' meetings of large corporations and at board meetings when there is dissension among the directors. Expert stenographers are sometimes brought to stockholders' meetings to take the notes.

In taking notes at a meeting, make no attempt to put everything down in full, but do take important statements verbatim. Also make a verbatim record of resolutions that are framed at the meeting. When someone at the meeting asks that his or her views be made a part of the record, the secretary should record those remarks in full. Do not hesitate to record in the minutes full details of what transpires at the meeting.

Do not permit the meeting to proceed to the next subject unless you have a clear understanding of what has been done. By prearranged signal let the chairman know that you do not have a clear understanding of an action that was taken or a statement that was made. It is helpful to have reports and other data handy from which you can quickly extract facts and figures, check spelling of names, and so on. At small meetings, a

```
                    SECRETARY'S MEMORANDUM

                MEETING OF BOARD OF DIRECTORS

                            Stated        Reg. Notice
                            Annual        Personal
    ORGANIZATION            Special       Waiver

    DATE           19—          Hour          Standard

    PRESENT        No. present  Necessary for quorum
    CHAIRMAN
    SECRETARY
    MINUTES
    STATEMENTS
    RESOLUTIONS
         #1    Proposed by      Seconded by
                                For
              Votes             Against


         #2    Proposed by      Seconded by
                                For
              Votes             Against


         #3    Proposed by      Seconded by
                                For
              Votes             Against
```

Figure 17.1. *Secretary's Memorandum for Entering Notes of Minutes at Meeting (Page 1).*

seating chart helps identify the people who are speaking during the meeting.

Make a separate notation of any action that is to be taken immediately after the meeting.

MINUTES

17.19 The minute book. Minutes of stockholders' meetings, directors' meetings, and committee meetings are often kept in separate books. For a small company, however, it is feasible to use one book, dividing it into distinct parts. Minute books are usually loose-leaf. After a sufficient number of pages have accumulated, they may be bound. The pages of a minute book may be numbered for convenience. Both sides of the sheet are written on. Standard paper for minute books is of a special quality—smooth, heavy, and durable, usually with an outside ruled margin. Manufacturers and stationers who specialize in corporate forms can supply it.

```
┌──────────────────┬──────────────────────────────────────────────────────┐
│ RESOLUTIONS      │                                                        │
│ CONTINUED        │                                                        │
│           #4     │ Proposed by              Seconded by                   │
│                  │                          For                           │
│                  │ Votes                    Against                       │
│                  │                                                        │
│           #5     │ Proposed by              Seconded by                   │
│                  │                          For                           │
│                  │ Votes                    Against                       │
│                  │                                                        │
│           #6     │ Proposed by              Seconded by                   │
│                  │                          For                           │
│                  │ Votes                    Against                       │
│                  │                                                        │
│           #7     │ Proposed by              Seconded by                   │
│                  │                          For                           │
│                  │ Votes                    Against                       │
│ NOTES            │                                                        │
│                  │                                                        │
│ ADJOURNMENT      │                                                        │
│                  │ Fees        Per member present                         │
│ DISBURSEMENT     │ Expenses     "     "    present   Sundries  Total      │
│                  │              (Signed).....................             │
│                  │                              Secretary                 │
└──────────────────┴──────────────────────────────────────────────────────┘
```

Figure 17.2. *Secretary's Memorandum for Entering Notes of Minutes at Meeting (Page 2).*

17.20. Arrangement of contents of combined minute book. The contents of a minute book should be arranged as follows:

1. Bind or paste a certified copy of the corporation's charter in the first pages of the book, or merely copy the charter into the book. Leave space to insert amendments later.

2. Beginning at the top of a right-hand page, copy the bylaws of the corporation. Again, leave space to insert amendments later.

3. After the bylaws, insert the minutes of the meeting of incorporators or of other organization meetings.

4. Continue with the minutes of the stockholders' meetings, beginning each set of minutes at the top of a new page.

5. After the minutes of stockholders' meetings, begin the section on minutes of directors' meetings.

17.21. Content of minutes. The content and form of minutes are fairly well standardized (see Form 1 on page 421). The order of the contents follows:

1. Begin with the time and place of the meeting.

2. Establish that the meeting was properly called and that notice was given or waived. When the bylaws do not require notice of regular directors' meetings, omit this item from the minutes.

3. Give the names of the chairman and secretary of the meeting.

4. List those present. Also list absentees at directors' meetings. In minutes of stockholders' meetings, list those represented by proxy as well as those present in person and, also, the amount of stock represented.

5. State that the minutes of the previous meeting were read and unanimously approved, or that reading was dispensed with.

6. Follow with a clear, accurate, and complete report of all business transacted, arranged in accordance with the order of business established in the bylaws.

17.22. Preparation of draft of minutes. Write the minutes immediately after the meeting while events are still fresh in your mind.

If you do not attend the meeting, write the minutes by expanding the lawyer's notes. For example, the notes will show that a certain resolution was unanimously adopted. The minutes will be expanded to read:

On motion duly made and seconded, the following resolution was unanimously adopted:
RESOLVED, That ....

To write minutes from notes made by another, you must have before you all papers, documents, and reports that were discussed at the meeting. If the lawyer takes notes on the memorandum form described in figures 17.1 and 17.2, the task of expanding the notes is simple.

Submit a draft of the minutes to the lawyer for review and correction. Enter minutes in the minute book only after a draft has been approved by the lawyer or appropriate corporate officer.

17.23. How to prepare minutes in final form. Some of the larger corporations have strict rules about the uniformity of arrangement of minutes. Independently of rules, a secretary should take particular pains with details about the typing, arrangement, spacing, and general appearance of the minute book. The following is a suggested list of rules relating to the form to be followed in typing the minutes into the minute book:

1. Capitalize and center the heading designating the meeting.
2. Indent paragraphs 10 spaces.
3. Indent names of those present or absent 15 spaces.
4. Double-space the text, including preambles to resolutions.
5. Single-space and indent, but do not quote, take-ins, such as

letters, waivers of notice of meetings, oaths of inspectors of election, and the like. Leave at least 4 spaces before and after the take-in. When the take-in is a printed paper, the text following the printed take-in should start on a new page.

6. Double-space between each paragraph, and triple-space between each item in order of business.

7. Indent resolutions 15 spaces and single-space them.

8. Capitalize the words *Board of Directors* and the word *Corporation* when reference is made to the corporation whose minutes are being written. References to specific officers of the corporation may be capitalized or in lower case, but the capitalization should be consistent.

9. Leave 1½ inch outside margin if the paper does not have a ruled margin.

10. Put captions in the margin in capitals or in red type.

11. Capitalize all letters in the words *Whereas* and *Resolved,* followed by a comma, and begin the word *that* with a capital.

12. When sums of money are mentioned in a resolution, write them first in words and then in figures in parentheses.

17.24. Correction of errors in minutes. As previously noted, the minutes of a meeting are usually approved at the next meeting. The chairman informally directs correction of simple errors. If the error can be corrected immediately, make the correction at the meeting and offer the minutes, as changed, for approval. If the error involves a revision of the minutes, report the corrections of the minutes of the previous meeting in the minutes of the current meeting. A form of resolution correcting the minutes of a previous meeting is shown on page 428.

Insering corrections in the minute book. Strike out the erroneous material by drawing a red line through each line of the incorrect material. Write the correct minutes in between the red lines. Make a reference in the margin of the corrected minutes to the minutes of the following meeting, to show where the correction was ordered.

When it is impractical to make the correction this way, strike out the erroneous material in red and make a note in the margin showing where the revised minutes appear. Insert the corrected minutes at the end of the original minutes. Do not throw away the pages that were incorrectly written. Retain the original pages and indicate that they are obsolete by reference to the minutes of the meeting at which the errors were corrected.

17.25. Certified extract of minutes. Directors authorize by resolution the transaction of various items of business on behalf of the corporation, and the resolutions passed by the directors are embodied in the minutes of the meetings. It is frequently necessary to produce evidence of the authority granted in the form of a *certified extract* of the minutes, or copy of the resolution. The certification is usuallyby the secretary of the corporation. Figures 17.3 and 17.4 illustrate a certified extract of minutes. It may be typed on plain letter-size paper or on the corporation's letterhead.

17.26. Indexing of minutes. If minutes of meetings are voluminous, keep a card index so any business that has been passed upon

CERTIFIED EXTRACT OF MINUTES

I, the undersigned, Secretary of GLASSER & SONS, INC.,

a corporation duly organized and existing under the laws of

the State of New York, and having its principal place of

business in the City of New York, hereby CERTIFY that the

following is a true copy of a certain resolution duly adopted

by the Board of Directors of the said corporation in accord-

ance with the Bylaws at, and recorded in the minutes of,

a meeting of the said Board duly held on   , 19   ,

and not subsequently rescinded or modified:

RESOLVED:

That an account be opened in the name of the Glasser & Sons, Inc., with the EAST RIVER SAVINGS BANK at 41 Rockefeller Plaza, in the Borough of Manhattan, City of New York, and that the funds of the said Glasser & Sons, Inc., may be deposited therein and that all drafts and other instruments for the payment of money shall be signed by the following officers:-

Jules MacDonald	President
Janet Lewis	Secretary & Treasurer
John Bennett	Asst. Secretary & Asst. Treasurer
Ellen Farnsworth	Vice-President
Joseph Hart	Asst. Treasurer of Committee of Managers

And the Bank is hereby authorized to pay such drafts and instruments when so signed (including those drawn to cash or bearer or to the individual order of the officer or officers signing the same) and also to receive the same

Figure 17.3. *Certified Extract of Minutes (Page 1).*

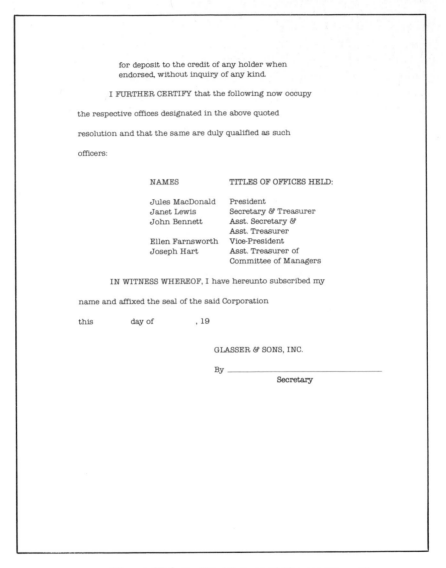

for deposit to the credit of any holder when endorsed, without inquiry of any kind.

I FURTHER CERTIFY that the following now occupy

the respective offices designated in the above quoted

resolution and that the same are duly qualified as such

officers:

NAMES	TITLES OF OFFICES HELD:
Jules MacDonald	President
Janet Lewis	Secretary & Treasurer
John Bennett	Asst. Secretary & Asst. Treasurer
Ellen Farnsworth	Vice-President
Joseph Hart	Asst. Treasurer of Committee of Managers

IN WITNESS WHEREOF, I have hereunto subscribed my

name and affixed the seal of the said Corporation

this   day of   , 19

GLASSER & SONS, INC.

By _____
                    Secretary

Figure 17.4. *Certified Extract of Minutes (Page 2).*

may be referred to easily and quickly. The making of the index is facilitated by marginal captions in the minutes. The index card contains the subject matter taken from the captions and a reference to the page on which the caption appears.

ISSUANCE AND TRANSFER OF STOCK
OF A SMALL CORPORATION

17.27. Authority to issue certificate. A large corporation has a transfer agent, usually a bank, that issues and transfers shares of stock. The lawyer frequently has this responsibility for a small corporation. He issues an original certificate of stock for a definite number of shares to a certain person when authorized to do so by resolution of the directors or of the stockholders.

17.28. Stock certificate book. A bound book of blank stock certificates is kept for each class of stock. The certificates and corresponding stubs are numbered consecutively. The number of shares is usually left blank so certificates may be issued for various amounts. Figure 17.5 is a reproduction of a stock certificate. In a small corporation with only a few stockholders, the stock certificate book usually serves as a transfer record and as a stock ledger.

17.29. Original issue and transfer of stock. An original issue of stock refers to a share of stock that has never before been issued. The certificate of incorporation authorizes the corporation to issue a stated number of shares. All of these shares need not be issued immediately, but as each is issued, it is considered an *original issue.* When the person to whom it is issued sells or gives it to someone else, it becomes a *transferred share.*

Taxes on stock. Federal stamp tax. The federal government no longer imposes a stamp tax on stock issues or transfers.

State transfer tax. Some states have a transfer tax on stock. Whether or not the state tax is payable depends upon the state in which the transfer is made. Thus, a transfer in New York of a Delaware corporation's stock is subject to the New York transfer tax, although Delaware does not have a tax. It is impractical to give the rate of taxation for each state here, but you can get the information from the state statutes.

Almost every law imposing these taxes gives some official the right to call for books and documents on a moment's notice. For example, state inspectors may call on New York transfer agents and ask to see the stock transfer books to ascertain whether the proper stamps have been affixed to meet stock transfer requirements. If you are the custodian of a corporation's books, it is your duty (1) to be most punctilious in seeing that the proper documentary stamps are affixed and (2) to present the books for inspection upon presentation of the proper credentials.

Figure 17.5. *Stock Certificate.*

17.30. Issuance of certificate of stock. Here are the steps necessary to issue a stock certificate:

1. Enter the name and address of the person to whom the certificate is issued and the number of shares for which it is issued on the stub.

2. Tear the certificate out of the stock book.

3. Type on the face of the certificate the name of the person to whom it is issued, the number of shares it represents, and the date.

4. Have the certificate signed by the officers whose signatures are required.

5. Impress the corporate seal in the space provided.

6. If possible, have the receipt on the stub of the certificate signed. If the person in whose name the certificate is issued is not present to sign the stub, type the receipt on a slip of paper the size and shape of the receipt printed on the stub. Be certain that the information on the receipt corresponds with the stub. Enclose the receipt with the certificate and request the person in whose name the certificate is issued to sign and return it. When it is received, paste it over the receipt portion of the stub.

7. Affix to the stub and cancel documentary stamps. (See page 443 for cancellation of stamps.)

8. Send certificates *by registered mail.*

17.31. Transfer of certificate. The back of the certificate has a form for an assignment or transfer of stock from one holder to another (figure 17.6). When shares of stock are transferred, the corporation issues a new certificate. The holder of a 100-share certificate might want to transfer, say, 50 shares and keep the other 50. In that case, two new certificates of 50 shares each are issued—one to the transferee and one to the original owner.

When a certificate is transferred, follow the procedure outlined on the preceding pages for the original issuance of a certificate. Notice that the stub to a transferred certificate calls for more information than the stub to an original issue. In addition, take the following steps:

1. Write "Canceled" in ink across the face of the old certificate.

2. Date and initial the canceled certificate.

3. Paste the canceled certificate to its stub in the bound stock certificate book, as nearly in the certificate's original position in the book as possible.

4. Affix the state documentary stamp to the canceled certificate and cancel the stamp. The stamp tax will apply *only to the shares that are transferred,* not to the certificate for the new shares that the original owner might keep. (See page 443 for cancellation of stamps.)

For Value Received, ——— *hereby sell, assign and transfer unto*

PLEASE INSERT SOCIAL SECURITY OR OTHER
IDENTIFYING NUMBER OF ASSIGNEE

——————————————————————— *Shares*
represented by the within Certificate, and do hereby
irrevocably constitute and appoint
——————————————————————— *Attorney*
to transfer the said Shares on the books of the within named
Corporation with full power of substitution in the premises.
Dated ——————— *19——*
In presence of

NOTICE THE SIGNATURE OF THIS ASSIGNMENT MUST CORRESPOND WITH THE NAME AS WRITTEN UPON THE FACE OF THE CERTIFICATE, IN EVERY PARTICULAR, WITHOUT ALTERATION OR ENLARGEMENT OR ANY CHANGE WHATEVER.

The designations and the powers, preferences and rights, and the qualifications thereof are as follows: The non-voting mana shares, as a class, shall be entitled to such dividends as from time to time may be declared by the board of directors of the Corporati irrespective of whether or not dividends are declared and paid on any and all classes of voting stock of Preferred Shares. The of the Management Shares can only be officers or employees of the Corporation and said shares are subject to call by the Board of Di at any time at the same price at which they were issued. The deposit at any bank in Puerto Rico to the credit of the registered ho any then outstanding Management Shares of an amount equivalent to the price at which said shares were issued, shall have the e making valueless and void any certificate or certificates representing any shares outstanding against which such deposit shall hav made. The holders of such Management Shares are not entitled to vote at any meeting of stockholders, have no interest whatsoever corporate surplus nor in the assets of the Corporation other than to the extent of the amount paid for said shares. The Management of this Corporation shall be issued from time to time as authorized by the Board of Directors of the Corporation, and the persons to said shares are issued, receive them subject to the conditions hereinabove mentioned and subject to the further condition that said must be surrendered at such time as when said officer or employee ceases to be an officer or employee of the Corporation, it being stood that if said Certificate or Certificate of Management Shares of the Corporation are not surrendered by a person who ceases t officer or an employee of the Corporation, said certificate shall be of no value in his possession and shall not be entitled to such di as therafter may be declared by the Corporation on the holders of Management Shares.

The amount of the authorized stock of the Company may be increased or decreased by the affirmative vote of the holders then outstanding Class A Voting Stock, Class B Non-Voting Stock. It shall not be required, for any amendment to these articles corporation, the vote of the then holders of Management Shares, irrespective of whether or not such amendment may affect the rig privileges of the holders of said Management Shares.

Figure 17.6. *Back of Certificate Showing Transfer Form.*

17.32. Separate form of assignment. When you handle the lawyer's personal securities, you will probably deal with a broker. Securities transferred through a broker are transferred in blank because the transferor does not know to whom they will be delivered. A transfer in blank might be made on a form of assignment separate from the stock certificate, instead of on the assignment that is printed on the back of the certificate. The broker will supply you with printed forms for this purpose. If the certificates are sent to the broker by mail, registered or otherwise, send the assignment in blank separately. The reason for this is that only nonnegotiable securities should be sent through the mail. A security endorsed on the back in blank or a security accompanied by a separate assignment in blank is negotiable. The wording of a separate assignment is similar to that of the assignment on the back of a certificate. Figure 17.7 illustrates an assignment separate from a stock certificate.

Figure 17.7. *Assignment Separate from Certificate.*

THE CORPORATION CALENDAR

17.33. Need for a corporation calendar. The need for a corporation calendar is evident to anyone whose office has the responsibility of seeing that certain acts of a corporation are done at certain times. The acts for which the lawyer is responsible generally relate to the following subjects:

1. Directors' and stockholders' meetings
2. Expiration and renewal of contracts, leases, and the like
3. Tax matters
4. Reports

In some cases, the lawyer attends to these matters personally; in others, he or she merely advises the corporation that the matter should be attended to by a certain date.

It is advisable to keep the follow-ups for the corporation on a calendar separate from the appointment and court diary (chapter 3). However, if the lawyer has these follow-up responsibilities for more than one corporation, one calendar will serve for the several corporations.

17.34. How to keep the corporation calendar. The most usual form of corporation calendar is a card index, 3 by 5 inches, arranged chronologically behind monthly tab cards. The card contains sufficient information, in addition to the date, to give the lawyer a correct idea of what he or she is to do, or what the secretarys and paralegal are to do. The cards are made up as a transaction occurs or as the need for the card arises. Thus, if the lawyer is custodian of the corporate documents and you are given a lease to put in the safe, you will note the expiration date of the lease and make up a card for that particular day.

Acts that are to be done at certain times but for which no definite day is specified may be entered on a monthly reminder card. For example, suppose that in a certain state the corporation is required to file a statement with the secretary of state each time a change in officers occurs. You will make a note of the requirement on a card without a date and at the beginning of each month move it along to the next month. If you prefer, you might make a note on 12 separate cards and file one for each month.

At the beginning of each month, examine all of the items in the calendar for the succeeding two months to allow ample time for taking action on the reminders furnished by the cards. Time-consuming tasks that must be done by a certain date should be entered sufficiently in advance to permit the work to be finished on time.

17.35. Where to get dates for the corporation calendar. You will have to ask the lawyer to give you the date for many of the calendar entries, but you can get some of them from the material in the information folder (see page 402) and from the sources indicated below. In any event, the lawyer should verify the dates, because severe penalties result from failure to perform some of these acts at the required time.

Annual stockholders' meeting. See the bylaws.

Regular directors' meeting. See minutes of first meeting of directors or stockholders.

Expiration and renewal dates. See the documents or abstracts of them in the information folder.

Annual report to stockholders. The annual report is published as soon after the end of the fiscal year as possible. Work on it begins considerably before the close of the fiscal year, the length of time depending upon the elaborateness of the report.

Annual report to state authority. Check the general corporation law for the state of incorporation, pamphlet copy of which should be in the information folder.

Tax matters and reports to federal and state governments. For accurate, up-to-date information, a loose-leaf tax service, such as those published by Prentice-Hall, Inc., would probably serve your purpose best. These services cover all taxes imposed by federal, state, and local governments and contain tax calendars. If your office maintains a corporation, its library will probably contain a service of this kind. If not, and if the service is not available in a nearby law library, write to the particular tax authority for the information desired.

CHANGE OF CORPORATE NAME

17.36. Details when corporate name is changed. The states provide by statute the manner in which a corporation may change its name and indicate the procedure to be followed. The attorney will give you detailed instructions about the legal procedure because the directions outlined by the statute must be strictly followed. Numerous other changes are made necessary by the adoption of a new name. The corporation personnel looks after many of them, such as changes in bank accounts, stationery, and the like, but some of the changes are handled in the law office. Matters to which you should attend include:

1. Changes in corporate seal
2. Change in contracts
3. Change in leases
4. Change in deeds to real property

If your office keeps the stock certificate book

5. Order new stock certificate book
6. Write to stockholders to send in certificates

Specimen Corporate Forms

No. 1

Minutes of first meeting of incorporators

of a Corporation.

[*Note.* The headings in brackets may appear as marginal notes in the minute book.]

[Time and place of meeting]

The first meeting of incorporators of the .... was held at ......, in the City of ...., State of ...., at ...... o'clock in the ...... noon of the .. day of ...., 19.., pursuant to a written waiver of notice, signed by all of the incorporators, fixing said place and time.

The following incorporators were present in person or by proxy:

Name of Incorporator	Name of Proxy*
....	....
....	....
....	....

being all of the incorporators named in the Certificate of Incorporation.

[Temporary officers]

On motion unanimously carried, Mr./Mrs./Miss .... was elected Chairman, and Mr./Mrs./Miss .... Secretary of the meeting.

[Waiver of notice]

The Secretary presented the waiver of notice of the meeting signed by all of the incorporators, and it was filed as part of the minutes. The Secretary was ordered to file as a part of the minutes any proxies that had been accepted.

[Certificate of incorporation reported filed]

The Chairman reported that the Certificate of Incorporation of the Corporation was filed in the office of the Secretary of State of the State of .... on the .. day of .... 19.., and a certified copy thereof was filed for record in the office of the recorder of Deeds in the County of ...., on the .. day of ...., 19.., and a copy of said Certificate of Incorporation was ordered to be inserted in the minute book as part of the records of the meeting.

[Adoption of Bylaws]

The Secretary presented a proposed form of Bylaws for the regulation and management of the affairs of the Corporation, which was read, section by section, and unanimously adopted and ordered to be made a part of the permanent records to follow the Certificate of Incorporation in the minute book.

[Election of directors]

Motions were then declared by the Chairman to be in order for the nomination of directors of the Corporation to hold office for the ensuing year and until their successors are elected and qualify, and the following persons were nominated: (*insert names of nominees*).

No further nominations having been made, a ballot was taken and all of the incorporators having voted, and the ballots having been duly canvassed, the Chairman declared that the above-named persons were elected directors of the Corporation by the unanimous vote of all the incorporators.

Upon motion duly made, seconded, and unanimously carried, it was

[Issuance of capital stock]

RESOLVED, That the Board of Directors be and it hereby is authorized in its discretion to issue the capital stock of this Corporation to the full amount or number of shares authorized by the Certificate of Incorporation, in such amounts and for such considerations as from time to time shall be determined by the Board of Directors and as may be permitted by law.

---

*If the incorporator was present in person, write "In person" in the column. If not, write the name of the person who represented him as proxy.

[Adjournment]

There being no other business to be transacted, the meeting was, upon motion duly made, seconded, and carried, adjourned.

....
Secretary of the Meeting

No. 2
Waiver of notice of first meeting of incorporators.

We, the undersigned, being all of the incorporators of the ...., a corporation organized under the laws of the State of ...., do hereby severally waive all the statutory requirements as to notice of the time, place, and purpose of the first meeting of incorporators of the said corporation and the publication thereof, and consent that the meeting shall be held at ...., in the City of ...., State of ...., on the .. day of ......, 19.., at .... o'clock in the ...... noon; and we consent to the transaction of any and all business that may properly come before this meeting.
Dated ...., 19...

....
....
....

No. 3
Waiver of notice of first meeting of directors

We, the undersigned, duly elected directors of ...., do hereby severally waive notice of time, place, and purpose of the first meeting of directors of said corporation, and consent that the meeting be held at ...., in the City of ...., State of ...., on the .... day of ...., 19.., at .... o'clock in the .... noon; and we do further consent to the transaction of any business requisite to complete the organization of the company, and to any and all business that may properly come before the meeting.
Dated ...., 19...

....
....
....

No. 4
Notice of annual meeting of stockholders.

........, ..., 19..

The annual meeting of the stockholders of the .... Company, for the election of directors and the transaction of such other business as may properly come before the meeting, will be held at the office of the Company on (*day of week*), ..., 19.., at ...... o'clock in the .... noon.

If you cannot be present at the meeting, please sign and return the accompanying proxy in the enclosed envelope.

....
Secretary

No. 5

Notice of special meeting of stockholders, indicating purpose of meeting.

NOTICE IS HEREBY GIVEN that a special meeting of the stockholders of the
.... Company, a corporation of the State of........., has been called and will
be held on ...., 19.., at .... o'clock .....M., at the registered office of the
Company, (*address*)........., City of........., State of........., for the following
purposes:

    1. (*Here insert purpose of meeting.*)

    2. To transact any other business that may come before the said meeting.

    If you are unable to be present in person, please sign the enclosed form of proxy
and return it in the enclosed stamped envelope.

    By order of the Board of Directors.

....
Secretary

Dated ...., 19...

No. 6

Affidavit of secretary that notice of annual meeting of stockholders was mailed.

STATE OF ....   } ss.:
COUNTY OF ....

.... , being duly sworn, on oath deposes and says: that he/she is the
Secretary of the .... Corporation, a corporation organized and existing
under the laws of the State of ...., having its principal office in the State
of .... ; that on the .. day of ...., 19.., he/she caused notice of the
annual meeting of the stockholders of the said Corporation, a copy of which is
hereto attached and is hereby made a part of this affidavit, to be deposited in
the United States Post Office at .... City, in a sealed envelope, postage
prepaid, duly addressed to each stockholder of record of the said Corporation
at his last-known post office address as the same appeared on the books of the
Corporation.

....

    Subscribed and sworn to before me
this .. day of ...., 19...

....
Notary Public

No. 7

Affidavit of secretary of publication of notice of stockholders' meeting.

STATE OF ....   } ss.:
COUNTY OF ....

.................., being duly sworn, on his oath says that he/she is the Secretary
of .... Corporation, a corporation organized and existing under the
laws of the State of.........; that pursuant to the order of the Board of Directors of
said Corporation, he/she caused the notice of the .... (*insert annual or
special*) meeting of stockholders, a copy of which is hereto annexed and made a

part of this affidavit, to be published in the ...., a newspaper published in the City of ...., and circulating in the County of ...., being the county in which said Corporation is located, for a period of ...., beginning the .. day of ...., 19.., as required by .... (*insert words "the laws of the State of ....," or "the Bylaws of the Corporation"*).

Sworn to before me this ....
.. day of ...., 19.. Secretary
....
Notary Public

No. 8

Proxy for special meeting of stockholders.

KNOW ALL MEN BY THESE PRESENTS, That ...., the undersigned, stockholder in the .... Company, does hereby appoint .... and ...., or either of them, true and lawful attorneys, with power of substitution for .... and in .... name to vote, as .... proxy, at the Special Meeting of the Stockholders in said Company, to be held at the City of ...., State of ...., on the .. day of ...., 19.., or at any adjournment thereof, with all the powers which .... should possess if personally present.

Dated this .. day of ...., 19...

....

No. 9

Notice of special meeting of directors, specifying purposes.

.... (*City*) .... (*State*)

To ...., ..., and ....,
Directors of .... Corporation:

NOTICE IS HEREBY GIVEN That, in accordance with the provisions of Article ...., Section .... of the Bylaws of the .... Corporation, and in accordance with the requirements of the laws of the State of ...., a special meeting of the Board of Directors of the said Corporation will be held at its office and principal place of business, ... (*Street*), ... (*City*), ... (*State*), on the .. day of ...., 19.., at .... o'clock in the .... noon, for the purpose of:

1. (*Here insert particular purpose of meeting.*)
2. To transact such other business as may lawfully come before said meeting.

....
Secretary

No. 10

Minutes of annual meeting of directors.

[*Note:* The headings in brackets ordinarily appear in the minute book as marginal captions.]

[Time and place of meeting] The .... annual meeting of the Board of Directors of the .... Corporation was held at the office of the Corporation, ..., in the City of ...., State of ...., on the .. day of .... 19.., at .... o'clock in the ..... noon, immediately following the adjournment of the annual meeting of the stockholders.

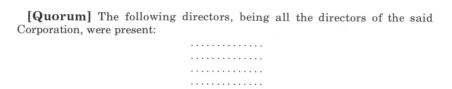

[Quorum] The following directors, being all the directors of the said Corporation, were present:

. . . .
. . . .
. . . .
. . . .
. . . .

[Chairman; Secretary] Mr./Mrs./Miss . . . ., President of the Corporation, presided, and Mr./Mrs./Miss . . . . acted as Secretary of the meeting.

[Notice of meeting] The Secretary presented the notice of the meeting pursuant to which the meeting was held. The same was ordered to be entered in the minutes and is as follows:

(Insert notice here.)

The Chairman laid before the meeting the minutes of the annual meeting of the stockholders of the corporation, held on the .. day of . . . ., 19.., showing the election of the following persons as directors of the Corporation, to hold office for the term of . . . . . . year(s), and until their successors shall be elected and shall qualify.

. . . .
. . . .
. . . .
. . . .
. . . .

[Election of officers] On motion duly made, seconded, and unanimously carried, the Board of Directors thereupon proceeded to elect the following officers of the Corporation, to wit: President, Vice-President, Secretary, and Treasurer.

Mr./Mrs./Miss . . . . was nominated for the office of President of the Corporation. No other nominations being made, upon motion duly made, seconded, and unanimously carried, Mr./Mrs./Miss . . . . was elected President of the Corporation, and was declared duly elected to the said office.

(Repeat the minutes given above for each officer.)

Each of the officers so elected was present and thereupon accepted the office to which he/she was elected.

Upon motion duly made, seconded, and unanimously carried, the Board of Directors proceeded to fix the salaries to be paid to the President, Vice-President, Secretary, and Treasurer for the year 19...

[Compensation of officers] The Chairman announced that the salary of each officer would be voted upon separately, and that the officer whose salary was under consideration would not participate in the vote. Mr./Mrs./Miss . . . ., President, thereupon left the room.

On motion duly made, seconded, and affirmatively voted upon by all the directors then present, it was

[Salary of President] RESOLVED, That the salary of Mr./Mrs./Miss . . . ., President of the Corporation, be fixed at $. . . . . for the year beginning . . . ., 19.., and ending . . . ., 19.., payable in semimonthly installments on the fifteenth day and the last day of each calendar month.

The vote having been taken, Mr./Mrs./Miss . . . . was recalled to the meeting.

The Vice-President then left the room.

(Repeat the minutes given above for each officer.)

[Adjournment] There being no further business to come before the meeting, the same was, upon motion, adjourned.

....
President

....
Secretary

No. 11

Resolution of directors authorizing sale and issue of stock to persons determined by executive committee.

RESOLVED, That this Corporation sell and issue .... (........) shares of the Preferred Stock of this corporation at par, and .... (........) shares of Common Stock having no par value at ...... dollars ($......) per share, payable in cash at the time of purchase, to such persons, firms, or corporations as the Executive Committee shall determine, and the President and the Secretary of this Corporation are hereby authorized to execute and deliver certificates of stock to purchasers upon receipt of full payment for shares purchsed.

No. 12

Resolution of directors amending a particular bylaw upon authorization of stockholders.

WHEREAS, The holders of more than two-thirds of the subscribed capital stock of the corporation have, by a resolution adopted at a meeting duly called upon notice, authorized and directed the Board of Directors of this corporation to amend Section .... of Article .... of the Bylaws, it is

RESOLVED, That the aforesaid Section .... of Article .... of the Bylaws be amended in accordance with the said resolution of the stockholders, to read as follows:

(Here insert new bylaw.)

IT IS FURTHER RESOLVED, That the Secretary of the corporation be and he hereby is authorized and directed to copy the said Section .... of Article .... of the Bylaws, as amended, in the book of Bylaws of the corporation, and properly to certify the same.

No. 13

Directors' resolution accepting resignation of a member of board.

RESOLVED, That the resignation of .... as a member of Board of Directors of the .... Corporation, as evidenced by his/her letter to the said Corporation, dated the .. day of ...., 19.., be and it hereby is accepted, and the Secretary of this Corporation is hereby instructed to notify the said .... of the acceptance of his/her aforesaid resignation.

No. 14
Directors' resolution accepting resignation of officer.

RESOLVED, That the resignation of Mr./Mrs./Miss .... as .... (*insert office*) be and it hereby is accepted to take effect on the .. day of ...., 19...

No. 15
Directors' resolution expressing gratitude for services of resigning officer.

WHEREAS, ... has, for the past ...... (....) years, been President of the Company, and whereas the said .... declines to be a candidate for re-election, this Board of Directors wishes to spread the following resolution upon the minutes.

RESOLVED, That we recognize the excellent, energetic, and intelligent service that .... has rendered the Company during his/her incumbency. We believe the high position the Company has attained has been in large measure due to his/her earnest efforts and untiring devotion.

RESOLVED FURTHER, That in recognition of his/her services to the Company, the aforesaid ...... be elected Chairman to preside at the meetings of the Board for the ensuing year.

No. 16
Blanket resolution of directors authorizing issuance of duplicate certificate in event of loss.

RESOLVED, That, in the event of the loss, multilation, or destruction of any certificate of stock of .... Corporation, a duplicate thereof may be issued, provided the owner makes a sufficient affidavit setting forth the loss, mutilation, or destruction of the original certificate, and gives a surety bond to the Corporation to such amount as may be determined by the .... (*indicate officer*).

No. 17
Excerpt of minutes showing adoption of minutes of previous meeting as corrected.

RESOLVED, That the minutes of the meeting of ...., held on the .. day of ...., 19.., be and they are hereby adopted and approved in their entirety, except that the words "..............." be eliminated from the resolution ...... (*specify subject matter of resolution for identification*) contained therein.

No. 18
Resolution of directors (or stockholders) extending sympathy upon death of associate.

WHEREAS, The directors of the .... Corporation wish to record their deep sorrow at the death on ...., 19.., of their esteemed associate ...., who since ...., 19.., served as director of this Corporation, be it

RESOLVED, That the Board of Directors of this Company hereby gives formal expression of its grievous loss in the death of................, and does hereby note in its records the passing from this life of someone who was esteemed by his/her associates, loved by his/her friends, and respected by all.

RESOLVED, FURTHER, That a copy of this resolution be tendered to his/her family as a humble expression of the Board's heartfelt sympathy in its bereavement.

18

Assisting in

Real Estate Practice

and Foreclosures

The legal secretary and paralegal are very valuable to a lawyer engaged in real estate practice. By becoming familiar with the various legal documents involved in real estate transactions, and the procedure necessary to consummate the transaction, they can relieve the lawyer of practically all routine work, with very little guidance.

In chapter 9, we gave basic information about legal instruments generally. In this chapter, we describe specific real estate instruments, with information and suggestions that will help you assume part of the responsibility for their preparation. Regardless of how capable you are, observe this rule: *Always get the lawyer's approval of an instrument both before it is signed and after it is executed, before placing it on record.*

The following sections will discuss deeds, mortgages, leases, purchase and sale agreements, closings, and foreclosure actions. Although realtors and bank mortgage departments handle many of these matters, the lawyer's secretary and the paralegal must be familiar with the various legal documents and procedures involved in real estate practice.

18.1. Pattern followed for each instrument. The following pattern is followed for each instrument:

Definition: The short, precise definition given for each instrument enables you to understand more thoroughly the purpose of it.

Parties: An understanding of the parties affected by an instrument—their connection with it—assists you in preparing the testimonium clause, signature, and certificate of acknowledgment, and enables you to fill in printed forms accurately.

Forms and kinds: The lawyer frequently will instruct you to prepare a specific instrument in a certain form.

Checklist of information needed to fill in printed forms: To complete the printed form of a specific instrument, you will need the information listed in the checklists. You can probably obtain it from the lawyer's notes and other papers in the file; otherwise, you will have to ask the lawyer, or, at his or her direction, the client.

Statements and clauses that the instrument contains: When a lawyer dictates an instrument, he or she will probably instruct you to substitute certain dictated material for a particular clause or statement in a printed form; or the lawyer might tell you to pick up a certain clause from a printed form. For example, if the lawyer is dictating a mortgage, he or she might say, "Substitute this for the priority privilege clause in this form"; or "Pick up the partial release clause from Sunnyside Subdivision mortgage." The explanation and examples of statements and clauses under each instrument will assist you.

Do's and don'ts: These summarize the procedure you should follow in the preparation of a specific instrument. To avoid repetition, references are made to prior chapters where detailed instructions about each item may be found, should you need to refer to them.

Illustrations: Illustrations show how instruments should look when typed and, also, how printed forms should look when completed.

REAL PROPERTY DESCRIPTIONS

18.2. How land is described. A description of real property appears in many legal instruments you prepare and constitutes an important part of the instrument. The descriptions are often complicated and difficult to follow when typing. Usually they are copies from some other document or from an abstract of title. An understanding of how these descriptions are evolved will make it easier for you to copy them and will lessen the possibility of an error. *Accuracy is essential.*

Land is identified according to section and township or by metes and bounds. In towns and subdivisions, lot and block identification is also used. Property is never identified solely by street and number because the names and numbers of streets might change.

18.3. Section and township description. In the eighteenth century, when the United States began to sell public lands, it was necessary to adopt some conventional method of describing the tracts that were sold. A *rectangular system of surveys* was devised. The survey divided the public lands into rectangular tracts, located with reference to base lines running east and west and *prime* or *principal meridians* running north and south. The prime meridians are numbered, as Third Prime Meridian, or named, as San Bernardino Meridian. The rectangular tracts are divided into six-mile squares, known as *townships*. A row of townships running north and south is called a *range*, and the ranges are numbered east and west from the prime meridians. The townships are divided into 36 sections, each one mile square or 640 acres. The sections are numbered from 1 to 36, beginning with the section in the northeast corner of the township, proceeding west to boundary of the township; the next row is numbered from west to east, and so on. (See figure 18.1) The sections in turn are divided into half and quarter sections, and the quarters into quarter-quarter sections, designated by their direction from the center as northwest, southwest, northeast, and southeast.

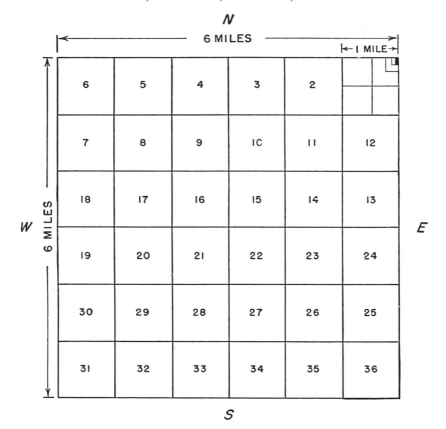

Figure 18.1. *Diagram of Township Divided into Sections.*

The description of a given five acres of land identified by the section and township (government survey) description might read:

The East Half of the Northeast Quarter of the Northeast Quarter of the Northeast Quarter of Section One, Township 39 North, Range 12 East of the Third Prime Meridian.

The shaded portion of the diagram in Figure 18.1 represents the parcel described above, assuming that the diagram is Township 39 North, Range 12 East.

Land identification in the 29 public land states in which government survey description is used is thus precise and orderly; it is possible to designate any plot of land as small as five acres with perfect accuracy; no two parcels are described in exactly the same terms because they are identified with reference to a specific prime meridian. The public land states are Alabama, Arizona, Arkansas, California, Colorado, Florida, Idaho, Illinois, Indiana, Iowa, Kansas, Louisiana, Michigan, Minnesota, Mississippi, Missouri, Montana, Nebraska, Nevada, New Mexico, North Dakota, Ohio, Oklahoma, Oregon, South Dakota, Utah, Washington, Wisconsin, and Wyoming.

18.4 Metes and bounds description. Before the government survey, the land in the area comprising the 13 colonies (18 states) was held under original grants from the Crown to the Colonists. In these states—Connecticut, Delaware, Georgia, Kentucky, Maine, Maryland, Massachusetts, New Hampshire, New Jersey, New York, North Carolina, Pennsylvania, Rhode Island, South Carolina, Tennessee, Vermont, Virginia, and West Virginia—and in Texas[1] each parcel of land is different in size and shape and is described by *metes and bounds*. A metes and bounds description is not correlated to any system of meridians and base lines, but each tract of land is described by the lines that constitute its boundaries. Metes are lineal measures and bounds are artificial and natural boundaries. A natural landmark, such as a tree or river, or an artificial landmark, such as a fence, stake, railroad, or street, often marks the corners and angles. These marks are known as *monuments*. A description by courses and distances constitutes part of a metes and bounds description. The direction from the starting point in which the boundary line runs is a *course*; the length of the line is a *distance*.

Figure 18.2 illustrates a metes and bounds description.

18.5. The plat system. Tracts of land described by metes and

---

[1]The United States never had original title to the land in Texas because it was annexed as an independent republic.

ALL that lot or parcel of land, situate, lying and being in the Town of Oyster Bay, County of Nassau, State of New York, bounded and described as follows:

BEGINNING at a point in the center line of Buena Vista Avenue distant two hundred sixty-one and thirty hundredths (261.30) feet southerly from the point of intersection of said line with the center line of Jones Road; running thence along the center line of Buena Vista Avenue South twenty-five (25) degrees thirty-three (33) minutes East four hundred fifty-two and seventy-eight hundredths (452.78) feet to a point; running thence North sixty-eight (68) degrees thirty-two (32) minutes East three hundred ten and eleven hundredths (310.11) feet to a point in the center line of a driveway; running thence generally along the center line of said driveway the following courses and distances:

    A.   North forty-five (45) degrees forty-two (42) minutes West, 50 feet;

    B.   North thirty-nine (39) degrees two (02) minutes West, 50 feet;

    C.   North thirty-four (34) degrees sixteen (16) minutes West, 50 feet;

    D.   North twenty-eight (28) degrees fifty-eight (58) minutes West, 40 feet;

    E.   North twenty-six (26) degrees seventeen (17) minutes West, 100 feet;

    F.   North Thirty-two (32) degrees six (06) minutes West, 50 feet;

    G.   North fifty-five (55) degrees thirty-four (34) minutes West, 50 feet;

    H.   North Sixty-one (61) degrees thirty-two (32) minutes West, 50 feet;

    I.   North eighty (80) degrees thirty-three (33) minutes West, 50 feet;

    J.   South seventy-nine (79) degrees eleven (11) minutes West, 50 feet;

    K.   South sixty-five (65) degrees thirty-two (32) minutes West, 50 feet; and

    L.   South sixty-four (64) degrees forty-seven (47) minutes West, 77 feet, to a point in the center line of Buena Vista Avenue, the point or place of beginning;

Containing, in area, approximately two and seven hundred seventy-four thousandths (2.774) acres;

Being and intended to be all of Plot No. 5, as shown on a map entitled "Plot Plan," Property of John Doe Estate, Town of Oyster Bay, Nassau County, New York, made by James Brown, Surveyor, November 1, 1940, as revised January 13, 1942, and December 31, 1945.

Figure 18.2. *Metes and Bounds Description.*

bounds or the rectangular survey system may be further divided into streets, blocks, and lots. Maps or plans of these divisions are called *plats*. A *plat book* is a record maintained showing the location, size, and name of the owners of each plat of real property in a given area. A *plat description* might read:

Lot Ten (10), Block Eight (8), Bay Shore Subdivision, as recorded in Volume 5 of Plats, Page 39, records of Blank County, State of ....

18.6 How to type real property descriptions. Unless otherwise instructed observe the following style in preparing descriptions of real property for use in deeds and other instruments:

1. Single-space, with double space between paragraphs.

2. Do not abbreviate *Street, Avenue, Road, Boulevard,* in the text.

3. Write the words *North, Northeast, South, West, Southwest,* and the like, with initial capitals, but do not capitalize the words *northerly, northeasterly,* and the like.

4. Capitalize *quarter, township, section,* and *range,* and the name or number of a prime meridian.

5. Write courses as follows: "South twenty (20) degrees, thirty-three (33) minutes, forty-five (45) seconds West." A single quotation mark stands for minutes, a double quotation mark for seconds (e.g., S 20° 33′ 45″ W).

6. Write distances as follows: "One hundred thirty-three and twenty-nine one hundredths (133.29) feet."

7. When several courses and distances are given in succession, introduced by a phrase such as "... the following several courses and distances ..." each of the courses and distances is written separately, indented and single spaced, separated one from the other by a double space, and each course and distance is ended with a semicolon. The sentence after the last course and distance is flush with the left-hand margin of the text preceding the itemized courses and distances. (See figure 18.2.)

8. It is preferable not to use figures, symbols, and abbreviations, but many law offices use them because of the limited space on a printed form. A description would then be written: "South 20° 33′ 45″ West, 50 ft." In law offices with extensive real estate practice, a special key is placed on the typewriter for the symbol of the word *degrees;* otherwise, the symbol is made by turning the platen up a half space and striking the small *o.*

18.7. How to check land descriptions. A typographical error in the description of land can cause trouble and even result in a law suit. The importance of checking the description cannot be overemphasized. It is easy to make an error in copying that is not always discernible from merely reading the description. For example, the government survey description on page 434 contains the phrase "of the Northeast Quarter" three times. It would be easy to omit the phrase once, but difficult to realize the omission in reading over the description; yet the omission would double the amount of land conveyed by the deed. Nor is it advisable for one person to compare the description line by line. The safest method of checking the typographical accuracy of a land description is to have someone read aloud to you the original copy, slowly enough to permit you to follow your typed copy carefully.

If you have a plat or diagram showing the location of the parcel described, you can check the accuracy of the description from that, especially if the identification is by government survey. To compare a government survey description with the map designation, read the parts of the description in reverse order—that is, begin with the township and range and work backward to the designated plot. A typewriter with an automatic memory is useful in these instances.

DEEDS

18.8. What is a deed? A *deed* is a formal written instrument by which title to real property is conveyed from one person to another. A *purchase and sale agreement* is an agreement to convey title, whereas a deed is the conveyance itself.

18.9 Parties to a deed. The parties to a deed are the *grantor,* who conveys his or her interest in the property, and the *grantee,* to whom the conveyance is made. The grantor is the seller, and the grantee is usually the purchaser, but not necessarily. The purchaser may buy the land for the grantee. Only the grantor signs the deed, unless the grantee makes special convenants (see page 442).

The *grantor* may be a natural person, a partnership, or a corporation. The individual must be of legal age and of sound mind. Frequently the grantor makes the deed in a representative capacity, for example, as the guardian of a minor. In such case, the first paragraph of the deed recites the capacity in which the grantor makes the deed. Whether or not the grantor's spouse must join in the deed depends upon the law of the state where the land is situated. Generally speaking, it is necessary for the spouse to join and for that reason the marital status of the grantor is stated in the deed, as *single, widow, widower,* or *divorced and not remarried.*

The *grantee* may be a natural person, a partnership, or a corporation. A minor or insane person may be a grantee, although he or she cannot be a grantor. In some states, a deed cannot be made to a partnership in the firm name, but must be made to the individual partners. For example, the conveyance would not be made to "Hillside Estates," but would be made to "Marcus Wylie and Joan Boyle, doing business as Hillside Estates." In some states foreign corporations are not permitted to acquire title to land unless they have received authority to do business in that state.

18.10. Forms of deeds. There are two standard forms of deeds: *indenture deed* and *deed poll.* The distinction is in the phraseology.The standard indenture deed opens with, "THIS INDENTURE (or DEED) made ...," whereas the standard deed poll opens with, "KNOW ALL MEN BY THESE PRESENTS:" or similar words. Also, the deed indenture is written in the third person, whereas the deed poll is written in the first person. In some states, only the indenture form is used; in others, only the deed poll; but in many states the indenture deed and deed poll are both used. The indenture is often signed by both parties.

To save the space required for recording deeds, many states provide by statute for a short form of deed, known as a *statutory form*. By statute, certain covenants and warranties are made part of the deed and, although not set forth in the deed, are binding on the grantor and his or her heirs. Since the statute is actually part of the deed and a state statute is not effective outside of the state enacting it, a statutory form of deed can be used only in the specific state that makes statutory provision for it.

18.11. Kinds of deeds. There are various kinds, as well as forms, of deeds. Those commonly used are the *warranty deed* and *quit-claim deed*. *Fiduciary deeds* executed by third parties, such as the executor of an estate, or a trustee, are also relatively common.

A warranty deed is the most desirable from the standpoint of the purchaser. It not only transfers title in fee simple but covenants and warrants that the grantor has the right to transfer the title to the property and that the grantee will enjoy the premises quietly, forever. Should anyone later make a claim against the property, the grantee can sue the grantor for breach of his or her warranty.

A quit-claim deed conveys title as effectively as a warranty deed, but it does not warrant the title against adverse claims. A quit-claim deed may also be used to obtain a release from a person who is believed to have some interest in or claim to the property, whether real or not. By this form of deed, the grantor "quits" any claim he or she might have to a given piece of real property. These deeds do not obligate the grantor in any way, but if he or she should have full title, the quit-claim deed will operate as a full and complete conveyance of title.

A fiduciary deed transfers title of real estate belonging to a deceased or incapacitated person. A trust deed conveys property held by a trust.

18.12. Printed forms of deeds. Printed forms of deeds are frequently used. Figures 18.3 and 18.4 illustrate a printed form of deed. Follow carefully the directions on page 227 for filling in printed forms. With the information called for by the following checklist, you will have no difficulty in filling in the printed forms without dictation. The lawyer will dictate any special clauses with reference to encumbrances, covenants, and the like.

1685—Warranty Deed with Full Covenants, Individual.
Statutory Form A with Lien Covenant.
One Side Recording.

JULIUS BLUMBERG, INC., LAW BLANK PUBLISHERS
80 EXCHANGE PLACE AT BROADWAY, NEW YORK

THIS IS A LEGAL INSTRUMENT AND SHOULD BE EXECUTED UNDER SUPERVISION OF AN ATTORNEY.

THIS INDENTURE, made the   day of   19

BETWEEN

grantor

grantee

WITNESSETH, that the grantor   , in consideration of

Dollars,

lawful money of the United States,
paid by the grantee   do   hereby grant and release unto the grantee

and assigns forever,

   ALL

TOGETHER with the appurtenances and all the estate and rights of the grantor   in and to said premises.
TO HAVE AND TO HOLD the premises herein granted unto the grantee
                                             and assigns forever. **AND** the said grantor   covenant as follows:
FIRST.—That the grantor   seized of the said premises in fee simple, and ha   good right to convey the same;
SECOND.—That the grantee   shall quietly enjoy the said premises;
THIRD.—That the said premises are free from incumbrances;
FOURTH.—That the grantor   will execute or procure any further necessary assurance of the title to said premises;
FIFTH.—That the grantor   will forever warrant the title to said premises;
This deed is subject to the trust provisions of Section 13 of the Lien Law.

IN WITNESS WHEREOF, the grantor   ha   hereunto set   hand   and seal   the day and year first
above written.

In presence of:

.... L. S.

.... L. S.

STATE OF   **COUNTY OF**   *ss.:*

   On the   day of   19   before me came

to me known and known to me to be the individual   described in, and who executed, the foregoing instrument, and acknowledged to me that   he   executed the same.

Figure 18.3. *Full Warranty Deed with Full Covenants.*

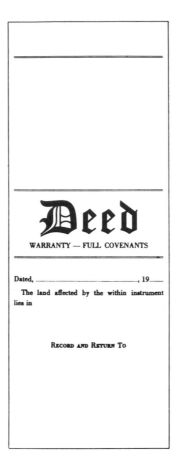

Figure 18.4. *Endorsed Back; Full Warranty Deed.*

Some printed forms are drawn especially for use by corporations, others for use by individuals.

Printed forms of deeds with special provisions, such as cutting of timber, or harvesting of crops, or oil rights, are also available in localities where there is a need for them.

18.13. Checklist of information needed to fill in form. 1. Whether grantor is an individual, a partnership, or a corporation

2. Full name and residence of grantor, including street address in large cities

3. Full description of the grantor's office and authority if he or she is conveying in a representative capacity

4. Marital status of grantor

5. Full name of spouse if spouse must join in the conveyance

6. Full name and residence of grantee
7. Date of deed
8. Description of property
9. Whether deed is to be a warranty, quit-claim, or other type of deed, the form for each being different
10. Consideration to be expressed in deed
11. When and where deed is to be acknowledged
12. Names and official positions of officers signing and acknowledging deed, if grantor is a corporation.

18.14. Typed deeds. Sometimes a printed form is not adequate for the special clauses and conditions that a deed must contain. The lawyer will then dictate the deed to you, probably telling you to copy various parts from a printed form or from another deed. When typing the deed, follow the general style of a printed form.

The lawyer might also dictate to you a deed to be printed after it is typed. These are for a special purpose, such as the sale of lots in a subdivision. Usually several drafts are written before the final typed copy is sent to the printer. They are set up in the same form as any deed. Chapter 8 tells how to prepare material for the printer.

18.15. Statements and clauses in deeds. *Consideration.* The consideration is the payment made by the purchaser for the property. It is usually a sum of money, but it might take some other form, such as the cancellation of debt owed by the seller to the purchaser. A deed frequently states a nominal consideration because the parties do not want the actual consideration to be known.

EXAMPLES:
WITNESSETH, That the Grantor(s), in consideration of five thousand dollars ($5,000), lawful money of the United States, paid by the Grantee, does hereby grant . . .
. . . for the sum of one dollar ($1), to me in hand paid, and other good and valuable consideration, do hereby grant ....
. . . That the Grantor(s), in consideration of her natural love and affection for the Grantee, does hereby . . .

Encumbrances. Frequently there is an indebtedness against property that is being sold, or taxes or assessments are owed on it. There are *encumbrances* against the property, and the deed recites the agreement between the parties regarding them. The person who holds the encumbrance is the *encumbrancer*. The statement of encumbrances, if any, either follows the property description or is made a part of the habendum (see below). It is usually dictated by the lawyer.

EXAMPLES:

The said premises are conveyed subject to a mortgage thereof in the sum of ten thousand dollars ($10,000), with interest, made by David Jones to Leon Holt, dated the fifteenth day of January, 19. ., and recorded in Book 27 of conveyances, page 359, in the office of the Clerk of said county.

Subject to a purchase money mortgage made by the Grantee to the Grantor delivered and intended to be recorded simultaneously herewith,

Habendum clause. The habendum clause derives its name from the Latin phrase *habendum et tenendum* and, accordingly, begins with the words *to have and to hold.* Its purpose is to define the extent of the interest conveyed. When special circumstances surround the transfer of the property, the lawyer dictates a substitute habendum.

EXAMPLE:

TO HAVE AND TO HOLD the premises herein granted unto the Grantee, his heirs and assigns, forever,

TO HAVE AND TO HOLD the granted premises, with all the rights, easements, and appurtenances thereto belonging, to the said William V. Croft, his heirs and assigns, to his and their own use forever,

SUBJECT, HOWEVER, to all rights of the lessees, tenants and occupants of, or in said granted premises, or in any part, or parts, thereof.

Covenants. The *covenants* are the promises made by the grantor and grantee. The usual covenants by the grantor, which are printed in the deed, relate to the title to the property and to its quiet and peaceful enjoyment by the grantee. The grantor might make special promises not included in the usual printed form, such as agreeing to construct and maintain roadways. Covenants by the grantee are less common than covenants by the grantor. The most frequent use of covenants by the grantee is in connection with the sale of lots in subdivisions; they usually relate to the type of structure that may be erected on the premises and the uses that may be made of the property. These covenants are not included in the usual printed form of deed, but special deeds that contain them are usually printed for the sale of lots in a specific subdivision.

EXAMPLE OF COVENANT BY GRANTEE:

And the said grantee does hereby for himself, his heirs and assigns, covenant with the said grantor, his heirs, executors, and administrators, that he will not, at any time hereafter, erect, or cause, or suffer, or permit, to be erected upon the hereby granted premises, or any part thereof, any building other than a brick or stone private dwelling house, not less than three stories in height.

Restrictions and conditions. Property is often sold subject to certain restrictions and conditions to be observed by the grantee. These usually relate to types of buildings that may be constructed, purposes for which the property may be used, and the subsequent sale of the property. The restrictions and conditions are not included in the usual printed form of deed, but are frequently included in specially printed forms.

Exceptions and reservations. Property is frequently sold subject to certain exceptions and reservations. These might relate to easements, rights of way, growing crops, timber, minerals, and the like. They are not included in the usual printed form of deed; the lawyer dictates them.

Testimonium clause. The testimonium clause to a deed is similar to the testimonium clause to any written instrument. (See page 196).

18.16. Revenue stamps and state taxes. Before 1968, a federal transfer tax, evidenced by revenue stamps, had to be paid when property was sold; the stamps had to be affixed to the deed and canceled. However, many states have imposed a similar *state tax*, as a source of revenue. If your state requires revenue stamps, they may be affixed at the registry of deeds at the time of recording or may be bought by either the purchaser's or seller's lawyer and affixed to the deed.

18.17. How to cancel the stamps. If state stamps are required, you probably will follow the cancellation procedure formerly used for federal stamps. To cancel a stamp, write your initials and the date on the face of the stamp, in ink. Also, make several parallel incisions through the stamp with some sharp instrument. This should be done after the stamp is affixed to the document. The stamps are usually affixed before the instrument is recorded.

Some states impose a tax on deeds, payable usually before the deed can be recorded.

18.18. Recording. The purchaser has the deed recorded for his or her own protection and pays the recording fee. If the purchaser is your firm's client, the lawyer will probably ask you to have the deed recorded. Follow the instructions on page 210.

18.19 How to prepare a deed. Unless instructed otherwise, follow these directions when preparing a deed. Obviously, some of them apply only to typed deeds, some to printed forms, and some to both.

1. Make three copies—the original for the grantee, a copy for the grantor, and a copy for your files.

2. Use legal cap or 8½"× 11" paper according to your office or the registry preference.

3. Follow carefully the directions for filling in a printed form. (See chapter 10.)

4. Do not forget the responsibility and distribution line at the top of the first page. (This goes on the office copy only of printed form.) (See chapter 10.)

5. Double-space.

6. Type the land description in accordance with directions on page 436.

7. Number all pages of typed deed.

8. If you are using a printed form, be sure to make the "Z" after the land description. (See chapter 10.)

9. Do not forget to have at least two lines of typing on the signature page. (See chapter 9.)

10 Prepare signature line for the grantor. (See chapter 9.) The grantee does not sign a deed except in special circumstances.

11. Affix the seal in accordance with directions in chapter 9, when it is required.

12. Remember that a corporation's seal is generally affixed to an instrument.

13. Type witness lines and attestation clause, when required. (See chapter 9.)

14. Prepare certificate of acknowledgment. (See chapter 9.)

15. Collate.

16. Check and double-check spelling of names.

17. Get someone to compare the land description with you. (See page 436.)

18. Endorse the back of a printed form as illustrated by figure 18.4. If the deed is typed, prepare legal back. (See chapter 10.)

19. Arrange for the grantor to come in and sign the deed and acknowledge it.

20. *Get the lawyer's approval of the instrument before it is signed.* Have the grantor sign the original only.

21. Does the grantor's signature agree with the name typed in the deed?

22. Have the deed notarized. If you are a notary, take the acknowledgment, following instructions in chapter 9.

23. Affix and cancel revenue stamps, if required.

24. Prepare closing statement. (See page 466, *et seq.*)

25. After signature and acknowledgment, conform copies to original. (See chapter 10.)

26. Get the lawyer's approval and then have the deed recorded. (See chapter 9.) Do not forget to put a notation on the back of the deed asking that it be returned to you. (The secretary to the lawyer for the grantee attends to the recording.)

27. When the deed is returned by the recorder, send it to the grantee with a covering letter. (See chapter 9.)

MORTGAGES

18.20 What is a mortgage? A mortgage is a *conditional* conveyance. It is given by a borrower or debtor to secure the payment of a debt, with a provision that the conveyance will become void on the payment of the debt by the date named. In early English times, the debtor actually turned over his property to the lender, who would keep the income and profits from it. The land was "dead" to the owner and gave him no return; hence the word *mort-gage*, meaning *dead pledge*. A mortgage may be given on real estate or on personal property, but a mortgage on personal property is referred to as a *chattel mortgage,* whereas a mortgage on real estate is referred to simply as a *mortgage.* Some mortgages cover both real and personal property, for example, a mortgage on a furnished apartment building.

The word *mortgage* also refers to the instrument used to make the conveyance. The debt is evidenced by promissory notes; the mortgage is the security instrument that secures payment of the notes. In some states, the debt is evidenced by a bond instead of a promissory note. The bond takes the place of the note. Frequently, the bond and mortgage are combined in one instrument, which is referred to as a *bond and mortgage.*

18.21. Parties to a mortgage. The parties to a conventional mortgage are the *mortgagor*, who is the debtor or borrower, and the *mortgagee*, who is the lender. The mortgagor owns the property that is being mortgaged and gives a mortgage to the mortgagee, usually in return for a loan; he or she is sometimes referred to in the instrument as the *party of the first part.* The mortgagee is sometimes referred to as the *party of the second part.*

The parties to a deed of trust are the mortgagor, party of the first part, and the trustee, party of the second part. Some states, Colorado for example, have designated officials, known as *public trustees,* to whom the estate is conveyed under a deed of trust.

18.22. Designation of the parties. Extreme care should be exercised to see that the name of the mortgagor appears exactly as it appears in the instrument under which he or she claims title to the land; otherwise, the mortgagee's title might be defective if it becomes necessary for him or her to foreclose. The mortgagor's name should be exactly the same in the body of the mortgage, in the signature, and in the acknowledgment. If the mortgage is a purchase money mortgage (see page 446), the names of both parties should be given precisely as they appear in the deed from the mortgagee to the mortgagor.

The requirements relative to the grantor and grantee in a deed apply generally to the mortgagor and mortgagee (see page 437).

18.23. Forms of mortgages. Practice has given rise to the use of forms that differ widely in detail in the various states. However, any instrument that is actually intended as security for a debt will generally ber construed as a mortgage.

The forms of mortgages most commonly used are the form that might be termed the *conventional mortgage* and the form variously called a *trust deed, deed of trust, trust indenture,* or *trust mortgage.*

A conventional mortgage is essentially a deed from the borrower to the lender, which contains a provision, known as the *defeasance clause,* that the mortgage will be void on payment of the debt. The additional provisions, which appear in fine print in the printed form, vary with the state.

A deed of trust conveys the land to a third party instead of directly to the lender. The third party holds the property in trust for the lender until the debt is paid in accordance with the terms of the trust deed. In some states, the deed of trust is *more commonly used* than the conventional mortgage deed: Alabama, California, Colorado, District of Columbia, Illinois, Mississippi, Missouri, Montana, New Mexico, Tennessee, Texas, Virginia, West Virginia, and Wisconsin. In the other states, a deed of trust is seldom used except in connection with large transactions, such as railroad mortgages, that involve a large number of creditors. It would be impracticable to convey part of the legal title to each lender or bondholder. A trust deed may be used when the lender is a government body such as the Federal Housing Administration.

Some states have short *statutory* forms of mortgages, which save space when recorded. Since these forms are amplified by statute, they are not used outside the state of origin. Many careful real estate practitioners feel the short statutory form does not protect the mortgagee sufficiently.

18.24. Purchase money mortgage. A *purchase money mortgage* is one that is given in part payment of the purchase price of the property. For example, if the purchase price is $50,000, the purchaser might pay $20,000 cash and give the seller a purchase money mortgage for $30,000. The deed and the purchase money mortgage are executed simultaneously. The grantee in the deed is the mortgagor; the grantor in the deed is the mortgagee. All names and descriptions of property in the purchase money mortgage must agree with those in the deed. A purchase money mortgage has certain priorities that other mortgages do not have. For example, it has preference over the dower rights of the mortgagor's wife, and she, therefore, does not have to sign it. It also has priority over existing judgments and other debts of the mortgagor. On the other hand, as a rule, the mortgagee cannot get a deficiency decree against the mortgagor when he or she forecloses a purchase money mortgage, which the mortgagee can usually get under other mortgages. (See sections 18.64-18.84 for foreclosure actions.) A purchase money mortgage may contain a statement similar to the following example, which distinguishes it from a mortgage given for an existing debt.

EXAMPLE:

This mortgage is a purchase money mortgage, which is given and intended to be recorded simultaneously with a deed this day executed and delivered by the mortgagee to the mortgagor, covering the property above described; this mortgage being given to secure a portion of the purchase price expressed in said deed.

18.25. Printed mortgages. Printed forms of conventional mortgages and deeds of trust are used extensively. Follow carefully the directions given on page 227 for filling in printed forms.

Upon instructions from the lawyer, you can complete the printed forms of the ordinary mortgage and deed of trust without dictation. The lawyer will dictate any special clauses that he or she wants to include in the instrument.

18.26. Checklist of information needed to fill in mortgage or deed of trust. To complete the printed form of mortgage or deed of trust, you will need the information listed here. You can probably obtain it from the lawyer's notes and other papers in the file; otherwise, you will have to ask the lawyer or, at his or her direction, the client.

1. Full name of mortgagor and mortgagee; also of trustee in the case of a trust deed
2. County and state of residence of mortgagor and mortgagee; in a large city, their street address; also residence of trustee in the case of a trust deed
3. Full description of the mortgagor's office and authority if he is conveying in a representative capacity
4. Marital status of mortgagor
5. Full name of spouse if spouse must join in the conveyance
6. If purchase money mortgage, is wife to join
7. Date of mortgage
8. Amount of mortgage
9. Period mortgage is to run; maturity date
10. Rate of interest and when payable
11. Description of property

12. Date and place mortgage is to be acknowledged

13. If mortgagor is corporation, name and title of officers signing and acknowledging

14. If mortgage contains power of sale, number of days notice to be given in newspaper (this is determined by statute) and where newspaper is published

15. If there is to be an affidavit of title, who is to make it

18.27. Typed mortgages and deeds of trust. Printed forms of mortgages and trust deeds are frequently inadequate for the special conditions of the transaction. The lawyer will then dictate the instrument to you. The dictation is usually lengthy and requires special care in transcription. Instead of dictating certain parts of the mortgage, the lawyer will probably tell you to copy from a printed form. For example, the lawyer might say, "Copy the defeasance clause from this form." Generally a dictated mortgage is typed in draft form before it is finally typed. When typing the instrument, follow the general style of a printed form.

Deeds of trust that are given to secure a bond issue are long and involved and are printed especially for a specific bond issue. The lawyer dictates the draft and revises it, usually several times. You can assist the lawyer in this laborious task by an especially careful and accurate transcription of your notes, thus enabling him or her to devote full attention to the content of the draft without the distraction of typographical errors. Law offices that do a large volume of real estate work often use automatic typewriters.

18.28. Statements and clauses in mortgages. *Description of debt.* A mortgage is given to secure a debt, and the mortgage instrument must describe and identify the debt with preciseness. The description includes the rate and time of payment of interest and clearly states the time of payment of the debt. Some forms call for a copy of the note secured by the mortgage to be copied in the body of the instrument.

EXAMPLE:

... an indebtedness in the sum of twenty thousand dollars ($20,000), lawful money of the United States, to be paid on the first day of November, 19.., with interest thereon to be computed from November 1, 19.., at the rate of nine percent (9%) per annum, and to be paid semiannually thereafter, according to a certain note bearing even date herewith, ...

Defeasance clause. The provision in the mortgage that it will become void upon payment of the debt is known as the *defeasance clause*—the mortgage will be defeated upon payment of the debt. Printed forms usually contain an adequate defeasance clause.

EXAMPLE:
Provided always, that if said mortgagor, ... shall pay ... a certain promissory note, a copy of which is on the reverse side hereof, and shall perform and comply with each and every stipulation, agreement and covenant of said note and of this mortgage, the estate hereby created shall be void, otherwise the same shall remain in full force and effect.
... provided, that if I shall punctually pay said notes according to the tenor thereof, then this mortgage shall be void.

Consideration. A mortgage recites the consideration for which it was given. Statement of the consideration might name the amount of the indebtedness, or it might recite a nominal consideration.

EXAMPLES:
... for and in consideration of the aforesaid debt of five thousand dollars ($5,000), and the better securing the payment of the same with interest .....
... for the better securing the payment of the sum of money mentioned in the said bond, or obligation, with the interest thereon, and, also, in consideration of one dollar ($1) paid by the Second Party, the receipt whereof is hereby acknowledged....

Acceleration clause. Mortgages contain a clause providing that if principal or interest payments are not made when due, or if any obligation on the part of the mortgagor is not fulfilled, the entire amount of the mortgage becomes payable immediately. The maturity date of the mortgage is *accelerated*, if the mortgagor defaults. This clause is the *acceleration clause.* It is usually printed in the instrument.

EXAMPLE:
That the whole of said principal sum shall become due after default in the payment of any installment of principal or of interest for .... days, or after default in the payment of any tax, water rate or assessment for .... days, after notice and demand.

Description of property. See page 432 for an explanation of land descriptions and how to type them. Accuracy in the description of mortgaged property is even more important in a mortgage than in a deed, because a purchaser takes possession of the premises purchased, thus giving notice to all the world of his rights; but a mortgagee must depend upon the recording of the instrument to give notice of his rights.

Prepayment privilege. The mortgagor sometimes likes to pay off the mortgage, or part of it, before maturity, but he does not have this right unless the terms of the mortgage specifically give it to him. Mortgages and mortgage notes frequently provide that the debt is payable *on or before* the maturity date, or they contain a specific clause giving the mortgagor this right. This clause is the prepayment privilege. A comparable provision in trust deeds securing issues of bonds permits *redemption* of the bonds before maturity dates. The privilege enables a mortgagor to refinance his or her debt when money is cheaper or to sell the property free and clear of any mortgage. Printed forms do not usually include the prepayment privilege.

EXAMPLE:
The mortgagor is hereby authorized and permitted to pay the debt hereby secured, or any part of it, not less than .... dollars at any one time, whenever and at such time and times as he may choose, and the mortgagee hereby agrees to accept such payment or payments, and thereupon the interest shall cease upon such part of the debt as may be so paid; and upon the full payment of said debt, with all interest up to the date of actual payment, he will discharge this mortgage.

Partial release. The mortgagor, in the course of his or her business, frequently wants to sell part of the mortgaged land. For example, the owner of a subdivision sells lots that are part of a subdivision covered by a blanket mortgage. The prepayment privilege (see above) does not release any of the mortgaged land from the mortgage until the entire mortgage is paid. Therefore, to permit the mortgagor to sell part of the land, some mortgages contain a *partial release* clause. The clause permits the release of a specified portion of the premises covered by the mortgage upon payment of a specified sum.

EXAMPLE:
Said mortgagor reserves the right to release all or any part of the said land from the operation of this mortgage, in case said land is subdivided, upon payment to mortgagee of a sum of money to be agreed upon for each lot, the sum to be determined according to the size and location of the lot as soon as the said land is subdivided.

Said mortgagee has agreed to sign a plat of said premises prepared by mortgagor.

Other statements and clauses. A mortgage might contain, also, some or all of the clauses in a deed, such as the habendum, or the convenants, or the testimonium clause. (See page 441 *et seq.*)

18.29. State tax. In some states, a mortgage registration tax is in effect. It is payable by the mortgagee at the time the mortgage is recorded. Some states do not permit the mortgagee to collect the tax from the mortgagor.

18.30. How to prepare a mortgage. Follow the instructions for perparing a deed in section 18.19, substituting "mortgagor" for "grantor," "mortgagee" for "grantee," and "mortgage" for "deed." Also see figure 18.5 for an example of an endorsed back. In addition, note the following: (1) If the mortgage is a purchase money mortgage, compare the names of the mortgagor and mortgagee with the names of grantor and grantee. (2) If the mortgage is not a purchase money mortgage, the mortgagor's spouse may also have to sign the document. (3) Revenue stamps, of course, are applied to a deed but not to a mortgage.

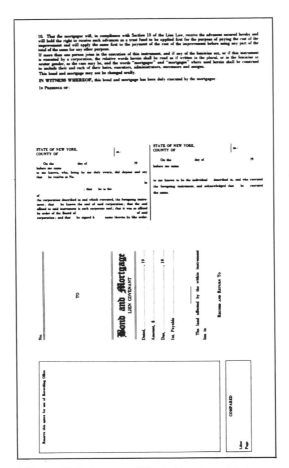

Figure 18.5. *Endorsed Back; Bond and Mortgage.*

LEASES

18.31. What is a lease? A *lease* is a binding contract, written or oral, for the possession of lands and improvements on the one side, and the recompense by rent or other compensation on the other side. When the lease is evidenced by a written instrument binding the parties to fulfill certain covenants or agreements, that instrument is known as a *lease*. Leases range from the letting of an apartment for 1 year to a 99-year lease on vacant property. They may cover real property, personal property, or both, but a lease of real property is most common. Leases of realty give the lessee a *leasehold estate in the premises*.

18.32. Parties to a lease. The parties to a lease are the *lessor*, who owns the property, and the *lessee*, who rents it. The lessor, or owner, leases the property *to* the lessee, or tenant; the lessee leases the property *from* the lessor.

A party to a lease may be a natural person, a partnership, or a corporation. Leases on behalf of minors or insane persons shoud be made by a guardian. The officers of a corporation enter into a lease on its behalf pursuant to authorization of the board of directors or stockholders. An administrator cannot make a lease because his or her function is to wind up the estate, not to lease real property. An executor or testamentary trustee must have specific authority given to him or her by the will to make a lease.

18.33. Classification of leases. *Duration.* Leases may be classified according to their duration as short-term or long-term leases. Although there is no definite duration that takes a lease out of the short-term class into the long-term class, a lease of 10 or more years is generally considered a long-term lease. In a number of states, a lease for more than 7 years must be recorded. The fundamental distinctions are in the responsibilities assumed by the lessee and in the bond and security requirements. Under a short-term lease, the lessor usually requires the lessee to deposit with him 1, 3, or 6 months' rental at the time the lease is executed, whereas under a long-term lease the lessee is required to furnish a bond or collateral in an amount equal to about 3 years' rental. The most common practice is for the lessee to deposit with a bank or other financial institution negotiable securities of the required amount.

A special type of long-term lease is the 99-year lease, which has been used extensively in the development of business districts in large cities. These leases are made on parcels of valuable real estate strategically located for business expansion. They contemplate the erection or improvement of buildings upon the property by the lessee.

Type of property. Leases may be classified as *commercial* or *residential*, according to the type of property covered by the lease. You are more likely to prepare commercial leases than residential leases. Short-term leases may be either commercial or residential leases, but long-term leases are almost exclusively commercial leases.

Rental. The majority of leases call for the payment of a definite amount of rental, which continues at a uniform rate throughout the term of the lease. The amount is called a *flat rental*. Other leases, especially long-term leases, provide that the rental will start at a comparatively low figure and gradually increase. A rental provision of this type is called a *graded rental*. Another method of fixing the amount of rental is to require the tenant to pay a specified percentage of the gross income from sales made upon the premises. A lease with this requirement is called a *percentage lease*. These leases generally cover premises occupied by retail businesses, such as chain stores and department stores. Percentage leases generally run for ten or more years.

18.34. Printed forms. Printed forms of leases covering almost any kind of property are available and are frequently used for short-term leases. Many concerns print their own leases, in a form prepared by the lawyer. The lawyer's secretary is more likely to be concerned with the drafting and printing of a form than with filling in the run-of-the-mill lease, such as a lease on an apartment. (See chapter 8 for preparation of material for the printer.)

Figures 18.6 and 18.7 illustrate the first and last page of a printed form of a commercial lease covering a loft. The back of the lease contains a proper endorsement and forms of acknowledgement for an individual and for a corporation.

18.35. Standard lease clauses. Usually the lawyer dictates both the short-term and long-term leases that are prepared in his office. Although many of the clauses are standard (see below), a variety of other clauses is necessary to express the agreement between the parties, especially in long-term leases. Ninety-nine year leases and many other long-term leases are extremely technical legal instruments, their preparation requiring a lawyer who is a specialist in the field. You will probably have to type several drafts before the lawyer and the client are satisfied. Some offices use automatic typewriters to reduce the amount of retyping required.

If the practice involves drawing commercial leases, the lawyer will probably have a work folder or loose-leaf notebook from which he or she dictates the lease. This folder will consist of each of the standard lease clauses in the form the lawyer prefers. (If the lawyer does not have a work folder of this kind, you might compile one.) Each clause will be pasted on a separate sheet, or half-sheet, and the lawyer will probably have written comments for guidance beneath the form. The folder, or notebook, will also contain clauses that are not standard or that do not appear in all leases. Occasionally the lawyer overlooks one of the standard clauses, even when he or she is using the notebook for guidance. You should become familiar with the standard clauses in commercial leases so you will be able to call the omission to the lawyer's attention. Furthermore, in

A 35—Lease, Business Premises.
Loft, Office or Store. 2-66

JULIUS BLUMBERG, INC., LAW BLANK PUBLISHERS
80 EXCHANGE PLACE, AT BROADWAY, NEW YORK

This Lease made the _____ day of _____ 19___, between

hereinafter referred to as LANDLORD, and

hereinafter jointly, severally and collectively referred to as TENANT.

Witnesseth, that the Landlord hereby leases to the Tenant, and the Tenant hereby leases and takes

from the Landlord

in the building known as

to be used and occupied by the Tenant

and for no other purpose, for a term to commence on _____ 19___, and to end

on _____ 19___, unless sooner terminated as hereinafter provided, at the ANNUAL RENT of

all payable in equal monthly instalments in advance on the first day of each and every calendar month during said term,

except the first instalment, which shall be paid upon the execution hereof.

THE TENANT JOINTLY AND SEVERALLY COVENANTS:

FIRST.—That the Tenant will pay the rent as above provided.

REPAIRS

SECOND.—That, throughout said term the Tenant will take good care of the demised premises, fixtures and appurtenances, and all alterations, additions and improvements to either; make all repairs in and about the same necessary to
ORDINANCES AND VIOLATIONS preserve them in good order and condition, which repairs shall be, in quality and class, equal to the original work; promptly
pay the expense of such repairs; suffer no waste or injury; give prompt notice to the Landlord of any fire that may
ENTRY occur; execute and comply with all laws, rules, orders, ordinances and regulations at any time issued or in force (except
those requiring structural alterations), applicable to the demised premises or to the Tenant's occupation thereof, of the
Federal, State and Local Governments, and of each and every department, bureau and official thereof, and
of the New York Board of Fire Underwriters; permit at all times during usual business hours, the Landlord and representatives of the Landlord to enter the demised premises for the purpose of inspection, and to exhibit them for purposes
of sale or rental; suffer the Landlord to make repairs and improvements to all parts of the building, and to comply with
INDEMNIFY LANDLORD all orders and requirements of governmental authority applicable to said building or to any occupation thereof; suffer the
Landlord to erect, use, maintain, repair and replace pipes and conduits in the demised premises and to the floors above and
below; forever indemnify and save harmless the Landlord for and against any and all liability, penalties, damages, expenses
and judgments arising from injury during said term to person or property of any nature, occasioned wholly or in part by
any act or acts, omission or omissions of the Tenant, or of the employees, guests, agents, assigns or undertenants of the
Tenant and also for any matter or thing growing out of the occupation of the demised premises or of the streets, sidewalks
or vaults adjacent thereto; permit, during the six months next prior to the expiration of the term the usual notice "To Let"
to be placed and to remain undisturbed in a conspicuous place upon the exterior of the demised premises; repair, at or
before the end of the term, all injury done by the installation or removal of furniture and property; and at the end of the
term, to quit and surrender the demised premises with all alterations, additions and improvements in good order and
condition.

MOVING INJURY SURRENDER

THIRD.—That the Tenant will not disfigure or deface any part of the building, or suffer the same to be done, except
so far as may be necessary to affix such trade fixtures as are herein consented to by the Landlord; the Tenant will not
NEGATIVE COVENANTS obstruct, or permit the obstruction of the street or the sidewalk adjacent thereto; will not do anything, or suffer anything
to be done upon the demised premises which will increase the rate of fire insurance upon the building or any of its contents, or be liable to cause structural injury to said building; will not permit the accumulation of waste or refuse matter,
OBSTRUCTION SIGNS and will not, without the written consent of the Landlord first obtained in each case, either sell, assign, mortgage or transfer
this lease, underlet the demised premises or any part thereof, permit the same or any part thereof to be occupied by
anybody other than the Tenant and the Tenant's employees, make any alterations in the demised premises, use the
AIR CONDITIONING demised premises or any part thereof for any purpose other than the one first above stipulated, or for any purpose
deemed extra hazardous on account of fire risk, nor in violation of any law or ordinance. That the Tenant will not obstruct
or permit the obstruction of the light, halls, stairway or entrances to the building, and will not erect or inscribe any sign,
signals or advertisements unless and until the style and location thereof have been approved by the Landlord; and if any
be erected or inscribed without such approval, the Landlord may remove the same. No water cooler, air conditioning unit
or system or other apparatus shall be installed or used without the prior written consent of Landlord.

IT IS MUTUALLY COVENANTED AND AGREED, THAT

FOURTH.—If the demised premises shall be partially damaged by fire or other cause without the fault or neglect of Tenant,
Tenant's servants, employees, agents, visitors or licensees, the damages shall be repaired by and at the expense of Landlord and the
rent until such repairs shall be made shall be apportioned according to the part of the demised premises which is usable by Tenant. But
FIRE CLAUSE if such partial damage is due to the fault or neglect of Tenant, Tenant's servants, employees, agents, visitors or licensees, without
prejudice to any other rights and remedies of Landlord and without prejudice to the rights of subrogation of Landlord's insurer,
the damages shall be repaired by Landlord but there shall be no apportionment or abatement of rent. No penalty shall accrue for
reasonable delay which may arise by reason of adjustment of insurance on the part of Landlord and/or Tenant, and for reasonable
delay on account of "labor troubles", or any other cause beyond Landlord's control. If the demised premises are totally damaged
or are rendered wholly untenantable by fire or other cause, and if Landlord shall decide not to rebuild the same, or
if the building shall be so damaged that Landlord shall decide to demolish it or to rebuild it, then or in any of such events Landlord may, within ninety (90) days after such fire or other cause, give Tenant a notice in writing of such decision, which notice shall
be given as in Paragraph Twelve hereof provided, and thereupon the term of this lease shall expire by lapse of time upon the third
day after such notice is given, and Tenant shall vacate the demised premises and surrender the same to Landlord. If Tenant shall
not be in default under this lease then, upon the termination of this lease under the conditions provided for in the sentence immediately preceding, Tenant's liability for rent shall cease as of the day following the casualty. Tenant hereby expressly waives
the provisions of Section 227 of the Real Property Law and agrees that the foregoing provisions of this Article shall govern and
control in lieu thereof. If the damage or destruction be due to the fault or neglect of Tenant the debris shall be removed by, and at
the expense of, Tenant.

EMINENT DOMAIN

FIFTH.—If the whole or any part of the premises hereby demised shall be taken or condemned by any competent authority
for any public use or purpose then the term hereby granted shall cease from the time when possession of the part so taken shall be
required for such public purpose and without apportionment of award, the Tenant hereby assigning to the Landlord all right and
claim to any such award, the current rent, however, in such case to be apportioned.

LEASE NOT IN EFFECT

SIXTH.—If, before the commencement of the term, the Tenant be adjudicated a bankrupt, or make a "general assignment,"
or take the benefit of any insolvent act, or if a Receiver or Trustee be appointed for the Tenant's property, or if this lease or the
DEFAULTS estate of the Tenant hereunder be transferred or pass to or devolve upon any other person or corporation, or if the Tenant shall
default in the performance of any agreement by the Tenant contained in any other lease to the Tenant by the Landlord or by any
corporation of which an officer of the Landlord is a Director, this lease shall thereby, at the option of the Landlord, be terminated
and in that case, neither the Tenant nor anybody claiming under the Tenant shall be entitled to go into possession of the demised
premises. If after the commencement of the term, any of the events mentioned above in this subdivision shall occur, or if Tenant
shall make default in fulfilling any of the covenants of this lease, other than the covenants for the payment of rent or "additional
rent" or if the demised premises become vacant or deserted, the Landlord may give to the Tenant ten days' notice of intention to
TEN DAY NOTICE end the term of this lease, and thereupon at the expiration of said ten days' (if said condition which was the basis of said notice
shall continue to exist) the term under this lease shall expire as fully and completely as if that day were the date herein definitely
fixed for the expiration of the term and the Tenant will then quit and surrender the demised premises to the Landlord, but the

Figure 18.6. *First Page of Commercial Lease Form.*

THE TENANT FURTHER COVENANTS:

IF A FIRST FLOOR TWENTY-SECOND.—If the demised premises or any part thereof consist of a store, or of a first floor, or of any part thereof, the Tenant will keep the sidewalk and curb in front thereof clean at all times and free from snow and ice, and will keep insured in favor of the Landlord, all plate glass therein and furnish the Landlord with policies of insurance covering the same.

INCREASED FIRE INSURANCE RATE TWENTY-THIRD.—If by reason of the conduct upon the demised premises of a business not herein permitted, or if by reason of the improper or careless conduct of any business upon or use of the demised premises, the fire insurance rate shall at any time be higher than it otherwise would be, then the Tenant will reimburse the Landlord, as additional rent hereunder, for that part of all fire insurance premiums hereafter paid out by the Landlord which shall have been charged because of the conduct of such business not so permitted, or because of the improper or careless conduct of any business upon or use of the demised premises, and will make such reimbursement upon the first day of the month following such outlay by the Landlord; but this covenant shall not apply to a premium for any period beyond the expiration date of this lease, first above specified. In any action or proceeding wherein the Landlord and Tenant are parties, a schedule or "make up" of rate for the building on the demised premises, purporting to have been issued by New York Fire Insurance Exchange, or other body making fire insurance rates for the demised premises, shall be prima facie evidence of the facts therein stated and of the several items and charges included in the fire insurance rate then applicable to the demised premises.

WATER RENT TWENTY-FOURTH.—If a separate water meter be installed for the demised premises, or any part thereof, the Tenant will keep the same in repair and pay the charges made by the municipality or water supply company for or in respect to the consumption of water, as and when bills therefor are rendered. If the demised premises, or any part thereof, be supplied with water through a meter which supplies other premises, the Tenant will pay to the Landlord, as and when bills are rendered therefor, the Tenant's proportionate part of all charges which the municipality or water supply company shall make for all water consumed through said meter, as indicated by said meter. Such proportionate part shall be fixed by apportioning the respective charge according to floor area against all of the rentable floor area in the building (exclusive of the basement) which shall have been occupied during the period of the respective charges, taking into account the period that each part of such area was occupied. **SEWER** Tenant agrees to pay as additional rent the Tenant's proportionate part, determined as aforesaid, of the sewer rent or charge imposed or assessed upon the building of which the premises are a part.

ELECTRIC CURRENT TWENTY-FIFTH.—That the Tenant will purchase from the Landlord, if the Landlord shall so desire, all electric current that the Tenant requires at the demised premises, and will pay the Landlord for the same, as the amount of consumption shall be indicated by the meter furnished therefor. The price for said current shall be the same as that charged for consumption similar to that of the Tenant by the company supplying electricity in the same community. Payments shall be due as and when bills shall be rendered. The Tenant shall comply with like rules, regulations and contract provisions as those prescribed by said company for a consumption similar to that of the Tenant.

SPRINKLER SYSTEM TWENTY-SIXTH.—If there now is or shall be installed in said building a "sprinkler system" the Tenant agrees to keep the appliances thereto in the demised premises in repair and good working condition, and if the New York Board of Fire Underwriters or the New York Fire Insurance Exchange or any bureau, department or official of the State or local government requires or recommends that any changes, modifications, alterations or additional sprinkler heads or other equipment be made or supplied by reason of the Tenant's business, or the location of partitions, trade fixtures, or other contents of the demised premises, or if such changes, modifications, alterations, additional sprinkler heads or other equipment in the demised premises are necessary to prevent the imposition of a penalty or charge against the full allowance for a sprinkler system in the fire insurance rate as fixed by said Exchange, or by any Fire Insurance Company, the Tenant will at the Tenant's own expense, promptly make and supply such changes, modifications, alterations, additional sprinkler heads or other equipment. As additional rent hereunder the Tenant will pay to the Landlord, annually in advance, throughout the term $........................, toward the contract price for sprinkler supervisory service.

SECURITY TWENTY-SEVENTH.—The sum of..Dollars is deposited by the Tenant herein with the Landlord herein as security for the faithful performance of all the covenants and conditions of the lease by the said Tenant. If the Tenant faithfully performs all the covenants and conditions on his part to be performed, then the sum deposited shall be returned to said Tenant.

NUISANCE TWENTY-EIGHTH.—This lease is granted and accepted on the especially understood and agreed condition that the Tenant will conduct his business in such a manner, both as regards noise and kindred nuisances, as will in no wise interfere with, annoy, or disturb any other tenants, in the conduct of their several businesses, or the landlord in the management of the building; under penalty of forfeiture of this lease and consequential damages.

BROKERS COMMISSIONS TWENTY-NINTH.—The Landlord hereby recognizes as the broker who negotiated and consummated this lease with the Tenant herein, and agrees that if, as, and when the Tenant exercises the option, if any, contained herein to renew this lease, or fails to exercise the option, if any, contained therein to cancel this lease, the Landlord will pay to said broker a further commission in accordance with the rules and commission rates of the Real Estate Board in the community. A sale, transfer, or other disposition of the Landlord's interest in said lease shall not operate to defeat the Landlord's obligation to pay the said commission to the said broker. The Tenant herein hereby represents to the Landlord that the said broker is the sole and only broker who negotiated and consummated this lease with the Tenant.

WINDOW CLEANING THIRTIETH.—The Tenant agrees that it will not require, permit, suffer, nor allow the cleaning of any window, or windows, in the demised premises from the outside (within the meaning of Section 202 of the Labor Law) unless the equipment and safety devices required by law, ordinance, regulation or rule, including, without limitation, Section 202 of the New York Labor Law, are provided and used, and unless the rules, or any supplemental rules of the Industrial Board of the State of New York are fully complied with; and the Tenant hereby agrees to indemnify the Landlord, Owner, Agent, Manager and/or Superintendent, as a result of the Tenant's requiring, permitting, suffering, or allowing any window, or windows in the demised premises to be cleaned from the outside in violation of the requirements of the aforesaid laws, ordinances, regulations and/or rules.

VALIDITY THIRTY-FIRST.—The invalidity or unenforceability of any provision of this lease shall in no way affect the validity or enforceability of any other provision hereof.

EXECUTION & DELIVERY OF LEASE THIRTY-SECOND.—In order to avoid delay, this lease has been prepared and submitted to the Tenant for signature with the understanding that it shall not bind the Landlord unless and until it is executed and delivered by the Landlord.

EXTERIOR OF PREMISES THIRTY-THIRD.—The Tenant will keep clean and polished all metal, trim, marble and stonework which are a part of the exterior of the premises, using such materials and methods as the Landlord may direct, and if the Tenant shall fail to comply with the provisions of this paragraph, the Landlord may cause such work to be done at the expense of the Tenant.

PLATE GLASS THIRTY-FOURTH.—The Landlord shall replace at the expense of the Tenant any and all broken glass in the skylights, doors and walls in and about the demised premises. The Landlord may insure and keep insured all plate glass in the skylights, doors and walls in the demised premises, for and in the name of the Landlord and bills for the premiums therefor shall be rendered by the Landlord to the Tenant at such times as the Landlord may elect, and shall be due from and payable by the Tenant when rendered, and the amount thereof shall be deemed to be, and shall be paid as, additional rent.

WAR EMERGENCY THIRTY-FIFTH.—This lease and the obligation of Tenant to pay rent hereunder and perform all of the other covenants and agreements hereunder on part of Tenant to be performed shall in nowise be affected, impaired or excused because Landlord is unable to supply or is delayed in supplying any service expressly or impliedly to be supplied or is unable to make, or is delayed in making any repairs, additions, alterations or decorations or is unable to supply or is delayed in supplying any equipment or fixtures if Landlord is prevented or delayed from so doing by reason of governmental preemption in connection with a National Emergency declared by the President of the United States or in connection with any rule, order or regulation of any department or subdivision thereof of any government agency or by reason of the conditions of supply and demand which have been or are affected by war or other emergency.

THE LANDLORD COVENANTS

QUIET POSSESSION FIRST.—That if and so long as the Tenant pays the rent and "additional rent" reserved hereby, and performs and observes the covenants and provisions hereof, the Tenant shall quietly enjoy the demised premises, subject, however, to the terms of this lease, and to the mortgages above mentioned, provided however, that this covenant shall be conditioned upon the retention of title to the premises by Landlord.

ELEVATOR **HEAT** SECOND.—Subject to the provisions of Paragraph "Fourteenth" above the Landlord will furnish the following respective services: (a) Elevator service, if the building shall contain an elevator or elevators, on all days except Sundays and holidays, from A.M. to P.M. and on Saturdays from A.M. to P.M.; (b) Heat, during the same hours on the same days in the cold season in each year.

And it is mutually understood and agreed that the covenants and agreements contained in the within lease shall be binding upon the parties hereto and upon their respective successors, heirs, executors and administrators.

In Witness Whereof, the Landlord and Tenant have respectively signed and sealed these presents the day and year first above written.

....[L. S.]
Landlord

IN PRESENCE OF:

....[L. S.]
Tenant

Figure 18.7. *Last Page of Commercial Lease Form.*

dictating, the lawyer might tell you to insert the usual insurance or liability clause, or some other standard clause, and you should be able to select the proper clause without further instruction from the lawyer.

18.36. Checklist of standard clauses in commercial leases. Here is a list of the standard clauses that appear in almost all commercial leases. Although each clause might not be in a separate paragraph, in all probability the lease will contain words covering each of these subjects.

1. Term of duration
2. Rent
3. Water, electricity
4. Alterations
5. Repairs
6. Damage or liability—that is, the provision fixing the liability for injury to persons or property
7. "To let" sign before expiration of lease
8. Assignment of the lease
9. Surrender of the premises upon expiration of the lease
10. Rules and ordinances
11. Fire—that is, the agreement about the respective rights of the parties if the building should be destroyed by fire or "other action of the elements"
12. Elevators and heat
13. Insurance
14. Default in payment of rent
15. Bankruptcy of lessee
16. Peaceful possession or quiet enjoyment of the premises
17. No waiver—that is, the provision that the consent of the lessor to a variation of the terms in one instance is not a waiver of terms and conditions of the lease
18. Subordination to mortgages
19. Sprinkler system
20. Condemnation or eminent domain proceedings—that is, the rights of the respective parties if the city, county, state, or federal authority should condemn or take possession of the premises
21. Security deposited by lessee
22. War—that is, the provision that the lessee is not exempt from payment of rent if lessor, because of shortages caused by war, is unable to supply services or equipment called for by the lease

18.37. Style of typed lease. When a lawyer drafts a lease, he or she simplifies the location of specific provisions by grouping them in a particular order. In planning the style in which to type the lease, your object should be to further simplify the location of specific provisions. You can do this by indicating the subject of each provision in the margin, as in the printed form illustrated in figures 18.6 and 18.7. Another style of typing the lease is to make side headings of the subjects and underscore them. Still another style is to center the subjects. Usually the clauses are numbered consecutively throughout the lease. The numbering may be any style that you choose: I, II, FIRST, SECOND; ONE, TWO; 1., 2.; (1), (2).

18.38. Execution, acknowledgment, and recording of lease. A lease of land or commercial property is executed with the formalities of a deed. The state statutes vary, but generally the following apply:

1. Both the lessor and lessee sign the lease.

2. A lease is sealed unless the state statute does not require a deed to be sealed.

3. A lease is witnessed unless the state statute does not require a deed to be witnessed.

4. If the duration of the lease is more than one year (longer in some states), the lessor and lessee acknowledge it, and the lessee should have it recorded.

5. A lease may be signed by an agent with written authority.

The execution of the run-of-the-mill short-term lease, such as a lease on an apartment, is not so formal. Both the lessor and lessee sign, and usually the signatures are witnessed. Otherwise there are no formal requirements. The directions about acknowledgments and recording apply only to leases that must be recorded.

18.39. How to prepare a lease. Follow the instructions for preparing a deed in section 18.19, substituting "lease" for "deed," "lessor" and "lessee" for "grantor" and "grantee," and so on. These special additional instructions apply to the preparation of leases: (1) Make four copies—an original for the lessee, a duplicate original for the lessor, a triplicate original for the broker, and a copy for your files. (2) Both the lessor and lessee must sign the lease. Therefore, you will need to prepare signature lines and certificates of acknowledgment for both lessee and lessor. Lessor and lessee should each sign three copies. (3) Revenue stamps, mentioned in section 18.19, are applied to deeds, not leases.

PURCHASE AND SALE AGREEMENTS

18.40. What is a purchase and sale agreement? In real estate sales, there is almost always an agreement to buy and sell before the actual conveyance is made. This agreement, called a *purchase and sale agreement*, may be an informal memorandum or merely a receipt for a deposit on the purchase price, which is not prepared in the lawyer's office. Often it is prepared on a printed form setting forth the customary terms of such an agreement. It is usually prepared by the real estate broker and signed by the buyer and seller. The seller's lawyer enters the picture when he or she is asked to draw the deed and purchase money mortgage, if any; the buyer's lawyer, when asked to pass upon the seller's title to the property and his or her right to convey it. But many times the lawyer is asked to draw a formal agreement, or contract, of sale. He usually draws the contract when the property is very valuable, if the property is income producing, or if it is to be sold on the installment plan. An agreement to enter into an important lease is also necessary, before the lease itself is entered into. Under the statute of frauds these agreements, whether formal or informal, must be in writing or they are not enforceable.

Purchase and sale agreements fix a date—called the *closing date*—at which time title to the property is actually conveyed. The lawyer's secretary and the paralegal will have many preparations to make for the closing. Since your preparations depend to a large extent upon the contents of the purchase and sale agreement, you should first become familiar with this document. Read carefully the form of contract used in your locality.

18.41. Necessity for a purchase and sale agreement. When an owner decides to sell and a buyer decides to purchase real estate, they agree upon the terms of sale—the purchase price, the amount of cash to be paid, how the balance will be paid, what will be done about mortgages on the property—and upon numerous other details. The transfer of the property cannot be effected immediately because the seller must produce evidence of his or her right to sell, and the buyer wants his or her attorney to examine this evidence; the buyer needs time in which to arrange the necessary financing; the seller must collect various data regarding insurance, taxes, rents, and the like; instruments of conveyance must be prepared. Neither party wants the other to back out of the deal in the interim. Therefore, they enter into a contract of sale, commonly called a purchase and sale agreement, that sets forth in detail the terms under which the property will be conveyed. Great care is exercised in the drafting and preparation of a purchase and sale agreement because the conveyance will be made upon the terms set forth in the agreement.

18.42. Types of contracts of sale of land. There are two principal types of contracts of sale of land. One type, the purchase and sale agreement, contemplates the immediate transfer of title to the buyer, the buyer to pay the entire purchase price in cash, or part in cash and part by a purchase money mortgage. The contract binds the parties while the buyer is having the title examined.

The other type of contract of sale is an *installment* contract. The purchase price is paid in installments, and the title remains with the seller until the entire purchase price has been paid, or until the unpaid purchase price has been reduced to an amount agreed upon in the contract of sale. This type of sale is now heavily regulated and has become less common.

18.43. Parties to a purchase and sale agreement. The necessary parties to a purchase and sale agreement are the seller or vendor and the buyer or purchaser or vendee. Both seller and purchaser sign the contract, because each has certain obligations to perform. Since the seller agrees to convey title, the seller must be a natural person or corporation with the power and ability to make a deed of conveyance (page 443). When a married person enters into a purchase and sale agreement, it is necessary for the spouse to sign the contract in those states where the spouse must sign the deed of conveyance.

The buyer must be an adult of sound mind or a corporation with power to purchase real estate. Although an infant or an incompetent may be the grantee of real property, he or she cannot enter into a purchase and sale agreement because he or she does not possess contractual powers. Trustees and executors rarely have power to buy land.

The broker who brings about the agreement is naturally interested in its consummation. Although the broker is not a party to the contract, provision is usually made in the contract for payment of his or her commission.

18.44. How to prepare a purchase and sale agreement. Each locality has a contract form approved by the local real estate board. Printed forms are available from stationery stores and, also, from abstract and title companies. The forms are easy to complete and require little explanation. The lawyer will give you a memorandum of the information necessary to complete the form.

Make four copies—original and duplicate original for the seller and buyer, a copy for the broker, and a copy for your file. Both the seller and the buyer sign the contract and, usually, the seller's spouse. Generally an acknowledgment is not necessary, because ordinarily the contract is not recorded. Unless you receive specific instructions from the lawyer, be guided by the form. If the form adopted in your locality has an acknowledgment printed on it, fill in the acknowledgment. The form will also indicate whether it should be witnessed.

When the lawyer dictates the contract, follow the instructions for typing deeds (page 443).

18.45. Checklist for information necessary to fill in form. 1. Date of contract

2. Name and residence of seller

3. Name of seller's spouse if spouse must join in deed that is to be delivered

4. Name and residence of the buyer

5. Description of property to be conveyed and evidence of title

6. Purchase price, the exact amount being named

7. Amount to be paid when contract is signed (earnest money)

8. Amount to be paid at closing, when deed is delivered

9. Whether existing mortgage, if any, is to be assumed or property purchased subject to it

10. How balance is to be paid, and when

11. Name of trustee in those states where a deed of trust is the security instrument

12. Unpaid taxes and assessments

13. Fire insurance data

14. Name of broker

15. Closing date

16. Expiration date of offer

17. Date of possession

18.46 Earnest money. An element of all purchase and sale agreements is a cash deposit by the buyer as an indication that he or she intends to go through with the purchase if the seller furnishes good title to the property. The deposit is designated *earnest money*. It is also referred to as a *binder*, although this term is more frequently applied to a deposit made under informal agreements than to deposits made in connection with formal contracts drawn up by the lawyer. If the buyer fails to consummate the deal, the earnest money is retained by the seller; if the buyer does perform his or her part of the contract, the earnest money is applied as part payment of the purchase price. If the seller cannot convey good title to the property, the deposit is returned to the buyer. The amount of earnest money depends upon the agreement between the parties. It is ordinarily sufficient to compensate the seller for the loss he or she might sustain should the buyer fail to go through with the deal.

18.47. Escrow for the sale of real property. One of the most common uses of escrow (see part 5, Glossary, for definition) is in connection with real estate transactions. Frequently the buyer's deposit is placed in escrow so there will be no difficulty about a refund should it prove impossible for the seller to deliver a clear title to the property. Sometimes the purchase and sale agreement is put in escrow so it cannot be recorded until the deal is consummated, because the recorded contract might be a cloud on the title. Sometimes, especially in transactions involving very valuable property, both the seller and the buyer deposit bonds in escrow to prevent either party from being damaged by the failure of the other party to consummate the sale. The ramifications of escrows for the sale of real property are manifold, but necessary components are:

1. A valid and enforceable contract for the purchase and sale of land.
2. An escrow agreement.
3. A disinterested third party, usually a bank, to act as escrow holder, *escrowee.* Neither buyer or seller nor their agents or attorney can act as escrowee.

When the lawyer in your office acts as escrow holder, you should deposit funds placed with him or her in escrow in the trust account, not in the firm's regular account. See chapter 6 for the method of entering the item in the books.

TITLE CLOSINGS AND EVIDENCE OF TITLE

18.48. What is a title closing? The purchase and sale agreement designates a certain day, and sometimes hour, when the deed will be delivered, the balance of the purchase price paid, and the mortages, if any, delivered. This transaction between the seller and purchaser, and their representatives, is known as the *title closing* or *closing of title.* All of the formalities necessary to the conveyance of property are attended to at the closing. It usually takes place at the office of the lawyer for the seller. Papers to be signed must be ready for signature; other papers, such as receipts and insurance policies, must be produced; and a closing statement must be prepared. The date on which the title closing takes place is known as the *closing date.* Before the closing, the purchaser must have proof that the seller has a good title to the land.

18.49. Evidence of title. Every purchaser insists upon satisfactory evidence that the seller has good title to the land that he or she is selling. Proof of good title is also just as important to a mortgagee. There are four kinds of evidence of title—*abstract and opinion, certificate of title, title insurance,* and *Torrens certificate.* To a great extent, the acceptability of a particular kind of evidence of title depends upon the local custom.

18.50. Abstract of title. The evidence of title most commonly used in the United States is the *abstract of title.* An abstract is a condensed history of the title to a particular tract of land. It consists of a summary of the material parts of every recorded instrument affecting the title. It begins with a description of the land covered by the abstract and then shows the original governmental grant and all subsequent deeds, mortgages, releases, wills, judgments, mechanics' liens, foreclosure proceedings, tax sales, and other matters affecting title.

Of course, only a summary of these items is shown. For example, a deed is summarized as follows:

DONALD HALL AND JANE HALL, HIS WIFE to KENNETH CLARKE	WARRANTY DEED Dated Sept. 15, 1860 Ack. Sept. 18, 1860 Rec. Sept. 20,. 1860 Bk. 21, page 23

Conveys a large plot of land including the premises under examination.

The abstract concludes with the abstracter's certificate. This discloses what records the abstracter has and has not examined. For example, if the abstracter certifies that he or she has made no search of federal court proceedings affecting the property, it will be necessary to write to the Clerk of the District Court, who will supply the search for a small charge.

Abstract companies, lawyers, and public officials prepare abstracts. Abstract companies do by far the greatest portion of the abstracting, except in a few states where there are no abstract companies.

Always keep the name, address, and telephone number of the abstract company, or other abstracter, used by your firm in your desk directory. If you are employed by the lawyer for the purchaser or the mortgagee in communities where abstracts are acceptable evidence of title, you will frequently have to order abstracts. When you order the abstract, make a follow-up entry in your diary or an extra copy of the letter for your follow-up file. It is important to get the abstract as soon as possible because the deal cannot be closed until the purchaser's attorney has examined the abstract of title. When the abstract is received, charge the cost to the client; the lawyer will pay the abstracter. (See chapter 6 for bookkeeping entry.)

You will find that purchase and sale agreements frequently provide that the seller will furnish an abstract of title. This usually means he or she will give the purchaser an abstract of title to the date that the seller obtained the property. The purchaser will have it brought down to date. You will then be asked to order a *continuation* or an *extension*. The original abstract is sent to the abstract company and the company *recertifies* its accuracy and brings it down to date.

Your letter ordering an abstract of title, or a continuation, might read as follows:

We are enclosing an abstract of title for the west three rods of Lots 30 and 31, Cecil Hedgwick's Addition to Saco, York County, Maine, according to the recorded plat thereof.

Please continue this to date for the land owned by Mary Hartz and return it to us as soon as possible.

18.51. Opinion of title. When the attorney receives the abstract, he or she examines it and prepares an *opinion* about the validity of the title. If the lawyer finds any difficulty, such as a deed that was improperly acknowledged, or a discrepancy in the description of the property, he or she states these defects. They constitute *clouds* upon the seller's title and must be removed by affidavits, quit-claim deeds, or court procedure to quiet title. The attorney also sets forth in his or her opinion any liens and mortgages on the property, because the title is subject to them. Usually the purchase and sale agreement mentions the liens and mortgages and provides for their disposition. The opinion will also refer to covenants or restrictions on the property that may affect the use the buyer may make of it.

The lawyer dictates the opinion of title, which is usually in the form of a letter. If there are no defects in the title, you might be asked to draft a routine opinion of title letter. A sample letter follows.

June 21, 19..

Mr. and Mrs. Harold Wallace
Box 600
Freeport, Maine 04032

Dear Mr. and Mrs. Wallace:

We have examined the abstract of title continued by the Saco Abstract and Title Company of Saco, Maine, to date of June 15, 19.. at 8:00 a.m., for the following described premises:

The west three (3) rods of Lots Thirty (30) and Thirty-one (31), Cecil Hedgwick's Addition to Saco, York County, Maine, according to the recorded plat thereof.

From such examination, we find the title thereto to be in Mary Hartz, subject to the following:

1. There are ancient and minor errors in this title, but we do not consider any of them sufficiently important to affect the merchantability of the title.

2. There are no liens or encumbrances against said premises.

3. The abstract shows no unpaid taxes for 19.. and prior years. The summer taxes for 19.. will be due July 1, 19.. and may be checked with the City Treasurer, as may also special assessments.

It is therefore our opinion that a merchantable title exists in said above-named titleholder, subject to the exceptions above noted. This opinion is based upon the abstract continued as aforesaid and does not cover rights of persons in possession, line fences, location of buildings, or any other matter or thing not contained in said abstract.

Respectfully submitted,

JC:F

18.52. Certificate of title. In some localities, an abstract is dispensed with. The attorney examines the public records and issues a *certificate,* which is merely the lawyer's opinion of title based on the public records he or she has examined. The lawyer does not guarantee the title, but is liable for damages caused by his or her negligence. For example, if the lawyer's certificate failed to show a mortgage that was recorded, he or she would be liable to a purchaser who relied upon that certificate and purchased the property without knowledge of the mortgage. Abstract companies also issue certificates of title. A certificate of title is not to be confused with title insurance policies issued by title companies.

18.53. Title insurance policies. Title guarantee companies issue title insurance policies, which guarantee against defects in title. They are called *title guarantee policies*, or *guaranty title policies*. They are issued to owners and to mortgagees. A title policy not only guarantees against defects in the title, but the company issuing it usually undertakes to defend at its own expense any lawsuit attacking the title. Of course, a title company will not insure a defective title.

The attorney for the buyer, or the mortgagee, orders the policy of insurance from the title company, and the title company then searches its records and makes any surveys necessary to the issuance of the title insurance.

18.54. Torrens certificate. In addition to the system of transferring title under the recording acts, there is a system known as the *Torrens system*, originated by Sir Robert Torrens. A landowner who wishes to register under the Torrens system first obtains a complete abstract of title to the land. He or she then files in the proper public office an application for the registration of title. After certain legal procedure, the court orders the registrar of titles to register the title. The registrar makes out a certificate showing the title as found by the court. These certificates are bound in books and are public records. The registrar delivers a duplicate certificate to the owner. When land that has been registered under the Torrens system is sold, the deed itself does not pass title to the land. The deed must be taken to the registrar's office, and he or she issues a new certificate to the grantee. The deed is not returned to the grantee but remains in the registrar's office. Likewise, a mortgage or judgment lien is not effective until a notation has been entered on the certificate of title in the registrar's office. The Torrens system is now rarely used. It is confined to only a few metropolitan areas.

18.55. Preparations for closing. As soon as you prepare or receive a purchase and sale agreement, the closing of which is of interest to a lawyer in your office, *enter the date of the closing in your diary.* The following checklists show some of the preparations you will have to make before the closing:

Checklist of preparation by staff of seller's attorney. (The asterisks indicate items that are to be delivered to the buyer at the closing.) *1. Prepare the deed (section 18.19).

2. Prepare the purchase money mortgage and bond or note, if any (section 18.30).

*3. Prepare, or obtain from the seller, a list of tenants, rents paid and unpaid, and due dates.

*4. Obtain from the mortgagee holding any mortgage the purchaser assumes a certificate, properly acknowledged, showing payment on account or the amount actually due at the closing date.

5. Prepare memorandum of closing figures (see page 466, *et seq.*) (A copy of the memorandum might be mailed to the attorney for the purchaser, thus saving time in adjusting figures at the closing.)

*6. Prepare letter to tenants advising them to pay future rent to the purchaser.

*7. Prepare assignment of any service contracts, such as exterminator's contracts, that are to be assigned to the purchaser.

8. Notify seller of the exact time, date, and place of the closing. Tell him or her to bring to the closing the following papers:

    a. Receipts for last interest payment on mortgages

    *b. Insurance policies and assignments of them

    *c. Last receipts for taxes, special assessments, gas, electricity, and water

    *d. Leases and assignments

    *e. Securities deposited by tenants as security for rent, which might be in the form of cash

9. If seller is an individual, tell the seller his or her spouse must also be present at the closing to sign the deed.

10. If seller is a corporation, indicate the two officers who are to sign the deed and who, therefore, should be present at the closing. Also, advise the officers to bring the corporation's seal.

11. Notify others who might be present in behalf of seller of closing date—broker, accountant, title closer (see figure 18.9).

Checklist of preparations by staff of purchaser's attorney.

1. Order abstract of title (see page 461).

2. Type opinion of title after lawyer dictates it (page 463).

3. Prepare a memorandum of closing figures (pages 466, *et seq.*) (This

might be mailed to the seller's attorney, thus saving time in adjusting figures at the closing.)

4. Notify purchaser of the exact time, date, and place of the closing. Tell him or her to bring to the closing the following:

    a. Certified check for approximate amount that will be due to the seller. (You can get the figure from the memorandum of closing figures.)

    b. Blank check (to be filled in at the closing for any additional amount owed the seller).

5. If purchaser is a corporation, indicate the two officers who are to sign the purchase money mortgage and who, therefore, should be present at the closing. Also advise the officers to bring the corporate seal with them.

6. Notify others who might be interested in behalf of the buyer of the closing date—accountant, insurance broker, title closer (see figure 18.9).

7. Prepare for the attorney a checklist of papers that are to be delivered to the buyer at the closing. This list will include the items marked with an asterisk in the foregoing checklist of preparations by the seller's staff.

PREPARATION OF CLOSING STATEMENT

18.56. What is a closing statement? A purchase and sale agreement, or a contract for lease, provides that certain charges against the property and the income from it should be adjusted or prorated. For example, if the seller has paid the insurance for a year in advance, he or she is entitled to receive an adjustment from the buyer. If the seller has collected the rents for a month in advance, the buyer is entitled to an adjustment. This prorating or adjustment results in credits in favor of each party and charges against each party. A statement of the charges and credits is known as a *closing statement,* sometimes called a *settlement sheet.*

Forms of closing statements vary. Printed forms are available and are widely used. When the printed forms do not provide for all the items that must be entered on the closing statement, the statement is typed. This situation frequently arises in large, complicated transactions. The statement cannot be prepared in final form until the closing is held, because all of the necessary information is not available. It is prepared on the basis of the figures agreed upon by all parties at the closing. However, the lawyer for each party usually calculates the adjustments and prepares a memorandum of them before the closing. You will probably have the responsibility of calculating the adjustments. The lawyer will tell you what items are to be adjusted and he or she will check your figures.

Figure 18.8 illustrates a printed form on the back of a contract that may be used for a memorandum of the closing figures. A form of this kind is frequently used as a closing statement. (See also the closing statement illustrated in figures 18.9 and 18.10).

18.57. How to calculate adjustments. The practice of computing adjustments and the date of adjustment varies with the locality. In many localities, adjustments are made as of the day immediately preceding the day on which title is closed. In other words, the buyer receives the income and is charged with the expenses incurred beginning with and including the day on which title passes to him.

It is much easier to compute interest, taxes, water rates, and insurance by the 360-day method, each month representing $\frac{1}{12}$ of the annual charge, and each day $\frac{1}{30}$ of the monthly charge, than by the 365-day method. This is the practice adopted by many local real estate boards. Rent is usually computed on the basis of the days in the particular month in which title is closed. Although the 360-day method of computing interest, taxes, water rates, and insurance is used, when the period for which computation is made is more than one month, the time is computed by full months and by the actual number of days in each partial month. For example, the period between March 15 and June 3 is 2 months (April and May) and 20 days (17 days in March, and 3 days in June).

Calculations of taxes, interest, insurance, and rents follow. Other adjustments are calculated in the same manner. For the purpose of the examples, we will assume that title closes June 8, 1970.

18.58. Example of calculation of tax adjustment. Taxes in the locality are payable semiannually, April 1 and October 1. The seller paid taxes on April 1 for the preceding 6-month period. During the current 6-month period, the seller is responsible for taxes from April 1 to, but not including, June 8, the closing date. He or she will have to allow the buyer the amount of the taxes for that period—2 months (April and May) and 7 days. Assuming that the taxes for the 6-month period amount to $1,500, the taxes for one month are $250 ($1,500 ÷ 6); for one day, $8.33 $\frac{1}{3}$ ($250 ÷ 30). An adjustment of $558.34 is made in favor of the purchasers [(2×$250) + (7×$8.33⅓)].

But suppose the seller had paid taxes 6 months in advance. He or she would be entitled to recover taxes from and including June 8 *through* September 30, or for a period of 3 months (July, August, and September) and 23 days (June 8 through June 30). Allowance of $941.67 would be made in favor of the seller [(3×$250)+(23×$8.33⅓)].

18.59. Example of calculation of interest adjustment. Suppose there is a mortgage of $20,000 on the property, with interest at 9 percent payable quarterly on 15th of December, March, June, and September.

CREDIT   FINANCIAL STATEMENT AS OF ..... *June 8* ..... 19......

Paid on signing Contract	5,000	00
Mortgage held by .. *N. C. B.*	20,000	00
Int. from *3/5* .... @ ...... *9* .....%	280	00
Mortgage held by ..... @ .....%		
Int. from ...... @ .....%		
Purchase money mortgage	25,000	00
Security on lease		
Rent from *June 8* *to June 30*	3,833	33
Taxes as adjusted *$3,000 for 6 mo.* *2 mo., 7 days*	566	67
Water charges as adjusted		
Sewer rents as adjusted		
Assessments		
Rent security	7,500	00
Total credit	$ 62,180	00
Disbursements by purchaser		
Revenue stamps		
Drawing papers		
Recording papers		
Title Company bill		

19......   DEBIT

Purchase Price	$100,000	00
Taxes as adjusted		
Water charges as adjusted		
Sewer rents as adjusted		
Insurance *Northwestern* *$360 paid 8/11 - for 3 years* *10 months, 7 days*	102	33
Fuel		
TOTAL DEBIT	100,102	33
TOTAL CREDIT, brought over	62,180	00
BALANCE PAID TO SELLER	$ 37,922	33
Disbursements by seller		
Revenue stamps		
Recording papers		

Closing of title under the within contract is hereby adjourned to   19   at   19   o'clock

at   all adjustments to be made as of

Dated,   19

For value received, the within contract and all the rights, title and interest of the purchaser hereunder are hereby assigned, transferred and set over unto and said assignee hereby assumes all obligations of the purchaser hereunder.

Dated,   19

IN PRESENCE OF

.... Purchaser

.... Assignee of Purchaser

Figure 18.8. *Memorandum of Closing Figures.*

CLOSING STATEMENT

1   Re: Sale of Premises located at 345 Fifth
           Avenue, New York, New York, known as
               The Professional Building
           _____

2   Seller: West Consultants, Inc.

3   Purchaser: Joel Archer, who conveys to Joel Archer, Inc.

4   Purchaser: Joel Archer, Inc.

Adjustments computed as of June 9, 19--.

Closing held at the office of Morris & Kennedy, 70

Fifth Avenue, New York, N.Y., at 3:00 p.m., Tuesday,

June 10, 19--.

5   PRESENT AT CLOSING

For the Seller

        James West and Roland Pickard, President and Secretary,
            respectively, of West Consultants, Inc.

        Benjamin Morris, Attorney.

        Patrick Heald, C. P. A.

For the Buyer

        Joel Archer and Henry Valden, President and Secretary,
            respectively, of Joel Archer, Inc.

        Boyd Hurst, Attorney.

        Paul Michaels, C. P. A.

        Jeanne Pauley, Insurance Broker.

Others Present

        Harold Fry, the only broker on the sale.

        Gene Postum, Closer for the Title Guarantee Co., under their
            title number 14587.

        Larry Voight, Attorney for Henry Valdem, holder of mortgage.

(The numbers in the margin do not appear on the statement. See text, page 472.)

Figure 18.9. *Closing Statement—Preliminary Information.*

When title closed on June 8, interest had been paid to but not including
March 15. The purchaser is entitled to an allowance for interest from and
including March 15 through June 7, or for a period of 2 months (April and

I   REAL ESTATE AND SUMMARY

6 SALES PRICE $100,000.00

7   Subject to the following mortgage:
         First mortgage, held by
         Henry Valdem.................... $20,000.000

         Mortgages assumed:
         None

             Total Mortgages .... $ 20,000.00

         BALANCE OF .... $ 80,000.00

         Payable as follows:
8   Paid on contract May
                 9, 19-- $10,000.00
9   Purchase Money Mort-
                 gage and Notes 20,000.00

                 Total $30,000.00

         Balance paid at closing* $50,000.00

   SUMMARY:

             *Payable on Real Estate at
              Closing $50,000.00
10   Adjustments in favor of
              Seller, per schedule
              II A 102.33

                     Total $50,102.33
              Less: Adjustments in Favor
              of Purchaser, per Sched-
              ule II B $12,180.00

   BALANCE DUE SELLER $37,922.33

   Paid as follows:

         By certified check dated June 8, 19--,
             drawn by Joel Archer, Inc., to the
             order of West Consultants, Inc., on
             the City Bank in the amount of $35,000.00
         Check dated June 8, 19--, drawn by
             Joel Archer, Inc., to the order of
             West Consultants, Inc., on the City
             Bank in the amount of .... $ 2,922.33

                     Total $37,922.33

SEF:r   1-2-1   5/7/--

(The numbers in the margin do not appear on the statement. See text, pages 472 and 473.)

Figure 18.10. *Closing Statement—Part I.*

May) and 24 days (17 days in March, 7 days in June). The interest on $20,000 at 9 percent per annum is $150.00 per month, $5 per day ($150 ÷ 30). The interest for 2 months 24 days is $420 [(2×$150)+(24×$5)]. An adjustment of $420 is made in favor of the purchaser.

18.60. Example of calculation of insurance adjustment. Suppose there is a fire policy on the property that had been paid up for three years. The expiration date of the policy is August 1, 1981. The seller is therefore entitled to an adjustment of insurance for 13 months and 23 days (June 8, 1980, the date of the closing, to August 1, 1981). The premium is $10 per month [$360÷(12×3)], or 33⅓¢ per day ($10÷30). An adjustment of $137.67 [(13×$10)+(23×33⅓¢)] is made in favor of the seller.

18.61. Example of calculation of rent adjustment. The seller had collected the rents in advance for the month of June. They amounted to $5,000. The purchaser is entitled to an adjustment for the period from and including June 8 through June 30, or 23 days. Since June has only 30 days, the rent per day is $5,000÷30, or $166.66 ⅔ per day. The purchaser is entitled to an adjustment of $3,833.33 (23×166.66 ⅔). If there is more than one tenant, you will have to prorate the rent for each separately, unless the rents had all been collected for the same period.

18.62. Miscellaneous payments. Certain miscellaneous items are paid by the seller and others by the purchaser. These items do not constitute part of the actual closing figures because they are not charges or credits to the property itself, and they are not included in the calculation of the amount due by the buyer to the seller. However, each party must be given a memorandum of the payments for which he is responsible.

Checklist for miscellaneous payments by seller. The seller is usually responsible for the following items:

1.   Broker's commission
2.   Attorney's fees (attending closing, etc.)
3.   Fee for drawing deed
4.   Recording tax on purchase money mortgage
5.   Revenue stamps on purchase money mortgage

Checklist of miscellaneous payments by purchaser. The purchaser is usually responsible for the following items:

1.   Abstract
2.   Fee for drawing purchase money mortgage (payable to seller's attorney)

3.   Attorney's fees (examination of abstract, attending closing, etc.)

4.   Recording fee and documentary stamps on deed

18.63. Suggested form of closing statement. Figure 18.9 illustrates the preliminary information and Part I of a closing statement, based on a form suggested by Mr. Samuel Kaplan, C.P.A., in his article "Standardization of Closing Statements for Real Estate Transactions," published in *The New York Certified Public Accountant*, Volume XVIII, No. 10. An explanation of the items will enable you to prepare a statement in any form. (The numbers appearing in the margins of the illustration do not appear on the statement but are for the purpose of this explanation.) Parts II A and II B and III of the closing statement are not illustrated here. Part II A is a list of "Adjustments in Favor of Seller"; Part II B is a list of "Adjustments in Favor of Purchaser." Part III is entitled "Supplementary Schedules and Information." It lists (1) miscellaneous payments by the seller; (2) miscellaneous payments by the purchaser (see above); (3) instruments delivered at closing, and other matters pertinent to the particular closing.

1. The description need not be the complete description given in the purchase and sale agreement and the deed. A street address is usually sufficient. A farm property might be described as "......... acres in the County of ...., State of ...., known as .... Farm."

2. Get the seller's name from the agreement. If the seller is an individual and the spouse also signed the agreement, both names should appear on the closing statement.

3. Sometimes the person who signs a purchase and sale agreement assigns the agreement before the sale is consummated. The assignee then becomes the purchaser. This item shows the name of the purchaser signed to the agreement. If he or she assigned it, the item shows, "......... who conveys to ...." Printed forms of contracts frequently provide for an assignment.

4. This is the name of the party who takes title at the closing.

5. Those present at the closing vary with the size and complexity of the transaction. The seller and buyer (or their representatives) and their lawyers are always present. Usually the broker attends the closing. If a mortgage loan is involved, the lender's representative usually attends. In localities where title insurance is customary, the title company's closer is present.

6. This is the purchase price indicated in the purchase and sale agreement.

7. The purchaser may purchase the property *subject* to an existing

mortgage, which constitutes a lien on the property, without personal liability on the part of the purchaser, or he or she may *assume* the mortgage, thereby becoming personally liable for the debt.

8. This is the deposit, or earnest money, mentioned in the agreement. If the agreement calls for additional payments between the signing of the contract and the closing, they should be listed here.

9. The purchase and sale agreement recites the amount of the purchase money mortgage, if any.

10. Calculation of adjustments was explained on page 467 *et seq.* You can get these figures from the memorandum of closing figures (figure 18.8) that you prepared, unless they were adjusted at the closing. List the adjustments in favor of the seller in one schedule, those in favor of the buyer in another.

The purchaser brings to the closing a certified check for the approximate amount and draws a check for the balance after the calculation of adjustments has been agreed upon by all parties.

FORECLOSURE ACTIONS

18.64. What is a foreclosure action? The forced sale of property to satisfy the payment of a mortgage (or deed of trust) or other default under the terms of the mortgage (or deed of trust) is a *foreclosure*. In some states the foreclosure is by advertisement and sale, held in accordance with the legal technicalities prescribed by the state statutes. In the majority of states, foreclosure is by litigation. The preliminary steps in foreclosure litigation are fairly similar in all jurisdictions, but the procedure between the commencement of the action and the sale vary considerably not only with the jurisdiction but with the circumstances of the case. For that reason, emphasis here is on the preliminary procedure.

18.65. Papers necessary for institution of foreclosure action. The lawyer will need the following papers and documents before starting a foreclosure action:

1. Bond or note
2. Mortgage or deed of trust
3. Assignment, if any
4. Abstract of title
5. Receipted bills for taxes, assessments, water rates, interest, insurance, and the like paid by the mortgagee or his or her assignee

These papers constitute the nucleus of your file in the case. As soon as you receive a new matter slip (chapter 1) about the case, ask the lawyer if you should get them from the client, so they will be on hand when he or she is ready to start the action.

18.66. Information needed to prepare papers in foreclosure action. You will need the following information to prepare the preliminary papers in a foreclosure action:

1. Venue
2. Parties plaintiff
3. Parties defendant
4. Description of property
5. Description of note or bond
6. Description of mortgage
7. How the mortgage is in default

18.67. Venue. You can get the *venue* from the description of the property in the mortgage. An action to foreclose a mortgage is always brought in the state and county in which the property is located. A foreclosure is an equity action and in those states that have separate courts for law and equity, the action is brought in the Chancery Court.

18.68. Parties to a foreclosure action. *Parties plaintiff.* The owner of the mortgage—the mortgagee, or his or her beneficiary or assignee—is the plaintiff in a foreclosure action. The suit must be brought in the name of the actual owner of the mortgage. For example, if the mortgage is held by William Walsh as Trustee for Carl Sloane, the action is brought by William Walsh, Trustee for Carl Sloane, not by William Walsh. If the mortgage is owned jointly, say by husband and wife, the action is brought in the name of both owners.

Parties defendant. Every person who has an interest in the property covered by a mortgage is made a *party defendant* to the foreclosure action. These might include the mortgagor; the mortgagor's heirs, devisees, or legatees; wife of the mortgagor; *cestui que trustent*; persons in possession as tenants or occupants; the People of the State; and others. You can get the names of known defendants from the Certification of Defendants (page 476); the lawyer will give them to you if there is no certification.

18.69. Fictitious names. Since someone frequently has an interest that the plaintiff does not know about, or someone whose name is unknown has an interest in the property, several *fictitious names* are added as defendants. The reason for adding the fictitious names is that additional defendants can be brought into the action without the necessity of serving an amended complaint on all defendants. Perhaps an interested party's last name is known but not his or her first; a fictitious first name is given to that defendant, thus:

"Gerald" Thomas, first name "Gerald" being fictitious, defendant's real first name being unknown to the plaintiff.

Sometimes an unknown person is identified by a description, thus:

"Abraham Bryant," name fictitious, defendant's real name being unknown to the plaintiff, person intended conducting a stationery store at No. 35 East 18 Street.

The complaint usually alleges that the names are fictitious. The true name is substituted for the fictitious name as soon as it is learned. *In all subsequent papers filed in the case, the caption reflects the substitution.*

18.70. Description of note or bond. The foreclosure complaint contains a complete *description of the note or bond* secured by the mortgage. A note is usually copied verbatim. Only the gist of the bond is set forth, including the name of the person signing it, the amount, the date, rate of interest and when payable, date of maturity. You can get the wording from a good form book, but unless your office does considerable foreclosure work, the lawyer will dictate the terms of the bond. Check the names, dates, and amounts against the original bond.

18.71. Description of mortgage. A *description of the mortgage* sufficient to identify it is set forth in the complaint, *lis pendens,* and other papers. The description includes the name of the mortgagor, name of mortgagee, date of execution, maturity date. The description also shows when and where the mortgage was recorded—the date, the clerk's office, book (*Liber*) and page number. In some jurisdictions a copy of the mortgage is attached to the complaint as an exhibit.

If the plaintiff is the assignee of the original mortgage, the foreclosure complaint alleges the fact of the assignment, thus showing plaintiff's right to sue.

18.72 Description of property. Get the *description of the property* from the mortgage. It is advisable to keep the copy in your file so you will have it handy whenever you prepare a paper in the case. Some offices use automatic typewriters with such information stored on magnetic cards or tapes. Follow the directions given on page 436 for copying land descriptions. Remember, whenever you copy the description, have someone read it back to you while you follow the description in the original mortgage. This is particularly important in a foreclosure action because the action is defective if the description has an error in it.

18.73. When is a mortgage considered in default. Failure of the mortgagor to meet any obligation under a mortgage is a *default*. The default may be in payment of principal, interest, taxes, insurance, or in the observance or performance of any of the conditions of the mortgage. For example, if the mortgagor fails to pay the taxes when due, he or she is in default. Under the acceleration clause (page 448), the entire amount of the mortgage then becomes due, and the owner may foreclose for the entire amount, not merely for the amount that is in default.

PROCEDURE IN FORECLOSURE ACTION

18.74. Title search for foreclosures. When the mortgagor delivered the mortgage to the mortgagee, he or she either turned over to the mortgagee an abstract of title to the premises or the mortgagee conducted his or her own *title search*. Banks taking mortgages have their own title-search requirements. Before the lawyer begins foreclosure proceedings he or she will want that abstract brought up to date. Write a letter to the abstract company similar to the letter ordering a continuation of abstract when a purchase and sale agreement is entered into (page 461). In those few states where there are no abstract companies, other arrangements are made for the title search.

Upon request, most title companies will also furnish a *certification of defendants*, or a *foreclosure report*, as it is called in some localities. The certification lists the necessary and proper parties defendant to the foreclosure action and the interest of each in the premises. It also discloses the legal capacity of each defendant. (See "Who may be parties to a law suit" on page 275, *et seq.*) When you order the continuation of abstract, ask the lawyer if he or she wants a certification of defendants. The lawyer might prefer to prepare the list of parties defendant from the abstract, rather than have the title company make the certification.

18.75. Preparation of complaint. The *complaint* in a foreclosure action is largely standardized. The lawyer will give you a form to follow, or refer you to one in a form book, for the standard parts and will dictate any unusual parts. The complaint is typed in the same style and on the same kind of paper as a complaint in any civil action (chapter 14).

Caption. The *caption* of the complaint includes the fictitious names as well as the names of the known defendants. The exact wording varies, but the following styles are typical.

HENRY MASON,

Plaintiff,

vs

JOHN MASON, doing business under the trade name or style of John's Stores, "JOHN DOE," "RICHARD DOE," and "EARL DOE," said three last named defendants being fictitious, said defendants' true names being unknown to plaintiff, they being intended to designate tenants of portions of the premises described in the complaint,

Defendants.

HENRY MASON,

Plaintiff,

against

JOHN MASON and HELEN MASON, husband and wife, DOE ONE, DOE TWO, DOE THREE, and DOE FOUR,

Defendants.

18.76. Number of copies. To know how many copies of the complaint to prepare, besides your office copy, you will have to know the answer to these practice questions:

1. How many copies are filed in court?
2. May we dispense with service against any group of defendants?

Foreclosure actions frequently have numerous defendants, and the preparation of a copy of a long complaint for each of them works a hardship on the plaintiff. To relieve the plaintiff, some jurisdictions have adopted practice rules that make it unnecessary to serve the complaint on every defendant.

18.77. Lis pendens. *Purpose.* Whenever a law suit involving property is commenced, a notice of *lis pendens* or "pendency of action," is filed. *Lis pendens* is Latin for "pending suit." A notice of *lis pendens* gives constructive notice to the world that the property described therein is involved in a law suit. The notice is filed with the proper official, such as the county clerk, recorder, or register of titles under the Torens system, at the time the complaint is filed.[1] The filing of the notice of *lis pendens* is a vital step in actions involving real property, such as foreclosures, actions to quiet title, condemnation proceedings, and partitions. If a defendant disposes of an interest in the property after suit is started, but before notice is filed, the plaintiff's suit is defective. On the other hand, any

---

[1] In New York Supreme Court, notice of pendency is filed before the complaint because in that court no pleadings have to be filed until issue is joined.

claim against, or interest in, the property arising subsequent to the filing of the *lis pendens* is subordinate to the interest of the plaintiff as determined by the law suit.

18.78. Preparation of notice of lis pendens. As soon as you receive the certification of defendants, or foreclosure report, from the title company, you can prepare the *notice of pendency* without waiting for the lawyer to give you instructions about the complaint. The lawyer will not dictate the notice; you will be expected to follow a form. The only parts that change are the names of the parties, the description of the mortgage, and the description of the property. Figure 18.11 illustrates a notice of pendency of action or *lis pendens,* but the wording varies with the state.

1. Use the same kind of paper that you use for any court paper.

2. Make an original and a file copy. Also make an extra copy for your loose-leaf notebook. Copy of the notice is not served on the defendants.

3. The caption is the same as the caption in the complaint. You may shorten the title by the use of *et al.* (see page 282), unless the wording of the notice makes this inadvisable. See 6 below.

4. The title of the document is "Notice of Lis Pendens," or "Notice of Pendency of Action."

5. Have someone compare the description with you against the description in the original mortgage. *This is most important.*

6. The notice illustrated in figure 18.11 contains a direction to the county clerk: "You are hereby directed to index the foregoing notice of pendency against the names . . . ." Insert the name of every *known* defendant as listed in the certification of defendants, but do not include fictitious names. If the form of notice that you follow refers to the defendants without listing them, the title of this case must contain the name of every known defendant and cannot be shortened by the use of *et al.* A *lis pendens* is no good unless it is indexed against each defendant, insofar as that defendant has an interest in the property.

7. Staple the original in an endorsed legal back (page 292).

8. The attorney for the plaintiff signs the notice.

18.79. Preparation of summons. The *summons* in a foreclosure action is prepared like the summons in any civil action. See the directions on page 301, *et seq.* As a foreclosure action usually has numerous defendants, you will probably have to type the summons instead of using a printed form.

18.80. Filing and service of summons, complaint, and lis pendens. After the summons, complaint, and *lis pendens* are prepared, proceed as in any civil action. See directions on page 304. File the notice of

IN THE DISTRICT COURT OF THE STATE OF IOWA

IN AND FOR POLK COUNTY

JACOB LAKEWOOD and
EVELYN LAKEWOOD,

	Plaintiffs,	No. 4896
vs.		NOTICE OF LIS PENDENS

DONALD FOSTER and SALLY FOSTER,
husband and wife, TIMOTHY BOYD, DOE ONE,
DOE TWO, DOE THREE, and DOE FOUR,

Defendants

NOTICE IS HEREBY GIVEN, That an action has been commenced and is pending in this Court upon a complaint of the above named plaintiffs against the above named defendants for the foreclosure of a mortgage, bearing date the twenty-first day of September, one thousand nine hundred and ...., executed by Donald Foster and wife, Sally Foster, to Jacob Lakewood and wife, Evelyn Lakewood, to secure the sum of Five Thousand Dollars ($5,000), and recorded in Liber 2063 of Mortgages, at page 25, in the office of the Recorder of Deeds of the County of Polk, on the twenty-second day of September, one thousand nine hundred and .... at ten o'clock in the forenoon;

AND NOTICE IS HEREBY GIVEN, That the mortgaged premises affected by the said foreclosure action, were, at the time of the commencement of said action, and at the time of the filing of this notice, situated in the County of Polk
in the State of Iowa, and are described in the said mortgage as follows, to wit:

(Insert description that appears in mortgage)

....
Jones & McArthur
Attorneys for Plaintiffs

(Continued on following page)

(Continued from preceding page)

To THE CLERK OF THE DISTRICT COURT OF POLK COUNTY:

You will please index the above notice to the name of each of the following defendants: Donald Foster, Sally Foster, and Jacob Lakewood.

Dated: May 7, 19–.

. . . .
Jones & McArthur
Attorneys for Plaintiffs

Figure 18.11. *Notice of Lis Pendens.*

lis pendens with the proper county official (the official varies with the jurisdiction) at the time the summons is issued and the complaint is filed with the clerk of the court. The summons and complaint must be served on the defendants within a specified time after the *lis pendens* is filed.

Do not forget to make your diary and suit register entries.

18.81. Follow-up of process service. Follow-up of *process service* is necessary in all civil actions, but is particularly important in foreclosure actions because of the number of defendants. Numerous foreclosure actions are delayed because service of process is lax. It is your responsibility to see that the process server makes every effort to effect service expeditiously on all defendants. Request weekly reports on the progress of service. Insist that you be informed immediately when, where, and upon whom service is made, and that the process server make affidavit of service as soon as service is made. The process server should inform you of any difficulties that may arise, such as questions with respect to identity. In those jurisdictions where process is served by the sheriff or other county official, you cannot follow the matter as closely as when your office employs the process server.

Make appropriate diary and suit register entries.

18.82. Party Sheet. Numerous parties defendant in a foreclosure action make it advisable to keep a special record, which might be called a *party sheet,* of service on and appearance by each defendant. (This record is not to be confused with the party sheet that is filed in court in some jurisdictions.) Use a wide sheet of paper for the record. Head the sheet:

PARTY SHEET
Action No. .... Plaintiffs .... Premises .. (brief description) ..
Office File No. ....

Rule the sheet into vertical columns, with the following columnar headings:

> Defendants (specify legal status, such as infant, corporation, trustee)
>
> Interest in premises (owner, tenant, etc.)
>
> Address where served
>
> When served
>
> How served
>
> By whom served
>
> Affidavit of service made before .... (*notary's name*)
>
> Last day to answer
>
> Appeared by .... (*name of defendant's attorney*)
>
> Address and telephone number of attorney
>
> Date appearance entered
>
> Remarks

A glance at the party sheet will tell the lawyer the status of service and appearance of each defendant.

18.83. Other steps in foreclosure proceedings. After the summons, complaint, and *lis pendens* have been filed and served, the procedure in foreclosure litigation varies. The following steps are among those that will have to be taken, depending upon the jurisdiction and the circumstances of the case.

1. Application for receivership. If the property involved is income producing, the plaintiff will ask for the appointment of a receiver to collect the income and make the necessary disbursements.

2. Application for appointment of guardian ad litem. If the parent of an infant defendant will not ask for the appointment of a guardian ad litem, the plaintiff does.

3. *Ex parte* motion to obtain leaver to sue "arm of court," such as a trustee in bankruptcy.

4. Entry of default judgment.

5. Reference to compute or reference to master in chancery.

6. Hearing before referee or master. The lawyer will want the following papers to take to the hearing:

    a. Referee's oath

    b. Referee's report ready for signature

    c. Bond or note

    d. Mortgage or deed of trust

    e. Assignments

    f. True or photocopies of (c), (d), and (e), so the originals may be withdrawn when the hearing is over

    g. Receipted bills for taxes, assessments, water rates, penalties or interest, if any, paid by mortgagee

    h. Receipt for payment of insurance if paid by mortgagee

    i. Summons with affidavit of service

    j. Check to order of referee

7. Judgment or decree of foreclosure and sale.

8. Publication of notice of sale.

9. Sale.

18.84. Checklist of what to do in foreclosure action. Here is a checklist of what you will have to do when your office handles a foreclosure action.

1. Make file and process as any other new matter (chapter 1).

2. *Keep diary entries* (chapter 3) and progress record (chapter 12).

3. Order abstract of title continuation.

4. Prepare all papers, as directed by the attorney.

5. See that summons, complaint, and *lis pendens* are filed and served.

6. Make sure to keep a record of all process served on defendants; if any are missed their interest in the property may not be foreclosed.

7. Have copies (typed or photocopy) made of mortgage or deed, trust, bond or note, and assignments.

8. Prepare party sheet and keep it up-to-date.

9. If a receiver is appointed, keep after him for regular reports.

10. Gather together papers for the lawyer to take to the hearing (see preceding paragraph).

11. Make bookkeeping entries of all disbursements and receipts, just as in any case (chapter 6).

19

Assisting with Probate

and Estate Administration

The property left when a person dies is known as a *decedent's estate*. Whether the deceased died *testate* (leaving a will) or *intestate* (without a valid will), it is usually necessary that a competent person or corporation be charged with the duty of administering the deceased person's estate. (See chapter 11 for instructions concerning the preparation of wills.) The objects of the administration are, first, to collect the assets of an estate and pay the claims against it; and, second, to determine the persons to whom any residue of the estate belongs and deliver it to them. The administration of an estate is under the jurisdiction of the probate court (known as the Surrogate's Court in New York), and it is only through proceedings in this court that the executor or administrator can function.

Proceedings in probate courts, although similar, vary in detail not only from state to state but from county to county. The courts have printed forms for almost all of the papers that are filed in the administration of an estate. You can prepare many of these without detailed instruction from the lawyer. Those that you might find difficult to fill in are reproduced in this chapter. The procedure described here and the illustrated forms are based upon practice in New York County. They are typical, with deviations, of the procedure and forms in many states.

19.1. Distinction between executor and administrator. The general term used to dscribe any person appointed to administer an estate, whether testate or intestate, is *personal representative* or *legal representative*. If the decedent leaves a valid will naming the person or corporation whom the testator wanted to administer the estate, the person or corporation named in the will is an *executor* (*executrix*, if a woman). The testator may name as many executors as desired. Often an individual names both the spouse and a bank as co-executors. The spouse thus has a voice in the administration of the estate and the bank can advise the spouse and handle the considerable amount of work involved in the administration. Frequently an alternate executor is named in case the first is unable to serve.

If the decedent died intestate, the court will appoint a person who is entitled to share in the estate as *administrator* (*administratrix*, if a woman). If the decedent left a will but did not nominate an executor, or if the person named is incompetent, or refuses to act, or dies, the court will appoint an administrator *cum testamento annexo* (with the will annexed).

There is little practical difference between the authority and duties of an executor and administrator, except that a will may confer on an executor powers in addition to those the law gives.The executor, although nominated by the testator, receives authority to act by petitioning the probate court for *letters testamentary*. The administrator receives authority to act by petitioning for *letters of administration*. The will controls the distribution the executor (or administrator c.t.a.) makes of the property, whereas state inheritance statutes control the distribution the administrator makes.

19.2. The lawyer's part in the administration of an estate. Almost every lawyer is at some time the executor or administrator of one or more estates. However, the lawyer's most common role in the administration of an estate is as counsel to an executor or administrator. Every executor and administrator, corporate or individual, requires the services of an attorney in the administration, settlement, and distribution of the estate. The attorney probates the will, files the petition for letters testamentary or letters of administration, institutes the necessary proceedings, such as tax proceedings and accounting proceedings, and advises the executor about the legality of his or her acts. The executor or administrator receives a commission from the estate, except when agreeing to serve without compensation. If executor or administrator as well, the attorney may perform the necessary legal services and receive proper compensation in addition to a commission.

PROBATE OF WILL

19.3. The executor's right to act. The executor named in a will cannot take over the administration of an estate without first indicating an intention to act and receiving the sanction of the court. Three documents are necessary to establish the executor's right to act: (1) the will itself, (2) the decree admitting it to probate, and (3) letters testamentary. The will is generally considered the source and measure of an executor's power, but the will must first be proved. It is proved by a legal proceeding in probate court known as *probate of will.* The proceeding culminates in a decree by the court admitting the will to probate and directing that letters testamentary issue to the executor. The letters testamentary are the evidence of the executor's authority.

19.4. Probate of will. The attorney for the estate generally prepares and submits to the executors the necessary papers in the proceeding to probate the will. The probate proceeding is initiated by the filing of the will itself, together with a copy of it, certified to be a correct and true copy. (Figure 19.1 shows entries made in the suit register record [chapter 12] in a probate proceeding.) A petition for the probate of the will is also filed with the will and the copy. Simultaneously, a transfer tax affidavit is filed. The inheritance tax is not based upon the affidavit. A special proceeding is needed for that. Legal notice of the probate proceeding must be served upon all interested parties and affidavit of service (or waiver of service) filed with the court. Sworn depositions of one or more witnesses to the will must also be filed. If there are no objections to the admission of the will within the time specified, the will is admitted to probate by a decree of the court to that effect. The person named as executor in the will then files a bond (unless waived in the will) and an oath, and letters testamentary as executor issue to the person who is named. A corporate fiduciary named as executor does not generally have to file a bond.

19.5. Parties to a probate proceeding. The proponent of the will, that is, the person or corporation seeking to have the will probated, is the *petitioner.* The petitioner is usually the person or corporation named in the will as executor. There are three groups of interested parties who must be informed of the probate proceeding so they may protect their interests:

1. The surviving spouse and the distributees. These are the heirs-at-law of the deceased who would have inherited if the decedent had died intestate. This group of distributees includes the heirs-at-law who are also named in the will as legatees, because they might take less by the will than they would have inherited if there had been no will.

2. The executors and trustees named in the will who do not sign the petition.

3. Legatees or devisees who are not distributees. These are the legatees or devisees named in the will who would not have inherited if the

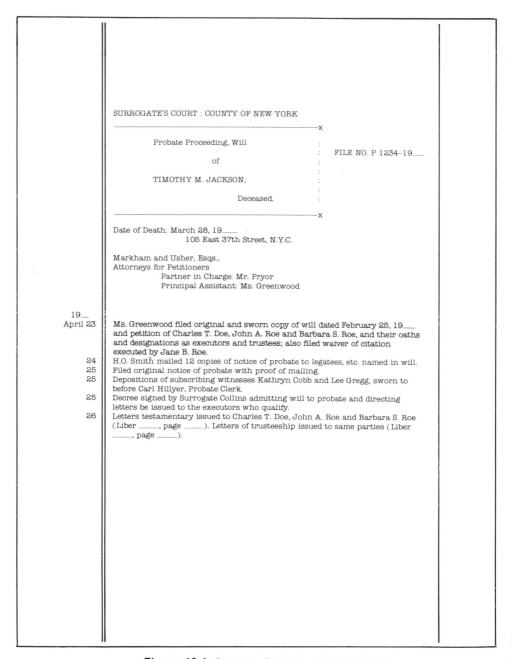

Figure 19.1. *Progress Record in Probate of Will.*

decedent had died intestate. They are interested in the proceeding because they lose their legacies if the will is not admitted to probate.

19.6. Copy of will and affidavit. Some states require a copy of the will to be filed in the probate court with the original will. In most jurisdictions a photocopy may be filed. In the administration of a large, complicated estate, where numerous copies of the will are needed, the will is sometimes duplicated or printed.

1. Make as many legible copies as you can in one typing.
2. Copy the will exactly, typing also the signature and data that are written in ink.
3. Have two adults (you may be one of them) compare one copy with the original and make an affidavit to that effect. They must both compare the same copy.
4. Fill in the blanks on the back of the affidavit. If you do not use a printed form of affidavit, make a legal back endorsed like the printed form illustrated in figure 19.2.
5. Staple the affidavit to the compared copy of the will, placing the affidavit beneath the copy.

19.7. Petition for probate of will. The petition sets forth certain factual data about the testator and the testator's heirs, legatees, and devisees, and prays that the will be admitted to probate and that letters testamentary be issued to the executor. If trustees are named in the will, the petition also prays for letters of trusteeship. Figures 19.3 to 19.6 illustrate a printed form of petition, properly completed.

1. Make an original for the court and a copy for your office file.
2. Be especially careful about names, addresses, and values of legacies and devises.
3. The lawyer will give you a memorandum of (a) the name and address of the petitioner or petitioners; (b) the name of the testator, the testator's residence at the time of death, and the time and place of his death; (c) the names, addresses, ages, and degree of kinship to the decedent of the heirs-at-law and of those interested in the will; (d) the addresses of the other legatees and devisees. This memorandum and the copy of the will give you the information necessary to fill in the form, unless the will is complicated. The lawyer will dictate any additional necessary information.
4. The relationship of the distributees (listed in Subdivision *a* through *g* of the illustration, page 1 of figure 19.3) shows how to fill in the information on surviving relatives. A surviving spouse always shares in a decedent's estate. The distributees, other than the surviving spouse, take in the following order:

Children and issue of deceased chidren

Father, mother

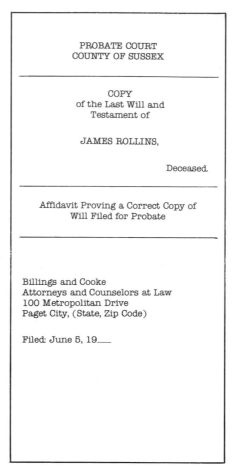

PROBATE COURT
COUNTY OF SUSSEX

COPY
of the Last Will and
Testament of

JAMES ROLLINS,

Deceased.

Affidavit Proving a Correct Copy of
Will Filed for Probate

Billings and Cooke
Attorneys and Counselors at Law
100 Metropolitan Drive
Paget City, (State, Zip Code)

Filed: June 5, 19___

Figure 19.2. *Back of Affidavit Proving a Correct Copy of Will Filed for Probate.*

Brothers, sisters, and issue of deceased brothers and sisters

Uncles, aunts, and issue of deceased uncles and aunts

There is no need to make an allegation concerning relatives of a deceased who are not entitled to inherit. Thus, in the illustration, only the spouse and children are listed as distributees. There is no need to make an allegation about a surviving mother or father, or others, because in this case they cannot inherit. If there were no surviving children or issue of a predeceased child, and no surviving mother or father, the brothers and sisters would be listed as distributees. It would then be necessary to allege that there were no surviving children or issue of a deceased child, and no surviving mother or father. It would not be necessary to allege that there were no surviving aunts or uncles and no issue of a deceased aunt or

Form UF-B-O Revised   9268-69 (C.S.)   ◄━━ 94

State of New York

Surrogate's Court: County of New York

Probate Proceeding, Will of	**Probate Petition**
EDGAR BROWN	
...., **Deceased.**	**File No...1234./.19..**

To the Surrogate's Court, County of New York   :

It is respectfully alleged:

(1) The name(s), domicile(s) (or, in the case of a bank or trust company, its principal office) and interest(s) in this proceeding of the petitioner(s) are as follows:

Name: .... **Elizabeth R. Brown**

Domicile or
Principal Office: .... **214 East 17 Street, New York, N.Y. 10003**
                                                        (Street and Number)

....
(City, Village or Town)   (State)

Name: .... **John Brown**

Domicile or
Principal Office: .... **214 East 17 Street**
                                                        (Street and Number)
                              New York, N.Y. 10003
(City, Village or Town)   (State)

Interest(s) of Petitioner(s):   ☒ Executor(s) named in decedent's Last Will
(*Check one*)   presented herewith
                                         ☐ Other (Specify) ....

(2) The name, domicile, date and place of death, and national citizenship of the above-named deceased are as follows:

(a) Name: .... **Edgar Brown**

(b) Date of death .... **December 25, 19__**

(c) Place of death .... **New York City, N.Y.**

(d) Domicile Street .... **214 East 17 Street**

City, Town, Village .... **New York City**

County .... **New York**

State .... **New York**

(e) Citizen: (Subject) of .... **United States**

(3) The Last Will, herewith presented, relates to both real and personal property and consists of an instrument or instruments dated as shown below and signed at the end thereof by the decedent and the following subscribing witnesses:

.... **November 23,19__** .... **John Mills** and **Thomas Crane** ....
(Date of Will)   (Witnesses to Will)

.... **NONE** ....
(Date of Codicil)   (Witnesses to Codicil)

(4) There is no other will or codicil of the decedent on file in the office of the court, and upon information and belief, there exists no will, codicil or other testamentary instrument of the decedent later in date to any of the instruments mentioned in paragraph (3) hereof, except

(5) The decedent left surviving:
(a) [☒] Spouse (husband/wife).
(b) [1] Child ....
(c) [no] Father/mother.
(d) [no] Brothers or sisters, either of the whole or half-blood; or descendants of such predeceased brothers or sisters.
(e) [no] Grandfather/grandmother.
(f) [no] Uncles or aunts.
(g) [no] Descendants of predeceased uncles or aunts.

(Information is required only as to those classes of surviving relatives who would take the property of decedent if there were no will. The term "child or children" includes adopted as well as natural children. State number of survivors in each such class. Insert "X" in all subsequent classes. Insert "NO" in all prior classes.)

Figure 19.3. *Petition for Probate of Will (Page 1).*

(6) The names, relationships and addresses of all distributees, of each person designated in the Last Will herewith presented as primary executor, of all persons adversely affected by the purported exercise by such Will of any power of appointment, of all persons adversely affected by any codicil and of all persons having an interest under any prior will of the decedent on file in the Surrogate's office, are hereinafter set forth in subdivisions (a) and (b):

(a) All persons and parties so interested who are of full age and sound mind, or which are corporations or associations, are as follows:

Name and Address	Relationship	Description of Legacy, Devise or Other Interest, or Nature of Fiduciary Status
Elisabeth R. Brown	Wife	Legacy of $75,000; beneficiary of residuary trust.
John Brown	Son	Legacy of $25,000; specific legacy of 100 shares of Edgar Brown, Inc.

(b) All persons so interested who are persons under disability, are as follows:

(Please furnish all information specified in NOTE below.)

None.

(Note: In the case of each infant, state (a) name, birth date, age, relationship to decedent, residence address, and the person with whom he resides; (b) whether or not he has a general or testamentary guardian, and whether or not his father, or if dead, his mother, is living; and (c) the name and residence address of any guardian and any living parent. In the case of each other person under disability state (a) name, relationship to decedent, and residence address; (b) facts regarding his disability, including whether or not a committee has been appointed and whether or not he has been committed to any institution; and (c) the names and addresses of any committee, any person or institution having care and custody of him, and any relative or friend having an interest in his welfare. In the case of person confined as a prisoner, state place of incarceration. In the case of unknowns, describe such persons in the same language as will be used in the process. In each case give a brief description of the party legacy, devise or other interest as in paragraph (6) (a) hereof.)

(7) The names and domiciliary addresses of all substitute or successor executors and of all trustees, guardians, legatees and devisees, and other beneficiaries named in the Last Will herewith presented, other than those named in Paragraph (6), are hereinafter set forth in subdivisions (a) and (b):

(a) All such other legatees and devisees who are of full age and sound mind, or which are corporations or associations, are as follows: None.

Name	Address	Description of Legacy, Devise or Other Interest or Nature of Fiduciary Status

(b) All such other legatees, devisees and other beneficiaries who are persons under disability, are as follows:

(Please furnish all information specified in NOTE to paragraph (6) (b) hereof.)

(8) There are no persons, corporations or associations, interested in this proceeding other than those hereinabove mentioned.

(9) To the best of the knowledge of the undersigned, the approximate total value of all property constituting the decedent's gross testamentary estate is more than $100,000 and less than $250,000.

(10) Upon information and belief, no other petition for the probate of any will of the decedent or for the granting of letters of administration on the decedent's estate has heretofore been filed in any Court.

Figure 19.4. *Petition for Probate of Will (Page 2).*

uncle, because they could not inherit, unless specifically named in the will.

5. You can always get the names of the legatees and devisees from the copy of the will.

WHEREFORE your petitioner(s) pray(s) (a) that process be issued to all necessary parties to show cause why the Last Will herewith presented should not be admitted to probate; (b) that an order be granted directing the service of process pursuant to the provisions of article 3 of the SCPA, upon the persons named in paragraph (6) hereof who are non-domiciliaries, or whose names or whereabouts are unknown and cannot be ascertained; and (c) that such Last Will be admitted to probate as a will of real and personal property and that letters issue thereon as follows:

(Check and complete appropriate request.)

☒ Letters Testamentary to .... **Elizabeth R. Brown and John Brown as coexecutors** ....

☐ Letters of Trusteeship to ....

Dated: .... **January 15, 19** ....

....
(Petitioner)

....
(Petitioner)

STATE OF NEW YORK }
County of **New York** } ss.:

COMBINED VERIFICATION, OATH
AND DESIGNATION

(For use when a petitioner to be appointed executor is not a bank or trust company)

We ⅀, the undersigned .... **Elizabeth R. Brown and John Brown** ....

being duly sworn, say:

(1) VERIFICATION: **We** ⅀ have read the foregoing petition subscribed by **us** and know the contents thereof, and the same is true of **our** own knowledge, except as to the matters therein stated to be alleged upon information and belief, and as to those matters ⅀ believe it to be true.

(2) OATH OF EXECUTOR: **We are each** over twenty-one (21) years of age and ⅀ citizens of the United States; **we are** not ineligible to receive letters; **we are** the executors named in the Last Will described in the foregoing petition and will well, faithfully and honestly discharge the duties of such executors, and **shall** duly account for all moneys or other property which may come into **our** hands.

(3) DESIGNATION OF CLERK FOR SERVICES OF PROCESS: ⅀ **We** do hereby irrevocably designate the Clerk of the Surrogate's Court of New York County, and his or her successors in office, as a person on whom service of any process issuing from such Surrogate's Court may be made, in like manner and with like effect as if it were served personally upon **us** whenever ⅀ cannot be found and served within the State of New York after due diligence used.

Our domicile **is** .... **are 214 East 17th Street, New York City, N.Y. 10003.** ....

....
(Signatures of Petitioners)

On .... **January 15,** ...., 19 ....., before me personally came ..... **Elizabeth R. Brown** ..... **and John Brown** .... to me known to be the persons described in and who executed the foregoing instrument. Such persons duly swore to such instrument before me and duly acknowledged that .... **they had** .... executed the same.

....
(Notary Public)

Figure 19.5. *Petition for Probate of Will (Page 3).*

6. The petition indicates the kind of legacy, as well as its value. You can get this information from the will. Thus, the testator might leave the residue of the estate in trust for the testator's spouse, the remainder to go to the children upon the death of the spouse. The petition would show that

I, the undersigned, a . . . . of
(Title)

. . . .
(Name of Bank or Trust Company)
being duly sworn, say:

(1) VERIFICATION: I have read the foregoing petition subscribed by me and known the contents thereof, and the same is true of my own knowledge, except as to the matters therein stated to be alleged upon information and belief, and as to those matters I believe it to be true.

(2) CONSENT: . . . . , a corporation/national banking association under the laws of . . . . hereby accepts its appointment as executor of the Last Will described in the foregoing petition and consents to act as such executor.

(3) DESIGNATION: . . . . , a corporation/national banking association under the laws of . . . . , having an office at . . . . hereby designates the Clerk of the Surrogate's Court of . . . . County, and his or her successor in office, as a person on whom service of any process issuing from such Surrogate's Court may be made, in like manner and with like effect as if it were served personally upon such corporation/national banking association, whenever one of its proper officers cannot be found and served within the State of New York, after due diligence used.

. . . .

. . . .
(Signature and Title)

. . . .
(Name of Bank or Trust Company)

By: . . . .
(Signature and Title)

ATTEST:

. . . .
(Signature and Title)

On . . . . ,19 . . . . ,before me personally came . . . .
. . . . , to me known, who duly swore to the foregoing instrument and who did say that he resides at . . . .
and that he is a . . . . of . . . .
the corporation/national banking association described in and which executed such instrument; that he knows the seal of such . . . . ;
that the seal affixed to such instrument is such seal and was so affixed by order of the Board of Directors of such . . . . and that he signed his name thereto by like authority.

. . . .
(Notary Public)

ATTORNEY

Name of Attorney . . . . Albert Anderson . . . . Tel. No. 212.971-1678. .
Address of Attorney . . . 393.Seventh Avenue, New York City, N.Y. 10001. . . . .

[Editor's note: When the petitioner seeking appointment as executor is a bank or trust company, the above form of combined verification, consent and designation is used.]

Figure 19.6. *Petition for Probate of Will (Page 4).*

the spouse was the *beneficiary of a residuary trust,* and that the children were given a *remainder interest in the residuary trust.*

If the testator does not place the residue of the estate in trust but leaves it outright to someone, the petition indicates that the person is the *residuary legatee.*

When specific personal property, rather than a sum of money, is bequeathed, the bequest is indicated in the petition as a *specific legacy.*

7. Arrange for the petitioners to come in and sign the petition.

8. Have the petitioners verify the petition. The illustrated petition has a form of verification by an individual printed on it (figure 19.6). When the petitioner, or one of them, is a corporation, use the form in figure 19.6.

9. Conform your office copy.

10. File the original of the petition, the original and certified copy of the will, and the transfer tax affidavit (see below) in the probate court.

11. Mark on your office copy the date the petition was filed.

12. Make entry to suit register.

19.8. Transfer tax affidavit. A *transfer tax affidavit* is filed with the petition. This is a sworn statement about the totals of realty and personality affected by the will and of the names, amounts of legacies, residences, and relationship of those who receive gifts under the will. The affidavit supplies the state taxing authorities with data to be used by them for taxing purposes. It is typed on a printed form supplied by the taxing commissioner.

19.9. Citation and waiver in probate proceeding. The Surrogate's Court Act of New York provides that the surviving spouse, distributees, and executors and trustees named in the decedent's will must be given notice of the petition for probate by service of a *citation*. Probate acts of other states have similar provisions. The citation is a legal writ citing those to whom it is addressed to appear in court on a certain date and show cause why the will should not be admitted to probate. It does not *command* an appearance like a summons does. Those who do not wish to contest the will need not appear in court. A citation is issued by the clerk of the court, but is prepared by the petitioner's attorney.

Any person over eighteen may serve a citation. Service is made by delivering a copy to the person upon whom it is served. If an infant is a distributee, the citation is addressed to the infant but is served upon the parent with whom the infant resides or upon the infant's guardian. If an infant is over fourteen, service is made upon the distributee, as well as the distributee's parent or guardian.

Service of citation by publication and mailing. If any of the distributees live outside the state, or if there are any heirs or next of kin whose names and place of residence are unknown, service is had upon them by publication and mailing. The procedure is similar to that in a civil action (page 592).

Adults may *waive* the issuance and source of a citation in the matter of proving the last will and testament of the deceased, but infants may not. Thus, before the citations are prepared, waivers are secured.

19.10. How to prepare a waiver of citation. Figure 19.7 illustrates a properly completed form of waiver.

UF Form C   9265-69 (C.S.)   94

State of New York
Surrogate's Court, County of New York

Probate Proceeding, Will of

EDGAR BROWN

Deceased.

}
Waiver and Consent

P 1234   19 _ _

To the Surrogate's Court, New York County:
We, Elizabeth R. Brown and John Brown

the undersigned, being of full age and residing at   214 East 17th Street, New York City, N.Y. 10003

distributee s of   Edgar Brown   , late of the County of New York, deceased, do   hereby waive the issue and service of a citation in the matter of proving the Last Will and Testament of said   Edgar Brown   , deceased, and consent that said instrument bearing date   November 23, 19 _ _ be admitted to probate forthwith.

Dated,   New York City, January,   19_ _

....
....
....
....

STATE OF NEW YORK }
     ss.:
COUNTY OF New York }

   On this   day of   January.........., 19_ _, before me personally came Elizabeth R. Brown and John Brown   , to me known and know to me to be the individuals described in and who executed the foregoing waiver and consent, and who acknowledged that   they   executed the same.

....
(Notary Stamp)

[N.B.—If the acknowledgment is taken outside the State of New York, a certificate of the officer's authority must be attached.]

Figure 19.7. *Waiver of Citation in Probate Proceeding.*

1. Make an original for the court and an office copy.

2. Have those who waive citation sign the original in the presence of two witnesses.

3. Take the acknowledgment of those signing the waiver.

4. Conform office copy, marking on it the date the original is filed.

5. File original in court.

6. Make entry in suit register.

19.11. How to prepare a citation. Figure 19.8 illustrates a properly completed form of citation in probate proceedings.

1. Make an original for the court, an office copy, and a copy for each person to be served. In the illustrated case 5 copies must be made—an original for the court; an office copy; a copy for service upon Robert Brown, an infant over fourteen; a copy for service upon his mother in his behalf; a copy for service upon the mother of Irene Brown, an infant under fourteen. The adult distributees waived citation.

2. The return date may be any date within the time allowed by the court rules.

3. Get the clerk of the court to sign the original.

4. Conform copies and give original and copies (except office copy) to person who is to serve the citation.

5. Prepare affidavit of service, which is usually printed on the back of the citation (figure 19.9), and have the person who served the citation sign and swear to the affidavit in the presence of a notary.

6. Conform office copy, marking on it the date the original is filed in court.

7. File original in court.

8. *Enter in diary* return date of citation.

9. Make entry in suit register.

19.12. Preparations for hearing. The hearing in an uncontested probate proceeding is rather informal. The lawyer for the petitioners appears before the clerk of the court with the witnesses to the will. The date of the hearing is the return day indicated in the citation. (In some jurisdictions the clerk of the court sets the date for hearing at the time the petition is filed.) You will have to make certain preparations before the hearing:

1. Prepare deposition of witnesses.

2. Notify witnesses to the will.

3. Prepare and mail notice of probate.

4. Prepare oath of executor.

Form 1   SURROGATE'S COURT PROCEDURE

Form No. 1

File No. _____, 19__.

CITATION

The People of the State of New York,
By the Grace of God Free and Independent,

To _____

A petition having been duly filed by _____, who is domiciled at _____,

YOU ARE HEREBY CITED TO SHOW CAUSE before the Surrogate's Court, _____ County, at _____ in the County of _____ on 19__, at __M., why a decree should not be made in the estate of _____, lately domiciled at _____, in the County of _____, [*state relief sought*]

Dated, Attested and Sealed, _____, 19__.

(L.S.)   Surrogate

                                            Clerk.

ATTORNEY

Name of attorney _____Tel. No._____

Address of attorney _____

This citation is served upon you as required by law.   You are not obliged to appear in person.   If you fail to appear it will be assumed that you do not object to the relief requested.   You have a right to have an attorney-at-law appear for you.

> Note.—If affidavit of service be made outside the State of New York, it must be authenticated in the manner prescribed by CPLR 2101, 2309.

Figure 19.8. *Waiver of Citation in Probate Proceeding.*

[Note.—If affidavit of service be made
outside the State of New York, it must be
authenticated in the manner prescribed
by CPLR Sec. 2309 (c).]

AFFIDAVIT OF SERVICE OF CITATION

State of New York
County of . New York..
                                                          ss.:

........Matthew. Davis..................

of . 33 Sylvia Lane, Mineola,.N.Y. 11501, being duly sworn, says that   he is over the
age of eighteen years; that   he made personal service of the within citation on the
persons named below, whom deponent knew to be the persons mentioned and described in
said citation, by delivering to and leaving with each of them personally a true copy of said
citation, as follows:

On the .29th........ day of ...January...................................... , 19 _ _

**[Specify clearly time and place of
service on each party served.]**

on .....Jacqueline Brown, in behalf of Robert Brown and Irene Brown, infants,........

at . 27 E. 40th Street, New. York City, N.Y. 10017....................................

On the ...29th......day of ...January.................................... , 196

on . Robert Brown, an infant over fourteen years of age,............................

at 27 E. 40th Street, New York City, N.Y. 10017..................................

On the .... day of .... , 19

on ....

at ....

On the .... day of .... , 19

on ....

at ....

On the .... day of .... , 19

on ....

at ....

Sworn to before me this 3rd

day of   February   , 19 _ _ .

(Notary Stamp)

[N.B.—The original citation together with the proof of service thereon must be
filed in the Probate Department not later than 1:00 P.M. on the day preceding the
return day of citation.]

Figure 19.9. *Affidavit of Service of Citation.*

5. Prepare decree.

6. Prepare letters testamentary; also letters of trusteeship if the petition prays for them.

19.13. Notice of probate. The legatees and devisees who are not heirs-at-law must be given *notice* that the will has been offered for probate. The printed form of notice calls for the name and address of the proponents (the petitioners) and for a list of the names and addresses of the legatees, devisees, and beneficiaries who have not been cited or have not waived citation.

1. Make an original for the court, an office copy, and a copy for each person listed in the notice.

2. The notices may be sent by mail. The attorney for the petitioners makes affidavit of service by mail on the back of the notice.

3. Notarize the affidavit made by the attorney.

4. Conform the office copy.

5. Place the original with the papers that the lawyer will take to the hearing.

6. Make entry in suit register that the notices were mailed.

19.14. Deposition of witnesses to the will. As soon as you know the date of the hearing, notify the witnesses to the will of the time and place of the hearing. You can get their names and addresses from the will. If the witnesses are not available, the lawyer will have to take other legal steps to prove the will. Make an entry of the notice in your suit register.

Printed forms of depositions are available.

1. Prepare an original and an office copy for each witness. Thus, if there are two witnesses, you will prepare two sets of depositions.

2. Do not date the depositions. They are signed and sworn to before an officer of the court, who dates them at that time.

3. Place the originals with the papers that the lawyer will take to the hearing.

4. Draw checks to witnesses for fee allowed by law. The lawyer will probably take the checks to the hearing and pay the witnesses at that time; otherwise mail the checks after the depositions are taken.

19.15. Oath of executor. An executor must take an *oath* to faithfully perform the duties of executor. Printed forms are available.

1. Prepare an original and an office copy for each executor. Thus if there are two executors, you will prepare two sets of oaths.

2. Each executor signs the original of the oath in the presence of a notary.

3. Conform your office copies.

4. Place the originals with the papers the lawyer will take to the hearing.

5. Make an entry in the suit register that the oaths have been executed.

19.16. Decree admitting will to probate. A *decree* in a probate proceeding serves the same purpose as an order or judgment in a civil action. A favorable decree admits the will to probate and directs that letters testamentary issue to the executor nominated in the will. The probate judge (the surrogate in New York) signs the decree, but the petitioner's attorney prepares it. Printed forms are available.

1. Make an original for the court and a copy for your office file.

2. Do not date the decree. It will be dated when the judge signs it.

3. Place the original with the papers the lawyer will take to the hearing.

4. The decree might not be signed for several days after the hearing. *Make a follow-up entry in your diary* for a few days after the hearing and inquire of the clerk of the court if it has been signed.

5. Mark on your office copy the date the decree was signed.

6. Make entry in the suit register.

19.17. Letters testamentary. After the judge signs the decree, the clerk of the court issues *letters testamentary* to the executor. The attorney for the executor prepares the letters. They are the evidence of the executor's authority to act. Anyone dealing with the executor as the representative of the estate will require a certificate to the effect that letters have been issued and are still in force. Certificates are available from the clerk of the court for a small fee.

1. Prepare an original, or duplicate original, for each executor, an office copy, and a sufficient number of copies to be certified by the clerk of the court. Thus, if there are two executors, prepare three copies in addition to the copies to be certified. There must be a certified copy for each bank account, each security issue, each safe deposit box, and the like.

2. If there are two or more executors, all of them are named in the letters.

3. Do not date the letters. The clerk of the court will date them when they are issued.

4. Place the original and duplicate original with the papers that the lawyer will take to the hearing. The clerk will sign a copy for each executor named in the letters and return them to your office.

5. Conform your office copy

6. Deliver a signed copy to each executor. If executor, the lawyer will retain one of the signed copies.

7. Make entries in suit register.

19.18. Notice to creditors. As soon as letters testamentary are issued, notice to creditors should be published in a local newspaper. Creditors of the decedent are given a certain time in which to file any claims they may have against the decedent. *Enter in your diary* the last day the creditors have to present claims.

Newspapers usually have a printed form of notice to creditors that you can fill in without any difficulty. Within a specified time after the last publication, affidavit of publication is filed with the clerk of the court. The publisher makes the affidavit of publication and delivers it to either the clerk of the court or the attorney. *Enter in your diary* the date by which the affidavit must be filed; also make entries in your suit register.

APPOINTMENT OF ADMINISTRATOR

19.19. Application for letters of administration. When a person dies without leaving a will, a person who is an adult (18 or older in most states) of sound mind, and entitled by law to share in his estate, may ask to be appointed administrator of the estate. He does this by applying to the probate court for *letters of administration.* The procedure is governed by statute but is more or less similar in all of the states.

19.20. Parties. The person who files an application for letters of administration is known as the *petitioner.* There are no plaintiffs and defendants—the petitioner does not bring a suit against someone else—but there are other necessary and interested parties. Those nearer of kin to the deceased than the petitioner have a prior right to be appointed; those of an equal decree of kinship have an equal right to be appointed. The kin of the decedent in these two categories are, therefore, necessary parties to the proceeding and are made parties to it by the service of a citation (see page 506), unless they waive citation.

All of those who are entitled by law to share in the intestate's estate— the *distributees*—are interested parties to the proceeding, although they may not be entitled to letters of administration. For example, a minor child of the deceased, or a minor child of his prior deceased child, are distributees of the estate and are interested parties. They are not served with citations because they cannot serve as administrators, but they are given notice of the application for letters of administration.

19.21. Who has prior right to letters of administration. The statutes provide the order of *priority* by which distributees of the decedent's estate are entitled to letters of administration. The usual order is:

1. Surviving spouse
2. Children
3. Grandchildren
4. Parents
5. Brothers and sisters
6. Nephews and nieces

19.22. Necessary papers in application for letters of administration. Printed forms of papers that must be prepared by the attorney and filed in an application for letters of administration are usually available, and the courts prefer that they be used. The forms are not uniform, varying even from county to county within a state, but they are similar. In every state, there is a petition for letters of administration, an oath of administrator, and a notice in some form to interested parties. In New York County, the papers consist of the following:

1. Petition for letters of administration ⎰ Frequently combined
2. Oath of administrator　　　　　　　 ⎱　　in one paper
3. Designation of the clerk of the court as a person on whom service of process may be made (sometimes combined with petition and oath)
4. Renunciation, if any
5. Citation
6. Notice of application for letters of administration, if necessary

19.23. How to prepare petition; oath; designation of clerk. Figures 19.10 to 19.13 illustrate a printed form, used in New York County, that combines a petition for letters of administration, oath of administrator, and designation of clerk of the court as a person on whom service of process may be made. The form is basically similar to forms used in other states.

The lawyer will give you a memorandum of the factual information necessary to fill in the form.

1. Prepare an original and one copy of the petition.
2. Fill in the blanks not only in the petition but also in the form of verification, oath, and designation of clerk, even if they are on separate forms.
3. The petition must be verified.
4. Arrange for the client to come in and sign the petition when it is ready.

Form 17   7734-66 (C.S.) ◄═══ 94

Surrogate's Court, County of New York

Proceeding for Letters of Administration,
                    Estate of
            JAMES PURCELL

....
                                          Deceased.

                              **Petition for
                              Letters of Administration**

                              File No. ..3636 - 19...............

To the Surrogate's Court, County of New York:

It is respectfully alleged:

(1) The name, domicile and interest in this proceeding of the petitioner, who is of full age, is as follows:

Name _____ **Peter Purcell** _____

Domicile __ **123 West 4th Street, New York City, N.Y. 10011** _____

_____

                         (Street and Number)

_____
        (City, Village or Town)   (State)

Interest of
Petitioner:
(check one)

(**x**) Distributee of decedent, to wit _____ **son** _____
                                          (Relationship)

( ) Other (specify) _____

Citizenship _____ **United States** _____

(2) The following are the particulars respecting the above named decedent:

(a) Name _____ **James Purcell** _____

(b) Date of Death: _____ **January 5, 19__** _____ Place of Death: _____ **New York City, N.Y.**

(c) Domicile: Street ___ **123 West 4th Street, New York City, N.Y. 10011.** _____

City, Village or Town: _____

County: ____ **New York** _____ State: ____ **New York** _____

(d) Citizenship _____ **United States** _____

(3) Your petitioner has made diligent search and inquiry for a will of the decedent and has not found any and has been unable to obtain any information concerning any will of the decedent and therefore alleges upon information and belief that the decedent died without leaving any last will.

(4) Search of the records of this court shows that no application has ever been made for letters of administration upon the estate of the decedent or for the probate of a will of the decedent and your petitioner is informed and verily believes that no such application has ever been made to the Surrogate's Court of any other county of this State.

(5) The decedent left surviving:
(a) (**1**) Spouse ~~(husband)~~(wife)
(b) (**1**) Child ~~or children or descendants of predeceased child or children.~~
(c) (**No**) Father/mother.
(d) (**No**) Brothers or sisters, either of the whole or half-blood; or descendants of such predeceased brothers or sisters.
(e) (**No**) Grandfather-grandmother.
(f) (**x**) Uncles or aunts.
(g) (**x**) Descendants of predeceased uncles or aunts.

(Information is required only as to those classes of surviving relatives who would take the property of decedent if there were no will. The term "child or children" includes adopted as well as natural children. State number of survivors in each such class. Insert "X" in all subsequent classes. Insert "No" in all prior classes.

Figure 19.10. *Petition for Letters of Administration, Oath, and Designation of Clerk (Page 1).*

(6) The decedent left surviving the following DISTRIBUTEES, whose names, degrees of relationship, domicile, post-office addresses and citizenship are as follows:

(a) The following who are of full age and sound mind:

Name	Relationship	Domicile and Post-office Address	Citizenship
Amy Purcell	Wife	123 W.4th St.,N.Y. City, N.Y. 10011.	United States
Peter Purcell	Son	Same	United States

(b) The following who are persons under disability:
(Please furnish all information specified in NOTE below.)

NONE

NOTE: In the case of each infant, state (a) name, birth date, age, relationship to decedent, domicile residence address and the person with whom he resides; (b) whether or not he has a guardian or testamentary guardian and whether or not his father, or if dead, his mother, is living and (c) the name and address of any guardian and any living parent. In the case of each other person under disability, state (a) name, relationship to decedent and residence address, (b) facts regarding his disability, including whether or not he has been committed to any institution and (c) the names and addresses of any relative or friend having an interest in his welfare. In the case of person confined as a prisoner, state place of incarceration. In the case of unknowns describe such persons in the same language as will be used in the process. In each case give a brief description of the party's interest in the estate.)

Figure 19.11. *Petition for Letters of Administration, Oath, and Designation of Clerk (Page 2).*

(7) Decedent was the owner of and died possessed of certain PERSONAL PROPERTY, the value of which ~~does~~ exceed~~s~~ the sum of $ 100,000

(8) Decedent died seized of REAL PROPERTY, in this state which is ~~improved/~~unimproved (strike out one), the estimated value of which does not exceed $ 25,000

The estimated gross rents for a period of eighteen months is the sum of $ none

A brief description of each parcel is as follows:

Approximately five acres of unimproved land lying in the Town of Port Jefferson, County of Suffolk, State of New York on the northeast corner of Setauket Highway and Terryville Drive.

(9) In addition to the value of the personal property stated in paragraph (7) hereof, the following right of action existed on behalf of the decedent and survived his death, or is granted to the administrator of the decedent by special provision of law, and it is impractical to give a bond sufficient to cover the probable amount to be recovered therein: (Write "None," or state briefly the cause of action and the person against whom it exists.)

NONE

(10) There are no other persons than those mentioned hereinbefore who have an interest in this application or proceeding.

WHEREFORE your petitioner respectfully prays: (Check and complete all relief requested.)

(a) (X) That process issue to all necessary parties to show cause why letters should not be issued as hereinafter requested;

(b) (X) That an order be granted dispensing with service of process upon those persons named in Paragraph (6) hereof who have a right to letters prior or equal to that of the person hereinafter nominated therefor, and who are non-domiciliaries of whose names or whereabouts are unknown and cannot be ascertained;

(c) (X) That a decree award Letters of Administration of the estate of the decedent to

Peter Purcell

or to such other person or persons having a prior right as may be entitled thereto ~~hereunder~~.

(d) ( ) That the authority of the representative under the foregoing letters be limited with

respect to _____

_____

_____

Dated: New York City, January 24, 19__

_____

_____
(Signature(s) of Petitioner)

Figure 19.12. *Petition for Letters of Administration, Oath, and Designation of Clerk (Page 3).*

STATE OF NEW YORK
COUNTY OF **NEW YORK** } ss.:

Combined Verification, Oath and Designation
(For Use When Petitioner Is To Be
Appointed Administrator)

I, the undersigned, the petitioner named in the foregoing petition, being duly sworn, say:

(1) VERIFICATION: I have read the foregoing petition subscribed by me and know the contents thereof, and the same is true of my own knowledge, except as to the matters therein stated to be alleged upon information and belief, and as to those matters I believe it to be true.

(2) OATH OF ADMINISTRATOR: I am over twenty-one (21) years of age and a citizen of the United States; and I will well, faithfully and honestly discharge the duties of Administrator (trix) of the goods, chattels and credits of said decedent according to law, and duly account for all moneys or other property which may come into my hands. I am not ineligible to receive letters.

(3) DESIGNATION OF CLERK FOR SERVICE OF PROCESS: I do hereby designate the Clerk of the Surrogate's Court of New York County, and his or her successor in office, as a person on whom service of any process issuing from such Surrogate's Court may be made in like manner and with like effect as if it were served personally upon me, whenever I cannot be found and served within the State of New York after due diligence used. If I shall change my address so stated I shall promptly notify the court of my new address.

My domicile is __123 West 4th Street, New York City, N.Y. 10011__
(State complete address)

_____

_____
(Signature(s) of Petitioner)

On __January 24,__ , 19___, before me personally came

__Peter Purcell__
to me known to be the person described in and who executed the foregoing instrument. Such person duly swore to such instrument before me and duly acknowledged that he executed the same.

_____
(Notary Public)

ATTORNEY

Name of Attorney __Gabriel Henry__ Tel. No. __212 - 516 - 7700__

Address of Attorney __521 Fifth Avenue, New York, N.Y. 10017.__

Estate of	File No.	Date of Death	Petition filed	Cit. returnable	Sup. cit. returnable	Decree signed	Bond filed	Bond Book L	Letters dated	Letters recorded L	Surety	Amount of Bond $	Bond No.
	, 19	, 19						P.		P.			

Figure 19.13. *Petition for Letters of Administration, Oath, and Designation of Clerk (Page 4).*

5. Have the petitioner sign on the line designated in the presence of a notary public; also immediately beneath the verification, immediately beneath the oath, and immediately beneath the designation of the clerk for service of process.

6. If you are a notary, ask the petitioner to swear to the petition and to the oath (see page 501 for administration of oath) and to acknowledge the designation of the clerk (see page 514 for taking an acknowledgment).

7. Notarize the instrument.

8. Conform your copy.

9. The original is filed in court.

10. Get court file number from clerk and enter on back of office copy.

11. Make entry in suit register.

12. In some states the clerk of the court set a hearing date when the petition is filed. If this is the practice in your state, *enter hearing date in diary*.

19.24. Renunciation. Many states provide that a person who is entitled to letters of administration may renounce this right. An individual does this by signing a simple printed form like the one illustrated in figure 19.14. The *renunciation* makes it unnecessary to serve a citation on those who renounced.

19.25. Citations. All interested parties must be notified of the application for letters. The method of notifying them varies. In New York State, parties who have a prior or an equal right with the petitioner to letters of administration are made parties to the proceeding by the service of a *citation*, except those who waive citation by renunciation of their right to letters of administration. The writ is signed by the clerk of the probate court (surrogate's court in New York), but is prepared by the attorney for the petitioner. It cites the person or persons upon whom it is served to appear before the court on a certain date and show cause why the letters of administration should not be granted to the petitioner. The person cited does not have to appear in court or reply in any way unless he opposes the appointment of the petitioner. Service is had in the same manner as service of citation in a proceeding to prove a will (see page 493). Printed forms of citations are available. They are similar to, but not the same as, the form used in a proceeding to prove a will.

1. The citation does not have a caption.

2. Address the citation to those distributees who have a right prior or equal to that of the petitioner to letters of administration. You can get the names and addresses of those to whom the citation is to be addressed from the petition.

Form 19   7733-68 (C.S.) ◄═══► 94

Surrogate's Court, County of New York

Proceeding for Letters of Administration,

Estate of

JAMES PURCELL

                                    Deceased.

Renunciation of
Letters of
Administration and
Waiver of Process

The undersigned, being of full age and a distributee of the decedent above-named being related as

_____wife_____ and whose domiciliary address is _123 West 4th Street, New York City,_
State relationship   Street and Number

New York 10011.
City, Village or Town   State

hereby personally appears in the Surogate's Court of New York County and

    (1) renounces all rights to Letters of Administration upon the estate of said decedent,

    (2) waives the issuance and service of process in this matter, and

    (3) consents that such Letters of Administration may be granted by the Surrogate to any other person or persons entitled thereto without any notice whatsoever to the undersigned.

Dated: _January 24, 19__   _____

State of____New York____ ⎫
                          ⎬ ss.:
County of____New York____ ⎭

On_____24th day of January_____, 19 __ , before me personally came

Amy Purcell
_____,

to me personally known to be the same person described in and who executed the foregoing instrument, and to me such person duly acknowledged that~~he~~ she executed the same.

_____
Notary Public

(NOTE: If acknowledgment taken outside New York State, Clerk's Certificate must be attached.)

Figure 19.14. *Renunciation of Letters of Administration and Waiver of Process.*

3. Make an original for the court, a copy for each person to whom the citation is addressed, and an office copy.

4. The return date of the citation may be any date within the time allowed by the court rules. In some jurisdictions the date is set by the clerk of the court when the petition is filed.

5. Get the court clerk to sign the original.

6. Conform the copies and serve.

7. Make affidavit of service.

8. *Enter return date in diary.*

9. Make entry in suit register, and follow the court calendar just as in a contested action.

19.26. Notice of application for letters of administration. In New York State, distributees who do not have a right to letters of administration equal to that of the petitioner are not served with a citation but are *notified* of the application. Printed forms are available.

1. Make an original for the court, a copy for each distributee entitled to the notice, and an office copy.

2. The notice of application may be dated at any time subsequent to the filing of the petition, before the issuance of the letters.

3. Have the petitioner sign the notice.

4. Mail copies of the notice to each distributee entitled to it at the address given in the petition.

5. Make affidavit that notice was mailed.

6. Conform office copy and file original in court.

7. Enter in suit register.

19.27. Letters of administration. If there is no opposition to the appointment of the petitioner as administrator, the court enters a decree directing that *letters of administration* issue to the petitioner. The letters of administration serve the same purpose for the administrator as letters testamentary do for the executor. The attorney for the petitioner prepares the decree and the letters in the same manner as when a will is admitted to probate and letters testamentary are granted (see page 499).

As soon as letters of administration are granted, notice to creditors must be published. See notice to creditors after letters testamentary are granted, on page 500. Be sure and make appropriate *diary entries* and suit register entries.

20

HANDLING COMMERCIAL COLLECTIONS

Commercial items, that is, past due accounts, that the lawyer undertakes to collect for others are referred to as *collections*. Collections may be turned over to the lawyer by local clients, or they may be forwarded from another town by a collection agency or by another lawyer. Commercial collections have become a specialty in the legal profession. Some law offices handle collections almost exclusively. Others handle few, if any, and refer most to the specialists. Unless suit is filed, collections are usually handled on a contingent fee basis at rates suggested by the Commercial Law League. Although some commercial items involve large amounts, the majority of them are for small sums, with a correspondingly small fee. It is, therefore, desirable in the case of small items to curtail the usual office procedure as much as is consistent with efficiency. Collections are usually segregated from the other cases and are handled in a special manner. The procedure is routine and, after it has been established, the secretary and paralegal can assume responsibility for the entire operation of the collection department.

20.1. Commercial law lists. Lawyers who want to handle the collection of commercial items obtain representation on one or more bonded commercial law lists. It is from these lists that out-of-town lawyers select an attorney in the debtor's locality to handle the claim. It is from these lists that the lawyers in your office will select attorneys to whom to forward accounts against debtors in another jurisdiction.

Usually the forwarder of an item will mention the law list from which the lawyer's name was obtained. Some lists produce better results than others. You, therefore, should keep a record of the items the lawyer receives through each list and the fees earned by reason of representation on that list. The lawyer can then determine whether continued representation on a special list is warranted. A simple record is sufficient. Keep a separate sheet for each law list and show on it the forwarder, the item (creditor, debtor, and amount), and, when the matter is closed, the amount of the fee. You might keep these sheets in a folder in the front of the file drawer in which the collection cases are filed.

    20.2. Office procedures affecting collections. The office procedures affecting collections involve the following:

1. Files
2. Follow-up system
3. Acknowledgment of claim
4. Letters to debtor
5. Reports to forwarder
6. Records of collections
7. Remittances to forwarder
8. Forwarding collection items
9. Suit

    20.3. How to file collection matters. As soon as a collection item is received, make a file folder for it. File the folders alphabetically under the debtor's name. The creditor-client is not given a number, nor is the case. In conformance with the policy of keeping office procedure at a minimum, file index cards are not made. If your office prefers that index cards should be made, use plain 3″ by 5″ cards and keep them separate from your other index cards. Show on the card the name of the creditor, the name of the debtor, and the name of the forwarder. When the numbering system of filing is used for collections, cross-reference index cards are, of course, essential.

    When suit is brought on a collection, the case is transferred to a legal folder and handled like any other litigated case. Since default judgment is obtained in the majority of collection cases, considerable clerical work can be saved by not transferring the file unless the suit is contested.

    20.4. Filing system. One method of following collections is to use a file folder that has the days of the month printed on the top edge of the

		5 part	ACR	PHONE:			
		1					
		2					
		3					
		4					
		5					
		6					
		7					
		9					
		10					
		11					
		12					
		13					
		14					
		15					
		16					

DISTRICT / CIRCUIT		PAID	AMOUNT	REC'D	AMOUNT			
/								
RE-ISSUE								
RE-ISSUE								
SUPERIOR								
ATTORNEY'S FEE								
ORDER TO RECORD/LIEN								
DOCKET ENTRIES								
SHERIFF								
SUP. PROCEEDINGS								
TESTIMONY								
RE-ISSUE								
CONTEMPT								
FI-FA								
FI-FA								
GARNISHEE								
GARNISHEE								
CERT. COPY OF JUDGMENT								
ASSIGNMENTS								
APPRAISAL								
TITLE REPORT								
FORECLOSURE								
AUCTIONER								

Courtesy Commercial Law League of America

Figure 20.1. *Front Page of Collection Folder Showing Extra Columns with Blank Spaces to Use for Follow-up.*

ARRANGEMENTS:

DATE	BANK	NO	DEBT	COSTS	FEE	OTHER	TOTAL

Figure 20.2. *Inside of Collection Folder Showing Columns for Various Financial Transactions.*

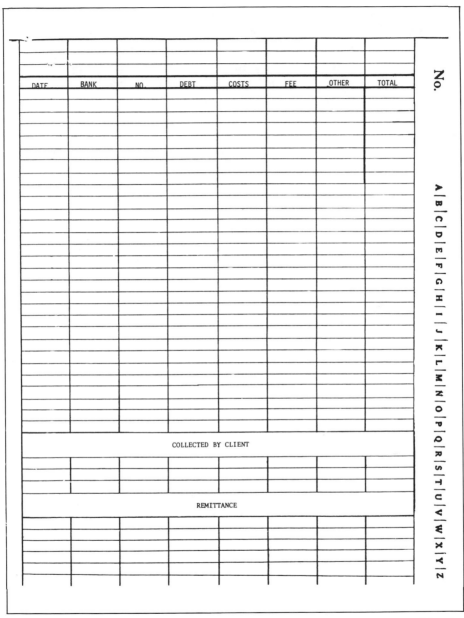

Figure 20.2. *Continued.*

folder. Folders without any printed matter except the days of the month are also obtainable. A metal tab is placed on the date that the file should come up for action, and the folder is filed alphabetically under the name of the debtor. Thus, regardless of the follow-up date, the folder is always in its proper alphabetical position in the filing cabinet. Each morning you pull all folders that have the metal tab placed on the current date. After the necessary action is taken, the metal tab is moved to the date on which the file again should come up for action.

Another popular method of follow-up for collections is a follow-up file with the folders tabbed so they can be located alphabetically. Figures 20.1 and 20.2 show a popular letter-sized folder that can be used for small- or large-volume collections. As you can see, the folder has several columns for follow-up dates, spaces for court records, executions, and so on, as well as the costs and payments involved. Inside the folder are more columns for the various financial transactions. A white tab with the debtor's name can be placed on the top back of the folder.

Each file drawer, if more than one is necessary, is arranged as a follow-up file, with guides for the months and dates. Each drawer is operated as a separate follow-up file, in the same manner as the follow-up system described in chapter 3. How can a folder be located if it is needed before the follow-up date? The letters of the alphabet printed near the top edge of the front leaf of the folder make this possible. A small gummed tab marked with the debtor's name is pasted on the back leaf of the folder, opposite the index letter printed near the top of the front leaf. Thus, the name *Jones* is on the folder opposite *J*; the name *Smith* is opposite *S*, and so on. It makes no difference under what date the folder is filed, the *J*'s are always in one line in one position in the file, and so is each letter of the alphabet. By looking at the proper line, you can easily find the proper folder at any time. The folder can be returned to the correct follow-up date, because the last date in the space for follow-up dates, on the front of the folder, shows where it is to be filed. This system simplifies the task of pulling the folders each morning, because all folders to be brought up on a certain date are together. It also eliminates moving the metal tabs, which are sometimes difficult to move without tearing the folder.

20.5. Acknowledgment of claim. Simultaneously with the preparation of the folder, the claim should be acknowledged. Promptness in acknowledging the collection is very important, because the forwarder is naturally interested in knowing that the matter is receiving immediate attention. The acknowledgment might read:

Dear Sir:

Re: Jones Brothers, Inc. v. F.M. Wilson
Amount $345

We acknowledge receipt of the above claim and accept the claim for collection on the basis of the terms and regulations of the Commercial Law League of America.

Since you are recognized as the client's agency, we will report developments and make remittances directly to you.

Sincerely yours,

Elwood & Adams

Firms that handle a large volume of collection accounts often use a snap-out form, with the firm's name and address printed at the top, for acknowledgments, initial collection letters, and file identification.

20.6. Collection letters. In a comparatively small community, the attorney frequently knows the debtor against whom there is a collection claim. Handling the collection is often tempered by the personal relationship, but in normal cases the lawyer proceeds promptly and vigorously. You will probably be called upon to draft collection letters. If so, keep these premises in mind:

1. The purpose of the letter is to collect money; therefore, do not hesitate to ask for a check.

2. Do not take the attitude that the account "probably has been overlooked," because numerous demands for payment are made before the account is given to an attorney.

3. Use *dated action*. That is, tell the debtor that a certain action is expected by a given date, or within a given number of days, not in the "near future."

4. The *divided urge* is a serious fault in a collection letter. Suggest only one course of action—do not mention an alternative. For example, do not tell the debtor that you expect a check by a certain date and then suggest that he should telephone if payment is impossible.

5. The period between letters should be short—from 5 to 10 days.

A first letter to the debtor from the attorney on May 3 might read:

Dear Mr. Wilson:

Jones Brothers, Inc. has retained us to collect your past due account in the amount of $345.

Since this account has been delinquent for six months, it is imperative that you give it your immediate attention. Please let us have your check in full by May 8.

Sincerely yours,

After this letter is written, mark your file for follow-up for May 10. If the debtor does not reply by that date, you might send another letter that reads:

Dear Mr. Wilson:

We have received no reply to our letter of May 3 concerning your past due account with Jones Brothers, Inc. in the amount of $345. We will be compelled, therefore, to bring suit against you for the above amount, together with costs, disbursements, and interest, unless your check in full payment is received at this office by May 15.

Sincerely yours,

20.7. Reports to the forwarder. The forwarder is interested in developments. As soon as contact is made with the debtor, write to the forwarder telling what the prospects for collection are. It is helpful to the forwarder to send reports in duplicate, especially those in which the lawyer recommends suit or some special arrangement. The forwarder can then send a copy to the client, thus saving the time and trouble involved in copying the report.

20.8. Installment payments. Suit to collect a small sum is a last resort. It is expensive, and the judgment may be as difficult to collect as the debt. For this reason, attorneys will "play along" with a debtor and accept partial payments. Usually the arrangement is that the debtor will pay a certain amount at regular intervals. As a matter of fact, an arrangement of this type is often made even after judgment is obtained against the debtor. It is your responsibility to bring up the file for attention on the dates that payments are due. If a payment is not made as promised, you should communicate with the debtor, either by telephone or mail and keep a record of such communications on your file folder (see figures 20.1 and 20.2).

20.9. Record of collections. A payment on an account, whether in full or part, is *noted on the file folder* (figures 20.1 and 20.2) as soon as it is received. If you use a plain folder, simply enter the date and the amount received. All entries should be made in ink. The payments are also entered in the journal and posted to the client's ledger account in the same manner as payments in any other kind of case. The amount of bookkeeping involved is one of the drawbacks to accepting partial payments.

When a collection is made, put it in the trust account (see chapter 6). It is the client's money and should not be commingled with the firm's funds. The fee may be deposited to the firm account.

20.10. Remitting. As soon as any money is collected, remit promptly to the forwarder, after deducting the fee. This is a "must" in handling collections. If it is necessary to collect an account in installments, report the details to the forwarder and have an understanding about when and how often an accumulation of small payments will be remitted.

20.11. Fees. Suit fees are not contingent, but other collection fees are. The Commercial Law League of America recommends a sliding rate schedule, which is generally adhered to by lawyers who handle collections. The recommended schedule follows:

20% on the first $300
18% on $300 to $2,000; 13% over $2,000
33⅓% up to $75
$25 on claims of $75 to $125

You will have to calculate the lawyer's fee before remitting to the forwarder, because only the net is remitted. Thus, if you collect $60 on a claim, you will deduct, according to the above schedule $20 for a fee and remit $40. The $20 fee is run through the books like any other fee (chapter 6). The fee is calculated on the basis of the collections in each case, not on the total of collections for a certain client. If a claim goes to litigation, the collections lawyer will expect a noncontingent suit fee of 5 to 10 percent of the claim before suit is filed.

20.12. Forwarding an item for collection. Sometimes a claim is received for collection against a debtor in another locality. The lawyer then consults the law lists and selects the name of an attorney in the debtor's locality, to whom the claim is sent. You will make up a file for a claim that is forwarded, just as you do for claims that were forwarded to your office, and follow them in the same manner. Your letter forwarding the claim should give the name and address of the creditor, name and address of the debtor, amount of the claim, law list from which the attorney's name was selected, and the terms upon which the claim is forwarded. Your letter might read:

Dear Sir:

    Client: Henderson Jewelers, Inc.
          West Palm Beach, Florida 33602
    Debtor: David Goldstein
          324 Fourth Street, N.W., Birmingham, Ala. 35215
    Amount: $284.36

We are forwarding to you for collection the above account. This claim is sent to you on the basis of two-thirds of our fee, which is the Commercial Law League rate.

    Please acknowledge and keep us informed of developments. If you are unable to handle this account, we will appreciate it if you return it promptly. Please do not institute suit before informing us.

    We obtained your name from the .... Law List.

                                                  Sincerely yours,

    The documentary evidence necessary to collect the account should be forwarded with your letter. The evidence depends upon whether the suit is upon open account or upon an instrument. In the case of suit upon open account, you should forward: (1) copies of the original written order for the merchandise, if any; (2) copies of the invoice; and (3) copies of the bills of lading. If the suit is upon an instrument, that is, upon a dishonored trade acceptance or promissory note, the necessary documents are: (1) the trade acceptance or note; (2) the bank's memorandum of nonpayment; and (3) copies of any notices of dishonor sent to the buyer and to accommodation endorsers, if any.

    When your office forwards a collection to an attorney whose name is taken from the law list, check the name on the law list. If the attorney handles the account satisfactorily, you will know to whom to forward the next claim that your office has against a debtor in that locality.

UNCONTESTED SUIT

    20.13. When the lawyer recommends suit. Lawyers seldom write more than two collection letters. If the debtor does not make some arrangement for payment, the lawyer recommends suit or returns the claim to the forwarder. This decision, of course, is the lawyer's, not yours. Tell the forwarder the prospects of collection by suit. Also indicate what advanced court costs will be required and what papers will be needed. The defendant in a suit on a collection item rarely has a defense against the claim and thus lets the suit go by default. It will save time if you get all papers that are needed in the ordinary course of a default judgment before suit is actually filed. These vary with the jurisdiction—the lawyer will tell you what papers are needed, or you can get the information from other collection files. The legal procedure is not complicated, and you should be able to draw the necessary court papers without detailed instructions from the lawyer.

Many collection suits are small enough to be filed as "small claims." The procedure in small claims court is simpler and less costly than the procedure used in suing for larger amounts. The small claims limit is about $500 in most states. Courts have special forms to be used in filing small claims actions. These can usually be obtained from the local clerk of court.

20.14. Summons and complaint. A short-form complaint is usually permissible. A brief statement of the indebtedness is alleged instead of a statement of the specific facts required by code pleading (chapter 14). The statement may be typed on the back of the printed form of summons. The causes of action, or counts, generally alleged in suits on collection items are for:

1. Goods sold and delivered

2. Account stated

3. Open book account

4. Account for services

20.15. Preparation and service of summons and short-form complaint. Use a printed form of summons and type the complaint in the space provided on the back for that purpose. When inserting the forms in the typewriter for endorsement of the back, be careful to endorse the original as the ribbon copy.

The service, affidavit of service, and filing of a short-form complaint in a collection suit is the same as in any other action (see chapter 14). If it is the practice in your office to make a litigation file of all collection suits in which summons is served, *enter return date of summons in diary* and open suit register sheet for the case. If your practice is not to transfer uncontested cases, *mark the file for follow-up on the return date of the summons.* Remember that the period of time to answer begins the date the summons is served, not the date it is prepared.

Keep in close touch with your process server and immediately recall the summons from him if the account is paid before service of the summons. If by any chance the summons is served on the defendant after the account is paid, the summons and affidavit of service should not be filed in court. The lawyer will depend upon you to keep track of these matters, and your records must be accurate and up-to-date to know the status of an account or an action at any time.

20.16. Checklist of information needed to draw summons and complaint in suit on a collection item. 1. *The court in which to bring* *the action.* This will depend on the amount of the claim and the jurisdiction of the local courts. Usually suit on a collection item may be brought in a municipal court or a justice of the peace court.

2. *The court district,* if the city is divided into districts with a municipal court in each.

3. *The amount of the debt.* A collection item is for a *liquidated amount*—that is, the amount is certain as distinguished from an indefinite amount to be determined by the court or jury, as in the case of an action for damages in an accident case. The file shows the amount of the debt.

4. *The rate of interest and the date from which it is to be charged.* The rate is the legal rate of interest in the state in which the debt was contracted, unless a lower rate had been contracted for. Interest runs from the date the debt became due.

5. *The wording of the complaint.* The wording varies with the jurisdiction and with the cause of action, but the counts are short and you will become familiar with the wording in your state very quickly. Examine the files on similar cases for the wording. You will notice that in an action on an account for merchandise, which is the most common action, the legal phraseology is "goods, wares, and merchandise," whether the merchandise is hardware, groceries, drugs or wearing apparel. Whenever you type a count for a new cause of action, make an extra copy for your loose-leaf notebook.

20.17. Judgment by default. If the defendant decides to contest the suit, a copy of his answer will probably be delivered to your office. However, in municipal court, the defendant may go to the court and make his answer orally, at any time before court closes on the return day of the summons. Therefore, you will not know until the day after the return day whether the defendant has answered or has defaulted. The day after return day, ask a law clerk to go to the court and find out if the defendant appeared. Or you can get the information yourself, by going to the court and looking at the papers in the court file under the index number of the case. If the defendant has not answered, prepare a *judgment by default.*

20.18. How to prepare a judgment by default. A printed form is generally available. You can get the necessary information from your file.

1. Make an original and two copies.

2. Calculate the interest at the legal rate, from the date indicated in the summons.

3. Itemize the cost disbursed by your office and include the total in the amount of the judgment.

4. Get the clerk of the court to sign the original and file it in court.

5. Conform the two copies.

6. Fill in the notice of entry of judgment in the space provided on the back of the judgment.

7. Mail one copy to the defendant. The other copy is for your office file.

After judgment by default is entered, the plaintiff is known as a *judgment creditor* and the defendant as a *judgment debtor*. If the judgment debtor does not pay the judgment, the attorney for the judgment creditor may ask the clerk of the court to issue execution. Should the execution be returned unsatisfied, the attorney will commence supplementary proceedings, if it appears that the judgment debtor has any assets out of which the judgment may be collected. If the debtor has no such assets, he is considered *judgment proof*.

Some states permit a court, on petition of the creditor, to inquire into the financial condition of the debtor. If the court finds the debtor is able to make payments at regular intervals, usually weekly, the court may order him to do so. Failure to obey such an order may result in a finding of contempt of court and the imposition of appropriate penalties.

PART 5

Legal Facts and Secretarial Aids

Forms of Address: Honorary and Official Positions

Latin Words and Phrases

Glossary of Legal Terms

State Requirements for Age of Testator and Number of Witnesses to Will

Courts of Record and Judicial Circuits

Authentication of Instruments

Notaries Public

Statutes of Limitations in Number of Years

Official Reports and How They Are Cited

Reporters of National Reporter System

Approved Method of Citing Compilations of Statutes and Codes

FORMS of AddRESS:
HONORARY ANd Official PosiTiONS

The chart in this section gives the correct forms of written address, salutation, and complimentary close for letters to persons holding honorary or official titles, whether of high or low rank. It also gives the correct form of referring to those persons in a letter and the correct form to use in speaking to, or informally introducing, them. (The form of informal introduction and the form of reference to a person are usually similar. Where they differ, the form of reference is shown in parentheses.)

To facilitate usage, the forms of addresses are presented in nine groups:

United States Government Officials, page 527
State and Local Government Officials, page 531
Court Officials, page 533
United States Diplomatic Representatives, page 535
Foreign Officials and Representatives, page 536
The Armed Forces, page 537
Church Dignitaries, page 540
College and University Officials, page 545
United Nations Officials, page 547

You should make every effort to learn the name of the person addressed, as well as his or her title. Use the name in writing, except in those few instances where the name is omitted in the chart. If you know the person's title only, address him by the title prefaced by *The*. For example, *The Lieutenant Governor of Iowa*. The formal salutation would be *Sir* or *Madam*.

When a person is acting as an official, the word *acting* precedes the title in the address, but not in the salutation or spoken address. For example, *Acting Mayor of Memphis, Dear Mayor Blank.*

A person who has held a position entitling him to be addressed as *The Honorable* is addressed as *The Honorable* after retirement. The title itself, such as Senator or Governor, is not used in the address or salutation. Even a former president is called *Mr.* An exception to this practice is the title of *Judge.* A person who has once been a judge customarily retains his title even when addressed formally. Retired officers of the armed forces retain their titles, but their retirement is indicated, thus, *Lieutenant General John D. Blank, U.S.A., Retired.*

In many cases the name in the address is followed by the abbreviation of a scholastic degree. If you do not know whether the addressee has the degree, you should not use the initials. Nor should a person be addressed by a scholastic title unless he or she actually possesses the degree that the title indicates.

The wife of an American official does not share her husband's title. She is always addressed as *Mrs. Blank.* When they are addressed jointly, the address is, for example, *Ambassador and Mrs. Blank.* Nor does a husband share his wife's title. When they are addressed jointly, if he does not have a title, the traditional address is *Mr. and Mrs. J.W. Blank,* regardless of any high-ranking title she may hold. Alternatives to the traditional address that include her title if her husband is untitled are: *Ambassador* Ruth Blank and *Mr.* J.W. Blank (the titled person preceding the untitled person), *Ambassador* Ruth and *Mr.* J.W. Blank, *Ambassador* and *Mr.* Blank.

Women in official or honorary positions are addressed just as men in similar positions, except that Madam replaces Sir, and Mrs., Miss, or Ms. replaces Mr. Ms. may be substituted for *Miss* or *Mrs.* in cases where the marital status of the woman is unknown or where the woman has stipulated that she prefers the title *Ms.*

Note: In the following chart, Correct Forms of Address, the form of address for a man is used throughout, except where not applicable. To use the form of address for a woman in any of these positions, use the substitution *Madam* for *Sir,* and *Mrs., Miss,* or *Ms.* for *Mr.* Thus, Dear *Madam; Mrs.* Blank, Representative from New York; The Lieutenant Governor of Iowa, *Miss* Blank; The American Minister, *Ms.* Blank. The *Mr.* preceding a title becomes *Madam;* thus, *Madam* Secretary, *Madam* Ambassador. Use *Esquire* or *Esq.* in addressing a man, where appropriate; some organizations are beginning to use *Esquire* in addressing a woman.

Forms of Address: Honorary and Official Positions

UNITED STATES GOVERNMENT OFFICIALS

Personage	Envelope and Inside Address (Add City, State, Zip)	Formal Salutation	Informal Salutation	Formal Close	Informal Close	1. Spoken Address / 2. Informal Introduction or Reference
The President	The President / The White House	Mr. President	Dear Mr. President:	Respectfully yours,	Very respectfully yours, / Very truly yours, / or / Sincerely yours,	1. Mr. President / 2. Not introduced (The President)
Former President of the United States[1]	The Honorable William R. Blank / (local address)	Sir:	Dear Mr. Blank:	Respectfully yours,	Sincerely yours,	1. Mr. Blank / 2. Former President Blank / or / Mr. Blank
The Vice-President of the United States	The Vice-President of the / United States Senate	Mr. Vice-President:	Dear Mr. Vice-President	Very truly yours,	Sincerely yours,	1. Mr. Vice-President / or / Mr. Blank / The Vice-President
The Chief Justice of the United States Supreme Court	The Chief Justice of the / United States / The Supreme Court of the / United States	Sir:	Dear Mr. Chief Justice:	Very truly yours,	Sincerely yours,	1. Mr. Chief Justice / 2. The Chief Justice
Associate Justice of the United States Supreme Court	Mr. Justice Blank / The Supreme Court of the / United States	Sir:	Dear Mr. Justice:	Very truly yours,	Sincerely yours,	1. Mr. Justice Blank / or / Justice Blank / 2. Mr. Justice Blank
Retired Justice of the United States Supreme Court	The Honorable William R. Blank / (local address)	Sir:	Dear Justice Blank:	Very truly yours,	Sincerely yours,	1. Mr. Justice Blank / or / Justice Blank / 2. Mr. Justice Blank

[1] If a former president has a title, such as *General of the Army*, address him by it.

Source: From the book, *Complete Secretary's Handbook*, 4th Edition, Mary A. De Vries, Rev'sor. © 1977 Prentice-Hall, Inc. Published by Prentice-Hall, Inc., Englewood Cliffs, New Jersey 0'632

UNITED STATES GOVERNMENT OFFICIALS *continued*

Personage	Envelope and Inside Address (Add City, State, Zip)	Formal Salutation	Informal Salutation	Formal Close	Informal Close	1. Spoken Address 2. Informal Introduction or Reference
The Speaker of the House of Representatives	The Honorable William R. Blank Speaker of the House of Representatives	Sir:	Dear Mr. Speaker: or Dear Mr. Blank:	Very truly yours,	Sincerely yours,	1. Mr. Speaker or Mr. Blank 2. The Speaker, Mr. Blank (The Speaker or Mr. Blank)
Former Speaker of the House of Representatives	The Honorable William R. Blank (local address)	Sir:	Dear Mr. Blank:	Very truly yours,	Sincerely yours,	1. Mr. Blank 2. Mr. Blank
Cabinet Officers addressed as "Secretary"[2]	The Honorable William R. Blank Secretary of State The Honorable William R. Blank Secretary of State of the United States of America (if written from abroad)	Sir:	Dear Mr. Secretary:	Very truly yours,	Sincerely yours,	1. Mr. Secretary or Secretary Blank or Mr. Blank 2. The Secretary of State, Mr. Blank (Mr. Blank or The Secretary)
Former Cabinet Officer	The Honorable William R. Blank (local address)	Dear Sir:	Dear Mr. Blank:	Very truly yours,	Sincerely yours,	1. Mr. Blank 2. Mr. Blank
Postmaster General	The Honorable William R. Blank The Postmaster General	Sir:	Dear Mr. Postmaster General:	Very truly yours,	Sincerely yours,	1. Mr. Postmaster General or Postmaster General Blank or Mr. Blank 2. The Postmaster General, Mr. Blank (Mr. Blank or The Postmaster General)

[2]Titles for cabinet secretaries are Secretary of State; Secretary of the Treasury; Secretary of Defense; Secretary of the Interior; Secretary of Agriculture; Secretary of Commerce; Secretary of Labor; Secretary of Health, Education, and Welfare; Secretary of Housing and Urban Development; Secretary of Transportation.

UNITED STATES GOVERNMENT OFFICIALS *continued*

Personage	Envelope and Inside Address (Add City, State, Zip)	Formal Salutation	Informal Salutation	Formal Close	Informal Close	1. Spoken Address 2. Informal Introduction or Reference
The Attorney General	The Honorable William R. Blank The Attorney General	Sir:	Dear Mr. Attorney General:	Very truly yours,	Sincerely yours,	1. Mr. Attorney General or Attorney General Blank 2. The Attorney General, Mr. Blank (Mr. Blank or The Attorney General)
Under Secretary of a Department	The Honorable William R. Blank Under Secretary of Labor	Dear Mr. Blank:	Dear Mr. Blank:	Very truly yours,	Sincerely yours,	1. Mr. Blank 2. Mr. Blank
United States Senator	The Honorable William R. Blank United States Senate	Sir:	Dear Senator Blank:	Very truly yours,	Sincerely yours,	1. Senator Blank or Senator 2. Senator Blank
Former Senator	The Honorable William R. Blank (local address)	Dear Sir:	Dear Senator Blank:	Very truly yours,	Sincerely yours,	1. Senator Blank or Senator 2. Senator Blank
Senator-elect	Honorable William R. Blank Senator-elect United States Senate	Dear Sir:	Dear Mr. Blank:	Very truly yours,	Sincerely yours,	1. Mr. Blank 2. Senator-elect Blank or Mr. Blank
Committee Chairman— United States Senate	The Honorable William R. Blank, Chairman Committee on Foreign Affairs United States Senate	Dear Mr. Chairman:	Dear Mr. Chairman: or Dear Senator Blank:	Very truly yours,	Sincerely yours,	1. Mr. Chairman or Senator Blank or Senator 2. The Chairman or Senator Blank
Subcommittee Chairman— United States Senate	The Honorable William R. Blank, Chairman, Subcommittee on Foreign Affairs United States Senate	Dear Senator Blank:	Dear Senator Blank:	Very truly yours,	Sincerely yours,	1. Senator Blank or Senator 2. Senator Blank

UNITED STATES GOVERNMENT OFFICIALS *continued*

Personage	Envelope and Inside Address (Add City, State, Zip)	Formal Salutation	Informal Salutation	Formal Close	Informal Close	1. Spoken Address 2. Informal Introduction or Reference
United States Representative or Congressman[3]	The Honorable William R. Blank House of Representatives The Honorable William R. Blank Representative in Congress (local address)(when away from Washington, DC)	Sir:	Dear Mr. Blank:	Very truly yours,	Sincerely yours,	1. Mr. Blank 2. Mr. Blank, Representative (Congressman) from New York or Mr. Blank
Former Representative	The Honorable William R. Blank (local address)	Sear Sir: or Dear Mr. Blank:	Dear Mr. Blank:	Very truly yours,	Sincerely yours,	1. Mr. Blank 2. Mr. Blank
Territorial Delegate	The Honorable William R. Blank Delegate of Puerto Rico House of Representatives	Dear Sir: or Dear Mr. Blank:	Dear Mr. Blank:	Very truly yours,	Sincerely yours,	1. Mr. Blank 2. Mr. Blank
Resident Commissioner	The Honorable William R. Blank Resident Commissioner of (Territory) House of Representatives	Dear Sir: or Dear Mr. Blank:	Dear Mr. Blank:	Very truly yours,	Sincerely yours,	1. Mr. Blank 2. Mr. Blank
Directors or Heads of Independent Federal Offices, Agencies, Commissions, Organizations, etc.	The Honorable William R. Blank Director, Mutual Security Agency	Dear Mr. Director (Commissioner, etc.):	Dear Mr. Blank:	Very truly yours,	Sincerely yours,	1. Mr. Blank 2. Mr. Blank
Other High Officials of the United States, in general: Public Printer, Comptroller General	The Honorable William R. Blank Public Printer The Honorable William R. Blank Comptroller General of the United States	Dear Sir: or Dear Mr. Blank:	Dear Mr. Blank:	Very truly yours,	Sincerely yours,	1. Mr. Blank 2. Mr. Blank

[3]The official title of a "congressman" is *Representative*. Strictly speaking, senators are also congressmen.

UNITED STATES GOVERNMENT OFFICIALS *continued*

Personage	Envelope and Inside Address (Add City, State, Zip)	Formal Salutation	Informal Salutation	Formal Close	Informal Close	1. Spoken Address 2. Informal Introduction or Reference
Secretary to the President	The Honorable William R. Blank Secretary to the President The White House	Dear Sir: or Dear Mr. Blank	Dear Mr. Blank:	Very truly yours,	Sincerely yours,	1. Mr. Blank 2. Mr. Blank
Assistant Secretary to the President	The Honorable William R. Blank Assistant Secretary to the President The White House	Dear Sir: or Dear Mr. Blank:	Dear Mr. Blank:	Very truly yours,	Sincerely yours,	1. Mr. Blank 2. Mr. Blank
Press Secretary to the President	Mr. William R. Blank Press Secretary to the President The White House	Dear Sir: or Dear Mr. Blank:	Dear Mr. Blank:	Very truly yours,	Sincerely yours,	1. Mr. Blank 2. Mr. Blank

STATE AND LOCAL GOVERNMENT OFFICIALS

Personage	Envelope and Inside Address (Add City, State, Zip)	Formal Salutation	Informal Salutation	Formal Close	Informal Close	1. Spoken Address 2. Informal Introduction or Reference
Governor of a State or Territory[1]	The Honorable William R. Blank Governor of New York	Sir:	Dear Governor Blank:	Respectfully yours,	Very sincerely yours,	1. Governor Blank or Governor 2. a) Governor Blank b) The Governor c) The Governor of New York (used only outside his or her own state)
Acting Governor of a State or Territory	The Honorable William R. Blank Acting Governor of Connecticut	Sir:	Dear Mr. Blank:	Respectfully yours,	Very sincerely yours,	1. Mr. Blank 2. Mr. Blank

[1]The form of addressing governors varies in the different states. The form given here is the one used in most states. In Massachusetts by law and in some other states by courtesy, the form is *His (Her) Excellency, the Governor of Massachusetts.*

STATE AND LOCAL GOVERNMENT OFFICIALS *continued*

Personage	Envelope and Inside Address (Add City, State, Zip)	Formal Salutation	Informal Salutation	Formal Close	Informal Close	1. Spoken Address 2. Informal Introduction or Reference
Lieutenant Governor	The Honorable William R. Blank / Lieutenant Governor of Iowa	Sir:	Dear Mr. Blank:	Respectfully yours, or Very truly yours,	Sincerely yours,	1. Mr. Blank 2. The Lieutenant Governor of Iowa, Mr. Blank or The Lieutenant Governor
Secretary of State	The Honorable William R. Blank / Secretary of State of New York	Sir:	Dear Mr. Secretary:	Very truly yours,	Sincerely yours,	1. Mr. Blank 2. Mr. Blank
Attorney General	The Honorable William R. Blank / Attorney General of Massachusetts	Sir:	Dear Mr. Attorney General:	Very truly yours,	Sincerely yours,	1. Mr. Blank 2. Mr. Blank
President of the Senate of a State	The Honorable William R. Blank / President of the Senate of the State of Virginia	Sir:	Dear Mr. Blank:	Very truly yours,	Sincerely yours,	1. Mr. Blank 2. Mr. Blank
Speaker of the Assembly or The House of Representatives[2]	The Honorable William R. Blank / Speaker of the Assembly of the State of New York	Sir:	Dear Mr. Blank:	Very truly yours,	Sincerely yours,	1. Mr. Blank 2. Mr. Blank
Treasurer, Auditor, or Comptroller of a State	The Honorable William R. Blank / Treasurer of the State of Tennessee	Dear Sir:	Dear Mr. Blank:	Very truly yours,	Sincerely yours,	1. Mr. Blank 2. Mr. Blank
State Senator	The Honorable William R. Blank / The State Senate	Dear Sir:	Dear Senator Blank:	Very truly yours,	Sincerely yours,	1. Senator Blank or Senator 2. Senator Blank

[2]In most states the lower branch of the legislature is the House of Representatives. The exceptions to this are: New York, California, Wisconsin, and Nevada, where it is known as the Assembly; Maryland, Virginia, and West Virginia—the House of Delegates; New Jersey—the House of General Assembly.

STATE AND LOCAL GOVERNMENT OFFICIALS *continued*

Personage	Envelope and Inside Address (Add City, State, Zip)	Formal Salutation	Informal Salutation	Formal Close	Informal Close	1. Spoken Address 2. Informal Introduction or Reference
State Representative, Assemblyman, or Delegate	The Honorable William R. Blank House of Delegates	Dear Sir:	Dear Mr. Blank:	Very truly yours,	Sincerely yours,	1. Mr. Blank 2. Mr. Blank or Delegate Blank
District Attorney	The Honorable William R. Blank District Attorney, Albany County County Courthouse	Dear Sir:	Dear Mr. Blank:	Very truly yours,	Sincerely yours,	1. Mr. Blank 2. Mr. Blank
Mayor of a city	The Honorable William R. Blank Mayor of Detroit	Dear Sir:	Dear Mayor Blank:	Very truly yours,	Sincerely yours,	1. Mayor Blank or Mr. Mayor 2. Mayor Blank
President of a Board of Commissioners	The Honorable William R. Blank, President Board of Commissioners of the City of Buffalo	Dear Sir:	Dear Mr. Blank:	Very truly yours,	Sincerely yours,	1. Mr. Blank 2. Mr. Blank
City Attorney, City Counsel, Corporation Counsel	The Honorable William R. Blank, City Attorney (City Counsel, Corporation Counsel)	Dear Sir:	Dear Mr. Blank:	Very truly yours,	Sincerely yours,	1. Mr. Blank 2. Mr. Blank
Alderman	Alderman William R. Blank City Hall	Dear Sir:	Dear Mr. Blank:	Very truly yours,	Sincerely yours,	1. Mr. Blank 2. Mr. Blank

COURT OFFICIALS

Personage	Envelope and Inside Address (Add City, State, Zip)	Formal Salutation	Informal Salutation	Formal Close	Informal Close	1. Spoken Address 2. Informal Introduction or Reference
Chief Justice[1] of a State Supreme Court	The Honorable William R. Blank Chief Justice of the Supreme Court of Minnesota[2]	Sir:	Dear Mr. Chief Justice:	Very truly yours,	Sincerely yours,	1. Mr. Chief Justice or Judge Blank 2. Mr. Chief Justice Blank or Judge Blank

[1] If his or her official title is *Chief Judge* substitute *Chief Judge* for *Chief Justice*, but never use *Mr., Mrs., Miss* or *Ms.* with *Chief Judge* or *Judge*.

[2] Substitute here the appropriate name of the court. For example, the highest court in New York State is called the Court of Appeals.

COURT OFFICIALS *continued*

Personage	Envelope and Inside Address (Add City, State, Zip, or City, Country)	Formal Salutation	Informal Salutation	Formal Close	Informal Close	1. Spoken Address 2. Informal Introduction or Reference
Associate Justice of a Supreme Court of a State	The Honorable William R. Blank Associate Justice of the Supreme Court of Minnesota	Sir:	Dear Justice Blank:	Very truly yours,	Sincerely yours,	1. Mr. Justice Blank 2. Mr. Justice Blank
Presiding Justice	The Honorable William R. Blank Presiding Justice, Appellate Division Supreme Court of New York	Sir:	Dear Justice Blank:	Very truly yours	Sincerely yours,	1. Mr. Justice (or Judge) Blank 2. Mr. Justice (or Judge Blank)
Judge of a Court[3]	The Honorable William R. Blank Judge of the United States District Court for the Southern District of California	Sir:	Dear Judge Blank:	Very truly yours,	Sincerely yours,	1. Judge Blank 2. Judge Blank
Clerk of a Court	William R. Blank, Esquire Clerk of the Superior Court of Massachusetts	Dear Sir:	Dear Mr. Blank:	Very truly yours,	Sincerely yours,	1. Mr. Blank 2. Mr. Blank

UNITED STATES DIPLOMATIC REPRESENTATIVES

| American Ambassador | The Honorable William R. Blank American Ambassador[1] | Sir: | Dear Mr. Ambassador: | Very truly yours, | Sincerely yours, | 1. Mr. Ambassador or Mr. Blank 2. The American Ambassador[2] (The Ambassador or Mr. Blank) |

[1]When an ambassador or minister is not at his or her post, the name of the country to which he or she is accredited must be added to the address. For example: *The American Ambassador to Great Britain.* If he or she holds ambassadorial rank, the diplomatic complimentary title *The Honorable* should be omitted, thus *General William R. Blank, American Ambassador (or Minister).*
[2]With reference to ambassadors and ministers to Central or South American countries, substitute *The Ambassador of the United States for American Ambassador or American Minister.*
[3]Not applicable to judges of the United States Supreme Court.

UNITED STATES DIPLOMATIC REPRESENTATIVES *continued*

Personage	Envelope and Inside Address (Add City, State, Zip, or City, Country)	Formal Salutation	Informal Salutation	Formal Close	Informal Close	1. Spoken Address 2. Informal Introduction or Reference
American Minister	The Honorable William R. Blank American Minister to Rumania	Sir:	Dear Mr. Minister:	Very truly yours,	Sincerely yours,	1. Mr. Minister or Mr. Blank 2. The American Minister, Mr. Blank (The Minister or Mr. Blank)
American Chargé d'Affaires, Consul General, Consul, or Vice Consul	William R. Blank, Esquire[3] American Chargé d'Affaires ad interim (or other title)	Sir:	Dear Mr. Blank:	Very truly yours,	Sincerely yours,	1. Mr. Blank 2. Mr. Blank
High Commissioner	The Honorable William R. Blank United States High Commissioner to Argentina	Sir:	Dear Mr. Blank	Very truly yours,	Sincerely yours,	1. Commissioner Blank or Mr. Blank 2. Commissioner Blank or Mr. Blank

[3]Do not use *Esquire* to refer to a woman in this position.

FOREIGN OFFICIALS AND REPRESENTATIVES

Personage	Envelope and Inside Address	Formal Salutation	Informal Salutation	Formal Close	Informal Close	1. Spoken Address 2. Informal Introduction or Reference
Foreign Ambassador[1] in the United States	His Excellency,[2] Erik Rolf Blankson Ambassador of Norway	Excellency:	Dear Mr. Ambassador:	Very truly yours,	Sincerely yours,	1. Mr. Ambassador or Mr. Blank 2. The Ambassador of Norway (The Ambassador or Mr. Blank)

[1]The correct title of all ambassadors and ministers of foreign countries is *Ambassador (Minister) of* _____ (name of country), with the exception of Great Britain. The adjective form is used with reference to representatives from Great Britain—*British Ambassador, British Minister.*
[2]When the representative is British or a member of the British Commonwealth, it is customary to use *The Right Honorable* and *The Honorable* in addition to *His (Her) Excellency* wherever appropriate.

FOREIGN OFFICIALS AND REPRESENTATIVES *continued*

Personage	Envelope and Inside Address (Add City, State, Zip, or City, Country)	Formal Salutation	Informal Salutation	Formal Close	Informal Close	1. Spoken Address / 2. Informal Introduction or Reference
Foreign Minister[3] in the United States	The Honorable George Macovescu Minister of Rumania	Sir:	Dear Mr. Minister:	Very truly yours,	Sincerely yours,	1. Mr. Minister or Mr. Blank 2. The Minister of Rumania (The Minister or Mr. Blank)
Foreign Diplomatic Representative with a Personal Title[4]	His Excellency,[5] Count Allesandro de Bianco Ambassador of Italy	Excellency:	Dear Mr. Ambassador:	Very truly yours,	Sincerely yours,	1. Mr. Ambassador or Count Bianco 2. The Ambassador of Italy (The Ambassador or Count Bianco)
Prime Minister	His Excellency, Christian Jawaharal Blank Prime Minister of India	Excellency:	Dear Mr. Prime Minister:	Respectfully yours,	Sincerely yours,	1. Mr. Blank 2. Mr. Blank or The Prime Minister
British Prime Minister	The Right Honorable Godfrey Blank, K.G., M.C., M.P. Prime Minister	Sir:	Dear Mr. Prime Minister: or Dear Mr. Blank:	Respectfully yours,	Sincerely yours,	1. Mr. Blank 2. Mr. Blank or The Prime Minister
Canadian Prime Minister	The Right Honorable Claude Louis St. Blanc, C.M.G. Prime Minister of Canada	Sir:	Dear Mr. Prime Minister: or Dear Mr. Blanc:	Respectfully yours,	Sincerely yours,	1. Mr. Blanc 2. Mr. Blanc or The Prime Minister
President of a Republic	His Excellency, Juan Cuidad Blanco President of the Dominican Republic	Excellency:	Dear Mr. President:	I remain with respect, Very truly yours, (formal general usage) Sincerely yours, (less formal)	Sincerely yours,	1. Your Excellency 2. Not introduced (President Blanco or the President)

[3]The correct title of all ambassadors and ministers of foreign countries is Ambassador (Minister) of _____ (name of country), with the exception of Great Britain. The adjective form is used with reference to representatives from Great Britain—British Ambassador, British Minister.

[4]If the personal title is a royal title, such as His (Her) Highness, Prince, etc., the diplomatic title His (Her) Excellency or The Honorable is omitted.

[5]Dr., Señor Don, and other titles of special courtesy in Spanish-speaking countries may be used with the diplomatic title His (Her) Excellency or The Honorable.

FOREIGN OFFICIALS AND REPRESENTATIVES *continued*

Personage	Envelope and Inside Address (Add City, State, Zip, or City, Country)	Formal Salutation	Informal Salutation	Formal Close	Informal Close	1. Spoken Address 2. Informal Introduction or Reference
Premier	His Excellency, Charles Yves de Blanc Premier of the French Republic	Excellency:	Dear Mr. Premier:	Respectfully yours,	Sincerely yours,	1. Mr. Blanc 2. Mr. Blanc or The Premier
Foreign Chargé d'Affaires (de missi)⁶ in the United States	Mr. Jan Gustaf Blanc Chargé d'Affaires of Sweden	Sir:	Dear Mr. Blanc:	Respectfully yours,	Sincerely yours,	1. Mr. Blanc 2. Mr. Blanc
Foreign Chargé d'Affaires ad interim in the United States	Mr. Edmund Blank Chargé d'Affaires ad interim⁷ of Ireland	Sir:	Dear Mr. Blank:	Respectfully yours,	Sincerely yours,	1. Mr. Blank 2. Mr. Blank

[6]The full title is usually shortened to *Chargé d'Affaires.*
[7]The words "ad interim" should not be omitted in the address.

THE ARMED FORCES/THE ARMY

Personage	Envelope and Inside Address (Add City, State, Zip, or City, Country)	Formal Salutation	Informal Salutation	Formal Close	Informal Close	1. Spoken Address 2. Informal Introduction or Reference
General of the Army	General of the Army William R. Blank, U.S.A. Department of the Army	Sir:	Dear General Blank:	Very truly yours,	Sincerely yours,	1. General Blank 2. General Blank
General, Lieutenant General, Major General, Brigadier General	General (Lieutenant General, Major General, or Brigadier General) William R. Blank, U.S.A.¹	Sir:	Dear General Blank:	Very truly yours,	Sincerely yours,	1. General Blank 2. General Blank
Colonel, Lieutenant Colonel	Colonel (Lieutenant Colonel) William R. Blank, U.S.A.	Dear Colonel Blank:	Dear Colonel Blank:	Very truly yours,	Sincerely yours,	1. Colonel Blank 2. Colonel Blank
Major	Major William R. Blank, U.S.A.	Dear Major Blank:	Dear Major Blank:	Very truly yours,	Sincerely yours,	1. Major Blank 2. Major Blank

[1]*U.S.A.* indicates regular service. *A.U.S.* (Army of the United States) signifies the Reserve.

THE ARMED FORCES/THE NAVY

Personage	Envelope and Inside Address (Add City, State, Zip, or City, Country)	Formal Salutation	Informal Salutation	Formal Close	Informal Close	1. Spoken Address 2. Informal Introduction or Reference
Captain	Captain William R. Blank, U.S.A.	Dear Captain Blank:	Dear Captain Blank:	Very truly yours,	Sincerely yours,	1. Captain Blank 2. Captain Blank
First Lieutenant, Second Lieutenant[2]	Lieutenant William R. Blank, U.S.A.	Dear Lieutenant Blank:	Dear Lieutenant Blank:	Very truly yours,	Sincerely yours,	1. Lieutenant Blank 2. Lieutenant Blank
Chief Warrant Officer, Warrant Officer	Mr. William R. Blank, U.S.A.	Dear Mr. Blank:	Dear Mr. Blank	Very truly yours,	Sincerely yours,	1. Mr. Blank 2. Mr. Blank
Chaplain in the U.S. Army[3]	Chaplain William R. Blank Captain, U.S.A.	Dear Chaplain Blank:	Dear Chaplain Blank:	Very truly yours,	Sincerely yours,	1. Chaplain Blank 2. Captain Blank (Chaplain Blank)
Fleet Admiral	Fleet Admiral William R. Blank, U.S.N. Chief of Naval Operations, Department of the Navy	Sir:	Dear Admiral Blank:	Very truly yours,	Sincerely yours,	1. Admiral Blank 2. Admiral Blank
Admiral, Vice Admiral, Rear Admiral	Admiral (Vice Admiral or Rear Admiral) William R. Blank, U.S.N. United States Naval Academy[1]	Sir:	Dear Admiral Blank:	Very truly yours,	Sincerely yours,	1. Admiral Blank 2. Admiral Blank
Commodore, Captain, Commander, Lieutenant Commander	Commodore (Captain, Commander, Lieutenant Commander) William R. Blank, U.S.N. U.S.S. Mississippi	Dear Commodore (Captain, Commander) Blank:	Dear Commodore (Captain, Commander) Blank:	Very truly yours,	Sincerely yours,	1. Commodore (Captain, Commander) Blank 2. Commodore (Captain, Commander) Blank

[1] *U.S.N.* signifies regular service; *U.S.N.R.* indicates the Reserve.

[2] In all *official* correspondence, the full rank should be included in both the envelope address and the inside address, but not in the salutation.

[3] Roman Catholic chaplains and certain Anglican priests are introduced as *Chaplain Blank* but are spoken to and referred to as *Father Blank*.

THE ARMED FORCES/THE NAVY *continued*

Personage	Envelope and Inside Address (Add City, State, Zip, or City, Country)	Formal Salutation	Informal Salutation	Formal Close	Informal Close	1. Spoken Address 2. Informal Introduction or Reference
Junior Officers: Lieutenant, Lieutenant Junior Grade, Ensign	(Lieutenant, etc.) William R. Blank, U.S.N. U.S.S. Wyoming	Dear Mr. Blank:	Dear Mr. Blank:	Very truly yours,	Sincerely yours,	1. Mr. Blank[2] 2. Lieutenant, etc., Blank (Mr. Blank)
Chief Warrant Officer, Warrant Officer	Mr. William R. Blank, U.S.N. U.S.S. Texas	Dear Mr. Blank:	Dear Mr. Blank:	Very truly yours,	Sincerely yours,	1. Mr. Blank 2. Mr. Blank
Chaplain	Chaplain William R. Blank Captain, U.S.N. Department of the Navy	Dear Chaplain Blank:	Dear Chaplain Blank:	Very truly yours,	Sincerely yours,	1. Chaplain Blank 2. Captain Blank (Chaplain Blank)

[2]Junior officers in the medical or dental corps are spoken to and referred to as *Dr.* but are introduced by their rank.

THE ARMED FORCES—AIR FORCE

Air Force titles are the same as those in the Army. *U.S.A.F.* is used instead of *U.S.A.*, and *A.F.U.S.* is used to indicate the Reserve.

THE ARMED FORCES—MARINE CORPS

Marine Corps titles are the same as those in the Army, except that the top rank is *Commandant of the Marine Corps. U.S.M.C.* indicates regular service, *U.S.M.R.* indicates the Reserve.

THE ARMED FORCES—COAST GUARD

Coast Guard titles are the same as those in the Navy, except that the top rank is *Admiral. U.S.C.G.* indicates regular service, *U.S.C.G.R.* indicates the Reserve.

CHURCH DIGNITARIES/CATHOLIC FAITH

Personage	Envelope and Inside Address (Add City, State, Zip, or City, Country)	Formal Salutation	Informal Salutation	Formal Close	Informal Close	1. Spoken Address / 2. Informal Introduction or Reference
The Pope	His Holiness, The Pope / or / His Holiness Pope ——— / Vatican City	Your Holiness: Most Holy Father:	Always Formal	Respectfully,	Always Formal	1. Your Holiness 2. Not introduced (His Holiness or The Pope)
Apostolic Delegate	His Excellency, The Most Reverend William R. Blank / Archbishop of ——— / The Apostolic Delegate	Your Excellency:	Dear Archbishop Blank:	Respectfully yours,	Respectfully,	1. Your Excellency 2. Not introduced (The Apostolic Delegate)
Cardinal in the United States	His Eminence, William Cardinal Blank / Archbishop of New York	Your Eminence:	Dear Cardinal Blank:	Respectfully yours,	Respectfully, or Sincerely yours,	1. Your Eminence or less formally Cardinal Blank 2. Not introduced (His Eminence or Cardinal Blank)
Bishop and Archbishop in the United States	The Most Reverend William R. Blank, D.D. / Bishop (Archbishop) of Baltimore	Your Excellency:	Dear Bishop (Archbishop) Blank:	Respectfully yours,	Respectfully, or Sincerely yours,	1. Bishop (Archbishop) Blank 2. Bishop (Archbishop) Blank
Bishop in England	The Right Reverend William R. Blank / Bishop of Sussex / (local address)	Right Reverend Sir:	Dear Bishop:	Respectfully yours,	Respectfully,	1. Bishop Blank 2. Bishop Blank
Abbot	The Right Reverend William R. Blank / Abbot of Westmoreland Abbey	Dear Father Abbot:	Dear Father Blank:	Respectfully yours,	Sincerely yours,	1. Father Abbot 2. Father Blank

CHURCH DIGNITARIES/CATHOLIC FAITH *continued*

Personage	Envelope and Inside Address (Add City, State, Zip, or City, Country)	Formal Salutation	Informal Salutation	Formal Close	Informal Close	1. Spoken Address 2. Informal Introduction or Reference
Canon	The Reverend William R. Blank, D.D. Canon of St. Patrick's Cathedral	Reverend Sir:	Dear Canon Blank:	Respectfully yours,	Sincerely yours,	1. Canon Blank 2. Canon Blank
Monsignor	Reverend Msgr. William R. Blank	Reverend Monsignor Blank	Dear Monsignor Blank:	Respectfully yours,	Sincerely yours,	1. Monsignor Blank 2. Monsignor Blank
Brother	Brother John Blank 932 Maple Avenue	Dear Brother:	Dear Brother Blank:	Respectfully yours,	Sincerely yours,	1. Brother Blank 2. Brother Blank
Superior of a Brotherhood and Priest[1]	The Very Reverend William R. Blank, M.M. Director	Dear Father Superior	Dear Father Superior:	Respectfully yours,	Sincerely yours,	1. Father Blank 2. Father Blank
Priest	With scholastic degree: The Reverend William R. Blank, Ph.D. Georgetown University	Dear Dr. Blank:	Dear Dr. Blank:	Respectfully,	Sincerely yours,	1. Doctor (Father) Blank 2. Doctor (Father) Blank
	Without scholastic degree: The Reverend William R. Blank St. Vincent's Church	Dear Father Blank:	Dear Father Blank:	Respectfully,	Sincerely yours,	1. Father Blank 2. Father Blank

[1]The address for the superior of a Brotherhood depends upon whether or not he is a priest or has a title other than superior. Consult the *Official Catholic Directory.*

CHURCH DIGNITARIES/CATHOLIC FAITH *continued*

Personage	Envelope and Inside Address (Add City, State, Zip, or City, Country)	Formal Salutation	Informal Salutation	Formal Close	Informal Close	1. Spoken Address 2. Informal Introduction or Reference
Sister Superior	The Reverend Sister Superior (order, if used)[3] Convent of the Sacred Heart	Dear Sister Superior:	Dear Sister Superior:	Respectfully,	Respectfully, or Sincerely yours,	1. Sister Blank or Sister St. Teresa 2. The Sister Superior or Sister Blank (Sister St. Teresa)
Sister	Sister Mary Blank St. John's High School	Dear Sister:	Dear Sister Blank:	Respectfully,	Sincerely yours,	1. Sister Blank 2. Sister Blank
Mother Superior of a Sisterhood (Catholic or Protestant)	The Reverend Mother Superior, O.C.A. Convent of the Sacred Heart	Dear Reverend Mother: or Dear Mother Superior:	Dear Reverend Mother: or Dear Mother Superior:	Respectfully,	Sincerely yours,	1. Reverend Mother 2. Reverend Mother
Member of Community	Mother Mary Walker, R.S.M. Convent of Mercy	Dear Mother Walker:	Dear Mother Walker:	Respectfully,	Sincerely yours,	1. Mother Walker 2. Mother Walker

CHURCH DIGNITARIES/JEWISH FAITH

Personage	Envelope and Inside Address (Add City, State, Zip, or City, Country)	Formal Salutation	Informal Salutation	Formal Close	Informal Close	1. Spoken Address 2. Informal Introduction or Reference

[3]The address of the superior of a Sisterhood depends upon the order to which she belongs. The abbreviation of the order is not always used. Consult the *Official Catholic Directory.*

CHURCH DIGNITARIES/JEWISH FAITH *continued*

Rabbi	With scholastic degree: Rabbi William R. Blank, Ph.D.	Sir:	Dear Rabbi Blank: or Dear Dr. Blank:	Respectfully yours, or Very truly yours,	Sincerely yours,	1. Rabbi Blank or Dr. Blank 2. Rabbi Blank or Dr. Blank
	Without scholastic degree: Rabbi William R. Blank	Sir:	Dear Rabbi Blank:	Respectfully yours, or Very truly yours,	Sincerely yours,	1. Rabbi Blank 2. Rabbi Blank

CHURCH DIGNITARIES/PROTESTANT FAITH

Archbishop (Anglican)	The Most Reverend Archbishop of Canterbury or The Most Reverend John Blank, Archbishop of Canterbury	Your Grace:	Dear Archbishop Blank:	Respectfully yours,	Sincerely yours,	1. Your Grace 2. Not introduced (His Grace or The Archbishop)
Presiding Bishop of the Protestant Episcopal Church in America	The Most Reverend William R. Blank, D.D., LL.D. Presiding Bishop of the Protestant Episcopal Church in America Northwick House	Most Reverend Sir:	Dear Bishop Blank:	Respectfully yours,	Sincerely yours,	1. Bishop Blank 2. Bishop Blank
Anglican Bishop	The Right Reverend The Lord Bishop of London	Right Reverend Sir:	My dear Bishop:	Respectfully yours,	Sincerely yours,	1. Bishop Blank 2. Bishop Blank
Methodist Bishop	The Very Reverend William R. Blank Methodist Bishop	Reverend Sir:	Mr dear Bishop:	Respectfully yours,	Sincerely yours,	1. Bishop Blank 2. Bishop Blank
Protestant Episcopal Bishop	The Right Reverend William R. Blank, D.D., LL.D. Bishop of Denver	Right Reverend Sir:	Dear Bishop Blank:	Respectfully yours,	Sincerely yours,	1. Bishop Blank 2. Bishop Blank

CHURCH DIGNITARIES/PROTESTANT FAITH *continued*

Personage	Envelope and Inside Address (Add City, State, Zip, or City, Country)	Formal Salutation	Informal Salutation	Formal Close	Informal Close	1. Spoken Address 2. Informal Introduction or Reference
Archdeacon	The Venerable William R. Blank Archdeacon of Baltimore	Venerable Sir:	My dear Archdeacon:	Respectfully yours,	Sincerely yours,	1. Archdeacon Blank 2. Archdeacon Blank
Dean[1]	The Very Reverend William R. Blank, D.D. Dean of St. John's Cathedral	Very Reverend Sir:	Dear Dean Blank:	Respectfully yours,	Sincerely yours,	1. Dean Blank or Dr. Blank 2. Dean Blank or Dr. Blank
Protestant Minister	With scholastic degree: The Reverend William R. Blank, D.D., Litt.D. or The Reverend Dr. William R. Blank	Dear Dr. Blank:	Dear Dr. Blank:	Very truly yours,	Sincerely yours,	1. Dr. Blank 2. Dr. Blank
	Without scholastic degree: The Reverend William R. Blank	Dear Mr. Blank:	Dear Mr. Blank:	Very truly yours,	Sincerely yours,	1. Mr. Blank 2. Mr. Blank
Episcopal Priest (High Church)	With scholastic degree: The Reverend William R. Blank, D.D., Litt.D. All Saint's Cathedral or The Reverend Dr. William R. Blank	Dear Dr. Blank:	Dear Dr. Blank:	Very truly yours,	Sincerely yours,	1. Dr. Blank 2. Dr. Blank
	Without scholastic degree: The Reverend William R. Blank St. Paul's Church	Dear Mr. Blank: or Dear Father Blank:	Dear Mr. Blank: or Dear Father Blank:	Very truly yours,	Sincerely yours,	1. Father Blank or Mr. Blank 2. Father Blank or Mr. Blank

[1]Applies only to the head of a Cathedral or of a Theological Seminary.

COLLEGE AND UNIVERSITY OFFICIALS

Official	Address	Formal Salutation	Informal Salutation	Formal Closing	Informal Closing	Informal Address
President of a College or University	With a doctor's degree: Dr. William R. Blank or William R. Blank, LL.D., Ph.D. President, Amherst College	Sir:	Dear Dr. Blank:	Very truly yours,	Sincerely yours,	1. Dr. Blank 2. Dr. Blank
	Without a doctor's degree Mr. William R. Blank President, Columbia University	Sir:	Dear President Blank:	Very truly yours,	Sincerely yours,	1. Mr. Blank 2. Mr. Blank or Mr. Blank, President of the College
	Catholic priest: The Very Reverend William R. Blank, S.J., D.D., Ph.D. President, Fordham University	Sir:	Dear Father Blank:	Very truly yours,	Sincerely yours,	1. Father Blank 2. Father Blank
University Chancellor	Dr. William R. Blank Chancellor, University of Alabama	Sir:	Dear Dr. Blank:	Very truly yours,	Sincerely yours,	1. Dr. Blank 2. Dr. Blank
Dean or Assistant Dean of a College or Graduate School	Dean William R. Blank School of Law or (If he holds a doctor's degree) Dr. William R. Blank, Dean (Assistant Dean) School of Law University of Virginia	Dear Sir: or Dear Dean Blank:	Dear Dean Blank:	Very truly yours,	Sincerely yours,	1. Dean Blank 2. Dean Blank or Dr. Bank, the Dean (Assistant Dean) of the School of Law
Professor	Professor William R. Blank or (If he holds a doctor's degree) Dr. William R. Blank or William R. Blank, Ph.D. Yale University	Dear Sir: or Dear Professor (Dr.) Blank:	Dear Professor (Dr.) Blank:	Very truly yours,	Sincerely yours,	1. Professor (Dr.) Blank 2. Professor (Dr.) Blank

COLLEGE AND UNIVERSITY OFFICIALS *continued*

Personage	Envelope and Inside Address (Add City, State, Zip, or City, Country)	Formal Salutation	Informal Salutation	Formal Close	Informal Close	1. Spoken Address 2. Informal Introduction or Reference
Associate or Assistant Professor	Mr. William R. Blank or (If he holds a doctor's degree) Dr. William R. Blank or William R. Blank, Ph.D. Associate (Assistant) Professor Department of Romance Languages Williams College	Dear Sir: or Dear Professor (Dr.) Blank:	Dear Professor (Dr.) Blank:	Very truly yours,	Sincerely yours,	1. Professor (Dr.) Blank 2. Professor (Dr.) Blank
Instructor	Mr. William R. Blank or (If he holds a doctor's degree) Dr. William R. Blank or William R. Blank, Ph.D. Department of Economics University of California	Dear Sir: or Dear Mr. (Dr.) Blank:	Dear Mr. (Dr.) Blank:	Very truly yours,	Sincerely yours,	1. Mr. (Dr.) Blank 2. Mr. (Dr.) Blank
Chaplain of a College or University	The Reverend William R. Blank, D.D. Chaplain, Trinity College or Chaplain William R. Blank Trinity College	Dear Chaplain Blank: or (If he holds a doctor's degree) Dear Dr. Blank:	Dear Chaplain (Dr.) Blank:	Very truly yours,	Sincerely yours,	1. Chaplain Blank 2. Chaplain Blank or Dr. Blank

UNITED NATIONS OFFICIALS[1]

Personage	Envelope and Inside Address (Add City, State, Zip, or City, Country)	Formal Salutation	Informal Salutation	Formal Close	Informal Close	1. Spoken Address 2. Informal Introduction or Reference
Secretary General	His Excellency, William R. Blank Secretary General of the United Nations	Excellency:[2]	Dear Mr. Secretary General:	Very truly yours,	Sincerely yours,	1. Mr. Blank or Sir 2. The Secretary General of the United Nations or Mr. Blank
Under Secretary	The Honorable William R. Blank Under Secretary of the United Nations The Secretariat United Nations	Sir:	Dear Mr. Blank:	Very truly yours,	Sincerely yours,	1. Mr. Blank 2. Mr. Blank
Foreign Representative (with ambassadorial rank)	His Excellency, William R. Blank Representative of Spain to the United Nations	Excellency:	Dear Mr. Ambassador:	Very truly yours,	Sincerely yours,	1. Mr. Ambassador or Mr. Blank 2. Mr. Ambassador or The Representative of Spain to the United Nations (The Ambassador or Mr. Blank)
United States Representative (with ambassadorial rank)	The Honorable William R. Blank United States Representative to the United Nations	Sir: or Dear Mr. Ambassador	Dear Mr. Ambassador:	Very truly yours,	Sincerely yours,	1. Mr. Ambassador or Mr. Blank 2. Mr. Ambassador or The United States Representative to the United Nations (The Ambassador or Mr. Blank)

[1]The six principal branches through which the United Nations functions are The General Assembly, The Security Council, The Economic and Social Council, The Trusteeship Council, The International Court of Justice, and The Secretariat.

[2]An American citizen should never be addressed as "Excellency."

LATIN WORDS AND PHRASES

Legal dictation in every field contains many Latin words and phrases. Those that you are most likely to hear are listed below. The list also contains a few French terms. The list will enable you to write the words and phrases correctly; the almost literal translations will enable you to understand the meaning of the dictation. Foreign words and phrases are frequently italicized in printing and underlined in typing. However, many of them have become completely Anglicized and are not generally printed in italic type or underlined. The words and phrases that are italicized in the list should be underlined when typed. Those in roman type should not be underlined. You will notice that some words are not underlined unless used in a phrase or expression. For example, "animus" is not italicized when written alone, but is italicized in the phrase *animus furandi.*

a fortiori. With stronger reason; much more.

a mensa et thoro. From bed and board.

a priori. From what goes before; from the cause to the effect.

a vinculo matrimonii. From the bonds of marriage.

ab initio. From the beginning.

actiones in personam. Personal actions.

ad faciendum. To do.

ad hoc. For this (for this special purpose).

ad infinitum. Indefinitely; forever.

ad litem. For the suit; for the litigation (A guardian *ad litem* is a person appointed to prosecute or defend a suit for a person incapacitated by infancy or incompetency.)

ad quod damnum. To what damage; what injury. (A phrase used to describe the plaintiff's money loss or the damages he claims.)

ad respondendum. To answer.

ad satisfaciendum. To satisfy.

ad valorem. According to value.

aggregatio menium. Meeting of minds.

alias dictus. Otherwise called.

alibi. In another place; elsewhere.

alii. Others.

aliunde. From another place; from without (as evidence outside the document).

alius. Another.

alter ego. The other self.

alumnus. A foster child.

amicus curiae. Friend of the court.

animo. With intention, disposition, design, will.

animus. Mind; intention.

animus furandi. The intention to steal.

animus revertendi. An intention of returning.

animus revocandi. An intention to revoke.

animus testandi. An intention to make a testament or will.

anno Domini (A.D.). In the year of the Lord.

ante. Before.

ante litem motam. Before suit brought.

arguendo. In the course of the argument.

assumpsit. He undertook; he promised.

bona fide. In good faith.

bona vacantia. Vacant goods. (Personal property that no one claims, which escheats to the state.)

capias. Take; arrest. (A form of writ directing an arrest.)

capias ad satisfaciendum (ca. sa.). Arrest to satisfy. (A form of writ.)

causa mortis. By reason of death.

caveat. Let him beware; a warning.

caveat emptor. Let the buyer beware.

cepit et asportavit. He took and carried away.

certiorari. To be informed of; to be made certain in regard to. (See glossary of legal terms.)

cestui (pl. cesuis). Beneficiaries. (Pronounced "setty.")

cestui que trust. He who benefits by the trust.

cestui que use. He who benefits by the use.

cestui que vie. He whose life measures the duration of the estate.

civiliter mortuus. Civilly dead.

Consensus, non concubitus, facit nuptias vel matrimonium. Consent, not cohabitation, constitutes nuptials or marriage.

consortium *(pl.* consortia). A union of lots or chances (a lawful marriage).

contra. Against.

contra bonos mores. Against good morals.

contra pacem. Against the peace.

coram non judice. In presence of a person not a judge. (A suit brought and determined in a court having no jurisdiction over the matter is said to be *coram non judice,* and the judgment is void.)

corpus. Body.

corpus delicti. The body of the offense; the essence of the crime.

corpus juris. A body of law.

corpus juris civilis. The body of the civil law.

Cujus est solum, ejus est usque ad coelum. Whose the soil is, his it is up to the sky.

cum testamento annexo (c.t.a.). With the will annexed. (Describes an administrator who operates under a will rather than in intestacy.)

damnum absque injuria. Damage without injury. (Damage without legal wrong.)

datum (*pl.* data). A thing given; a date.

de bonis non administratis. Of the goods not administered. Frequently abbreviated to *de bonis non.*

de bono et malo. For good and ill.

de facto. In fact; in deed; actually.

de jure. Of right; lawful.

De minimis non curat lex. The law does not concern itself with trifles.

de novo. Anew; afresh.

de son tort. Of his own wrong.

dies non. Not a day (on which the business of the courts can be carried on).

donatio mortis causa. A gift by reason of death. (A gift made by a person in sickness, under apprehension of death.)

duces tecum. You bring with you. (A term applied to a writ commanding the person upon whom it is served to bring certain evidence with him to court. Thus, we speak of a *subpoena duces tecum.*)

dum bene se gesserit. While he shall conduct himself well; during good behavior.

durante minore aetate. During minority.

durante viduitate. During widowhood.

e converso. Conversely; on the other hand.

eo instanti. Upon the instant.

erratum (*pl.* errata). Error.

et alii (et al.). And others.

et alius (et al.). And another.

et cetera (etc.). And other things.

ex cathedra. From the chair.

ex contractu. (Arising) from the contract.

ex delicto. (Arising) from a tort.

ex gratia. As a matter of favor.

ex necessitate legis. From legal necessity.

ex officio. From office; by virtue of his office.

ex parte. On one side only; by or for one party.

ex post facto. After the act.

ex rel (short for *ex relatione*). On information of; on behalf of a party or parties.

et uxor (et ux.). And wife.

et vir. And husband.

felonice. Feloniously.

feme covert. A married woman.

feme sole. A single woman (including one who has been married but whose marriage has been dissolved by death or divorce).

ferae naturae. Of a wild nature.

fiat. Let it be done. (A short order or warrant of a judge, commanding that something shall be done.)

fieri. To be made up; to become.

fieri facias. Cause to be made. (A writ directed to the sheriff to reduce the judgment debtor's property to money in the amount of the judgment.)

filius nullius. The son of nobody; a bastard.

filius populi. A son of the people.

flagrante delicto. In the very act of committing the crime.

habeas corpus. You have the body. (See glossary of legal terms.)

habendum clause. Clause in deed that defines extent of ownership by grantee.

habere facias possessionem. That you cause to have possession. (A writ of ejectment.)

habere facias seisinam. That you cause to have seisin. (A writ to give possession.)

honorarium (*pl.* honoraria). An honorary fee or gift; compensation from gratitude.

idem sonans. Having the same sound (as names sounding alike but spelled differently).

Ignorantia legis neminen excusat. Ignorance of the law excuses no one.

illicitum collegium. An unlawful association.

Impotentia excusat legem. Impossibility is an excuse in law.

in bonis. In goods; among possessions.

in esse. In being; existence.

in extremis. In extremity (in the last illness).

in fraudem legis. In circumvention of law.

in futuro. In the future.

in loco parentis. In the place of a parent.

in pari delicto. In equal fault.

in personam. A remedy where the proceedings are *against the person,* as contradistinguished from those against a specific thing.

in praesenti. At present; at once; now.

in re. In the matter.

in rem. A remedy where the proceedings are *against the thing,* as distinguished from those against the person.

in rerum natura. In nature; in life; in existence.

in specie. In the same, or like, form. (To decree performance *in specie* is to decree specific performance.)

in statu quo. In the condition in which it was. (See *status quo.*)

in terrorem. In terror.

in toto. In the whole; completely.

in transitu. In transit; in course of transfer.

indebitatus assumpsit. Being indebted, be promised, or undertook. (An action in which plaintiff alleges defendant is indebted to him.)

indicia. Marks; signs.

infra. Below.

innuendo. Meaning.

inter. Among; between.

inter vivos. Between the living.

interim. In the meantime.

intra. Within; inside.

ipse dixit. He himself said (it). (An assertion made but not proved.)

ipso facto. By the fact itself.

ita est. So it is.

jura personarum. Rights of persons.

jura rerum. Rights of things.

jurat. Portion of affidavit in which officer administering the oath certifies that it was sworn to before him. (See p. 230.)

jure divino. By divine right.

jure uxoris. In his wife's right.

jus (pl. jura). Law; laws collectively.

jus accrescendi. The right of survivorship.

jus ad rem. A right to a thing.

jus civile. Civil law.

jus commune. The common law; the common right.

jus gentium. The law of nations; international law.

jus habendi. The right to have a thing.

jus proprietatis. Right of property.

levari facias. Cause to be levied; a writ of execution.

lex loci. Law of the place (where the cause of action arose).

lex loci rei sitae. The law of the place where a thing is situated.

lex mercatoria. The law merchant.

lis pendens. Litigation pending; a pending suit.

locus delicti. The place of the crime or tort.

locus in quo. The place in which.

locus sigilii (L.S.). The place for the seal.

mala fides. Bad faith.

mala in se. Wrongs in themselves (acts morally wrong).

mala praxis. Malpractice.

mala prohibita. Prohibited wrongs or offenses.

malo animo. With evil intent.

malum in se. Evil in itself.

mandamus. We command. (See glossary of legal terms.)

manu forti. With a strong hand (forcible entry).

mens rea. Guilty mind.

nihil dicit. He says nothing. (Judgment against defendant who does not put in a defense to the complaint.)

nil debet. He owes nothing.

nisi prius. Unless before. (The phrase is used to denote the forum where the trial was held as distinguished from the appellate court.)

nolle prosequi. To be unwilling to follow up, or to prosecute. (A formal entry on the record by the plaintiff or the prosecutor that he will not further prosecute the case.)

nolo contendere. I will not contest it.

non compos mentis. Not of sound mind.

non est factum. It is not his deed.

non obstante. Notwithstanding.

non prosequitur (non pros.). He does not follow up, or pursue, or prosecute. (If the plaintiff fails to take some step that he should, the defendant may enter a judgment of *non pros.* against him.)

nudum pactum. A nude pact. (A contract without consideration.)

nul tiel record. No such record.

nul tort. No wrong done.

nulla bona. No goods. (Wording of return to a writ of *fieri facias.*)

nunc pro tunc. Now for then.

obiter dictum. Remark by the way. (See *dictum* in glossary of legal terms.)

onus probandi. The burden of proof.

opus (*pl. opera*). Work; labor.

ore tenus. By word of mouth; orally.

pari delicto. In equal guilt.

particeps criminis. An accomplice in the crime.

pater familias. The father (head) of a family.

peculium. Private property.

pendente lite. Pending the suit; during the litigation.

per annum. By the year.

per autre vie. For another's lifetime. (See also *pur autre vie.*)

per capita. By the head; as individuals. (In a distribution of an estate, if the descendants take per capita, they take share and share alike regardless of family lines of descent.)

per centum (per cent). By the hundred.

per contra. In opposition.

per curiam. By the court.

per diem. By the day.

per se. By itself; taken alone.

per stirpes. By stems or root; by representation. (In a distribution of an estate, if distribution is *per stirpes*, descendants take by virtue of their representation of an ancestor, not as individuals.)

postmortem. After death.

postobit. To take effect after death.

praecipe or *precipe.* Command. (A written order to the clerk of the court to issue a writ.)

prima facie. At first sight; on the face of it.

pro. For.

pro confesso. As confessed

pro forma. As a matter of form.

pro hac vice. For this occasion.

pro rata. According to the rate or proportion.

pro tanto. For so much; to that extent.

pro tempore (pro tem.). For the time being; temporarily.

prochein ami. Next friend.

publici juris. Of public right.

pur autre vie. For, or during, the life of another. (See also *per autre vie.*)

quaere. Query; question; doubt. (This word indicates that a particular rule, decision, or statement that follows it is open to question.)

quantum meruit. As much as he deserved.

quantum valebant. As much as they were (reasonably) worth (in absence of agreement as to value).

quare. Wherefore.

quare clausum fregit. Wherefore he broke the close. (A form of trespass on another's land.)

quasi. As if; as it were. (Indicates that one subject resembles another, but that there are also intrinsic differences between them. Thus, we speak of quasi contracts, quasi torts, etc.)

quid pro quo. What for what; something for something. (A term denoting the consideration for a contract.)

quo warranto. By what right or authority. (See glossary of legal terms.)

quoad hoc. As to this.

quod computet. That he account.

reductio ad absurdum. Reduced to the absurd.

res. A thing; an object; the subject matter.

res gestae. Things done; transactions.

res ipsa loquitur. The thing speaks for itself.

res judicata. A matter adjudicated.

scienter. Knowingly.

scilicet (SS. or ss.) To wit. (sc. is not used in legal papers)

scintilla. A spark; the least particle.

scire facias. Cause to know; give notice. (A writ used to revive a judgment that has expired.)

se defendendo. In self-defense; in defending oneself.

semper. Always.

semper paratus. Always ready. (A plea by which the defendant alleges that he has always been ready to perform what is demanded of him.)

seriatim. Severally; separately.

sigillum. A seal.

simplex obligato. A simple obligation.

sine die. Without day. (Without a specified day being assigned for a future meeting or hearing.)

situs. Situation; location.

stare decisis. To abide by decided cases.

status quo. State in which (the existing state of things at any given date.) See *in statu quo.*

sub judice. Under consideration.

sub modo. Under a qualification; in a qualified way.

sub nom. Under the name.

sui juris. Of his own right (having legal capacity to act for himself).

supersedeas. That you supersede. (A writ commanding a stay of the proceedings.)

supra. Above.

terminus a quo. The starting point.

ultra vires. Without power; beyond the powers of. (See glossary of legal terms.)

venire facias. That you cause to come (a kind of summons).

Verba fortius accipiuntur contra proferentem. Words are to be taken most strongly against the one using them.

versus (vs., v.). Against.

vi et armis. By force and arms.

via. A road; a right of way; by way of.

vice versa. On the contrary; on opposite sides.

videlicet (viz.) (contraction of *videre* and *licet*). It is easy to see (that is, namely).

virtute officii. By virtue of his office.

viva voce. By the living voice; by word of mouth.

voir dire. To speak the truth. (Denotes a preliminary examination to determine the competency of a witness.)

Glossary of Legal Terms

The following pages give clear and concise definitions and explanations of words and terms that you will hear in your daily work in a law office. Many of the words are not, strictly speaking, law terms, but are used in the preceding text with special legal significance. The words in the texts of the definitions that are in caps and small caps are defined in their respective alphabetical positions in this glossary. Also included here are some miscellaneous practices and procedures that are not covered elsewhere in the text.

Abrogation. The annulment or repeal of a law or obligation. The COMMON LAW, for example, is abrogated by statute.

Acceleration clause. A clause in contracts evidencing a debt, such as mortgages and installment contracts, that results in the entire debt becoming immediately due and payable when a condition of the contract is breached. Without an acceleration clause, the mortgagee or seller would have to sue for the amount of each payment as it became due, or would have to wait until the entire debt matured.

Account stated. An account balance, as determined by the creditor, that has been accepted as correct by the debtor. In law, the *account stated* operates as an admission of liability by the debtor. He is barred from disputing the accuracy of the computation, the bar being raised either by the debtor's explicit approval of the account or by his failure within a reasonable time to indicate any exception to it.

Acknowledgment. The act by which a person who has signed an instrument goes before an authorized officer, such as a notary public, and declares that he executed the instrument as his free act and deed. *See also Index.*

Adjective law. See SUBSTANTIVE LAW.

Administrative law. The rules and regulations framed by an administrative body created by a state legislature or by Congress to carry out a specific statute. For example, the federal income tax law is administered by the Internal Revenue Service. The bureau issues regulations and rules that have the weight of law as long as they keep within the scope of the income tax statute. Frequently such regulations interpret in a specific way the legislature's general intent when it enacted the statute. Thus, administrative bodies that are primarily executive in nature may also have powers that resemble legislative or judicial authority.

Administrator. A person appointed by the court to settle the estate of a deceased person who has left no valid will or whose named executor fails to serve. *See also Index.*

Affidavit. A written statement signed and sworn to before some person authorized to take an oath; frequently required as proof when no other evidence of a fact is available. *See also Index.*

Affirmance. See RATIFICATION.

Agency. The relationship that exists when one person authorizes another to act for him. The one granting the authority is the *principal;* the one authorized to act is the *agent.* For an agent to act, a *third party,* with whom he contracts, is necessary. An agency relationship is created when a person gives a POWER OF ATTORNEY or a PROXY, and in other situations. An agency may be *general*—the agent has broad powers to represent the principal; or the agency may be *special*—the agent represents the principal for a specific purpose or for a series of routine tasks. The principal is liable for the acts of the agent within the scope of the agency.

Alien corporation. A business organization incorporated outside the United States and its territories. The state statutes make no distinction between an alien and a FOREIGN CORPORATION, except in a few states that do not recognize alien corporations.

Allegation. A statement made by a party who claims it can be proved as fact. *See also Index.*

Allonge. (French.) A piece of paper attached to a bill of exchange or a promissory note, on which to write endorsements when there is no room on the instrument itself.

Ancillary. Auxiliary; subordinate. The term *ancillary letters* is used to apply to letters testamentary or letters of administration (see Index) that are taken out in a state other than that of the decedent's domicile, but in which he had assets or debts. Those letters are subordinate or supplementary to the letters issued in the decedent's domicile. The term *ancillary* also applies to court proceedings that are auxiliary to the main action—for example, a bill of discovery is ancillary to the principal action.

Antitrust laws. Laws designed to prevent restraint of trade, monopoly, and unfair practices in interstate commerce. The antitrust statutes are the Sherman Act (Antitrust Act of 1890); the Clayton Act; the Federal Trade Commission Act; the Robinson-Patman Act; the Miller-Tydings Act; the Wheeler-Lea Act.

Assault and battery. An assault is a threat made with the apparent intention of doing bodily harm to another. An essential element of assault is real or apparent ability on the part of the person making the threat to do bodily harm to another. Mere words do not constitute an assault. A *battery* is the wrongful touching of another's person or clothing as a result of assault. A battery always includes an assault, but an assault may be made without a battery. A person guilty of assault and battery is liable for damage to the injured party. Assault and battery may also be a crime punishable by the state.

Assignment. The transfer of property or some right or interest in property to another. Assignments are made (a) by the act of the parties, as in the case of a tenant assigning his lease to another; or (b) by operation of law, as in the case of death or bankruptcy. The party transferring his right is the *assignor;* the party to whom the rights are transferred is the *assignee.* To be valid, an assignment must be executed by a party having legal capacity, and it must be supported by consideration.

Attestation. The act of signing a written instrument as witness to the signature of a party, at his request; for example, witnessing signatures to a contract or a will. *See also Index.*

Attorney-in-fact. One who is appointed by another, with the authority to act for him in matters specified in the terms of the appointment. (see AGENCY; *also Index.*)

Bailment. A delivery of personal property for some particular purpose, upon a contract, express or implied, that the property will be returned to the person delivering it after the accomplishment of the purpose for which it was delivered. An essential of a bailment is that return of the property or an accounting in accordance with the terms of agreement is contemplated. The person delivering the property is a *bailor*; the person receiving it is a *bailee.* If under the terms of the contract the bailee is obligated to pay a sum of money instead of returning the goods, the obligation is a debt and not a bailment. Thus, a conditional sale is distinguished from a bailment in that the purchaser must pay the purchase price at which time he acquires title to the property. The parties to a consignment of goods expect that the goods will be sold for the account of the consignor or returned to him; a consignment is therefore considered a bailment. A bailee is liable for breach of his contract to keep the property in a particular manner in a particular place for a particular purpose. The following transactions are bailments: lease of a car for hire; deposit of goods for storage or safekeeping; pledge of stocks as collateral. Title to the property remains in the bailor.

Bankruptcy. *Bankruptcy* is a state of insolvency in which the property of a debtor is taken over by a receiver or trustee in bankruptcy for the benefit of the creditors. This action is taken under the jurisdiction of the courts as prescribed by the National Bankruptcy Act.

Voluntary bankruptcy. Voluntary bankruptcy is brought about by the filing of a petition in bankruptcy by the debtor. The form of the petition is prescribed by the act. By filing a voluntary petition, the debtor seeks, first, to have his assets equally distributed among all his creditors but on the basis of established priorities and, second, to free himself of his debts. He is thus able to begin his business life anew, free of those debts discharged in bankruptcy.

Voluntary bankruptcy is open to all individuals, firms, partnerships, and corporations, except banking and building and loan associations, and insurance, railroad, and municipal corporations. No special amount of indebtedness is required; a person owing one dollar or several million dollars may file a petition in voluntary bankruptcy.

Involuntary bankruptcy. Involuntary bankruptcy is brought about by the filing of a petition by the creditors against an insolvent debtor. If there are fewer than 12 creditors, 1 creditor may file the petition; if there are more than 12, 3 creditors must join in the filing. Before creditors can throw a debtor into bankruptcy, these conditions must exist:

1. The debtor must owe at least $1,000.

2. The creditor or creditors filing the petition must have provable claims aggregating $500.

3. The debtor must have committed an act of bankruptcy within four months preceding the filing of the petition.

Involuntary bankruptcy proceedings cannot be brought against a wage earner, a farmer, or a banking or building and loan association, or an insurance, railroad, or municipal corporation.

Steps in bankruptcy proceedings. After a petition is filed in the federal courts, in a form prescribed by the United States Supreme Court, the basic steps are: (1) application for receiver, (2) adjudication of the bankrupt, (3) referral to bankruptcy judge, (4) filing of schedules by the bankrupt, (5) meetings of creditors, (6) election of trustee in bankruptcy, (7) proof and allowance of claims, and (8) discharge of the bankrupt.

Bankruptcy judge. When the court signs a decree of adjudication it refers the case to a bankruptcy judge. The judge, who is a lawyer, acts in place of the bankruptcy court, conducts all the usual proceedings, and grants the final discharge of the bankrupt from further liability for his debts. He presides over all creditors' meetings.

Filing of schedules by the bankrupt. Within five days after the debtor has been adjudged bankrupt he must file, in involuntary cases, a schedule of his assets and liabilities on a form prescribed by the United States Supreme Court. If the debtor files a voluntary petition, he must accompany the petition with similar schedules.

What the secretary and paralegal do. Open a file and process a bankruptcy matter just as you do any new matter. *Make diary entries* and keep a progress record sheet. The petition, application, schedules, and the like are prepared on forms prescribed by the United States Supreme Court. You will have no difficulty filling them in.

Bill of sale. A formal document issued by a seller to a buyer, as evidence of transfer to the latter of title to the goods described in the instrument. A bill of sale may be used in the case of any sale of PERSONAL PROPERTY.

Blue-sky laws. Laws that have been enacted by most of the states to protect the public from fraud in the offering of securities. Such laws are an exercise of the POLICE POWER of the states; they supplement interstate regulation of securities offerings, securities exchanges, and speculative practices, through the Securities and Exchange Commission. Protection is achieved through (1) specific legislation—blue-sky laws; and (2) through enforcement of the statute of frauds.

Breach of contract. The failure or refusal by one of the parties to a contract to perform some act the contract calls for without legal excuse. A contract may also be breached by preventing or obstructing performance by the other party; or by "anticipatory" breach, as the unqualified announcement by a seller, before delivery date, that he will not deliver the goods.

Breach of a contract by one party may discharge the other from performance. Or the injured party may sue for damages representing the loss directly incurred from the breach. Damages cannot be obtained for speculative or possible losses that cannot be shown to have resulted directly from the breach.

Breach of warranty. When a WARRANTY made by a vendor proves to be false, the warranty is said to be breached. For the breach, the buyer has a choice of four remedies: (1) accept or keep the goods and set up the breach to reduce the purchase price; (2) keep the goods and recover damages for the breach of warranty; (3) refuse to accept the goods if title has not passed and bring an action for damages for breach of warranty; (4) rescind the contract, or if the goods have been delivered, return them, and recover any part of the purchase price that had been paid. The buyer can claim only *one* of these remedies.

Business trust. See MASSACHUSETTS TRUST.

Bylaws (corporate). Rules adopted by a corporation to regulate its conduct as a corporate entity and to define and determine the rights and duties of its stockholders and the rights, powers, and duties of the directors and officers. They are permanent, except in so far as they may be amended. They are never public laws or regulations, hence the term *bylaws. See also Index.*

Caveat emptor. (Latin for "let the buyer beware.") This COMMON LAW doctrine or maxim imposes on the buyer the duty of examining what he buys. It is applied where the seller makes no express warranty and is not guilty of fraud. Exceptions to the *caveat emptor* doctrine are made under the following circumstances: (1) A fiduciary relationship exists between the parties, as between principal and agent, attorney and client, trustee and beneficiary. (2) The defects are not obvious and the buyer has not had an opportunity for thorough inspection. (3) The sale was made by sample or by description. (4) The sale was for a specific purpose.

Certificate of stock. See CORPORATION; *also Index.*

Certiorari. A writ issued by a superior court to an inferior court directing it to send to the former court the record of a particular case. A *writ of certiorari* is an extraordinary remedy resorted to in cases obviously entitled to redress where no direct appellate proceedings are provided by law. A writ of certiorari cannot be used as a substitute for an appeal or a writ of error. It is distinguished from an appeal in that it brings up the case on the record, whereas on appeal a case is brought up on the merits. A litigant is entitled to a writ of error as a matter of right, but a writ of certiorari lies within the court's discretion.

The dissatisfied party in the lower court petitions the appellate court for a writ of certiorari. If, on the face of the record, the appellate court determines that the lower court has not proceeded in accordance with the law, it will consent to issue the writ and hear the case. If the record itself does not indicate that the petitioner has been wronged by the proceeding, the court will deny the petition for writ of certiorari. The denial is, in effect, an affirmance of the lower court's decision on the point of law before the appellate court, but the issuance of the writ does not mean that the appellate court will decide in favor of the petitioner. The court may then order the certiorari dismissed; or return it to the lower court with instructions; or render a final judgment which must finally govern the case.

Chattel. An article of tangible PERSONAL PROPERTY, as distinguished from real property (land and improvements) and intangibles (stocks, bonds, and the like).

Chose in action. PERSONAL PROPERTY that is not susceptible to physical possession and that requires some form of action to acquire or recover possession.

Some of the most important choses in action are contracts, promissory notes, checks, trade acceptances, stocks, bonds, bank accounts, and the right of legal action to recover money or property.

Civil law. The law of the Romans under Emperor Justinian was condensed and digested into a code known as Corpus Juris Civilis. The laws of Justinian were lost in the Western Empire during the early Dark Ages, but a complete copy was found about 1137. The laws were then revised and became the basis of jurisprudence for most of continental Europe. The present law on the Continent is therefore referred to as the Roman or civil law. See COMMON LAW for development of law in England.

Civil wrongs. Concern the relationship between individuals as such, as distinguished from wrongs against the public (see CRIMINAL LAW). Civil wrongs infringe on private rights and duties; remedy against them is sought by private action. TORT and BREACH OF CONTRACT are among the more common civil wrongs.

Close corporation. A corporation whose capital stock is held by a limited group, in contrast to one whose stock is generally sold to the public. Frequently the owners are also the managers. Usually a close corporation is small, although some are large. Ford Motor Company, until 1956 for instance, was a close corporation.

Common law. A system of law, or body of legal rules, derived from decisions of judges based upon accepted customs and traditions. It was developed in England. It is known as the *common law* because it is believed that these rules were generally recognized and were in full force throughout England. Common law is now the basis of the laws in every state of the United States, except Louisiana, which bases its laws upon the early laws of France. Statutes have been enacted to supplement and supersede the common law in many fields; the common law, however, still governs where there is no statute dealing with a specific subject. Although the common law is written, it is called the *unwritten law* in contradistinction to STATUTORY LAW enacted by the legislatures.

Common law trust. See MASSACHUSETTS TRUST.

Community property. In some states a system exists whereby all earnings of either husband or wife constitute a common fund of the husband and wife. The property is known as *community property*. The central idea of the system is the same in all states where community property exists, but statutes and judicial decisions have directed the development of the system along different lines in the various states. For example, is some states only property that is acquired by the exertion or labor of either party is *common*, whereas in other states income from separate property is also considered community property. Generally, either husband or wife may have "separate" property, such as that belonging to either of them at the time of marriage, real estate acquired in a state that does not recognize community property, or property given to or inherited by either at any time. Property acquired in exchange for separate property is separate property; that acquired in exchange for community property is community property. In some states the husband may dispose of or encumber the community property, but the wife may not; nor may community property be attached for the wife's debts, except for those contracted for necessities for herself and her children.

Competent parties. See CONTRACTS, 2.

Conditional sale. An installement sale. The buyer usually gives the seller a promissory note secured by a conditional sale contract or a chattel mortgage. A *conditional sale contract* is a contract for the sale of goods under which the goods are delivered to the buyer but the title remains in the seller until the goods are paid for in full, or until the conditions of the contract are fulfilled. When a chattel mortgage is used, the seller transfers the goods to the buyer who, in turn, executes a chattel mortgage in favor of the seller. This instrument gives the seller a lien on the goods.

The seller's choice of a security depends upon the laws in his state. He studies the laws and selects the type of instrument that provides the most protection with the least inconvenience. The instrument usually includes a provision that if an installment is not paid when due, the entire debt becomes payable at once. This clause, called the ACCELERATION CLAUSE, is essential in any installment contract. Otherwise the seller would have to sue for the amount of each installment as it became due, or would have to wait until the entire debt matured.

Constructive. The term *constructive* generally applies to that which amounts in the eyes of the law to an act, although the act itself is not necessarily performed. The law presumes an act to have been performed, and applies the term to many situations to prevent a miscarriage of justice.

Some of the circumstances under which the law will presume an act are indicated by the following: constructive abandonment, constructive delivery, constructive desertion, constructive eviction, constructive fraud, constructive gift, constructive notice, constructive possession, constructive process, constructive receipt of income, constructive service, and constructive trusts. A few of these are explained.

Constructive delivery. Arises when actual, or manual, delivery is impossible or undesirable. Constructive delivery includes those acts that are equivalent to actual delivery although they do not confer real possession. Acts that bar a lien or a right to stoppage in transit, such as marking and setting apart goods as belonging to the buyer, constitute constructive delivery.

Constructive notice. Notice that arises from a strictly legal presumption that cannot be controverted. The presumption is one of law and not of fact, as distinguished from implied notice that arises from an inference of facts. The presumption of constructive notice is conclusive against the actual facts. Thus, a mortgage recorded with the proper public authorities is constructive notice of the mortgagee's interest in the property.

Constructive receipt. Constructive receipt of income usually constitutes taxable income under the various tax laws. For example, any time during the year commissions may be credited on a firm's books to a salesman who may draw upon the firm to the amount of the credit. The commission is said to be constructively received. Whatever amount is credited to the salesman would have to be reported by him as income in the year the amount was credited on the books, even if the money was not drawn until the following year.

Contracts. An agreement, enforceable at law, by which two parties mutually promise to give some particular thing, or to do or abstain from doing a particular act. A contract may be formal or informal; it may be oral or written, sealed or unsealed, except that state statutes, usually designated as the STATUTE OF FRAUDS, require certain agreements to be in writing. A contract may be *executed*—one that has been fully carried out by both parties; or *executory*—one that is yet to be performed. It may be executed on the part of one party and executory on the part of the other. For example, the purchase of merchandise on credit, followed by delivery, is executed on the part of the seller and executory on the part of the buyer. A contract may be *express*—all the terms definitely expressed in the oral or written agreement; or *implied*—the terms not expressed but implied by the law from the actions of the parties. For example, when a person gets on a bus, his action implies a contract with the transit company.

To be enforceable at law a contract must have the following four elements:

1. *Offer and acceptance.* Before a contract can be formed, there must be an offer by one party, called the *offeror,* to do or to refrain from doing a certain thing, and an acceptance of the proposal by another party, called the *offeree.*

An offer is considered open until it is revoked, rejected, or accepted, or until after the lapse of a reasonable time. The only case in which an offeror cannot withdraw an offer before acceptance is the case in which he has entered into an OPTION contract, which is an agreement supported by the payment of a sum of money, or for some other consideration, to hold an offer open for a definite period. As a general rule, an offer, once accepted, cannot be withdrawn or revoked.

An acceptance is an indication by the offeree of his willingness to be bound by the terms of the offer. The acceptance may take the form of an act, the signing and delivery of a written instrument, or of a promise communicated to the offeror. Silence on the part of the offeree is not an acceptance unless the previous dealings between the parties create a duty upon the part of the offeree to accept or reject the offer. The acceptance must be unequivocal and must show an intention to accept all the terms of the offer. In the language frequently used by the courts, there must be a "meeting of the minds" of the offeror and the offeree.

2. *Competent parties.* All persons are presumed to have unlimited power to contract—except infants, insane persons or persons with impaired mental faculties, intoxicated persons, married women, and corporations.

Under common law, a person is in his infancy until he reaches the age of 21, although some states provide that women become of age at 18, and other states provide that marriage removes the infancy status. Contracts by infants are not void, but generally they may be disaffirmed by the infant. An infant is not bound by an executory contract unless he affirms the contract after coming of age; failure to affirm implies disaffirmance. An infant may disaffirm an executed contract during infancy or within a reasonable time after he attains his majority; failure to disaffirm within a reasonable time implies affirmance. Contracts for necessities, as food, clothing, shelter, medical care, education, and the like, may be binding upon an infant.

Like infants, insane persons are not absolutely incapable of making contracts; their contracts are voidable, not void, and they may be held liable for necessities. A person who is so drunk that he is deprived of his reason and does not understand the nature of his acts is in the same position as a mental incompetent: he may disaffirm his contracts if the disaffirmance does not injure third persons, and provided he disaffirms immediately upon restoration of his faculties.

Under the COMMON LAW a married woman was deemed incapable of binding herself by contract, her contracts being regarded as void rather than voidable. But the statutes in most states have modified the common law. In general, a married woman may now contract as freely as a single woman, but in some states she cannot contract with her husband, enter into partnership with him, or act as surety for him.

A corporation's ability to contract is limited by its charter and by various statutes.

3. *Legality of subject matter.* A contract is illegal if it calls for the performance of an act forbidden by law or against public policy. Gambling and wagering contracts, and usurious contracts (see USURY), for example, are generally held to be illegal. In some states any contract entered into on Sunday is illegal. Federal and state laws make those contracts illegal that restrain trade, fix prices, or result in unfair practices.

4. *Consideration.* Something of benefit to the person making a promise must be given, or some detriment must be suffered by the person to whom a promise is made to make a contract binding. *Consideration* is the price, motive, or matter inducing the contract; it may consist of (a) doing some act that one is not obligated to perform; (b) refraining from doing something that one would otherwise be free to do; (c) giving some money or property; (d) giving a promise. The value of the consideration is generally immaterial.

5. *Contracts under seal.* The placing of a SEAL on a contract has lost the significance formerly attached to it, but it is still customary, and required in some states, on contracts of major importance. Deeds, mortgages, and other conveyances of real estate are among the contracts requiring a seal.

Conversion. The unlawful taking or possession of another's CHATTEL. When a seller has passed title but refuses to make delivery, the buyer may sue him for conversion. Conversion may also take the form of unauthorized destruction or alteration of another's property.

Corporation. An organization formed under a state statute for the purpose of carrying on an enterprise in such a way as to make the enterprise distinct and separate from the persons who are interested in it and who control it; ".... an artificial being, invisible, intangible, and existing only in contemplation of law." *The Trustees of Dartmouth College* v. *Woodward* (1819) 17 U.S. 518, 636.

The ownership of the corporation is represented by its capital stock, which is divided into identical units or groups of identical units called *shares*. These shares are represented by written instruments called *certificates of stock*. The owners of the shares are called the *stockholders*. Every stockholder has the right to transfer his shares—a right based on the inherent power of a person to dispose of his property. Since the shares of stock of a corporation can be transferred by sale or otherwise from one owner to another without affecting the corporate existence, the corporation enjoys continuous succession. The existence of the corporation is not disturbed by death, insanity, or bankruptcy of individual stockholders or by change of ownership. *See also Index.*

Counterclaim. A defendant may take advantage of a suit against him to ask the court for relief against the plaintiff, when otherwise he would be compelled to institute an action of his own. For example, the maker of a note might claim that the payee is indebted to him for certain sums in connection with a matter not related to the note. The cause of action set up by the defendant, to be tried at the same time as the cause of action alleged by the plaintiff, is a counterclaim.

Court bond. Litigants at law are required many times to file a bond or other security guaranteeing that, if unsuccessful in litigation, they will pay to the other party the monetary damages awarded by the court. These bonds are known as *court* or *judiciary* bonds. Another class of court bonds are known as *probate bonds*. They are issued to executors, administrators, and other fiduciaries to guarantee the faithful performance of their legal duties.

Criminal law. The statutes and general dicta that forbid certain actions or conduct as detrimental to the welfare of the state and that provide punishment therefor. Criminal acts are prosecuted by the state, as oppposed to CIVIL WRONGS, which are prosecuted by an individual. A wrong may be both a criminal wrong and a civil wrong; for example, ASSAULT AND BATTERY. A crime may be a *treason,* a *felony,* or a *misdemeanor.* The Constitution states that treason "shall consist only in levying war against them or in adhering to their enemies, giving them aid and comfort." *Felonies* are crimes punishable by death or by imprisonment in a federal or state prison. They include murder, grand larceny, arson, and rape. *Misdemeanors* are crimes of lesser importance than felonies and are punishable by fine or imprisonment in the local jail. They include petty larceny, drunkenness, disorderly conduct, and vagrancy. Violation of traffic ordinances, building codes, and similar city ordinances are not crimes but are termed *petty offenses, public torts,* or *mala prohibita.*

Cumulative voting. A system of voting for directors of a corporation under which each stockholder is entitled to a number of votes equal to the number of shares he owns multiplied by the number of directors to be elected. He may cast all the votes for one candidate—cumulate them—or he may distribute his votes among the candidates in any way he sees fit. This system enables the minority stockholders to elect one or more of the directors. The right to cumulative voting cannot be claimed unless provided for (1) by statute, (2) by the corporation's charter or bylaws, or (3) by contract among all the stockholders, provided the agreement is not otherwise illegal.

Cy pres doctrine. (French for "as near as.") An ancient doctrine applicable to the construction of instruments in equity, whereby the intention of the party making the instrument is carried out as nearly as possible when it is impossible to carry out his precise intention. The doctrine, though ancient, is especially useful in modern times as a device to render charitable trusts useful. For example, if funds left to a charitable trust are insufficient to carry out the provisions of the testamentary trust, the fund does not necessarily revert to the estate, but may be used for a charitable purpose similar to that provided for in the trust. The doctrine is not accepted in all states.

Damages. The sum allowed by law as compensation for an injury or loss caused by the unlawful act or negligence of another. The amount of damages to be recovered is usually a matter for the jury to determine.

Decree. The court's decision in EQUITY. A decree usually directs the defendant to do or not to do some specific thing, as opposed to a judgment for damages in a court of law. A decree is *final* when it disposes of the case, leaving no question to be decided in the future; for example, a decree ordering SPECIFIC PERFORMANCE of a contract. A decree is *interlocutory* when it leaves unsettled some question to be determined in the future; for example, a temporary INJUNCTION. *See also Index.*

Deed. A formal written instrument by which title to real property is conveyed from one person to another. The parties to a deed are the *grantor,* who conveys his or her interest in the property, and the *grantee,* to whom the conveyance is made. *See also Index.*

Defamation. See LIBEL AND SLANDER.

Del credere. (Italian.) A term applied to an agent who, for a higher commission, guarantees his principal that he will pay for goods sold on credit if the buyer does not. Del credere agencies are common in businesses that employ commission merchants or agents whose relatively independent financial status enables them to guarantee their customers' accounts.

Dictum. An opinion expressed by a court that is not necessary in deciding the question before the court. When, in addition, such opinion does not relate to the questions before the court, it is called *obiter dictum* (Latin for "remark by the way"). Dicta carry legal weight in courts deciding subsequent questions but not to the extent that court decisions do. Court decisions are binding precedents; the dicta expressed in the opinion are not.

Disaffirmance. The act by which a person who has entered into a voidable contract indicates that he will not abide by the contract. (See VOID; VOIDABLE.) For example, an infant may refuse to honor a contract by disaffirmance when he reaches majority.

Discharge of contract. The release of the parties to a contract from their obligations under it. Contracts may be discharged by the following methods: (1) *Performance.* The carrying out of the terms of the contract. (2) *Agreement.* The parties may agree to discharge one another from further liability under the contract. There must be sufficient consideration for the agreement. (3) *Impossibility of performance.* When a contract is based on an implied condition that certain factors shall continue to exist during the life of the contract, and those factors cease to exist, performance is impossible and the contract is discharged. (4) *Operation of law.* A change in the law in effect at the time the contract was made may bring about a discharge of the contract, or a law itself may operate as a discharge. Thus, a contract to build a garage on a certain site would be discharged by a zoning ordinance forbidding the erection of a garage within that zone. (5) *Breach.* If one party breaches a contract the other may be discharged. (See BREACH OF CONTRACT.)

Discovery. A procedure designed to obtain facts known by the defendant, or referred to in papers in his possession. The information is obtained by means of a bill of discovery.

Dishonor. Refusal to pay a NEGOTIABLE INSTRUMENT when due. Notice of dishonor is usually given to endorsers and drawers, who, in addition to the maker, are liable on the instrument. Notice of dishonor may be given orally or in writing. If it is not given, endorsers and drawers are discharged from liability. (See also PROTEST.)

Doing business. See INTERSTATE COMMERCE; INTRASTATE COMMERCE.

Domestic corporation. A corporation organized under the laws of a particular state is a domestic corporation in that state. When this corporation does business in another state, it's a *foreign* corporation there. (See FOREIGN CORPORATION.)

Duress. Coercion causing action or inaction against a person's will through fear. Duress may take the form of physical force, imprisonment, bodily harm, improper moral persuasion, or the threat of any of these. Threat of criminal prosecution constitutes duress, but threat of civil prosecution does not. A contract made under duress is voidable at the option of the party subjected to duress.

Earnest (earnest money). The payment that one contracting party gives to another at the time of entering into the contract to bind the sale, and that will be forfeited by the doner if he fails to carry out the contract. The money is applied to the purchase price if the doner lives up to his bargain. *See also Index.*

Eminent domain. The power of federal, state, and local governments to appropriate property for public use or the public welfare. When such property is taken, the owner is reimbursed according to a fair appraisal, and has the right to sue for a greater amount. PUBLIC UTILITY (public service) corporations are also given the power of eminent domain.

Endorsement. (*See Index* for typed endorsement on back of legal documents.) *On negotiable instrument.* Writing one's name, either with or without additional words, on a NEGOTIABLE INSTRUMENT or on a paper (called an ALLONGE) attached to it. By an endorsement, the endorser becomes liable to all subsequent holders in due course for payment of the instrument if it is not paid by the maker when properly presented, and if he is given notice of dishonor (see DISHONOR).
Blank endorsement. The writing of one's name on an instrument, or an allonge, without any additional words, is a blank endorsement. Its effect is to make the paper payable to the bearer. Thus, a finder or thief might transfer the note to a third party for a consideration, and the third party might then enforce payment against the maker or the endorser.
Special endorsement. The designation of a certain person to whom the instrument is payable is a special endorsement. Thus, if an instrument is endorsed "Pay to John Jones," or "Pay to the order of John Jones," followed by the endorser's signature, no one but John Jones can receive payment for the instrument or transfer it.
Restrictive endorsement. An endorsement that transfers possession of the instrument for a particular purpose is a restrictive endorsement. Examples: "Pay to John Jones only. Sam Brown." "Pay to National City Bank for collection. Sam Brown." "For deposit only. Sam Brown." A restrictive endorsement terminates the negotiability of the instrument.
Qualified endorsement. An endorsement that qualifies or limits the liability of the endorser is a qualified endorsement. If an endorser endorses an instrument "without recourse," he does not assume liability in the event the maker fails to pay the instrument when due.

Conditional endorsement. A special endorsement with words added that create a condition which must happen before the special endorsee is entitled to payment is a conditional endorsement. The endorser is liable only if the condition is fulfilled. Example: "Pay to Greenwood Cotton Growers Association upon delivery of warehouse receipt for twenty-five standard bales cotton, strict to middling. John Jones."

Irregular or accommodation endorsement. An endorsement made for the purpose of lending the endorser's credit to a party to the instrument is an irregular or accommodation endorsement. It is also called an *anomalous* endorsement. A regular endorsement transfers title to the instrument, whereas an accommodation endorsement is for additional security only. An accommodation endorser is never the maker, drawer, acceptor, payee, or holder of the instrument he endorses.

Equity. 1. *Legal. See Index.*

2. *Accounting and finance.* The value of the owner's interest in property in excess of all claims and liens against it. Examples: (a) An owner's equity in his home is its present value less the amount of the mortgage. (b) The equity of the stockholders of a business is its net worth; hence, the interest of the stockholders as measured by capital and surplus, or the value of the assets of the business in excess of its liabilities. Sometimes, however, equity refers to the unlimited interest of common stockholders. (c) The equity of a person who has bought securities on margin is the present market value of the securities less the sum borrowed from the broker to make the purchase.

Escheat. The return of land to the state if the owner dies without legal heirs. Unclaimed personal property may also go to the state. Escheated personal property is called *bona vacantia.*

Escrow. A conditional delivery of something to a third person to be held until the happening of some event or the performance of some act. To place an instrument or a fund in escrow is to deliver the instrument or fund to a person charged with its custody and disposition under the terms of a specific agreement, known as the *escrow agreement.* For example, a grantor may deliver a deed in escrow to a trust company until the grantee makes certain payments on the purchase price, at which time the trust company delivers the deed to the grantee. *See also Index.*

Estate by the entirety. See TENANCY BY THE ENTIRETY.

Estoppel. A bar raised by law preventing a person from taking a position, denying a fact, or asserting a fact, in court, inconsistent with the truth as established by judicial or legislative officers or by his own deed or acts, either express or implied. Example: *A* sells *B* a house that he *(A)* does not own, giving *B* a covenant and warranty deed, in which he warrants that he has title to the house. Later, *A* obtains title from the actual owner and attempts to eject *B* on the ground that *A* is now the true owner and *B* is not. *A* would be estopped from disputing what he formerly warranted, namely, that he was the true owner when he sold the house.

Ex parte. (Latin for "of the one part.") Done for or on behalf of one party only. The term is applied to a proceeding, order, or injuction that is taken for the benefit of one party only. An injuction is granted *ex parte* when only one side has had a hearing. When *ex parte* appears in the title of a case, the name following is that of the party upon whose application the case was heard.

Execution. 1. *Of judgment.* A legal writ directing an officer of the law to carry out a judgment is an execution of judgment. *See also Index.*
   2. *Of instrument.* The signature and delivery of a written instrument constitutes execution of the instrument. *See also Index.*

Fee simple. The absolute ownership of real property. It gives the owner and his heirs the unconditional power of disposition and and other rights. (See REAL PROPERTY.)

Felony. See CRIMINAL LAW.

Force majeure. (French.) Superior or irresistible force. Corresponds in a general way to "Act of God"; for example, an earthquake, or the sudden death of a person. If a party to a contract is prevented from executing it by a *force majeure,* he may not be held liable for damages.

Foreign corporation. A corporation doing business in a state of the United States other than the state in which it was created or incorporated. It must comply with certain terms and conditions imposed by the state. The state statutes make no distinction between a foreign and an alien corporation (a corporation organized outside the United States and its territories); both are regarded as foreign, except in those few states that do not recognize alien corporations.

Garnishment. The right of a creditor to compel a third party owing money to, or holding money for, a debtor to pay the money to the creditor instead of to the debtor. (See EXECUTION.) The third party against whom the proceedings are brought is called the *garnishee.* Not only wages and salaries, but trust funds, insurance disability payments, and the like, may be garnisheed. The laws that govern the right of garnishment differ considerably in the various states, and in some states it is referred to as a *factoring process* or a *trustee process.*

Guaranty. The term is used interchangeably with suretyship by courts and lawyers as well as laymen, although there may be a distinction about the degree of liability wherein the surety is primarily liable upon the engagement and the guarantor is secondarily liable and not chargeable with nonperformance until notice is given. A contract of guaranty or of suretyship is a contract whereby one person agrees to be responsible to another for the payment of a debt or the performance of a duty by a third person. It must be in writing and is not enforceable if made orally.

The term *guaranty* (or *guarantee*) is often loosely used in the sense of WARRANTY. In a strict legal and commercial sense, it is of the essence of a contract of guaranty that there should be a principal, liable directly to perform some act or duty. An agreement by a third party guaranteeing the honest and faithful performance of a contract of sale is a contract of guaranty; an agreement in a sales contract "guaranteeing" the efficient performance of a product for a certain number of years is a contract of warranty.

Habeas corpus. (Latin for "You have the body.") A writ commanding the person having custody of another to produce the person detained at a certain place and time so the court may determine if the detention is lawful.

Holder in due course. The transferee of a NEGOTIABLE INSTRUMENT who acquires the instrument under the following conditions: (1) The paper must be complete and regular on its face. (2) It must be purchased before maturity. (3) The purchase must be in good faith for a valuable consideration. (4) The purchase must be made without notice of defects in the title or of defenses against payment to the transferor. A holder in due course may enforce collection of the instrument against prior parties regardless of their claims, defenses, and offsets against one another. A transferee may acquire the rights of a holder in due course without being one himself. *Example: A,* the holder in due course of a note procured by the payee through fraud, endorses the note to *B,* who knew of the fraud and hence was not a holder in due course. *B,* however, acquires *A's* right as a holder in due course to collect the note regardless of the fraud, provided *B* had no part in the fraud.

Exception: Some states have amended their consumer protection laws to allow a buyer of goods to assert *any defenses* he would have against the seller, as against seller's assignee, even though the latter has met the above criteria as a holder in due course.

Inchoate. Begun but not completed, as a contract not executed by all the parties. An instrument that the law requires to be recorded is an *inchoate instrument* until it is recorded, in that it is good only between the parties and privies (see PRIVITY). A wife's interest in her husband's lands that becomes a right of dower upon his death is an *inchoate right of dower* during his lifetime. An interest in real estate that may become a vested interest unless barred is an *inchoate interest.* Other phrases are *inchoate equity, inchoate lien, inchoate title.*

Indemnity. An undertaking, either express or implied, to compensate another for loss or damage, or for expenses or trouble incurred, either in the past or in the future. Under a contract of indemnity, the indemnity is the obligation or duty resting upon a particular person or company to make good any loss or damage another has suffered or may suffer, upon the happening of a specific event. The person giving the indemnity (agreeing to indemnify) is the *indemnitor,* corresponding to an insurer; the person who receives the indemnity or protection is the *indemnitee,* corresponding to the insured. The term *indemnity* also applies to the sum paid as compensation or remuneration in the event of loss or damage to the indemnitee. The indemnity may be payable to the indemnitee or to someone else in behalf of the indemnitee. For example, the payments that are made to an injured workman under workman's compensation insurance are indemnities. They are payable to the workman in behalf of his employer, who is the indemnitee.

Indenture. A formal written instrument between two or more parties that involves reciprocal rights and duties, such as a lease. In ancient times, the practice was to write two or more copies of the instrument on the same piece of parchment. The copies were then separated by tearing the parchment in irregular fashion, so the indentations of each torn part would fit the other. Hence, the name *indenture. See also Index.*

Infant's contract. See CONTRACTS, 2.

Injunction. A writ issued by a court of equity restraining a person or corporation from doing or continuing to do something that threatens or causes injury, or requiring the defendant to do a particular act. Injunctions may be classified as *prohibitory* and *mandatory.* A *prohibitory injunction* restrains the commission or continuance of an act. Thus, a prohibitory injunction may restrain a board of elections from placing a certain candidate's name on the ballot. A *mandatory injunction* commands acts to be done or undone. For example, a mandatory injunction may compel a property owner to open a road that he had closed by constructing a fence across it, thus depriving another property owner of the use of the road.

Injunctions may also be classified as (1) restraining orders, (2) temporary injunctions, and (3) permanent injunctions. A *restraining order* may be granted without notice to the opposite party, for the purpose of restraining the defendant until the court has heard an application for a temporary injunction. A *temporary injunction* is granted on the basis of the application, before the court has heard the case on its merits. It restrains the defendant during the litigation of a case, and may be either dissolved or made permanent when the rights of the parties are determined. Temporary injunctions are also called preliminary, interlocutory, or injunction *pendente lite. Permanent injunctions* are granted on the merits of the case. They are often called final or permanent injunctions.

Insurable interest. A person has an insurable interest if he might be financially injured by the occurrence of the event insured against. Under American law if an insurable interest is not present, the contract is a mere wager and is not enforceable.

In property. Insurable interest must exist at the time the loss occurs. Title to the property insured is not necessary; an owner, lessee, mortgagee, or purchaser has an insurable interest. Thus, the interest (1) may be contingent, as the interest of a purchaser under a contract of sale; (2) may be conditional, as the interest of a seller under a contract of CONDITIONAL SALE until the conditions of the sale have been met; (3) may arise from possession as in the case of a bailee (see BAILMENT).

In life. Insurable interest must exist at the time the policy is written but need not exist at the time death occurs. Every person has insurable interest in his own life and may name anyone he chooses as beneficiary. Other examples of relations giving rise to an insurable interest are those of (1) employer and valued employee; (2) several partners of a partnership; (3) creditor and debtor; (4) corporation and its officers; (5) wife and husband; (6) dependent children.

Interlocking directorates. Boards of directors of two or more corporations have one or more directors in common. Through this method of control, the will of the common dominant stockholders is executed.

Interlocutory decree. See DECREE.

Interstate commerce, intrastate commerce. The Constitution gives the federal government power to regulate "commerce among the several states" (Art. I, Sec. 8). But it does not define either commerce or interstate commerce. The courts decided originally that commerce meant buying and selling. Hence, if the buying and selling is part of an interchange of commodities or intangibles between states, it is *interstate commerce.* Today, interstate commerce includes transportation of persons and property, transmission of power, and communication—radio, television, telephone, and telegraph.

Interstate commerce also comprises general movements of commodities. For example, on different occasions, the courts have upheld the regulation of both buying and selling of livestock at the stockyards, and the buying and selling of grain futures. Both operations, even though local, are part of the general flow of commerce that supplies produce to the consumer markets.

A company is engaged in *intrastate commerce* as distinguished from interstate commerce if the bulk of its business (isolated cases of interstate commerce do not count) takes place entirely within a state, and is not part of an interchange or movement of tangible or intangible commodities.

As a general rule, a state cannot prohibit foreign corporations (corporations chartered in other states) from doing interstate business within its borders; however, it can prohibit them from doing intrastate business unless they meet certain qualifying conditions. Usually, the conditions include: (1) registration and filing of certain documents with state officials; (2) designation of an agent to accept service of summons; (3) payment of certain fees and taxes. If a corporation "does business" in a state without "qualifying," that is, meeting the state's requirements, it may become subject to certain fines or it may lose the right to sue in state courts on contracts made within the state.

What constitutes "doing business" is an important technical question that has come up in almost all of the state courts. A company that is engaged only in interstate commerce cannot be considered as "doing business" in a state even though it actually gets business in the state. For example, sending salesmen into a state to secure business, but filling the orders from outside of the state, is not considered "doing business." This is interstate commerce. But if the orders are turned over to a local wholesaler within the state to be filled from the wholesaler's stock, the firm is "doing business" in the state and must qualify. These simple examples should not mislead one into thinking that it is easy to determine whether a company is or is not "doing business" in a state.

It is important to differentiate between intrastate and interstate commerce under most of the federal regulatory laws as well. For example, the Fair Labor Standards Act (1938) (Wage-Hour Law) regulates labor conditions in industries not only "engaged in commerce" but also in the "production of goods for commerce," or "in any process or occupation necessary to the production." The Supreme Court held that the act covered an owner who employed personnel to service his building in which tenants produced goods for interstate commerce. The services rendered by the employees were necessary for the production of goods for interstate commerce.

The regulatory laws are not consistent in their definition of what is interstate commerce, although the tendency is toward uniformity.

Issue of execution. When a judgment is obtained by one party against another, the successful party is known as a *judgment creditor* and the other party as a *judgment debtor*. If the judgment debtor does not pay the judgment, the attorney for the judgment creditor may get the clerk of court to issue execution to a designated officer of the law, usually the sheriff, constable, or marshal. The execution is a printed form, easily filled out upon the basis of the information in the file. If the officer to whom the execution is issued can find no property of the judgment debtor against which to levy, he returns the execution "unsatisfied." The lawyer may then commence a SUPPLEMENTARY PROCEEDING.

Joint adventure (venture). An association of two or more persons for a given, limited purpose, without the usual powers, duties, and responsibilities that go with a PARTNERSHIP. Thus, if two people buy a specific piece of real estate for resale at a profit, they become parties to a joint adventure; but if they enter into a agreement whereby each contributes money and services in establishing and carrying on a real estate business, they become members of a partnership.

Joint and several. An obligation or liability incurred, either under contract or otherwise, by two or more parties together and separately is said to be *joint and several*. The parties may be held jointly responsible or severally responsible. Thus, partners are jointly and severally liable on partnership transactions, whereas a subscriber to a charity is severally liable—the subscriber is not jointly liable with the other subscribers for their subscriptions. Or a bond may be joint and several, in which case the obligors are liable either individually or together, at the option of the obligee.

Joint estate. See JOINT TENANCY.

Joint stock company. A form of business organization created by an agreement of the parties. This agreement is commonly called articles of association. This type of company is similar to the CORPORATION in the following respects: (1) the ownership is represented by transferable certificates; (2) management is in the hands of a board of governors or directors elected by the members (shareholders); (3) the business continues for its fixed term notwithstanding the death or disability of one or more of the members. It is unlike the corporation and like the PARTNERSHIP in that each shareholder is personally liable for the company's debts.

In many states the laws affecting taxation and regulation of corporations make the definition of a corporation broad enough to include joint stock companies. These states regard a joint stock company organized in another state as a FOREIGN CORPORATION. In other states, a joint stock company may conduct business in the state without being subject to restrictions imposed upon corporations.

Joint tenancy. If two or more persons acquire the same estate at the same time, by the same title or source of ownership, each having the same degree of interest (including right of survivorship) as the others, and each having the same right of possession as the others, the estate is called a *joint estate* or *tenancy*. The distinguishing characteristic of a joint tenancy is that upon the death of one of the joint tenants, his or her interest automatically passes to the others by survivorship. The courts do not favor joint tenancies, and in many jurisdictions permit joint tenants to defeat the right of survivorship by mortgage or conveyance. Some of the states have passed retroactive statutes making existing undivided interests TENANCY IN COMMON unless a contrary intent plainly appears in the instrument sufficient to negate the presumption of a tenancy in common. (See also TENANCY BY THE ENTIRETY.)

Judgment. An adjudication by a court after a trial or hearing, of the rights of the parties. Broadly speaking, an adjudication by a court of law or of EQUITY is considered a judgment, but technically an adjudication by a court of equity is a DECREE. The sentence in a criminal case is the judgment. If, following judgment, the debtor fails or refuses to pay the award of the court, the judgment or debtor may direct that a writ of execution be issued by the clerk of court. Pursuant to the terms of the writ, the sheriff may seize and sell any property of the debtor not exempt by law in satisfaction of the judgment. If the party against whom a judgment is rendered appeals to a higher court, execution of the judgment is stayed pending the higher court's decision. *See also Index.*

Judgment by default. After a SUMMONS has been served by the sheriff and returned to the court, the court has JURISDICTION over the defendant. If the defendant fails to defend a civil case by filing proper pleadings, or fails to appear within a definite time, a judgment is given against him in his absence. This judgment is called *judgment by default. See also Index.*

Jurisdiction. *See Index.*

Laches. Unreasonable delay in bringing suit or seeking remedy in an equity court. For a defendant to plead laches as a defense to a suit, he must show that he suffered from the plaintiff's delay in bringing suit.

Letters patent. See PATENTS, APPLICATIONS FOR.

Libel and slander. That which tends to injure the reputation of a living person or the memory of a deceased person and to expose him to public hatred, disgrace, ridicule, or contempt, or to exclude him from society, is known as *defamation. Slander* is *oral* defamation of one person by another in the presence of a third person or persons; *libel* is *written* or *printed* defamation of one person by another, published before a third person or persons. A corporation is a person in this sense. For a slanderous statement to be actionable, it must be false and must cause injury to the person to whom the statement refers. In libel actions, no injury need be proved, although, of course, proved injury will affect the amount of damages awarded. (See also LIBELOUS LETTERS.)

Libelous letters. For a letter to be libelous (see LIBEL AND SLANDER), it must have been read by someone other than the person defamed. The reader may be a stenographer who takes the libelous writing by dictation and transcribes the notes, although some courts have taken the view that publication to a stenographer does not subject the writer to liability unless the letter was prompted by actual malice.

License, business. Federal, state, or city approval and permission are necessary to engage in certain businesses that are of sufficient concern to the public to justify regulation. Permission and approval are issued in the form of a license, for which a fee is charged.

Lien. A charge imposed on property by which the property is made security for the discharge of an obligation. Some liens, particularly those on personal property, must be accompanied by actual possession of the property: a *lienor* (the holder of a lien) who parts with possession loses his lien. Other liens, particularly those on real estate, need not be accompanied by possession: the lienor gives notice of the lien he claims by a public record of it. Some of the common liens are vendor's lien, MECHANIC'S LIEN, mortage lien (see Mortgage, in *Index*), and TAX LIEN.

Life estate. An interest in property, real or personal, that lasts only for the duration of the owner's life. A life estate may also be for the duration of another's life or may terminate with the happening of a certain contingency. For example, a life estate may terminate upon the marriage of the owner. This estate may be created by an act of the parties, as by deed, will, or gift, or by operation of law, as by dower or curtesy. The owner of a life estate (called the LIFE TENANT) has the current use of the property and is responsible for its maintenance, including taxes and carrying charges. He also gets the income from the property but cannot ordinarily sell the property or do anything to impair its permanent value. However, the life tenant may be allowed to sell or consume property to support himself if the deed or will so provides. He cannot dispose of the property at his death. The person or persons to whom the estate passes upon termination of the life estate is determined when the life estate is created. The estate that is left at the termination of the life estate is called a *remainder;* the person to whom it passes is a *remainderman* (plural, *remaindermen*).

Life tenant. The owner of a LIFE ESTATE. Beneficiaries with life interests under trusts are sometimes called equitable life tenants.

Limited partnership. A partnership in which the liability of one or more special partners for debts of the firm is limited to the amount of his investment in the business. Special partners have no voice in the management of the partnership. They merely invest money and receive a certain share of the profits. There must be one or more general partners who manage the business and remain liable for all its debts.

A limited partnership is organized under state statutes, usually by filing a certificate in a public office and publishing a notice in a newspaper. The statutes, codified in many states as the Uniform Limited Partnership Law, must be strictly observed. A limited partnership is regarded as a general partnership in states other than the state in which it is organized; therefore, it must register and form a limited partnership with the same firm members under the laws of each state in which it wishes to do business.

As in a general partnership, the death, insanity, or bankruptcy of any one of the general partners dissolves the limited partnership. (See PARTNERSHIP.)

Liquidated damages. An amount the parties to a contract have agreed upon that shall be paid in satisfaction of a loss resulting from a BREACH OF CONTRACT. The amount must be in proportion to the actual loss; otherwise the agreement is unenforceable.

Mandamus. (Latin for "We command.") A writ issued by a court of superior jurisdiction to a public or private corporation, or an official thereof, or an inferior court, commanding the performance of an official act, which the person or body named in the writ had failed or refused to perform. It is an extraordinary WRIT, which is issued in cases where the usual and ordinary procedures do not afford remedies to the party aggrieved. The writ of mandamus is known as a remedy for official inaction. It was introduced to prevent disorder from a failure of public officials to perform their duties and is still an important legal remedy for the protection of the public and of individual against exploitation and abuse by official inaction. Mandamus is frequently applied for to control the letting of public contracts.

A mandamus may also enforce a private right. It compels the performance by a corporation of a variety of specific acts within the scope of the corporation's duties. For example, a stockholder may institute a mandamus proceeding to compel a corporation to submit to an inspection of its books and records.

The writ is either peremptory or alternate. The peremptory mandamus compels the defendant to perform the required act; the alternate mandamus compels him to perform the act or show cause on a certain day why he should not perform it. The alternate writ is usually issued first.

Massachusetts trust. A business association formed under a deed of trust, which is really a contract between the trustees and beneficiaries. It is also known as a business trust or a common-law trust. Its structure closely resembles that of a CORPORATION. The interests of the beneficiaries are represented by certificates, frequently called certificates of stock, which may be divided into several classes of common and preferred stock and may be listed on stock exchanges. The trustees correspond to the directors and the certificate holders to the stockholders. The trustees manage the property and pay dividends out of the profits. They usually appoint and remove the officers. Unlike a corporation, the management is permanent. The trustees are personally liable in dealing with outsiders unless they clearly indicate that they are acting as trustees and that the creditors shall look only to the trust property for all payments.

Massachusetts trusts are regarded as corporations under many taxing statutes and federal acts.

The duration is limited by statute in most states, but the parties interested at the time the trust expires can agree to another trust.

Mechanic's lien. The statutory lien of a contractor, subcontractor, laborer, or materialman, who performs labor or furnishes material for the permanent improvement of real property for hire or with the consent or at the request of the authorized agent. The lien attaches to the land and improvements. A mechanic's lien is for the amount of the contract plus interest. Notice of the lien must be filed in the public filing place prescribed by statute. If a mechanic's lien is not discharged, it may be foreclosed subject to all prior liens. Like a mortgage, a mechanic's lien may be released or waived.

Merger. The absorption of one or more corporations by another existing corporation, which retains its identity and takes over all the rights, privileges, franchises, properties, and liabilities of the absorbed companies. The absorbing corporation continues its existence, whereas the other companies terminate their existence. For example, companies *A, B,* and *C* agree to combine so companies *A* and *B* are absorbed by *C*. When the plan becomes effective, companies *A* and *B* go out of existence and company *C* remains. The remaining company takes care of the creditors of the constituent companies.

The procedure designated by statute to bring about the merger must be followed. The percentage of the stockholders fixed in the law must approve the agreement. Where the statute so provides, stockholders who dissent to the plan may obtain cash for the appraised value of their shares, instead of shares in the remaining company.

Minutes of corporate meetings. A *minute* is the official recording of proceedings at a meeting. Specifically, in the plural, the word means the official record of the proceedings at a meeting of an organized body, such as the stockholders or directors of a corporation. It is not essential to the validity or binding effect of acts done by an organized body that minutes be kept, but accurate minutes avoid future misunderstandings. They are particularly useful if the corporation institutes suit or is sued upon a matter recorded in the minutes. Ordinarily minutes are PRIMA FACIE EVIDENCE of what transpired at the meeting; frequently they are the best evidence. *See also Index.*

Misdemeanor. See CRIMINAL LAW.

Muniments of title. Written evidence by which title to real property may be defended. The word *muniments* is derived from the Latin verb *munio,* meaning *to fortify.* Hence, muniments of title fortify or strengthen rights in property. The expression as generally defined refers to deeds of conveyance, wills, legislative grants, and other documents relating to the title to land.

Negotiable instrument. A written instrument, signed by a maker or drawer, containing an unconditional promise or order to pay a certain sum of money, which can be passed freely from one person to another in a manner that constitutes the transferee the holder. If payable to bearer, the instrument may be negotiated simply by delivery; if payable to order, it is negotiated by endorsement of the holder, completed by delivery.

The Uniform Commercial Code governs negotiable instruments in all states and territories except those few states that still retain the older Uniform Negotiable Instruments Law. The code states the manner in which a negotiable instrument shall be transferred, and it fixes the rights and duties of the maker, the payee, the holder, and the endorser. For example, under the law an endorser of a negotiable instrument vouches for its genuineness. If it is a forgery, the endorser is liable to a HOLDER IN DUE COURSE of the instrument after delivery.

Strictly speaking, documents of title (such as order bills of lading and warehouse receipts) are not negotiable instruments because they do not contain an order to pay a sum of money. However, various statutes have given certain documents of title the quality of negotiability. These are known as quasi-negotiable instruments.

Negotiation. The transfer of a written instrument in a manner that makes the transferee the holder of the instrument. If payable to order, an instrument is negotiated by endorsement and delivery; if payable to bearer, by delivery alone.

An instrument is not negotiated until it is transferred by the person to whom it is issued. Thus, *A* makes a note payable to *B* and delivers it to him. Subsequently, by negotiation, *B* transfers to note to *C*, and *C* to *D*, and so on. As opposed to transfer by ASSIGNMENT, the innocent transferee by negotiation takes the paper free of defenses that are good against the transferor.

Novation. The substitution of a new contract, or debtor or obligor, for an existing one. The substitution must be agreed to by all the parties.

Example: A sells a car to *B*, who makes a small down payment and agrees to pay the balance in installments. Finding himself unable to make the payments, *B* sells the car to *C*, who agrees to make the payments to *A*. If *A* agrees to release *B* from the contract and to look to *C* for payment, a novation is created.

Obiter dictum. See DICTUM.

Offer and acceptance. See CONTRACTS, 1.

Omnibus. A term applied to that which contains two or more independent matters. The term is applied, for example, to a legislative bill that relates to two or more subjects.

Option. An agreement, usually in consideration for the payment of a certain sum of money by the offeree, to hold an offer open for a definite period. The offer ceases to be an offer and becomes a contract of option; it cannot be withdrawn until the option period expires. Although an option is generally based upon a consideration, a few states require no consideration if the contract is in writing. Others recognize an option under seal as binding because a seal, at COMMON LAW, indicates consideration. The consideration for an option is not returnable to the optionee if he fails to take up the option; it is, however, usually applied to the purchase price if the offer is accepted.

Ordinance. A law or statute. The word is commonly used to apply to enactments of a municipality.

Partnership. "An association of two or more persons to carry on as co-owners a business for profit."[1] A partnership is organized by oral or written agreement among the parties. Agreement may also be implied from the acts and representations of the parties. Partnerships are governed by fairly uniform laws, which are codified in many states by the Uniform Partnership Law. A partnership may carry on business in any state without paying greater taxes than residents of the state pay.

Each partner of a general partnership is fully liable personally for all partnership debts regardless of the amount of his investment. (See LIMITED

---

[1] Uniform Partnership Law.

PARTNERSHIP.) All types of capital produced or acquired by the partnership become partnership property. Real estate is generally acquired in the individual names of the partners or in the name of one partner who holds the property in trust for the partnership.

In the absence of a specific contract, partners share profits and losses equally. It is customary, however, to provide in the partnership agreement that profits and losses shall be distributed pro rata according to the amount of capital contributed by each or in any other ratio to which they agree. Partners have no right to salaries unless they are agreed upon, even though one partner may devote all of his time to the business and the other may devote little or none. The agreement may provide for the division of profits after allowing each of the partners an agreed-upon salary.

Partnerships are dissolved without violation of the partnership agreement by (1) withdrawal of one of the members under some circumstances; (2) operation of law through death or bankruptcy of one of the partners or a change in the law that makes the partnership's business illegal; (3) court decree granted because of incapacity or insanity of one of the partners, gross misconduct, or neglect or breach of duty.

Patents. A *patent* is an exclusive right granted by the federal government for a fixed period, to make, use, and sell an invention. A person who perfects a new machine, process, or material, or any new and useful improvement of them, or who invents or discovers and reproduces a distinct and new variety of plant, may make application to the government for a patent for it. The person to whom a patent is granted is called the *patentee.* Patent rights are issued in the form of *letters* and run to the patentee, his heirs and assigns, generally for a period of 17 years. A *design patent,* which is an ornamental design to be placed upon an article of manufacture, runs for 3½, 7, or 14 years, according to the application made by the patentee. A patent is not renewable. Anyone using a patented product without the owner's consent may be compelled to pay damages.

Application Procedure. When a client wants to obtain a patent, he brings, or sends, the details of his invention or discovery to the lawyer in the form of a *disclosure.* The disclosure may be a picture, a sketch, or a working model. An idea is not patentable; only the device for carrying out an idea can be patented.

The patent lawyer must make a *search* to learn what patent or patents have already been issued on that idea. Copies of other patents issued on an idea are called *prior art,* and they may be inspected at the Patent Office. The patent lawyer studies the art before preparing the application. Copies of patents and trademarks may be obtained from the Patent Office for a nominal charge. The patent lawyer sends the application to the Commissioner of Patents in Washington, D.C., who sends it to the appropriate division; the next step will be an *official action.* The official action may be an *allowance,* which means that the Patent Office deems the application ready to issue into a patent. In almost every case, however, the official action is a response by the Patent Office in which the Patent Office Examiner points out the items in the application he considers objectionable, for one reason or another. It sometimes takes several years to get an official action. After receipt of the official action, the attorney has six months in which to file an amendment. In the amendment the lawyer takes each point objected to by the examiner and either deletes it from the application or argues for it. There is no definite time by which the Patent Office responds to the amendment. If the first amendment does not make the application ready for allowance, there must be another amendment and so on until the examiner states that the next amendment must be final. The average number of amendments is three or four. If the patent lawyer does not think the examiner has a clear view of the whole idea, he may go to Washington and interview the examiner. Sometimes this facilitates the allowance.

Parts of the application. The application consists of:

1. *Specification.* This is a written description of the invention or discovery and the manner and process of making it.

2. *Claims.* These are the assertions made for the invention. Each individual part of the invention is written up as a claim. A design patent has only one claim, but other patents may have many claims. These claims are numbered 1, 2, 3, and so on. A patent application might begin with 40 claims and have only 15 when it is finally allowed. Some claims will be "stricken" because the claim has been covered by a prior invention.

3. *Drawings of the invention.*

4. *Petition.* This gives the name, residence, and post office address of the inventor and the title of the invention sought to be patented.

5. *Oath or affirmation.* The applicant swears or affirms that he believes himself to be the first inventor or discoverer of the invention sought to be patented.

6. *Power of attorney.* The applicant usually gives his lawyers power of attorney (see chapter 11) to transact all business in the Patent Office connected with the patent.

What the secretary and paralegal do. 1. The lawyer will dictate the specification and claims. Make an original, a copy for each inventor, and a file copy on plain paper.

2. The oath, power of attorney, and petition are printed forms that you can easily fill in. They are frequently combined in one document. Make an original and the same number of copies as you made of the specification and claims.

3. The applications must be signed and verified before a notary public by the inventor, or inventors if there is more than one. When there is more than one inventor, there must be a separate verification for each if the inventors do not sign the application at the same time, or if they are at different locations when signing.

4. Have photoprints made of the drawings of the invention, send one copy to the inventor (or a copy to each inventor), and keep one for your files. The originals made by a draftsman accompany the application to the Patent Office for filing.

5. The Patent Office issues rules about how the papers are arranged, the backing, and the like.

6. As soon as the application is typed and assembled, send it to the applicant

for signature and verification. If there is more than one inventor, you will have to send the application to each in turn for his signature and verification.

7. Make a diary or calendar entries with reference to any action that must be taken at a future date. Although an application for a patent is not a legal action, it is advisable to keep a progress record sheet (chapter 12). You might keep the sheet in the file folder. If litigation developes from the application, keep the same records that you do in any litigated matter.

Assignment of application for patent. Frequently an inventor agrees to assign his patent rights before he applies for the patent. When he does, he makes an *assignment of application* simultaneously with his application. A printed form is usually used. Make an original, a copy for each applicant, and a copy for your file. Send the original to the inventor (or inventors) for signature and acknowledgment before a notary public. When original has been executed by each inventor, forward it to the Patent Office to be recorded. The Patent Office will return the assignment after it has been recorded; forward it to the assignee.

Covering letters. Whenever the lawyer sends papers to the client or to the Patent Office you can write the covering letters without dictation. Here are three sample letters.

Letter forwarding application to Patent Office.

The Commissioner of Patents
United States Patent Office
Washington, D.C. 20231
Sir:

We are enclosing, for filing, the application of .. (inventor or inventors).... for Letters Patent covering an improvement in .... (title)..., Case ..... We are also enclosing our check for $ ...... to cover the first government fee.

Sincerely yours,

Letter forwarding assignment to Patent Office for recording.

The Commissioner of Patents
United States Patent Office
Washington, D.C. 20231
Sir:

We enclose for recording assignment of.... (patentee or patentees).... transferring unto .... (assignee)..., a (an).... (name of state).... corporation, all right title and interest in and to his (their) application for .... (title)...., Case ......, executed .... and transmitted for filing of even date herewith.

Our check for $... to cover the recording fee is also enclosed.

Sincerely yours,

Letter sending issued patent to patentee.

Dear ....:

We are enclosing original United States Letters Patent No. ...., issued to you on .... (date)...., covering an improvement in .... (title)..... .

Please acknowledge receipt of the patent. Thank you.

Sincerely yours,

Perjury. The act of wilfully giving, under oath, false testimony. A statement that one does not remember certain facts when he really does is perjury; conversely, swearing one remembers something when in fact he has no recollection of it is also perjury. Honest but erroneous expression of opinion is not perjury. A statement substantially true but literally false is not necessarily perjury. Federal and some state statutes provide for punishment for perjury by fine or imprisonment.

Personal property. A right or interest, protected by law, in something that is not land or anything permanently attached to land and is capable of ownership (see REAL PROPERTY). Personal property is generally movable. It may be tangibles (also called *chattels*), such as money, gold, merchandise, or any movable object susceptible to physical possession, or intangibles, such as contracts, stocks, and the like (see CHOSE IN ACTION). Personal property may be an interest in land: a 99-year lease may be personal property. Products of the soil become personal property when severed from the land: trees and crops that are sold while attached to the land constitute real property, but when severed from the land they constitute personal property.

Title to personal property may be acquired by the following methods: (1) *Appropriation or original possession:* although almost all property today belongs to someone, there are still some kinds of property, such as wild game and fish, that may be appropriated. (2) *Discovery:* the finder of lost property acquires a title that is good against everyone except the rightful owner. (3) *Creation:* a person is entitled to that which he produces by his physical or mental labor, unless the product is produced during the course of his employment or under some other contract; then it belongs to his employer or the party for whom he contracted to create the property. (4) *Gift.* (5) *Sale or exchange.* (6) *Will.* (7) *Operation of law:* when a person dies without making a will, his property passes by operation of law to certain relatives. Or if a person becomes bankrupt, his property, with certain exceptions, passes to a trustee for the benefit of creditors. A person's property may also be taken from him by legal process (see EXECUTION, 1).

Pleadings. *See Index.*

Pledge. The placement of personal property by the owner with a lender as security for a debt. Pawned articles and stocks and bonds put up as collateral for a loan are the most common pledges. Essentials of a pledge are (1) a debt or obligation to be secured; (2) the thing pledged; (3) the pledgor (the one who gives the pledge) and the pledgee (the one who receives the pledge); (4) transfer of possession of the property (if actual physical possession is practically impossible, the pledgee may acquire CONSTRUCTIVE possession); (5) retention of title in the pledgor; (6) the pledgor's right to redeem the pledge; (7) a contract, express or implied, covering the transaction.

When stock is pledged as collateral, the pledgee has the right and is bound to collect the dividends and apply them to the loan, in the absence of an agreement to the contrary between the pledgor and pledgee. This is the legal theory. As a matter of practice, the stockholder makes an assignment of the stock in blank and the stock is not transferred on the books of the corporation unless the pledgor defaults; the stockholder-pledgor therefore continues to collect the dividends.

Police power. That power which any governmental body has to protect the property, life, health, and well-being of its citizen by legislation. State minimum wage laws have been held by the United States Supreme Court to be a proper exercise of the states' police powers. Under police powers states license doctors and lawyers, barbers and beauticians, and the like, and only those who obtain a license are authorized to practice their profession or trade. City ordinances that require certain standards of cleanliness in restaurants, or that impose building restrictions, are regulations issued under police power. The extent of a governing body's police power is limited by the state constitutions and by the Fourteenth Amendment to the Constitution of the United States, which protects personal liberties and freedoms. The power of Congress to regulate and control business activities is not a police power but is a power granted by the several states and by the Constitution.

Power of attorney. A written instrument in which the principal (the person giving the power of attorney) authorizes another to act for him. The instrument may be a blanket authorization, but more commonly it authorizes the agent to represent the principal in one specific transaction, as the closing of a real estate deal, or to do a certain act continuously, as the signing of checks. The person appointed is commonly called an ATTORNEY-IN-FACT. A power of attorney may be revoked at the will of the principal, unless it was given to the agent for a consideration. The death of the principal constitutes an instantaneous revocation, but there is no revocation when consideration was given for power.

Preemptive right. The right of each stockholder, upon the issuance of additional shares by the corporation, to purchase his proportion of the new stock in order to maintain his relative interest in the corporation. *Example:*

If *A* owns $10,000 of the $100,000 worth of stock issued and outstanding, and the corporation increases its authorized capital stock of $200,000, *A* will have a right to purchase 1/10 of the new issue, or an additional $10,000 worth of stock, before the stock may be offered to outsiders. The stockholder has a right to purchase the stock at the price fixed by the corporation, and if he fails to take it, it cannot be offered to anyone else upon more favorable terms. He must be given reasonable notice of his right to subscribe and a reasonable opportunity to exercise the right. Stockholders who are not in a position to take and pay for the stock to which they are entitled may sell the rights to anyone who can. A stockholder may also waive his preemptive right by agreement with the corporation.

The preemptive right is governed by statute in many states. Frequently the certificate of incorporation regulates the preemptive right in accordance with the governing statute. In the absence of regulating statute and charter provisions, the court decisions determine under what circumstances the preemptive right exists; these decisions in many instances are conflicting.

Pretrial. A system to expedite the progress of a case. Before the trial of a case, the judge calls counsel for both sides into conference for the purpose of settling issues that are either unnecessary or not disputed. Counsel agree on undisputed and indisputable facts common to both parties; on exhibits, about the authenticity of originals and accuracy of copies; and on various other matters that ordinarily consume considerable time in the trial of a case. For example, in an automobile accident case, the ownership of the car is admitted, without the necessity of putting a witness on the stand to testify about the ownership.

Pretrial has not yet been accepted officially in all states, but some judges use it in jurisdictions where court rules neither require nor specifically sanction it. Rule 16 of Federal Rules provides for pretrial, making the use of it optional with each judge. There is no set form for pretrial, the procedure varying from state to state and from judge to judge.

At the end of the pretrial conference, the judge prepares an order embodying the results of the conference. There is no uniformity in the method of preparing it. The order is official and controls the case to the same extent as any other order.

Prima facie evidence. Evidence deemed by law to be sufficient to establish a fact if the evidence is not disputed. For example, the placement of a corporate seal on an instrument is prima facie evidence that the instrument was executed by authority of the corporation.

Private law. See PUBLIC AND PRIVATE LAW.

Privity. Mutual or successive relationship to the same right of property, or the power to take advantage of and enforce a promise or warranty. Identity of interest is essential. There must be a connection or bond of union between parties about some particular transaction. Thus, privity of contract exists between a lessor and lessee, because the parties are mutually interested in the lease. Privity of contract also exists between a lessor and an assignee of the lease, because the assignee succeeded to the rights of the lessee. Heirs, executors, and assigns succeed to the rights and liabilities of a contract whether or not it so states. They are thus *privies* to the contract.

Privity affects legal rights and duties and, in many cases, determines whether a party may sue or be sued. Thus, a privy has the same right to relief against mistake of fact as the original party to a contract. A stranger to a contract has no right to sue for fraud, but a privy does. An injuction extends to all persons in privity with the parties enjoined. Evidence may be admissible or inadmissible because of privity. Privity may be an element in an action for negligence or in the substitution of parties in a legal action.

Probate bond. See COURT BOND.

Proprietorship, sole. One of the three most common forms of business organization. Ownership of the business is vested in one proprietor. The other two common forms of business organization are PARTNERSHIP and CORPORATION.

Protest. A formal certificate attesting the DISHONOR of a NEGOTIABLE INSTRUMENT after NEGOTIATION. A protest is usually made by a notary public but may be made by a responsible citizen, in the presence of two witnesses. The certificate states the time and place of presentment, the fact that presentment was made and the manner thereof, the cause or reason for protesting the bill, and the demand made and the answer given or the fact that the drawee or acceptor could not be found. The protest is attached to the dishonored instrument or a copy of it. Notice of protest is then sent to the parties who are secondarily liable (drawer and endorser). Protest is required only when a bill of exchange or check drawn in one state (or country) and payable in another is dishonored, but as a matter of business practice domestic instruments are often "protested." The word *protest* is loosely applied to the process of presenting an instrument for payment, demanding payment, and giving notice to the drawer or endorser.

Example:

Buyer accepts a trade acceptance drawn by Seller. Seller endorses and discounts the acceptance at Doe Bank, which sends it to Roe Bank for collection. Roe Bank's notary public (usually an employee) presents the instrument to Buyer for payment, which is refused. The notary then *protests* (using the term loosely): he makes out the certificate, attaches it to the instrument, and sends notice of protest to Seller, who is secondarily liable, through Doe Bank. In this case, Seller is the drawer and the endorser.

Public and private law. *Public law* is the law that relates to the public as a whole, rather than to a specific individual. It involves the authority of the federal and state governments to make laws and of federal and state executives to issue orders, as well as ADMINISTRATIVE LAW and CRIMINAL LAW. *Private law* is that body of the law that pertains to the relationship between individuals as such. It includes laws relating to contracts, sales, agency, negotiable instruments, and business organizations.

Public utility (public service corporation). A private corporation that renders service to an indefinite public, which has a legal right to demand and receive the service or commodities of the corporation. Public utilities are subject to special laws that do not apply to other corporations, and they are closely supervised by governmental agencies. They owe a duty to the public that they may be compelled to perform. For example, a railroad company cannot abandon part of its route without authority from the Interstate Commerce Commission. On the other hand, public utilities are given certain powers of a public nature, for example, the power of EMINENT DOMAIN. Public utilities include railroads, bus lines, airlines, gas and electric companies, hydroelectric, water, and irrigation corporations.

Quasi. (Latin.) Almost; like; resembling. Thus, we speak of certain federal agencies, such as the Federal Trade Commission, as being "quasi-judicial" bodies because they have powers, resembling those of a judicial body, to enforce certain rules and regulations. Or we speak of certain documents of title as being "quasi-negotiable instruments"—they are invested by statute with certain characteristics of negotiability but are not NEGOTIABLE INSTRUMENTS as that term is defined by the Uniform Commercial Code.

Quiet title, action to. An equity proceeding to establish the plaintiff's title to land by bringing into court an adverse claimant and compelling him either to establish his claim or to be estopped from asserting it. Whenever a deed or other instrument exists that may throw a cloud over the complainant's title or interest, a court of equity will clear the title by directing that the instrument be cancelled or by making other decree required by the rights of the parties. For example, when a real estate mortgage is valid on its face but has ceased to be a lien, it may be cancelled as a cloud on the title by an action to quiet title.

Quit-claim deed. *See Index.*

Quo warranto. (Latin for "by what authority.") A WRIT of inquiry as to the warrant or authority for doing the act complained of. The writ tests the right of a person to hold an office or franchise or to exercise some right or privilege derived from the state. Quo warranto affirms an existing right to an office, or it sets aside wrongful claims of a pretender. An information in the nature of a quo warranto has replaced the old writ, but the terms *information in the nature of a quo warranto* and *quo warranto* are used interchangeably and synonymously and have substantially the same purpose. The power to file a quo warranto is incident to the office of the attorney general, but the privilege of instituting the proceeding upon the refusal of the attorney general to act has been granted to private individuals in their capacity as taxpayers and citizens.

Quorum. The number of persons who must legally be present at a meeting to transact corporate business or the business of any assembly of persons. When the membership of the assembling group or body consists of a *definite* number of persons as required by law—for example, a board of directors or the United States Senate—a majority (more than half) of the members are required to make a quorum, unless the controlling law expressly states that another number constitutes a quorum. At COMMON LAW, when the membership of the assembling body consists of an *indefinite* number of persons (that is, the law requires no definite number)—as the stockholders of a corporation—any number constitutes a quorum; however, the BYLAWS, and frequently the statutes or charter, customarily make an express provision concerning a quorum. In the case of a stockholders' meeting, the designated quorum usually relates to the amount of stock represented at the meeting, and not to the number of stockholders.

Ratification. The approval of an act that had not been binding previously; ratification, or affirmance, reverts and becomes effective as of the date the act was performed. An infant may ratify, or affirm, his contracts after he reaches his majority; a principal may ratify, or affirm, the unauthorized acts of an agent; a corporation may ratify, or affirm, the unauthorized acts of its officers. A corporation could not ratify or affirm the acts of its incorporators before the corporation was formed because it was not in existence and could not possibly have entered into a contract at that date. It may, however, *adopt* the acts of the incorporators.

Regulations. See ADMINISTRATIVE LAW.

Real property. *(See also Real estate, in Index.)* The land, APPURTENANCES, and man-made improvements attached to it. All other property is PERSONAL PROPERTY. Hence, in addition to the land, real property includes the buildings, natural growth, minerals, and timber that have not been separated from the land, and the air space above the land. Apples on the tree constitute real property, whereas harvested apples become personal property.

An interest in real property is an *estate*, and runs the entire gamut of varying rights from an estate in FEE SIMPLE (absolute ownership) to a LEASEHOLD (the right to use property during a fixed term for a specific consideration). An *estate* is only a designation of a particular type of interest in property; it is not a legal entity. Other forms of estates are modifications and limitations of a fee simple estate. (See LIFE ESTATE; TENANCY BY THE ENTIRETY; JOINT TENANCY; TENANCY IN COMMON.)

Remainderman. See LIFE ESTATE.

Replevin. A court action to recover possession of property unlawfully taken or detained. Title to the property must be in the person bringing the action. Thus, if title passes to the buyer and the seller refuses to deliver the goods, the buyer may bring an action in replevin to get possession of the goods. Or the seller, under a conditional sale contract by which he retains title to the goods until payment is made, may recover the goods by an action in replevin if the buyer does not make the payments called for by the contract.

Rescission. An action in equity whereby a court is asked to annul a contract entered into through fraud, misrepresentation, or excusable error. For example, if a person enters into a contract of partnership and then discovers that material facts were misrepresented, he brings an action in rescission. Rescission may be absolute or qualified. Thus, in *rescission* of a contract of sale, the seller resumes title and possession of the goods as though he had never parted with them, but he has no claim for damages. In *qualified rescission* he resumes title and possession but does not rescind the entire contract because he reserves the right to sue for damages. A contract may also be rescinded by mutual consent.

Residuary estate. That part of a testator's estate remaining after payment of the legacies and debts. The testator usually makes certain bequests and then names the person or institution who shall receve the remainder, or residue, of his estate. That person or institution is the *residuary legatee.*

Restrictive covenant. A provision in an agreement limiting or restricting the action of one of the parties to the agreement. Thus, a seller of a business may agree not to engage in the same business within a certain number of years. Or a deed may contain a covenant restricting the type of building that may be placed upon the property. A restrictive covenant of this type is said to "run with the land"—subsequent purchasers are bound by the covenant whether or not it is expressly set forth in the deed to them.

Royalties. Payments or rentals made to the owner of a patent for the privilege of manufacturing or renting the patented article. The term is also applied to payments made to authors and composers for the sale of copyrighted material and to payments under gas, oil, mining, or mineral leases.

Service of process. The law compels the giving of notice of a suit to a defendant, which makes him a party to the suit and compels him to appear in court or suffer JUDGMENT BY DEFAULT. The means of compelling in court is called *process*. (See SUMMONS and SERVICE BY PUBLICATION; also *Index*.)

Service by publication. Generally service of process or other notice is personal or upon the agent of the party to be served, but where personal service is impossible, service may be had in many cases by *publication*. The paper to be served is published in a designated newspaper a required number of times. Certain other legal formalities are also observed, such as mailing the paper to the party's last known address. Usually service by publication is permitted if the party to be served is a nonresident or is absent from the jurisdiction, or if his address is unknown. *Proof of publication* is made in the form of an affidavit by the publisher.

Silent partner. A partner who has no voice in the management of the partnership business. Unless he is also a special partner (see LIMITED PARTNERSHIP), a silent partner is equally responsible with the other partners for the debts of the partnership.

Slander. See LIBEL and SLANDER.

Special partner. See LIMITED PARTNERSHIP.

Specific performance. The performance of a contract according to its exact terms. A court of EQUITY will enforce specific performance, whereas a court of law awards damages to the injured party to a contract. Specific performance is never enforced in contracts for personal services. It is usually confined to sales of REAL PROPERTY and unique personal property, for instance an antique.

Star page. The line and word at which the pages of a first edition of a law book begin are frequently indicated by a star in differently paginated later editions. The original page number is indicated in the margin. In citing a few well-known works, the edition is left out and the star page is referred to, thus, 1 Bl. Comm. *150.

Statute of frauds. A statute, enacted with variations in all the states, providing that certain contracts cannot be enforced unless they are in writing signed by the party against whom the contract is sought to be enforced. The writing need not be a formal document signed by both parties—a written note or memorandum of the transaction signed by the party to be bound by the agreement is sufficient. The laws in the various states are fairly uniform in requiring the following contracts to be in writing:

1. A special promise to be responsible for the debt or default of a third person.

2. An agreement by an executor or administrator to become liable out of his own property for the debts of the estate.

3. A contract, the consideration for which is marriage. Engagement contracts are not included.

4. Contracts for the sale of real estate or any interest therein.

5. Contracts that cannot be performed within one year.

6. Contracts involving the sale of personal property in excess of a certain amount (which varies in the different states), when no part of the property has been delivered and no part of the purchase price has been paid.

In addition, many states require the following contracts to be in writing:

1. An agreement to bequeath property or to make any provision for someone by will.

2. An agreement to pay upon attaining legal majority a debt contracted during infancy.

3. The creation of a trust of real estate (*Note:* Few states require a writing for trusts of personal property).

4. The promise to pay a debt that has been outlawed by the statute of limitations or barred by bankruptcy.

5. An assignment of wages to be earned in the future.

6. A mortgage of personal property.

7. The employment of real estate brokers to negotiate the sale or purchase of real estate.

Statute of limitations. A state statute that limits the time within which legal action may be brought, either upon a contract or TORT. State and federal statutes also limit the time within which certain crimes can be prosecuted. The purpose of the time limitation is to make it impossible to bring suit many years after a cause of action originates, during which time witnesses may have died or important evidence may have been lost. When a debt is involved, it is possible to interrupt (or "toll") the running of the statute—that is, to lengthen the period in which action may be brought—by obtaining a payment on the debt or a promise to pay. A promise to pay a debt that has been barred by the statute of limitations does not require new consideration (see CONTRACTS, 4) but many states require such a promise to be in writing. The statutes often differentiate between oral and written contracts. (See also Statutes of Limitations in Number of Years, page 614.)

Statutory law. Rules formulated into law by legislative action. The Constitution of the United States and the constitutions of the various states are the fundamental written law. All other law must be in harmony with the constitutions, which define and limit the powers of government. State constitutions must be in harmony with the Constitution of the United States.

Congress, cities and towns, and other governmental units find in the constitutions their authority, either express or implied, to enact certain laws. These legislative enactments are called *statutes* and constitute the greater part of the written or statutory law. Statutory law supplements and supersedes COMMON LAW. (See also ADMINISTRATIVE LAW.)

Subornation. The crime of procuring another to commit perjury. Thus one speaks of *suborning* witnesses.

Subpoena. A writ or order commanding the person named in it to appear and testify in a legal proceeding.

Subrogation. The substitution of one person in another's place.
Example: A's car is insured by an insurance company against collision. A's car is negligently damaged by B. The insurance company pays $150 for repairs to A's car. The insurance company is subrogated to A's position and may prosecute the claim for damages against B.

Substantive law. The part of the law that creates, defines, and regulates rights and duties. Substantive law is opposed to *adjective* or *procedural* law, which provides the method of administering and protecting the rights, duties, and obligations created by substantive law. All statutes of a general nature are substantive law; those regulating administrative and court proceedings are adjective law. All case law, except the decisions interpreting administrative regulations, codes of procedure, and court rules, are substantive law. For example, the right of administration of an estate is substantive; the procedures by which the estate can be administered are adjective law. The line of distinction between the two is narrow and often hard to define.

Summary proceeding. A form of legal proceedings in which the established procedure is disregarded, especially in the matter of trial by jury. The term is applied to the process by which a landlord may dispossess a tenant instead of having to resort to eviction, which is a long drawn-out proceeding.

Summons. A legal notice requiring a person to answer a complaint within a specified time. A copy of the summons must be left personally with (served upon) the person against whom it is directed. A corporation is served with process when a copy of the summons is left with an agent of the corporation found in the county. In a few jurisdictions the summons may be left with an adult member of the defendant's household or with some person at the defendant's place of business. An attorney-at-law is often authorized to accept service of a summons for a client. When the summons is served, the process server endorses the summons when, where, and upon whom served, with an affidavit to that effect. This procedure is called the "return of the summons." After return of the summons, the court has jurisdiction over the defendant. *See also Index.*

Supplementary proceeding. When an execution of judgment is returned unsatisfied, the judgment creditor has the right to force the judgment debtor to submit to an examination for the purpose of discovering any assets that may be applied to the payment of the debt. The legal procedure by which the judgment creditor exercises this right is known as a *supplementary proceeding*—it is supplementary to the execution of judgment. (see ISSUE OF EXECUTION).

Suretyship. See GUARANTY.

Syndicate. An association of individuals formed to conduct and carry on some particular business transaction, usually of a financial character. A syndicate more nearly resembles a JOINT ADVENTURE than any other business organization. Syndicates in general are temporary associations or firms. They usually terminate automatically when the purpose for which they were formed has been accomplished.

Tax Court practice.[1] All papers filed with the Tax Court, including petitions, motions, briefs, and replies, should conform to the following standards (references are to "Rules of Practice, Tax Court of the United States," U.S. Government Printing Office, Washington, D.C.):

1. PRINTED OR TYPEWRITTEN. All papers shall be either printed or typewritten (Rule 4(a)).
2. PRINTED PAPERS (Rule 4(b)).
   a. *Type.* Using 10- or 12-point type.
   b. *Paper.* Use good, unglazed paper, 5⅞ inches wide by 9 inches long.
   c. *Margin.* Inside margin not less than one inch.
   d. *Spacing.* Double-leaded text and single-leaded quotations.
   e. *Citations.* Italicize citations Rule 4(d)).
3. TYPEWRITTEN PAPERS.
   a. *Typing.* Type on one side only (Rule 4(c)).
   b. *Paper.* Use plain white paper, 8½ inches wide by 11 inches long, weighing not less than 16 pounds to the ream (Rule 4(c)), except for copies which may be on any weight paper (Rule 4(h)).
   c. *Covers.* Attach no backs or covers (Rule 4(a)).
   d. *Citations.* Underscore citations (Rule 4(d)).
   e. *Copies.* Copies shall be clear and legible (Rule 4(h)).
4. FASTENING. Papers shall be fastened on the left side only (Rule 4(a)).
5. CAPTIONS. All papers shall have the proper caption. In the case of an individual petitioner, the caption shall set forth the full given name and surname, without any prefix or title, such as "Mrs.," "Dr.," and so forth. In the case of a fiduciary, the caption shall set forth the name of the estate, trust, or other person for whom he acts, followed by his own name and pertinent title, for example:

---

[1]*Acknowledgment:* Sidney Roberts, Samuel Schultz, and Gerhard Mayer, *Annotated Forms for Tax Practice,* 1948, 1951, Englewood Cliffs. N.J.: Prentice-Hall, Inc.

THE TAX COURT OF THE UNITED STATES

Estate of John Doe, deceased, Richard Roe, Executor, Petitioner, v. Commissioner of Internal Revenue, Respondent.	Docket No. _____ (Rule 4(e)).

6. SIGNATURES.

    a. Original copy. The original of all pleadings, motions, and briefs shall be signed in writing by either the petitioner or his counsel.

    b. Firm name. The signature shall be in the individual and not in the firm name, except that in the case of a petitioner that is a corporation, its signature shall be in the name of the corporation by one of its active officers, for example:

John Doe, Inc.

By /s/ Richard Roe, President

    c. Name and address. The name and mailing address of the signatory petitioner or counsel shall be typed or printed immediately beneath the written signature (Rule 4(f)).

7. NUMBER OF COPIES.

    a. Except in case of papers filed in more than one proceeding, the number of copies to be filed is tabulated below. Rule 4(g) provides for an original and four conformed copies, except as provided otherwise in the Rules; but the exceptions are numerous, as the following tabulation of the more common papers filed by taxpayers indicates:

Paper	*Number To Be Filed*	*Rule No.*
Petition	"original and four complete, accurately conformed, clear copies"	7(a) (1)
Reply	"original and four conformed copies"	15
Request for Place of Hearing	"original and two copies"	26(b)
Brief (Typewritten)	"original and two copies"	35(d)
Brief (Printed)	"20 copies"	35(d)
Stipulation of Facts	"in duplicate"	31(b)
Computation for Entry of Decision Under Rule 50	"original and two copies"	50
Entry of Appearance	"in duplicate"	24
Application for Subpoena	"only the original"	44(b)
Application to Take Depositions	"verified application and two conformed copies"	45(a)
Interrogatories and Cross-Interrogatories	"original and five copies"	46(a)
Motions (generally)	"four conformed copies with the signed original"	4(g)
Motion for Changing Place Designated for Hearing	"motion with four copies"	26(d)

Whenever a copy is required, it is advisable to submit conformed copies (see page 222). Of course, if the papers are to be submitted "in duplicate," both the original and duplicate should be executed.

b. When papers are to be filed in more than one proceeding, add to the number of copies otherwise required one additional copy for each such additional proceeding. For example, in the case of a motion to consolidate two proceedings, it is necessary to file a signed original and *five* conformed copies. (Motions generally require *four* conformed copies and the original. See above.) After the proceedings have been consolidated, all papers subsequently filed in the consolidated proceedings should be filed with the signed original and five conformed copies. (Rule 4(g)).

Tax lien. A claim against REAL PROPERTY that accrues to the taxing agency (municipality, township, city) from taxes that are assessed against the property. If the lien is not paid when due, the taxing agency may sell the property at a TAX SALE.

Tax sale. A sale of property, usually at auction, for nonpayment of taxes.

Tenancy in common. An estate held by two or more persons by separate and distinct title, with unity of possession only. If a deed is made to two or more persons who are not husband and wife, and nothing is said in the deed concerning the character of the estate created by the deed, the estate created is a *tenancy in common.* The co-owners are tenants in common. They need not have acquired their titles at the same time or by the same instrument. Their shares need not be equal. For example, one co-owner may have an undivided one-tenth interest and the other the remaining undivided nine-tenths interest. Tenants in common are entitled to share the possession of the property according to their shares in the property. Except for their sharing of possession and income, however, the situation is almost as if each tenant in common owned a separate piece of real estate. Each tenant in common may convey or mortgage his share, and the share of each is subject to the lien of judgments against him. Upon the death of one of the tenants in common, his interest passes to his heirs and legatees, and not to the other tenant in common.

Tenancy by the entirety. An estate held by husband and wife by virtue of title acquired by them jointly after marriage. Upon the death of either spouse, his or her interest automatically passes to the other by survivorship. A tenancy by the entirety cannot be terminated without the consent of both parties. Thus, neither spouse can defeat the right of survivorship by mortgage or conveyance without the consent of the other. The courts do not look with disfavor upon a tenancy by the entirety as they do upon a JOINT TENANCY. Not all states recognize tenancy by the entirety or "tenancy by the entireties," as it is sometimes called.

Testamentary trust. See TRUST.

Tort. A civil wrong inflicted otherwise than by a breach of contract. Elements of tort are (1) a wrongful act or a wrongful failure to act, and (2) an injury to some person. Tort gives the injured party the right to sue for any damages resulting from the defendant's breach of some duty. Persons (including minors) and corporations are liable for torts. *Example of tort:* A visitor to a department store (even one having no expressed intention to make a purchase but intending merely to examine the merchandise) can recover damages from the proprietor for injuries caused by the negligent maintenance of the store premises. Action arises not from breach of contract but from breach of duty.

Treason. See CRIMINAL LAW.

Trespass. The common meaning of trespass is the unauthorized entry upon the land of another. It also means an unlawful and violent interference with the person or property of another. In the practice of law an *action in trespass* is brought to recover damages for injuries sustained by the plaintiff as the immediate result of trespass.

Trust. A holding of property subject to the duty of applying the property, the income from it, or the proceeds for the benefit of another, as directed by the person creating the trust. A trust is created when *A* transfers property to *X*, the trustee, and *X* undertakes to apply the property and income from it for the purposes and in the manner directed by *A*. The elements of an ordinary trust are (1) the trustor (also called settlor, donor, or grantor), who furnishes the property to be put in trust; (2) the subject matter or property that is put in trust (called the trust principal, corpus, or res); (3) the trustee, who holds the property and administers the trust; and (4) the beneficiaries, for whose benefit the trust exists. A trust may be created by oral declaration, by writing, or by operation of law. It may be established by will (testamentary trust) or by deed (*inter vivos* or living trust). Many men put property in trust to pay the income to their wives for life and then to pay the principal to their children. In these situations the wives would be *income beneficiaries* (or "equitable life tenants") and the children would be *remaindermen.* (See LIFE ESTATE.)

Ultra vires. Without power; beyond the powers of. A term used to apply to a contract or act beyond the powers of a corporation as expressed or implied in its certificate of incorporation or by statute. For example, if a corporation contracts a debt in excess of the maximum allowed by statute, the contract is *ultra vivres*—beyond the power of the corporation. If neither party to the contract has performed, either the corporation or the other party may declare the contract void. After both parties have performed, the courts will not rescind the contract; the weight of authority is to the effect that after one party has performed the other party cannot repudiate the contract by claiming that it was *ultra vires.* Directors may be held personally liable for loss to the corporation occasioned by an *ultra vires* act.

An *ultra vires* contract made by a municipal corporation is not binding upon the municipality, although the other party has performed.

Uniform Laws. Conflicting state statutes have led to the adoption, in many fields of business and commercial interest, of similar laws by the various states. The laws are known as *uniform laws.* Some of the more important uniform laws are the Uniform Commercial Code, the Uniform Partnership Act, the Uniform Stock Transfer Act, and the Uniform Warehouse Receipt Act.

Usury. Contracting for or receiving something in excess of the amount of interest allowed by law for the loan or forbearance of money, as in the sale of goods on credit or under the installment plan. In the majority of states, a lender who charges a usurious rate of interest loses his right to collect any interest, although a few states permit him to collect the legal rate. In some states, both principal and interest are forfeited. Service charges, investigation fees, and commissions charged by an agent are not usually considered interest and may be added to the legal rate without usury. In some states the parties to a contract may agree upon a rate of interest higher than the legal rate but within a statutory limit; in a few states, they may agree on any rate. In some states loans to corporations, but not to individuals, may be made at more than the legal rate. Certain types of loans, such as small personal loans, are not covered by the usury law but are subject to special laws.

Void; voidable. That which is void is of no legal force or effect; that which is voidable may be rendered void. For example, a gambling or wagering contract is void (see CONTRACTS, 3); whereas an infant's contracts are merely voidable at his election (see CONTRACTS, 2).

Voting trust. A method devised for concentrating the control of a company in the hands of a few people. A voting trust is usually organized and operated under a *voting trust agreement.* This is a contract between the stockholders and those who manage the corporation, called the voting trustees. The stockholders transfer their stock to the trustees, giving them the right to vote the stock during the life of the agreement. The trustees, in turn, issue certificates of beneficial interest, called *voting trust certificates,* to the stockholders, who are entitled to the dividends. All stockholders may become parties to the agreement, which is generally subject to statutory regulation. The trust is usually for a definite period. When it is terminated, the certificate-holders are notified to exchange their trust certificates for certificates of stock.

Waiver. The surrender, either expressed or implied, of a right to which one is entitled by law. Thus, a stockholder might sign a waiver of notice of meeting, or he might impliedly waive that notice by participation in the meeting. The essence of waiver is conduct that indicates an intention not to enforce certain rights or certain provisions of an agreement. A widow may waive her right to share in the estate of her husband; a buyer may waive delivery on a certain date by accepting the goods at a subsequent date. *See also Index.*

Warranty. Affirmation of a material fact or promise by the seller, which acts as an inducement for the buyer to make a purchase. A warranty may be *express* (a direct statement made by the seller) or *implied* (one that is indicated by the nature of the contract). The Uniform Commercial Code has added a class of warranties, neither express nor implied, consisting of warranties of title and against infringement. Warranties relate to many things: fitness of the goods sold for a special purpose; merchantability of the goods; title to real or personal property (see specific titles in *Index*); and quiet enjoyment of premises. All representations made by an applicant for insurance, whether material or not, are deemed warranties. The term *guaranty* is loosely used in the sense of warranty. The common guaranty of a product is, strictly, a warranty and not a guaranty. (See GUARANTY.) Any warranty made by a seller that proves to be false gives the buyer a right of legal action.

Without recourse. A phrase used in an ENDORSEMENT that relieves the endorser from assuming liability in the event the maker fails to pay the instrument when due.

Writ. An order issued by a court, or judge, in the name of the state, for the purpose of compelling the defendant to do something mentioned in the order.

"Yellow-dog" contract. An oral or written contract under which either party, as a condition of the employment relationship, agrees to join or remain a member of some *specific* labor organization or some *specific* employer organization or agrees not to join *any* labor organization or *any* employer organization. It is illegal under the Norris-LaGuardia Act and under many state anti-injunction laws.

State Requirements for Age of Testator and Number of Witnesses to Will (not applicable to holographic wills)

State	Real Property	Personal Property	Witnesses
Alabama	21	18	2
Alaska[1]	18	18	2
Arizona	18	18	2
Arkansas	18	18	2
California	18	18	2
Colorado	18	18	2
Connecticut	18	18	3
Delaware	18	18	2
District of Columbia	21 (18 female)	21 (18 female)	2

[1] Persons must be 19 or more years of age to execute an anatomical gift.

continued

State	Real Property	Personal Property	Witnesses
Florida	18	18	2
Georgia	14	14	2
Hawaii	18	18	2
Idaho[2]	18	18	2
Illinois	18	18	2
Indiana[3]	18	18	2
Iowa[4]	21	21	2
Kansas	21	21	2
Kentucky	18	18	2
Louisiana[5]	16	16	3
Maine[7]	18	18	3
Maryland	18	18	2
Massachusetts	18	18	3
Michigan	18	18	2
Minnesota	18	18	2
Mississippi	18	18	2
Missouri	18	18	2
Montana	18	18	2
Nebraska	18	18	2
Nevada	18	18	2
New Hampshire[8]	18	18	2
New Jersey[9]	21	21	2
New Mexico	18	18	2
New York	18	18	2
North Carolina	18	18	2
North Dakota	18	18	2
Ohio	18	18	2
Oklahoma	18	18	2
Oregon[8]	18	18	2
Pennsylvania	18	18	2
Rhode Island	21	18	2
South Carolina	18	18	3
South Dakota	18	18	2
Tennessee	18	18	2
Texas[11]	18	18	2
Utah	18	18	2
Vermont	18	18	3
Virginia	18	18	2
Washington	18	18	2
West Virginia	18	18	2
Wisconsin	18	18	2
Wyoming	21	21	2

[2] No age requirement if emancipated minor.
[3] No age requirement if in the armed forces.
[4] No age requirement if ever married.
[5] Minors over 16 only in anticipation of death. The age of majority is 18 years.
[6] One of which is a notary.
[7] No age requirement if married or a widow or a widower.
[8] No age requirement if married.
[9] 18, if in active military service in time of war.
[10] 18, if married.
[11] No age requirement if in the armed forces or ever married.

Note: Some states' statutes permit wills to be self-proved when certain formalities are followed. States that permit self-proved wills include Alaska, Arizona, Colorado, Delaware, Florida, Idaho, Indiana, Kansas, Kentucky, Minnesota, Montana, Nebraska, New Mexico, North Dakota, Oklahoma, Texas, and Utah.

COURTS OF RECORD AND JUDICIAL CIRCUITS
(TABLES I, II, III AND IV)

I. FEDERAL COURTS OF RECORD IN THE UNITED STATES AND THEIR MEMBERS

Court	Members
Supreme Court of the United States	Chief Justice
	Associate Justices
United States Court of Appeals for the District of Columbia	Circuit Justice
	Chief Judge
	Circuit Judges
United States Court of Appeals for the (First) Circuit	Circuit Justice
	Chief Judge
	Circuit Judges
United States District Court for the (Southern) District of (New York)	Chief Judge
Or where the state is all in one district	District Judges
United States District Court for the District of (Maryland)	
United States Court of Claims	Chief Judge
	Associate Judges
United States Court of Customs and Patent Appeals	Chief Judge
	Associate Judges
United States Customs Court	Chief Judge
	Judges
United States Court of Military Appeals	Chief Judge
	Associate Judges
The Tax Court of the United States	Chief Judge
	Judges
Temporary Emergency Court of Appeals of the United States	Chief Judge
	Associate Judges

II. STATE COURTS OF RECORD IN THE UNITED STATES AND THEIR MEMBERS
(Asterisks indicate intermediate appellate courts. Municipal courts are not included.)

State	Court	Members of Court
Alabama	Supreme Court	Chief Justice
		Associate Justices
	*Court of Appeals	Presiding Judge
		Associate Judges
	Circuit Courts	Judges
	Probate Courts	Judge

continued

II. State Courts of Record—*continued*

State	Court	Members of Court
Alaska	Supreme Court	Chief Justice
		Associate Justices
	Superior Court	Judges
Arizona	Supreme Court	Chief Justice, Justices
	Court of Appeals	Judges
	Superior Courts	Judges
Arkansas	Supreme Court	Chief Justice
		Associate Justices
	Circuit Courts	Judges
	Chancery Courts	Chancellors
	Probate Courts	Judges
California	Supreme Court	Chief Justice
		Associate Justices
	*Courts of Appeal	Presiding Justice
		Justices
	Superior Courts	Judges
Colorado	Supreme Court	Chief Justice, Justices
	Court of Appeals	Judges
	District Court	Judges
	Superior Courts	Judges
	County Courts	Judges
	Probate Courts (Denver only)	Judges
Connecticut	Supreme Court	Chief Justice
		Associate Justices
	Superior Court	Judges
	Courts of Common Pleas	Judges
	Probate Courts	Judges
Delaware	Supreme Court	Chief Justice
		Associate Justices
	Court of Chancery	Chancellor
		Vice Chancellor
	Superior Court	President Judge
		Associate Judges
	Registers' Courts	Register of Wills
District of Columbia	U.S. District Court	Chief Judge
		Judges
	District of Columbia Superior Court	Chief Judge
		Associate Judges
Florida	Supreme Court	Chief Justice, Justices
	*District Courts of Appeal	Chief Judge, Judges
	Circuit Courts	Judges
	County Courts	Judges
	Probate Courts	Judges

continued

II. State Courts of Record—*continued*

State	Court	Members of Court
Georgia	Supreme Court	Chief Justice
		Presiding Justice
		Associate Justices
	*Court of Appeals	Chief Judge
		Presiding Judge
		Judges
	Superior Courts	Judges
	Probate Courts	Probate Judges
Hawaii	Supreme Court	Chief Justice
		Justices
	*Circuit Courts	Judges
	District Courts	District Judges
Idaho	Supreme Court	Chief Justice
		Justices
	District Courts	Judges
Illinois	Supreme Court	Chief Justice
		Justices
	*Appellate Courts	Judges
	Circuit Courts	Judges
	Court of Claims	Chief Judge
		Judges
Indiana	Supreme Court	Chief Justice
		Associate Judges
	*Court of Appeals	Chief Judge
		Presiding Judge
		Associate Judges
	Superior Courts	Judges
	Circuit Court	Judges
	Probate Courts	Judges
Iowa	Supreme Court	Chief Justice
		Justices
	*Court of Appeals	Judges
	District Courts	Judges
Kansas	Supreme Court	Chief Justice
		Justices
	*Court of Appeals	Judges
	District Court	Judges
Kentucky	Supreme Court	Chief Justice
		Associate Justices
	*Court of Appeals	Commissioners of Appeals
		Special Commissioners
	Circuit Courts	Judges
	District Courts	Judges

continued

II. State Courts of Record—*continued*

State	Court	Members of Court
Louisiana	Supreme Court	Chief Justice
		Associate Justices
	*Court of Appeal	Judges
	(New Orleans only)	
	District Courts	Judges
Maine	Supreme Judicial Court	Chief Justice
		Associate Justices
	Superior Court	Justices
	State District Courts	Chief Judge, Judges
	Probate Courts	Judges
Maryland	Court of Appeals	Chief Judge
		Associate Judges
	Court of Special Appeals	Judges
	Circuit Courts	Chief Judges, Judges
	Orphans' Courts	Judges
Massachusetts	Supreme Judicial Court	Chief Justice
		Associate Justices
	*Appeals Court	Justices
	Superior Court	Chief Justice
		Associate Justices
	Probate Courts	Judges
	Land Court	Judge, Associate Judges
Michigan	Supreme Court	Chief Justice
		Associate Justices
	Court of Appeals	Justices
	Circuit Courts	Circuit Judge
		Judges
	Court of Claims	Judge
	Probate Courts	Judges
Minnesota	Supreme Court	Chief Justice
		Associate Justices
	District Court	Judges
	County Courts	Judges
	Probate Courts	Judges
Mississippi	Supreme Court	Chief Justice
		Associate Justices
	Circuit Courts	Judges
	Chancery Courts	Chancellors
	County Courts	Judges
Missouri	Supreme Court	Chief Justice
		Presiding Judge
		Associate Judges
	*Courts of Appeals	Presiding Judge
		Associate Judges

continued

II. State Courts of Record—*continued*

State	Court	Members of Court
Missouri (con't.)	Court of Common Pleas	Judges
	Circuit Courts	Judges
	Probate Courts	Judges
Montana	Supreme Court	Chief Justice
		Associate Justices
	District Court	Judges
Nebraska	Supreme Court	Chief Justice
		Associate Justices
	District Court	Judges
	County Courts	Judges
Nevada	Supreme Court	Chief Justice
		Associate Justices
	District Court	Judges
New Hampshire	Supreme Court	Chief Justice
		Associate Justices
	Superior Court	Chief Justice
		Justices
	Probate Courts	Presiding Judges
New Jersey	Supreme Court	Chief Justice
		Justices
	*Superior Court,	Senior Judge
	Appellate Division	Judges
	Superior Court,	Judges
	Chancery Division	
	Superior Court,	Judges
	Law Division	
	County Courts	Judges
	Surrogate's Courts	Surrogates
New Mexico	Supreme Court	Chief Justice
		Justices
	*Court of Appeals	Chief Judge
		Judges
	District Court	Presiding Judge
		Judges
	Probate Courts	Judges
New York	Court of Appeals	Chief Judge
		Associate Judges
	*Supreme Court,	Presiding Justice
	Appellate Division	Justices
	Supreme Court	Justices
	County Courts	Judges
	Surrogates' Courts	Surrogates
	Court of Claims	Judges
	City and District Courts	Judges
	(in larger cities and	
	counties)	

continued

II. State Courts of Record—*continued*

State	Court	Members of Court
North Carolina	Supreme Court	Chief Justice
		Associate Justices
	*Court of Appeals	Judges
	Superior Courts	Judges
North Dakota	Supreme Court	Chief Justice
		Judges
	District Court	Judges
	County Courts	Judges
Ohio	Supreme Court	Chief Justice
		Justices
	*Courts of Appeals	Judges
	Court of Claims	Judges
	Courts of Common Pleas	Judges
Oklahoma	Supreme Court	Chief Justice
		Vice Chief Justice
		Justices
	*Criminal Court of Appeals	Presiding Judge
		Judges
	*Court of Appeals	Judges
	District Courts	Judges
Oregon	Supreme Court	Chief Justice
		Associate Justices
	*Court of Appeals	Judges
	Tax Court	Judges
	Circuit Courts	Judges
	County Courts	County Judges
Pennsylvania	Supreme Court	Chief Justice
		Justices
	Superior Court	Presiding Judge
		Judges
	Commonwealth Court	Judges
	Courts of Common Pleas	Judges
Rhode Island	Supreme Court	Chief Justice
		Associate Justices
	Superior Court	Presiding Justice
		Justices
	Family Court	Judges
	District Court	Judges
	Probate Courts	Judges
South Carolina	Supreme Court	Chief Justice
		Associate Justice
	Circuit Courts	Judges
	County Courts	Judges
	Probate Courts	Judges

continued

II. State Courts of Record—*continued*

State	*Court*	*Members of Court*
South Dakota	Supreme Court	Presiding Judge
		Judges
	Circuit Courts	Judges
Tennessee	Supreme Court	Chief Justice
		Associate Justices
	*Court of Appeals	Presiding Judge
		Associate Judges
	*Court of Criminal Appeals	Judges
Tennessee	Chancery Courts	Chancellors
(Continued)	Circuit Courts	Judges
	County Courts	Judges
	Probate Courts, Shelby	
	and Davidson Counties	Judge
Texas	Supreme Court	Chief Justice
		Associate Justices
	*Court of Civil Appeals	Chief Justice
		Associate Justices
	Court of Criminal	Presiding Judge, Judges
	Appeal	Commissioners
	District Courts	Judges
	County Courts	Judges
Utah	Supreme Court	Chief Justice
		Justices
	District Court	Judges
	Circuit Courts	Judges
Vermont	Supreme Court	Chief Justice
		Associate Justices
	Superior Courts	Judges
	Probate Courts	Judges
Virginia	Supreme Court	Chief Justice
		Justices
	Circuit Courts	Judges
Virgin Islands	District Court	Judge
	Territorial Courts	Judges
Washington	Supreme Court	Chief Justice
		Associate Judges
	Court of Appeals	Judges
	Superior Courts	Judges

continued

II. State Courts of Record—*continued*

State	Court	Members of Court
West Virginia	Supreme Court of Appeals	President
		Judges
	Circuit Courts	Judges
	County Commissions	Commissioners
Wisconsin	Supreme Court	Chief Justice
		Associate Justices
	*Court of Appeals	Judges
	Circuit Courts	Judges
	County Courts	Judges
Wyoming	Supreme Court	Chief Justice
		Associate Justice
	District Courts	Judges

III. JUDICIAL CIRCUITS AND THE STATES AND TERRITORIES IN EACH CIRCUIT

District of Columbia Circuit	District of Columbia
First Circuit	Maine, Massachusetts, New Hampshire, Puerto Rico, Rhode Island
Second Circuit	Connecticut, New York, Vermont, Virgin Islands,
Third Circuit	Delaware, New Jersey, Pennsylvania, Virgin Islands
Fourth Circuit	Maryland, North Carolina, South Carolina, Virginia, West Virginia
Fifth Circuit	Alabama, Canal Zone, Florida, Georgia, Louisiana, Mississippi, Texas
Sixth Circuit	Kentucky, Michigan, Ohio, Tennessee
Seventh Circuit	Illinois, Indiana, Wisconsin
Eighth Circuit	Arkansas, Iowa, Minnesota, Missouri, Nebraska, North Dakota, South Dakota, Territory of Guam
Ninth Circuit	Alaska, Arizona, California, Hawaii, Idaho, Montana, Nevada, Oregon, Washington
Tenth Circuit	Colorado, Kansas, New Mexico, Oklahoma, Utah, Wyoming

continued

IV. STATES AND TERRITORIES AND JUDICIAL CIRCUIT IN WHICH EACH IS LOCATED

State	Circuit	State	Circuit
Alabama	Fifth Circuit	Montana*	Ninth Circuit
Alaska*	Ninth Circuit	Nebraska*	Eighth Circuit
Arizona*	Ninth Circuit	Nevada*	Ninth Circuit
Arkansas	Eighth Circuit	New Hampshire*	First Circuit
California	Ninth Circuit	New Jersey*	Third Circuit
Canal Zone*	Fifth Circuit	New Mexico*	Tenth Circuit
Colorado*	Tenth Circuit	New York	Second Circuit
Connecticut*	Second Circuit	North Carolina	Fourth Circuit
Delaware*	Third Circuit	North Dakota*	Eighth Circuit
Florida	Fifth Circuit	Ohio	Sixth Circuit
Georgia	Fifth Circuit	Oklahoma	Tenth Circuit
Guam	Eighth Circuit	Oregon*	Ninth Circuit
Hawaii*	Ninth Circuit	Pennsylvania	Third Circuit
Idaho*	Ninth Circuit	Puerto Rico	First Circuit
Illinois	Seventh Circuit	Rhode Island*	First Circuit
Indiana	Seventh Circuit	South Carolina	Fourth Circuit
Iowa	Eighth Circuit	South Dakota*	Eighth Circuit
Kansas*	Tenth Circuit	Tennessee	Sixth Circuit
Kentucky	Sixth Circuit	Texas	Fifth Circuit
Louisiana	Fifth Circuit	Utah*	Tenth Circuit
Maine*	First Circuit	Vermont*	Second Circuit
Maryland*	Fourth Circuit	Virginia	Fourth Circuit
Massachusetts*	First Circuit	Virgin Islands	Second Circuit
Michigan	Sixth Circuit	Washington	Ninth Circuit
Minnesota*	Eighth Circuit	West Virginia	Fourth Circuit
Mississippi	Fifth Circuit	Wisconsin	Seventh Circuit
Missouri	Eighth Circuit	Wyoming*	Tenth Circuit

*Only one district court.

AUTHENTICATION OF INSTRUMENTS

State	When an instrument is notarized outside the state for recording within the state, must it be authenticated if notary affixes his seal?	Who authenticates acknowledgments taken by notary public in state for use in another state?
Alabama	No	Clerk of Circuit Court
Alaska	No	Lieutenant Governor
Arizona	No	Clerk of Superior Court
Arkansas	Yes[1]	Superior Court Clerk
California	Yes	Clerk of Court of Record
Colorado	No[1]	Secretary of State
Connecticut	Customary[1]	Clerk of Superior Court, Waterbury District Clerk
Delaware	No	Prothonotary
District of Columbia	No	Secretary of District Council
Florida	No	Secretary of State
Georgia	No	Clerk of Superior Court
Hawaii	No	Clerk of Circuit Court
Idaho	No	Clerk of District Court
Illinois	No	County Clerk or Secretary of State may grant certificates of magistracy to notaries
Indiana	No	Clerk of Circuit Court
Iowa	Yes	Secretary of State
Kansas	No[1]	Clerk of Court of Record
Kentucky	No[1]	Clerk of County (District) Court
Louisiana	No	Clerk of District Court
Maine	No[1]	Clerk of Court
Maryland	No	Clerk of Circuit Court (Clerk of Superior Court of Baltimore City)
Massachusetts	No	State Secretary; Clerk of Superior Court
Michigan	No	Clerk of County
Minnesota	No[1]	Clerk of District Court, Secretary of State
Mississippi	No	Chancery Clerk, Secretary of State
Missouri	No	Clerk of County Court (Clerk of Circuit Court for City of St. Louis)
Montana	No	Secretary of State or County Clerk
Nebraska	No[1]	County Clerk
Nevada	No[1]	County Clerk
New Hampshire	No[1]	Secretary of State or Clerk of Court of Record
New Jersey	Yes	County Clerk
New Mexico	Not required but customary	County Clerk
New York	Yes	County Clerk
North Carolina	No	Secretary of State or Register of Deeds
North Dakota	No[1]	Clerk of District Court
Ohio	No[1]	Clerk of Common Pleas Court

continued

Authentication of Instruments—*continued*

State	When an instrument is notarized outside the state for recording within the state, must it be authenticated if notary affixes his seal?	Who authenticates acknowledgments taken by notary public in state for use in another state?
Oklahoma	No[1]	Secretary of State
Oregon	No	County Clerk or Secretary of State
Pennsylvania	No[1]	Prothonotary of Common Pleas Court
Rhode Island	No	Superior, Supreme, and District Court Clerks
South Carolina	No[1]	Clerk of Court
South Dakota	No	Clerk of Circuit Court
Tennessee	No	Clerk of County, Secretary of State for Notaries at Large
Texas	No	County Clerk
Utah	No	Secretary of State
Vermont	No (banks usually request authentication)	County Clerk
Virginia	No[1]	Clerk of Court
Virgin Islands	No	Clerk of District Court
Washington	No	Secretary of State or County Clerk
West Virginia	No[1]	Clerk of County Court
Wisconsin	No[1]	Clerk of Circuit Court
Wyoming	No	County Clerk

1. Uniform Recognition of Acknowledgements Act adopted.

NOTARIES PUBLIC

State	Appointments made by	Length of term	Notary must affix		Record of acts required	Bond required
			Seal	Date commission expires		
Alabama	Judges of Probate	4	Yes	No	Yes	Yes
Alaska	Secretary of State	4	Yes	Yes	Yes	Yes
Arizona	Secretary of State	4	Yes	Yes	Yes	Yes
Arkansas	Governor	4	Yes	Yes	Yes	Yes
California	Secretary of State	4	Yes	No	Yes	Yes
Colorado	Secretary of State	4	Yes	Yes	Yes	Yes

continued

Notaries Public—*continued*

State	Appointments made by	Length of term	Notary must affix		Record of acts required	Bond required
			Seal	Date commission expires		
Connecticut	Secretary of State	5	Yes	No	No	No
Delaware	Governor	2	Yes	No	No	No
District of Columbia	D.C. Commissioners	5	Yes	No	Yes	Yes
Florida	Governor	4	Yes	Yes	No	Yes
Georgia	Clerks of Superior Court	4	Yes	No	No	No
Hawaii	Atty. Gen.	4	Yes	Yes	Yes	Yes
Idaho	Governor	4	Yes	No	Yes	Yes
Illinois	Secretary of State	4	Yes	No	No[2]	Yes
Indiana	Governor	4	Yes	Yes	No	Yes
Iowa	Secretary of State	3	Yes	No	Yes	Yes
Kansas	Secretary of State	4	Yes	Yes	No	Yes
Kentucky	Secretary of State	4	No	Yes	No[1]	Yes
Louisiana	Governor	Indefinite	No	No	Yes	Yes
Maine	Governor	7	Yes	No	No[3]	No
Maryland	Governor	4	Yes	Yes	Yes	No
Massachusetts .	Governor	7	No	Yes	No	No
Michigan	Governor	4	No	Yes	No	Yes
Minnesota	Governor	7	Yes	Yes	No[1]	Yes
Mississippi	Governor	4	Yes	Yes	Yes	Yes
Missouri	Secretary of State	4	Yes	Yes	Yes	Yes
Montana	Governor	3	Yes	Yes	No[1]	Yes
Nebraska	Governor	4	Yes	Yes	No	Yes
Nevada	Secretary of State	4	Yes[6]	Yes	No	Yes
New Hampshire	Governor	5	Yes[4]	Yes	No	No
New Jersey	Secretary of State	5	No	No	Yes	No
New Mexico	Governor	4	Yes	Yes	Yes	Yes
New York	Secretary of State	2	Yes	Yes	No	No
North Carolina	Secretary of State	5	Yes	Yes	No	No
North Dakota ..	Secretary of State	6	Yes	Yes	No[1]	Yes
Ohio	Governor	5	Yes[4]	No	No[1]	Yes
Oklahoma	Secretary of State	4	Yes	Yes	Yes	Yes

continued

Notaries Public—*continued*

State	Appoint-ments made by	Length of term	Notary must affix		Record of acts required	Bond required
			Seal	Date commis-sion expires		
Oregon	Governor	4	Yes	Yes	No[1]	Yes
Pennsylvania ..	Secretary of the Common-wealth	4	Yes	Yes	Yes	Yes
Rhode Island ..	Governor	5	No	No	No	No
South Carolina .	Governor	10	Yes	Yes	No	No
South Dakota ..	Governor	8	Yes	Yes[4]	No[1]	Yes
Tennessee	Governor	4	Yes	Yes	Yes	Yes
Texas	Secretary State	2	Yes	Yes	Yes	Yes
Utah	Governor	4	Yes	Yes	No[1]	Yes
Vermont	Judges of the County Court	2	Yes	No	No	No
Virginia	Governor	4	No	Yes	No	Yes
Washington	Governor	4	Yes	No	No	Yes
West Virginia ..	Governor	10	No	Yes	No	Yes
Wisconsin	Governor	4	Yes	Yes	No	Yes
Wyoming	Governor	4	Yes	Yes	Yes[5]	Yes

[1.] Except with reference to commercial papers.
[2.] Except with reference to negotiable instruments.
[3.] Except with reference to mercantile and marine protests.
[4.] In practice, but not by statute.
[5.] For official acts required by law to be recorded.
[6.] Stamp, rather than seal.

STATUTES OF LIMITATIONS IN NUMBER OF YEARS

State	Open Accounts	Notes	Written Contracts	Contracts Under Seal
Alabama	3	6[7]	6[7]	10
Alaska	6[7]	6[7]	6[7]	10
Arizona	3	6[1]	6[7]	6[1]
Arkansas	3	5	5[7]	5
California	4	4[2]	4	4
Colorado	6	6	6[3, 7]	6[3, 7]
Connecticut	6	6	6[7]	17
Delaware	3	6	3[7]	--
District of Columbia	3[7]	3[7]	3[7]	12
Florida	3	5	5[7]	20
Georgia	4	6	6[7]	20

continued

Statutes of Limitations—*continued*

State	Open Accounts	Notes	Written Contracts	Contracts Under Seal
Hawaii	6[7]	6[7]	6[7]	6
Idaho	4	5	5	5
Illinois	5	10	10[7]	10[4]
Indiana	6	10	10-20	20
Iowa	5	10	10[7]	10
Kansas	3	5	5[7]	5
Kentucky	5	15[5]	15[7]	15
Louisiana	3	5	10	10
Maine	6	6[6]	6[7]	20
Maryland	3[7]	3[7]	3[7]	12
Massachusetts	6	6[6]	6[7]	20
Michigan	6[7]	6[7]	6[7]	6[7]
Minnesota	6	6[7]	6[7]	6
Mississippi	3	6	6	6
Missouri	5	10[7]	10[7]	10[7]
Montana	5	8	8[7]	8
Nebraska	4	5	5[7]	5
Nevada	4	6[7]	6[7]	6[7]
New Hampshire	6[7]	6[7]	6[7]	20
New Jersey	6[7]	6[7]	6[7]	16
New Mexico	4	6	6[7]	6
New York	6[7]	6[7]	6[7]	6[7]
North Carolina	3	3	3	10
North Dakota	6[7]	6[7]	6[1, 7]	6[3]
Ohio	15	15	15	15
Oklahoma	3	5	5	5
Oregon	6[7]	6[7]	6[7]	--
Pennsylvania	6	6	6[7]	20
Rhode Island	6[7]	6[7]	6	20
South Carolina	6	6	6	20
South Dakota	6[7]	6[7]	6[7]	20
Tennessee	6[7]	6[7]	6[7]	6[7]
Texas	2	4	4	4
Utah	4	6	6[7]	6
Vermont	6	6[8]	6[7]	8
Virginia	3	5	5[7]	10
Washington	3	6	6[7]	6
West Virginia	5	10	10[7]	10
Wisconsin	6[7]	6[7]	6[7]	10-20
Wyoming	8	10	10[7]	10

[1] Executed without the state, 4 years.
[2] Corporate notes, 6 years.
[3] Contracts affecting real property, 10 years.
[4] Vendor's lien, mortgage, 20 years.
[5] 5-year period applies if note is placed on the footing of a bill of exchange.
[6] Witnessed notes, 20 years.
[7] Sales contracts, 4 years (Uniform Commercial Code).
[8] Witnessed notes, 14 years.

OFFICIAL REPORTS AND HOW THEY ARE CITED

Official report	Cite as
Alabama Reports	Ala.
Alabama Appellate Reports	Ala. App.
Alaska Reports	P. 2d
Arizona Reports	Ariz.
Arkansas Reports	Ark.
California Appellate Reports	Cal. App.
California Appellate Reports, Second Series	Cal. App. 2d
California Reports	Cal.
California Reports, Second Series	Cal. 2d
Colorado Reports	Colo.
Connecticut	Conn.
Delaware Reports	By name of Rep.
Delaware Chancery Reports	Del. Ch.
Florida Reports[1]	Fla.
Georgia Reports	Ga.
Hawaii Reports	H.
Idaho Reports	Idaho
Illinois Reports	Ill.
Illinois Appellate Court Reports	Ill. App.
Indiana Reports	Ind.
Indiana Appellate Reports	Ind. App.
Iowa Reports	Iowa
Kansas Reports	Kan.
Kentucky Reports[2]	Ky.
Louisiana Reports	La.
Maine Reports	Me.
Maryland Reports	Md.
Massachusetts Reports	Mass.
Michigan Reports	Mich.
Minnesota Reports	Minn.
Mississippi Reports	Miss.
Missouri Reports	Mo.
Missouri Appeal Reports	Mo. App.
Montana Reports	Mont.
Nebraska Reports	Neb.
Nevada Reports	Nev.
New Hampshire Reports	N.H.
New Jersey Equity Reports	N.J. Eq.
New Jersey Reports	N.J.
New Jersey Superior Court Reports	N.J. Super.
New Mexico Reports	N.M.
New York Appellate Division Reports	N.Y. App. Div.
New York Miscellaneous Reports	N.Y. Misc.
New York Reports	N.Y.
North Carolina Reports	N.C.

continued

Official Reports—*continued*

Official report	*Cite as*
North Dakota Reports	N.D.
Ohio Appellate Reports	Ohio App.
Ohio State Reports	Ohio St.
Oklahoma Reports	Okl.
Oklahoma Criminal Reports	Okl. Cr.
Oregon Reports	Or.
Pennsylvania Reports	Pa.
Pennsylvania Superior Court Reports	Pa. Sup.
Rhode Island Reports	R.I.
South Carolina Reports	S.C.
South Dakota Reports	S.D.
Tennessee Reports	Tenn.
Tennessee Appeals Reports	Tenn. App.
Texas Reports	Tex.
United States Reports	U.S.
United States Court of Appeals, District of Columbia	U.S. App. D.C.
Utah Reports	Utah
Vermont Reports	Vt.
Virginia Reports	Va.
Washington Reports	Wash.
Washington Reports, Second Series	Wash. 2d
West Virginia Reports	W. Va.
Wisconsin Reports	Wis.
Wyoming Reports	Wyo.

[1] Up to Vol. 160 only. Now the Southern Reporter is official.
[2] Up to Vol. 314 only. Now the Southwestern Reporter is official.

REPORTERS OF NATIONAL REPORTER SYSTEM

Name of reporter	Cite as	Courts covered
Supreme Court Reporter	S. Ct.	United States Supreme Court
Federal Reporter	F.	United States Circuit Courts of Appeals and the District Courts
Federal Reporter, Second Series	F. 2d	United States Courts of Appeals, United States Court of Customs and Patent Appeals, United States Emergency Court of Appeals
Federal Supplement	F. Supp.	United States District Courts, United States Court of Claims
Atlantic Reporter Atlantic Reporter, Second Series	A. A. 2d	Connecticut Delaware Maine Maryland New Hampshire New Jersey Pennsylvania Rhode Island Vermont District of Columbia
New York Supplement New York Supplement, Second Series	N.Y. Supp. N.Y.S. 2d	New York Court of Appeals Appellate Division of the Supreme Court Miscellaneous Courts
Northeastern Reporter Northeastern Reporter, Second Series	N.E. N.E. 2d	Illinois Indiana New York Massachusetts Ohio
Northwestern Reporter Northwestern Reporter, Second Series	N.W. N.W. 2d	Iowa Michigan Minnesota Nebraska North Dakota South Dakota Wisconsin

continued

Reporters of National Reporter System—*continued*

Name of reporter	Cite as	Courts covered
Pacific Reporter Pacific Reporter, Second Series	P. P. 2d	Alaska Arizona California Colorado Hawaii Idaho Kansas Montana Nevada New Mexico Oklahoma Oregon Utah Washington Wyoming
Southeastern Reporter Southeastern Reporter, Second Series	S.E. S.E. 2d	Georgia North Carolina South Carolina Virginia West Virginia
Southern Reporter Southern Reporter, Second Series	So. So. 2d	Alabama Florida Louisiana Mississippi
Southwestern Reporter Southwestern Reporter, Second Series	S.W. S.W. 2d	Arkansas Kentucky Missouri Tennessee Texas

APPROVED METHOD OF CITING COMPILATIONS OF STATUTES AND CODES

State	*Title of compilation*	*How cited*
Ala.	Code of Alabama, Recompiled 1958	Code of Ala. Tit. 10, § 101
Alaska	Alaska Statutes 1962	A.S. § 08.04.310
Ariz.	Arizona Revised Statutes Annotated	ARS § 10-101
Ark.	Arkansas Statutes Annotated 1947	Ark. Stats. (1947) Sec. 10-101
Calif.	Deering's California Codes (Code of Civil Procedure)	CCP § 101
Colo.	Colorado Revised Statutes, 1963	101-1-7, C.R.S. '63
Conn.	General Statutes, Revision of 1958	Conn. G.S. 1958 Sec. 101
Del.	Delaware Code Annotated, 1953	10 Del. C. § 110
D.C.	District of Columbia Code Annotated, 1961	D.C. Code 1961, Title 26, § 703
Fla.	Florida Statutes, 1967	Florida Statutes, 1967, § 101.011
Ga.	Code of Georgia, Annotated	Ga. Code Ann. § 10-1010
Hawaii	Revised Laws of Hawaii, 1955	R.L.H. 1955 § 172-1
Idaho	Idaho Code	Idaho Code, Sec. 26-1850
Ill.	Illinois Revised Statutes 1951	Ill. Rev. Stat. 1951 Ch. 10, §101
	Smith-Hurd Illinois Annotated Statutes	S.H.A. Ch. 10, § 101
	Jones Illinois Statutes Annotated	Jones Ill. Stat. Ann. Ch. 10, § 101
Ind.	Burns Annotated Indiana Statutes	Burns Ann. St. Sec. 25-101
Iowa	Code of Iowa, 1966	Code of Iowa, 1966, § 110.10
Kan.	Kansas Statutes Annotated, 1963	K.S.A. 48-101
Ky.	Kentucky Revised Statutes, 1962	KRS 101.010 (1)
La.	Louisiana Revised Statutes of 1950	R.S. 10:101
Maine	Revised Statutes of Maine, 1964	R.S. of Maine 1964, T. 10 § 51
Md.	Annotated Code of Maryland, 1957	Md. Code (1957), Art. 10, Sec. 101
Mass.	Annotated Laws of Massachusetts, 1966	A.L., C. 8 § 10
Mich.	1948 Compiled Laws of Michigan	C.L. 1948, § 10.101
	Michigan Statutes Annotated	Stat. Ann. § 10.101
Minn.	Minnesota Statutes 1967	Minn. Stat. 1967, Sec. 101.51
Miss.	Mississippi Code, 1942, Annotated	Miss. Code, 1942, Ann., § 101

continued

Citing Compilations—*continued*

State	Title of compilation	How cited
Mo.	Missouri Revised Statutes, 1959	R.S. Mo. 1959, § 101.010
Mont.	Revised Codes of Montana, 1947, Annotated	RCM 1947, § 10-101
Nebr.	Nebraska Revised Statutes, 1943	Sec. 1-101, R.S. Nebr., 1943
	Reissue Revised Statutes of Nebraska, 1943	Sec. 1-101, R.R.S. Nebr., 1943
Nev.	Nevada Revised Statutes	NRS § 19.010
N.H.	1966 New Hampshire Revised Statutes Annotated	RSA 101:1
N.J.	Revised Statutes of New Jersey, 1937	N.J.R.S., 10:101-10
	New Jersey Statutes Annotated	N.J.S.A., 2A: 4-30.1
N.M.	New Mexico Statutes Annotated, 1953	NMSA Comp., 3-7-16
N.Y.	McKinney's Consolidated Laws of New York	Business Corporation Law, § 101
N.C.	General Statutes of North Carolina, 1965	G.S. § 10-101
N.D.	North Dakota Century Code, Annotated, 1961	N.D.C.C.A. § 9-08-05
Ohio	Baldwin's Ohio Revised Code, Annotated	R.C. § 1110.10
Okla.	Oklahoma Statutes, 1961	10 O.S. 1961 § 101
Ore.	Oregon Revised Statutes	ORS 11.010
Penn.	Purdon's Pennsylvania Statutes Annotated	10 P.S. § 101
R.I.	General Laws of Rhode Island of 1956	Gen. Laws 1956, 1-1-10
S.C.	Code of Laws of S.C. 1962	1962 Code, § 10-101
S.D.	South Dakota Code of 1939	SDC 10.1010 (10)
	South Dakota Code Supplement of 1960	SDC 1960 Supp. 11.0111
Tenn.	Tennessee Code Annotated	T.C.A., § 10-101
Tex.	Vernon's Texas Statutes, 1948	Vernon's Texas St. 1948, Art. 101
	Vernon's Texas Statutes, 1962 Supplement	Vernon's Texas C.C.P., 1962 Supp., Art. 5728
Utah	Utah Code Annotated, 1953	UCA 1953, 10-10-1
Vt.	Vermont Statutes Annotated	VSA, Title I, § 51
Va.	Code of Virginia, 1950	Code, § 10-101
Wash.	Revised Code of Washington, 1968 Supplement	RCW 10.11.101
W. Va.	West Virginia Code Annotated (1966)	Michie's § 17-3-6
Wis.	Wisconsin Statutes 1967	Stats. § 84.12
Wyo.	Wyoming Statutes 1957	WS, § 10-10

Index

A

Abbreviations:
  citations, 375
  law degrees, 27
Abstract company, 72
Abstracts of indentures, 402
Acceptance, letters, 137-138
Accounting department, 39
Accounts Payable, 142, 143
Accounts Receivable, 141, 143, 155
Accrued Federal Insurance Contributions, 143
Accrued Withholding Tax, 143
Accumulated Depreciation, 143
Acknowledgment:
  authentication, 207
  certificates, 201, 202, 203, 204
  date, 205
  date of expiration of commission, 205
  definition, 201
  designation of person making, 205
  distinct from affidavit, 229-230
  essentials, 203-206
  how and where to type, 206
  importance, 201
  laws governing, 201, 202, 203
  notary's seal, 205-206
  principle of law governing, 202

Acknowledgment *(cont'd)*
  signature and designation of officer
    taking, 205
  ss., 204-205
  venue, 203-205
  who may make, 206
  who may take, 206-207
Acknowledgments of documents,
  requests, 72
Action number, 262
Address:
  business titles or position, 106-107
  checking, 178
  forms, 104-106, 525-547
  honorary and official positions,
    525-547
  street, 107-108
  women, 107
Administration material, office, 80
Administration of estate, 483-508
  (see also Estate administration)
Administrators, 275, 483
Admission to bar, 26-27
Advance sheets, 371
Advertisements, 87
Advertising, 28
Advice over phone, 62
Affiant, 229, 230, 277

Affidavit:
  affiant, 229
  authentication, 230
  averment of oath, 230
  definition, 229
  deponent, 229
  distinct from acknowledgment, 229-230
  double-space, 231
  essentials, 230
  jurat, 230, 231
  name of affiant, 230
  preparation, 230-232
  service by mail, 358
  signature line, 231
  signature of affiant, 230
  signature of notary, 231
  statement of facts, 230
  "sworn to" clause, 230
  venue, 230
Affidavit for use in court:
  analysis, 339
  content, 340
  how to prepare, 340
  in opposition, 341
Affirm, word, 281
Agenda, meeting, 406
Agent, power of attorney, 232
Alias summons, 303
Alien corporations, 384
Allegations, 298
Alphabetical filing, 85-86
  (*see also* Files)
Alternate citations, 168-169
American court system, 253-255
American Digest, 170, 171
American Federal Tax Report, 169
American Jurisprudence, 176
American Labor Cases, 169
American Law Reports, 176, 373
Amicus curiae, 274
Ampersand, 104
Anniversary, business, 135
Annotated compilation, excerpt, 167
Announcements:
  changes in law firms, 87
  entering practice, 28
  law school, 87
  mailing list, 29-30
  removal of offices, 29
  resuming practice, 29
Annual report:
  state authority, 420
  stockholders, 420
Annual stockholders' meeting, 420

Answer:
  analysis, 305
  caption, 305
  counterclaims, 305
  defendant's first pleading, 305
  denial, 305
  endorsed back, 309
  how to prepare, 305, 307, 308
  introduction, 305
  service on plaintiff's attorney, 308-309
  signature of attorney, 305
  verification, 305
  what to do about, 310
  "wherefore" clause, 305
Appeal, 354
Appellant, 355
Appellee, 355
Appointment:
  client calls without, 51
  diary, 69
  early client, 53
  hysterical client, 53-54
Appreciation, letters, 131-132
Argument, 361
Article, congratulations, 134
Articles, will, 236
Articles of association, 387
Articles of incorporation, 387-390
Assets, 143
Assignment of errors, 357, 359
Assistants, legal, 33
Association, 385
Attention line, 112
Attestation, 200
Attestation clause:
  execution, 199-200
  will, 238
Attested seal, 199
Attorney-in-fact, 232
Attorneys, 252
Authentication:
  acknowledgments, 207
  affidavits, 230
  instruments, 611-612
Author's alterations, 187
Automated legal research systems, 177
Automatic typewriters, 35
Averment of oath, 230

                          B

Bachelor of Civil Law, 27
Bachelor of Laws, 27

Bad Debts, 143
Bailiffs, 252
Ballentine's Law Dictionary, 177
Bank accounts:
  list, 402
  resolution opening, 397-398
Banks, 383, 385
Bar, admission, 26-27
Barristers, 261
Beneficiaries, will, 235
Bequest, will, 237
Bibliographies, copy, 180-181
Bill in equity, 250, 298
Billing the client, 161, 163-164
Bill of complaint, 250, 298
Bill of particulars:
  how to prepare, 328
  parts listed, 328
  style, 329
  what to do about, 328
Black's Law Dictionary, 360
Blind-copy notation, 113-114
Block style, 99
"Bluebook," 30, 90, 168
Boldface, 183, 184
Book, congratulations, 135
Booklets, 80
Books, references, 165-178
  (*see also* References)
Books and records:
  billing the client, 161, 163-164
    calculating the amount, 163
    charges made to clients, 163
    petty cash fund, 163-164
    preparation of bill, 161
  bookkeeping, 139-158
    Accounts Payable, 143
    Accounts Payable, credit, 142
    Accounts Payable, debit, 142
    Accounts Receivable, 141, 143
    Accounts Receivable, credit, 141
    Accounts Receivable, debit, 141
    Accrued Federal Insurance Contributions, 143
    Accrued Withholding Tax, 143
    Accumulated Depreciation, 143
    Assets, 143
    Bad Debts, 143
    basic principles, 140
    books required, 139-140
    capital account, 158
    Capital (Proprietorship), 143
    Cash (Firm Bank Account), 143
    Cash (Firm Bank Account), credit, 141

Books and Records *(cont'd)*
    Cash (Firm Bank Account), debit, 141, 158
    cash journal, 141-142
    cash journal entries and posting, 145-154
    cash payments, 141
    cash received, 141
    "control" account, 143
    Depreciation, 143
    "double-entry" system, 139
    drawing account, 158
    Expense, 143
    Fees Earned, 142, 143
    general ledger, 142-143
    General Ledger, credit, 142
    General Ledger, debit, 142
    Income, 143
    Insurance, 143
    Liabilities, 143
    Miscellaneous Expense, 142, 143
    Office Supplies, 143
    Overhead expenses, 142
    payroll record, 158
    Petty Cash, 143
    posting to general ledger, 145
    Profit and Loss, 143
    profit and loss statement, 155, 158
    Rent, 143
    rules, 140-141
    Salaries, 143
    Services charged, 143
    Service Charged, credit, 142
    Services Charged, debit, 142
    Services Charged, account, 141
    subsidiary ledger, 143, 145
    taking trial balance of accounts receivable, 155
    Tax Expense, 142, 143
    Telephone, 143
    trial balance, 154-155
    Trust Fund Account, 143
    Trust Fund Account, credit, 141
    Trust Fund Account, debit, 141
    professional services, 158
    daily time sheet, 159
    posting time charges, 159, 161
    time and cost, 158-159
Books of index, 170
Brief:
  application for oral argument, 363, 367
  Argument, 361
  cover, 367, 368
  cover and binding, 362

Brief *(cont'd)*
  draft, 361-362
  filing and serivce, 362-363
  format, 362
  index to, 362, 365
  list of authorities cited, 362, 366
  manuscript marked for printer, 369
  nature, 360-361
  number of copies, 362
  page from, 364
  preliminaries to preparing, 361
  preparation, 361-363
  procedure when having printed, 367, 369, 370
  time element, 361
Bulletins, 80, 87
Business titles or position, 106-107, 109
Buyer, 197
Bylaws:
  information folder, 402
  preparation, 395-396

C

Cables, 121
Calculator, 35
Calendar:
  corporation, 419-421
  court, 363
Calendar call, 263-264
Calendar number, 263
Call, calendar, 263-264
Calls *(see* Telephone)
Canons of Ethics, 28
Capital account, 158
Capital (Proprietorship), 143
Capitalization:
  legal papers, 221
  will, 244
Captions, court papers, 282-292
Cards, diary, 67
Case in brief, 251
Cases:
  decided, 166, 168-170
  not accepted, 80
Cash (Firm Bank Account), 141, 143, 158
Cash journal, 141-142
Cash journal entries and posting, 145-154
Cash payments, 141
Cash received, 141
Catalogues, 87
Certificate of incorporation, 387, 389
Certification, will, 243-244
Certified extract of minutes, 412-413, 414

Certiori, 354
Chambers, 250
Chancery courts, 258
Change of corporate name, 421-429
Character count, 185
Charges:
  collection, 32
  made to client, 163
Charters, 387
Chinese copy, 221
Circuit court, 254
Citations:
  accuracy, 370-371
  Advance Sheet, 371
  alternate, 168-169
  American Law Reports, 373
  date, 373
  definition, 370
  estate administration, 506
  federal court, 373
  how to cite, 371
  illustrations, 376
  jurisdiction and court, 373
  Law Reports Annotated, 373
  law reviews, 375
  legal newspapers, 375
  marking copy, 183
  named reporters, 374
  names of parties, 372-373
  National Reporter System, 371
  official reports, 371
  official reports and reporters, 372-373
  parallel, 373
  placement, 375-376
  probate of will, 493-497 *(see also* Probate of will)
  "2¢," 373
  selective case series, 373
  shorthand, 370
  slip decision, 374
  sources, 370
  spacing of abbreviations, 375
  spot page reference, 373
  star page, 374
  statutes and codes, 372
  string, 374
  sub nom, 373
  treatises, 374
  underscoring and italicizing, 375
  Uniform System of Citation, 370
  unpublished case, 374
  volume and page, 373
Citing compilations of statutes and codes, 620-621
Claim, acknowledgment, 514-515

Classmates, 30
Clauses, recurring, 43
Clerk of court, 252, 261-263, 501-506
Clients:
  asking fee, 63
  billing, 161, 163-164
  calls without appointment, 51-52
  charges made to, 163
  contacts in person, 50-56
  early, 53
  hysterical, 53-54
  introduction to, 49
  invitations from, 54
  irate, 62
  job hunters, 55
  law book salesmen, 55
  lawyer's instructions about, 50
  names on announcement list, 30
  placing toll calls, 59
  presents and payment for work, 54
  stranger wanting legal advice, 52-53
  wants to see file, 54-55
Clients' files, 79, 80-86 (*see also* Files)
Close corporation, 383
"Closed" files, 84, 85
Closing arguments, 251
Closings, title, 461-466 (*see also* Title
  closings)
Closing statement:
  calculation of adjustments, 467, 469, 471
    insurance, 471
    interest, 467, 469, 471
    rent, 471
    tax, 467
    miscellaneous payments, 471-472
  settlement sheet, 466
  suggested form, 472-473
  what it is, 466-467
Code of Professional Responsibility, 28
Codes, 165-166, 372, 620-621
Codicil, 245
Cold type, 183, 185
Collating, 222
Collection charges, 32
Collection letters, 72
Collections:
  acknowledgment of claim, 514-515
  commercial law lists, 509-510
  fees, 517
  filing, 510, 514
  forwarding an item, 517-518
  installment payments, 516
  judgment by default, 520-521
  judgment creditor, 521
  judgment debtor, 521

Collections *(cont'd)*
  judgment proof, 521
  letters, 515-516
  office procedures, 510
  record, 516-517
  remitting, 517
  reports to forwarder, 516
  uncontested suit, 518-521
    summons and complaint, 518
    when lawyer recommends suit, 518-519
"Coming-back," 73
Commercial law lists, 509-510
Company, 385
Compilations of laws, 165
Compilations of statutes and codes, citing,
  620-621
Complainant, 273
Complaint:
  analysis, 298-299
    allegations, 298
    body, 298
    caption, 298
    counts, 298
    introduction, 298
    prayer, 298
    signature, 299
    verification, 299
    "wherefore" clause, 298
  bill in equity, 298
  bill of complaint, 298
  collections, 519
  declaration, 298
  designation of first pleading, 250
  petition, 298
  plaintiff's first pleading, 297-298
  preparing, 299-301
  term, 298
  what to do about, 304-305
  writ, 298
Complaint in intervention, 274
Complimentary close, 110
Compositor, 179
Computers, 35
Confidential, 112
Conforming, 222
Congratulations:
  letters of, 133-135
  letter of appreciation, 132
Consistency, manuscript, 181, 183, 188
Constitution, how to cite, 371
Contacts:
  basic precepts, 50
  in person, 50-56
    client calls without appointment, 51
    client wants to see file, 54-55

Contacts *(cont'd)*
 early client, 53
 hysterical clients, 53-54
 invitations from clients, 54
 job hunters, 55-56
 law book salesmen, 55
 other salesmen, 55
 presents and payment, 54
 stranger wanting legal advice, 52-53
 with clients, 50-51
 introduction to client, 49-50
 telephone, 56-64
 answering calls for lawyer, 59
 clients placing toll calls, 59
 finding purpose of call, 61-62
 importance, 56
 irate client, 62
 law business numbers, 63-64
 lawyer's personal numbers, 64
 legal advice over phone, 62
 lists, desk, 63-64
 long distance, or toll, calls, 57-59
 notes of incoming calls, 59-60
 office administration numbers, 64
 placing calls, 56-57
 quoting fees, 63
 rules of courtesy, 56
 screening calls, 60-61
 your conversation, 63
Contingent fee, 31
Continuation sheets, 37, 114
Contractor, 194
"Control" account, 143
Copy distribution notation, 113-114
Copyholder, 35
Copying, 221
Corporate name, change, 421-429
Corporate seal, 199, 222
Corporate secretary:
 change of corporate name, 421-429
 corporate meetings, 402-409
 agenda, 406
 directors' fees, 406-407
 drafting resolutions before, 407-408
 folder, 403
 kinds, 402
 material to take, 407
 notice of directors' meeting, 405
 notice of stockholders', 403
 preparation for taking notes, 408
 preparations, 402
 preservation of notice, 405
 proxies and proxy statement, 404-405
 quorum, 404
 quorum at directors' meeting, 405

Corporate secretary *(cont'd)*
 reservation and preparation of room, 406
 taking notes, 408-409
 waiver of notice of stockholders', 403
 corporation calendar, 419-421
 annual report to state authority, 420
 annual report to stockholders, 420
 annual stockholders' meeting, 420
 expiration and renewal dates, 420
 how to keep, 420
 loose-leaf tax service, 421
 need, 419
 regular directors' meeting, 420
 where to get dates, 420-421
 information folder, 402
 minutes, 409-414
 certified extract, 412-413
 contents, 410-411
 contents of minute book, 410
 correction of errors, 412
 how to prepare in final form, 411-412
 indexing, 413-414
 minute book, 409
 preparation of draft, 411
 stock, 415-418
 authority to issue certificate, 415
 certificate book, 415
 issuance of certificate, 417
 original issue and transfer, 415
 separate form of assignment, 418
 state transfer tax, 415
 taxes, 415
 transfer of certificate, 417
Corporation:
 articles of association, 387
 articles of incorporation, 387
 association, 385
 alien, 384
 bank, 385
 business, 383
 certificate of incorporation, 387
 charters, 387
 clear the name, 386
 close, 383
 company, 385
 defined, 382
 domestic, 384
 dummies, 384
 execution of incorporation papers, 390-392
 filing papers, 392
 foreign, 384
 for profit, 383
 incorporated, 385
 incorporation papers, 387

Corporation *(cont'd)*
  incorporators, 384
  litigant, 276
  moneyed, 383
  not for profit, 382
  organization meetings, 393-398
    corporate outfit, 393-394
    incorporators, 393
    incorporators and subscribers, 393
    minutes, 396-397
    necessity and purpose, 393
    preparation, 393
    preparation of bylaws, 395-396
    preparation of stock certificates, 398
    resolution opening bank account,
      397-398
    shareholders or stockholders, 393
    waiver of notice, 394
  payment of fees, 392
  preliminary memorandum, 384-385
  preparation of articles of incorporation,
    387-389
  private, 383
  professional, 383
  professional association, 383
  public, 382
  publicly owned, 383
  public service, 383
  public utilities, 383
  purpose clause, 385
  reservation of name, 385-387
  shareholders, 385
  state of incorporation, 384-385
  steps in organization, 383
  stock clause, 385
  stockholders, 385
  trust, 385
  who may form, 384
Corporation calendar, 419-421
Corpus Juris Secundum System, 174-176
Corrections:
  bound pages, 226
  galley and page proofs 187
  legal papers, 220
  lengthy, 181
  manuscript, 181, 183
  short, 181
Correspondence *(see also* Letters)
Cost, professional services, 158
Counterclaim, 274, 305
Counts, 298
County courts, 258
County officials, 30
Court:
  action number, 262

Court *(cont'd)*
  American system, 253-255
  attorneys, 252
  authorized assembly, 249
  bailiffs, 252
  barristers, 261
  bill in equity, 250
  bill of complaint, 250
  calendar, 263
  calendar call, 263-264
  calendar number, 263
  case in brief, 251
  chambers, 250
  chancery, 258
  circuit, 254
  clerk, 261-263
  clerk of court, 252
  closing arguments, 251
  complaint, 250
  county, 258
  court reporter, 252
  criminal, 258
  daily call, 263
  declaration, 250
  defendant, 250, 253
  diversity of citizenship, 255
  docket, 262, 264
  docket number, 262
  equity, 259-260
  expert witnesses, 253
  federal, 254-255, 602
  index number, 262
  index system, 262
  inferior, 257
  intermediate review, 258
  judge, 252
  judges and justices, 260-261
  judge or judges, 249
  jurisdiction, 255-257
    definition, 255
    in personam, 256
    in rem, 256
    litigants, 256
    sphere of court's authority, 256
  jury, 252
  juvenile, 258
  libel, 250
  minute book, 263
  municipal, 258
  opening statement, 251
  oyer and terminer, 258
  personnel, 252-253
  persons assembled, 249
  petition, 250
  place where court is held, 250

Court *(cont'd)*
  plaintiff, 253
  pleadings, 250
  probate, 258
  procedure, 250
  progress record, 264-271
  prosecution, 253
  "Ready," 264
  "Ready subject to engagement," 264
  recross-examination, 251
  redirect examination, 251
  register, 262-263
  register of actions, 264
  sessions, 264
  "Settled," 264
  solicitors, 261
  special jurisdiction, 257-258
  state, 253-254, 602-609
  suit register, 264-271
    closing the record, 271
    file folder, 265
    filing record sheets, 265-266
    form and sufficiency, 267, 270-271
    loose-leaf binder, 265
    opening case, 267
    physical features, 265
    portable tray or cabinet, 265
    record, 268-269
    what to enter, 267
  superior, 257
  supreme appellate, 258-259
  term, 264
  trial lawyer, 261
  United States district, 255
  weekly call, 263
  what happens, 250-252
  witnesses, 253
  word, 249-250
Court order, 342
Court papers:
  administrators, 275
  affiant, 277
  affidavit for use in court, 339-341
  affirm, word, 181
  alias summons, 303-304
  amicus curiae, 274
  answer, 305-310
  bill of particulars, 328, 329
  called pleading, 193
  complainant, 273
  complaint, 297-301
  complaint in intervention, 274
  corporations, 276-277
  Curator, 275
  defendant, 273

Court papers *(cont'd)*
  demand for bill of particulars, 324-328
  demurrers, 319-324
  deponent, 277
  et vir, 276
  executors, 275
  ex uxor, 276
  findings of fact and conclusions (or rulings) of law, 346-347
  guardian *ad litem,* 275
  husband and wife, 276
  incompetents, 275
  instructions to jury, 348
  interrogatories, 328, 330
  intervenor, 274
  judgments and decrees, 348-352
  litigation papers, 273
  minors, 275
  motion and notice of motion, 336-339
  motion to make pleading more definite, 330, 331
  notice of appearance, 310-313
  notices, 330-336 (*see also* Notices)
  notice of trial: note of issue, 313-317
  orders, 342-346
  parties on appeal, 274
  parties to an action, 273-277
  parties to cross action, 274
  partnerships, 276
  party bringing law suit, 273
  party defending law suit, 273
  party intervening, 274
  plaintiff, 273
  pluries summons, 304
  practice and procedure, 295-296
    secretary's responsibility, 295-296
    variations, 296
  stipulations, 317-319
  summons, 301-305
  sworn to, word, 181
  third-party plaintiff, 274
  trustees, 275
  Tutor, 275
  typing, 282-295
    caption, 283-292
    captions on papers filed in federal district courts, 292
    conforming copies, 292
    endorsement, 293-295
    et al., et ux., et vir., 282
    folding, 295
    heading or caption, 282-283
    indentations, 292
    index number, 282
    jurisdiction and venue, 282

Court papers *(cont'd)*
  legal backs, 292-295
  numbering pages, 292
  number of copies, 292
  paper, 282
  printed litigation blanks, 295
  title of case, 282
  title of pleading, 283
  verifications, 277-282 *(see also* Verifications)
  who may be parties to law suit, 275-277
Courts of record and judicial circuits, 602-610
Court work, diary, 69
Covering letter, 72
Creative Legal Secretary, 170
Criminal courts, 258
Cross action, parties to, 274
Curator, 275
Current Legal Forms, 176

D

Daily call, 263
Daily time sheet, 159
Dateline, typing, 104
Date of printing, 227
Death, letter of sympathy, 133
Debts, will, 237
Decennial Digest, 171
Decided cases:
  other publications, 169
  reports, 166, 168-170
Declaration, 250, 298
Declination, letters, 138
Decree, probate proceeding, 499
Decrees, judgments and, 348-352 *(see also* Judgments and decrees)
Deeds, 437-445 *(see also* Real estate)
Default, judgment by, 520-521
Defendant, 250, 253, 273
Degrees:
  abbreviations or initials, 106
  law, 27
Deletions, 181
Demand for bill of particulars:
  abolished, 324
  caption, 325
  dateline, 325
  details demanded, 325
  how to prepare, 325, 327
  introduction, 325
  name and address of attorney, 325

Demand for bill of particulars *(cont'd)*
  parts, 325
  salutation, 325
  signature of attorney, 325
  what to do about, 327-328
Demurrers:
  analysis, 319-320
  attorney's certificate of good faith, 320
  caption, 320
  first page, 321
  grounds, 320
  how to prepare, 320, 324
  introduction, 320
  last page, 322
  motion to dismiss, 319
  points and authorities, 320, 323
  raises issue of law, 319
  signature of attorney, 320
  what to do about, 324
Deponent, 229, 277
Deportment, 34
Depreciation:
  accumulated, 143
  bookkeeping, 143
Descriptions, real property, 432-437
  (see also Real estate)
Desks, 35
Desk telephone lists, 63-64
Devise, will, 237
Devisee, will, 235
Diary:
  advance entries, 67
  advance notice of large payments, 68
  appointments, 69
  checklist of entries, 69
  court work, 69
  family dates, 69
  holidays, 69
  how to make, 67-68
  important days, 67
  litigation, 69
  making entries about legal work, 68
  making entries immediately, 68
  meetings, 70
  obtaining information, 68-69
  page from, 66
  payment dates, 70
  permanent record, 65
  presents or cards, 67
  recurring items, 67
  renewal dates, 70
  separate page for each day, 65
  tax dates, 70
  tickler card file, 70-71
  time-consuming task, 67

Diary *(cont'd)*
  two diaries, 67
  what it is, 65-67
  work accomplished, 71
  work done and time consumed, 65-66, 71
Dictating equipment, 35
Dictation and typing, 40-48 (*see also* Typing and dictation)
Directors' fees, 406-407
Directors' meeting:
  agenda, 406
  directors' fee, 406-407
  drafting resolutions before, 407-408
  material to take, 407
  meeting room, 406
  notice, 405
  preparation for taking notes, 408
  preservation of notice, 405
  quorum, 405
  taking notes, 408-409
Dispositive clauses, 237
Distribution, 215-216
District court, 255
Ditto marks, 222-223
Diversity of citizenship, 255
Dividends, 402
Divorcee, 107
Docket, 262-263, 264, 267
Docket envelopes, 93-95
Docket number, 262
Doctor of Both Laws, 27
Doctor of Civil Law, 27
Doctor of Jurisprudence, 27
Doctor of Juristic Science, 27
Doctor of Law, 27
Doctor of Laws, 27
Domestic corporation, 384
"Double-entry" system, 139
Doubling, 119
Dr., 109
Drafting resolutions before meetings, 407-408
Drawer labels, 89
Drawing account, 158
Dummies, 384
Duplicate original, 213, 214
Duties, secretary's 33-34

E

Early client, 53
Electric typewriters, 35
Electronic innovations, 96
Enclosure mark, 113

Enclosures:
  enclosure mark, 113
  larger than letter, 114-115
  omission, 130
  size of letter, 114
  smaller than letter, 115
Endorsement, 223
Entering practice, announcement, 28
Envelopes, 37, 111-112
Environmental Law Reporter, 170
Equipment:
  correspondence about, 80
  law office, 35
Equity, 259-260
Errors:
  assignment, 357, 359
  dictation, 41
  in account, 128
  legal papers, 218, 220
  minutes, 412
Esquire, 105
Estate administration:
  administrator, 484
  appointment of administrator, 500-501, 506, 508
    citations, 506, 508
    designation of clerk, 501, 506
    distributees, 500
    letters of administration, 500, 501, 508
    oath, 501, 506
    parties, 500
    petition, 501, 506
    petitioner, 500
    prior right to letters of administration, 500-501
    renunciation, 506
  decedent's estate, 483
  executor, 484
  intestate, 483
  lawyer, 484
  letters of administration, 484, 500, 501
  letters of testamentary, 484
  personal representative, 483-484
  probate of will, 484-500 (*see also* Probate of will)
  testate, 483
Et al., 282, 293
Ethics, 25
Et vir, 276, 282
Execution of instrument, 196-200
Executive letterheads, 37
Executor, 237, 275, 483, 484
Executrices, 237
Executrix, 237

Ex parte attachment, 336
Ex parte motions, 338
Expense, 143
Expert witnesses, 253
Expiration dates, 420
Extra copies, 90
Extracted material, manuscript, 180
Ex uxor, 276, 282

F

Family dates, diary, 69
Family Law Reporter, 170
Fast telegram, 120
Federal courts, 254-255, 373, 602
Federal Energy Guidelines, 170
Federal Insurance Contributions, Accrued, 143
Federal Practice Digest, 171
Fees:
  collection, 517
  contingent, 31
  forwarding, 32
  quoting over phone, 63
Fees Earned, 142, 143
File department, 39
File folder, progress records, 265
Files:
  advertisements, 87
  alphabetical, 85-86
    how to transfer, 86
    how to use, 85-86
    what it is, 85
  announcements, 87
  arranging papers in folders, 89-90
  case lawyer does not accept, 80
  catalogues, 87
  "catch-all," 80
  classification, 79-80
  clients', 79-86
  client wants to see, 54-55
  closing, 90
  collections, 510, 514
  commercial collections, 80
  control of materials taken from, 90, 96
  correspondence about office equipment, 80
  correspondence with law book publishers, 80
  drawer labels, 89
  electronics, 96-97
  extra copies, 90
  folder labels, 89
  follow-up, 71-74 (*see also* Follow-up files)

Files *(cont'd)*
  general correspondence, 80, 87
  guide labels, 89
  hold papers, 89, 90
  inactive, 80, 85
  information storage and retrieval, 96-97
  litigation filing envelope, 91-92
  "memory" filing, 79
  misplaced paper, 79
  numerical, 80-85
    assigning numbers, 84
    auxiliary card index, 80
    closed and *retired,* 84, 85
    how to use, 81-84
    key number for client, 81
    retirement or storage, 85
    storage, 85
    transfer, 84-85
    what it is, 80-81
  office administration material, 80
  out of date material, 87
  periodicals, bulletins, etc., 80, 87
  personal, 80, 86
  personnel applications, 80
  physical setup, 87-96
  preparation of material, 87-88
  printed papers, drafts, 90
  record sheets, 265
  sample legal blanks, 80
  subsidiary, 80
  tickler, 70-71, 73
  typing index tabs and labels, 88-89
Filing, distinct from recording, 210
Fill-ins, space, 217, 227
Findings of fact and conclusions (or rulings) of law:
  how to prepare, 347
  what they are, 346-347
  what to do about, 347
Firm letterheads, 37
First Party, 197
First pleading, 297
Folder labels, 89
Folders:
  arranging papers, 89
  meeting, 403
Folding, court papers, 295
Follow-up files:
  arrangement of folders, 72
  checklist of material, 71-72
  collection letters, 72
  "coming-back," 73
  correspondence awaiting answer, 72
  covering letter, 72
  daily, handling material, 73

Follow-up files *(cont'd)*
  diagram, 74
  equipment for system, 72
  "Future Years" folder, 72
  letters enclosing papers for recording, 72
  letters to abstract company, 72
  matters referred, 72
  necessity, 71
  operation of system, 72-73
  receipts for documents, 72
  requests for acknowledgements, 72
  small scale, 73
  tickler card file, 73
Follow-up letters, 130-131
Footnotes, copy, 180
Foreclosure actions:
  checklist, 482
  complaint, 476-477, 478
  definition, 473
  description of mortgage, 475
  description of note or bond, 475
  description of property, 475-476
  fictitious names, 474-475
  follow-up of process service, 480
  information needed, 474-476
  lis pendens, 477-478
  mortgage in default, 476
  notice of pendency, 478
  other steps, 481-482
  papers necessary, 473-474
  parties defendant, 474
  parties plaintiff, 474
  party sheet, 480-481
  procedure, 476-482
  summons, 478, 480
  title search, 476
  venue, 474
Foreign corporation, 384
Form books, 40, 176-177
Forwarder collections, 516
Forwarding fee, 32
Forwarding item for collection, 517-518
Front matter, 180
Full-block style, 99
Full partner, 398
Full-rate message, 121
Funeral expenses, will, 237
Furniture, 35
"Future Years" folder, 72

G

Galley proofs, 186-187
General correspondence files, 80, 87

General Digest Series, 171
General ledger, 142-143, 145
General power of attorney, 232
General practitioners in law, 27
Glossary, 557-600
Government bulletins, 87
Guardian:
  minors or incompetents, 275
  will, 238
Guardian *ad litem,* 275
Guide labels, 89

H

Habeas corpus, 354
Heading, court papers, 282
Heading on succeeding pages, 114
Headnotes, 166
Hearing, probate proceeding, 495
Hold papers, 89, 90
Holidays, diary, 69
Holographic will, 235
Honorary positions, address, 106, 109, 525-547
Hospitality:
  letter accepting, 137
  letter of appreciation, 132
Hotel reservations, 127
Hot type, 183
Husband and wife, 276
Hysterical clients, 53-54

I

Identification line, 112
Illness, letter of sympathy, 133
Inactive files, 80, 85
Income, 143
Incoming calls, 59
Incompetents, 275
Inconsistencies, proof, 188
Incorporation *(see Corporation)*
Incorporators, 384
Indentations, court papers, 292
Indented material, 218
Indentures, 402
Index brief, 362, 365
Indexing of minutes, 413
Index number, 262, 282, 293
Index system, clerk's, 262
Index tabs and labels, 88-89
Individual's seal, 199
Inferior courts, 257

Information storage and retrieval equipment, 35, 96-97
Injury, letter of sympathy, 133
In personam, 256
In re, 104
In rem, 256
Installment payments, 516
Instructions:
  about certain clients, 50
  lawyer's, 43-44
Instructions to jury, 348
Instruments:
  authentication, 611-612
  legal, 193-211 (*see also* Legal instruments)
Insurance, 143
Insurance companies, 383
Interlocutory decree or judgment, 348
Interrogatories, 328, 330
Intervenor, 274
Intestate, 483
In testimony whereof, 197
Introduction:
  copy, 180
  letters, 135-136
  to client, 49
Introductory paragraph, will, 236
Invitations:
  from clients, 54
  letters, 136
In witness whereof, 197
Irate client, 62
Issue, 313 (*see also* Note of issue)
Italics:
  citations, 375
  legal papers, 218
  marking copy, 183, 184
Items, will, 236

J

Job hunters, 55-56
Joint testators, 235
Jr., 105
Judge, 252, 260-261
Judge's order, 342
Judgment by default, 520-521
Judgment creditor, 521
Judgment debtor, 521
Judgment proof, 521
Judgments and decrees:
  decree, word, 348
  final, 348
  how to prepare, 349
  interlocutory, 348, 351

Judgments and decrees *(cont'd)*
  judgment, word, 348
  number of copies, 349
  on the pleadings, 349
  stayed, 349
  what they are, 348-349
  what to do about, 349, 352
Judicial circuits, 609-610
Jurat, 230
Juris, meaning, 27
Juris Civilis Doctor, 27
Jurisdiction, 255-257, 282
Juris Doctor, 27
Jurum Doctor, 27
Jury, 252
Justices, 260-261
Juvenile courts, 258

L

Labels, 88-89
Labor Law Reporter, 170
Latin words and phrases, 549-556
Law blanks, printed, 227-228
Law book publishers, correspondence, 80
Law book salesmen, 55
Law business numbers, 63-64
Law degrees, 27
Law Dictionary for Non-Lawyers, 177
Law office, 34-37 (*See also* Office)
Law-office team, 25
Law Reports Annotated, 373
Law report series, 373
Law reviews, 375
Law school, 26
Law Week, 170
Lawyer:
  admission to bar, 26-27
  advertising, 28
  announcements, 28-30
  appointments for month, 75
  building a practice, 28-30
  collection charges, 32
  contingent fee, 31
  court work, 78
  daily time sheet, 159, 160
  entering practice, 28
  ethics, 25-26
  finding cost of time, 158-159
  forwarding fee, 32
  law degrees, 27
  law-office team, 25
  outside activities, 30
  personal telephone numbers, 64

Lawyer *(cont'd)*
  posting time charges, 159
  relationship with clients, 31-32
  reminders, 75, 78
  removal of offices, 29
  resuming practice, 29
  service ledger sheet, 158, 161
  single retainer, 31
  specialization, 27-28
  things to be done, 75
  training, 26
  trial, 261
  yearly retainer, 31
Layout, 34-35
Leases, 451-457 *(see also* Real estate)
Legacy, will, 237
Legal backs, 223-226, 292-295
Legal blank cabinet, 35
Legal cap, 36
Legal forms, books of, 176-177
Legal instruments:
  acknowledgments, 201-207 *(see also* Acknowledgments)
  agreement between two corporations, 196
  attestation, 200
  attestation clause, 196, 199-200
  authentication, 207
  Buyer, 197
  contractor, 194
  court paper, 193
  definition, 193
  execution, 196-200
  First Party, 197
  fit signatures on page, 198
  how to type, 194-196
  in testimony whereof, 197
  in witness whereof, 197
  notaries public, 207-209
    definition, 207-208
    details to observe, 209
    following letter of law, 208-209
    "L.S." or "Seal," 209
    "under seal," 209
  notary's seal, 205
  parties, 193-194
  Parties of First Part, 197
  pleading, 193
  recording, 210-211
    distinction between recording and filing, 210
    purpose, 210
    secretary or paralegal, 210-211
  sealing, 198-199
    attested, 199
    corporation's seal, 199

Legal instruments *(cont'd)*
    individual's seal, 199
    sealed instruments, 198
    sealing the instrument, 198
    seal or L.S., 199
  seller, 194, 197
  signatures, 197-198
  ss., 204-205
  testimonium clause, 194, 196-197
  venue, 203-205
  witness clause, 196, 199
Legal newspapers, 375
Legal papers, 213-228 *(see also* Papers)
Legal representative, 483
Legal Research in a Nutshell, 177
Legal Secretary's Encyclopedic Dictionary, 177
Legal size paper, 36
Legatee, will, 235
Letterheads, 37, 222
Letters:
  abstract company, 72
  acceptance, 137-138
    banquet, luncheon, entertainment, 137
    invitation to serve, 138
    membership, 138
    overnight visit, 137
    speaking invitation, 137-138
  address, 104-108
    business titles or position, 106-107
    degrees and other honors, 106
    divorcee, 107
    Esquire, 105
    firm composed of women, 107
    forms, 104-106
    forms for women, 107
    married woman, 107
    Mesdames or Mmes., 107
    Messrs., 105
    Miss or Ms., 107
    Mr., Mrs., Miss, or Ms., 106
    Mrs., 107
    name of company, 104
    official or honorary positions, 107
    person's name, 104
    professional women, 107
    Sr. or Jr., 105
    street, 107-108
    titles, 105-106
    unmarried woman, 107
    widow, 107
    wife of titled man, 107
  appreciation, 131-132
    assistance to firm or club, 131
    hospitality, 132

Letters *(cont'd)*
    message for sympathy, 132
    message of congratulations, 132
  attention line, 112
  big words, 120
  collection, 72, 515-516
  complimentary close, 110
  congratulations, 133-135
    business anniversary, 135
    outstanding community service, 134
    professional or civic honor, 133
    promotion, 134
    retirement from business, 134
    seasonal good wishes, 135
    speech, article or book, 134
  copy distribution notation, 113-114
  dateline, 104
  declination, 138
  enclosing papers for recording, 72
  enclosure mark, 113
  enclosures, 114-115
    larger than letter, 114-115
    size of letter, 114
    smaller than letter, 115
  envelopes, 111-112
  favorite words and expressions, 119-120
  heading on succeeding pages, 114
  identification line, 112
  introduction, 135-136
    business or professional associate, 136
    personal friend, 135
  invitation, 137-138
    banquet, luncheon, entertainment, 136
    to give address or talk, 136-137
  mailing notation, 113
  opinion, 102-103
  over secretary's signature, 123-131
    acknowledging letters received
      during employer's absence, 123-126
    error in account, 128-129
    follow-ups, 130-131
    making reservations, 126-128
    regarding omission of enclosures, 130
    reply to notice of meeting, 129-130
  personal notation, 112
  postscript, 114
  punctuation, 103-104
  reference line, 112-113
  Register of Deeds, 72
  salutations, 108-110
    addressed to women, 109-110
    business title or designation, 109
    company or group, 109
    firm of lawyers, 109
    forms, 109

Letters *(cont'd)*
    honorary and official titles, 109
    organization of men and women, 109
    plural, 109
    singular, 109
    typing, 108-109
  secretary may write for employer's signature, 131-138
  secretary writes, 123
  sentence length, 120
  signature, 110-111
  style of setups, 99-102
    block, 99
    full-block, 99
    official, 101-102
    semiblock, 100-101
  subject line, 104
  sympathy, 132-133
    death, 133
    personal injury or illness, 133
  telegrams, 120-123 *(see also* Telegrams)
  trite terms, 115-118
  unnecessary words and phrases, 118-119
  words with same meaning, 119
Letters of administration, 484, 500, 501
Letters testamentary, 484, 499
Letter telegram, 121
LEXIS, 177
Liabilities, 143
Libel, 250
Limited partner, 398
Limited power of attorney, 233
Line spacing, legal papers, 216, 218
Litigants, 256
Litigation, time limits, 69
Litigation papers, 273-296, 297-352 *(see also*
  Court papers)
Litigation filing envelope, 91-92
Local bar, members, 30
Long distance calls, 57-59
Loose-leaf formbook, 40
Loose-leaf services, 169-170, 421
L.S., 199

                    M

Mailgram, 120
Mailing notation, 113
Managing partner, 32
Mandamus, 354
Manuals, practice, 176
Manuscript:
  author's alterations, 187
  bibliographies, 180-181

Manuscript *(cont'd)*
 boldface, 183, 184
 capitals, 184
 checking, 181-183
 circle instructions, 185
 citations, 183
 cold type, 183
 consistency, 181, 183
 continuity, 189
 corrections, 183, 187
 correct page reference numbers, 180
 covers, 36
 deletions, 181
 double spacing, 179
 errors to look for, 188
 estimate length of copy, 185-186
  character count, 185
  word count, 185-186
 extracted or quoted material, 180
 footnotes, 180
 front matter, 180
 galley proofs, 186, 187
 headings, 180, 184
 hot type, 183
 inconsistencies, 188
 indenting paragraphs, 4
 italics, 183, 184
 kind of type, 183
 lengthy corrections, 181
 lowercase a capital letter, 181
 margin on four sides, 180
 marking copy, 183-185
 numbering pages, 182
 numerical code for types, 185
 or *copy*, 179
 page numbers, 189
 page proofs, 186-187
 pica, 183, 185
 planning, 183
 preface or introduction, 180
 procedure, 186-187
 proofreader's marks, 181, 182, 185
 punctuation, 188
 quotations, 183
 reading proof, 187-189
 retaining material crossed out, 182
 right-hand margin, 179
 rules for typing, 179-181
 separate two words, 181
 short corrections, 181
 six inch typed line, 179
 size and name of body type, 184-185
 size of type area, 183
 small caps, 183, 184
  spelling, 188

Manuscript *(cont'd)*
 starting new paragraph, 181
 stet, 182
 subheadings, 180
 superior figures, 180
 table of contents, 180
 tables, 179, 181
 title page, 180
 transpositions of lines, 189
 uniform length pages, 180
 use one side of sheet, 180
 windows or short lines, 187
 working with others, 186
Marginal and tabular stops, 215
Margins:
 legal papers, 214, 218
 manuscripts, 180
Marking copy, 183-185
Martindale-Hubbell Law Dictionary, 30
Master of Laws, 27
Meetings:
 agenda, 406
 corporate, 402-409 (*see also* Corporate
  secretary)
 diary, 70
 directors', 405
 directors' fees, 406-407
 drafting resolutions before, 407-408
 folder, 403
 kinds, 402
 material to take, 407
 meeting room, 406
 notes, 408-409
 preparations, 402
 preservation of notice, 405
 proxy statement, 404-405
 quorum, 404, 405
 reply to notice, 129-130
 stockholders', 403
Membership, letter accepting, 138
Members of local bar, 30
Memorandum setting for trial, 313
Mesdames, 107, 110
Message memo, 59-60
Messrs., 105
Microfilming, 97
Minors, 275
Minute book, 263
Minutes:
 certified extract, 412-414
 content, 410-411
 correction of errors, 412
 final form, 411
 first meeting of directors, 396-397
 first meeting of incorporators, 396

Minutes *(cont'd)*
  indexing, 413
  minute book, 409-410
  preparation of draft, 411
Miscellaneous Expenses, 142, 143
Mixed punctuation, 103
Mmes., 107
Monarch size envelopes, 37
Moneyed corporations, 383
Mortgage, 445-451 *(see also* Real estate)
"Motion day," 338
Motion to dismiss, 297, 319
Motion to make pleading more definite, 330, 331
Ms., 106, 107, 109
Municipal courts, 258

N

Names:
  checking, 178
  corporate, change, 421-429
  forms of address, 104
National Reporter Blue Book, 168
National Reporter System, 371, 618-619
New matter:
  new case report, 37
  routing new case report, 38, 39-40
  what secretary does, 37-38
Newspapers, legal, 375
Night letter, 120
Noncupative wills, 235
Notarial seal, 222
Notaries public, 207-209, 612-614
Notary, signature, 230
Notary's seal, 205-206
Notation:
  blind-copy, 113-114
  "Confidential," 112
  copy distribution, 113-114
  Enclosure, 113
  mailing, 113
  "Personal, " 112
Note of issue:
  issue, definition, 313
  issue of fact, 313
  issue of law, 313
  joined issue, 313
  preparation, 313-314
  what to do about, 315, 317
  when it must be served, 313
Notes, meetings, 408-409
Notice of appeal, 356

Notice of appearance:
  analysis, 310
  caption, 310
  common law case, 311
  equity case (federal court), 312
  how to prepare, 310, 313
  never verified, 313
  no statements of fact, 313
  original, 310
  responsibilities, 313
  signature line, 310, 313
  what to do about, 313
Notice of entry, 344
Notice of meeting, reply, 129-130
Notice of motion:
  based upon affidavit, 339
  change of venue, 338
  information needed to prepare, 338-339
  leave to amend, 338
  motion, term, 336
  new trial, 338
  return day, 338
  set cause for trial, 338
  strike, 338
Notice of Settlement, 344
Notice of trial:
  after issue is joined, 313
  back, 315
  front, 314
  issue, 313
  preparation, 314
  trial calendar, 313
  what to do about, 315, 317
  when served, 313
Notices:
  analysis, 330
  appearance, 311, 312, 332
  backing and binding, 332
  directors' meetings, 405
  filing and entry, 332, 333-334
  how to prepare, 330
  motion, 332, 336-339 *(see also* Notice of motion)
  service, 332
  settlement, 332, 334-335
  stockholders' meetings, 403
  to take deposition upon oral examination, 332, 335-336
Number:
  action, 262
  calendar, 263
  copies, court papers, 292
  docket, 262
  index, 262, 282, 293
  law business, 63-64

Number *(cont'd)*
  lawyer's personal, 64
  manuscript pages, 182
  office administration, 64
  page, 189, 214-215, 292
  page, legal papers, 214-215
Numerical filing, 80-85 *(see also* Files)

O

Oath:
  administration, 280
  executor, 498, 501
Office:
  equipment, 35
  furniture, 35
  layout, 34-35
  legal blank cabinet, 35
  stationery supplies, 36-37
Office administration material, 80
Office administration numbers, 64
Office docket, 267
Office Supplies, 143
Official positions, forms of address, 525-547
Official reports, 371, 616-617
Officials, county, 30
Official seal, 222
Official style, 101-102
Omissions, legal papers, 218-220
Opening statement, 251
Open punctuation, 103-104
Opinion letters, 102-103
Oral wills, 235
Order and Notice of Entry, 344, 346
Orders:
  analysis, 342
  court, 342, 344
  how to prepare, 342, 344
  judge's, 342, 345
  "settle order on notice," 342
  "submit order," 342
  what to do about, 344, 346
Organization, 32
Overhead expenses, 142
Overseas Telex service, 121
Oyer & terminer, 258

P

Page numbers:
  correcting galley or page proofs, 189
  legal papers, 214-215
Page proofs, 186-187

Pamphlets, 80
Paper, 36, 282
Paper file, 90
Papers:
  "annexed" or "attached," 332
  asterisks, 218, 219
  capitalization, 221
  Chinese copy, 221
  collating, 222
  conforming, 222
  copying, 221
  correction of errors, 220
  corrections on bound pages, 226
  court, 273-296, 297-352 *(see also* Court
    papers)
  crossing-out, 220
  ditto marks, 222-223
  drafts, 220
  duplicate original, 213
  endorsement, 223
  errors, 218
  indented material, 218
  italics, 218
  legal backs, 223-226
  letterheads, 222
  line spacing, 216, 218
  litigation back, 224, 225, 226
  marginal and tabular stops, 215
  margins, 214
  margins and paragraphs, 218
  notarial seal, 222
  numbering pages, 214-215
  number of copies, 213
  official or corporate seal, 222
  omissions, how to show, 218-220
  paper, 213-214
  paragraphs, 214
  points, 218, 219
  printed law blanks, 227-228
  punctuation, 221
  quotation marks, 218
  registration of printing, 227
  responsibility and distribution line,
    215-216
  retyping, 221
  retyping corrected draft, 220
  Signed, 222
  small blanks, 227-228
  space for fill-ins, 217
  standard rules for spacing, 216-217
  tabulated items, 215
  tabulated material, 215
  test-writing, 221-222
  triplicate original, 213
  typing on ruled lines, 227

Papers *(cont'd)*
  underscoring, 217
  "Z" ruling, 228
Paragraphs:
  legal papers, 214, 218
  recurring, 43
Paralegals, 33, 35, 210-211, 261
Parallel citations, 373
Parties:
  appointment of administrator, 500
  power of attorney, 232
Parties of First Part, 197
Parties to an action, 273-277 *(see also* Court
  papers)
Parties to instrument, 193
Partnership:
  full partner, 398
  how formed, 398
  limited partner, 398
  parties to law suit, 276
  partnership agreement, 399
  what it is, 398
Party of first part, 194
Payment dates, diary, 70
Payment for work, 54
Payments, installment, 516
Payroll record, 158
Periodicals, 55, 80, 87
Personal files, 80, 86-87
Personal notation, 112
Personal representative, 483
Personal telephone numbers, 64
Personnel:
  court, 252-253
  law office, 32-33
Personnel applications and records, 80
Petition, 250, 298, 501
Petitioner, 355, 485
Petty Cash, 143
Petty cash fund, 163-164
Photocopiers, 35
Phrases, recurring, 43
Plaintiff, 253, 273
Plane reservations, 127
Pleading, 193, 250, 283
Pluries summons, 304
Posting:
  cash journal entries, 145-154
  general ledger, 145
  time changes, 159, 161
Postscript, 114
Poverty Law Reporter, 170
Power of attorney:
  agent, 232
  attorney-in-fact, 232

Power of attorney *(cont'd)*
  beginning, 232
  collate, 233
  conveyance of real estate, 233
  directions for preparation, 233
  distribution, 233
  double-space, 233
  endorsed legal back, 233
  forms, 232
  general, 233
  limited, 232
  original, 233
  paper, size, 233
  parties, 232
  principal, 232
  principal's signature, 233
  recording, 233
  responsibility marks, 233
  signature line, 233
  signature page, 233
  statements and clauses, 232
  testimonium clause, 232
  what it is, 232
  witnessed and acknowledged, 233
Practical Manual of Standard Legal Citations, 373
Practice manuals, 176
Prayer, 298
Precatory provisions, will, 238
Preface, 180
Prentice-Hall Federal Tax Service, 170
Presents:
  diary, 67
  for work done, 54
Principal, 232
Printed law blanks, 227-228
Printed materials, manuscript preparation,
  179-189 *(see also* Manuscript)
Printed papers, 90
Private corporations, 383
Privileged communication, 31
Probate courts, 258
Probate of will:
  beneficiary of residuary trust, 492
  citation and waiver, 493
  copy of will and affidavit, 487
  decree, 499
  deposition of witnesses to will, 498
  executor's right to act, 484-485
  how to prepare citation, 495
  letters testamentary, 499-500
  notice, 498
  notice to creditors, 500
  oath of executor, 498-499
  parties to proceedings, 485-486

Probate of will *(cont'd)*
  petition, 487-488, 490-493
  petitioner, 485
  preparations for hearing, 495, 498
  preparing waiver of citation, 493, 495
  remainder interest in residuary trust, 492
  residuary legatee, 492
  specific legacy, 492
  transfer tax affidavit, 493
Professional association, 383
Professional corporation, 383
Professional services, time and cost, 158-161
Professional women, 107
Profit and Loss, 143, 155, 158
Progress record, court matters, 264-271
Prohibition, 354
Promotion, congratulatory letter, 134
Proofreader's marks, 181, 182, 185
Proofs, 186-187
Proposed Order and Notice of Settlement, 346
Prosecution, 253
Proxies and proxy statement, 404
Public corporations, 382
Publicly owned corporations, 383
Public service corporations, 383
Public utilities, 383
Publishers, law book, 80
Punctuation:
  legal papers, 221
  mixed and open, 103-104
  proof, 188
  will, 244
Purchase and sale agreements:
  binder, 460
  closing date, 458
  defined, 457-458
  earnest money, 460
  escrow for sale of real property, 460-461
  how to prepare, 458
  information to fill in, 458-460
  installment, 457
  necessity, 458
  parties, 458
  types, 457-458
Purpose clause, 385

Q

Quorum:
  directors' meeting, 405
  stockholders' meeting, 404

Quotations:
  copy, 180, 183
  legal papers, 218-220
Quo warranto, 354

R

Radio photo service, 121
Re, 104
Reading the proof, 187-189
Real estate:
  closing statement, 466-473 (*see also* Closing statement)
  deeds, 437-445
    consideration, 441
    covenants, 442
    definition, 437
    encumbrances, 441
    exceptions and reservations, 443
    fiduciary, 438
    forms, 437-438
    grantee, 437
    grantor, 437
    habendum clause, 442
    how to cancel stamps, 443
    indenture, 437
    kinds, 438
    lawyer's approval, 444
    parties, 437
    poll, 437
    preparation, 443-445
    printed forms, 438, 440, 441
    quit-claim, 438
    recording, 443
    restrictions and conditions, 443
    revenue stamps, 443
    statements and clauses, 441-443
    state taxes, 443
    statutory form, 438
    testimonium clause, 443
    typed, 441
    warranty, 438
  descriptions, 432-437
    accuracy, 432
    course, 434
    distance, 434
    how land is described, 432
    how to check, 436-437
    metes and bounds, 434, 435
    monuments, 434
    plat system, 434-435
    prime or principal meridians, 433
    range, 433
    rectangular system of surveys, 433

Real estate *(cont'd)*
    section and township, 432-434
    typing, 436
  foreclosure actions, 473-482 *(see also* Fore-
    closure actions)
  leases, 451-457
    acknowledgment, 457
    classification, 452-453
    commercial, 452
    definition, 451-452
    duration, 452
    execution, 457
    how to prepare, 457
    leasehold estate in premises, 452
    lessee, 452
    parties, 452
    percentage, 453
    printed forms, 453
    recording, 457
    rental, 452-453
    residential, 452
    standard clauses, 453-456
    typed, style, 456-457
    type of property, 452
  mortgage, 445-451
    acceleration clause, 449
    bond and, 445
    chattel, 445
    conditional, 445
    consideration, 449
    conventional, 446
    dead pledge, 445
    deed of trust, 446
    defeasance clause, 446, 448-449
    definition, 445
    description of debt, 448
    description of property, 449
    designation of parties, 445
    forms, 446
    how to prepare, 450-451
    information to fill in, 447-448
    mortgagee, 445
    mortgagor, 445
    partial release, 450
    party of first part, 445
    pàrty of second part, 445
    prepayment privilege, 449-450
    printed, 447
    public trustees, 445
    purchase money, 446-447
    statements and clauses, 448-450
    state tax, 450
    trust deed, 446
    trust indenture, 446
    trust mortgage, 446

Real estate *(cont'd)*
    typed, 448
    pattern for each instrument, 431-432
    purchase and sale agreement, 457-461
      (See also Purchase and sale agree-
      ment)
    title closings and evidence of title, 461-466
      (see also Title closings)
Receipts for documents, 72
Reciprocal wills, 235
Recording legal instruments, 210-211
Record of collections, 516-517
Record on appeal:
  assignment of errors, 359
  binding, volumes and title, 360
  certification, filing, service, 360
  directions to clerk, 359
  format and make-up of record, 360
  how to prepare, 359-360
  preparation, 359
  what it is, 357
  who prepares, 359
Records *(see* Books and records)
Record sheets, 265-266
Recross-examination, 251
Recurring phrases, clauses and paragraphs,
  43
Red-inking, 245-246
Redirect examination, 251
Reference line, 112-113
References:
  American Digest, 171
  books of index, 171-176
  classifying the law, 170-176
  Corpus Juris Secundum System, 174-176
    alphabetical arrangement, 175-176
    American Jurisprudence, 176
    American Law Reports, 176
    analysis preceeding each title, 175
    fact, or descriptive, word index, 175
    how to cite, 176
    how to use, 175-176
    scope and organization, 174-175
  form books, 176-177
    basic reference books, 177
    computerized legal research, 177
    legal forms, 176-177
    practice manuals, 176
    treatises, 177
  names and addresses, checking, 178
  reports of decided cases, 166, 168-170
    finding alternate citations, 168-169
    headnotes, 166
    loose-leaf services, 169-170
    other publications, 169

References *(cont'd)*
  scope and organization, 166, 168
  selected case series, 169
  subject reports, 169
  syllabus, 166
  using reports and reporters, 168
  Shepard's Citations, 172-173
    how to use, 172
    illustrative case, 172, 174
    page, 173
    purpose, 172
  statutes and codes, 165-166, 167
    compilations of laws, 165-166
    excerpt from annotated compilation, 167
    how to find law, 166
Referred materials, 72
Register, 262-263
Register of actions, 264
Register of Deeds, 72
Registration of printing, 227
Regular directors' meeting, 420
Reminders:
  appointments, 69
  court work, 69
  diary, 65-71 *(see also* Diary)
  family dates, 69
  follow-up files, 71-74 *(see also* Follow-up files)
  holidays, 69
  important days, 67
  lawyer, 75, 78
    appointments for month, 75
    court work, 78
    how to remind of appointments, 75
    necessity, 75
    things to be done, 75
  litigation, 69
  meetings, 70
  payment dates, 70
  payments of large sums, 68
  presents or cards, 67
  recurring items, 67
  renewal dates, 70
  tax dates, 70
  tickler card file, 70-71, 73
  time-consuming tasks, 67
  work done, time consumed, 65-66, 71
Remitting, collections, 517
Removal of offices, announcement, 29
Renewal dates:
  corporation calendar, 420
  diary, 70
Rent, 143
Renunciation, 506

Reporter:
  court, 252
  named, 374
  National Reporter System, 618-619
Reports, decided cases, 166, 168-170
Reports to forwarder, 516
Requests for acknowledgements, 72
Research, references, 165-178 *(see also* References)
Reservations, 126-128
Residuary clause, will, 237
Residuary trust, 492
Resolution opening bank account, 397-398
Resolutions, drafting before meetings, 407-408
Respondent, 355
Responsibility and distribution line, 215-216
Resuming practice, announcement, 29
Retainers, 31
Retired, term 84
Retirement, congratulations, 134
Return day, 303
Retyping unsigned draft, 221
Review by higher court:
  appeal, 354
  appealing a case, 354
  appellant, 355
  appellee, 355
  certiori, 354
  change in caption of case, 355
  designation of parties to an appeal, 355
  diary entries, 354-355
  habeas corpus, 354
  mandamus, 354
  methods, 354
  notice of appeal, 356-357
  petitioner, 355
  prohibition, 354
  quo warranto, 354
  respondent, 355
  rules, 353-354
  service on opposing counsel, 357
  stay writs, 354
  taking an appeal, 354
  writ of error, 354
Reviews, law, 375
Revocation clause, will, 236
Routing new case report, 38-40
Rule days, 303
Ruled lines, typing on, 227

S

Salaries, 143

Salesmen, 55
Salutations:
  forms, 109
  how to type, 108-109
  letters to women, 109-110
Sample legal blanks, 80
Screening calls for lawyer, 60-61
Seal:
  will, 245
  word, 199
Sealed instrument, 198
Sealing an instrument, 198-199
"2d," 373
Second Series, 371
Second sheets, 114
Secretary, duties, 33-34
Selected cases series, annotated, 169
Seller, 194, 197
Semiblock style, 100-101
Sentence length, 120
Service:
  congratulations, 135
  salesmen, 55
Services Charged, 141, 142, 143
Settle order on notice, 342
Shareholders, 385, 393
Shepard's Citations, 168, 169, 172-173
Ship-to-shore radio, 121
Shore-to-ship radio, 121
Shorthand, citations, 370
Short lines, 187
Signature:
  affiant, 230
  execution of instrument, 197-198
  notary, 230
  typing, 110-111
  witnesses, will, 238
Signature clause, will, 238
Signature page, will, 240-242
Single retainer, 31
Slip decision, 374
Small caps, 183, 184
Solicitors, 261
Special jurisdiction, courts, 257-258
Specialization in law field, 27-28
Speech, congratulations, 134
Spelling, proof, 188
Spot page reference, 373
Sr., 105
Standard Federal Tax Reporter, 170
Star page, 374
State and Local Tax Services, 170
State courts, 253-254, 602-609
State examination, 26
Statement of facts, 230

State of incorporation, 384
Stationery supplies, 36-37
Statutes, 165-166, 372, 620-621
Statutes of limitations in number of years,
  614-615
Stay writs, 354
Stet, 44, 182
Stipulations:
  analysis, 317
  body, 317
  caption, 317
  dateline, 317
  extending time to answer, 318
  how to prepare, 317, 319
  meaning, 317
  signatures of attorneys, 317
  what to do about, 319
Stock:
  authority to issue certificate, 415
  certificate book, 415
  issuance of certificate, 417
  original issue, 415
  preparation of certificate, 398
  separate form of assignment, 418
  state transfer tax, 415
  taxes, 415
  transfer, 415
  transfer of certificate, 417
Stock clause, 385
Stockholders, 385, 393
Stockholders' meetings:
  drafting resolutions before, 407-408
  material to take, 407
  notice of, 403
  preparations for taking notes, 408
  proxies and proxy statement, 404-405
  quorum, 404
  taking notes, 408-409
  waiver of notice, 403
Storage, 85
Street address, 107-108
String citations, 374
Subject line, 104
Subject reports, 169
Submit order, 342
Sub nom, 373
Subsidiary files, 80
Subsidiary ledger, 143, 145
Suit register, 264-271 (*see also* Court)
Summons:
  alias, 303
  body, 301
  caption, 301
  collections, 519
  conform copies, 304

Summons *(cont'd)*
  default judgment, 305
  file, 304
  how to prepare, 301, 303
  on top of complaint, 304
  original, 304
  pluries, 304
  printed form, 302
  return day, 303, 304, 305
  rule days, 303
  signature and seal of clerk, 301
  space for sheriff's return, 304
  what to do about, 304
Superior courts, 257
Supplies, stationery, 36-37
Supreme appellate courts, 258-259
Supreme Court Digest, 171
Supreme Court Reports, 371
"Sworn to" clause, 230
Syllabus, 166
Sympathy, letters, 132-133

T

Table of contents, 180
Tables, manuscript, 181
Tabs, index, 88
Tabulated material, 215
Tabular stops, 215
Take-ins, 43
Taking an appeal, 354
Taking trial balance of accounts receivable, 155
Tax dates, diary, 71
Tax Expense, 142, 143
Tax matters and reports, 421
Team, law-office, 25
Telegrams:
  fast, 120
  full-rate message, 121
  how to send, 120-121
  how to type, 121
  letter, 121
  mailgram, 120
  mixed letters and figures, 122
  night letter, 120
  overseas Telex service, 121
  paragraphing, 122
  punctuation, 122
  radio photo service, 121
  recipient on plane, 122
  recipient on train, 122
  same message to multiple addresses, 121
  ship-to-shore radio, 121

Telegrams *(cont'd)*
  shore-to-ship radio, 121
  typing when work is in machine, 122-123
Telephone:
  answering for lawyer, 59
  caller wants legal advice, 62
  courtesy, 56
  finding purpose of call, 61-62
  general ledger, 143
  importance of contacts, 56
  irate caller, 62
  law business numbers, 63-64
  lawyer's personal numbers, 64
  long distance, or toll, calls, 57-59
  message memo, 59, 60
  notes of incoming calls, 59
  office administration numbers, 64
  placing calls for lawyer, 56-57
  quoting fee , 63
  record of toll call, 57, 58
  screening calls, 60-61
  up-to-date directory, 63-64
  when client places toll calls, 59
  your conversation, 63
Term of court, 264
Testament, 233 *(see also* Will)
Testamentary trusts, will, 237
Testate, 483
Testator:
  only party to will, 234
  state requirements for age, 600-602
Testatrix, 234
Testimonium clause:
  execution of instrument, 194, 196-197
  power of attorney, 232
  will, 238
Testimony, 44-48
Test-writing, 221-222
Text, or body of will, 236-237
Third-party plaintiff, 274
Tickler file:
  description, 70
  follow-up, 73
  use with diary, 70-71
Time, professional services, 158
Time sheet, daily, 159
Title:
  case, typing, 282
  forms of address, 105, 106-107, 109
  will, 236
Title page, 180
Title closings:
  abstract of title, 461-463
  certificate of title, 464
  definition, 461

Title closings *(cont'd)*
evidence of title, 461
opinion of title, 463
preparations, 464-466
title insurance policies, 464
Torrens certificate, 464
Toll calls, 57-59
Trade Regulation Reporter, 170
Training, legal, 26
Train reservations, 127
Transfer tax affidavit, 493
Transposition of lines, 189
Treaties:
form books, 177
how to cite, 374
Trial balance, 154-155
Trial calendar, 313
Trial lawyer, 261
Triplicate original, 213, 214
Trite terms, 115-118
Trust, 385
Trustees, 275
Trust Fund Account, 141, 143
Trust provisions, will, 237
Tutor, 275
Type, 183 *(see also* Manuscript)
Typewriters:
automatic, 35
electric, 35
Typing and dictation:
confusing pairs of words, 42-43
errors in dictation, 41-42
recurring phrases, clauses and para-
graphs, 43
secretary's loose-leaf formbook, 40
special outlines for unusual words, 43
take-ins, 43-44
understanding dictated material, 40-41

U

Uncontested suit, 518
Underscoring: 217, 375
Uniform Acknowledgment Act, 201
Uniform Partnership Act, 381
Uniform System of Citation, 177, 370, 373
United States district court, 255
U.S. Law Week, 170

V

Venue:
acknowledgments, 203-205

Venue *(cont'd)*
affidavit, 230, 231
court papers, 282
Verification:
administering oath, 280-282
affirm, word, 281
answers, 277
bills of particulars, 277
complaints, 277
deponent or affiant, 277
forms, 277-278
how to type, 278-280
sworn to, 281
what it is, 277
who may verify pleading, 277

W

Waiting room, 34
Waiver of citation, 493, 495
Waiver of notice of stockholders' meetings,
403
Webster's Collegiate Dictionary, 177
Weekly call, 263
WESTLAW, 177
"Wherefore" clause, 298
Widow, 107
Wife, husband and, 276
Will:
appointment of guardian, 238
articles, 236
attestation clause, 238, 245
beneficiaries, 235
bequest or legacy, 237
bind, 245
capitalization, 244
certify copies, 245
certifying copies, 243-244
codicil, 245
collate, 245
debt and funeral expenses, 237
definition, 233
devisee, 235
dispositive clauses, 237
do's and dont's, 244-245
draft form, 244
endorse, 245
executor, appointment, 237-238
executrices, 237-238
executrix, 237
final typing, 244
first page, 239
first witness line, 245
former, 245

Will *(cont'd)*
  forms and kinds, 235
  holographic, 235
  institution named executor, 245
  introductory paragraph, 236
  items, 236
  joint testators, 235
  last page, 240
  legatee, 235
  lines on page, 244
  numbering pages, 244
  number of witnesses, 600-602
  nuncupative, 235
  oral, 235
  original in envelope, 245
  page length, 242
  paper, 244
  parties, 234-235
  pattern of contents, 235-236
  precatory provisions, 238
  printed forms, 235
  probate, 484-500 *(see also* Probate of will)
  punctuation, 244
  real estate, 245
  reciprocal, 235
  red-inking, 245-246
  residuary clause, 237
  responsibility line, 244
  revocation clause, 236
  seal, 245
  signature clause, 238
  signature line, 244
  signature page, 240
  spacing, 244
  spelling of names, 245
  testament, 233
  testamentary trusts, 237
  testator, 234
  testatrix, 234
  testimonium clause, 238
  text, or body, 236
  title, 236

Will *(cont'd)*
  trust provisions, 237
  typing, 238-240
  witnesses' signatures, 238
  witnessing, 242-243
Windows, 187
Withholding tax, accrued, 143
Witness clause, 196, 199
Witnesses:
  court, 253
  expert, 253
  signatures, 238
  will, 242-243, 498, 600-602
Women:
  addressing, 107
  salutation in letters addressed to, 109-110
Word count, 185-186
Words:
  big versus one syllable, 120
  confusing pairs, 42-43
  favorite, 119-120
  Latin, 549-556
  sentence length, 120
  trite terms, 115-118
  two with same meaning, 119
  unnecessary, 118-119
  unusual, special outlines, 43
Work accomplished, 71
Workroom, 34
Writ, 298
Writ of error, 354

                          Y

Yearly retainer, 31

                          Z

"Z" ruling, 228